News Clippings from Cedar City, Utah 1851 - 1924

Includes Hamilton, Kanarraville, Summit, Enoch, Sahara &

Nada

Compiled from the Deseret News, Iron County Record & Washington County News with contributions from other regional papers.

Often while working on family history (genealogy) I wonder about more than is listed on the pedigree sheets and am so grateful for their sacrifices and love for the generations to follow.

Some of the names include:Adams, Ahstrom, Alldridge, Anderson, Armstrong, Aucill, Bauer, Baugh, Bell, Bennett, Birkbeck, Bladen, Brown, Bosnew, Bowman. Bullock, Burkholder, Canfield, Chaffin, Chamberlain, Chancey, Chatterly, Condie, Corlett, Corry, Cossett, Cox, Crowther, Dover, Duncan, Eddards,Esplin, Fife, Find, Fordsham, Fretwell, Gilbert, Gower, Granger, Green, Haight, Hamilton, Hansen, Harris, Hayborne, Hopkins, Hunter, Isom, Jenson, Jessop, Johnson,Knell, Lambeth, Laney, Lee, Leigh, Little, Lunt, Martineau, McFarlane, Meise, Merrill, Middleton, Morgan, Morris, Muir, Muria, Murry, Nelson, Nixon, Palmer, Parker, Pearsall, Perkins, Perry, Pinnock, Pogson, Popkess, Pryor, Role, Rollo, Sheppersop, Sherratt, Shuratt, Slack, Stapley, Smith, Spiking, Stephens, Stones, Stubbs, Talt, Thomas, Thorley, Togua, Unthank, Urie, Walker, Watson, Webster, West, Whittaker, Whitter, Wiley, Willden, Wilkinson, Williams, Willis, Wingate, Wixom and many, many more.

Some of the articles are easier to read than others, please consider that they are nearly 100 years old.

Copyright 2015

ISBN-13: 978-1515266211

ISBN-10: 1515266214

EXTRACTS of a letter from Elder George A. Smith, dated

Cedar City, Iron County, }
March 25, 1851. }

PRESIDENT BRIGHAM YOUNG:—By the express which starts to-day for your city, I send you a few items regarding our situation, location, and the facilities which surround us for our operations; though by the brethren you may learn many minute particulars I have not space to give you: for these I refer you to Bro. Anson Call and Capt. A. L. Fullmer. We are progressing rapidly in our farming operations, having already sown four hundred acres of wheat, and they will probably amount to one thousand. The soil is considered of the first quality, both upland and wire grass, by our best farmers—no division of opinion regarding soil. There have been about sixteen hundred acres surveyed, and the probability is that it will nearly all be cultivated this season. Our fencing and public buildings are in a state of progression, as well as private buildings composing the fort. This will be enclosed either by buildings or pickets by the first of July. It is in a good state of forwardness, considering the amount of labor bestowed upon making roads into kanyons, and our farming operations.

There seems to be a good feeling pervading the camp. We have done but little in making explorations; but from what we have found of lime, stone, alum, and timber, the easy access to each give indications of this becoming a rapid growing settlement. Our saw-mill is also in a state of forwardness, and will soon be in operation; but we need a good mill-wright here very much.

The weather, since our arrival, has been very favorable; but at present the ground is dry. The health of the camp is good, and two children have been added to our numbers; they are doing well.

If some thirty or more could be induced to come on this spring, before high water, we could then be secure; and I would recommend Bro. Call as a suitable person to bring the company through as captain or pilot.

Many of the brethren are very anxious to return early and get their families before winter; and if this addition could be made to our numbers, they could be released. I had some thoughts of coming through to conference myself; but a violent cold prevents, and I trust to the brethren to give you much information: some of them, however, will plead very hard to be released from returning; but I see no reason why a man who can live like a prince at home, should be released any more than a poor man; but each fill his mission.

Some in camp complain of their bread stuff being short. I presume it will be before harvest, though the harvest will probably be early. There is considerable wheat up; some barley, and looks well. Those who come on will do well to bring a supply of provisions, as we may have to subsist on meat alone before our harvest.

Walker informs us that Brown was killed by Toquan's band of Pictes on Big Muddy. In the fight with Capt. Winters, (an emigrant company), there were two Indians killed, and two wounded.

I have only been called upon to lay hands upon two persons since I left the city, and one of these was from pain from the bite of a dog; the other from over exertion and loss of strength;—they were immediately relieved. How different from times at Nauvoo!

GEO. A. SMITH.

MARRIED,

On the 12th of March, 1852, at Cedar City, Iron county, by Elder Matthew Carruthers, Mr. ROBERT HENRY and Miss MARY Ross, all of Cedar City; this being the first marriage ceremony celebrated in Iron county; (not the last.)

MARRIED,

On Thursday, March 25th, 1852, Parowan, Iron Co., by bishop Lewis, Mr. HENRY LUNT, of Birmingham, Eng., to Miss ELLEN WHITTAKER, late of Bolton, Eng. Both are residents of Cedar City.

Can earth present a lovelier sight,

And more like heaven than this?

Kind angels love to view the scene;

E'en oft would drop a kiss.

In North Kanyon Ward, Sunday, April 4, 1852, by John Stoker, GEORGE W. HANCOCK and EMMA HANCOCK, both of this place.

Their union be sweet, their hearts joined in one,
And love, pure, celestial, endure with the sun.

Dear Bro. Richards:—A few days ago we had a visit from the Toquer Captain, (or Black Chief,) so called by the South Pah Eed Indians, with about thirty of his warriors. They were from the Santa Clara and Rio Virgin country, and wished to hold a council with me upon the subject of forming a settlement in their country. I was absent from Parowan at the time, which to them was quite a disappointment, but fortunately, though accidentally, I fell in with them on their return near Coal Creek. They met me with the greatest warmth of Indian friendship, they all recognized me on sight, and said that I had been in their country, and promised to settle there. They wished to know if I still intended to comply with my promises, and how soon; I replied, whenever the Big Captain told me to go, perhaps it would be within four moons. They expressed great anxiety to have us settle among them, so they could "manika" (work) for the Mormons, like the Pah Eeds at Parowan.

The settlements at Parowan and Cedar City are in a flourishing condition; crops of almost every kind look well. The Iron company have labored under many disadvantages which are common in every new country, which has caused the work to move on slowly, yet the most of the brethren are determined never to cease their exertions until iron is made, and I believe they will accomplish it. The health of the saints is good in general. The spirit that led them to form this colony in the depth of winter, and that too under many adverse circumstances, is still here to unite the people together in their exertions to build up the Kingdom of God.

The natives in general are peaceable and well disposed, though some few are reckless and have need to be looked after. On Saturday, the 7th inst., one of those characters, a brother to Ow-wan-nop the Chief, came into my house in my absence, and was very saucy. Mrs. Lee bid him leave which he took as an insult, and instead of going out, struck her over her left eye with a piece of plank, leaving the skull bare about four inches. He struck her three blows, which used up his present weapon; he then seized a stick about three inches over, and aimed the fatal blow, when she was rescued by br. Wm. Barton, who caught the blow with one hand, and struck him two licks with the other hand, almost dislocating his neck; this ended the affray.' It is but due to Mrs. Lee to say that she fought like a heroine to the last moment, although her face and clothes were bathed in crimson gore. This transaction caused a doleful sensation throughout the camp for a little season.

This morning Ow-wan-nop, the chief, and a Pahvante chief, together with a few of their leading men met in council at my house. President Smith, Br Steele, Br. Lunt, and myself told them through my boy, who was our interpreter, that we were not mad with all the Indians, but were not pleased with the Indian who had abused our squaws, and if they wanted to be our friends, they must bring and tie him to the liberty pole, and give him forty lashes, well put on, and we would then be satisfied for that and other offences which he had previously committed on other females. We sat in council about two hours, and fully explained our intentions and feelings toward them. They readily promised to comply with our proposition and be friendly.

Accordingly, about sun-down the two chiefs, with twenty-two of their braves, marched the criminal to the spot appointed, armed with their bows and arrows. We told them that if they were our friends, they would leave their weapons at their camps as a token of their sincerity; they were disarmed in a moment, and two men were appointed to convey them without the Fort. The victim was then stripped and tied to the liberty pole, and with a raw hide lash doubled five times, received thirty-eight lashes, pretty well tucked on. He was whipped by his own brother the chief, who, while repeating the blows, said, "you would not hear, your ears were stopped up, but now I will open them so that they will always stay open." He then told him that if he attempted to shoot our cattle in retaliation, he would kill him. We told the chief to stop, that we were satisfied.

The pipe of friendship was then smoked, though previously a prayer was offered to the Great Spirit by one of their chiefs, as an evidence of their innocence of the misdemeanor alleged to one of their tribe. In return for their prompt compliance with our request, the chiefs were presented with a shirt each and the braves with bread. A greater degree of fidelity in the performance of their promises was never before witnessed among any of the Indian tribes, and they set an example worthy to be followed by many of the more civilized and enlightened whites.

With grateful feelings, I subscribe myself your friend and brother in the new and everlasting Covenant,

JOHN D. LEE.

Deseret News
October 24, 1852

PAROWAN, IRON COUNY, U. T.,
October 24th, 1852.

MR. EDITOR.—We are happy to inform you that all is health, peace and prosperity in this County; the people continue to enjoy a friendly intercourse with the Indians.

The California Emigrant companies have generally left for California in good spirits. J. D Lee has commenced building a Fort and cattle Corral, on Ash Creek, a tributary of the Rio Virgin, some 22 miles South of Cedar City.

H. G. Sherwood the Ex. Surveyor General and company left this city for California, on Wednesday.
Very respectfully, yours &c.,
GEO. A. SMITH.

Deseret News
November 10, 1852

MARRIED.
At Cedar City, November 10th, 1852, by Henry Lunt, Mr. DAVID MURIA, and Miss MARY MUIR, both late from Scotland.

EDITOR OF THE NEWS:—

Dear Sir,—I left Parowan February 20th., and arrived in this city on the first day of March, in company with President Henry Lunt, Col. James A. Little, Major J. D. Lee, Samuel West, James H. Martineau, Silas and Jesse Smith, and others.

We arrived in safety, having had a prosperous journey to this place, although we encountered several storms and severe cold. The roads were very bad on account of deep snow on the mountains and mud in the valleys. The past winter has been the coldest we have had in Iron County since its settlement; the thermometer fell to 16 degrees below zero.

It is a general time of health in Iron County, there having been but one death at Parowan for the last six months, and that was the death of sister Sarah Morse, relict of Dr. William A. Morse, who died at Parowan, January, 1853. There have been but two or three deaths at Cedar City during the last winter, one of which I will note, namely, the death of bro. Cyrus Wingate, one of the missionaries appointed at the October Conference.

The saints are well united in Iron County, trying to carry out the instructions from headquarters. We held meetings on Sunday, in the day and evening, and on Thursday evenings. We have also set apart the first Thursday of each month for fasting and prayer. Our meet-ings have been well attended during the winter, and a great number of the brethren and sisters have renewed their covenants by baptism. We have day and evening schools at Parowan and Cedar City, for learning the English, Spanish, German, and Indian languages.

The brethren that were sent to Iron County last fall to strengthen the settlements, and learn the Indian language, have enjoyed the spirit of their mission and manifested a spirit to build up the kingdom. They have all prepared themselves with comfortable houses. The Pi-edes have been friendly, as usual, and manifest a desire to live in peace with the saints. Ammon and about twenty-five of the Utes have been with us most of the time during the winter. When they first came among us they wished us to buy their friendship with provisions, clothing, &c., but finding we would not come to their terms, they concluded to trade their buck-skins and work for their bread. They have mani-fested a friendly disposition towards us.

On the 6th of February the man on the look-out at Parowan reported a company, supposed to be Indians, coming into the north end of the valley, twenty miles distant from Parowan, about eleven o'clock on the morning of the 7th. Colonel John C. Fremont, with nine white men and twelve Delaware Indians, arrived in Paro-wan in a state of starvation; one of his men had fallen dead from his horse the day previous, and several more must inevitably have shared his fate had they not had succour that day. They reported that they had eaten twenty-seven bro-ken down animals; that when a horse or mule could go no farther, it was killed and divided out, giving one-half to the Delawares, and the other to the Colonel and his men; the hide was cut in pieces and cast lots for. After the bones had been made into soup, they were burned, and car-ried along by the men for luncheon. The en-trails were shaken, and then made into soup, together with the feet and eyes; thus using up the whole mule. They stated they had travelled forty-five days living on this kind of fair.

Although Colonel Fremont was considered by the people an enemy to the saints, and had no money, he was kindly treated and supplied on credit with provisions for himself and men, while at Parowan, and fitted out with animals and provisions to pursue his journey, and went on his way rejoicing on the 20th of February.

The Colonel was sanguine, in his opinion, that he had found the best route for the Great National Railway.

The Honorable Secretary A. W. Babbit ar-rived here on the evening of the 7th, and left on the 8th, having been out five days and a half.

Your brother in the gospel covenant,

J. C. L. SMITH.

MARRIED:

At Box Elder on the 13th of April, 1854, by Elder John Morgan, JEREMIAH W. THOM-AS of Cedar City, and Miss MARY THOMAS of Box Elder, both natives of Wales.

Iron County.

Elder T. D. Brown writes from Cedar City to Elder Joseph Cain, under date of December 30th, that six coke ovens were in full operation, and at date the new furnace was receiving its first charge, and the blast was to be put on that evening; also, that Snow and Boznell's grist mill would soon be in operation. Peace, prosperity, union, and plenty are enjoyed by the residents of that region.

During the past week the weather has been delightful, and the snow is rapidly and constantly wasting under the warm rays of the sun.

Up to noon of the 17th inst. no word from Eas...

MARRIED:

In Cedar City, Dec 30, 1854, by Elder Isaac C. Haight, Mr. JOHN McFARLANE—from Scotland—and Miss ANN CHATTERLY—from England:—Also

AGENTS.

The following persons are requested to act as Agents for the Deseret News Vol. 5:

GREAT SALT LAKE COUNTY.

Kanyon Creek Ward	A. O. Smoot.
Gardner's Mill, Mill Creek	Robt. Gardner.
Mill Creek	Alex. Hill.
Big Cottonwood	Lyman Stevens.
South Cottonwood Ward	And'w. Calhoon.
Union	S. Richards.
Drapersville	Wm. Draper.
West Jordan Ward	Joseph Harker.

TOOELE COUNTY.

Richville	J. Rowberry.
Tooele City	Eli B. Kelsey.
Grantsville	Thos. H. Clark.

DAVIS COUNTY.

Stoker	John Stoker.
Centerville	A. B. Cherry.
Farmington	Jas. Leathead.
Kaysville	Saml. Henderson.

WEBER COUNTY.

Ogden City	J. G. Browning.
Bingham's Ward	E. Bingham.
South Weber	Thomas Kington.
East Weber	A. Wordsworth.
North Ogden Ward	Thomas Dunn.
North Willow Creek	C. W. Hubbard.
Youngsville	Eli H. Pierce.

UTAH COUNTY.

Provo City	D. Carter.
Springville	Aaron Johnson.
Lehi City	David Evans.
Mountainville	Isaac Houston.
Cedar Valley	Allen Weeks.
American Fork	L. E. Harrington.
Pleasant Grove	Wm. G. Sterrett.
Palmyra	John W. Berry.
Payson	Chas. B. Hancock.
Juab County	T. B. Foot.
San Pete County	George Peacock.
Millard County	S. P. Hoyt.

IRON COUNTY.

Parowan	J. C. L. Smith.
Cedar City	Isaac C. Haight.
Washington County	John D. Lee.
San Bernardino, Cal.	D. M. Thomas.

GRASSHOPPERS, &c.—Hon. Calvin C. Pendleton, arrived in this city from Iron co., on the 24th.; general health among the people; the grasshoppers have destroyed all the grain at Paragoonah, nine-tenths at Parowan; all the wheat at Fort Johnson, and about one-tenth of the grain at Cedar city; the grain at Harmony is uninjured.

The bursting of a cloud on the mountains about the first of June, washed away the house of Elder Benjamin R. Hulse in Cedar city, and injured several others. The fields look like a desert and every separate bench appears to be hatching out fresh crops of grasshoppers. Several companies have started to the 'Pangwitch' lake, on fishing excursions. The water is lower than has ever been known before, and but a small portion of the land resown can possibly be watered. A small party has also started to the Santa Clara mission to plant corn. The people of Iron co. are in first rate Spirits. The Public Square at Parowan city (10 acres) has been planted with potatos in the hopes that the united efforts of men, women, and children, chickens, ducks, turkies, &c., &c., may save a sufficiency to have occasionally a little potato soup next winter.

At Cedar city, Jan. 4th, 1856, by Bishop Philip K. Smith, Mr. NEPHI JOHNSON and Miss MANDANA R. MERRILL, both of that city.

Improvements in the South.

In Washington county John Hamblin and company are building a stone fort on the Santa Clara, and intend entering at once into raising cotton in the warm rich bottoms bordering on that stream, and probably, at an early day, sugar cane, olives and other fruits of warm climes.

Jehu Blackburn & Co. have erected a splendid saw mill in Pine valley, about 25 miles S. W. from Cedar city and near an extensive tract of pine timber of superior quality, equal to that at Parowan.

Peter Shirts is erecting a grist mill at Canarra. The above named substantial improvements speak well for the energy of the settlers in our most southern county.

In Iron county Messrs. J. C. Haight and Simpkins are hurrying forward the work upon their carding machine and woolen factory in Cedar city, and anticipate having it in readiness for this season's clip of wool.

Another saw mill, on an extensive scale, is in progress at Cedar, and the iron on hand is being cast into flat-irons and other useful articles.

The Iron Company have cast some beautiful machinery, intended to supercede the use of Coal creek for motive power, and are accumulating a large amount of material, in readiness for future operations.

Deseret News
April 16, 1856

Cedar City, Iron County.

During the past winter, snow has fallen as follows:

Nov. 1st, 6 inches; 14th, 1 inch; 15th, 2 inches; 23rd, 3 inches.

Dec. 2nd, 1 inch; 7th, 2 1-2 inches; 12th, 4 inches; 22nd, 3 inches; 23rd, 2 inches.

Jan. 24th, 3 inches; 25th, 2 inches;.

Feb. 1st, 1 inch; 4th, 2 inches; 5th, 1 inch; 21st, 6 inches; 26th, 10 inches.

Observations by　　SOLOMON CHAMBERLAIN.

Deseret News
April 1, 1857

MARRIED:

At Grantsville, March 22d, by Bishop Thomas H. Clark, Mr. JAMES WRATHALL and Mrs. MARY MONRO, from Preston, Lancashire, England.

[Millenial Star, please copy.]

At Cedar city, Feb. 11th, by Elder I. C. Haight, RICHARD PALMER and ANN WILEY, both of that place.

Deseret News
August 4, 1858

MARRIED:

In Cedar City, on the 20th ult., by Prest. Isaac C. Haight, Mr. BERIAH BAUGH and Miss MARY ANDERSON, alias Christina Maria Togur, both of the above city.

Toquerville.

From a letter written by J. T. Willis, dated March 11th, we learn that the people in that small settlement, consisting of only 19 families, were prospering remarkably well, and busy in getting in wheat and other kinds of grain, fencing, etc.

It has been represented that the best molasses from Chinese sugar cane made in the Territory was produced at that place last season, and preparations are being made to cultivate that useful and remunerative article very extensively the coming season.

This settlement was commenced last year, and is about 40 miles from Cedar city, on the new road to Washington and the Santa Clara.

On looking over our mail lists, we find that every family in this new and thriving little settlement has subscribed for the current volume of the *Deseret News*.

Died:

In Cedar city, Iron county, on the 14th of October, LYDIA, wife of Charles Hopkins, Esq.

FROM CEDAR CITY.

CEDAR CITY, Iron co., Feb. 2, 1860.

EDITOR DESERET NEWS:

*　　*　　*　　*　　*　　*　　*

On the morning of the 15th ult. we received two slight shocks of an earthquake. The winter thus far has been mild and pleasant—there having been only two small snow storms. A great deal of out door work has been done, and the people are quite busy hauling fencing for our new field. We should like Uncle Sam to let us have a mail route through this country, for we want to know how things are moving in other parts of the world.

M. SLACK.

Married:

In Cedar city, Iron co., on March 26, by Prest. Henry Lunt, CHARLES WILLDEN, jun., and Miss EMMA SMITH.

Information Wanted.

Frank Pitman, of this city, late from Southampton, England, wishes to learn the whereabouts of his uncle, David King, also from Southampton, who came to this Territory four or five years since. Any information that will disclose the place of residence of the said King, will be thankfully received by the young man, who wishes to find his relative.

R. V. Morris, of Cedar city, Iron co., Utah, also wishes to hear from Mr. George Davies, late of Dowlais, Glamorganshire, Wales; if he communicates with him, it will be to his advantage.

Married:

In this city, on the 27th, by Elder Levi Stewart, Mr. CHARLES ADDISON NORTH, of Mill creek, and Miss ALBERTINA JOSEPHINE BATTLESON, of this city.

In Cedar city, Iron co., U. T., 25th Dec., 1860, by Bishop Henry Lunt, Mr. WM. WALKER and Miss JEANETTE CORRY.

FROM IRON COUNTY.

CEDAR CITY, Iron Co., U. T. }
January 30, 1861. }

EDITOR DESERET NEWS:

DEAR SIR—I take pleasure in dropping a few lines to you to inform you how we are getting along as a settlement. We have good health generally and blessed with peace and plenty. We enjoyed ourselves well during our Christmas festivities, and nothing occurred to disturb the peace of the community—the best of feelings prevailing throughout.

The weather was very mild until Christmas, but since then we have experienced very severe cold weather, and there has been some eight or ten inches of snow on the ground till recently. Within the last few days, it has been thawing considerably in the day time.—At Harmony, the snow has been two feet deep on the level and, on the north side of the fort, the snow drift was level with the roofs of the houses.

The brethren here are now very busily engaged pulling down the old meeting house in the old fort, hauling rock and preparing for the erection of a Social Hall, which, when completed will be used for a meeting house until we can build one, which we expect to do next fall, as we have none to meet in at present, except a school room, in this new town.

Not having seen any report from the corresponding secretary of the Southern Auxiliary of the Deseret Agricultural and Manufacturing Society, I will just say that there was a Fair held in Parowan the latter end of October last, in which there was a good display of home manufactured cloth and other articles; also, fair specimens of stock as well as a good variety of vegetables.

There are about 700 head of sheep in the settlement, and about 3,000 yards of cloth has been spun and wove within the last year.— We have over a 1,000 bushels of wheat in the Lord's Store House and near y 500 belonging to the News office; so you see we are greatly blessed in this far off settlement. Our meetings are well attended, and the people feel exceedingly well as a general thing. I pray that we may have wisdom and listen to the counsels of the servants of God to store up and take care of our grain, so that we may not see want, should a day of famine come and that we may ever feel to realize that we are dependant upon our Heavenly Father for every blessing we enjoy.

Your brother in the Gospel,

HENRY LUNT.

Deseret News
April 17, 1861

A MOTHER'S WISH.—Mrs. Spiking wishes to hear from her son, BENJAMIN SPIKING, who has been absent many years, and is supposed to be in California, if living. Any information that will enable her to discover his whereabouts, will be thankfully received by his mother at Cedar City, Iron county, Utah Territory. California papers please copy.

Deseret News
January 29, 1862

Married:

In Cedar city, on the 13th inst., by Bishop Henry Lunt, JOHN L. JONES and RACHEL SIMKINS.

Deseret News
February 26, 1862

SNOW STORM IN SOUTHERN UTAH.—Reports and letters from the South represent that after the floods in that part of the Territory subsided, there was a big snow storm the last of January, or first of February, extending throughout Iron and Washington counties, which at Cedar City fell to the depth of from twelve to fifteen inches, and in places below the rim of the basin, where snow seldom falls to any considerable depth; it is represented as having been nearly a foot deep, but it soon melted away.

Deseret News
May 28, 1862

Married:

In Great Salt Lake City, May 16th, by Elder D. H. Wells, Mr. WILLIAM SCOGGING and Miss SUSAN PAGE, late of London. [Millennial Star, please copy.

At Cedar City, Iron county, April 27th, by Bishop Henry Lunt, JAMES BULLOCK and MARY BLADEN.

Deseret News
June 8, 1864

Died:

In Cedar city, Iron county, May 19, SARAH JOYCE COX, aged 45 years.

Deseret News
June 18, 1862

Mail Lettings.

The route 14603, from Cedar city, by Summit, Hamilton Fort, Harmony, Toquerville, Washington and Tonaquint, to Santa Clara, 70 miles and back once a week, to O. P. Rockwell, $800.

Deseret News
July 27, 1864

Died:

In Cedar city, July 8, of inflammation, HENRY ANDERS, son of Haugt and Ellen Neilsen, aged 5 months and 5 days.

Deseret News
January 25, 1865

Married:

At Cedar city, Iron co., by Bishop Henry Lunt, Mr. JOSEPH S. HUNTER Jr. and Miss ELIZA CATHERINE PINNOCK, formerly of London. [Mil. Star please copy.

Deseret News
February 22, 1865

In Cedar City, Jan. 2, of child-bed fever, MARY, wife of James Frodsham and daughter of William and Elizabeth Shepperson. She was born in Nottingham, England, Sep. 15, 1828.

Deseret News
June 7, 1866

In Cedar City, Iron Co., May 12, ELIZA B., daughter of John V. and Mary Ann Adams, aged 3 years and 12 days.

Deseret News
June 28, 1866

In Cedar City, Iron Co., (date not given) MARY ANN, daughter of John and Cristenna Sherratt, aged 4 years, 4 months and 9 days.

Deseret News
April 17, 1867

Died.

In Cedar City, Iron County, March 17, MARY, wife of Joseph H. Smith, aged 11 years and 10 days—[Mil. Star please copy.

CEDAR VALLEY, June 11, 1868.

Editor Deseret News.—We have had an abundance of rain this last Spring. Three or four days ago it turned warm, and it seems that Summer has set in in good earnest. The brethren seem to be in good spirits, in spite of the destruction the locusts are making. It is thought there will be some grain raised here; although some that have planted will not raise anything.

The farmers are planting all the corn they can; thinking perhaps that it will escape the ravages of those little pests if the wheat does not. Our meetings have been well attended this Spring. Brothers Geo. A Smith and A. M. Musser visited us a few Sundays ago and preached to us. There is nothing that seems to do so much good, or strengthens our faith more, than to have our brethren, who stand in authority over us to visit us, and preach the words of life and salvation to us. The Sunday after Bros. Geo. A. Smith and Musser were here, our Bishop David Evans and Br. Karren, of Lehi City, held a two days' meeting with us. They spoke upon the various texts given to us to preach from; more particularly upon Home Manufacture, and emigration. We all enjoyed ourselves exceedingly well.

Last Sunday, the High Priests held meeting here. Jas. Rodeback is President of the High Priests here, and at Fairfield also. The sisters have organized a Relief Society, and are taking hold with a spirit, that is calculated to do a vast amount of good. God bless the sisters in their efforts to relieve the poor and suffering of God's people, everywhere where it may be their lot to labor. Our Sunday School is prospering finely; we have over one hundred scholars that attend regularly.

There is some little stir in regard to the Railroad. Some are making arrangements to go to work immediately on the road. We are decidedly in a prosperous condition in this place. In consequence of the prospect of obtaining material, for building purposes, at very low figures; several of the brethren are making arrangements to build frame houses this summer and fall. Higly, Phippin & Dayton are running a Blandy's sawmill in the North Cañon eight miles north of here. Bro. Wilcox is building a stationary saw mill here, and expects to have it running by the first of September. Lumber can be obtained for one half what it could be had for heretofore.

There is nothing that seems to afford us so much pleasure as the reading of your valuable paper, and there is nothing that seems to create as much grumbling and dissatisfaction as to call at the Post Office, at the time our paper should be there, and find that, through the carelessness of somebody, our papers have gone to Cedar City or some other place. Such is the case often. Sometimes our papers are a month coming here from Salt Lake City. It is very annoying to us indeed. Still, we live in hopes that the time will come when our mail matter will come to us when it is directed properly.

Yours truly,

GEO W. THURMOND.

Deseret News
December 19, 1869

At Cedar City, December 19th, 1869, at 2 a.m., of cold on the lungs, George William, infant son of James and Mary Davis, from London, England, aged 1 year, 1 month and 25 days.
Mill. Star please copy.

Deseret News
March 26, 1872

At the residence of his son Homer, Cedar City, Iron County, March 20th, JOHN DUNCAN, at the age of 92 years and 20 days. He was a member of Zion's Camp.

Deseret News
February 20-22, 1873

At Cedar City, January 20, of consumption, SARAH, wife of David Williams, aged 50 years.

At Cedar City, Feb. 22nd, MARY ISOM, (formerly of Birmingham, England,) wife of Smith B. Thurston, in the 30th year of her age.

She leaves a husband and four children. She was much respected by all who knew her.—COM.

Deseret News
August 20, 1873

OBITUARY.

PETER MUIR FIFE was born near Pathlad, Scotland, April 5th, 1805; died at Hamilton's, six miles south of Cedar City, Iron county, Utah Territory, July 31st, 1873, aged 68 years and 3 months.

Bro. Fife embraced the gospel when first introduced in Scotland, and shortly afterwards left Scotland and came to Nauvoo, where he walked, talked and became acquainted with the Prophet of the last dispensation, Joseph Smith. In company with Elder Geo. D. Watt he spent a short time preaching the gospel in the State of Virginia; passed through the mobbings and drivings of the Saints in Illinois; gathered to Winter Quarters; was one of the Mormon Battalion, and when released in California wended his way with others to Salt Lake City; a short time afterwards, with Elder George Q. Cannon and others, was very successful in accomplishing a short mission to California; on his return was called upon to locate in Iron county in 1850, but through ill health did not respond till 1851, in which county he remained until the day of his death, honored and respected by all who were familiar with his life; he died in full faith, believing in and awaiting a glorious resurrection. He had failings, as we all have, but his good works live in the hearts of the Saints, whilst his failings are forgotten. His great faith and confidence in the Prophet Joseph, President Young and the leaders generally remained unwavering. He left a wife and six children. A great number of the brethren and sisters from Cedar City, with the choir, went to Hamilton's and followed the remains of Brother Fife to the cemetery in Cedar City, where they were deposited.—COM.

Deseret News
March 25, 1874

DIED.

Suddenly, at her residence, Cedar City, March 3rd, CAROLINE ELIZA, wife of Christopher J. Arthur, and daughter of Isaac C. and Eliza Anne S. Haight.

Her death was so sudden and unexpected that her sisters living but a few rods distant from the house of deceased failed to arrive in time to see her expire. Sister Caroline was born December 5th, 1837, in the old town of Sempranius (afterwards called Moravia), Cayuga County, New York. She was fifteen months old when her parents embraced the gospel. Two years afterwards her parents moved to Nauvoo. She was baptized when eight years old.

Traveled with the Saints in their drivings from Nauvoo to Winter Quarters, and in 1847 came to Salt Lake City in President B. Young's company. In 1853, with her parents, moved to Cedar City, her father being called to superintend the iron works at this place. Was married to C. J. Arthur

in December, 1854. She was the mother of eight children, four of whom have passed behind the vail, and four remain with their father. She was a sister of unimpeachable character, a kind and affectionate wife and mother, and was much appreciated, which was exemplified at the funeral by the large concourse in attendance.—COM.

At Cedar City, April 14th, after an illness of about three months, ABEL LAMB, aged 73 years.

Brother A. Lamb was the son of Enes and Anna Lamb; born March 9th, 1801, in Rowe, Vermont; joined the Church of Jesu Christ of Latter-day Saints in 1833, in Livana, Livingston Co., New York; soon after was appointed to preside over the Church in that place, where he remained until 1836; then moved with his family to Kirtland, Ohio; there was ordained a High Priest under the hands of Don Carlos Smith; in 1888 removed with the Saints into Davis Co., Missouri; soon after was driven by mob violence from that State, then settled in Illinois; soon after received a call to preach the Gospel twenty miles east of Quincy, near Columbus, Adams Co., and built up a branch of the Church of 725 members; a stake of Zion was organized there, called Mount Hope, over which he presided for about three years; about that time the stakes of Zion were broken up, and the Saints were called into Nauvoo; was one of twenty-five that were at the dedication of the Temple in Nauvoo; in the Spring of 1846, with his family, left the State of Illinois and worked his way to Salt Lake City, reaching that place, September 10, 1850; moved to Cedar City about three years ago; in July, 1873, was ordained a Patriarch, under the hands of President B. Young, G. A. Smith and G. Q. Cannon. He died as he had lived, rejoicing in the principles of the Gospel, expiring seemingly without a struggle or groan. His funeral was numerously attended.—COM.

Deseret News
June 16, 1874

At the residence of his father, Hamilton, near Cedar City, Iron County, June 16, of consumption, SAMUEL HAMILTON, of Harrisburgh, Washington Co., son of John and Mary Hamilton.

Deceased was born at Hillsborough, County Down, Ireland, June 13, 1832; emigrated to Nauvoo in the Spring of 1843, with his father, mother and brother; in the Fall of 1850 arrived in Salt Lake City; the same Fall, in President George A. Smith's company, went down and settled Parowan, Iron Co.; from that time to the present, with the exception of three and a half years in California, spent his days in Iron and Washington counties, and was much respected by those who associated with and knew him. He has left two wives, seven children, father, mother, and brother, and a large circle of friends for a season, who anticipate a glorified re-union through faithfulness and fidelity to the principles of the Gospel of Christ.

The funeral ceremonies were held at Father Hamilton's, and were attended by several of the brethren and sisters of Cedar City and Kanarra.—Com.

Deseret News
November 9, 1874

DIED.

At Cedar City, Iron County, November 9th, 1874, of inflammation of the bladder, JaMES BULLOCH, formerly of Paisley, Scotland, aged 65 years.

Bro. Bulloch embraced the Gospel in his native land in 1839; emigrated to the United States in 1848, and settled in Iowa, where he remained a short time; then moved to Gravoi, near St. Louis, where he lost his wife by cholera; in 1851 emigrated with his two sons and one daughter to the Valley of Salt Lake, where he resided one month; then moved down to Cedar City, as one of the pioneers of its first settlement, where he remained up to the time of his death.

Brother Bulloch was one of the faithful Latter-day Saints, ever trying to perform his part in the good work. He had many friends. His enemies were unknown.—Com.

Deseret News
February 10, 1875

CEDAR CITY, Feb. 10, 1875.

Editor Deseret News:

This is one of the most open winters that we have had since Cedar was settled, with hard frosty nights, and clear, pleasant, sunny days, with scarcely any snow or rain up to date.

Quite a number are engaged in hauling rock for our new meeting house, while others are hauling fire wood as if it were October.

There is much sickness in the city at the present time, mostly among the young. Two were taken to an early grave last week, one a fine, promising daughter of Amos Thornton's, of Pinto Creek, who was here attending school and learning to play the piano; the other an infant son of David Williams. The old proverb says—"A green Yule makes a fat kirkyard."

Last summer was a dry season here, with but little rain in the valley, while on the mountains there was heavy and continuous showers, causing fierce destructive floods, which rolled down our canyons, sweeping everything before them, destroying roads, bridges, and crossings and making travel up the canyon for a time almost impossible, except on horse back; doing considerable damage to the farming interest, in washing away or choking up the main ditches leading from the creek to the fields; also to the mill company, in preventing them from hauling the greater portion of their lumber, there being at the present time over one hundred thousand feet piled up near the saw mill.

Most of our crops were very light last season, corn and potatoes not being more than one-fourth of what was raised the year before; wheat, oats and barley were about two-thirds of a crop. We had an excellent season for fruit of all kinds, the trees being so heavily laden that they had to be propped up to enable them to bear their precious burdens. Cedar at that time was one dense mass of foliage of fruit and shade trees, presenting a pleasing contrast to the bold, rugged precipitous hills on the east, and the wild uninviting sage plain stretching for miles westward. It seems but as yesterday that the sight of an apple caused joy and rejoicing to our children, but now, thanks to a kind Providence, good counsel, and perseverance, our orchards are a source of much profit and many luxuries.

We do not hear so much talk of late about silver mines and their alluring prospects of great wealth with but little labor, the making of iron and the extension of the Utah Southern occupying the people's attention the more. One of the best mines we own here is our sheep herd: the total income from which last year, in wool and lambs, was nineteen thousand (19,000) pounds of wool, and two thousand six hundred and nine (2,609) lambs. The above number of lambs was raised from two thousand four hundred (2,400) ewes. When the manager of our sheep-herd, Mr. Francis Webster, was in Salt Lake City, last fall, he bought from Mr. Kilpatrick, of Vermont, nine head of full blooded Spanish Merino sheep, seven bucks and two ewes, and there is a very good prospect of further improvement in our sheep.

We have two good day schools and a Sunday school here, which are doing much good among the young. Respectfully,
THOMAS THORLEY.

DIED
Deseret News
March 3, 1875

At Cedar City, Iron County, February 6th, 1875, of inflammation of the lungs, DAVID HENRY, son of David and Amelia Williams, aged 11 months.

Also at the same place, February 9th, of the same complaint, WILLIAM ALIGUR, son of William and Margaret Unthank, aged 2 years, 6 months, and 10 days.

The Lee Trial.—Our correspondent at Beaver reports by telegraph last evening that the jury in the Lee case is full and sworn in chief. Their names are Josephus Wade, J. C. Herston, David Rogers, Isaac Duffin, James C. Robinson, Joseph Knight, Paul Price, George F. Jarvis, John Brewer, Wilton Daley John C. Duncan, Ute Perkins, Sen.; eight "Mormons" and four "Gentiles." The prosecution were to proceed to introduce testimony today. If the verdict should be "guilty," Lee's counsel rely upon the fact that the indictment does not appear by record to have been presented in open court, and the changing of the February term to July by the governor.

BEAVER, July 23.

Editor Deseret News:

Carey opened the Lee case to the jury this morning, stating that the facts they expected to prove were that, eighteen years ago, a train of emigrants, consisting of nearly 150 persons was wending its way westward to find a home in California. It was said to be the best equipped and richest train that ever crossed the Rocky Mountains. About September 1st they arrived in Salt Lake City, camped on the Jordan, and tried to purchase supplies, which were refused them, and were ordered to leave their encampment. They passed south from Salt Lake, but were met with the answers at all the settlements that they could buy no supplies, till they reached Corn Creek.

Here they enquired where they might get supplies and a place to recruit their stock, they were answered at Mountain Meadows, at Parowan they were forbidden to enter the town, and they reached Mountain Meadows and camped about the 7th of September. Shots were fired into their camp, killing seven men and wounding fifteen. They looked out and saw the hills full of Indians, and immediately formed their wagons into a circle and dug a rifle pit. All day shots rattled into their wagons. These Indians were gathered from all the regions round. Who was the Indian Agent or Superintendent at that place? John D. Lee, and he gathered them up and influenced them to consummate this massacre.

The Indians, finding that they were fortified, sent a message to Cedar City that they must have aid. At Cedar a military order was issued, commanding men to Mountain Meadows, ostensibly for the purpose of burying the dead, whom it was said the Indians had massacred, but really to complete the foulest crime. On reaching the scene of conflict they raised the American flag, and then a white flag of truce, and decoyed the emigrants from their stronghold under a promise of protection from the Indians. They took them about half a mile and then, with their Indian allies, who were secreted for the purpose, murdered them all but seventeen children.

Who was commanding the militia in Utah at that time? Geo. A. Smith. From Fillmore down Wm. N. Dame, Col., of the Iron Military district, immediately under him.

Issac C. Haight, and J. M. Higbee, and these are to blame for it. Two or three hundred head of the cattle were turned out, branded with the mark John D. Lee. Part of the stock was driven to Salt Lake and sold. Lee and others went to Brigham Young, who told what disposal was to be made of the property, and also that they were to keep secrecy, not even to talk among themselves. But the secrets were too heavy to be borne and some of the guilty ones have divulged all this, which Carey says he has witnesses to prove. The defense will not open to the jury till they commence to introduce evidence.

Deseret News
July 30, 1875

DEPOSITIONS OF PRESIDENTS BRIGHAM YOUNG AND GEO. A. SMITH CONCERNING THE MOUNTAIN MEADOW MASSACRE.

Territory of Utah, } s.s.
Beaver Co.

In the Second Judicial District Court of the Territory of Utah, Beaver County.

The People &c ,
vs.
John D. Lee, Wm. } Indictment for murder, Sept. 16, 1857.
H. Dame, Isaac C.
Haight, et al.

Questions to be propounded to Brigham Young, on his examination as a witness in the case of John D. Lee and others on trial at Beaver City, this 30th of July, 1875.

1. State your age, the present condition of your health, and whether in its condition you could travel to attend, in person at Beaver, the court now sitting there? If not, state why not?

2. What offices, either ecclesiastical, civil or military, did you hold in the year 1857?

3. State the condition of affairs between the Territory of Utah and the Federal Government in the summer and fall of 1857.

4. Were there any United States judges here during the summer and fall of 1857?

5. State what you know about trains of emigrants passing through the Territory to the West, and particularly about a company from Arkansas en route for California, passing through this city in the summer or fall of 1857?

6. Was this Arkansas company of emigrants ordered away from Salt Lake City by yourself, or any one in authority under you?

7. Was any counsel or instructions given by any person to the citizens of Utah not to sell grain to or trade with the emigrant trains passing through Utah at that time; if so, what were those instructions and counsel?

8. When did your first hear of the attack and destruction of this Arkansas company at Mountain Meadows in September, 1857?

9. Did John D. Lee report to you at any time after this massacre what had been done at that massacre, and if so, what did you reply to him in reference thereto?

10. Did Philip Klingen Smith call at your office with John D. Lee, at the time of Lee making his report; and did you at that time order Smith to turn over the stock to Lee and order them not to talk about the massacre?

11. Did you ever give any direction concerning the property taken from the emigrants at the Mountain Meadow massacre, or know anything as to its disposition?

12. Why did you not as Governor institute proceedings forthwith to investigate that massacre and bring the guilty authors thereof to justice?

13. Did you, about the 10th of September, 1857, receive a communication from Isaac C. Haight or any other person of Cedar City, concerning a company of emigrants called the Arkansas company?

14. Have you that communication?

15. Did you answer this communication?

16. Will you state the substance of your letter to him?

The answers of Brigham Young to the interrogatories, hereto appended, were reduced to writing and were given after the said Brigham Young had been duly sworn to testify the truth in the above entitled cause and are as follows—

1. To the first interrogatory, he saith—

I am in my seventy-fifth year. It would be a great risk, both to my health and life, for me to travel to Beaver at this present time. I am and have been for sometime an invalid.

2. He saith—

I was the Governor of this Territory and ex-officio Superintendent of Indian affairs, and the President of the Church of Jesus Christ of Latter-day Saints during the year 1857.

3. He saith—

In May or June, 1857, the United States mails for Utah were stopped by the Government, all communication by mail was cut off. An army of the United States was *en route* for Utah with the ostensible design of destroying the Latter-day Saints, according to the reports that reached us from the East.

4. He saith—

To the best of my recollection there was no United States Judge here in the latter part of 1857.

5. He saith—

As usual emigrant trains were passing through our Territory for the West. I heard it rumored that a company from Arkansas, *en route* to California, had passed through the city.

6. He saith—

No, not that I know of—I never heard of any such thing, and certainly no such order was given by the then Acting Governor.

7. He saith—

Yes. Counsel and advice was given to the citizens not to sell grain to the emigrants to feed their stock, but to let them have sufficient for themselves, if they were out. The simple reason for this was that for several years our crops had been short, and the prospect was at that time that we might have trouble with the United States army, then en-route for this place, and we wanted to preserve the grain for food. The citizens of the Territory were counselled not to feed grain to their own stock. No person was ever punished or called in question for furnishing supplies to the emigrants, within my knowledge.

8. He saith—

I did not learn anything of the attack or destruction of the Arkansas company until sometime after it had occurred, then only by floating rumors.

9. He saith—

Within some two or three months after the massacre he called at my office and had much to say with regard to the Indians, their being stirred up to anger and threatening the settlements of the whites, and then commenced giving an account of the massacre. I told him to stop, as, from what I had already learned by rumor, I did not wish my feelings harrowed up with a recital of details.

10. He saith—

No. He did not call with John D. Lee, and I have no recollection of his ever speaking to me, nor I to him, concerning the massacre or anything pertaining to the property.

11. He saith—

No. I never gave any directions concerning the property taken from the company of emigrants at the Mountain Meadow massacre; nor did I know anything of that property or its disposal, and I do not to this day, except from public rumor.

12. He saith—

Because another governor had been appointed by the President of the United States, and was then on the way here to take my place, and I did not know how soon he might arrive; and because the United States judges were not in the Territory. Soon after Governor Cumming arrived I asked him to take Judge Cradlebaugh, who belonged to the Southern District, with him and I would accompany them with sufficient aid to investigate the matter and bring the offenders to justice.

13. He saith—

I did receive a communication from Isaac C. Haight or John D. Lee, who was then a farmer for the Indians.

14. He saith—

I have not. I have made diligent search for it, but cannot find it.

15. He saith—

I did, to Isaac C. Haight, who was then the acting President at Cedar City.

16. He saith—

Yes. It was to let this company of emigrants and all companies of emigrants pass through the country unmolested, and to allay the angry feelings of the Indians as much as possible. (Signed)

Deseret News
August 13, 1875

A Severe Hail Storm.

CEDAR CITY, Aug. 13.

Editor Deseret News:

A hail storm yesterday at Fort Hamilton, did serious damage; it destroyed about fifty acres of grain, besides damaging corn and potatoes. Some of the hail stones were as large as pigeon eggs.

HENRY LUNT.

Deseret News
November 12, 1875

Anniversary of the Settlement of Iron County.

CEDAR CITY, Nov. 12, 1875.

Editor Deseret News:

Bishop Henry Lunt, with his usual hospitality and kindness, for which he is proverbial throughout Southern Utah, invited to his house the few remaining pioneers of Cedar and also all that were pioneers to Iron County living in this place, to a pic-nic last evening, as it was the 24th anniversary of the settling of this place, and we had the substantials of life, but above all an interchange of good feelings, reminiscences of suffering and amusements, which generally happen in settling a new country among this people, with remembrances of the energy, kindness, fatherly love and masterly power of the late Bro. Geo. A. Smith, in opening up Southern Utah, also the prophecy of Elder P. P. Pratt in the winter of 1850 and 1851, as to the future prosperity of Southern Utah, which has been fulfilled to the very letter and more too. Peace to their remains until the glorious day of the resurrection. All seemed to rejoice in being spared to enjoy the blessings of God, through his kindness and goodness to them. Many were the expressions of thanksgiving for the goodness of God in preserving his people through all the many plots and schemes that his enemies have laid for his Saints, and also for our bishop's good wishes and feelings. All felt "God bless our Bishop" for his good feelings and anxiety to build up the kingdom of God, which all know is his desire.

All is peace and prosperity and a bright future before us.
With due respect,
ONE OF THE PIONEERS
of Cedar.

DIED.

At the residence of Bishop Henry Lunt, Cedar City, December 31st, 1875, of asthma, WILLIAM PEARSALL.

Deceased was born August 29th, 1817, in Birmingham, England; embraced the Gospel in his native town, in March, 1844; was baptized by Elder James Bailey; labored assiduously to promulgate the principles of our holy religion in the streets and by-ways, and many remember him for his integrity and zeal; emigrated to Utah in the fall of 1862; after a short rest in Salt Lake City he continued his journey south to Cedar City, where he arrived November 27th, same year, at the residence of Bishop Henry Lunt, who received him gladly, Brother Pearsall being the first person who introduced the principles of the gospel to Brother Lunt. He remained with the Bishop to the day of his death and was numbered and treated as one of his family. Elder Pearsall was firm and steadfast to the truth, nothing doubting; had strong desires to live to go through the Temple of the Lord and officiate for his dead friends; was a constant teacher at the Sunday-school; loved to attend to every known duty, ever at meeting when permitted by health; was ordained a High Priest March 25th 1866, under the hands of Elder Erastus Snow; passed to his rest calmly, as one going to sleep, sitting in an easy chair, with full dress, and his hat upon his head; was beloved by all in the city. A large concourse of friends attended his funeral.

C. J. ARTHUR.

At Cedar City, Jan. 4th, 1876, after a lingering illness, WILLIM PERKINS.

Deceased was born in the Parish of Swansea, South Wales, in the year 1807; was one of the first in that region of country to embrace the Gospel as revealed through the Prophet Joseph Smith, being baptized by Elder Abel Evans soon after the Gospel was introduced into Wales by Elder William Henshaw, and ever since that time until the time of his death was a firm and zealous supporter of the principles of the Gospel; emigrated with a portion of his family to this Territory in 1869, and ever since that time has resided in Cedar; was ordained a High Priest last fall. His integrity and unassuming manner won for him the respect and esteem of a large circle of friends.[COM

At Cedar City, May 26th, from the result of an accident, WILLIAM CORLETT, eldest son of William C. and Mary Ann Stewart, aged 15 years and 3 months.

Deceased had started, with another lad, from home about 2 p.m. on Wednesday, May 24th, to drive up a band of horses, and when about three quarters of a mile out the mule he was riding acted a little contrary and finally reared up on its hind feet, fell over with the boy and rolled over him.

The boy with him immediately rode back and informed Willie's mother, who with some of the neighbors took a team and brought the injured boy home. He was apparently unconscious. The sympathy of the people of the settlement was wrought out and everything thought of and wished for was done to save his life. He died 48 hours after the accident still unconscious. It is supposed his spine, lungs and left arm were injured. The accident has cast a gloom over the city and caused many a heart to mourn the loss of this youth, as exhibited by the large concourse of all ages and both sexes which attended his burial.

Deseret News
December 15, 1876

At her mother's residence in Hamilton, six miles south of Cedar City, December 15, MARY CONDIE, wife of Elder William Laney, of Harrisburgh, Washington County, and daughter of Mary H. Fife, spouse of Peter Muir Fife, deceased.

Sister Mary was born in Clackmanan, Scotland, December 26, 1843, where she also embraced the principles of the everlasting Gospel, to which she was ever true.

The funeral services were performed at the house of Sister Fife, and her body was interred in the cemetery at Cedar City. A large number of the Saints from Cedar attended the service and burial. Peace to her remains.—COM.

Deseret News
March 28, 1877

LEE'S STATEMENT.

(From the Beaver Square-Dealer, March 20.)

The New York *Herald* and San Francisco *Chronicle*, the two enterprising papers, *par excellence*, of America, are moving things generally to obtain John D. Lee's statement of the Mountain Meadows Massacre. Lee's first statement, and we believe the only one that he has made, was written a couple of years ago in the Beaver County jail, soon after he was arrested by Marshal Stokes. When it was known that the leader of the massacre was writing a history of it, great anxiety was felt in Beaver and elsewhere to know the character of his statement. It was popularly believed that Lee knew it all, and that he could not attempt a statement without telling all that he knew. We are not prepared to say that Lee did not tell all that he, himself, knew, but we are quite sure that he did not tell all that the public wanted to know. His statement did not satisfy anybody in Utah, and we opine that it will hardly meet the expectations of the two greatest sensational papers of this or any other age.

Lee's account of the massacre is an exceedingly meagre and contemptible history of an affair of immense proportions. In it he skulks and hides and appears to have but one motive in view, viz., the shielding of himself from the fierce indignation of the public.

He did not kill anybody; he went to the Meadows with a view of restraining the Indians, which he did for a number of days, when their savage natures getting full rein, they broke over all restraint and murdered the helpless emigrants. He knew nothing of any concerted plan on the part of the whites to murder the emigrants. If there was any, Haight, Higbee, Klingensmith and others were the ringleaders. He held an inferior rank in the Utah Militia, and in all that he did, simply obeyed the orders of his superiors.

Not only has Lee's confession been most unsatisfactory for paucity of narration, but he has been contradictory in his general statements from the first, disgusting his own lawyers and confusing the prosecution in search of the main threads of the deeply concealed plot.

One particular statement he has adhered to from the first. He had at all times declared that Brigham Young and the Church leaders had nothing to do with the massacre. His hopeful statement made at the time of his arrest and reiterated for several weeks, that he would place the saddle on the right horse, was found to refer solely to John M. Higbee who Lee said succeeded him as major of the Iron County Militia, some time before the massacre. Lee's statement does not even reach Col. Dame of the Nauvoo battalion. He knows nothing affecting any body higher in the Church than Haight and Klingensmith. The value of Lee's statement accrues chiefly to the Church leaders whom it exonerates completely.

Standing on the eve of the execution after a searching investigation which has been prolonged for two years, not a jot or tittle of evidence has been elicited connecting the Mountain Meadows slaughter with Brigham Young or any leading Church official. Everything which Klingensmith and Lee have told goes to prove that the conspiracy was hatched at Cedar City. * * *

Lee has told nothing because he had nothing to tell. The country will be satisfied after the execution that he died with no secret in him affecting Brigham Young. If he held such a fearful lodgment, Attorney Howard would be in possession of it to-day and Lee's sentence commuted.

A few facts warrant our statements: John D. Lee was tried by a Mormon jury, who, on the testimony of Mormon witnesses, brought in their verdict of murder in the first degree. Years ago Young severed Lee from his Church, thus challenging the exposition of any orders, written or otherwise, which he may have held from him as the head of the Church.

The conviction of Lee by a Mormon jury and his silent execution will be a receipt for Brigham Young for all time to come as against the massacre of the Arkansas emigrants.

DIED.

Of pneumonia, in Cedar City, March 23, 1877, EDWARD CHANCEY, son of Edward and Margaret Parry.

Deceased was born March 14th, 1872; he was a bright, intelligent and affectionate child, being a general favorite throughout this place for his kind, amiable and winning manner. It is a heavy bereavement to his sorrowing parents, who have the sympathy of a large circle of friends.—

At Cedar City, I on County, May 1, 1877, after a lingering illness of between four and five years, THOMAS GOWER, aged 60 years and 11 months.

Deceased was a native of Stourbridge, Worcestershire, England; joined the Church of Jesus Christ of Latter-day Saints about the year 1849, and soon after emigrated to St. Louis, Missouri, where he buried his wife and two children, who fell victims to the ravages of the cholera. In 1850 he married Martha Stockdale; crossed the plains in Captain Field's company in 1854; resided in the Eleventh Ward, Salt Lake City for a short time; then removed to Jordan Mills and resided there until the fall of 1855, when he was called to go to Cedar City to help make iron. Here he labored faithfully until the works were stopped. Since that time he toiled hard to help build up the settlement and to sustain a large family; was a member of the sixty-third Quorum of Seventies. Brother Gower was a man of unflinching integrity to the cause of truth. He leaves a large family to mourn his loss. The remains were followed to the cemetery by a large concourse of relatives and friends.—COM.

Deseret News
February 14, 1878

DIED

In Cedar City, Iron County, Utah, Feb. 14th, 1878, of old age, ARAMANTA ANN GILBERT, wife of Jonas Gilbert, and daughter of John Musgrove and Nancy Goldman. Deceased was born May 9th, 1786, in Hatchfield County, South Carolina. She lived and died a faithful Saint and has gone to rest in the hope of a glorious resurrection.—[Com.

DIED

Deseret News
April 18, 1878

At Cedar City, Iron County, April 18th, 1878, of disease of the kidneys, Elder HENRY THOMAS, aged 67 years. Deceased was a native of Monmouthshire, England, embraced the Gospel in the early days, and was for several years president of the Crumlin Branch. Emigrated to Utah in 1867, and has resided in this place ever since.

DIED

Deseret News
August 8, 1878

In Cedar City, Iron County, at 3 a m., Aug. 8th, of consumption, JOHN HARRIS who was born Dec. 17, 1813. When he was 34 years old, he heard the gospel, and obeyed the same in June, 1848, was ordained to the priesthood and labored faithfully in the Monmouthshire Conference as a traveling preacher; sailed from Liverpool for this country in 1851, and after much sickness with cholera and ague, emigrated to these valleys in 1853, since which time he has helped to build up southern Utah. He was full of integrity, and faithful and zealous in his religion. He died in full faith of a glorious resurrection, leaving a wife and six children.—[Com

DIED

Deseret News
January 1, 1879

At Hamilton, six miles south of Cedar City, Iron County, Utah Territory, January 1st, 1879, of disease of the liver and kidneys, after an illness of two years. MARY HUNTER CONDIE FIFE, daughter of William Hunter and Mary Snedden, born April 5th, 1823, in Newtownshaw, county of Clackmannan, Scotland. She was baptized in her native village in 1847; emigrated to Utah in 1861, accompanied by her five children, and settled in Cedar City, where she

was married to Elder Peter Muir Fife, by whom she had a son and daughter. She was a woman of exceeding faith, and was particularly prompt in the performance of every duty.—[COM.

DIED

Deseret News
March 15, 1879

At Cedar City, Iron County, Utah, March 15th, 1879, of heart disease, JANE PERKINS, wife of the late William Perkins.

Deceased was born at Treboth, Parish of Llangelach, Glamorganshire, South Wales, on the 27th day of May, 1814; was baptized into the Church of Jesus Christ of Latter-day Saints, in 1844, among the first who obeyed the gospel in that region; emigrated to Utah in 1869. She was ever faithful to the cause of truth, respected and loved by all who knew her, and passed away in the sure and certain hope of a glorious resurrection.—COM.

DIED

Deseret News
April 1, 1882

In Cedar City, Iron County, GEORGE HUNTER, son of William Hunter and Mary Snaddon; born in Clackmanan, Scotland, March 30, 1828; died on April 1st, 1882, of liver complaint and pneumonia.

DIED

Deseret News
March 25, 1883

ROE—At Kanarra, Iron County, Utah, March 25th, 1883, Mary Francis Young Roe, wife of John Charles Roe. Born in Cedar City, May 14th, 1856. Aged 26 years, 10 months and 11 days.

Deceased was a kind and affectionate wife and mother, a faithful and exemplary Latter-day Saint, and leaves a husband, one child, (a daughter) and a large number of relatives and friends to mourn her loss.

Deseret News
April 23, 1884

LOSS OF CATTLE SOUTH.

THE deep snows of last winter have played sad havoc among stock in Southern Utah, and the end is not yet. Messrs. Robert & David Bullock, of Cedar City were the owners of nearly 400 head of animals, besides having had charge of about 400 more for a person who resides in Pioche, making in all a herd of between 700 and 800. A few day ago Mr. Robert Bullock returned from the mountains where the cattle were wintering and reported that 500 of them had perished. The snow had been from five to seven feet deep in the mountains; it is now two feet. In order to reach home Mr. Bullock was compelled to make a circuit through the mountains of a hundred miles, most of the way on snowshoes.

DIED

Deseret News
May 20, 1884

PALMER--At Cedar city, Iron County, at 2.30 p. m., May 20th, 1884, of inflammatory rheumatism and consumption, Julius Rees, son of Richard and Johannah Palmer, aged 10 years, 1 month and 20 days.

Deseret News
July 2, 1884

Accidentally Shot.—A special dispatch to the NEWS, from Cedar City, received to-day reports that Dan Parker, of this city, about eighteen years of age, teamster for Bishop Thomas Taylor, whilst on his way from Parowan to Iron City, last evening with a load of grain, accidentally shot himself when within two miles of the latter place. He was in the act of taking his shot gun out of his wagon to shoot a rabbit, when the contents lodged under the thigh bone, a little above the knee. He drove on to Iron City, and two of his friends immediately started with him to Milford, on his way to Salt Lake City for surgical aid.

DIED

Deseret News
May 31, 1885

FIFE.—At Cedar City, Iron County, Utah, May 31st, 1885, Sarah Jane Leigh, wife of Peter B. Fife and daughter of Samuel and Mary Leigh; born February 24th. 1854; lived and died a faithful Latter-day Saint; leaves a husband and four children and many friends to mourn her loss.—COM.

Deseret News
March 27, 1886

HUNTER.—In Cedar City, March 27, 1886, of general debility, Elder Joseph Hunter, son of William and Mary Sneddon Hunter all of Alloa, Clackmanan, Scotland; born August 20, 1818; baptized October 30, 1846, by Prest. James Burnett, confirmed by Elder Wm. C. Dunbar, and ordained a Priest by Elder Ephraim Tomkinson.

He was an ardent, earnest laborer in the cause of truth, traveled much to proclaim the message to his countrymen and was eminently successful in converting many to the principles of the Gospel he proclaimed. He left his native land for his future home in the West on the 29th of October, 1849, with his family of a wife and five children. Tarried in St. Louis and other parts of the State of Missouri for two years, and before leaving there buried his wife and two of the children; arrived in Salt Lake City in the fall of 1852, and soon afterwards journeyed to and settled in Cedar City. He was much

attached to co-operation and placed a goodly portion of his means in the various institutions of that nature in the southern part
of the Territory. Shortly after his arrival
in the mountains he was ordained a Seventy. A few days before his death he sent
for his children, together with his wife,
talked of his condition and anticipated early
release from mortality. He also made a
satisfactory distribution of his property,
after which he felt perfectly resigned, and
soon passed away to the sphere beyond, his
features presenting a placid and pleasant
expression. He died as he had lived, firm
in his religious convictions.

His funeral was largely attended by the
people of the ward and neighboring settlements, when appropriate and eulogistic remarks were made on the occasion by some
of his friends.

Deseret News
April 11, 1886

HAMILTON.—In Hamilton, near Cedar
City, Iron County, April 11th, 1886, Mary,
wife of John Hamilton, Sr., born in Saintfield, County Down, Ireland, September
28th, 1807; baptized November 5th, 1840;
emigrated to Nauvoo in 1843, was driven
from that city in September, 1846, with many
others by the crusaders of that period; and
arrived at Salt Lake City in September, 1850.

In 1852 the family moved south to Iron
County, first settled in Parowan, then in
Cedar City, and for the past 30 years have
made their home in Hamilton, named after
her faithful husband.

The robes in which she was clothed for
burial were made of flax spun by her own
hands, some 50 years ago, in her native land.

She loved the principles of the Gospel and
defended them whenever occasion offered.
She had many friends, as fully exemplified
by the numerous attendance at the funeral
services, which were held at her late residence.—COM.

DEATHS.

PIGSON.—James Walker Pogeon, born February 25th, 1819, in Slackwnith, Yorkshire, England; died February 6th, 1888, in Cedar City, Iron County, Utah; baptized December 11th, 1842; ordained a Deacon March 28th, 1847; ordained a Teacher in 1848; ordained a Priest April 29th, 1849; ordained an Elder April 15th, 1851; ordained a Seventy February 22nd, 1865.

Millennial Star please copy.

HAIGHT.—Arabella Sinclair Haight, relict of the late Isaac C. Haight, of Cedar City, Iron County, Utah; born April 20th, 1811; died February 10th, 1888. Deceased emigrated from Glasgow, Scotland, in 1854; settled in Cedar City in the fall of 1855, where she lived until her death. She leaves two sons, thirty four grandchildren and a large number of great grandchildren.—COM.

Arrests in the South.

Joseph P. Barton was arrested by Marshal Dyer and brought to Beaver on Wednesday last. An indictment charging Mr. Barton with irregularities in postal accounts, was found by the last grand jury, and on this charge he was arrested.

The following have been arrested for unlawful cohabitation: Francis Webster, of Cedar City; Cornelius McReavy, of Washington, and Milton L. Lee, of Panacca, Nevada. The latter was arrested at St. George.

Postmaster Hammond, of Toquerville, was arrested on a postal indictment found by the last grand jury.—*Beaver Utonian, June 39.*

Deseret News
October 31, 1888

FATAL ACCIDENT.

Christian D. Barnston is Crushed to Death.

Advices from Cedar City, Iron Co., state that on Monday evening a fatal accident occurred in Cedar Cañon, resulting in the death of Christian D. Barnston, of Cedar City. The deceased left his home on Monday for the purpose of getting a load of poles which he had secured, and on his way down the mountain the reach of his wagon broke, causing the load to capsize, he falling underneath the same. The accident happened about sundown. Some persons who were working at the coal mines about two miles from the scene of the accident, becoming alarmed at the non-arrival of Mr. Barnston, who anticipated camping with them for the evening, immediately went in search of him and found him as before stated, at 9 o'clock in the evening, his head and part of his shoulders being bare. They immediately extricated him and found his limbs powerless. He requested them to rub his legs and try to produce circulation, but this did not avail. They carried him to their camp, and did all in their power for his comfort, immediately dispatching a messenger to his residence for assistance to take him home. He died about 2 a. m. yesterday, in the camp before mentioned, and before the conveyance reached him. His body arrived home at 8:50 a. m. A coroner's inquest was held, and a verdict rendered in accordance with the above facts. His wife and relatives are stricken with grief at the sad affair. He was 32 years old, and leaves a wife and two children. He was highly respected in the community. It is supposed he laid under the load about four hours before assistance reached him.

Deseret News
December 11, 1889

ARTHUR.—December 8th, at Cedar City, Iron County, Utah, Jeannette C., daughter of C. J. and Jane Arthur; born August 8th, 1888. Her death resulted from cold, teething, and canker.

Deseret News
February 1, 1890

ALLDRIDGE.—At Cedar City, Iron County, Utah, February 1st, 1890, Ann Blunt Alldridge, wife of Richard Alldridge, and daughter of John Blunt and Jane Gordon; born August 16th, 1820, at Northampton, England. She joined the Church at Birmingham in 1847; emigrated in 1851. She lived and died a true Latter-day Saint.

Father John Hamilton, of Hamilton, near Cedar City, Iron County, Utah (a name widely known among the early settlers of this Territory, and especially those of the southern portion, among whom he has lived for the past thirty-nine years) passed away on the 3rd inst., at the age of 83 years, 4 months and 21 days.

The deceased was born at Saintfield, County Down, Ireland, on the 12th of July, 1807. He embraced the Gospel in his native land, and was baptized by Elder Theodore Curtis in 1840. He left Ireland on Dec. 31st, 1842, and arrived in Nauvoo, Ill., April, 1843, where he labored at his trade as a blacksmith, working for the Temple, and especially on the baptismal font. He often spoke with unbounded respect of the Prophet Joseph coming into his shop, picking up a sledge-hammer and striking the hot iron he was working upon, by way of help. His love for Joseph and his brother Hyrum, when talking of them, often filled his heart to overflowing, and tears would even trickle down his cheeks. The last words the Prophet uttered on his leaving was when on his way to Carthage. The brethren were all flocking around him receiving his parting "God bless you!" Father Hamilton could not reach his side, but stood off and bowed to the good man, who acknowledged the humble offering and said, "All is well as yet." These words Father Hamilton never forgot. He remained in Nauvoo during the trials of the Saints, traveled in Warren Foot's company to Salt Lake City in 1850 and the year following to Iron County.

In 1852 he moved on to Shirts Creek in said county, six miles south of Cedar City. The Indians manifesting a warlike disposition, in 1853 he removed his family and effects to Cedar City, remaining there for four years till all was quiet and peaceful. He then returned to his place at Shirts Creek (now Hamilton), where he spent the remainder of his life.

Father Hamilton was a man of sterling integrity, never deviating from the faith which he espoused fifty years ago—always the same strong-minded, devoted Christian. He loved God, the Gospel, and his people. He was kind, benevolent, hospitable, reverent and humble, unassuming, but firm as the rock in his convictions, and conservative in his manners. He had no enemies, but a host of friends mourn his death.

Although on the day of the funeral the weather was very unfavorable, this did not prevent his friends from all parts of this Stake participating in the last tribute of respect towards him.

C. J. ARTHUR.
CEDAR CITY, Dec. 6, 1890.

Deseret News
March 5, 1891

CHAFFIN.—March 5th, at Cedar City, Iron County, Utah, Louis R. Chaffin. Brother Chaffin was born at Salem, Mass., December 3, 1806; embraced the Gospel in Illinois, under the hands of Zenos H. Gourley in March, 1840, and settled at LaHarp, where he was postmaster and justice of the peace. He suffered with the Saints in their expulsion from Illinois; reached Utah in 1852 and settled in Salt Lake City. In 1856 he filled a mission to Australia, being absent four years. In 1861 he was called to the Dixie mission, and was one of the pioneers of St. George. From St. George he went to help build up the settlements on the Muddy. Meeting with losses there by fire, he was counseled to locate at Cedar city, where he was a useful citizen, filling the position of justice of the peace and notary public. He died as he had lived, faithful to the Gospel.—Com.

Iron County News
March 14, 1891

The report from Pioche and Panaca is very discouraging. From a private source we learn that in the early part of this week the disease, called called the La Grippe, had seized upon every man and woman in the two places. The only doctor there succumbed during the latter part of last week. This leaves the people in a rather precarious condition. It is said that deaths are occuring every day, and a sadness and gloom prevails that are really depressing.

The following have been appointed deputy registrars for Iron county. Paragonah precinct, D. W. Lamoreaux; Parowan precinct, S. R. Burton Summit precinct, John White; Cedar City, James Corlett; Kanarra precinct Samuel J. Pollock.

CHAFFIN—August 2, 1891, at Cedar City, Utah Sarah Maria Cossitt Chaffin, relict of Father Louis Rice Chaffin.

Sister Chaffin was born June 2, 1815, at Mercer, Mercer County, Pennsylvania, and was married to Louis R. Chaffin on the 3rd of December, 1837. They lived together over fifty years. She was the mother of six sons and three daughters, eight of whom are still alive. There are also 54 grandchildren and twelve great-grandchildren. Sister Chaffin was baptized by Zenos H. Gurley and confirmed by J. Savage, in March, 1840, the same day that her husband was baptized. She passed through the persecutions of Illinois and was compelled to leave her home with her babe, five

days old. The notice given them by the mob was at midnight, and they were to leave at sunrise on the succeeding day. She drove her own team in 1852 from Winter Quarters, on the Missouri River, to Salt Lake City, was one of the pioneers to St. George in 1861, and with her husband moved to Cedar City in 1869. She employed herself for many years in Cedar City teaching a primary class under the supervision of the District Trustees, and was very successful in her labors in that direction. Sister Chaffin was a woman of strong nerve, an earnest and zealous worker in all duties entrusted to her and remained faithful to the end, having "fought the good fight and kept the faith." She had a lingering sickness of six months duration, and survived her husband only five months.—[COM.

PUCILL.—August 17, 1891, on the Mountain east of Cedar City, Robert Pucill; born in England, December 3 1855.

He was the son of William and grandson of the Pucill family that received kindly the Apostles that introduced the Gospel into England in 1837. President Brigham Young in his lifetime exhibited and extended true Christian charity and practical help towards them. Robert leaves a wife and six children.

URIE.—At Cedar City, Iron County, Sept. 14, 1891, Sarah Ann, wife of John Urie, born Oct 2, 1826, in County Waterford, Ireland. Deceased was baptized into the Church of Jesus Christ of Latter day Saints in Sydney, Australia, May 12th, 1854, by Augustus Farnham, emigrated to Utah December 20th, 1857. with five orphan children; had sixty-three grandchildren and seven great-grandchildren. Twelve of her children are still alive, the youngest being twenty-two years of age. Was president of the Relief Society for a number of years and acquitted herself honorably.

At the funeral services, President Thomas J. Jones and Bishops Arthur and Carry were the speakers.

OFF FOR MEXICO.

A Utah Pioneer Who Makes His Home in the Southern Republic.

Henry Lunt, of Colonia Pacheco, Mexico, is bidding good-bye to his friends in this city, and expects to start for his home this week. Elder Lunt was a pioneer in Southern Utah, and is continuing his worthy labors in the new settlements of Chihuahua. He is in his seventieth year, and is in excellent health and spirits. About 20 years ago his sight was partially impaired, but it has not grown any worse during the past few years. In conversation with a News representative, he said: "We have got a nice little place at Pacheco, where there are about thirty families. The place is under the presidency of Jesse N. Smith Jr. It is 7,000 feet above the level of the sea, in the Sierra Madre mountains, and the climate is most delightful. The summers are cool and pleasant and the winters mild. Water is not very plentiful, and there is not much farming.

"The country is a good place for plenty of hard work. The chief crops near Pacheco, are corn and potatoes. The locality is also a good place for stockraising. Down at Dublan, Diaz and Juarez they do not raise good keeping potatoes, and those from Pacheco bring about three cents a pound. The fruit crop at Juarez has been mostly destroyed by frost this spring, I am told. There is a good tannery down there, established by

Jacob Walser, formerly of Payson. We also have a grist mill, and contemplate building a woolen factory soon. We have two saw mills. It is a good country for sheep. There were no sheep in that section until the Mormons brought some to the mountains last year. There is a good wheat crop at Dublan, and at Diaz W. W. Galbraith, formerly of Davis county, has a farm of 300 acres which is the finest in that section. His prospects are better now than they ever have been. The customs duties seem a drawback to us, but they compel us to sustain ourselves, and such a policy might be better for the people here. The Lord opened that country for the Saints, and it is going to be a good place to live, though it will take lots of hard work. I put the first shingle roof on a house in Pacheco, and my son was the first child born in that town.

"I left there on the 25th of March, to come to conference. From here I went to visit relatives in the south, as far as St. George, and had a most pleasant time. At Cedar City, my old home, I was accorded a most hearty reception, being met by the brass band and choir. I commanded the first company of settlers that went to Cedar City. We left here December 7, 1850, with President George A. Smith. There were 101 wagons and two carriages in the company. From 1854 until late in the fall of 1857 I was on a mission to Great Britain, and then went back to Cedar City, where I remained till I went to Mexico a few years ago. I came back Monday from my trip to Southern Utah."

Elder Lunt is full of reminiscences of his pioneer experience in the south, and exerts a cheerful and happy influence in his conversation.

Deseret News
July 2, 1894

Cedar City Coal.

Mr. W. A. Cooper, who has just returned from Cedar city was exhibiting a fine specimen of coal brought by him for that place from one of the new claims just being developed. The article is dug from the ground four miles from Cedar city and sells at $5.50 per ton there.

Deseret News
October 25, 1894

Land Office.

The following filings were made in the local land office under date of Oct. 25th:

Amelia A. Popkess, of Cedar City, coal entry, north half of the southwest quarter, and the south half of the northwest quarter of section 24, township 37 south, range 11 west.

John E. Popkess, of Cedar City, coal entry, southeast quarter of section 24, township 37 south, range 11 west.

Wm. Purser, of Hyde Park, homestead entry, northeast quarter of section 12, township 12 north, range 1 east.

Delbert Ahlstrom, of Tropic, Utah, desert entry, unsurveyed tract of 80 acres, approximately in section 2, township 37 south, range 2 west.

CEDAR CITY, Utah, Feb. 17.—Anders Jenson, of Cedar City, passed peacefully away at 12:30 p.m., January 10, 1895, after a severe illness of six weeks. He was born in Sweden, near Rysgard, May 3, 1832, joined the Church of Jesus Christ of Latter-day Saints February, 1854, labored as a missionary in Sweden and Denmark for six years and emigrated to Utah in 1862, arriving at Salt Lake City the same year. He continued his journey south to Cedar City, and here he has resided ever since. He was ordained into the Sixty-third quorum of Seventies at its organization on April 18, 1863, and was a faithful member of that quorum. He has since been ordained a High Priest and held that Priesthood at his death. He was a hard-working man, faithful in all his transactions in life, has held many positions in this ward, both spiritual and temporal, and was faithful in all his duties. In whatever he was called upon to do, he was an honorable, upright man, true to his covenants that he has made with his God, true to his family and friends. He lost his first wife some fifteen years ago, and was left with six children, the youngest being but one month old. In all his trouble and sorrow he has never been known to murmur, and he died as he had lived, a good Latter-day Saint. He leaves a wife and ten children with numerous relatives and friends to mourn his loss.

The Brigham Young Memorial association acknowledges receipt of the following contributions to assist in the building of the Pioneer monument:

From Cedar City, Parowan Stake:

Mary Ann B Unthank	10
Walter Granger	50
Nellie Granger	5
Emma Granger	5
Walter K Granger	5
C G Bell	25
Samuel C Bell	15
Nellie S Dover	10
Leah M Dover	14
Wm D Leigh	1 00
Elizabeth W Leigh	1 00
Wm H Leigh	25

S G Leigh	75
Rufus Leigh	20
Baby Leigh	15
Elias Leigh	15
Mary Ann Adams	1 00
Wm V Adams	1 00
George A Adams	1 00
John A Adams	1 00
Kate Adams	1 00
William Dover	50
Mary Ann Dover	50
Horace Dover	20
May Dover	15
Total	$10 60

JANE JEWKES CROWTHER.

Died at Sanford, Conejos county, Col., Jane Jewkes Crowther, wife of Thomas Crowther; born at Kateshill, Dudley, Worcestershire, England, April 2, 1832; baptized into the Church of Jesus Christ of Latter-day Saints April 7, 1850, by Elder George Hill in the Tipton branch of the Birmingham conference. She emigrated to Utah in 1855 and was married to Thomas Crowther November 25th of the same year, at Cedar City, Iron county, Utah; from this place she moved with her husband in 1860 to Ephraim, Sanpete county, and in 1861 removed to Fountain Green of the same county, where she took a prominent part in the Relief Society, holding the office of first counselor to the president of that ward. In 1890 she removed with her family to Sanford, Col., where she continued her labors, holding the office of second counselor to the president of the Relief Society of the San Luis Stake.

Sister Crowther was the mother of twelve children, two of whom have gone before her. She leaves an aged husband, ten children, forty-nine grandchildren, one brother, one sister and a host of friends to mourn her loss. She had been failing in health about eighteen months, but of late had appeared to be improving, and on May 1st was at a birthday party of one of her daughters. On the morning of May 2nd Brother Crowther left her sleeping while he went out to feed his stock, being out about fifteen minutes, and on returning to the house found she had passed away apparently without a struggle. She had been a loving and devoted wife and mother and died in full faith of the Gospel, with the hope of a glorious resurrection.

May 4, at 10 a. m., the cortege went from the family residence to the meeting house where the services were conducted by Bishop Soren C. Berthelsen. Bishops Marcus Funk, Soren C. Berthelsen and Stake President Albert R. Smith were the speakers. The funeral was one of the largest ever seen in Sanford.

J. F. CROWTHER.

Deseret News
September 12, 1896

David John returned from Goshen Monday forenoon, where he had attended the funeral of Elder John Morgan, one of Utah county's leading citizens, who died last Friday afternoon at 6 o'clock. The deceased was born in Merthyr, South Wales, February, 22, 1833, and became a member of the Church of Jesus Christ of Latter-day Saints December 16, 1850. He emigrated to America in the spring of 1854, and was married to Emma Richards in Kansas City, Missouri, May 1, 1854, while they were on their way to Utah. He arrived in Salt Lake City on the 5th of October of the same year, and shortly after settled in what is now known as Cedar City in Iron county. He was one of the first settlers there, and fenced the first city lot in the place. After living there three years he moved to Beaver, where he lived for two years. He then moved to Goshen valley and was among the first settlers of that locality. He has taken a leading part in the development of the county, and has been prominently identified with all movements having for its object the financial and religious progress of the community. He has

Deseret News
March 24, 1897

ELIZA ANN ADAMS.

St. George, March 24th, 1897.—Sunday, March 21st, 1897, was a solemn day in the city of St. George, as on the evening previous Samuel L. Adams Jr, and nine of his children arrived here bringing with them the lifeless body of his beloved wife and the mother of his family, who had died at Eureka, on the 16th of March, 1897, after a short illness. As this was their home in life they could not consent to lay her away in any other place, but brought her to where her many deeds of love had caused all to admire her; for it can in truth be said that to know her was to love her.

Eliza Ann, daughter of Isaac C. and Eliza Ann Price Haight, was born at Cedar City, on the 8th of May, 1858, and was married to Samuel L. Adams Jr., on the 20th of May, 1875; she died on the 16th of March, 1897. She leaves an aged mother, an affectionate husband, ten living children (one has preceded her to the spirit world), and a large number of relatives and friends to mourn her departure. May He who has said that a sparrow shall not fall to the ground without His notice be a father in very deed and raise up friends to the motherless children.

The funeral services over the remains of Sister Adams were held in the St. George tabernacle Sunday, March 21st, 1897, Bishop Andrews presiding. Elder James G. Bleak was the first speaker. He was followed by Elders Thomas Judd and John E. Pace, Bishop Andrews, and President David H. Cannon, each having known her from her youth. All bore testimony of her firm integrity to the truth of the Gospel and also to her good example in all her walks in life. The tabernacle was well filled and a feeling of love was shown to the bereaved family. About 700 people viewed the remains, and although it was a bitter cold day a large procession followed the remains to the St. George cemetery.

W. A.

AFTER CEDAR COAL.

WHY THE SOUTHERN PACIFIC IS SURVEYING A RAILROAD TRACK THROUGH SOUTHERN UTAH.

[Salt Lake Tribune.]

One of the most interesting features of the present local railroad situation is the presence in southern Utah of the Southern Pacific surveying party. From time to time The Tribune has detailed the route being followed by the transit and levelmen, and it has been shown that the company is certainly at work on securing a line from the heart of Utah to its own line.

The Tribune has information at hand giving another reason for the Southern Pacific's activity in this State. Briefly, it is to secure a new coal supply, and the vast deposits a few miles southeast of Cedar City are being sought after by the big California corporation, whose purpose, it is stated, is to build a line south through the coal fields to the Southern Pacific.

There is no doubt but that the Southern Pacific is looking out for more sources of coal supply. This is positively announced in messages from San Francisco. Vice-President Crocker will leave there on the 20th to go to Carbon, the company's coal mine on the Northern Pacific, and at the same time a party of engineers leaves for Sonora, Mex., to examine coal properties there.

Two years ago the Southern Pacific examined the coal supply at Cedar City and found the lignite good for steam purposes, but not so good for commercial putposes. The company went into the matter carefully, but nothing was definitely decided upon. Now, however, it is absolutely necessary for the road to have a new coal supply. On the desert east of Mohave alone the road uses 2000 to 3000 tons a day, and it has to be hauled great distances. It is asserted as a positive fact that the Southern Pacific is bent on developing the Cedar City mines and making them the source of supply for all its lines in Arizona and southern California.

The Tribune's informant gives the whole plan in a very plain way. The new line is being surveyed, exactly as heretofore told in The Tribune, but below St. George the road will follow the Virgin river straight down to the Colorado river. It is not generally known, but the southern Pacific operates a steamer line, called the Colorado Steam Navigation company, from Yuma up the Colorado river a considerable distance.

For the present a temporary connection will be made to the point on the river as far north as boats can be navigated, and coal will be loaded there to be shot down the rapids to Yuma.

This is no new arrangement, but boats have been plying up the river for many years. No definate arrangement of this kind will be made, it is said, but a temporary connection will be made with the boat line.

The vast coal fields of Iron county have frequently been fully described. It is the nearest fuel supply to all points in southern California and has ever been one of the features of the Salt Lake-Los Angeles projects. That the Southern Pacific has been quietly figuring on the property and is now hard at work on the surveys for its railroad, puts an entirely new phase on the railroad situation in southern Utah.

Deseret News
January 3, 1899

Cedar City, Jan. 3.—A grand program ball was given last Friday in honor of Brother and Sister Richard P. Birkbeck on the fiftieth anniversary of their wedding day. Several hundred people assembled at the ward hall to do honor to the aged couple. A purse was made up by the guests amounting to $20, and presents and good cheer were in evidence. Owing to the long dry season, considerable sickness is prevalent—scarlet fever, pneumonia.

Owing to vacation at the branch normal, the city has been more quiet than usual. The Young People's Dramatic company presented "The Bottle," to a very creditable house last night.

Deseret News
June 12, 1899

Cedar City, Iron Co., June 12.—The Iron county board of equalization met in Parowan June 5th, continuing in session three days. Quite a number of changes were made in the ownership of real estate in the northern part of the county.

WEDDING OF MISS HOUCHEN.

Lorenzo Adams and Miss Nellie Houchen of this place were in Parowan last wednesday morning, and after procuring some legal papers from the county clerk, were married by County Attorney Jos. F. McGregor. The bride has been one of the teachers in the district school here for the past five years.

Deseret News
July 13, 1899

Cedar City, Iron County, July 13.—Considerable interest was taken in the school election here on Monday the 10th inst., there were two candidates in the field: Robert W. Heyborne and Dr. George W. Middleton; Mr. Heyborne was elected by a majority of thirty-seven votes.

SERIOUS GUN ACCIDENT.

James Walker of this place sustained quite a serious accident on the mountain east of here, last Monday; he was in the act of throwing a cartridge from the magazine into the gun with which he was hunting, when the cartridge exploded and with it seven others in the magazine, tearing the gun to pieces and filling his eyes with powder and inflicting some very severe wounds on his face. Dr. Middleton has the case in hand and the patient is slowly recovering.

The 4-year-old son of Stephen Gower succumbed to an attack of pneumonia last Friday and was buried on Saturday.

F. C. Ellison has the contract for painting and calcimining the branch normal school building, he began work last Saturday, and intends to have it completed by the 1st of September.

Deseret News
October 8, 1899

Cedar City, Iron Co., Oct. 8.—A few days ago a 11-year-old son of Charles Stapley, Jr., was stung in the night by some venomous insect, and after many days' suffering, expired Wednesday evening and was buried Friday.

Many young men are emigrating from this part to Mexico and Canada. Others contemplate going to Arizona. Early frosts and unprecedented dry weather prove very discouraging.

Deseret News
November 27, 1899

Pres. U. T. Jones returned from the metropolis the first of the week, where he went on business connected with the disposition of the Cedar City Furniture Company's coal properties in Coal Creek canyon, says the Iron County Record. Mr. Jones reports that no sale was made of the properties, but they will be handled by the Church officials in connection with their holdings here, and that it will be the policy of the Church to encourage the development of our resources, by offering their property at a reasonable figure to persons who will be likely to push its development. Mr. Jones seemed quite encouraged over the prospects for the early utilization of our matchless resources.

Deseret News
March 19, 1900

Coal Creek Meadow and Northwest Field Irrigation Company.

Articles of Incorporation of the Coal Creek Meadow and Northwest Field Irrigation company were filed with the secretary of State today. The company was organized at Cedar City, Iron county, having for its object the irrigation and reclamation of arid and other lands, and the acquiring of water for domestic purposes. The limit of the capital stock agreed upon is $9,161, with shares at $1 each. The officers are Lehi W. Jones, president; Andrew Corey, vice president; John Chatterley, secretary, and Edward Parry, treasurer, who, along with John Parry, Henry Leigh and Thomas Thorley, also comprise the directorate. The company is owner of certain water rights, ditches and canals in Iron county.

DEATH OF RICHARD LAMBETH.

Last week we were called upon to mourn the loss of one of our citizens, Elder Richard Lambeth, who has resided here some fourteen years, coming to this country from England. The deceased exposed himself to the recent stormy weather and contracted a severe cold, bringing on pneumonia, which proved fatal. Elder Lambeth was kind-hearted, industrious and honest. He leaves a wife and several children. With the exception of a few colds caused through the dampness of the weather general good health prevails here, and now that the drouth is broken we are looking forward for better times and greater encouragement in our agricultural pursuits.

Considerable sickness prevails in our little town among little children, caused by the excessive hot weather. Little Delroy Walker was brought down from the mountains quite sick yesterday and expired this morning, the cause being diabetes. The funeral is announced for Tuesday, the 18th. His parents have the sympathy of the entire community, he being the eldest son.

Considerable suffering with stock and sheep for lack of water is being felt in our county and southern Utah, yet the indications are now somewhat favorable for rain which would be of incalculable benefit to this part of our county.

SHERIFF FROYD WAS STABBED.

Assaulted by George M. Hunter, Whom He Had Arrested for Assailing One of Cedar City's Citizens—Wound a Dangerous One in Neck.

[SPECIAL TO THE "NEWS."]

Cedar City, Utah, July 27.—A serious and almost fatal stabbing affray occurred here last evening. George M. Hunter assaulted one of our citizens, for which Sheriff Froyd arrested him, and the sheriff was about to place him in the cell when Hunter drew a knife and cut the officer, who received a very dangerous wound across the neck, as well as some other minor cuts. Hunter, it is claimed, was drunk and is very quarrelsome at that time. He was thrown down the cell steps and his head was injured after the sheriff was cut.

A telegram to Prof. Clark, principal of the Cedar City Branch Normal school, now visiting in this city, announced this afternoon that Prof. Claude Lewis and bride were detained at Lund by the health authorities of Iron county today on account of failing to take a medical certificate with them, making it clear that they had not been exposed to smallpox while in Salt Lake.

Such a certificate was telegraphed this afternoon, and the young couple resumed their wedding tour.

Notwithstanding the percaution taken by our health board we have one family quarantined with the smallpox; the disease was introduced here by a citizen of Kanarra who had for some time been laboring in Mercur, on his return home he was feeling unwell and stayed here for the night with some friends residing in our city, on consulting the doctor next morning it was found he had the smallpox. It is now stated that there is another case in the family.

Last Saturday Samuel T. Leigh lost a bright child of two years by pneumonia. Services over the remains were held in the tabernacle on Sunday.

On January 14th our people were called together to pay their last respects to the earthly remains of Broth-

er Horace Gower, a young man of 26 years. Brother Gower has been in poor health for a number of years, being troubled with acute rheumatism and heart disease. The deceased was held in high esteem by our citizens as was demonstrated in the large attendance at the funeral services as well as the long cortege that followed his remains to their last resting place.

WILFORD, IDAHO.

Sad Death of Mrs. Margaret Jack — Babe Given to Sister.

Special Correspondence.

Wilford, Idaho, March 21.—Mrs. Margaret Jack, wife of Wm. R. Jack, died from childbirth March 13, 1901. Deceased was born in Springburg, Scotland, in 1861; came to Utah in 1868, and has lived in Beaver, Cedar City and South Cottonwood, Utah; was married to Wm. R. Jack, by whom she had fourteen children, in December, 1876; moved to Wilford, Idaho, in 1887, and died as above stated. The babe is a nice boy baby, and has been given to her sister, Mrs. Violet Urie, who will take it with her to her home in Salt Lake City.

Cedar City, Iron Co., March 29.—The early part of the present month was very favorable for farm labor, and farmers took advantage of the same, the result is small grain is now about all planted; now a return of winter greets us, for the past week very cold and frosty weather prevailed with an occasional light fall of snow. The warm and pleasant days of the early part of the month caused many fruit trees to bloom and we are now wondering if the present cold snap will not be very injurious. For two years Cedar City has been deprived of its fruit crop, the loss of which is felt very materially.

The prospects for a good supply of water the coming season has been an incentive to our farmers to cultivate a greater amount of land than has been done for the past two years.

We have had somewhat of an epidemic of whooping cough that has annoyed the small children very much lately, however, we are pleased to be able to report that only one death has occurred from its effect, the little 5-year-old son of Albert Nelson of this place, being the victim. This case finally developed membraneous croup, which is reported to be the immediate cause of the death.

UTAH IRON MINES ATTRACT NOTICE.

The extent to which the iron interests in and around Cedar City are attracting attention is well illustrated by the developments of the past few days. The heirs of the late Thomas Taylor, who inherited his iron properties have reluctantly given an option on them for $250,000, in favor of eastern parties, and John C. Cutler, Jr., agent of the heirs, has gone to New York to meet the principals in the proposed purchase. The option has several months yet to run, but Mr. Cutler said to a "News" representative Saturday evening just before taking his train for the east, that he felt little doubt of being able to make the sale as two other parties stood ready to take another option the instant the present one expired.

DIED

ENTERPRISE--At Cedar City, Iron Co., May 6, 1901, of heart failure, Lucy Philenor Canfield, beloved wife of John Day Enterprise.

Deceased was born in Provo, January 21, 1853; she was the daughter of David and Elizabeth Canfield; came with her parents to Dixie in 1861. She leaves a husband and seven children and many friends and relatives to cherish her memory. She was a faithful Latter-day Saint.

On Sunday last Cedar City experienced one of the severest thunder storms in its history. No fatalities are reported but the damage done is considerable. Branches of trees were thrown over two hundred yards after being struck by lightning. About five miles northeast of the city a great thunderbolt struck in the middle of a farm. A large volume of smoke and fire issued from the spot where it struck. One lady was felled to the ground by the force of the shock. She struck on her head, resulting in a rather severe abrasion of the skull.

For several hours the terrific peals of thunder and the incessant dashes of lightning kept the animals and their owners also in a constant state of terror.

The quarantine that is over the city will be raised on Friday or Saturday.

Cedar City, Iron Co., July 3.--We have enough breadstuffs to tide over until harvest and have not imported any the past year, but our bins will all be cleaned out. Our cheese surpasses all imported cream cheese from State or eastern factories. Butter imported is hardly to be mentioned. Hay has held out nicely.

Good beef and mutton in the shop are home produced; wish we could say the same of hams and bacon, but sorry to report an importation of five tons a year. Wool and lamb products excellent, prices low.

Field crops are fairly good, water is eking out nicely. The heat is intense.

Smallpox trifling, but have a few cases of typhoid. Health generally good.

Dairies are in full running order. A dull business spring, now improving.

Cedar City, Iron Co., July 19.—A painful accident befel the 16-year-old son of Orson Fretwell. The boy was coming home from the field on a load of lucern, when the load slipped, letting him off backward. The pitchfork slipped after him, sriking him in the thigh. One tine passed through the leg, another pierced to the bone, and another grazed along the abdomen. The boy is doing nicely.

Attorney S. A. King has been secured by James Glendenning to defend him in his preliminary hearing for the shooting of Jim Hedges. Mr. King happened to be in the vicinity of Stateline when the tragedy occurred. When he passed through the camp on Tuesday he was told there was bad blood between Hedges and Glendenning and that it would be certain to end in a shooting duel. Mr. King expressed the hope that nothing so serious would occur, and then went out a few miles to look over some mining claims. When he was returning he met a man who told him that Glendenning had shot and killed Hedges. The former heard that Mr. King was in the camp and sent for him. The result of the interview was a promise on the part of Mr. King to defend the prisoner.

Glendenning is in prison at Cedar City and is said to be suffering considerable from his wounded arm. Mr. King thinks there is no question of his discharge when the preliminary hearing is held.

One of Jim Hedges' sons attended the Salt Lake Business college last spring and was a very exemplary young man.

Cedar City, Iron Co., Jan. 1.—News reached this city this morning by telegraph from De Lamar, Nevada, of the accidental death of Mr. James Corlett, yesterday. The deceased has followed the occupation of freighter for a number of years and was engaged in that business between Callentes (the present terminus of the Oregon Short Line railroad), and De Lamar, Nevada, when he was run over by a loaded wagon and killed. Particulars of the accident have not yet reached his family, who reside here. Men and vehicles have been sent to Lund, where the remains will arrive tonight by rail, to bring the body home to his sorrowing wife and family. The sad news, coming as it did on New Year's day, has turned joy and pleasure into gloom and sadness, as Mr. Corlett was a respected and honorable citizen of our town, and was one of the early pioneers of Iron county, arriving here in his early boyhood, accompanied by his widowed mother, two sisters and a brother. He leaves a wife and three children as well as a host of friends to mourn his demise.

The festivities connected with Christmas and New Year's day are now things of the past, and old and young are settling down to a normal condition. Social parties and family gatherings have been frequent, and last evening a grand character ball and supper at midnight closed the eventful history of the year 1902.

Snow in the valley has almost disappeared. The weather for the past week has been very cold, but indications for more snow are very favorably this evening. Stock and sheep are reported to be doing reasonably well on the ranges and have not yet suffered by the heavy fall of snow thus far this winter.

Our merchants report doing an unusually heavy business during the holidays.

Work on the iron mines at Iron Springs is going on and it is rumored that a large force of men will be employed at an early date developing some of the many claims now secured in that vicinity. A representative of the Colorado Fuel & Iron Co. seems to take the lead in developing these immense deposits.

Kanarra Kinks.

Dec. 31st, 1902.

John Stapley, and Mrs Martha Ford, who have been very ill for the past two or three weeks are recovering their health.

Elders Parkinson and Cox, Mutual Improvement missionaries, are making a house to house visit in the interest of those associations.

About 75 of our people attended the wedding supper given by Bp. William Ford and lady in honor of the marriage of their daughter Rebecca, with Mr. Jas E. Anderson.

The Dramatic company that was organized here a short time ago, with the intention of presenting a play for the holidays, is in a dangerous state of coma, from which if they cannot be aroused death is likely to ensure.

A pleasant surprise for the Ford families was the arrival of Mr. John Ford the eldest son of Bp Ford, who came to his old home recently to spend the holidays. He was in time to partake of the wedding supper of his sister a welcome though unexpected guest.

Cedar City, Iron Co., Feb. 6.—Sister Cathrine Evans Middleton, one of our aged faithful and industrious citizens, departed this life this morning of general debility. Deceased came to Utah in the year 1860, emigrating from Aberdare, South Wales, a widow accompanied by one daughter. Soon after her arrival in Salt Lake City she married Brother William Middleton, a widower, both coming to Cedar City soon after. One son is the result of her last marriage. Sister Middleton was 85 years of age. She joined the Church in her native land in the year 1847, and took an active part in assisting the Elders to establish the doctrines of the Latter-day Saints in her native land. Sister Middleton leaves a daughter and son and 25 grandchildren and 24 great-grandchildren, and many friends, to cherish her memory. Funeral services will be held tomorrow in the tabernacle.

Since the heavy fall of snow we are having exceedingly cold weather, the temperature falling to 7 degrees below zero.

Lucern hay is now selling at $10 and $12 per ton, and hard to obtain at that price. Unless the weather moderates soon, it is feared stock and sheep will suffer, as the ranges are covered with snow to a depth of from one to two feet, making it impossible for animals on the ranges to procure feed.

Kanarra Kinks.

March 31, 1903.

Work has begun in the fields, some are plowing, others sowing.

The Grammar department of our district school closed last Friday.

We had a fine rain Saturday night, and the prospects for more are good.

Henry Pollock has bought a house and lot in the Eastern part of town from Myron Davis.

Brick hauling has commenced on the new school house, and the trench for the foundation is being dug.

Riley G. Williams has bought Priscilla Roundy's real estate for $1200, and sold the town part of it to W. R. Davis.

Another very young boy has made his appearance at the home of Mr. John Platt. If the Platt family never contains any more girls than it does now, John will never have the pleasure of kicking his would be son-in-law out at twelve o'clock at night.

Deseret News
April 2, 1903

Cedar City, Iron Co., April 2.—Carl Arrick Hallman, a highly esteemed citizen of this place, died somewhat unexpectedly yesterday. Deceased had been ill recently and while feeling poorly contracted a severe attack of la grip, which caused his death. Deceased was a native of Sweden and was born in the town of Askireta, in September, 1837. He left his native land for Utah in the year 1888 and with a family of two sons and a daughter located here. He was an honorable and industrious citizen, modest and unassuming in his manner, and faithful to the cause he espoused.

Deseret News
May 2, 1903

(Special to the News.)

Cedar City, Utah, May 2.—A sad accident took place in our city yesterday afternoon about 4 o'clock. Sarah Whittaker Chatterley was making soap, when suddenly her clothes caught fire and before help reached her she was badly burned from the feet to the chest. She did not appear to suffer much, but died at 6 o'clock this morning. She was one of the stalwart women in Church work in this ward and a pioneer of Iron county.

Iron County Record
May 2, 1903

Mr. Edwin R. Cox and Miss Mary Hamilton of "Hamilton's Fort" formed a life partnership this week, the contract being ratified in the St. George Temple. They bear an excellent reputation, and have the good wishes of all their friends, among whom The Record editor classes himself.

Summit Sumups.

President Uriah T. Jones with his counselors visited this ward last Saturday. We always appreciate these visits.

Elder John S. Woodbury of the Stake superintendency of the Y. M. M. I. A. met with the young people here Saturday evening.

Herbert White is preparing to move his house which stands on the back part of his lot, up to the front. As it is a three-roomed frame structure, Mr. White is likely to have quite a job to move it without injuring it.

Miss Esther Dalley was called home from school last week to assist her mother owing to the illness of little Mable who has been very sick. To-day the little one is sufficiently recovered to allow Miss Esther to return to her studies.

Iron County Record
May 29, 1903

Summit Sumups.

May 27, 1903.

The farmers are elated over the showers that have fallen lately.

We are pleased to welcome our students home again for a short time.

After a long absence from her native town, Mrs. Hannah Sadler is visiting relatives here.

The Summit and Enoch boys, regardless of the busy times sheared J. B. Dalley's sheep at the Pass pens last week.

Mrs. Thrine Dalley and her two daughters, Ida Hulet, and Lillian White, left for Salt Lake City this morning. They will attend conference and visit relatives.

Elder Heber Dalley, who has been taking a missionary course at Provo, received a call for a mission to the south western state. He is to leave Salt Lake City on the tenth of June but will visit at home until then.

Iron County Record
June 17, 1903

Kanarra Kinks.

June 17th 1903.

Mr. and Geo. Davis were blessed with another son last Sunday.

Richard Bryant of Cedar is finishing the painting of the meeting house.

Mrs. Emma Daugherty was in our town last Sunday on professional business.

Wm. Williams and family will move to their ranch on the Laverkin this week.

Richard Palmer of Cedar City and William Williams occupied the time in meeting last Sunday.

Thomas Perry is expected here this week to finish the Belfry on the meeting house which will require a little alteration to prevent the rain from coming into the building.

Deseret News
June 25, 1903

Cedar City, Iron Co., June 25.—Funeral services over the remains of Elder Robert Bulloch were held in the tabernacle of this city this afternoon, attended by a large concourse of citizens. Appropriate and consoling remarks were made by a number of Elders. In February, 1902, Brother Bulloch left his home in obedience to a call to take a foreign mission. On his arrival in England he was assigned to the Scottish mission, where he labored faithfully until June, 1903, when he was honorably released, through sickness, to return home, where he arrived on the 25th departing this life three days later. While in Scotland he was seized with a very severe attack of la grippe, which developed into a serious case of dropsy that proved fatal.

Deceased was born in Kilmarnock, Scotland, Jan. 5, 1838. He, with his parents, one brother and sister, started for Utah in 1848, burying his mother at St. Louis, where the family remained till 1851, when they came on to Utah. They came with the pioneers to Cedar City, where they have taken a prominent part in building up this city and developing the resources of the county. Elder Bulloch was an enterprizing, energetic and self-made man, manifesting great faith in the cause he had espoused; ever ready with his means and moral support to defend and advance the work of God in the earth, and although somewhat advanced in years for missionary labor, he frequently expressed, since his return, the satisfaction he had realized in being honored with the privilege of visiting his native land as a missionary, and regretted the fact of not being permitted to remain the allotted time. Deceased was the father of nine children, four of whom are married, who, together with his wife, mourn the loss of a kind, indulgent father and affectionate husband, and all of whom desire through the Deseret News to express their heartfelt gratitude to the Saints and Elders of the British mission who may have contributed in any manner to the comfort of their husband and father during his sickness while abroad.

Iron County Record
July 17, 1903

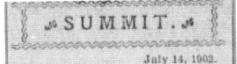

❧ SUMMIT. ❧

July 14, 1903.

A light shower of rain fell here Wednesday.

The hay is now nearly all harvested.

Miss Mae Dalley has gone to Circleville for an outing.

The families of Wm. Smith and S. C. Hulet, Jr., have moved to their ranches on the mountains. No doubt butter will be more plentiful now.

Monday a very pleasant surprise was given Mrs. Tweedie in honor of her birthday. A score or more of her friends joined in wishing her many happy returns of the day and in furnishing a sumptuous feast.

Iron County Record
July 24, 1903

The Bennett-Stewart Reception.

The wedding reception given at the home of Mrs. Adelia Murie last Saturday evening in honor of Harry Bennett and Miss Maggie Stewart, who were joined in the holy bonds of matrimony at Salt Lake City a short time since, was a very pleasant affair. The company was not especially large, but was congenial. The bride and groom appeared at their best and were the recipients of a number of nice presents and hearty congratulations.

The supper was dainty and all in good taste. An immense wedding cake ornamented one of the tables and before the party broke up it was divided among the guests, to dream over. Tea, coffee, lemonade, beer and wine constituted the liquid refreshments. The viands were all tasty and served in the most approved style.

The bride was attired in a white swiss trimmed with white satin ribbon and all-over lace. The evening was pleasantly spent in listening to vocal and instrumental music, reciting and in games.

KANARRA

Grain is ripening very fast this weather.

Mr. R. J. Williams and family moved to their mountain ranch last Tuesday.

M. T. and W. R. Davis moved their families to the mountain last Saturday.

Mrs. Rebecca Berry and daughter Minnie have gone to Provo, where Mrs. Berry will be treated for goiter.

Bp. Berry is buying sheep and intends running a bunch again this winter. He recently purchased 200 head from Mr. Kesler of Virgin City.

Mr. James Stapley and family moved today to their ranch on the mountain and will spend a couple of months there making butter and cheese.

The Twenty-fourth will not be celebrated with very much vim in Kanarra this year, on account of so many people being on the mountains and for other reasons.

James L. and George A. Davis have been prepareing their adobe yard this week preparatory to making the brick for the Store, which is to be moved to a new site.

John Platt went to Pinto Monday, making the trip on foot. He returned today with a team and wagon and a binder mounted on the wagon. John is a man who can walk when there is no chance to ride.

Iron County Record
August 14, 1903

TELEPHONE IS HERE

Connection Established With Cedar Tuesday.

The next maps issued by the Bell Telephone Co. will show connections with a few more Utah towns. At noon Tuesday Cedar City was placed in communication with all the principal towns of Utah, Montana, Idaho and other states.

The poles of the company have been erected along the centre of Main street, obstructing the shale grade which had been constructed at a considerable cost ... adverse criticisms were made ... the action of the council ... In the ... phone co ... well ha... been located eight or ... feet ... geographical centre of the street, with ... inconvenience to the company ... the city. However, there is no use ... ing over spilled milk, and we are glad the phone is here.

It is likely that Cedar City will be the southern terminus of the line until February or March of next year, but it is not out of the range of possibilities that work may be recommenced next October. Contracts have been let for the delivery of the poles between Cedar and St. George next February, but it is understood that should the company decide to continue the work this

fall and winter, the contractors would gladly furnish the poles this year.

About 30 to 35 men have been employed on the extension from Beaver, and the work has been under the supervision of S. S. Arrowsmith. The cost is reported to have been about $300 per mile. The poles are all large sturdy looking fellows, and the cross bars are constructed to receive six wires, although only two will be in use at present. Copper wire of the standard guage is being used.

Four rings calls up Cedar City and three designates Parowan. Beaver is a switch office where "central" is located. Connection has also been made at Paragoonah and Summit.

Only one phone has yet been placed in Cedar, which is the toll phone and is installed in the Cedar City Drug Store. Cedar has been greatly enthused over the arrival of the telephone and the workmen have been constantly "rubbered." Cedar has advanced one more step in the scale of civilization.

Iron County Record
September 17, 1903

Last Tuesday Mrs. Lewis Balser of Kanarra had her thigh broken by the falling on her of a heavy gate. As near as we have been able to learn, the lady was in the corral at the time, for the purpose of milking the cows, and in attempting to close the gate it fell from its hinges on the unfortunate woman. Mr. John Smith was called in and set the limb, which at date of our information was doing as well as could be expected under the circumstances. Mr. and Mrs. Balser have a family of small children which makes the situation still more distressing.

Iron County Record
November 14, 1903

We are sorry to learn Mrs. H. A. Andelin is ill with pneumonia.

Mrs. Isaac Haight is enjoying the rare pleasure of a visit from her mother Mrs. Clineman, whom she has not seen for twenty years.

Iron County Record
November 20, 1903

KANARRA

Nov. 20 1903.

Mrs. Louise Balser with her broken leg is mending slowly.

Tons of coal are being hauled from the mine daily and it is of a fine quality.

C. Parker's house and George Williams store are under construction.

Prin. Jno. W. Platt is trying with all his might to bring about a better state of affairs in the school.

Evening meetings for the past week have almost been a failure. Why? Because, who can see when the lights go out?

Jos. S. Williams, whose arm is swinging (not in a grapevine swing,) but in a sling, is coming around alright.

Photographer Rance is in town and he seems to be the center of attraction. There must be some pretty people here, especially girls.

Henry Pollock had another bad spell today, but at present is some better. Elders are frequently called in to his assistance.

Councilor J. W. Berry, accompanied by Mrs. Jessie Berry, left for Loa yesterday to receive his sheep of W. W. Taylor of that place.

Bp. Berry arrived home Thursday night from a trip to Dixie. Can't imagine what kept him so long. Don't think they have coolers down there.

The new school building is growing rapidly. Four masons are at work. Hard to tell how many overseers and tenders. Lime, lumber, sand and brick is being brought in pretty quick.

Iron County Record
December 5, 1903

Mrs. Sarah A. Bulloch is contemplating a trip to southern Arizona for the purpose of visiting her relatives in that section of country, especially her mother, Mrs. Eunice Higbee, who is in poor health. Mrs. Bulloch will leave soon after New Years, going by way of California.

Reception given last week Wednesday evening at the home of the groom's parents over at Washington to celebrate the marriage of Israel T. Nielson of that place to Miss Annie Reese of Cedar City, was quite a pretentious affair. A large number of young people were present, and a bountiful repast was served.

KANARRA

(Received too late for last issue.)

Dec. 17, 1903.

Wm. R. Williams has returned home again, and in good spirits, judging from his looks.

Father and son George Wood, were down to see their old friend Jno. Steel and to console him if possible.

A few more days will wind the mason work up—on the school building, then boys what must we do to be busy?

Coal hauling will be done for, if it snows, and this blessed South wind is apt to bring it. But Cedar needen't look for any cause the wind don't blow up there. It simply whistles.

Last Sunday was Ward Conference here, the Stake Presidency and stake Sunday School presidency were present in full. Orlando Bracken of the M. I. A., was also present.

We are pleased to recall the statement in last week's issue concerning Granfather Steele, and say: He is surprisingly smart at the age of 82 and were it not for his foot he could no noubt as he says, walk a mile in ten minutes. He is now at the residence of Jas Stapley of this place.

ARTHUR DALLEY DROPS DEAD.

Slightly Hurt by the Overturning of His Cart.

LAST WORDS, "MY GOD! I'M DYING!"

While Cutting Hay to Feed His Horse The "Grim Reaper" Gathers Him In.

Arthur Dalley son of W. W. Dalley of Summit died suddenly at that place Thursday evening while feeding his horses.

We have not been able to find any one who has been in direct communication with the young man's parents or his wife since the tragedy, but as near as we have been able to learn the circumstances are as follows: Mr Dalley and his wife visited relatives in Cedar last Thursday. While returning the cart in which they were riding was overturned and Mr. Dalley was slightly hurt, but nothing serious as far as he was able to judge at the time. They righted the cart and continued their journey home. Upon their arrival Mr. Dalley assisted his wife to alight from the cart, took his horse to the stable and put him up, and began to cut hay from the stack to feed him with, when suddenly the young man threw up his hands exclaming "My God I'm dying," he fell on the ground and expired in a few minuets. It is quite possible that this account may not be an entirely correct one, but that Mr. Arthur Dalley is dead and that he died suddenly and in something like the manner we have told, there is no reason to doubt. Deceased leaves a young bride of six or seven months standing, the daughter of Mrs. Bell of Enoch, to mourn his loss. The Record extends sympathy to the bereaved.

Cedar City, Iron Co., Jan. 4.—Another storm period is upon us, although the downfall is very light up to the present time. Farmers are becoming quite uneasy over the prospects for water the coming summer. Enough snow has fallen thus far to allow our sheep herds to move out from the various water courses where they have been compelled to stay for water.

The holiday season has passed off quietly. The usual dances and family gatherings have been indulged in.

Sister Louise Adams, wife of Timothy Adams of this city, departed this life on the 2nd inst., after an illness of several weeks. Deceased was born in the village of Thompson, near Walton, Norfolk, England, February, 1846; emigrated to Utah in 1866, coming across the plains with ox teams, leaving all her relatives in England for the Gospel's sake. On her journey over the plains she made the acquaintance of her husband, and on their arrival in the valley were married.

Sister Adams was an affectionate wife, an indulgent mother and a conscientious Latter-day Saint; unassuming in her manner, but kind and devoted to her friends and neighbor. She leaves a husband and four children.

Yesterday another of our veterans passed peacefully away in the person of Richard R. Birkbeck, who had been confined to his home for several months through general debility. Deceased was born in Cullin Row, County Durham, England, March 25, 1828; baptized Aug. 25, 1849, and came to Utah in 1862, crossing the ocean on that notable vessel the Ellen Maria, arriving in Salt Lake City, Oct. 4, 1862. In 1857 he was called by President Brigham Young to go to Iron county, in charge of a steam engine, to be used in the manufacturing of iron. Brother Birkbeck having been employed in his native land as a locomotive engineer. In 1865 he left his wife and home in Cedar City to fill a two-year mission to England. His aged wife survives him.

The Record extends sympathy to Mr. and Mrs. Henry Eddards, whose infant child died Thursday night.

Miss Hazel Haight, who has been very ill lately, is recovering slowly, but is still far from well.

Sheriff Froyd and wife added another to their bevy of girls last week. The count on the last general election showed that the sheriff was a popular man, and the possession of four pretty daughters is not at all likely to detract from his popularity.

Iron County Record
February 24, 1904

Feb. 24, 1904

We are pleased to welcome Mrs. Fannie Farrow, home again.

Miss Sebriskie of Minersville is in town visiting her friend Miss Marie Farrow.

Last Sunday evening the Mutual was favored with a visit from Pres. Randal Jones, Jos. H. Armstrong and Wm. Hunter.

The speakers in our sacramental meeting last Sunday were Elders Charles E. Jones, Silvester F. Jones and Hyrum Jones of Enoch. Also Bp. Dalley; who has been away from home for several weeks.

Miss Letty Dalley gave a party to a company of about 25 children on the evening of the 22nd in honor of little Thurza's birthday. The children say it was the best time of their life and each one came home with a beautiful souvenir of Letty's own handiwork.

Iron County Record
March 3, 1904

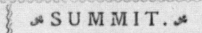

March 3, 1904.

Mr. Roy Simkins of Circleville is in town, a guest of Maroni Dalley.

The Deacons gave a Ball last evening which was in every way a success.

The farmers are busy putting in grain. The nice storm last Sunday has made them feel more encouraged.

We are sorry to report the death of Chief, the pure bred Clidesdale Stallion of S. C. Hulet Jr., valued at about $500 The cause of his death was distemper.

Iron County Record
March 10, 1904

March 10, 1904.

John Farrow new house is almost ready for occupancy.

William Smith has built an addition to his home and otherwise improved it.

On Monday, March 7th, there was a fine baby girl came to the home of Oscar Hulet. Mother and child are doing well.

We are sorry to learn of the illness of Mrs. Theressa Dalley, who has been in Cedar since holidays. We hope she will soon be able to come home.

The water owners have been busy the past week cleaning and making new ditches from the mouth of the canyon down through town hoping to increase the water.

Iron County Record
March 17, 1904

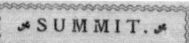

⚘SUMMIT.⚘

(Received too late for last issue.)
March 17, 1904.

W. H. Dailey leaves for Milford in the morning.

The Relief Society had its first lesson on Mothers' Class work today. The subject of pre-existence was treated.

We are pleased to have Niels Madson at home again. He has been working on the Bell Telephone line the past month.

Our town people have been afflicted with Lagrippe the last week or ten days. There is scarcely a home but what it has visited, and some families have all been down at once.

Iron County Record
March 23, 1904

Iron County Record
March 24, 1904

⚘SUMMIT.⚘

March 31, 1904.

The farmers are rejoicing over the beautiful fall of snow of yesterday and today.

S. S. Hulet of Alta, Wyo., is in town visiting relatives and friends. He will leave for his home in the north in a few days.

Mrs. Martha Dailey and her daughter Ann came home from Stateline last Sunday. They are both feeling and looking well.

While Mrs. John Farrow was standing at the wash tub with her back toward the stove one day last week the front leg of the stove gave way, causing a boiler full of boiling water and clothes to tip off of the stove, scalding Mrs. Farrow's quite baddly. The lady, however, is improving nicely.

On Tuesday March 29th, while Bro. James Dailey was moving around out of doors for exercise and fresh air he went to the stock yard to watch his son W. W. repairing his fence. Two cows were in the yard, and one hooked the other, causing her to run against the old gentleman, knocking him down. On being carried to the house it was found that his right leg had been very painfully injured so much so that he has been confined to his room.

Deseret News
April 5, 1904

Cedar City, April 5.—Mr. and Mrs. Richard H. Palmer are called upon to mourn the loss of their eldest child Virrona which occurred on March 15, 1904. She was nearly 11 years of age. She was a beautiful child and very popular with her school mates and social companions. This was pathetically shown in the beautiful floral offerings that were made at the funeral services which were very impressive. Remarks of consolation were made by local speakers and every effort was made by sympathizing neighbors and friends to lessen the sorrow of the bereaved parents.

There is said to be fully four feet of snow in the hills thus insuring considerable water for the farms, etc.

Iron County Record
April 28, 1904

♫ SUMMIT. ♫

April 28, 1904.

The Young Men of this ward have discontinued their meetings for this season.

There was a fall of about eight inches of snow last Saturday. The heavy frost after the storm damaged the fruit a great deal.

Miss Mattie Davis of Circleville is in town staying with her grandmother, Mrs. Sarah Davis. The old lady is still very ill.

The number of men was very few at our religious services last Sunday, owing to so many being employed at the shearing pens in Parley's Pass.

Last Monday about a dozen Relief Society workers took their picnic and gave Mrs. Marguretta Dalley a surprise. It was a very pleasant as well as profitable affair, because they sewed all of Sister Dalley's carpet rags for her.

Mr. C. S. Wilkinson and Lafe McConnell have been in town this week repairing the old telegraph line and converting it into a telephone line. We are pleased to see this. It made a person homesick to see the old faithful poles lying on the ground and the wire stringing around the street after so many years of good service.

Deseret News
April 30, 1904

Cedar City, Iron Co., April 30.—Another of our pioneer veterans, William Unthank, passed peacefully away on the 28th inst, after an illness of three months. Deceased was born in Cumberland, England, in 1827. In early boyhood he left his native land for Australia, where he joined the Church of Jesus Christ of Latter-day Saints in the city of Sydney, in which branch he took an very active part. In the year 1855, in company with some 200 Saints, emigrated from Sydney to America, landing at San Pedro, Cal., after a journey of some two months over the Pacific ocean. In the year 1856 Brother Unthank married Miss Mary Ann Barns, who had accompanied him from Australia, and in the year 1858 arrived in Cedar City, from San Bernardino, Cal., where he has resided up to the time of his death, leading a quiet, industrious, peaceful life, serving as a Teacher in this ward for a number of years, as well as a member of the choir.

Deceased leaves two wives and eight children, with numerous friends to mourn his demise.

Iron County Record
May 7, 1904

Yesterday at about midday, Elder Walter Granger formerly of St. George, and for many years a resident of the village of Enoch in this county, finished a well spent life at the ripe age of eighty two years. The old pioneer resided in Cedar City the fore part of the winter, but since the accident which deprived his granddaughter Mrs. Dalley of her husband last winter he went back to Enoch with his daughter Mrs. Bell, and has lived there ever since. Father Granger was one of the early settlers in St. George, and was for a number of years bishop of the second ward in that City. He was prominent in many other public matters and always bore the reputation of being a man of most excellent character. The direct cause of his death was lagrippe, although his advanced years made him a much easier victim than he would otherwise have been.

Iron County Record
May 23, 1904

On Wednesday Mr. Ernest Webster and Katherine Nelson of Cedar City, were granted a license and joined in and happy bonds of wedlock before leaving the Clerk's office.

Iron County Record
June 10, 1904

❧ SUMMIT. ❧

June 10, 1904

Uncle Wm. Dalley is very ill.

Stake President Annie M. Dalley is expected home this evening from Salt Lake where she has been attending the Mutual conference.

The Dalley boys, Vet and Ras, will stay and attend the teachers' institute and summer school at Salt Lake City.

Wm. Hales and wife are in town visiting relatives and friends.

Sylvester C. Jones, graduate of the U. of U., is a guest of O. W. Hulet. He returns home from Salt Lake in the best of health and spirits, having enjoyed his school work very much.

Iron County Record
June 18, 1904

The first operation in the new hospital was performed by Dr. Middleton last Saturday. The patient was Miss Emily Banks of Minersville and the operation was for appendicitis.

The disease was in the quiescent stage and the exterior appearance of the appendix caused the doctor a shade of uneasiness lest he should have made an error of diagnosis. The history of the case being so plain, however, it was decided to remove the appendix, which was done. On being dissected, the interior was found to be ulcerated, and to contain a part of a tooth-pick, which without doubt was responsible for the attack.

The case is a most interesting one to medical students, and it is doubtful if another such is to be found in the history of this peculiar disease.

The hospital now contains two patients, which are as many as the present accommodations will admit of, but work is being pushed on the upper floor and it will be placed in readiness as soon as possible, when it is believed there will be ample room for all probable requirements for a number of years.

It will take some little time for the people of Cedar City and the surrounding settlements to fully appreciate the advantage of having a hospital established here, with so competent a practitioner in charge.

Iron County Record
June 24, 1904

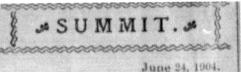

❧ SUMMIT. ❧

June 24, 1904.

Haying has begun.

Professors Giles and Cosslett were in town yesterday selling organs.

S. C. Hulet, Jr., has greatly improved his place by putting a new fence all round it.

The people of Enoch will join us in celebrating the Fourth of July, for which a nice program has been arranged.

Hon. E. L. Clark called on James Dalley one day this week. Although his visit was short it was very much appreciated. Though Father Dalley has practically lost the use of his speech and limbs he still enjoys a visit from a friend or neighbor.

There arrived at the home of Mr. and Mrs. Bert Robb, son No. 2. Parties concerned doing nicely.

KANARRA

August 11, 1904.

The health of the people is good.

We have had some heavy rains and a few floods, but no serious damage has resulted.

Attendance at religous gatherings is slim, owing to so many being on the mountain and other places.

We are sorry to report the death of the little babe of Mr. and Mrs. Henry Pollock, which occurred some two weeks ago.

At the mass meeting of the people held about a month ago, but very few were present to hear the report of the district school trustees. It was read, however, and accepted, after which the meeting was open for the voting to the board of their compensation for the year's hard labor. There were two voters present, one representing the pocrer class and the other the more wealthy position. One was liberal-minded and advocated giving $75; the other more conservative and thinking that $60 was sufficient. The latter won by one vote and the last named amount was fixed as the compensation.

Cedar City, Iron Co., Aug. 23.—Funeral services over the remains of John Williams were held in the tabernacle yesterday, when a large number of relatives and friends paid their respects to the departed young man. Deceased was the son of David Williams and Amelia Webster Williams, and was born in Cedar City. Nov. 28, 1875; died Aug. 21, 1904, of heart trouble, superinduced by rheumatism. He was exceptionally kind to his widowed mother, brothers and sisters; led an exemplary life and was active in the discharge of his Church duties, being a prominent member of the lesser Priesthood in this ward.

Since the stormy and unsettled weather considerable sickness prevails in our midst, mostly mild attacks of typhoid fever.

Weather conditions are very unfavorable for farm labor, and showers of rain are of daily occurrence. Some threshing of grain has been done, principally to bridge our citizens over the flour famine that usually prevails at this time of the year. However, most of the grain still stands in the shock in the field, waiting more favorable weather for hauling and stacking. The second cutting of lucern is ready for cutting, and where the recent floods have not damaged it, bids fair for a good yield.

Times are unusually dull with but little labor obtainable outside of the farming industry.

⚘ SUMMIT. ⚘

September 8, 1904.

Clarence McMullin is the honored guest of Mrs. Eliza Hulet.

W. W. Dalley, wife and daughter, have gone to Dixie to put up fruit.

R. H. Dalley of Preston, Idaho, arrived in town today, and will spend a week or ten days with his parents and other relatives.

On September 1 Mr. and Mrs. Herbert White were made happy by the advent of another son into their domicile. Mother and child are doing well.

Erastus B. Dalley and wife started to Fredonia last Saturday. They were accompanied by J. S. and Jos. B. Dalley and daughter, who expect to be absent about a week.

The inhabitans of our little community feel that they have sustained a great loss in the death of Sister Annie M. Dalley. The Mutual workers realize that a pillar of strength has gone from them. The Relief Society will also miss her greatly, as she was an able and willing worker in that organization, and the people as a whole deeply sympathize with her husband and daughter, and feel that we have all lost a friend in very deed.

KANARRA

September 16, 1904.

Bishop Wm. Ford has just returned from the Sevier and reports everything as being prosperous in that locality.

The home of Mr. and Mrs. Myron T. Davis was made happy by the advent of a beautiful baby girl a week ago today.

A Dixie threshing machine will do our work this year, as the Ford, Middleton and Prince machine has failed to put in an appearance.

Quite a number of our youngsters are intending to attend the Normal this winter, despite the awful reports that have gone out about the typhoid at Cedar.

The cheapest way to get your fruit is to go to Dixie yourselves and put it up, instead of buying from peddlers, says one of our citizens, who has been there.

Cedar City, Iron Co., Oct. 24.—Another sad death occurred in our city on the 22nd inst., when the spirit of Sister Clara Cram Bullock was released from its mortal tabernacle. The deceased had been in delicate health since the birth of her youngest child, some three months ago, but no serious apprehensions were had by her family until two or three days before her death. Deceased was born in Salt Lake City, December, 1868. Shortly after her birth she moved south with her parents, who settled in Kanab, Kane county, where she held many positions of honor in the young people's associations. In January, 1892, she was married to David C. Bullock of this place. She leaves a husband and six small children to mourn her demise, the oldest being now bedfast with typhoid fever. Funeral services were held in the tabernacle in this city Sunday, Oct. 23, when the building was filled with relatives and friends, who deeply sympathize with the family in their sad bereavement.

On Sunday, the 16th inst., funeral services were held in the same building over the remains of Sister Caroline Keturah A. Jones, widow of William Trehorne Jones, and daughter of Christopher and Caroline Haight Arthur of this city, who departed this life on the 14th inst., after a lingering illness. Deceased was born Aug. 11, 1861, in this city, was a faithful and consistent Latter-day Saint, a most dutiful daughter, an affectionate wife and devoted mother. She leaves three sons and three daughters, with her father, brother and sisters, and many relatives and friends, to mourn her departure. Consoling remarks were made on the occasion of her funeral, and a long cortege followed the remains to the cemetery.

✄ SUMMIT. ✄

Summit, Utah, Nov. 2, 1904.

A bounteous crop of potatoes was harvested here this year.

Mrs. William Hales is here visiting her parents and will remain a few weeks.

At our regular Sabbath meeting N. B. Dally and family were made members of the Summit ward.

The people of Summit extend their deepest sympathy to M. H. Dally and family in their great bereavement.

Mrs. Amelia D. Green came in from Lund today. She has come to stay with her mother while her husband is away on a mission to the Middle States.

Dr. Middleton and Mrs. Perry, the nurse who assisted him, left Thursday to return to Cedar City, accompanied by Mrs. Jessie Foster. The doctor was kept very busy while here, having performed ten surgical operations during his three days' stay. He was assisted by Dr. F. J. Woodbury of St. George. The most important cases are those of Bishop James McArthur, Raymond Cannon and Irvin Carter. All of the patients are doing very well.

❧ SUMMIT. ❧

Summit, Utah, Nov. 30, 1904.

The heatlh of the people of this place is, generally speaking, good at present.

The Mutuals gave a very nice party on the night of Thanksgiving, with which all who attended were very much pleased.

Hyrum Dalley has been released from the presidency of the Y. L. M. I. A. on account of having too many labors of a public character to alow him to give them all the necessary time and attention, and J. S. Dalley has been chosen to succeed him.

The Mutual Improvement associations are in a very prosperous condition, and are very popular among the young folks, nearly all of whom attend their meetings. Moroni Dalley has added two new rooms to his house, which has greatly improved his home.

We are sorry to learn that John Dover of this place has three children down with typhoid fever. One of them has been ill five weeks and is now beginning to recover. Dr. Green is in attendance. The other little ones are doing as well as could be expected.

R. H. Palmer and family were released from quarantine for smallpox, a few days since. Mr. Palmer suffered a severe attack of quinsy while housed up and looks as if he had been the most serious sufferer, though his daughter Gladys was the only member of his family that took smallpox.

Miss Jennie Angell is still very ill at Enoch and her parents are both by her bedside. Dr. Middlton is in attendance and has made several visits during this week.

About a week ago the son of Rees J. Williams of Kanarra had the misfortune to run a rusty nail in his foot, and the result is a badly swollen foot and some danger from blood poisoning. Dr. Middleton has been called in to take charge of the case.

KANARRA

Kanarra, March 15, 1905.

The Relief Society intend having a good time next Friday at the annual celebration of its organization.

It was decided tonight by the Y. M. M. I. A. to leave the manual and take up the Articles of Faith by Talmage.

The district school teachers, John W. Platt and Mae Stapley, attended the teachers' institute at Parowan on the 11th inst.

A pleasant evening was spent at the home of Mae Stapley last night, it being her birthday. She says she is "sweet 16"

Miss Eliza Williams, a teacher in the Cedar City district schools, came down and spet a weekly vacation visiting old time friends.

Bert Davies is looking forward with anxious eyes to Saturday when the race between him and Lowe Prince of Harmony is to come off.

Last week was a busy one with the farmers. This one is marked with quite a heavy rain fall, hence the saying, "More rain more rest."

We regret the absence of our friend Rees Jas. Williams, who two weeks ago had the misfortune to run a nail in his foot and is now under the doctor's care at Cedar City. Hope to have him with us soon.

David Bulloch has completed his contract with the Utah Construction Company for furnishing beef to the railroad camps along the new route, and reports that the business was very satisfactory, at least so far as he was concerned. He has now taken a contract for furnishing beef to the new town of Las Vegas.

⚘ SUMMIT. ⚘

Summit, Utah, May 3, 1905.

The people here have had very good health all winter, nothing more serious than colds and la grippe, but Mrs. Ann White is not so well or strong as we should like to see her.

Our town has been almost destitute of the male population for the last two weeks, and it is with pleasure that we notice they are again in their usual haunts, having just returned from sheep-shearing.

Our young townsman, Thos. Lawrence, is kept very busy these days, putting in lawns and gardens. He has very much improved the premises of Bp. O. W. Hulet, Herbert White and Thrine Dalley.

We were pleased to welcome the stake officers of the Relief Society last Sunday. Sisters Ollorton, Bayless, M. Wimmer and M. Halterman from Parowan were here and gave some very reasonable advice to parents.

James Dalley passed away early this morning. He has been a great sufferer for the last two years. Further particulars next week. Brother William Dalley, although 84 years of age, is able to be around. His youngest son, Heber, returned from a two year's mission today. He has been laboring in Texas and we are sorry to learn has been suffering much from rheumatism lately.

Cedar City, Iron Co., May 18.—The funeral services over the remains of Lamont Lunt Jones, the eldest son of Representative T. J. Jones, and who died May 17, were held in the tabernacle here today.

THE LATE LAMONT L. JONES.

The young man was one of Cedar City's brightest sons—genial, noble hearted and faithful in all his duties. The circumstances connected with his death called out great sympathy from all who knew him. For three years past he has been a constant sufferer from rheumatism. He bore his trial uncomplainingly, maintaining to the last such hope and cheer as were a lesson and inspiration.

Lamont was one of the charter students of the Branch Normal and the students and teachers attended the funeral in a body. The speakers, Prof. Howard R. Driggs, Dr. Middleton, President Henry Leigh and Elder Joseph Armstrong, all paid high tribute to the memory of the young man. Their words were full of consolation for those bereft. In addition to the good music furnished by the ward choir, Mrs. Driggs sang the solo "Calvary."

The deceased was born in Cedar City Feb. 16, 1879. He performed a faithful mission in California between June, 1899, and January, 1901, when he was forced to return home by the illness which has finally resulted in his death.

HARVEST OF GRIM REAPER.

The grim reaper has been unusually active in our city during the past week, four deaths having occurred. On the 8th inst. Mrs. Sarah Wain Pogson passed peacefully away at the ripe age of 88 years, of general debility. Mrs. Pogson was born in Huclaw, England, Oct. 25, 1817; was married to James Pogson, and some time after both joined the Church and came to Utah. They settled in Parowan, Iron county, Utah, where they lived several years, afterwards moving to this city. Her husband preceded her to the other side some 17 years. They had no children. The deceased was an active worker in Church affairs as long as her physical condition would permit, and was an earnest advocate of the religion she had espoused.

On the 11th inst. the infant son of George and Fanny Jones Corry died of acute Bright's disease.

On the 16th inst. Mrs. Margaret Adamson Condie, wife of George Condie of Hamilton's Fort, Iron county, and Cedar City ward, died of valvular heart disease. Deceased was a native of Scotland, born Oct. 12, 1840, and came to Utah in early days, crossing the plains with ox teams. She married Elder George Condie some few years after her arrival, and lived for a short time at Hamilton's, from which place they moved to Knosh, Millard county, returning to Hamilton's, Iron county, where they have resided since. Mrs. Condie was the mother of nine children, six of which have preceded her to the other side. She was an earnest and faithful Latter-day Saint. Funeral services were held in the Cedar City tabernacle on the 17th inst.

Iron County Record
May 19, 1905

At 7 o'clock, a. m. last Sunday, Mrs. Sarah Wain Pogson departed this life at the ripe old age of 88 years. With her death prishes the last, so far as known, of her family. Not a living realtive remains to bear the name of Pogson. Her husband preceded her to the other side some seventeen years ago, being killed by a large water-wheel, near this city. She was the mother of four children, two of whom died in England before the family immigrated to this country, one in Salt Lake City, and one in Cedar City.

The funeral services were held in the tabernacle Monday at 3 p. m., the attendance being large.

Mrs. Pogson was born in Huclaw, England, Oct. 25, 1817. She had little if any schooling. Was married to James Pogson in her native country, and some time after both joined the Church of Jesus Christ of Latter-day Saints.

Upon coming to Utah the family located in Parowan, where they lived for some years. From Parowan they came to Cedar City. From here they moved to Washington, Utah, where they resided five years, after which they returned to this place. The deceased was a teacher in the Relief Society for a number of years, and died as she lived, an earnest advocate of the religion she had espoused.

SUMMIT.

Summit, Utah, May 17, 1905.

We had neither Sunday School nor meeting on Sunday, every able bodied man being off shearing.

James Tweedie was home for a short visit last week and brought as his guest Roy Dalton of Circleville.

The Y. L. M. I. A. closed for the season last Sunday evening. The lecture "Baptism and Temptation of the Savior," was given by Cedenia Williams.

Amy Dalley returned this week from Dayton, Idaho, where she has been teaching school. She brings the news that Mrs. Charles Hulet has another son.

We are gald to note the spirit of improvement is still with our people. Wm. H. Dalley has had his house shingled, and Hyrum Dalley will build an addition to his house in the near future.

We hear that Obediah Farrow has been appointed fruit tree inspector for Summit and Enoch. We hope he will enforce the rules and see that the trees are regularly sprayed and taken care of.

The funeral of Bro. James Dalley was held last Friday. Although the weather was very inclement—the most stormy day we had had in six months—a number of visitors were presnt to pay their last respects to the deceased. The singing was beautifully and effectively rendered by Bro. Thos. Durham and a picked choir from Parowan, to whom many thanks are due. The speakers were Elders George Spilsbury from Toquerville, Thomas Durham, Wm. Mitchell and Charles Adams from Parowan, all of whom spoke of the sterling character and strong integrity of the deceased. Many showed the esteem in which they held Bro. Dalley by bringing beautiful wreaths of flowers, the casket being covered with roses and other flowers.

Bro. Dalley was born in England, Dec. 20, 1822. He accepted the gospel in his native land in 1841, and came to America in 1848. He has had four wives and was the father of 44 children. He has held all the offices in the Priesthood from Deacon to Patriarch, and was always faithful in the discharge of his duties.

Iron County Record
May 24, 1905

KANARRA

Kanarra, Utah, May 24, 1905.

The boys who were shearing sheep at Enoch are home again.

Roy Grant and his best girl were over from Harmony Sunday.

Mrs. Conger of Washington was here last week spending a few days with her husband.

We have recently been favored with a few days of pleasant weather favorable to the planting of corn and potatoes.

Dr. Conger, who has been here for about three weeks doing dental work, was joined last week by his partner, Mr. Finlea. They are now loacted in Cedar City.

Cedar City, Iron Co., June 4.—The past week has been a continual round of exercises, profitable and pleasurable, at the branch normal. Since Tuesday last the various classes have vied with one another in furnishing entertainment for their parents and friends, who have been in constant attendance. A great number of visitors from the surrounding towns came into Cedar City and have remained the whole week. They cannot but go away filled with the wholesome enthusiasm for education that characterizes the branch normal.

It is gratifying to say that this year the largest class in the history of the school has been graduated, and the quality of those who receive their certificates is as high as ever.

Among those who attended the exercises were President Riter of the board of regents and President Kingsbury. This is President Riter's first visit to Cedar City since he helped to pioneer the "Dixie" country in the sixties. He seemed delighted with the spirit of the school, and expressed himself as profoundly impressed with the marvelous changes wrought since his first visit here. The people and students were made to feel that in him as well as in President Kingsbury they have a father and a friend.

The commencement exercises were begun Tuesday evening, when the second years had much fun at the expense of the graduating class. On Wednesday afternoon a short but interesting program was carried out by the first year class. During Wednesday evening the third years—the graduating class—appeared in a very successful program. Every member of the class was given a chance, and the result was an excellent variety of music, addresses, original poetry, and reciting and witty burlesques. Thursday was filled with interesting events. The teachers gave a reception to the graduates during the forenoon. The specials carried out an entertaining program during the afternoon, and the alumni association was given a chance on the same day, beginning at 5 p. m. It furnished a series—business meeting, banquet, program and ball. More alumni were in attendance than ever before, and a happy reunion spirit prevailed.

On Friday morning the regular commencement program was carried out as follows:

Music .... Branch Normal Band
Music ......Branch Normal Orchestra
Invocation .... Dr. Geo. W. Middleton
Solo .... Mrs. Ada Wood Webster
"The Civic Problem" ...... Deslie Lowe
Cornet and Trombone Duet ....
...Wesley Taylor and John Webster
"My Say".............. Rupert Wixon
Address .... Prest. W. W. Riter
Solo .... Mrs. H. R. Driggs
Address ...... Prest. J. T. Kingsbury
Presentation of Certificates............
Chorus, "Hail Smiling Morn".........
Branch Normal Choral and Orchestra

A ball in the evening was the grand finale to a very successful year at the branch normal.

NAMES OF GRADUATES.

Parley Dalley, Sadie Hulet, Summit; Clarence Jones, Jennie Corry, Henrietta Jones, Irene Canfield, Zina Higbee, John Bladen, Hunter Lunt, John Webster, Cedar City; Deslie Lowe, Wesley Taylor, Junius Taylor, Albenia Hyatt, Parowan; Mary Urie, Hamilton's Fort; Esther Parker, Kanarra; Seth Jones, Enoch; John Page, Little Pinto; Josephine Seaman, Ranch, Kane county; Rose Jepson, Virgin; Albert Anderson, Mabel Naegle, Toquerville; Rupert Wixom, Circleville.

☙ SUMMIT. ☙

Summit, Utah, June 14, 1905.

Our conference visitors returned tonight, tired but happy.

The hearts of Mr. and Mrs. Wm. Hales were made glad by the advent of another bouncing boy, born June 10th.

J. S. Dalley has gone to Salt Lake City for Summer School. We understand he intends studying for a degree, presumably that of B. A.

Miss Sadie Hulet accompanied Dena Williams to the graduating exercises at Parowan, and afterwards took the teachers' examination.

It is very gratifying to know that so many of our young people in this small town are to the front along the lines of education. This year Parley Dalley made the second highest per cent in the Cedar Normal, 94 1-7, Mr. Wixom making 95. We also heard some time ago that Miss Dena Williams, our "sweet girl graduate" from the 8th grade, made the highest per cent in the county schools. By the bye, why does no one sing the praises of our dear, rough, shy, teasing, lovable boy graduates?

We offer Niels Madsen and bride our most sincere good wishes for their future health, happiness and prosperity, and we congratulate Niels on the prize he has won, for Norah is one of our most lovable and noble girls. We are glad the young couple have decided to make their home in Summit, for we could ill spare Norah, holding the position she does. In our SundaSy school she is teachre of the 1st intermediate, also secretary of the Relief Society, and Stake aid to the Y. L. M. I. A. Niels by his genuine good nature and good will to all, has won a place in all our hearts.

☙ SUMMIT. ☙

Summit, Utah, June 21, 1905.

Mrs. Nellie D. Dalley of Cedar is visiting the family of Wm. W. Dalley.

Cards are out announcing a reception on the 23rd inst. at the home of Mrs. Elzyna Hulet in honor of Mr. and Mrs. N. C. Madsen.

Mr. Alec Davis of Circleville is visiting his Mother, Mrs. Sarah Davis, and employing the time by putting a fence around her premeises.

Mrs. Letty B. Dalley gave a very enjoyable party last week in honor of Mr. and Mrs. Niels C. Madsen. Dainty refreshments, consisting of ice cream, cake, etc., were served.

Hyrum Dalley and wife are entertaining a very young lady, who will make an indefinite stay with them. She arrived yesterday morning and seems quite contented with here surroundings.

Cedar City, Iron Co., June 30.—An accident befell one of our respected citizens on Monday last, the 26th inst., which terminated fatally at 4 p. m. today. Charles M. Ahlstrom with his son Alonzo were engaged hauling hay from one of the fields close by and after loading their wagon were crossing a water ditch when the father was thrown from the wagon violently to the ground, breaking his thigh bone and injuring him internally, resulting as stated above, notwithstanding that all that the best of medical skill and kind nursing was done. The deceased was born in Malmo, Sweden, July 20, 1847 and in his early life came to Utah with his widowed mother and her family. In the year 1864 he came to Iron county. Mr. Ahlstrom was a devoted Latter-day Saint, a kind father and loving and affectionate husband; was of a jovial and happy disposition, held in high esteem by his friends. He is the father of 14 children, ten boys and four girls, 11 of whom survive him, with a brother believed to reside in Rush Valley and a sister residing in Salt Lake City.

During the session of the last legislature Mr. Ahlstrom was doorkeeper of the house branch of that body, and at the time of his death was the justice of the peace of the precinct.

A fair crop of lucern hay is being harvested. Grain is looking promising and if our irrigation water holds out we anticipate fair grain crops.

Arrangements are well under way for the observance of the nation's birthday.

Business is reported somewhat dull by our merchants, and outside of the farming industry but little if any labor can be procured.

Iron County Record
June 30, 1905

SHOCKING ACCIDENT.

Prominent Citizen of Cedar City Dies of the Injuries

Sustained by Fall From a Load of Hay—Charles M. Ahlstrom is the Victim.

A most shocking accident occurred in Cedar last Monday forenoon, which resulted in the death of one of our prominent and much esteemed citizens—Charles M. Ahlstorm.

The accident occurred while Mr. Ahlstrom and two of his sons were hauling hay from their land in the South field to town. The unfortunate man was standing up on the load driving the team across a ditch, which caused the load to lurch to one side and then suddenly and violently to the other. No one seems to have seen the man fall, and it will prehaps never be known exactly how he came in contact with the earth, but he was dazed for a few seconds, after which he suffered great pain. There were some men at work on a neighboring field and they assisted his older son, who was on the opposite side of the wagon when his father fell, to convey the sufferer to town. Dr. Middleton was summoned and did all that could be done for the patient. It was found that one of his shoulders was injured, his right hip broken and partially dislocated and there were internal injuries the extent of which it was impossible to ascertain at the outset.

The injured man, who was 63 years old, suffered intensely from the time of the accident until death released him, his only relief being found in the administration of morphine. During his brief illness his faithful wife kept close vigil at his bedside and neighbors rendered all the assistance within their power. Death was the result of his internal injuries.

The deceased was possessed of a remarkably strong constitution or he could not have withstood his injuries as long as he did. He lingered through Tuesday and Wednesday, the end finally coming at about 3:30 a. m. o'clock June 29th.

BIOGRAPHICAL.

Charles M. Ahlstrom was born July 20, 1842, in Sweden. He emigrated to the United States when a boy and has resided in Cedar City nearly all his life.

He was a member of the Church of Jesus Christ of Latter-day Saint, in good standing, although not prominen as a church worker. He was noted for his cheerful manner and his kind-heartedness. Conceiled beneath a rugged—almost uncooth—exterior, was a nature as tender and sympathetic as a woman's. In cases of sickness and death no one was more willing to render assistnace. He was always ready to share his last crust with a fellow being in want, and made the world about him glow with a warmer, more cheerful light by his pleasant and jocular disposition. The temperament of the man is shown by a number of incidents that have occurred since his injury. While being examined by the physician in attendance, he asked the doctor to feel of his shoulders to find if there was not something growing there. The doctor made the examination and replied in the negative. "Oh," said the sufferer between groans of pain; "I thought probably my wings were starting."

The deceased has been married twice and leaves in all nine children. Some of the older boys could not be located and did not know of their father's injury until he was dead. Most of the children, however, were at the deathbed.

For sevral years past the deceased has served as justice of the peace, either in a city or precinct capacity, and was the precinct justice at the time of his taking off. During the recent session of the state legislature he acted as door-keeper o the house of representatives and made many new acquaintances in Salt Lake City, who will be pained to learn of his untimely death.

"Charlie" Ahlstrom, as he was familiarly called, will be missed from the community. He will be mourned by his family and by a wide circle of associates, for in the warmth of his nature he made many fast rie nds.

Iron County Record
July 14, 1905

David Webster is crippling around this week as a result of stepping on a nail a few days ago. His foot has been badly swollen and quite painful.

Mr. and Mrs. Marion Millett have an increase in their family. The new arrival is of the feminien persuasion and put in an appearance yetaerday morning.

Mr. Hezekiah Simkins gave birth to a child last Saturday night. The infant lived only until Monday morning and was buried Tuesday. There were some complications at the birth and Dr. Green was called in. The parents have the sympathy of The Record in their beravement.

Frank Walker has rented Harry Hunter's old barber shop for a carpenter shop and seems to find no trouble in keeping busy.

Mr. J. F. Younger is going to launch a restaurant and feed stable business at Lund in a short time. He states that he was unable to make the salt business pay.

SUMMIT.

Mrs. Philip Dalley and family arrived here on Friday from Prestor, Idaho. They intend visiting friends and relatives here during the next two months.

Mrs. Thruie Dalley has been ill and suffering much pain the last three days.

Iron County Record
August 11, 1905

James W. Condie is the happiest man in town this week. On the 8th his wife presented him with his first girl baby. The Condie family comprises two boys, but this is the only girl. On the strength of it, Jim set up the cigars to a representative of The Record and paid his subscription a year in advance. He is a first-rate fellow, and deserves the good luck that has come to him.

Deseret News
August 27, 1905

DANIEL M. PERKINS DEAD.

On the 27th inst the community lost an esteemed citizen, in the death of Daniel Morgan Perkins. Deceased was a native of South Wales and emigrated with his grand-parents and their families to Utah in 1871. He was born March 15, 1865. He has resided in Cedar City since coming to Utah, and leaves a devoted wife and four children with many relatives and friends. Funeral services were held today in the Tabernacle.

Many of our young men tried their luck at the drawing of land for the settlement of the Uintah reservation, but did not draw lucky numbers.

Business here is quite dull. Some improvement by way of building is noticeable, principally the building of the boiler house, to be used for the heating of the Branch Normal, the old site having been condemned as unsafe and in too close proximity to the main buildings. This when complete will make quite an addition to the appearance of the university property.

Iron County Record
October 6, 1905

A baby boy arrived at the home of Mr. and Mrs. John Perry last Saturday morning.

Miss Nellie Hunter, who is one of the typhoid fever patients, is convalescing nicely.

We learn today that Edward Fife, who has been critically ill with disentery is much better.

There is a new-comer at the home of Mr. and Mrs. David Sherratt this week, of the feminine gender.

Rev. E. M. Landis will preach in the City Hall Sunday evening at 7:-30. Everybody cordially invited.

The two cases of typhoid fever at the home of Joseph Bauer are convalescing. The patients are a son and daugter of the family.

Iron County Record
October 27, 1905

Wednesday evening a few friends congregated at the home of Mr. and Mrs. Henry Leigh and tendered an informal reception to Mr. and Mrs. Samuel W. Leigh The bride and groom were in a happy mood and the evening passed by pleasantly.

Cedar City, Iron Co., Nov. 22.—Impressive funeral services were held in the tabernacle on the 17th inst., over the mortal remains of Mrs. Jane Cousins Birkbeck who departed this life on the 15th inst., after 14 days' illness. Deceased was born in Derby, England, July 13, 1822, and with her husband (who preceded her some two years ago) emigrated to Utah in 1852. In 1857 they were called with many others to settle in Iron county and assist in making iron. She was a very prominent figure in the ward Relief society and possessed lovable characteristics which endeared her to all who had the pleasure of her society.

The district schools were closed by order of the local board of health some four weeks ago on account of an epidemic of scarlatina breaking out here. It is understood they will remain so during the year as the disease seems to crop out in all parts of the town. Up to the present but two cases have proved fatal. As a precautionary measure those under 15 years of age are prohibited from attending public gatherings.

Jane Cousins Birkbeck Laid Away at Ride Age of 83 Years.

Last Friday the funeral services were held over the remains of Sister Jane Cousins Birkbeck, an aged and long-time resident of Cedar City, who departed this life Nov. 15th, at the ripe old age of 83 years. Bronchitis was the direct cause of her death, and she was a remarkably spry old lady for her years up to the time of her short and fatal illness.

The speakers at the funeral were Elders John Urie, Samuel T. Leigh, Wm. H. Corry, M. H. Dalley and Lehi W. Jones. Having no children of her own and having been preceded to the other shore by her husband some two years, the only relative in attendance was her adopted daughter, Sister Ella Mitchell. There were, however, a host of warm friends present to show their last respects.

The deceased was born in Duly, England, July 13, 1822. She was married to Richard Birkbeck in England, 1848, and they joined the Church of Latter-day Saints in their native country August 26, 1849, and emigrated to Utah, crossing the ocean in the sailing vessel, "Ellen Maria." The journey from Liverpool to Utah consumed eight months, and they arrived in Salt Lake City October 3, 1852.

Her husband was a locomotive engineer and came to this country to take charge of the engine at the primitive iron works established in this county in 1857, and the family has resided here ever since.

The deceased has been an active member of the Relief Soicety of this ward almost ever since she came here and was always ready and willing to do anything to relieve suffering or want.

With other pioneers of this county she passed through all the hardships and privations incident to the settlement of a new country. She has always been highly respected in the community and has certainly gone to inherit a rich reward for her many good deeds.

KANARRA

Kanarra, Utah, Dec. 27, 1905.

Ball playing and dancing are the principal amusements these holiday times. Of course, there are family and company dinners, occasionally.

Nearly all the young people are at home spending the time allotted to them by the vacation, and it is not ~~reasonable to suppose~~

Sister Samantha Parker, who has passed her 80th year, the last few days has been very ill but is now feeling some better.

The family of Wm. R. Williams has for the past few days been quarantined for scarletina, Lorenzo being the victim of the disease. He, however, is not very sorely tried.

Sunday services, both of the Sunday school and afternoon sessions, were carried on extemporaneously in commemoration of the one hundredth birthday of the Prophet Joseph Simth. A number of young women were called to speak.

Joel J. Roundy left yesterday morning for Lund, where he is to meet Mr. and Mrs. Dewellyn Taylor. They are no duobt coming to visit Mrs. Taylor's mother and aunt, and to assist the latter in her illness.

JURY LIST.

Following is the list of names selected by the Jury Commissioners of Iron County, Utah, to serve as jurors for the year 1905, as required by sections 1306 to 1309, Revised Statutes of Utah, 1898.

PARAGOONAH.

S. S. Barton, Jonathan Prothero, Thomas W. Jones, D. A. Lamoreaux, E. Robb, James C. Robinson, E. M. Owens, John B. Topham.

PAROWAN.

Charles D. Adams, Sidney Orton, L. N. Marsden, W. W. Pendleton, J. O. Decker, S. A. Matheson, Joseph Mickelsen, Hans J. Mortensen, John S. Hyatt, Henry W. Taylor, Richard Rowley, J. H. Gurr, E. L. Clark, John Stevens, John L. Lowder, W. C. Mitchell, Jr., Owen Matheson, Thomas Durham, John T. Bayles, W. H. Holyoak, Oscar M. Lyman, William Stubbs, John Davenport, M. M. Decker, Thomas Munford.

SUMMIT.

Charles R. Dailey, Obediah Farrow, Oscar Hulett.

CEDAR CITY.

M. H. Dailey, Charles Heyborne, James A. Bryant, Samuel B. Jones, Bengt Nelosn Jr., Thomas J. Webster, August Mackelprang, James Parry, Alfred K. Smith, Evan E. Williams, Charles N. Corry, Joseph T. Wilkinson, Myron D. Higbee, O. P. W. Bergstrom, George A. Wood, Randle W. Lunt, Frank A. Thorley, Frank W. Middleton, Henry Leigh, Daniel Stephens, Andrew Hansen, William P. Hunter, Everard A. Cox, William R. Palmer, William E. Pryor, Donald C. Urie, John Balden, Hyrum L. Perry, William D. Leigh, Isaac C. Macfarlane, Joseph Rosenberg.

KANARRA.

John Platt, George A. Williams, James Stapley, Rees J. Williams, Joel J. Roundy.

MODENA.

Robert C. Lund.

STATELINE.

Emanuel Jacobson, Joseph Johnson.

Bull Valley Iron.

James Canfield was in Cedar City this week and reports that work on the Bull Valley iron mines has been discontinued for the present. The annual assessment necessary to hold part of the claims was duly performed, and now they will wait for better weather before prosecuting the required labor for patenting the properties.

Mr. Canfield stated to a Record representative that the deposits developed to be larger with every stroke of the pick. In places where there were scarcely any indications a cut exposed ledges thirty or forty feet in thickness. Practically all of the iron is a Bessemer product, too.

Just as soon as the weather gets fit in the spring a large force of men will be set to work on the properties and Bull Valley will become a lively camp.

Henry Eddards came up from Manee, Nye county, Nevada, last Friday. He has been engaged in mining at that place and will return within a day or two to continue the work.

Mr. and Mrs. Julius Rosenberg have a child very sick with typhoid fever. The little one is some better at this writing. Dr. Middleton has the case in hand.

Notice.

The quarantine will be four weeks from now on and the flag will remain up for five weeks.

Parties who violate the quarantine law will be prosecuted.

To stamp out the prevailing disease strict measures are necessary, and the public are requested to assist the board.

E. SCHOPPMANN,
Sec. Board of Health.

DISASTROUS WRECK

Collision of Freight Cars Kills Three and Injures Two.

David Bulloch of Cedar in Critical Condition—Wreck Occurred Near Beryl Sunday Morning.

Latest advices from Salt Lake are to the effect that David Bulloch is slowly rallying from his injuries and is now practically out of danger. It is welcome news to his many friends in southern Utah.

A most disastrous wreck occurred on the San Pedro, Los Angeles and Salt Lake Railway last Sunday morning at 5:30, which resulted in the death of three men and serious injury of two others, one of the latter being David Bulloch of Cedar City.

The dead are:

Conductor G. W. Myres of Black Rock, Utah.

Extra Brakman W. T. Engles, Black Rock.

Brakeman W. F. Setphens, Black Rock.

The latter died as a result of his injuries while en route to Salt Lake.

THE INJURED.

The injured are David Bulloch of Cedar City, who is lying in the Holy Cross hospital at Salt Lake in a critical condition, and E. N. Hugiuni, a jeweler of Salt Lake City, who though severely bruised is not seriously injured.

DAVID BULLOCH.

HOW WRECK OCCURRED.

The wreck was due to the first section of the regular freight train, known as No. 81, breaking in two when one and one-half miles east of Beryl, and leaving nine cars on the track, which were crashed into by the second section of the train, there being a heavy fog a the time.

Mr. Bulloch was acompanying a shipment of live stock to the camps of Nevada, and at the time was asleep in the caboose, as were probably members of the train crew, who were killed.

The injured were at once placed on a special train and dispatched to Salt Lake City, while the authorities of Iron county were notified and County Attorney Ryan and Precinct Justice Herbert C. Adams of Cedar City at once repaired to the scene to hold inquest over the dead men.

FAMILY ADVISED.

The family of Mr. Bulloch was communicated with as early as possible, and David C. Bulloch, son of the injured man, hastened to Milford to join his father and accompanied him to the hospital, as did also Mrs. Sarah Ann Bulloch. Tuesday Robert W. and John T., also sons of the unfortunate man, accompanied by their mother, took train for the metropolis.

Warren Bulloch, the eight-year-old son of Mr. Bulloch, who accompanied his father to Lund and whom it was understood was going on with his father, fortunately remained behind and was not in the wreck. Warren arrived home Monday.

A PROMINENT MAN.

Mr. Bulloch is a prominent figure in southern Utah. He is a man of affairs, and has accumulated a considreable fortune in the raising of cattle and sheep. He carried considerable life insurance, and should the worst happen he would leave his family in comfortable circumstances. During the construction of the Salt Lake Route, on which he received his injuries, he had the contract of supplying the camps with beef, and made frequent shipments over the road. When the road was completed he made a contract to furnish some of the Nevada mining camps with steers and he was accompanying one of these shipments at the time of the accident.

Mr. Bulloch is a pioneer of Iron county, and was one of the two representatives who accepted of the hospitality extended by Senator Clark to the pioneers last summer. He has eight children living in Cedar City.

Iron County Record
March 9, 1906

Another matrimonial bark was launched for better or worse when Frank Lambeth and Mary Bladen of Cedar were married in Parowan Tuesday. Both are estimable young people, and the Record wishes them all kinds of prosperity.

Iron County Record
April 6, 1906

A new son arrived at the home of Jethro Palmer last Friday.

Mr. and Mrs. James Parry have moved to their cottage just north of Edward Parry's residence.

Mr. and Mrs. Joseph Thompson of St. George are in Cedar on a visit to Mrs. Thompson's mother, Mrs. Lucy Jones.

Deseret News
April 11, 1906

Cedar City, Iron Co., April 11.—A telephone message received here yesterday afternoon from Modena, a railroad station in this county on the line of the Salt Lake Route, conveys the sad intelligence of the dead of Frank Brown, a resident of Hamilton Fort, a small village connected with this ward, located some six miles south of this city, but particulars of the tragedy are not yet obtainable.

The deceased was a man of genial bearing, a respected citizen, a kind and indulgent father and husband, and honest and straightforward in his business deals. He leaves a wife and eight children, some of whom are in honorable positions in the community. The family is overcome at the sad end of their respected husband and father. Men and teams started last night to bring the body home, which they expect to meet on the desert west of this place. It is expected it will arrive some time today.

Iron County Record
April 27, 1906

The household of Mr. and Mrs. John Taylor Bulloch has been augmented by the arrival of a son last Wednesday.

A wedding reception was given by Mr. and Mrs. William Corry at their home Wednesday evening in honor of their newly married son and daughter-in-law, Mr. and Mrs. Willard Corry. A goodly number of the older friends of the family were present. A nice luncheon was served during the evening and the time passed enjoyably in music, reading, etc. A social for the younger friends of the family was held Thursday evening.

Iron County Record
May 15, 1906

The entire eighth grade class of the Cedar public schools has been graduated this week from the public school course. The members are Vivian Decker, Harrison Green, Myron Higbee, Irene Jones, Lillian Higbee, Cora Jones, Carrie Leigh, Manie Middleton, Pearl Benson, Caroline Leigh, Margaret Melling, Della Perry, Hazel Dalley, and Edna Brown of Hamilton's.

Cedar City, Iron Co., May 16.—On the 12th inst. Patriarch Francis Webster departed this life after a lingering illness of six months, the cause of death being dropsy and heart trouble. Deceased was born in Sutton, near Wymondham, Norfolk, England, Feb. 8, 1830; embraced the Gospel in 1848; in 1855 he married Miss Ann Elizabeth Parsons and in 1856 they emigrated to Utah, crossing the plains in Capt. Edward Martin's famous hand cart company, arriving in Salt Lake City November 30, and coming to Cedar the following year, where he has resided up to the time of his death.

Elder Webster was one of the prominent citizens of Iron county, and particularly interested in the building up of Cedar City. He has labored faithfully by example as well as precept to build up and develop the resources of Iron county. His labors in a Church capacity have extended from the position of ward teacher to the first counselor in the stake presidency, from which he was honorably released through failing health some few years ago, and ordained a Patriarch in this stake of Zion. In the temporal affairs of Cedar City he took a prominent part, and was generally recognized as the leader in any move to unite the people. His prominent part taken in the establishing and building of the branch normal in this city stands out as a monument of his indefatigable labors and will power in the establishing of that institution in this city. In the days of the introduction of the United Order he was elected president of that company and labored faithfully for its permanency for upwards of a year, when by mutual consent the company was dissolved. He served Iron county in the capacity of representative to the territorial legislature for one term, and acted as mayor and councilor in Cedar City for a period of 30 years.

Services over his remains were held this afternoon in the tabernacle, which was tastefully decorated for the occasion. Elder James G. Bleak of the St. George stake of Zion, (an old time friend of the deceased), and Elders Mitchell and Durham of Parowan City, whom the deceased had labored with for many years, President U. T. Jones of the Parowan stake of Zion, Bishop Henry W. Lunt and other intimate associates of the deceased, eulogized the life and worth of the deceased and offered words of comfort and consolation to the bereft family, which consists of two wives and 13 children, most of whom are married. The eldest son is now doing missionary service in the eastern states.

Delightful weather now prevails; garden and field crops are growing and the prospects for a bountiful harvest were never more promising. Shearing is now in full force, and reports are quite favorable for the crop of wool. Cattle on the range wintered without serious loss. The local stream of water is higher than has been recorded for a number of years at this season of year and farmers will have plenty of irrigating water.

James and Joshua Walker and Henry Eddards have returned from Nye county, Nevada, where they have be mining for some time.

Dr. Green is the proud papa of a daughter, which put in its appearance at the family residence Wednesday morning. This is the first arrival of feminine gender to apply for lodgings in the Green family, and doubtless received a hearty welcome.

David Haight is the proud grandfather of his first grandchild, a son having been born this week to Mrs. Caroline Esplin of Orderville. Miss Lottie Haight has left for the center of interest to see that the little stranger is well cared for.

A shocking accident occurred on Kolob Mountain Wednesday, which cost Wallace Williams, son of John D. Williams of Kanarra, his life. But few particulars are obtainable, except that the young man while out hunting was accidently shot through the lungs. Whether the shot was fired by himself or a companion, we have not at this writing been able to learn.

Dr. Middleton was summoned early yesterday morning and made all haste to reach the unfortunate young man who was still alive at that time, but died before the doctor arrived. Dr. Middleton is expected home this afternoon.

The deceased has been herding sheep on the Kolob mountain, and presumably had taken his gun and gone out for a little recreation when the fatal shot was fired. The remains will doubtless be taken to Kanarra for burial.

This is the second death caused by accidental shooting of young men from Kanarra during the past two or three years, Robert Davis, who was killed at Kelsey's ranch, being the other victim.

Deseret News
June 21, 1906

Rupert Lee Wixom and Miss Sarah Middleton of this city returned from St. George City today, where they were united in the holy bonds of matrimony. A family reunion was held in honor on the event last evening.

Cedar City, Iron Co., June 21—The mortal remains of Evan Williams were consigned to the grave today. The deceased departed this life on the 19th inst., after a lingering illness. He was stricken with paralysis over a year ago, which rendered him almost helpless, and has lingered in that condition until his demise. The funeral was held in the tabernacle, and was largely attended. Those who addressed the congregation spoke eulogistically of the life and general character of the deceased, who has been a model man in this community; honest with his fellows; exemplary in his course and progressive in his daily life. Mr Williams was born at St. Brides-Minor, Glammiorganshire, Wales, in 1827; emigrated to Utah with his wife, four sons and three daughters, in 1878, settling in Cedar City. One daughter had preceeded him to Utah, and one son followed him the year after. He was the father of nine children. Deceased was a very zealous advocate of the religion he had espoused in his early life, and was a gifted poet.

Iron County Record
July 6, 1906

The marriage of Frank Armstrong and Nellie Hunter was consummated in the St. George temple last week and a family reception in their honor given last Friday evening at the home of Mr. and Mrs. Jos. Armstrong. The young people are both highly respected in Cedar, and have our warmest wishes for a happy and prosperous married life.

Dr. Middleton's home is again under quarantine, little four year old Richard being down with scarletina. The case is not a serious one.

Deseret News
July 10, 1906

Cedar City, Iron Co., July 10.—The annual election for school trustee for this school district for the term of three years passed off quietly yesterday, three tickets being in the field as follows: Republican candidate, W. R. Palmer; Democratic candidate, Alexander Mathewson; Socialist candidate, Wm. McFarlane. Mr. Mathewson was elected by a large majority.

Last week while ex-Bishop Wm. Ford of Kanarra was hauling hay he was thrown from his loaded wagon while crossing a ditch. He was unconscious for several hours. Dr. Middleton was hastily summoned and gave the sufferer medical assistance. The bishop is badly bruised and shaken up but will pull through all right.

Iron County Record
July 13, 1906

David Bulloch, who was so frightfully injured in a wreck on the Salt Lake Route some months ago, is slowly regaining his usual health and strength, though he is still far from sound. He retains his usual jovial disposition, however, and is gradually beginning to resume his business responsibilities. His eyes still give him some trouble, and his back is affected.

Deseret News
July 25, 1906

Cedar City, Iron Co., July 25.—The feature of Pioneer day was a banquet tendered the pioneers of Cedar City and all the aged over 65. A program was well rendered at the tabernacle in the morning, but the afternoon was devoted to making the veterans happy.

The sudden and unexpected death of Mrs. Catherine J. Gibson Lunt, wife of Randall Lunt of this city, which occurred July 23, has cast a gloom over the community. Some three weeks ago Mrs. Lunt with her family moved to their summer ranch, some 12 miles from the city, in the Cedar canyon. She was taken suddenly ill and before medical assistance reached her she had crossed the dark river. Mrs. Lunt was the daughter of David and Catherine Grundfer Gibson, and was born in St. George, Washington Co., Dec. 12, 1868, being 37 years, 7 months and 11 days old. She was a kind indulgent mother, an affectionate wife, and devoted Latter-day Saint. A husband and eight children mourn her demise. The body arrived here last night and impressive obsequies were held in the tabernacle today at 4:30 p. m.

Iron County Record
August 3, 1906

The report comes from Kanarra that Bp. William Ford is still bedfast but slowly improving. His many friends throughout the county will be very glad to see him up and around again.

Iron County Record
August 10, 1906

Robert Knell is back in Cedar again after his summer's visit at Pinto.

Daniel Perkins has completed the walls of his new residence and is now putting the roof on.

Iron County Record
September 7, 1906

Cards are out announcing the marriage of Samuel L. Fife to Miss Letty Dally of Summit. The reception will be held at the home of the bride's father Bp. Jos. B. Dalley, in Summit, September 12. The young people will be married in the St. George Temple.

Mr. John Condie of Hamilton's Fort and Miss Nellie Grant of Harmony were married in the St. George temple Wednesday.

Iron County Record
September 21, 1906

We take pleasure today in reporting the arrival of a son and heir at the home of Attorney Ryan, which was added to the family circle last night. Mr. and Mrs. Ryan now have as great a variety of sex as anybody.

Iron County Record
September 28, 1906

Mr. and Mrs. George Millett have a new baby boy a their home, which arrived Sunday evening.

Iron County Record
October 26, 1906

Uncle Thos. Jessup is able to be around the streets again after his sick spell. He is hardly up to his former weight yet, however.

Mr. and Mrs. Frank Knell of Pinto have been in Cedar a few days as the guests of Mrs. Knell's mother, Mrs. Page.

S. F. Leigh, Rone and Will Corry and Henry Eddards are out doing assessment work on their mining property Iron Springs.

Mrs. Warren Taylor and Mrs. James Stapley of Loa are visiting with relatives in Cedar and Kanarra.

A pair of twin girls appeared at the home of Mr. and Mrs. Sam B. Jones last Friday, swelling the family from seven to nine. Mrs. Jones has been quite seriously ill during the week, but is greatly improved. The little ladies are well and seem to be quite favorably impressed with their new home.

Iron County Record
November 23, 1906

Francis and Mrs. Middleton of Hamilton's Fort have an addition to their family circle in the form of a fine girl, which came last Monday. The parents have our congratulations.

Mr. and Mrs. David Webster gained the title of papa and mamma yesterday when their first infant, a son and heir, was ushered into the world. Mother and babe are reported as doing well.

KANARRA

Since my last writing quite a number of things have happened, one of which,—the wedding of Wm. J. Williams and Amanda E. Reeves,—is the most important, they say. Now they are fairly settled down to housekeeping opposite his father's residence.

On the 3rd a farewell party was given in honor of Riley G. Williams, who left the following Wednesday for New Zealand, where he will do missionary work, it being the second time he has labored in that capacity. He was accompanied as far as Salt Lake City by Louis J. Balser, who has just returned home from visiting his mother and other relatives and friends.

Mr. George Williams' family is now enjoying their newly finished house on the corner of the public square.

Deseret News
November 24, 1906

Cedar City, Iron Co., Nov. 24.—On the 20th inst. Cedar was called to mourn the loss through death of Olivia Clark Jones, wife of Samuel Bell Jones. The deceased was born in Parowan in 1872, when she spent her girlhood days and was the daughter of the Hon. E. L. Clark of that city. In disposition she was very attractive and her kindly demeanor endeared her to a host of friends, who with her grief-stricken husband and children, and father, sincerely mourn her demise. In her home town she was a central figure, where her death will be keenly felt. Her funeral was held in the tabernacle here on the 22nd inst. and notwithstanding the unusual stormy weather, many friends of the family from Parowan, Summit and the village of Enoch were present. Bishop Morgan Richards of Parowan was the principal speaker at the funeral services when he related some of the many loveable traits of disposition possessed as by the deceased. She is the mother of seven children, was an indulgent mother and a devoted wife.

HEAVY SNOWSTORM.

Cedar has had one of the heaviest snowstorms ever known to visit this section of country so early in the season. It is estimated that 18 inches of the "beautiful" fell during the storm period. The conditions now prevalent are anything but favorable for wood and coal hauling, and many are left with scanty woodpiles and empty coal-bins. Mail service is very irregular and for a week mail has been 12 hours late.

Cedar City, Dec. 12.—Funeral services over the mortal remains of Mrs. Rachel Simpkins Jones, who departed this life on the 9th inst., were held in the tabernacle yesterday. The building was appropriately decorated, and many relatives and friends were present to pay their respects to the departed. Mrs. Walker and Mrs. Armstrong, who had been intimately acquainted with the deceased during her life, and Elders Armstrong, Heyborne, and Bishop Lunt, each bore testimony of her faithful labors and devotion to her religion and fidelity to her husband and numerous family.

Deceased was the daughter of James Simpkins and Jane Kirkbride and was born in England on the 3rd day of November, 1845. Her parents emigrated to Utah early in the '60s. While en route her mother was stricken with cholera, of which she with many others fell a victim, leaving the father and daughter to continue their journey Zion-ward. After arriving in Salt Lake City, the father was called to assist in the settlement of Iron county and develop the iron industry. The daughter accompanied her father to Cedar City, and although young in years, she took an active part in the arduous labors of establishing settlements in southern Utah. She subsequently married John L. Jones by whom she has raised a numerous and honorable posterity, all of whom are active members in the Church of which their mother was a devoted member.

In the death of Mrs. John L. Jones, who died at the home of her son, Samuel B. Jones, in this city last Sunday, Cedar City and Iron county loses a useful woman, and one who held the respect of all her acquaintances. Death was the result of chronic catarrh of the stomach, from which the deceased had been a sufferer for years, but she was only severely ill for four or five days. The end came suddenly and unexpectedly.

Funeral services were held from the Cedar tabernacle Tuesday afternoon, a large number of friends and relatives being present to show their last respects.

The speakers were R. W. Heborne, Mrs. Charlotte Walker, Mrs. Mary Ann Armstrong, Joseph Armstrong and Bishop Lunt. All spoke in the highest terms of the departed sister. Mrs. Walker had been especially well acquainted with the deceased, living close neighbor to her for a number of years, and bore eloquent testimoy to her chastity and sterling qualities of character. Professor Coslett and the choir were in attendance and furnished pathetic music.

President U. T. Jones dedicated the grave.

One houndred dollars changed hands Christmas Day on a horse race between Dave C. Bulloch's bay and the Henry Mackelprang horse—Glass Eye. The distance was half a mile and Mackelprang's horse completely ran way from his contestant.

The arrival of another fine daughter is reported at the home of Prin. and Mrs. O. W. Decker. The late addition was subtracted last Monday morning, and will tend to mutliply the Decker family until it is divided by the successful suit of some X in the matrimonial algebraic equasion a score or so of years hence. Until that time, at least, the Deckers have our (a)cute congratulations, notwithstanding this reference to their good fortune may be deemed to be decidedly obtuse.

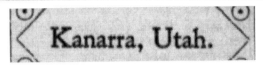

Kanarra, Utah.

The funeral of father John J. Davies took place this morning at 11 o'clock. A host of relatives surrounding his remains. Others of his family were unable to be present. He was born in South Wales on Dec. 28, 1831; embraced the gospel while there and imigrated to the land of the saints; was an early settler of this place, and leader of the choir in which he took great delight until his health disqualified him for the position.

Lorenzo Davis and his sister Mrs. Eleanor Pollock have been bedfast for some time, but it is hoped they will soon be making a speedy turn for the better.

Deseret News
January 8, 1907

Taylor, Navajo Co., Ariz., Jan. 8.—Llewellyn Harris a well known and faithful member of the Snowflake stake, passed away at his home in Shumway, Tuesday, Dec. 18, after an illuess of a year.

He was born in 1832, near Llandovery, Carmarthenshire, South Wales, he left Wales when about eight years of age with his widowed mother and came to America. He came to Utah in 1853 and the following October moved to Cedar City, Iron county, where he helped to build the old fort at that place, as a defense against the Indians, and helped in building up several towns in the southern part of Utah, and took an active part in all of the Indian wars there for over 20 years.

In the winter of 1862, 3 and 4 he went with Jacob Hamblin and others to explore the territory of Arizona to look out homes for the Saints. They visited several Indian tribes and made friends with them.

He married Patience Sibyl Groves, in October, 1865 and six children were born to them, one son and five daughters.

In October, 1878, he was called to go on a mission among the Indians and native races of Arizona, New Mexico and other places, where he labored faithfully among the Lamanites, many sick among them being healed under his administration by the laying on of hands.

In the fall of 1895, he moved with his family from Escalante, Utah, to Arizona, locating at Shumway where he has since resided.

The funeral services were held at Taylor in the ward meetinghouse, Dec. 20, presided over by Bishop James S. Shumway, most of the Saints, from Shumway, and many from Taylor and Snowflake were in attendance, where testimonies of Bro. Harris' faithfulness were born by Elders Joseph W. Smith, William H. Solomon, Littleton L. Perkins, William G. Shumway, F. P. Denham, William J. Flake, James L. Shumway.

Cedar City, Iron county, Jan. 26.—This section has had a seige of stormy weather, which ended today.

On Tuesday the 22nd inst, John Stephens a highly respected citizen of this city, passed away. Funeral services over his remains were conducted in the tabernacle here on the 24th inst., when appropriate remarks were made by some of his intimate friends who bore record of the good character, industry and liberality of the deceased. The deceased joined the Church of Jesus Christ of Latter-day Saints in Carmerthanshire, Wales, where he was born April 28, 1843, he followd the labor of collier in his native land. Before emigrating to Utah, he married Miss Elizabeth Perkins and then came to Utah in 1868. Ten children have been born to them, eight of whom and the wife survive him.

Notwithstanding the anxiety felt for the sheep and cattle interests on account of the severity of the winter, it is generally believed that these interests will come out with little loss. Snow is melting fast and in consequence the roads are reported almost impassable.

Cedar City, Iron Co., March 4.—The funeral of Mrs. Mary Davis Wood, one of the pioneers of Iron county, was held in the tabernacle in this city on the 1st inst., death having occurred on the 27th of February last. Deceased was born in Hainsley, Shropshire, England, April 26, 1834, where she with her parents, three sisters and two brothers, joined the Church of Jesus Christ of Latter-day Saints. The family shortly after immigrated to Utah, arriving in Salt Lake City in the fall of 1849. In 1859 deceased married George Wood in Salt Lake City, and they came to Iron county with the first settlers, settling in Parowan City. Shortly afterward Cedar City was selected as the most suitable place for the establishing of iron works. Mr. Wood was one of the first to establish himself in Cedar City with his family, where they have been prominent up to the present time in assisting to develop the innumerable resources of this county. The deceased endured all of the suffering and privations incident to pioneer life. She was the mother of nine children, all but two of whom survive her. Mrs. Wood was highly esteemed by all who knew her for her kindly disposition, modesty and considerate regard for the comfort of others. The casket containing the remains of the deceased was profusely decorated with flowers, most of which were brought from California by her daughter. Eight of her grandsons acted as pallbearers and carried the remains from her late residence to the tabernacle.

The funeral services were impressive, appropriate solos and quartets were rendered by members of the ward choir, and many encomiums were paid to her memory by a number of speakers who had been intimate and close friends of the deceased during her sojourn in Cedar City. Her aged husband, one son and six daughters survive her.

DEATH OF CHAS. WESTERHOLD.

On the 5th inst. the mortal remains of Charles Westerhold were consigned to the grave, he having departed this life on the 2nd inst. The cause of death being pneumonia. Deceased was born Feb. 10, 1855, in Prussia. He came to Cedar City from California in 1857. After a sojourn of a few years here he went to Pennsylvania to visit some friends, returning shortly with a young lady whom he afterward married. Before doing so, however, they both joined the Church of Jesus Christ of Latter-day Saints. Some four children blessed the union, when the grim reaper took from him his devoted wife. He married his second wife several years ago, who survives him. One child blessed the second marriage, but preceded its father to the great beyond. The deceased was an exceptionally quiet, industrious and inoffensive man, faithful to the cause he had espoused, ever ready with a cheerful disposition to perform his religious as well as secular duties, with a character above reproach. The funeral services were held from the tabernacle on the 5th inst. Consoling remarks were made by neighbors and intimate friends of the deceased, who testified to his honesty, integrity and excellent moral life.

DIED IN MEXICO.

Information by telephone brought the

sad intelligence to Peter B. Fife of this city of the death of his son, Edward L. Fife, which occurred in the City of Mexico, March 3, of smallpox. The young man had been a great sufferer from rheumatism, and at the urgent solicitation of his father and friends had gone to Mexico in the hope of bettering his physical condition by a change of climate. His father and relatives are almost distracted over the sad end of their son, who was a most exemplary youth.

Last week news was conveyed to the relatives of James C. Stewart, residing here, that he had been accidentally killed while working in a mine near Kingman, Ariz., but particulars of the accident have not yet reached the family. Arrangements have been made to embalm the body and have it forwarded here for burial. The deceased was the son of William C. Stewart and Mary Ann Corlett; was born in Cedar City and had followed the occupation of mining for several years.

Iron County Record
March 22, 1907

Henry Eddards returned from Southern Nevada last Monday, after a few weeks absence, brings back some fine samples of ores from the properties in which he is interested. He states that the outlook is bright for the section he has visited, and that the owners will soon commence shipping ore. It cost him over fifty dollars and a week's time to get home.

They hired outfits and made the trip overland as far as St. George, and when they reached that place it was found that the mail route had been changed, and as it was impossible to hire a man and team to make the drive to Cedar, Mr. Eddards was compelled to return via Modena and Lund.

Born, to Mr. and Mrs. William Macfarlane last Saturday, a son. Congratulations are in order.

Mrs. John Stezer presented her husband with a fine son last Sunday. All concerned are doing nicely.

Iron County Record
May 3, 1907

Dr. Robison officiated at the birth of a daughter at the home of I. C. Macfarlane last Monday. Mother and child are reported to be doing nicely.

A son was born to Mr. and Mrs. Jos. Melling last Sunday afternoon. The young gentleman arrived just too late for the regular afternoon services, but seems to be making the best of the matter, now that he is here.

Eleven-year-old Junior McConnell has been in bed this week with a badly lacerated leg. Last Sunday he was riding on a wagon loaded with baled hay. The wagon wheel dropped into a chuck, dislodging the bale on which Junior was sitting and both fell to the ground. The front wheel of the wagon passed over the calf of one of the boy's legs, cutting a nasty gash four or five inches long. Dr. Green closed the wound with 13 stitches, and the patient is doing as well as could be expected, though he has suffered much pain all week.

A son was born to Mr. and Mrs. James Parry last Saturday. Mother and infant are progressing nicely.

Mr. and Mrs. Wm. R. Palmer are the proud parents of a fine son. The little one was received last week, too late to be announced in our last issue.

Miss Lottie Haight is at home once more, having completed a course in obstetrics at Salt Lake City. Miss Haight informs us that she intends remaining here for a time, at least.

James Whittaker, an early pioneer of Utah, died Saturday evening, and tomorrow morning the remains will be shipped to Circleville, Utah, for burial. He is survived by a widow and nine children.

The deceased was born at Bolton, England, April 27, 1833. He joined the

JAMES WHITTAKER.

Church in 1849, and the following year came to Utah, crossing the plains with an ox team. He settled first at Cedar City, and later made his home in Circleville, until coming to Salt Lake to reside, three years ago. He was engaged in the sheep and cattle business and in merchandizing.

Mr. Whittaker was a very faithful and energetic man in every phase of life, unassuming, but at all times making an impress for good upon the community. For many years he was a choir leader, first at Cedar City, and afterwards at Circleville.

The remains may be viewed this afternoon, at 849 Alma avenue, Second North, between Eighth and Ninth West. Funeral services and interment will take place at Circleville.

CEDAR CITY.

DEATH OF ROBT. W. HEYBORNE.

Prominent Pioneer Citizen of Iron County Succumbs to Brief Illness.

Special Correspondence.

Cedar City, Iron Co., June 7.—The sudden death of Robert W. Heyborne, which occurred Wednesday night, June 5, is greatly lamented by the people of Cedar as the deceased was a prominent figure in the community since pioneer days and was highly esteemed by all. On Tuesday evening he was stricken with paralysis, when pneumonia developed and death quickly followed.

Mr. Heyborne was born in Kilkenny, Ireland, 63 years ago and when he was very young his parents took him with them to Australia, where his father died, leaving his mother a widow with six children, of whom the deceased was the eldest. In 1857 the family arrived in Cedar City, where Mr. Heyborne has resided ever since.

Early in life Mr. Heyborne was called into public service, beginning with the office of city marshal, from which he was promoted to the city council, where he served three terms. Later he filled the office of mayor for four years. He has also been city recorder for six years. He was assessor and collector of Iron county for eight years and a member of the territorial legislature four years. He has also been a member of two constitutional conventions and represented Iron county in the first state legislature. He crossed the plains twice to assist with immigration. He also held many Church positions which he filled with fidelity. He is survived by his wife and five daughters, two of whom are married.

LATE ROBERT W. HEYBORNE.

DIED IN THE MISSION FIELD.

Elder Geo. Wm. Wood of Bluff Falls Victim of Typhoid Fever.

After eight weeks of illness with a malignant case of typhoid fever, Elder George William Wood died in the mission field, Sunday July 21, at Harrold, Wilbarger Co. Texas. Elder Wood's home was at Bluff, San Juan county, Utah, to which place his remains were brought for burial, June 26. Prest. Samuel Bennion of the Central states mission and Elder August L. Nelson accompanied the remains as far as Thompson's Springs, where they were met by the brother of the deceased and taken overland to his home town.

Elder Wood was born Feb. 23, 1885, in Cedar City, and was in his 23rd year. He was the son of Samuel and Josephine C. Chatterly Wood. He had been in the mission field since the last of April, but had shown himself an earnest, faithful worker, quiet and unassuming, but always willing to do his part in the mission work. During his entire illness he was devotely nursed and cared for by Elder August L. Nelson, and part of the time by his conference president, Henry J. Bodily, and all was done for him that could be, but all to no avail. His parents and relatives have the heartfelt sympathy of all the elders in the Central mission field and the people at home.

Cedar City, Iron Co., Nov. 15.—William Haslam, over 97 years of age, one of the pioneer settlers of southern Utah, and an earnest and conscientious Church worker, died at his home here yesterday morning, after a strenuous and honored career as a pioneer and frontiersman. He will be buried at Virgin, in Washington county, in accordance with his request.

Mr. Haslam was twice married, both wives preceding him some years ago. He is survived by two sons and three daughters, one of the latter is living in Mexico.

When the California emigrants were passing through the country, they got into difficulty with the settlers and also with the Indians, and brought down the ill will of the people of all classes which threatened serious trouble. There was no telegraph in those days and Mr. Haslam was sent post-haste on horseback to notify President Brigham Young, then the governor of the territory of the impending trouble. Without letting the messenger rest, Gov. Young sent him back in all haste with a message to let the emigrants go through unharmed and unhindered. Mr. Haslam rode back, never stopping for rest, day or night, except long enough to change horses and made the journey of nearly 280 miles in a little over three days. But he was too late. When he arrived the tragedy had already been enacted.

Cedar City, Iron Co., June 4.—Mrs. Martha Gower of this place died today in her eighty-second year, being survived by five of her 11 children, four daughters and one son.

Mrs. Gower was born Nov. 1, 1826, in Northorum, England; baptized in 1845; married John Stockdale Sept. 17, 1848, and left for America on the 31st day of the same month, coming as far as St. Louis, where Mr. Stockdale died in 1849. The year following she was married to Thomas Gower, coming to Utah shortly after. They were among the first settlers of Iron county, and participated in the hardships of the pioneers. She has been a widow for 30 years, and was ever a devoted Latter-day Saint.

Born—To Mr. and Mrs. Heber Jensen, a girl, Monday.

It is reported that Wilford, the little son of Henry Leigh, is suffering from an attack of typhoid.

Mrs. Alice S. Smith is the happy mother of a fine baby girl born last Thursday. All concerned are feeling fine.

Miss Jemima Hamilton after improving somewhat from her attack of typhoid has now developed some form of lung trouble.

We are pleased to welcome Miss Verna Bowman of Ogden into our midst. Miss Bowman is conducting Domestic Science at the Branch Normal in Miss Eastwood's place.

Mr. and Mrs. Elias Hansen have taken up house keeping in part of J S. Woodbury's residence. Mr. Hansen is the history, mathematics and law instructor at the B. N. S.

Deseret News
October 2, 1908

Cedar City, Iron Co., Oct. 2.—Nathaniel Pryor of this city, died last night of typhoid fever with other complications. He was about 22 or 23 years old. Mr. Pryor's mother has been a widow for two or three years, her husband was frozen to death upon the desert west of Cedar.

Cedar was visited by the fiercest wind storm of months, last night.

The sheepmen of Iron county have left the summer range on the mountains, for the winter range on the great Escalante desert.

Deseret News
October 17, 1908

Funeral services over the remains of T. Harry Bennett were held yesterday afternoon at the undertaking parlors of Joseph William Taylor, there being a large number of friends in attendance. The services were conducted by Bishop Edward Hunter of the Eighth ward, and a number of addresses were delivered, in which the deceased was eulogized as an honorable and upright man.

Mr. Bennett was a native of England, where he was born 43 years ago. He had been a resident of Utah for 19 years, coming here from Canada. He was a pharmacist and lived at various times in Beaver, Cedar City and Garland. It was while conducting a business in the latter place that Bright's disease attacked him, and he passed away at a hospital in this city, Oct. 14. He is survived by his wife, formerly Miss Maggie Stewart, and one child, a son 15 months old.

Deseret News
October 30, 1908

Cedar City, Iron Co., Oct. 30.—On last Wednesday, Oct. 28.—Robert F. Bullock, a very prominent, esteemed and popular young man of 25 years, passed away from the effects of typhoid, combined with bronchial troubles. He was a member of the Seventy's quorum.

The old people over 60 were royally entertained by the people of Cedar, headed by the old folk's committee on Oct. 28, when a most enjoyable time was had in a fine program, banquet and ball.

SAHARA
Iron County Record
November 6, 1908

Yesterday afternoon word was received over the phone from Lund that Fred Houchen of this place had been accidently shot in the hip at a place called Sahara, a few miles north of Lund.

The word received is very meagre, and as near as can be made out the young man was sitting in a sheep wagon about one o'clock. In moving he accidently discharged a shotgun that was behind him, the charge striking him in the hip, tearing a ghastly hole clear through the young man and striking one of his hands, badly shattering it.

Word was sent at once to Cedar for medical help, and the father of the unfortunate young man and a physician started at once for the scene of the accident. They landed there about 12 o'clock last evening and found that the young man had lost considerable blood and was in a critical condition.

As we go to press later word has been received over the phone taht the young man succumbed to the injuries he received and his father immediately started to Cedar with the corpse.

Deseret News
February 8, 1909

The city health board was notified of five new cases of smallpox yesterday afternoon. They are as follows: Annie Leticia Steward, aged 4; Samuel Steward, aged 4; Ruby I. Steward, aged 16 months, 1261 east Seventh South street; Clara Willetts, aged 18, 1261 east Seventh South street; Katie Bar, aged 16, 755 east Third South street.

Dr. Middleton of Cedar City has communicated with the State health board with reference to the recent outbreak of smallpox at Parowan, and says there are no indications of precautions having been made to meet the emergency. Dr. Beatty has directed that the town be quarantined.

Seventeen cases of the disease have been reported from Green River by State Medical Inspector Baker, and he has been directed by the State board to quarantine the place.

It is reported that Indian Agent Myton of the White Rocks agency has been successful in getting most of the Indians there to submit to vaccination.

Deseret News
March 9, 1909

Cedar City, Iron Co., March 9—On Friday last Cedar lost one of its pioneers in the death of Mrs. Christina Sherratt.

Mrs. Sherratt came to Cedar with the first colony to settle in this valley. She was the first girl to cross Cedar creek, and lived here until her death, suffering all of the privation and trials incident to the early settlement of this section of the state. She was a devoted Latter-day saint and after a life of activity and suffering passed away as one going to sleep at the ripe age of 71 years and nearly two months.

Continues to Come.

Our Millinery continues to come every week with the changing styles of the advancing season.

Our Embroidery Waistings, Flouncings and Allover are of the prettiest, best and most reasonable prices.

We are now prepared to supply ladies with the new style, straight waist, long hipped corset in the famous Henderson make. Empire and Princess gowns cannot be properly worn without this corset.

Our Bargain Counter still carries children's hosiery and summer vests at reduced prices. Lace hosiery in black and white reduced from 25 cents to 15 cents per pair. Other notions at lowest prices.

Call and see for yourself at
E. CRANE WATSON'S
Cedar City, Utah.

Summit, Utah, June 8.

Mr. Wallace Hulet of Summit and Miss Sarah Stevens of Parowan have announced their engagement. The wedding takes place at St. George June 16, 1909. The young couple are both well respected and have the good wishes of the community.

Mr. Thomas Lawrence, Jr., recently of Summit, but now of Cedar City, has surprised his wife by presenting her with a brand new Singer sewing machine.

Alex Dalley is contemplating fencing his homestead with poultry fence. His intentions are to engage in hog and poultry raising on a large scale.

Marriage Licenses

County Clerk Woodbury has issued the following marriage licenses this week:

Seth M. Jones, of Enoch and Miss Clarissa H. Adair, of Enterprise, on May 31st.

David C. Urie and Miss Martha J. M. Perkins, both of Cedar City, on June 1st

Casper A. Bryner of St. George and Miss Sarah Maud Bergen, of West Jordan, June 2nd.

Militia History.

Dear Editor:—I believe the following bit of Cedar City history will interest some of your readers, containing as it does one of the militia companys of the Nauvoo Legion, mustered in Cedar City, Utah in 1857 and 8.

MUSTER ROLL OF COMPANY G —5TH BATTALION.

10th Regiment Nauvoo Legion.

COMPANY OFFICERS.—Eleazer Edwards, captain; Christopher J Arthur, adjutant; James Timmins and John Stoddard, musicians.

1st PLATOON—John H. Willis, 2nd lieutenant; Peter Nelson, sergent; John White, Josiah Reeves, Lemuel Willis, privates.

2ND PLATOON.—Samuel Leigh, 2nd lieutenant; George Horton, sergent; George Munro, Wm. W. Richards, Wm. Thomas, David Williams, David Morgan, Evan Owens, John Harris, Benjamin Rowland, privates.

3RD PLATOON.—John P. Jones, 2nd lieutenant; Daniel, Simpkins sergent; Watkin Rees, William Unthank, Thomas Gower, Benjamin Smith, Robert Smith, Wm. Walker. John S. Walker, Joseph Walker, John Lee Jones, Privates.

4TH PLATOON—Peter M. Fife, 2nd lieutenant; Wm. Bateman, sergent; Charles Wilden, Sr., Fergus Wilden, John Wilden, Thomas Muir, Robert Easton, Charles P. Smith, Robert Bullock, David Stoddard, privates.

5TH PLATOON—Wm. Willis, 2nd lieutenant; George Corry, sergent; Joseph Hunter, Henry Elliker, Wm. Davidson, John Bradshaw, Jr., James Bullock, Ashael Bennett, George Bennett, privates.

ACOUTREMENTS—15 muskets, 1 bayonet, 19 rifles, 7 Holster pistols, 2 swords.

AMMUNITION—12½ pounds of powder, 22½ pounds of lead.

MUSIC—3 bugles.

Respectfully,

C. J. ARTHUR,
Adjutant.

In 1859 I was promoted to be aid-de-camp to Regimental Col. Wm. H. Dana.

FOR A RAILROAD

Southern Company Men Return From Grand Canyon Trip And Meet With Citizens

The railroad people, Messrs. Dudley, Inman, Burke, Brown, and others, a total of twelve, who had been out to the Grand Canyon making a preliminary run over the proposed line from Lund to the Grand Canyon arrived in this city Tuesday evening Mrs Dudley, who was accompanied by Mrs. E. M Brown of this city, took the trip with the party and says she enjoyed the outing and the sublime scenery of the Grand Canyon exceedingly. Mr. R. K. Brown who was with the party is the division engineer of the Salt Lake Route.

To decide the amount of saw timber on the Kiabab plateau, Mr. F. W. Read, the assisting forester of the 4th district with headquarters at Ogden, and Mr. D. F. Scerey, the forest service expert lumberman, accompanied the party; the result of the foresters investigation showed that there is four billion feet of saw timber immediately available.

The engineers say that the route is feasible, but that there are two places where steep grades will be necessary, viz: the climb from Bellevue ridge on to the Hurricane plateau, and from Fredonia on to the Kiabab plateau.

Mr. Dudley when seen today stated that the proposed line would cost between five and ten million dollars; that it included a spur to Cedar City, and a spur from Bellevne ridge to St. George, 23 miles That he considered the route a fairly good one; that it would run via Pipe Springs to Fredonia, thence on to the Kiabab plateau and end at the Grand Canyon opposite to the terminus of the Williams branch of the Santa Fe. Mr Dudley stated that the Southern Company was simply organized for the purpose of exploiting the scheme, and for making all preliminary arrangements for the organization of the railroad company.

A meeting between the railroad people and leading citizens was held last evening for the purpose of deciding what this county would guarantee to the company to build the line The sense of the meeting was that Washington county guarantee $100,000 in work and material, to be expended within the county, free right of way and depot sites, the Commercial Club backed by the citizens giving the guarantee. The railroad company on their part agrees to commence construction within two years and have the railroad in operation within five years.

Iron County Record
September 17, 1909

Tribute to Owen Walker.

Last week we were compelled to omit an article handed to us by a friend of Owen Walker in which the young man's character is portrayed. We gladly give space to it this week because of the fact that it will show the readers how much he was respected by those who had the pleasure of his acquaintance:

Cedar City, Sept. 17, 1909.

Editor Record:—

In the death of Owen Walker Cedar has lost a striking young man of kind disposition, strictly good and moral.

He was born in Cedar City July 24, 1874, and died Sept. 9, 1909. He has always been exemplary in his conduct, and ever had a kind word for all, especially so for his parents, brothers, sisters and friends. Whatever means he accumulated he liberally gave to his parents and members of the family. He never indulged in bad habits, was naturally reserved in demeanor, and was a quiet student of whatever would improve his mind.

Owen had a premonition that he was going to pass away, and so expressed himself a number of times. As his father has been afflicted for some time he was ever solicitous of his welfare and comfort, and always thoughtful for the well being of all who were not feeling well.

He was of undoubted courage and indomitable will in all that concerned the best interests of the family.

May we all meet him on the morning of the first resurrection.

Iron County Record
December 17, 1909

A gloom fell over Cedar last Tuesday when word was given out that Mrs. Florence Lunt Webster had passed to the great beyond, after months of intense suffering.

Mrs. Webster was born here January 20, 1870, and has lived here all her life. In March of the year 1891 she was married to Herbert Webster and seven children resulted from the union, two of whom have preceded their mother to their last resting place.

She was a model wife and mother and her married life has been almost ideal.

She had a most beautiful soprano voice and was very well known and loved in musical circles. She has been a member of the choir for years and was always on hand to do her part to help entertain, and all who heard her sing were loud in their praise of her beautiful gift.

Mrs. Webster leaves a husband, a mother, brothers and sisters, five children and a host of friends to mourn her departure.

The entire community joins in mourning the loss of so lovable a woman and extend sincerest sympathy to the bereaved family.

Deseret News
December 17, 1909

WEBSTER, FLORENCE LUNT—At Cedar City, Iron Co., Utah, Dec. 14, death summoned Mrs. Florence Lunt Webster, wife of Herbert Webster, and one of Cedar City's most popular ladies. She was a member of the ward choir and has taken part in many of the musical functions of the city. She was gifted with a most beautiful voice and, had the opportunity of study presented itself would probably have been heard of in a much wider sphere. She leaves her husband with the care of five children, some of them quite young, the oldest being about 17.

Cedar mourns this week in the death of Joseph Cosslett, which occurred last Monday morning at about 9 o'clock.

He was stricken with pneumonia last Friday, and compelled to take to his bed. Medical assistance was summoned and all done for him that could be, and it seemed up to Sunday evening he was improving. But during the night he took a sudden turn for the worse and continued so till death came to relieve him Monday morning.

Joseph has been a man whom the people have loved and have relied upon him for 40 years in the matter of conducting the singing for religious services. He was a faithful man in the performing of his duty in this line and was always at his post on every occasion, rain or shine. The people appreciated his ability and relied upon him entirely to furnish singing for all occasions, and whenever a funeral was held it was he who notified the choir members and conducted the singing. It mattered not who was the person over whom services were held, he was always more than willing to assist to the utmost of his ability.

He was of a jovial disposition, always ready to cheer a friend up with his genial way, ready to sympathize with friends in misfortune, and always pleased at any one's success, nd encouraged all with whom he was acquainted by his ever ready fund of humor and good fellowship.

Funeral services were held yesterday at which a large congregation was present to show their last respects to a well deserving, and faithful Latter-day Saint. The tabernacle was beautifully decorated for the occasion, and the speakers eulogized the many good qualities of the deceased.

A very impressive part of the service was an organ selection played by George Durham of Parowan, composed by his father.

BIOGRAPHICAL.

Joseph Cosslett was born in Glamorganshire, South Wales, on the 29th day of July, 1850. He emigrated to Utah in 1868, arriving in Salt Lake City the 28th of August 1868.

He moved to Cedar City in the year 1869 and took charge of the Sunday school choir in 1870. In 1781 he was appointed to lead the ward choir which position he has held until his demise.

He was married to Miss Emmeline R. Haight on the 18th day of January 1877. He was 59 years old. He leaves a wife and an adopted daughter, as well as a brother to mourn his departure.

Deseret News
January 17, 1910

CEDAR CITY, Utah, Jan. 17.—The citizens of Cedar City mourn the recent death of three of its beloved inhabitants.

The first was Mrs. Sarah J. Cossett, who died on Wednesday, Dec. 29, 1909. She was a little over 50 years old and the mother of 10 children, four of whom preceded her to the great beyond. She was born in Coventry, Warwickshire, England, and came to America, and moved to Cedar in the early sixties.

On Jan. 10, the deaths of Mrs. Ellen J. Nelson and Joseph Cossett shocked the people.

Mrs. Nelson was born in Sweden, Aug. 20, 1835; joined the Church in 1854, and in 1856 came to Cedar City, where she lived until death called her away. She is the mother of eight children, five of whom and her husband survive. On Dec. 31 she fell and broke her thigh bone, and never in any way recovered.

Joseph Cossett was born in Glamorganshire, South Wales, July 29, 1850; came to Utah in 1863, and to Cedar in 1869. He took charge of the Sunday school choir in 1870, and the ward choir in 1871, which he had charge of until his death. He was 59 years old, leaving his wife and adopted daughter to mourn his demise, with many friends and distant relatives.

Iron County Record
January 28, 1910

Another Southern Utah Boy Makes Good.

Our readers are familar with the name Randall Jones and no doubt will be pleased to know that he has made good in the Valparaiso University. He had been in this University but a short time before he received marked recognition and was promoted

We append hereto a photo of Randall and a comment by the Valparaiso University Herald, and also a letter received from him in answer to a request for the cut below:

Randall L. Jones, M. T., '10 is a native of Cedar City, Utah, and a graduate of the Normal school of the same city. Before entering Valparaiso University he spent a year in the University of Utah at Salt Lake City. At the beginning of the second term he will be an Assistant in the M. T. department of this University, which fact shows the quality of his work and speaks for his ability.

Iron County Record
February 2, 1910

Summit Briefs.

Summit, February 2.

Bishop Chas. R. Dalley and Mrs. Martha Dalley left here for Lund Sunday morning, where they expected to take the train for Preston, Idaho, to be present at the funeral of their nephew, Allen Dalley, 15 year old son of Phillip and Jawetta Allen Dalley, former residents of Summit.

Word was received here Saturday over the phone announcing the death of the young man but the particulars have not reached here yet. He was buried at Preston on Monday the 31st.

Iron County Record
April 1, 1910

Mr. Jos. T. Wilkinson has been appointed census enumerator for Cedar City, Enoch, Hamilton's Fort, Kanarra and Lund. He will begin his work about the middle of the month.

Evan E. Williams will leave for his mission about the 14th of April. He will go to Salt Lake City to be set apart a few days before that time. It is understood that his wife will accompany him as far as Salt Lake.

Evan Hunter, Treborne Leigh and Thomas Bullock, who have spent the winter at Provo attending the missionary school, returned last Saturday. The boys feel well and have enjoyed themselves while learning some of the principles of the gospel.

Iron County Record
May 13, 1910

And now Eddie Smith holds his head a notch or two higher, and for the same reason that so many other men do, that of being a recipient of a beautiful girl baby. It came Monday and of course Ed has a perfect right to feel proud. Congratulations.

Eva Lunt of Cedar City arrived in Milford Sunday and on Monday, in company with Marion Matthews, went to Beaver where they were united in marriage. Both the bride and groom are well known to many Milford people all of whom join in extending congratulations and best wishes. Mr. and Mrs. Matthews will make their home in Milford.—Beaver Co. News.

Miss Irene Canfield is home again after having spent the winter up north teaching school.

Last Friday Mr. and Mrs. Sam Heyborne welcomed their first baby daughter to their home.

After an absence of over two years Trehorne Jones, son of Pres. U. T. Jones returned home Tuesday evening. He has been on a mission in South Africa.

CEDAR CITY, June 1.—The twelfth annual commencement of the Branch Normal school was held in Cedar City this week. Dr. William C. Ebaugh, of the state university, delivered the baccalaureate sermon, and Prof. Howard R. Driggs, an old time teacher at the normal, gave the address to the graduates.

There were 28 graduates in all; five from the four-year high school course, and 23 from the three-year normal course. The names of the graduates are as follows:

Four-year Course—Vivian Decker, Lillian Higbee, Margaret Melling, Dick Tweedie, Mart Robinson.

Three-year Course—Arthur Fife, John Fletcher, Gwen Higbee, Myron Higbee, Parley Ipson, Jessie Jessings, Leigh Ruby, Leigh Webster, Lunt Ray, Ross Macfarlane, Gladys McConnell, Irvin McQuarrie, Luella Mickelson, Caesar Myers, Ruby Naegle, Donald Simuitz, Claude Sevy, A. Nevada Watson, Annette Webster, Janie Wilkinson, Clara Williamson, Leon Winsor, Irene Jones.

Eighth Grade Graduation Exercises.

The following Eighth grade graduation exercises will be held in the Parowan opera house, June 18, 7:30 p. m.

Selection, Parowan school orchestra.

Prayer.

Song Parowan school.

Talk, Vera Pace, Cedar City.

Fancy club swinging, Julius A. Taylor, Parowan.

Song, Cedar City.

Paper, Paragonah school.

Vocal solo under direction of Prof. Durham.

Address to Graduates.

Presentation of certificates, Deputy Sup't. E. R. Dalley.

Selection, School Orchestra.

Dancing.

Benediction.

Superintendent Dalley must meet the graduates for arrangements at the opera house at five o'clock of the above date. Every graduate must be there at that time.

Exercises have been delayed in order to hear from Superintendent Nelson but it is not yet known that he will be with us on the date mentioned

Following is the list of graduates of Iron County:

Paragonah—Karl Topham, Ray Robinson, Mary Jones, Evelyn McBride.

Parowan—Julius A. Taylor, Grant A. Lowe, Earl R. Morris, Lawrence Miller, John R. Adams, Twenty T. Orton, Maggie D. Marsden, Lucille Adams, Mary Belle Benson, Maud Mickleson, Laura Gurr, Florence Lyman, Libbie Halterman, Belle Mitchell, Verda Lyman, Albateen Myers, Fay Ollorton, Emma B. Morris.

Cedar City—Vera Pace, Verena Wood, Emma Daugherty, Ruth Macfarlane, Annie Bauer, Genevieve Ford, Myrtle Smith, Lauretta Perry, Cora Haight, Mary Urie, Katie Thorley, Fanie Nelson, Ella Matheson, Manetta Bauer, Cassidy Roof, Lester Thorley, Gordon Hunter, Ray Haight, Sherman Haight, Parson Webster, Della Bullock, Jennie McConnell, Moroni Urie, Orion Jones, Nan Brown,

Zelma Jones, Lula Corry.

Kanarra—Kumen Williams.

The following students will be graduated and receive certificates at the same time as the others upon their principal's recommendation: Florine Watson, Louie Perry, Murl Gibson, Cedar City; Pearl Jones, Enoch.

Vera Pace of Cedar City passed with the highest per cent in the county and will be nominated for the "Normal scholarship."

Iron County Record
June 24, 1910

Iron County Record

PUBLISHED EVERY FRIDAY AT

CEDAR CITY, UTAH.

ALEX. H. ROLLO

LESSEE

ESTABLISHED DECEMBER, 1893.

ENTERED AT THE CEDAR CITY POST-OFFICE AS SECOND CLASS MATTER.

SUBSCRIPTION $1.50 PER YEAR

ALWAYS IN ADVANCE.

Friday, June 24, 1910.

Deseret News
August 6, 1910

MRS. CATHERINE WINGOT, who lives in Monroe, Utah, has for 70 years been a member of the Church of Jesus Christ of Latter-day Saints and is probably the oldest female member. She reached her ninetieth year on March 12, last, and although her hearing is poor and her eyesight impaired, she has a sound memory, and relates with accuracy and detail some of the stirring times she passed through in her younger days when the Saints were driven about from place to place and suffered many hardships. She is the mother of eight children, all living, and has more than 120 direct descendants. Besides a host of grandchildren, she has great-grandchildren and one great-great-grandchild.

This week she dictated the story of her life for The Deseret News, as follows:

"I am the daughter of Charles and Margaret Noah Hewlett, born March 12, 1820, at Nelson, Portage county, O. In 1830 the Prophet Joseph Smith and Parley P. Pratt came to my father's house and desired to hold a meeting there. Father gave him the privilege. The prophet bore testimony to finding the plates containing the Book of Mormon. Although being but 10 years of age I well remember it. A short time after this the prophet moved to a place called Hyrum, about seven miles from my house, and I used to attend meetings there and enjoyed hearing him talk on the principles of the gospel. I heard him preach the Sunday after the mob had tarred, feathered and beaten him and Sidney Rigdon so badly.

Oldest Woman Member of Church Relates the Thrilling Story of Her Life

FIVE GENERATIONS OF THE WINGOT FAMILY.

"In February, 1831, my parents embraced the gospel, and a few months later I was baptized. In 1832 my parents moved to Jackson county, Mo., father having sent money ahead with which to purchase a farm. We were, however, only permitted to stay there a short time, as the enemies of our Church were so hostile that they drove us from our home. One day Brother Lyman Wight, our neighbor, was working in his corn field and a number of the mob saw him and rode across the field after him. He concealed himself in a small shock of corn in the bottom of the field. They searched for him in vain and swore that he could not possibly be in that shock, the one in which he was hiding, for it was too small. I remember father hiding in a shock of corn to keep out of the way of a mob, and we carried him food while he was there.

ENCOUNTERS WITH MOBS.

"In the fall of 1833 we were driven from our homes and were not able to take many provisions, as four or five families went with one wagon. One beautiful night when we were camped out we witnessed a beautiful sight. Stars fell and the whole heaven seemed to be alive with them. This was just after the battle that was fought in Jackson county between the Saints and the mob. The same battle in which Philo Dibble was badly wounded and others of our brethren killed. We went about 60 miles from Jackson county and camped in a grove, and remained there until February, until we were obliged to go back to Jackson county for want of provisions. A day or two after we got there my uncle and broth-

er, Orin Hewlett, were coming into town when they were met by a mob. One of the mob struck my uncle with a revolver, breaking one of his ribs, while my brother was struck on the head with a club.

"While we were in Jackson county, Lyman Leonard was badly beaten by the mob. He was laid up for some time from the effects of the beating. A man by the name of Brace was also beaten by the mob. Barrett Cole and Hyrum Abbott were also beaten.

"The mob would often come and order us off, telling us that if we were not away within a given time they would shoot us down like rabbits. One day a man on horseback came riding up to the house. My brother and I were alone. Mother was some distance from the house and came walking up to the house and seemed to be as unconcerned as though nothing had happened. Her demeanor seemed to awe the peace-breakers and they rode away without making any trouble.

ZION'S CAMP.

"After staying here about six weeks we crossed the Missouri river and went over into Clay county. Soon after our arrival Joseph and Hyrum Smith came up with what was known as 'Zion's Camp,' thinking that they would be able to get the people back to their homes.

"The people of Clay county became very unfriendly and desired us to go. We accordingly took with us a few belongings and provisions and made our homes in Far West, Caldwell county. The Saints were still harassed and it seemed as if they were never left in peace. The people had to gather together as many as possible in one house. Two or three families were usually found in one building.

"While we were here the mob took the Prophet Joseph and Hyrum and intended to shoot them at 8 o'clock but instead of shooting them they put them in Liberty jail. Several others were placed in the jail. The Saints agreed to give up their arms and leave Missouri the next spring. An embankment was built around the village to protect themselves against the mob.

"It was at this place that I first saw Brigham Young. I was acquainted with all the Whitmers, Oliver Cowdery, Hyrum Page, all the witnesses of the Book of Mormon except Martin Harris.

"In the spring of 1839, we moved from Far West and went to Nauvoo, Ill. While I was in Nauvoo, I visited the Prophet Joseph. He had three Egyptian mummies in his chamber. In 1840 I became acquainted with a young man named Cyrus Wingot and in the fall of 1841 we were married by Nathan Hess. We moved to Burton, 60 miles from Nauvoo, and about two years later moved back to Nauvoo. In 1843 we were obliged to seek another home and accordingly went to Golden Point, seven miles from Nauvoo. While we were living there in 1844, the Prophet Joseph and Hyrum were murdered in Carthage jail.

DRIVEN FROM HOMES.

"In 1846 we had to leave our homes once more. This time we went to Iowa where we remained one year living in a tent. While we were there, the battle was fought between the Saints and the mob. We stayed in Des Moines for one year, my husband working at his trade, coopering, in order to get money to purchase an outfit to go farther west.

"We started to go to a camp called Pisgah in 1847 where some of the Saints were staying who had been driven from their homes. When we got there the company was ready to start for the valleys of Salt Lake. They were desirous that we should go with them. With their assistance we were fitted out and we started with a big yoke of oxen and a yoke of cows. We arrived in Salt Lake in 1847 about Oct. 1.

"After we came to the valley we suffered from hunger, living on roots and herbs. We were finally forced to kill our oxen for food during the first winter.

"We remained in Salt Lake City about three years and then moved to Springville. While there the Indians were unfriendly and my husband had to stand guard, with the other minute men.

"Later we were called to go south to Cedar City, Iron county, to strengthen the place against the Indians. While keeping guard and doing duty, my husband contracted a cold from which he never recovered. He died Jan. 14, 1854. I was then left alone with a family of seven children. After my husband's death the people of Cedar City were kind to me which I appreciated very much. In 1854 I returned to Springville. In later years I thought that I could do better elsewhere and moved to Manti, Sanpete county. With the assistance of my children in spinning and hat-making we were able to get along fairly well.

"Here I joined the Relief society and held interesting meetings. We spun cloth and made hats. In 1871 we moved to Monroe, Sevier county. I joined the Relief society there and was chosen as treasurer. I am the mother of eight children all living. Their names are as follows: Zenos, Mrs. Malvina W. Demille, Alphonzo, Mrs. Fidelia Demille, Cyrus, Alvira D. Leeks, Mrs. Catherine E. Yergensen and Mrs. Mary Ann Clyde."

FIRST SURVEY

Of Iron Mountain, St. George and Grand Canyon Road—Will Be Direct Route to Kingman

Much has been said of the Iron Mountain, St. George & Grand Canyon railroad, and now that the preliminary survey has been completed and the first map drawn, the details will be of interest. The line leaves the Salt Lake Route at Thermo and runs to Cedar City via Enoch. From Cedar it goes to Kanarra and at a point a few miles east of New Harmony it branches

The Kingman branch is projected to run through the following places Belleview, Silver Reef, Leeds, Harrisburg, Washington, Middleton, St. George, where it makes a turn up Santa Clara Creek to a point near Santa Clara and then makes another turn to the southwest, effecting an easy grade in crossing the Beaver Dam mountains, thence thence to Littlefield, Bunkerville, St Thomas. The Colorado river is crossed at Stone Ferry, a few miles west of Rioville. This is a pioneer landing in the old river steamboats, fully and interestingly described in Sunday's Tribune Then the line runs due south to Kingman, Ariz,

where it connects with the Santa Fe

Returning to the point of divergence near New Harmony, the other line runs southeast through Virgin, Canaan Spring, Short Creek and east to Pipe Springs and Mangum Springs in Arizona. Between Pipe Springs and Mangum Springs the third branch runs to the rim of the Grand Canyon of the Colorado in Arizona, at a point about fifty miles south of Kanab That town is north of the railroad line between Pipe and Mangum Springs but a few miles.

A distinct feature of the whole project is that it penetrates an entirely new and virgin field and at no point after leaving Thermo does it compete or aim to compete with any other railroad or branch The entire region is rich in products of mines, the soil, of forests, of animals, while the scenic attractions, headed by the Grand Canyon, would make it the most wonderfully attractive railroad in the world As a retreat for campers, hunters and fishermen it would be a paradise

Engineer Burgess has completed a map which is a most thorough one in setting forth the exact geographical outline of the country, as well as the geological and industrial possibilities It shows one of the most extensive empires not reached by a railroad that can be found in the whole west —Tribune.

Deseret News
August 20, 1910

Little Tot Lost in Wilderness Is Found by Indian Searcher

SNAPSHOTS OF THE SEARCH FOR LOW SHURATT.

Upper Picture Shows a Portion of the Big Searching Party After the Boy Was Found. Lower Picture Shows the Happy Father and Son Reunited, the Boy Seated on the Knees of the Indian Who Found Him.

Toddling off from the roadside in the whim of childish fancy, little Low Shuratt, the barely 5-year-old son of James Shuratt of Cedar City, Utah, was lost for over 36 hours beginning last Tuesday afternoon, in the Cedar Bottoms. During the daylight hours and the darkness of the night a searching party of 250 men, half of them mounted on horses, scoured the country in a wide area of miles, but the search was fruitless until "Seth," an Indian from Kanab, stumbled upon the little tot lying weary and tired under the scanty shade of under brush.

On Tuesday James Shuratt, with his two boys, Low and the older brother of 8 years of age, went into the Cedar bottoms to secure a wagonload of wood. Towards noon he told the older boy to drive the wagon to a point along the road. Little Low who was playing in the roadway, was told to follow the wagon.

When the wagon reached the designated point the little chap was found missing. Mr. Shuratt retraced the roadway, but found no trace of the boy. The assistance of people living in the bottoms was called for, and then word was sent into Cedar City, and the answer to the call for help brought out 250 searchers, including a party of Indians.

All during the evening and through the night the searching party, spread out in fan-like formation, beat through the bottoms, now and then coming upon the trail of the lost boy, but only to lose it on the sun-baked ground. After an hour's rest in the early morning of Wednesday the search was renewed and continued through the greater part of the day.

With the characteristic trait of the Indian trailing scent, the Indians hung onto the trail of the wandering boy, and towards sunset, "Seth" with exultant cry to his nearby companions in the child-hunt leaped forward into a clump of bushes and held up the sought boy.

A few minutes later little Low was clutched in the grip of his father's arms and laughing in the glee of boyish happiness.

In the 36 hours of being lost the boy had traversed in his bewildered wanderings some 29 miles. In boyish way he told of how he "had just walked." During the night he had been "fraid" till sleep closed his eyes, and cuddling down into his own arms he had slept on the hard ground.

In the morning he had again started out bravely to find the road that would lead him to his home, but after the first hour had tired out his little limbs he sat down frequently to rest. Wandering about, here and there, and never knowing where he was, he had sunk down in weariness when the Indian found him.

Despite the terror of the night, being hungry for hours and lost in what was to the child a wilderness, little Low came out of his experience unharmed and is the hero of Cedar City.

Washington County News
August 26, 1910

Lawrence Snow, and Miss Mattie McArthur returned home Wednesday from Cedar mountain where they have been for an outing bringing with them the former's sisters Misses Lola and Leona Snow of Cedar City and Arthur Anderson of Emery who will visit here a few days. —Washington County News.

Iron County Record
October 10, 1910

Presbyterian Meetings.

In the City Hall, Cedar City, Utah, I will preach as follows on Sunday, October 9th. At 11 A. M. "On the Foundation Laws of the human soul." At 7:15 P. M. I will give a second Sermon on the same subject.

Come and hear both and get a firm grip and understanding of these laws.

Next Saturday or Tuesday I will finish the first verse of Genesis and explain that the Creation of the earth was finished, that it was the most beautiful period of this earth with the exception of the garden of Eden period.

I will then take up the second verse of Genesis and explain why this great Catastrophe overtook this earth.

Except on Mondays and when the City Hall is required for some Public meeting I will lecture there every night at 7:15 P. M. Every person is most earnestly, cordially and heartily invited to attend every Sunday and week night service.

ALEXANDER MURRAY,
Presbyterian Clergyman.

Summit, Nov. 30th, 1910

We were visited on the 26th inst by a taste of winter. About three inches of beautiful snow fell on that date. It has all disappeared, however and we are again enjoying the beautiful, balmy days as of yore.

B. R. Lawrence has returned from Lund. His mother, Mrs. Thos Lawrence Sr. of Erda, Tooele Co. returned with him, and will visit with her son and family for the next few days, when she will visit in Cedar City with her son Thos. Lawrence Jr.

Summit is soon to have another handsome cottage, as Alex Dalley is contemplating execting a neat frame house in the near future.

Brother Sam Fife is here, plowing and preparing for farming for the next seed time.

A son was born to Mr. and Mrs. John Naegle on Jan. 11th. All concerned progressing favorably.

Socialist Party February 14th.

As was stated in last week's Record the Socialists of Cedar City will hold a grand ball February 14th, and they have invited every body to attend.

Saturday morning the people of the city were notified that John R. Wood had died, which cause a feeling of sympathy for the young wife and children of the diseased.

He has been a victim of a weak heart for years and was also suffering with Bright's disease, which became aggrivated Saturday morning early and at eight o'clock reached the acute stage and resulted in death.

At the time of the attack there was no one with him but his wife and little ones, and the wife was compelled to leave him and the children while she run for assistance, which was immediately secured, a physician called in and all done that was possible to relieve him. The diseases with which he suffered, however, were so far advanced that they refused to respond to medicines and he gradually sank until relieved of his sufferings at the hour above stated.

Funeral services were held Monday afternoon in the tabernacle at which there was a large attendance of relatives and friends. The tabernacle was beautifully decorated for the services and the speakers spoke many words of condolences to the mourners. They also referred to the upright and manly qualities of the deceased and

...uraged the wife, mother, father ... ...brothers and sisters to emulate ...example which he has set all his life.

John R. Wood was born in Cedar City March 16, 1880 and has lived here all his life. His character has always been above reproach, and he was a strong and faithful member of the Church of Jesus Christ of Latter Day Saints. He was an active worker in the church whenever his health would permit, being secretary of the Elders quorum and a ward teacher for many years.

He leaves a loving wife and four children to mourn his loss as well as father, mother and 13 brothers and sisters. The blow comes very hard to them as this is the first death in the family.

The Record joins with the many friends of the deceased in extending heartfelt sympathy to all who mourn, especially to the wife and little ones.

Iron County Record
May 5, 1911

Mrs. May Thompson Dead.

Word was received the fore part of the week that Mrs. May Thompson of St. George, daughter of Mr. and Mrs. Byrum Jones of Cedar City, died Monday from acute kidney trouble.

Mrs. Thompson was a lovable woman, a good wife and mother. She was prominently identified in the various public happenings of Cedar when a girl and held the love and esteem of her friends and acquaintance. She was about 28 years of age and just in the prime of womanhood, and will be sadly missed by her husband and three small children, and those of her relatives and friends in Cedar will also miss her as she was wont to make periodical visits home and always was pleased to meet them.

The parents, brothers and sisters of Mrs. Thompson have the sympathy of all who knew her, and hope that the time will act as a balm upon the torn heart strings.

Iron County Record
May 12, 1911

Hilman Dalley went to Provo this week to join a government surveying corps and will be gone from Cedar about seven months.

Last night Miss Alice Wood, who has been teaching school at Hamilton's Fort, gave the closing exercises. A number of the young people from Cedar were in attendance.

James E. Anderson, proprietor of the Cedar City Drug Store, has gone to Dixie to receive 1000 head of cattle which he had contracted for some time ago.

Miss Marget Melling and Arthur Fife have returned home after having completed a very successful school year at Kanarra.

CEDAR CITY ALIVE

Elsewhere in this issue may be found an article copied from the Iron County Record giving the status of the railroad situation there. It appears from it that the Cedar City Commercial Club is alive and actively working to get the right of way sought from the government granted at an early date. We believe they will be successful and certainly hope for success, for we want to see The Dixie Route have every opportunity and incentive to build its line, which would be so great an advantage to southern Utah

* There is one part of the Record's article which we do not clearly comprehend, wherein it states that a petition is being circulated in the two counties (which we understand to mean Iron and Washington) "which is being signed by all the business men and everybody interested in the road" So far we have failed to learn anything of any such petition in this county, and, further, we do not know that any action has been asked of the people here in the matter. We feel certain that the people of Washington County would readily respond to any call made upon them, but without any authority to act they would not feel like "butting" in

POPULATION OF UTAH CITIES AND TOWNS

[Special to WASHINGTON COUNTY NEWS]

Washington, March 9 —The census bureau issued today the first recapitulation of the results of the thirteenth census for the incorporated cities and towns of Utah. The following table shows the figures for 1900 and 1910

Cities and Towns	County.	1910	1900
Alpine (city)	Utah	496	520
American Fork (city)	Utah	2,797	2,732
Bear river (city)	Boxelder	463	362
Beaver City.	Beaver	1,890	1,701
Bingham (town)	Salt Lake	2,881	
Bountiful (city)	Davis	1,677	1,442
Brigham City	Boxelder	3,685	2,859
Castledale (town)	Emery	693	559
Cedar City	Iron	1,705	1,425
Charleston (town).	Wasatch	283	234
Clarkston (town)	Cache	564	
Coalville (city)	Summit	976	808
Corinne (city)	Boxelder	231	323
Elsinore (city)	Sevier	656	625
Emery (town)	Emery	525	
Ephraim (city)	Sanpete	2,296	2,086
Escalante (town)	Garfield	846	
Eureka (city)	Juab	3,416	3,085
Fairview (city)	Sanpete	1,218	1,119
Farmington (city)	Davis	1,231	968
Ferron (town)	Emery	651	
Fillmore (city)	Millard	1,202	1,037
Forestdale (town)	Salt Lake	1,549	
Fountain Green (town)	Sanpete	875	755
Garland (town)	Boxelder	600	
Glenwood (town)	Sevier	359	422
Goshen (town)	Utah	470	645
Grantsville (city)	Tooele	1,154	1,058
Green River (town)	Emery	628	
Gunnison (town)	Sanpete	950	829
Heber City	Wasatch	2,031	1,534
Helper (town)	Carbon	816	
Hinckley (town)	Millard	553	
Huntington (town)	Emery	800	653
Hyde Park (town)	Cache	699	
Hyrum (city)	Cache	1,833	1,652
Kanab (town)	Kane	733	710
Kanosh (town)	Millard	513	
Kaysville (city)	Davis	887	1,708
Lehi (city)	Utah	2,964	2,719
Levan (town)	Juab	722	
Lewiston (town)	Cache	989	
Logan (city)	Cache	7,522	5,451

Manti (city)	Sanpete	2,423	2,408
Mapletown (town)	Utah	534	
Meadow (town)	Millard	831	
Mendon (city)	Cache	459	494
Mercur (city)	Tooele	1,047	2,351
Midvale (city)	Salt Lake	1,760	
Midway (city)	Wasatch	838	719
Milford (town)	Beaver	1,014	
Millville (town)	Cache	353	
Minersville (city)	Beaver	591	437
Moab (town)	Grand	615	
Monroe (town)	Sevier	1,227	1,057
Morgan (city)	Morgan	756	600
Moroni (city)	Sanpete	1,223	1,224
Mt Pleasant (city)	Sanpete	2,280	2,372
Murray (city)	Salt Lake	4,057	
Nephi (city)	Juab	2,759	2,208
Newton (town)	Cache	515	429
Ogden (city)	Weber	25,580	16,313
Ophir (town)	Tooele	254	
Orangeville (town)	Emery	648	
Panguitch (city)	Garfield	1,338	883
Paradise (town)	Cache	620	
Park City	Summit	3,439	3,759
Parowan (city)	Iron	1,156	1,039
Payson (city)	Utah	2,397	2,636
Pleasant Grove (city)	Carbon	1,618	2,460
Price (city)	Carbon	1,021	539
Providence (town)	Cache	1,020	877
Provo (city)	Utah	8,925	6,185
Randolph (town)	Rich	533	
Redmond (town)	Sevier	547	451
Richfield (town)	Sevier	2,559	1,969
Richmond (city)	Cache	1,562	1,111
St George (city)	Washington	1,769	1,600
Salem (town)	Utah	693	894
Salina (town)	Sevier	1,082	847
Salt Lake (city)	Salt Lake	92,777	53,531
Sandy (city)	Salt Lake	1,037	1,030
Santaquin (city)	Utah	915	889
Scipio (town)	Millard	546	578
Smithfield (city)	Cache	1,865	1,494
Spanish Fork (city)	Utah	3,464	2,735
Spring City	Sanpete	1,100	1,135
Springville (city)	Utah	3,356	3,422
Stockton (town)	Tooele	258	
Tooele (city)	Tooele	2,753	1,200
Tremonton (town)	Boxelder	303	
Tropic (town)	Garfield	358	
Vernal (city)	Uintah	836	661
Wales (town)	Sanpete	294	
Washington (town)	Washington	424	529
Wellington (town)	Carbon	358	
Wellsville (city)	Cache	1,195	908
Willard (city)	Boxelder	577	580

Iron County Record
June 16, 1911

Wm. Elliker and Miss Ethel Hall, both of Cedar City, were quietly married in Parowan Wednesday.

Iron County Record
June 30, 1911

John Hunter is the proud father of a bouncing baby boy which his wife presented him with last Friday.

Vera, the little daughter of Mr. and Mrs. Wm. Adams, is suffering with an attack of rheumatism.

The wife of Frank McConnell, who has been quite ill for some time with pneumonia, is now recovering.

Iron County Record
September 22, 1911

Macfarlane —Palmer.

Saturday evening Menzies Macfarlane of St George, and Miss Kate Palmer of Cedar City were married at the home of W. R. Palmer.

The event was not altogether un looked for, but was not expected for some time yet, because of the fact that Mr Macfarlane goes back to Chicago to finish his schooling. However their friends were pleased to know of the marriage; and are wishing them success and happiness in the bonds of wedlock

Miss Palmer is one of Cedar's prominent and progressive young

women, highly connected and respect

Normal

Mr. Macfarlane is a product of St. George, bright and capable and is held in high esteem by all who know him. He was an instructor of the Branch Normal a couple of years ago, resigning his position there to go to Chicago to complete a course of study in which he is highly proficient.

The Record extends hearty congratulations to the young couple and wish them a long, happy and useful life in double harness.

An Unexpected Summons.

In the sudden death at an early hour last Wednesday morning of Miss Clara Emily Tucker, Cedar City lost a useful worker in public affairs and a conspicuous member of society among the younger class of the community. Endowed with a natural genius or music, and with an exceptionally good voice, she had improved her talents and was frequently called into requisition for the entertainment of the public, both in religious and social affairs.

The deceased was only ill a little more than a week, and the announcement of her death came as a complete surprise to the greater portion of the community. Many persons were not even aware that she was sick. Apparently of a robust physique, and of a jovial disposition, it was hard to realize the seriousness of her condition, even by the family and attending physician.

The direct cause of death was a general peritonitis, probably induced by some form of kidney complaint.

Deceased was 22 years of age. Funeral services will be held from the Tabernacle this afternoon at 2 o'clock.

* Summit, Utah, Oct. 11.

School commenced on the 9th inst., with Prof. John H. Dalley as Principal.

Mrs. Beecroft of New Mexico is here visiting with her mother, Mrs. Farnsworth.

Mrs. Mary C. Dalley and family have moved to Cedar City for the winter, to afford the opportunity of superior school facilities. Summit feels very keenly the loss occasioned by the absence of Sister Dalley, owing to the active part which she always took in the Primary and Sunday School work, being naturally endowed for that special work, as also that of ward chorister.

Mrs. Martha Alexander, who has been spending some little time in Cedar City with her daughter, Mrs. C. S. Wilkinson, is now paying a visit to her sister in Paragoonah, Mrs. Johnathran Prothero.

In the death of Henry Mc-Connell, which occurred at his home in this city Sunday afternoon at between 4:00 and 5:00, p. m., Cedar City looses an intelligent, honorable and upright citizen, and one of the well-known landmarks. Death was caused by pneumonia, supplemented by old age and the incident lack of vitality to combat the disease. The patient was ill only about a week, and suffered but comparatively little. All of the children of deceased were at his bedside when the last change came, and he did not want for tender and willing hands to nurse and care for him. The funeral services were held in the tabernacle Tuesday afternoon at 2 o'clock. The speakers were John V. Adams, Wm. H. Corry, John Parry, Rufus Allen and Alex G. Matheson. All bore testimony as to the good character of the deceased and spoke words of comfort and consolation to the bereaved family.

BIOGRAPHICAL.

Henry McConnell, son of Jehial and Nancy McConnell, was born in Posey county, Indiana. From there the family moved to Iowa, where they joined the Church of Latter-day Saints, and in the year 1849, emigrated to Utah. At this time he was 14 years of age, and ... family resided in the ... ward at Salt Lake City, and then they ... deceased was the first city marshal, and the family was prominently identified with the early history of that place, and during the past year deceased has furnished considerable information concerning the early settlement of that place, which is to be used in the preparation of a pioneer history of Lehi.

Deceased first came to Cedar City in the fall of 1854, and spent the winter here, but returned the following spring to Lehi, and resided there until 1862, when he moved to Cedar City to live, and has resided here ever since. From Lehi he was called to go with a company to Salmon City, Idaho, to afford relief for the saints there against the Indians, and to conduct them back to Utah. The expedition was fraught with considerable adventure, but was successful, and the saints were returned to Utah in safety. At Lehi, in 1858, he was married to Eliza Williams, and eight children resulted from the union, six of whom are still living.

In Cedar City deceased has served as city marshal, city councilman, etc. At one time he was prominently allied with the sheep industry in this county, and lost heavily from the depredations of Indians. With his frugal and industrious wife,

he was the first to establish a dairy on the Cedar Mountains, and for a number of years the products of their dairy stood pre-eminent on the local market.

Henry McConnell was of a quiet, retiring disposition, even-tempered, and made few, if any enemies. Yet, withal, he was firm and courageous in his support of right and justice.

He performed a creditable work on earth, and has gone to a well-earned rest.

The surviving children are, Mrs. Wm. F. Sawyer, William J., LaFayette, Thomas F. and George B. McConnell, and Mrs. Robert W. Bulloch. His faithful wife also survives him. There are also a number of grandchildren and three great-grandchildren.

To the bereaved family The Record extends condolence.

Iron County Record
November 10, 1911

History of Cedar City.

The Pioneers started from Parowan November 11, 1851 about noon. They had what was known as the dog wagons which they hauled their dogs in. They had a great number of dogs which were mostly all sheep dogs.

They stopped in Summit to feed their cattle. They got here in the night and camped in the cedars south west of the cemetery. This is how Cedar got its name. They built brush wigwams to live in until they could get houses built. They first lived in the Old Field, then they moved to the Old Fort, then to where we are living now.

Not long after the Pioneers got here Bishop Lunt had his team stolen by the Indians. A little while later the indians were brought back and whipped severely. They were tied to the liberty pole and the Chief of the Indians gave them each nineteen lashes on the bare back.

The pioneers served a big dinner and invited the Indians to attend. This was to make friends with them.

The fort they were in was something like this: Three houses then a Bastian to shoot from. These houses served as part of the wall and with all this they had to have day guards and night guards.

President Young told the people to move farther West because the Indians were so bad. The people left their homes again and _____ lived in cellars in th ____ which was known as ____ old ____

When the people wanted white flour they had to send to San Pete Valley. They sent to Salt Lake about once a year for a pound of sugar. This they used only when some one special came. They ground the most of their flour in coffee mills.

The people had three houses built by Christmas. These houses were owned by James Chatterley, James Bosnew and another man. They also had a meeting house and school house built by Christmas. Their first school teacher was William Caruthers.

In the summer of 1855 a great flood came through the town. It came down from the Hogsback.

Mr. Chatterley asked his daughter Anna Chatterley if she could make a flag for the fourth of July. Anna got Mary Whitter, and Mary Stones to help her make the flag and with a red silk dress of Anna's and a white one and some blue sateen they made the first flag that was ever put up in Cedar.

The people had lots of their cattle stolen by the Indians.

There was a large smelter ninety feet high and it would hold ninety tons of fuel.

Mr. and Mrs. Tait taught the second school.

The people lived in cellars in the winter of 1853.

Mr. Morris had a little Indian boy by the name of Isaac. This little boy herded cattle for the pioneers. Quince knowing that Isaac was out herding the cattle went to him and killed him. His idea of killing Isaac was so that his little boy would have some one to go to the hunting grounds with.

President Young was the man that laid off the blocks.

Leona Bauer.

Iron County Record
December 4, 1911

Summit, Utah, Dec. 4 , 1911.
"It is too bad! We will not be able to see "Santa Claus" at Cedar again this year. Summit has placed a strict quarantine against Enoch, Cedar City, and Hamilton's Fort. Allowing no-one to visit Summit, from those towns or anyone residing in Summit to visit those places and return, This is owing to our love of good health for ourselves and families.

Some of our worthy brethern have been honored with souven-irs from Box B. The ones thus favored are O. W. Hulet, and Charles Pratt, and Ronald Dalley. All are good workers for whom the Ward is proud.

Iron County Record
December 29, 1911

Only one birth reported in Summit for this week, that being the arrival of a baby girl at the home of Mr. and Mrs. B. R. Lawrence.

Iron County Record
January 12, 1912

In the Salt Lake temple Jan-uary third there was consummat-ed a marriage between J. Clayton Mitchell of Parowan, and Irene Canfield of Cedar City. The young couple are highly respect-ed in the two places and both have been quite prominent in public. Mr. Mitchell is cashier of the Bank of Iron County at Parowan and holds the respect and esteem of his employers. He is a bright and progressive young man with a bright future before him.

Miss Canfield is the neice of Mr. and Mrs. B. F. Knell, and is a charming young woman. She for the past few years has been a school teacher and has made a success of that calling She has a host of friends in Cedar all of whom hold her in the highest esteem.

Married,

Last Friday here was consummated at Milford a marriage by which John Fretwell of Cedar City secured one of Beaver's daughters, Miss Lucile Fennimore.

The groom is well known here and is the son of Mr. and Mrs. Orson Fretwell. The bride is connected with one of Beaver's well-known families, and is reported to be a charming young lady.

The friends of John wish him every success and happiness in wedded life, and will welcome his bride to Cedar.

Summit, Feb. 14.

The wedding of a popular young couple took place here on the 10th inst at 8 p. m., the ceremony being performed by Bp. Charles R. Dalley. The groom is John H. Beecroft and hails from Mexico, and the bride is Mrs. Thrine Dalley of this place.

Summit, Utah.

Born to Mr. and Mrs. Frank Jones, a baby girl, March 21. All concerned doing well.

Mr. and Mrs. B. R. Lawrence and family are moving to Cedar City to make their home for a while.

Summit Notes.

The general health of the people is good.

Isaac F. Langford is slowly recovering from a severe illness.

Mr. and Mrs. James H. Dalley have returned to their home in Spry, Garfield Co. They were here to attend the funeral of Mr. Dalley's mother.

Mr. Edward Dalley and family are now occupying the home of R. R. Lawrence who, has gone to Cedar City to spend the summer.

Mr. Lyman Johnson and wife of Junction were in attendance at the funeral of Sister Dalley. They are now visiting relatives and friends. Mrs. Johnson is not in the best of health but is improving slowly since her arrival here.

The funeral services of Sister Mandana Dalley were held Friday, in the New Hall, with a good attendance. President Marsden and Day, Bp. Adams and Bro. William H. Holyoak of Parowan were present and each spoke of the sterling qualities of Sister Dalley. She is the last of our number who saw and was acquainted with the Prophet Joseph Smith. She having lived in his family.

The following sketch of the life of Mandana Dalley, who recently passed away at Summit, will be of interest to all who were acquainted with her:

Mandana Dalley, daughter of Mayhew and Sarah Hillman, was born Dec. 3, 1820, at Spafford, Onondago County, New York. In her early childhood her parents joined the Latter-day Saints and removed to Nauvoo, Illinois. During the time of the mobbings in Nauvoo her father died and her mother was left a widow with four small children. While in Nauvoo she made her home a portion of the time with the family of the Prophet Joseph Smith and was well acquainted with his two wives who were living together at that time. Being driven with the Saints from Nauvoo, her mother settled for a short time at a place called Pisga; from there they moved to Trading Point, Iowa. At this place, September 4, 1846 she was married to William Dalley, a native of Leominster, Herefordshire, England, who joined the Latter Day Saints in his native land and came to America on account of his religion. With her husband and small family of children she moved westward with the body of Saints who were seeking homes in the West and was among ~~the~~ ~~family~~ ~~als in~~ ~~Burden: is the increase~~ finally settling at Pleasant Grove, Utah County, Utah. Her husband being called by the authorities of the Church to settle Iron County moved his family to Cedar City and later moved to and built a home at the place now known as Johnson's Fort. About the year 1858 she made her last move with her husband and family and was among the first settlers of the town of Summit in Iron County. During her late sickness she always expressed her willingness to depart this life as she felt that her life work was completed; and she passed away peacefully, on the morning of March 27, 1912. The funeral services were held in the new Summit tabernacle on the afternoon of March 29, and was followed to her final resting place in Summit cemetery by a goodly number of relatives and friends.

Mrs. Dalley was the mother of a large family of children: one son and three daughters preceed, and seven sons and one daughter, survive her. All her surviving children except one, and a number of her grand children and great grand children attended the funeral. All speakers at the funeral services spoke in the highest terms of praise of Grandma Dalley as a model mother, a faithful and devoted wife, a true Latter Day Saint, and one who had paid especial attention to her home duties in the training and caring for her children. She passed through the many hardships incident to pioneer life and was always willing to lend a helping hand and give words of encouragement to those in need and to all who became discouraged and disheartened on account of the many hardships and trials experienced by the early pioneers.

Kanarra Letter.

Kanarra, April 10.

Last Sunday we were surprised by a reorganization in the Primary Association. Sister Johanna Ford was chosen President with Sarah E. Roundy and Eva J. Reeves as counsellors. We are in hopes of having a change in the work, as the preceeding President has been away for several months, also one of her assistants. Our ward is in need of having vacancies filled.

Monday morning a boy was born to Mr. and Mrs. John H. Williams.

James Stapley is slowly recovering from an attack of La-Grippe.

We are still having wet weather. Yesterday it rained and last night and today it has snowed, giving the lately planted crops a fair show for yielding.

Kanarra, May 15.

Charles Parker, Jr., Constable, went to Cedar City today taking Wesley Groves to be examined as to his sanity.

Wm. Stapley, son of Jas. S. Stapley, arrived here from Hinckley last night to assist his brothers and father with their farms.

Tuesday morning of this week a baby girl arrived at the home of Mr. and Mrs. Millard Watson.

Miss Cora Jones has returned to her home in this city after having spent the winter teaching in Nevada.

A baby girl arrived at the home of Mr. and Mrs. Jas. Bullock Thursday moring. The Record extends congratulations.

Mr. and Mrs. Edward Stubbs are the proud parents of a new baby boy which arrived during the past week.

Mr. and Mrs. Carl Burkholder are the proud parents of a bouncing baby boy who came to the home Friday of last week and announced his intention of taking up permanent quarters with them.

COAL AND IRON FIELDS

Much Interest Being Manifested In The Rich Deposits of Iron County. Land Being Rapidly Taken Up

J H Arthur, chairman of the board of commissioners of Iron county is in the city and says that much greater interest is being mani fested in the coal and iron fields of that section since the announcement was made that a railroad line would be provided The promoters of the Utah & Grand Canyon railroad have expressed a willingness to start with their construction work just as soon as suitable arrangements can be made with the Salt Lake route for a contract for handling through freight This concern completed its surveys some time ago and obtained valuable concessions including ex tensive terminals It has extended considerable money in this work and appears to be anxious to com plete the line and get some return on the investment

The people of Cedar City and vicinity are much pleased over the recent announcement made by Sen ator Clark to the effect that he was prepared to construct a branch line through the iron fields on to St George as soon as he received assur ances of a tonnage that would give him a fair return on his investment They feel confident that they can give this assurance and say that their agricultural lands are being taken up rapidly and with a rail road line the country would settle up within a short time Mr Arth ur says that he has inquiries in every mail relative to their farm lands, mostly from western people living in California Oregon and Washington People of the middle west are coming into that section, the largest number thus far being from Kansas and Missouri

More work is being conducted by mineral land owners at this time than usual The Chloride Canyon Mining company a Salt Lake con cern is doing some exploratory work in its properties situated in Chlor ide canyon about twenty five miles west of Cedar City Several other concerns are proving up on their ground and the country has the ap pearance of an active season in all lines Some results are looked for that will have an important bearing upon the future of that southern country —Evening Telegram

Mrs. Anna Cox of Moapa, Nevada, arrived in the city Monday to spend the summer with her mother, Mrs. Jane Middleton, and other relatives.

Mrs. C. G. Bell, the genial proprietor of the Cedars hotel, accompanied Mr. Walter Granger and Miss Hazel Dalley to Salt Lake to be present at the wedding of the latter two, she being a sister of the groom.

Last Saturday a dog belonging to T. J Jones severely bit a little son of Thomas Wade. The boy was severly injured about the face but hopes are entertained that no permanent injury will result.

At about 2 o'clock Sunday afternoon, the spirit of Mrs. Caroline Height Esplin took its flight, and another life was cut short in the very prime of womanhood.

During the winter, Mrs. Esplin consented to act as a subject before the nursing class that was being conducted under the direction of an experienced nurse, and following a vigorous massage caught a severe cold which grew worse until it developed into incurable pulmonary trouble. All that the ministering hands of loving relatives and the skill of physicians could do, was of no avail, and after four months of suffering, death mercifully relieved her from pain.

Deceased was born in Cedar City April 26, 1882, and grew to womanhood here. She was married to Geo. W. Esplin, September 5, 1905, and for several years resided with her husband at Orderville, this state, removing to this city some three years since.

From early childhood she has been a member of the Latter Day Saints church, and died a firm believer in the saving power of God. The funeral was held in the tabernacle Tuesday, June 4, the services being under the direction of Counselor Jethro Palmer. The speakers were Prof. G. W. Decker, Bishops Alex Matheson and Wm. H. Corry.

A husband, three children, a father and mother, other relatives, and a host of sorrowing friends, are left to mourn her departure. "Like a flower, she grew and blossomed, only to be cut down in the midst of life."

Iron County Record
June 21, 1912

A boy baby arrived at the home of Mr. and Mrs. Lon Ahlstrom Wedensday morning.

The John L. Jones family of Enoch is holding a family reunion today. The festivities began yesterday and will close tonight.

Iron County Record
July 12, 1912

Frank Nixon of Kanarra came to Cedar City Tuesday. He would have been welcome had he not proceeded to take on too much "fire water." The result was that he started to create a disturbance in the west part of town, frightening women and children, and Marshal Urie was called to make an investigation. Nixon did not take kindly to the officer's interference and struck him a blow. The representative of the law got busy with his club with the result that his opponent was soon "hors de combat." He was locked in the "cooler" until Wednesday morning when he was arraigned before Justice Palmer and assessed $5 for the benefit of the city.

Iron County Record
July 19, 1912

Mr. and Mrs. David Murie are parents of a new baby boy who took up his residence with them Wednesday morning.

Jos. T. and Ray A. Wilkinson departed this morning for Hurricane to visit with their son and brother, Jos. T. Wilkinson, Jr.

Mrs. Lottie Perkins, Mr. and Mrs. Roy Heap, Mr. Joshua Walker, Mrs. Nettie Macfarlane, Principal G. W. Decker, Mr. J. W. Barton, Mr. Arthur Jones and Miss Urania Jones, went to Parowan Thursday to attend the funeral of Julius Taylor.

Iron County Record
August 2, 1912

Mrs. Edith Gregory became the mother of a fine son last Monday. Congratulations to the proud parents.

A baby girl was born to Mr. and Mrs. F. J. Green of Hamilton's Fort on the 1st day of the present month.

Wednesday morning Mrs. Anna Lunt and daughter Ellen, with her four children, arrived in this city from Pachdo, Mexico, from which place they were forced to flee, along with hundreds of other American colonists, from the Mexican rebels who are engaged in pillaging and destroying property and threatening the lives of the people.

After leaving their homes they finally reached El Paso, Texas, where they remained for a week before securing transportation to this city. From them The Record learns that the former homes of the colonists have been completely deserted almost without exception. The women and children were sent ahead across the border, the men remaining in the hope that they might be able to retain their property. Among those who remained were six sons of Mrs. Lunt.

When the refugees reached El Paso they learned that the men who had been left behind had abandoned the farms and were hurrying toward the United States border, in constant danger of attack from the rebels, and were due to arrive last Tuesday.

This is the first visit Mrs. Lunt has made to Cedar City since leaving here twenty-three years ago. Her daughter who is with her was a child when she removed to Mexico. Both are pleased with the changes and improvements in the city and will hereafter make their home here. They do not care to longer risk the uncertainties of Mexican government.

Many relatives and old friends in this city will be glad to welcome them again to citizenship in this community.

Iron County Record
August 16, 1912

A baby son was born to Mr. and Mrs. Andrew Rollo last Sunday.

Elson Morris of St. George, brother of Mrs. S. J. Foster of this city, was a visitor in town a couple of days last week.

Mr. and Mrs. Evelyn Parry are the proud parents of a baby boy who put in his appearance at the Parry home Monday morning.

The wife and 13-year-old daughter of Lorenzo Davis of Kanarraville are suffering from typhoid fever. From the attending physician, Dr. C. M. Clark, we learn that conditions are not the most favorable for the proper handling of a trouble of such seriousness but that he anticipates no difficulty in controlling the disease.

Vilate, the beloved two-year-old daughter of Mr. and Mrs. Wm. R. Palmer, died at the family home last Satruday morning about 11:30 o'clock after an illness of but three days, from a spasmodic affection of the throat.

The little one was first seized with an attack of tonsilitis which later developed into a complication in which symptoms of membraneous croup were plainly evident. Some of the indications of diptheria were also present and the physicians were unable to state positively the exact cause of death. As a precaution, the public were advised not to permit children to attend the funeral.

Summit, September 4.
Part of the family of Thomas Walker of Cedar City, including Miss Fannie and several of her brothers, are now occupying Hyrum Dalley's house. They will stay here until the boys get through with their fall work on the farm

Samuel S. Fife has been confined to his bed since last Friday. Dr. Leonard of Cedar was called to attend him a few days ago. He is still quite ill but is thought to be on the improve.

Watson Family Reunion

The Watson family reunion, which was held in this city last week, was a most successful and gratifying event to those attending. There were present 37 of the family, who came from Salt Lake, St. George, Beaver and Cedar City to meet and associate with each other for a short time amid the scenes of their childhood at the old home. That all enjoyed this brief but happy mingling of brothers and sisters, many of whom had not seen each other for a number of years, with their mother, need hardly be said. The home was kept continually enlivened with the happy voices of the 21 grandchildren who came to cheer the heart of grandma Watson.

The most important event of this family gathering was the erecting of the Watson monument at the cemetery in honor of the father Lorenzo D. Watson and the three children, Clare, Lorenzo and Talula, that their last resting place might show that their memory is ever living in the hearts of those left to mourn their loss.

The dedication took place Wednesday, August 28th, at 11 a. m., Bishop Morgan Richards offering the dedicatory prayer, and the beautiful sentiments expressed found grateful response in the hearts of all present; especially the one wherein the desire was expressed that the spirit of the father might know of this action and work of love by those who honor his memory. After the prayer Miss LaVerd Watson, youngest daughter of the deceased parent, dressed in white, wearing white carnations removed the white crape from the monument and there was revealed a beautiful stone, the base of which was of Utah granite, the cap of highly polished Vermont granite, bearing the simple inscription "Watson." Markers, also of Vermont granite, indicated the graves of the dead, and the family burial ground thoroughly cleaned, was covered with black gravel which blended well with the color of the monument.

Iron County Record
September 13, 1912

A daughter was born to Mr. and Mrs. S. J. Foster last Friday.

Tuesday in the temple in Salt Lake City, Mr. H. Gordon Matheson and Miss Gwen Higbee were united in marriage, at the same time Miss Rheda Matheson, sister of the groom, was made the wife of Mr. Wm. Wood .

The announcement of the marriage will no doubt be a surprise to the many friends of these young people, the fact of their approaching wedding being kept a profound secret from even their closest friends.

Mr. Matheson is the son of Bishop A. G. Matheson of this city, and last week was given a ball in the Ward Hall in honor of his departure on a mission to Germany. The bride is one of Cedar City's most talented and winsome young ladies, and a daughter of Alonzo Higbee, one of the best known citizens of the county.

Within a few days the groom will leave for Germany to spend two years in the mission field for the church, and the bride will return to her home in this city where she will continue to teach in the city schools, a position which she now holds.

Mrs. Jos. S. Fife, and Mr. and Mrs. Peter B. Fife attended the funeral of Mrs. Margaret Pace at New Harmony Thursday.

Mrs. Lottie Perkins, Mr. and Mrs. Edwin Walker and Mrs. Nettie Macfarlane are visiting in St. Geoage.

Mr. and Mrs. Harry Thorley are rejoicing over the arrival of a bouncing baby girl at their home last Saturday. Dr. C. M. Clark was in attendance.

LIGHT COMPANY TO INCREASE SERVICE

Hereafter, the Cedar City Light & Power Co. will give an all-day service four days of each week, Tuesdays, Wednesdays, Thursdays and Saturdays.

This improvement in the service will be welcomed by the public and will be of inestimable benefit to the people in many ways, and will no doubt result in the installation of many additional motors for power purposes, in addition to increasing the use of current for various other pur-

Mr. David Pryor of this city and Miss Mame Robertson of Alton were united in marriage at Panguitch Friday of last week. The young couple have the wishes of a host of friends for a long, contented married life.

A boy was born to Mr. and Mrs. James Hunter last Wednesday.

The Record regrets to announce that Mrs. William Walker, whose serious illness was announced some weeks since, died at her home in this city Christmas day, at 12 o'clock, at the age of 75 years.

She had been ill for more than two months, her affliction being chiefly due to the effects of advanced age, and for several days loved ones had been keeping a vigilant watch, fearing the worst.

Mrs. Walker was one of those sweet, christian souls, whose very presence made others better, and none knew her but to love her. Quiet and unassuming in her manner, she went quietly about doing good at every opportunity, and many there are who will remember her kindly ministrations.

In addition to her aged husband, Mrs. Walker leaves three sisters and three brothers, and eight children, as follows: former bishop Wm. V. Walker, George, Frank, Edwin, Ernest, Joshua, and one daughter, Mrs. Nettie Macfarlane, all of whom are residents of Cedar City.

Marriages Galore

County Clerk Woodbury has is-
sued marriage licenses as follows
Dec 19—Ben Sorenson and Rebecca
Coates both of St George Paul
Miner of Springville Utah, and
Ethel Bunker of Bunkerville Nev-
ada Dec 21—Ellis Pickett and
Ruth Morris both of St George
Dec 23—Dolph Andrus of Wash
ington and Irene Jones of Cedar
City, S R Wilkinson of Cedar City
and Veda Bringhurst of Toquerville
Jeff W Button and Cornelia Christ
enson both of Hurricane Charles
A Stratton and Kate N Angell
loth of Hurricane Lemuel W
Willis of Kanarra and Rhoda M
Bladen of Cedar City Dec 24—R
Joseph Farnsworth and Mary J
Foremaster both of St George
Floyd Edward Manges of Pittsburg
Pa and Hortense McQuarrie of St
George George H Olsen and Marie
McMullin both of Leeds

Kanarraville.

If you don't want the chicken-pox, you better not come here for a while.

Born Dec. 31st to Mr. and Mrs. W. J. Williams a girl. This is the 3rd birth, but the first girl. Bill says he has as many kinds as the most of people have now.

Principal and Mrs. E. B. Dalley are rejoicing over the arrival last Friday of a baby daughter.

Summit.

(Received too late for last issue.)

Lucy Dalley of Summit and Martin Walker of Cedar City were married New Year's Eve at the home of the bride's parents, by Bishop C. R. Dalley.

Arthur Dalley of Park City was a visitor here for two days last week. It is ten years since his last visit here.

Mrs. Eliza Farnsworth has been very sick with pneumonia the last week.

Miss Ella Hulett is spending her vacation at home. She brought a ____ d with her, Miss Farnham of Chicago, who has been enjoying herself in the holiday vacations here.

Hyram Dalley and family have moved home from Cedar again.

Angus Riggs, W. W. Dalley, N. B. Dalley, Charles Pratt, Isaac Chamberlain and J. P. Dalley will leave Friday morning to go out west to work.

We now have two new stores running in Summit. The proprietors are C. R. Dalley and Miss Marie Farrow.

F. E. Fletcher, the contractor, returned Saturday from Salt Lake City, where he had gone in response to a call summoning him to the bedside of his father. When he left his father was slightly improved but still in a very serious condition.

Leonard Green, son of Dr. E. F. Green, is now employed at the Cedar City Drug Store.

David Bullock is making a business trip through Nevada. His first stop will be at Pioche.

Miss Mae Lunt has accepted a position with the Cedar City Co-op, entering upon her duties last week.

Mrs. Eliza Ann Hansen while stepping from the door of her home last Wednesday fell and badly sprained her ankle.

Mr. George Esplin and Miss Lottie Haight of this city left for St. George Sunday where they were united in marriage in the temple on Wednesday. The Record joins their many friends in wishing them a long and happy wedded life.

A baby girl arrived at the home of Mr. and Mrs. Rufus Johnson Tuesday night . Mr. Johnson has just gone into business and says he intends to do all he can to "build up Cedar."

Monday the Matheson Bros. struck a flow of water of some two gallons a minute on the Higbee farm, where they are sinking a well, at a depth of about 88 feet.

Daniel, a son of Bishop J. J. G. Webster, fell from the roof of a neighbor's home several days since and suffered a badly sprained leg.

Summit.

Mrs. Laurena Langford was up from Cedar City last Friday visiting her mother and other relatives.

Bishop Charles R. Dalley who has been ill for some time is now able to be around again.

Joint funeral services were held Thursday over the remains of the infants of Joseph Haslem and George A. Lunt. A large concourse of relatives and friends was in attendance.

Kanarraville.

(Received too late for last issue.)

We are having the storm of the season. Snow commenced falling Monday morning about 8 o'clock and has been coming ever since with very short intervals and it is very wet.

Miss Bell Williams is at home for a few days taking a rest.

Born on February 21, a girl to Mr. and Mrs. John W. Platt, which only lived about 45 minutes. It died very suddenly and was buried on the 23rd.

Will J., Lorenzo J., and Jos. S. Williams went to Cedar on business.

Summit.

Mrs. Mary Simkins is on the sick list this week.

Dr. E. F. Green of Cedar City made a visit here on Monday to make a call on his patients.

Samuel L. Fife made a flying trip to Salt Lake City last week and on his return home stopped off at Lund to see the demonstration car.

The rabbit hunt between Summit and Enoch came off all O. K., the latter gaining the victory and they will be right royally entertained here in a dance next Friday night.

Leo Farnsworth who was accidently shot in the arm some time ago in a rabbit hunt has so far recovered that he can use his arm practically as well as ever.

Made Gallant Ride To Prevent Massacre

Wellsville, March 15 —James H. Haslam 87 years old, a resident of Utah since 1851, and the man who carried to President Brigham Young in Salt Lake City the express message concerning troubles in the southern part of the state, which culminated in the Mountain Meadow massacre, and who carried President Young's message back to the disturbed section in an effort to prevent injury to the emigrants, died at his home here last Thursday of old age.

Mr. Haslam was born in England, Sept 16. 1825, and came to America in his nineteenth year, sailing directly to New Orleans. Seven years later, in 1851, he came to Utah, and has been affiliated with the Church since that time. He was a high priest at the time of his death. He leaves a widow, Mrs Ann R. Haslam, 12 children, 44 grandchildren and 22 great grandchildren. Funeral services will be held in the Wellsville tabernacle next Tuesday afternoon at 2 o'clock.

In the early days of the state Mr. Haslam lived in Cedar City and just prior to the Mountain Meadow massacre in 1857, he was chosen by Col. Isaac C. Haight, commanding the militia of that place, to carry dispatches to President Brigham Young in this city detailing the provocation to hostilities that had been given to Indians, and the indignant fury of the savages toward the emigrants who were passing through. Leaving Cedar City Monday afternoon, Sept 7, and riding express, changing horses frequently, he reached Salt Lake City Thursday morning, the 10th, having covered in this time the distance of between 250 and 300 miles gave this message to President Young, and received orders a few hours later to carry back at utmost speed and without sparing horseflesh the word that the "Indians must be kept from the emigrants at all cost if it took all of Iron county to protect them." There was no lack of effort on his part, but when he reached Cedar City on the following Sunday, the massacre had already taken place —Deseret News

Wednesday last Mr. John M. Chatterley and Ellen Lunt, two of Cedar City's popular citizens, were united in marriage at the home of the groom's father west of the city.

The groom is one of the substantial men of the city, highly respected by every one, and the bride is a member of one of the best families in the county, being a daughter of Henry Lunt, one of the first pioneers to settle in this community.

We extend our heartiest good wishes for a long and happy wedded life.

Sherratt-Davis.

Mr. Wm. Sherratt and Miss Jessie Davis are to be married in this city today, and tomorrow they will leave for Monticello where they will make their home in future. Mr. Sherratt has sold the greater portion of his property in Cedar City and will locate permanently at Monticello

The little son of Marion Millet, after undergoing a second operation within a period of ten days is getting along splendidly, with every prospect of complete recovery.

Peter B. Fife, Miss Belle Armstrong, Mrs. Graff and son of Kanarra, and Mr. and Mrs. Henry Clark, were among those leaving yesterday for Salt Lake.

Uncle John Urie of Hamilton's Fort was in town Monday and while here took occasion to pay "ye editor" a pleasant visit. This was the first trip to Cedar City that Uncle John has been able to make for more than three months, or since he was seriously injured by a fractious colt last fall. Come again, Uncle John, and make The Record office your headquarters.

Next Wedesday in the Salt Lake temble Mr. L. A. Thorley and Miss Mame Parry will be united in marriage. The contracting parties are two of the best known and most popular citizens of Cedar City and Iron county.

The groom is one of the most highly respected and successful business men of the city, and a member of one of the leading families of this part of the state. He was born and reared in this city but for almost ten years, until last fall, resided in Wyoming, where he was successful in acquiring extensive land and live stock interests. At the last election he was elected to the Wyoming legislature as representative from Big Horn county, that state. At the close of the session of the legislature he returned to Cedar City and expects to make his home here in the future.

The bride is one of the city's most charming daughters, who numbers her friends by the hundreds. She was born and grew to womanhood here. Her father is Edward Parry, known as "Uncle Ed," and who has been a leading figure in the political and industrial affairs of the county for many years. She has been a leader in the social activities of the city, no social function being quite complete if "Mame" were absent. She has been the Manager of the Equitable Co-op store for more than a year and under her guidance the business has grown until it is one of the foremost establishments in the city. She will retain her position for a short time, until the owners can secure a new manager.

The happy couple will depart for Salt Lake City Saturday afternoon. They will remian in Salt Lake for about a week or ten days after which they will go to California to spend their honeymoon. They exepct to be absent about four weeks, returning to this city about the first of May, when they will be at home to their host of friends.

The Record extends congratulations—congratulations to the groom, congratulations to the bride. May your married life be strewn with joys like unto the fragrance of roses, the essence of sweet perfume.

HIGH WIND DOES CONSIDERABLE DAMAGE

Monday an exceedingly high wind visited Cedar City which resulted in considerable property damage, principally to barns. Some nine barns were overturned or wrecked by the gale, some of the losers being Walter Jones, Lehi W. Jones, Kumen Leigh, and R. A. Thorley. So fierce was the wind that pedestrians on the streets were in danger of being blown down and injured.

NEW POSTOFFICE FOR IRON COUNTY

Washington, May 10.—Congressman Johnson has recommended the establishment of a postoffice at Nada, Iron county, Utah.

Nada is a new town on the Salt Lake Route, north of Lund, and the postoffice is to accommodate the many new homesteaders who have settled there.

Thorley—Williams Nuptials.

Tuesday Mr. Stewart Thorley and Miss Mary Williams of this city left for St. George, where they will be united in marriage in the temple.

Both are popular residents of Cedar City, Miss Williams having been until recenly employed as assistant to Postmaster C. S. Wilkinson.

Congratulations and best wishes a host of friends go with them.

Mrs. Wm. Unthank's mother, formerly Mrs. Jessup, arrived in the city Wednesday to be present at the bedside of her daughter, who is at the hospital.

R. W. Spice, who came from California to be present at the marriage of his sister, Miss Zella, to Oscar Carlson, returned to his home in Los Angeles Sunday.

Washington County News
June 26, 1913

Marriages

Mr. W W. McAllister of this city and Miss Keturah Dalley of Cedar City obtained a marriage license on the 23rd inst and were married in the St. George temple the 24th. The bride is one of Cedar City's charming daughters and comes of a well and favorably known family of that city; the groom is a son of Mr. and Mrs J. W. McAllister of this city, a highly respected young man who has been engaged as school teacher for some years A reception was had at the McAllister home.

Marriage licenses were obtained here the 25th inst by Mr Jos. B Dalley of Summit and Miss Sara Heyborn of Cedar City, Mr Ether Wood of Hurricane and Miss Augusta B Carter of this city. The two latter couples intend being married in the St George temple today

Iron County Record
July 4, 1913

Mr. and Mrs. P. A. Clark are the proud parents of a new baby which came to their home Wednesday.

Samuel Fife has been on the sick list the last few days, but is better now.

Mr. O'Donnell and Frank Jones, with their wives, came down from Thornton's saw mill to spend the 4th.

Born to Mr. and Mrs. Angus Riggs a girl, on the 26th of June, and to Mr. and Mrs. William Allen, a girl, on the 2nd of July.

The following births have been reported within the last week: To Mr. and Mrs. Dan Barney, New Harmony; Mr. and Mrs. Thos. Carlett, Hamilton's Fort; Mr. and Mrs. A. E. Leonard and Mr. and Mrs. Jas. Parry, Cedar City.

Mrs. Lawrence Clark is recovering rapidly from the effects of the recent operation which she underwent at the hospital.

The recent hot spell was the hottest weather experienced in Cedar City within the last eight years, according to Voluntary Observer Parley Dalley. The temperature on Sunday, July 6th reached 97, and for the six days following ranged above 90. While these temperatures would have caused great suffering in the lower altitudes, but little inconvenience was experienced here, owing to the stiff breezes and cool nights.

A baby girl weighing 11½ pounds was born to Mr. and Mrs. Henry Watts Saturday night.

Iron County Record
August 8, 1913

A daughter was born to Mr. and Mrs. George Corry last Saturday.

R. J. Wiliams, justice of the peace of the domain of Kanarra, was among the visitors from Kanarra Monday.

Iron County Record
August 29, 1913

A baby girl was born to Mrs. Nancy Lunt Monday night.

Mrs. Laura Clark of Parowan arrived in Cedar City yesterday morning for a visit with her son and wife, Mr. and Mrs. P. A. Clark.

Iron County Record
September 19, 1913

Wednesday last, in the temple at Salt Lake City, the ceremony was performed which made Mr. John A. Booth of Nephi and Miss Mattie Hunter of this city man and wife.

Mr. Booth is a young man who has been attending the Argicultural College at Logan, and who is highly esteemed in his home town. Miss Hunter is one of the most charming young ladies of this city, one who has always been prominently identified with social activities. Last year she taught in the public school, and has been active in church work, her diligence in ecclesiastical lines being due to a conscientious desire to do her duty. She is a daughter of Mrs. Eliza Hunter, and a member of one of the oldest and most estimable families of Iron county.

Before leaving Monday afternoon for Salt Lake, Miss Hunter stated to a representative of The Record that she and her husband would reside in Logan the coming winter, where he will continue his studies in the Agricultural College. Mrs. Booth expects to return to Cedar City to spend the summer of 1914.

The Record joins in wishing them a long and happy married life.

Mitchell—Mackleprang.

Last week in Parowan the wedding ceremony was performed which made Harry Mitchell of Los Angeles and Miss Minnie Mackleprang of Cedar City man and wife.

The groom is a candy maker in Los Angeles and has a high standing in his community.

The bride is the daughter of Mr. and Mrs. Peter Mackleprang of Cedar City and is very highly esteemed in her home town. The happy couple will spend their honeymoon at the home of the groom.

Iron County Record
September 26, 1913

Uncle Benjamin Knell and Frank Knell, his son, father and brother respectively of B. F. Knell of this city, were visitors in Cedar City the first part of the week.

A. W. Brouse, foreman of The Record office, returned from Salt Lake City Wednesday after an absence of a week, to which place he went to procure treatment for his eyes.

Last Wednesday in this city, Mr. John A. Batt and Miss Jennie Bauer were united in the bonds of matrmony. The young couple have long resided here and are well and favorably known to a majority of our citizens.

HOW IT WAS ORGAN. IZED IN THE YEAR 1869

C. J. Arthur has handed us a list of those who organized the Cedar City Co-operative Sheep Association on May 24, 1869. The number of sheep each subscriber put into the association and the cash allowance made will be of interest to the present generation. The price allowed was according to the condition of the sheep.

	Head	Value
James Whitaker	112	$540 00
Samuel Leigh	59	285 00
Geo. Wood	69	337 00
Sage Jones	51	248 00
Bengt Nelson	68	344 50
John Parry, Sr	30	147 00
Jos. H. Smith	36	165 00
Cedar Tithing office	34	144 50
Jas. Bulloch	96	467 00
J. P. Jones	54	271 00
John Urie	46	234 50
Geo. Perry	76	395 50
John McConnell	52	265 00
Thos. Gower	98	485 50
Wm. Middleton	74	359 00
Isaac C. Haight	50	245 00
Joseph Walker	118	537 00
Geo. Hunter	87	424 00
J. M. Higbee	60	297 50
Thos. Perkins	135	647 50
Jos. Hunter, Sr	89	431 00
Frank Webster	87	410 00
W. G. Sheppesson	52	230 00
John Chatterley	24	119 00
Wm. Unthank	22	104 00
Social Hall	4	20 00
R. R. Bukbeck	7	37 00
J. Christopherson	9	44 00
Margaret Lloyd	7	36 00
Mary Bladen	25	106 00
Wm. Leigh	11	55 00
David Williams	21	101 00
R. Heyborne	30	133 00
Wm. Tait	11	49 00
Rich. Alldridge	14	70 00
J. E. Adams	21	102 00
Peter Mackleprang	20	95 00
Alouis Bauer	32	145 00
Chas. Lord	11	56 00
Jens Anderson	1	5 00
Timothy Adams	1	5 00
Wm. Pearcell	8	37 00
Henry McConnell	8	35 00
Rees	16	73 00
C. J. Arthur	10	44 00
Jane Spiking	7	34 00
Henry Lunt	4	20 00
Samuel Connell	2	10 00
Sister Miller	2	10 00
Alice Bennett	3	15 00
Henry Leigh	4	18 00
Jno Parry Jr.	3	12 00
Joseph S. Hunter	10	43 00
S. Bauer	8	40 00
A. Sylvester	25	117 00
Joseph Armstrong	9	42 00
Andrew Jensen	7	34 00
William White	1	5 00
Thos. Thorley	1	5 00
Joseph Melling	2	10 00
Henry Elliker	7	32 00
Jas. Dutton	2	11 00
Chat. McConnell	35	90 00
Robert Smith	80	441 00
Sundries	15	79 00
	2183	$10439 50

Miss Janet Rollo is spending the week in Beaver visiting friends.

Mr. and Mrs. Thos. Bulloch are rejoicing over the arrival of a girl baby last week.

Miss Joice Millett entertained her young friends at a candy pull last Friday evening.

Wm. Houchen, Attorney Fife and Sheriff Froyd were in Parowan this week on business.

Randall L. Jones and A. D. McGuire went to Beaver Monday on business, returning home Wednesday.

H. H. Lunt, county game warden, also candidate for city councilman, etc., was among those who succeeded in bagging a deer the fore part of the week. There appears to be some question as to whether or not he had a hunting license, and the jealousy that his success has caused among more unfortunate hunters may prompt an investigation to be made.

A daughter was born to Mr. and Mrs. R. S. Gardner on Tuesday last. This is the first daughter and consequently there is great rejoicing in the Gardner household.

Tonight from 6 to 9 o'clock, Mr. and Mrs. Richard Palmer will celebrate their fiftieth wedding anniversary at the home of a son, Jethero Palmer, in this city.

Some 85 invitations have been sent out to old friends and associates of former years of the aged couple, and a large attendance is expected. Refreshments will be served and an appropriate program rendered.

Mr. Palmer was one of the pioneers in this part of the state, being delegated by President Brigham Young to come to Cedar City to perform work in the line of a blacksmith for the people of the southern part of the state, he being a blacksmith by trade.

He came to Iron county in 1851, since which time he has resided here continuously. Mr. and Mrs. Palmer have a number of children who have grown to maturity here and who are among the county's leading citizens, standing high in the public estimation. The Record joins in wishing these good people the

greatest of happiness on this
their wedding anniversary, and,
with their host of friends,
wishes for them many more
similar occasions.

Iron County Record
October 17, 1913

Last Sunday a baby daughter
was born to Mr. and Mrs. C.
G. Goddard.

David Urie is a visitor in Cedar
City, having recently arrived
from Australia. He is a nephew
of Uncle John Urie of Hamilton's
Fort. Mr. Urie is a sailor and
has traveled the high seas for
several years, finally deciding to
pay his relatives here a visit.
He will probably remain here
until spring.

Iron County Record
October 24, 1913

A baby son was born to Mr.
and Mrs. Arthur Nelson last
Friday.

Uncle John Urie of Hamilton's
Fort was in town Tuesday for
the purpose of settling his tax
account with deputy collector S.
J. Foster. He says he does not
understand what disposition the
county and state proposes to
make of the large tax collec-
tions, in view of the large increase over previous years.

There are a great many more
who are beginning to think that
our legislators are altogether too
liberal in the making of appro-
priations, and that it is about
time something should be done
to save the people from the tax
burden, especially the enormous
state tax.

Died, at her home in Cedar City, Sunday, October 26, at 11 o'clock p. m., Jane Withers Middleton, one of the pioneers of Utah and one of the earliest settlers in Cedar City, at the age of 73 years, 1 month and 4 days.

Deceased was born September 22, 1840, in the town of Ayr, Scotland, and came to America in 1852, crossing the plains to Salt Lake City with one of the first ox-team immigrant companies that came to Utah, walking the greater portion of the distance.

She arrived at Salt Lake City September 22, 1862, and shortly thereafter was married to John Middleton. Soon after their marriage, Mr. and Mrs. Middleton came to Cedar City, where they resided for a year, removing to Hamilton's Fort, where they resided until her husband's death which occurred in 1895. After the death of her husband, Mrs. Middleton rerurned to Cedar City, where she has since resided.

Deceased leaves six children, as follows: Dr. George W. Middleton of Salt Lake City, Mrs. Anna M. Cox of Moapa, Nevada, Mrs. W. H. Pace of Price, and Name Ann Brown Middleton of Cedar City. In addition, deceased leaves thirty living grand-children.

Before leaving her native land Mrs. Middleton was converted to and joined the Church of Jesus Christ of Latter Day Saints, and ever since has lived a faithful christian life and remained a devoted member of the church. She was a person who loved books, and until the closing hours of her life, took a great delight in reading. As a child she received much of her instruction from the Bible and Burns, and always had a deep desire for spiritual readings and the poems of the poet of her native land, practically every one of which she knew "by heart." An exalted sense of honesty and a desire to be independent were, perhaps, the strongest points in her character.

Funeral services were held in the tabernacle in this city Wednesday afternoon at 3 o'clock.

Millard Watson is seriously ill from an attack of pneumonia.

Wm. S. Musser made a business trip to Milford Thursday.

A baby boy was born to Mr. and Mrs. J. T. Kerr Sunday night.

Dr. George W. Middleton of Salt Lake City came down to attend the funeral of his mother.

Miss Agnes Brown, formerly connected with The Record, was a visitor in Cedar City from Tuesday until Thursday, having come down to attend the funeral of her grandmother, Mrs. Jane W. Middleton.

Iron County Record
November 7, 1913

Menzies Macfarlane, M. D., Decides to Locate in Cedar

Dr. Menzies Macfarlane, recently from St. Marks hospital of Salt Lake City, and a graduate of the Jefferson Medical College of Philadelphia, has taken up his abode in Cedar City, and will open offices here.

The doctor, familiarly known as Menzies, is by no means a stranger to Cedar City, having spent a number of years here before entering a medical college, as a student of the Branch Normal, and later as teacher in the same institution.

His wife was selected from among Cedar's winsome daughters, being Miss Kate Palmer, before marriage.

Menizes is a good, clean, energetic young man, and will no doubt make a success of his chosen profession.

Mrs. Anna Cox, who has been in Cedar City since the death of her mother, Mrs. Jane Middleton, leaves today for her home in Moapa, Nevada. She was preceded by her husband immediately after the funeral.

Yesterday afternoon the funeral services over the remains of the one-year old child of Mr. and Mrs. John R. Fretwell were held from the family residence. The little one died Wednesday at 5:00 a. m. The bereaved parents have the sympathy of the community.

Iron County Record
November 14, 1913

Pete Bulloch has sold out his sheep herd and retired from the wool-growing business. He turned over about 5,000 head to Mr. Keyser of Ogden the first of the week.

Iron County Record
November 21, 1913

Dr. A. N. Leonard reports the birth of a son to Mr. and Mrs. C. D. Barnum last Wednesday.

Dr. A. N. Leonard reports three births recently: Mr. and Mrs. F. W. Middleton, a girl Sunday; Mr. and Mrs. Henry Jones, a boy, and Mr. and Mrs. E. M. Corry a girl. All interested are doing well.

Iron County Record
November 28, 1913

This afternoon, commencing at 2:00 p. m., in the tabernacle, funeral services over the remains of Mrs. Eliza C. Pinnock Hunter were conducted, under the direction of Bishop S. J. Foster of the East Ward.

Sister Hunter passed away at an early hour Wednesday morning, after a comparatively short illness, and until only a day or two before her demise her condition was not regarded as serious. Kidney disorders, coupled with a weak heart and general debility, caused her death.

The speakers at the funeral were Elders Jos. H. Armtsrong, L. W. Jones, H. W. Lunt and W. H. Corry.

Vocal solos were rendered by Miss Annette Webster and Mr. E. M. Corry.

There were many beautiful floral tributes, and the tabernacle was appropriately decorated.

The grave was dedicated by Elder Jos. H. Armstrong.

Relatives in attendance from a distance included the deceased's daughters, Mrs. William Dotson and Mrs. John Booth, with their husbands of Provo; Mrs. Rose Poll and Mrs. Precilla Milner, sisters of the deceased, and Mr. Arthur Dunford, a brother-in-law, all of Salt Lake City.

BIOGRAPHICAL.

Miss. E. C. Pinnock was born Mar. 4, 1846, in Coventry, England. Emigrated in 1862, one year before her parents. Walked across the plains in A. P. Hammon's company. Taught school the winter of 1862-3 in Salt Lake county. Moved to Cedar City in the fall of 1863, where she met Joseph S. Hunter, and they were married January 1, 1865, by Bishop Henry Lunt. Ten children, seven of whom survive her, were born to them. Her husband preceded her to the other side by 9 years and 5 months.

Sister Hunter was always a prominent worker in the ward organizations, particularly the Relief Society, and was well kuown for her charity and benevolence.

Deseret News please copy.

Manager Woodbury of the Iron County Telephone company, accompanied by Ed. Houchen as line man, went out on the southern line Tuesday to make repairs before the severe winter weather sets in. It was their intention to go over the line as far as Harmony, and look into business conditions at that place and Kanarraville.

Born to Mrs. John M. Chatterley on Dec. 23rd a boy, which explains the reason for the smile that wont come off which John M. is wearing these days.

Born, to Mr. and Mrs. Robert Mumford Wednesday night, Dec. 17, a baby girl. Dr. Macfarlane officiating. All concerned doinng well.

Mrs. Claude Morris of Milford is spending the vacation with her mother Mrs. Macfarlane. While here Mrs. Morris is receiving the professional services of Dr. Leigh.

Mrs. Lottie Perkins, Mrs. Nancy Walker, Mrs. Nellie Haight, Mrs Mary Gower and Mr. James Chatterly attended the funeral of Mrs. James Knell last week at Pinto.

Janet, the fourteen year old daguhter of Albert Nelson, is gradually sinking and neither Dr. Green nor Dr. Macfarlane give any hopes of her recovery. She has been a sufferer from Bright's disease for some time and has made a brave fight, but is unable to withstand the ravages of the dread malady. The Record extends sympathy.

Dr. Green was in attendance at the following births: Mr. and Mrs. Henry Pollock, Kanarra, boy on Dec. 25; Mr. and Mrs. Thos. A. Lunt, girl, Dec. 26; Mr. and Mrs. William Elliker, girl, Jan. 1. All the ladies and babies are reported as doing well.

Miss Janet Nelson, who is suffering from acute bright's disease, resulting from scarlet fever, and who was reported by The Record last week as being in a very hopeless condition, appears to be slowly recovering and Dr. Macfarlane, the attending physician, has hopes for her recovery.

Last Tuesday Warren Bulloch and LaPrele Neilson, the former a son of Mr. David and Sarah A. Bulloch of this city, and the latter a daughter of Mr. and Mrs. Peter Neilson of Washington, made a trip to Parowan for the purpose of procuring a permit to wed, and no doubt the ceremony has been performed before this time, though the family declined to state where, when and by whom.

Wednesday the young people accompained by the bride's sister, Miss Carrie Neilson, who has been clerking in the Co-op store here for some time past, and Mr. D. G. Bulloch, a half brother to Warren, left for St. George and vicinity. As the elder Mr. Bulloch has been very attentive to Carrie for some months past, it is only fair to assume that a double wedding is anticipated, which will probably be solemnized in the St. George temple. New Years will of course be spent with the brides' family, after which all will return to Cedar City to make their homes.

The young people are all well respected in the community, and have the hearty congratulations of The Record.

Iron County Record
January 16, 1914

On Sunday, January 11th, at 2:30, p. m., Ann Gower Lunt passed away at the home of her daughter, Mrs. Jos. H. Hunter, after 22 years of ill health, in which she suffered frequent attacks, many of which were so severe that they were thought to be her last. But possessing an unusually strong constitution and will power, she had lived to see her seventieth birthday, and the fiftieth anniversary of her wedding day, the last twelve years a widow.

Deceased was born in a small town in the county of Worcester, England, Oct. 10, 1843, her parents, Thomas and Jane Gower, embraced the Gospel and left their native land for America when she was but six years old. When the family reached St. Louis, it was stricken with cholera, which claimed mother, brother and sister, leaving the subject of this sketch alone with her father. Three years later her father married again, and the girl was raised by her stepmother.

She shared the hardships incident to the crossing of the plains with ox teams, arriving in Salt Lake in 1854, where they remained for a time when they shared the call to settle Iron county, and located at Cedar City, or as known now as the Old Fort.

Being the oldest child, she was her father's chief dependence for help, and spent much of her time in the field, doing a man's work. She was also an employee of the primative woolen factory, on which the early settlers depended for their clothing.

On the 11th day of April, 1863, has entered the holy bonds of matrimony, becoming the wife of Bishop Henry Lunt. She was a faithful wife, and labored unceasingly with him to provide themselves with a comfortble home, but remained to enjoy it only a comparatively short time, leaving Cedar City in the fall of 1889 to join in the colonization of Mexico, and being compelled to commence her life work over again.

Finding the country in a wild state and isolated from civilization, food became scarce and the hardships of this second pioneering proved too much for her at this stage of life. Her health was broken down, yet she stood it all uncomplainingly, working and living to see the colonies develop until the country became dotted over with modern American homes, though surrounded with the semi-civilized Mexicans, who, however, partook to a certain extent of the thrift of their Mormon neighbors and advanced along the lines of civilization.

Yet these comforts, so hard earned, were not to last. The uprising and civil war that broke out in Mexico afforded an opportunity for the covetuous anti-American element surrounding them to demand their homes and property, and they were given summary orders to leave the country. Though an invalid of many years standing, and unable to ride in any kind of a vehicle, nerved by the excitement she made the journey of 25 miles to the nearest railroad station in a lumber wagon, and with the members of her family and other refugees boarded the train that carried them to El Paso, Texas.

A week later with her widowed daughter and her four little ones, Sister Lunt arrived in Cedar City. Though the builder of two homes she was now homeless, but found a warm welcome with her daughter, and her husband. Mr. and Mrs. Jos. H. Hunter.

She was a faithful and devoted member of the church of Latter-day Saints, and her last dying words to her children who surrounded her bedside were an exhortation to remain true to the faith.

She is survived by eight children, three sons and five daughters, all of whom are married. Six reside in Cedar City, one in San Diego, Cal., and one in Dublan, Mexico.

Funeral services were held in the tabernacle Monday, Jan. 12, the following speakers occupying the time: David Bulloch, Henry Leigh, George Naegle and Bishop Matheson.

The first two speakers referred to incidents in the past life of Sister Lunt in the early days of Cedar City, and bore eloquent testimony to the good character and characteristics of the deceased. Elder George Naegle having been closely connected with the family during its sojourn in Mexico, recalled many thrilling incidents with this period of their lives.

The singing was most beautiful and appropriate, and greatly appreciated by the family.

Iron County Record
January 23, 1914

New goods are arriving at the Cedar City Drug Store.

Mrs. Mary A. Dover has been ill the past week with la grippe and bronchitis. Dr. Green is attending her.

Mrs. Jane Lambeth is very ill of acute cystitis. Dr. Green has her case. The patient is improving at this writing.

The Cedar City Drug Store will open in a few days with the greatest assortment of Drugs and sundries ever carried in this city.

Dr. J. A. Smith, veterinary surgeon, is suffering from severe ulceration of the stomach, and has endured a number of severe hemorrhages recently.

Mrs. John Dutton is reported very ill by Dr. Green. General debility, coupled with an acute attack of bronchitis makes her condition most critical.

Jean Schoppman, who has been very bad off with another attack of his old trouble, is reported some better since taking Dr. Macfarlane's rest teatment.

The Cedar City Drug Store will open in a few days under the management of H. P. Pettigrew, and experienced phamaist, with 25 years experience in the drug business.

As we go to press we learn that the homes of Ed. Cox and Joseph Thompson of Hamilton's Fort have been quarantined for scarlet fever by Dr. Leonard who was down there today.

Another good storm last Sunday, which causes the dry farmers and stockmen to smile. On the whole this has been a most delightful winter, mild, yet with a good fair amount of precipitation.

Miss Lillian Walker, who was operated on recently for peritonitis, is much better. Her temperature has returned to normal, and the symptoms of peritonitis have entirely disappeared, reports Dr. Macfarlane.

Miss Hilma Halman has been confined to her home this week by a severe attack of tonsilitis. At last report she is improving and we hope soon to see her smiling face behind the counter of the Sheep Store again.

Iron County Record
January 30, 1914

Six-year-old Willie Palmer is reported quite sick with what may prove to be pneumonia.

Little Howard Wilkinson, our baby boy, has pneumonia. The little sufferer is doing as well as could be hoped for.

Dr. Macfarlane was called to Kanarraville last evening to attend the little 11 year old daughter of Mr. and Mrs. Wallace Williams who is suffering with pneumonia.

A case of scarlet fever is reported at the home of Mr. and Mrs. Harry Thorley, the patient being their little three-year-old boy. The patient is reported to be progressing favorably.

Miss Maxine Froyd, the 8 year old dauhgter of Mr. and Mrs. Alfred Froyd, has passed the crisis in an attack of pneumonia and is now recovering nicely. Dr. Macfarlane in attendance.

Iron County Record
February 6, 1914

Mr. and Mrs George Corry have a little boy seriously ill with pneumonia.

A boy baby arrived at the home of Mr. and Mrs. John T. Bulloch on the 2nd inst.

Among other cases of pneumonia has developed, this time at the home of Bp. Matheson, and there is a suspected case at the home of Thomas Dix. Both patients are children.

Health officer Dr. A. N. Leonard reports this morning that a case of scarlet fever has developed at the home of Chris Ashdown and is now under quarantine, and a case of chicken-pox at the home of John A. Adams, which has also been quarantined. The latter case is directly traceable to St. George, and it is stated that there are a number of cases there and that no quarantine is maintained.

R. W. Bulloch was called home this week on account of the serious illness of his oldest boy. He made the entire trip from Modena on horseback, arriving here Monday evening. At last reports the boy was convalescing nicely.

Jean Woodbury, who has undergone a seige of pneumonia, is now on the rapid road to recovery.

Little Kelvin Findlay, Dr. Leonard reports, is now convalescing rapidly from his attack of pneumonia.

Mrs. William Macfarlane presented the constable with a girl baby last Friday night, Dr. Macfarlane in attendance.

Mrs. J. R. Rickards is reported by Dr. Macfarlane suffering from broncho pneumonia, and while seriously ill, is some better at this writing.

Mrs. Andrew Corry is reported ill with the influenza that is so prevalent this winter. Dr. Macfarlane states that she is quite seriously afflicted.

Mary, the oldest daughter of Mr. and Mrs. William Dix, Jr., was taken down with pneumonia Wednesday and is now passing through the serious stages of the disease. Dr. Leonard is in charge of the case.

The youngest child of Mr. and Mrs. Randall L. Jones has pneumonia. Dr. Macfarlane is attending it and reports that it is doing as well as can be expected.

Another boy, the fifth one in this particular family, came to Mr. and Mrs. Reuben Walker yesterday, and is receiving a warm welcome, notwithstanding a girl would have been their preference. Dr. Leonard in attendance.

Dr. Leonard reports the arrival of a fine boy at the home of Mr. and Mrs. William Mendenhal, last Wednesday. Except for the fact that the mother is afflicted with a most distressing cough, everything is going nicely. It is presumed, of course, that the father is wearing the proverbial smile, but the doctor neglected to advise us specifically in relation to this very important phase of the case.

The little three-year-old girl of Mr. and Mrs. Thomas Dix has been desperately ill with pneumonia this week, but we are pleased to be able to report that she has apparently passed the crisis in her disease, and with a normal temperature this a. m. and an appetite for food appears to be on the rapid road to recovery. Dr. Leonard has had charge of the case.

Miss Bell Williams, who went to Kanarraville to nurse her mother and sister through sieges of pneumonia, was hurriedly called home on Wednesday to be at the sick-bed of her sister, Mrs. Percy Wilkinson, who was taken suddenly and dangerously ill.

Wedding Bells.

Mr. Clifton McConnell and Aleen Bladen had business at the county seat last Tuesday, which it now transpires, was the procuring of a license to enter the holy bonds of matrimony. The ceremony was performed in the Clerk's office in Parowan. The young people's parents are well known residents of Cedar City, the groom being the eldest son of Mr. and Mrs. W. J. McConnell, and the bride a daughter of Mr. and Mrs. Thomas Bladen.

We wish the happy couple a long and prosperous journey through life. May all their troubles be little ones.

Iron County Record
February 18, 1914

SUMMIT.

Summit, Utah, Feb. 18, 1914.

Summit has been visited by another snow storm.

Men and women here are much enthused over the Farmers' Round-Up and Housekeepers' Conference to be held in Cedar City, and nodoubt there will be a large number attend.

Mr. and Mrs. Frank Williamson of Paragonah are guests of Mrs. O. Farrow.

At the services last Sunday afternoon the time was occupied by Bro. Hyrum Jones, Bro. Stevens and his two sons of Enoch, who came in the interests of the Round-Up. Their talks were instructive and interesting, and will nodoubt have the desired effect.

Mr. Sam L. Fife and family are now comfortably located at the home of Heber Dalley.

Mrs. Jesse Gifford is here with her parents, Mr. and Mrs. Wm. H. Dalley.

Summit is taking quite a boom in the building line just now. Several homes are being improved and a number of hay sheds are being erected.

Mrs. Jos. B. Dalley is home again. She has spent some time at Cedar, where she could secure medical treatment. Her health is some better now.

Last Wednesday Wells Williams, a student of the B. A. C. developed severe cramps in the region of his stomach, and it was at first believed that had in some way been poisoned, perhaps from eating vitrolled wheat. His sickness grew so severe that Dr. Leonard was called in and found Mr. Willams to be suffering from an acute attack of appendicitis. The acute stage has now been passed and no operation will be performed at present.

Born, to Mr. and Mrs. Henry Froyd last Thursday, a boy. Dr. Leonard as "godfather," and everything going nicely.

Mrs. Hannah Ahlstrom is now gaining rapidly and will soon be around again after her attack of pneumonia.

Henry Houchen's little boy who has been so ill, has now taken a marked change for the better and is convalescing rapidly.

Irving Jacobson, whose serious illness was mentioned in the last issue of The Record, died this morning at 5.05 o'clock.

The young man was born in Pine Valley twenty years ago the first day of last May. He was the son of Mr. and Mrs. James Jacobson of Pine Valley, and this is the third winter he has spent in Cedar City doing high school work. He was an earnest, ambitious student, well respected and esteemed by all who knew him.

He was stricken about a week ago with apendicitis. The case was so acute that an operation was advised at once and as soon as arrangements could be made he was removed to the local hospital where the operation was performed but the conditions were so bad that very little hope was etertained from the first, though everything possible was done to prolong his life, Specialists were called from Salt Lake City, who gave the best advice in their power and said the attending physicians were doing all there was to be done.

A father and mother, three brothers and two sisters and a betrothed wife are left to mourn his loss. The remains will be taken to Pine Valley sometime today for interment.

A beautiful casket was constructed by the boys in the carpentry department of the school, and one of the instructors from the College will be present and speak at the funeral services.

John Dover's wife presented him with twins Sunday night, a boy and a girl. God Father Leonard is getting partial with his gifts. Divide them up a little Doctor.

Dr. Macfarlane reports a fine boy at the residence of Edwin Smith born Wednesday morning and a girl to Mr. and Mrs. Walter Harris. All the interested parties doing well.

A Narrow Escape.

Dr. Leonard was called to Kanarraville to officiate at a birth at the home of Lorenzo J. Williams. He reports the arrival of a fine boy. Returning home in the night and driving without lights, the doctor met with an accident just at this side of Hamilton's Fort. He was skimming along in his car at the rate of about 60 miles an hour by the light of the moon and found the cement culvert that spans a deep wash too narrow for the track he was making. He jumped the chasm all right, but when the car alighted on the opposite side there was not sufficient resilence in the tires to absorb all the shock, and Mr. Kopp, the garage man now has a good job which will last for some time.

Fortunately neither the doctor nor George Palm, who was accompanying him were injured.

Mr. and Mrs. John Dover have a new pair of twins at their home, which were ushered in by Dr. A. N. Leonard last Monday.

Ronald Dalley Weds.

Mr. and Mrs. Peter Hiskey desire to announce the marriage of their daughter Marjorie M. Hiskey of Mona to Mr. Ronald J. Dalley of Cedar City, Saturday, Feb. 28. They will make their home for a time at least in Teasdale, where Mr. Dalley is teaching school.—Juab County Times.

A ten-pound baby girl is reported by Dr. Green at the residence of Mr. and Mrs. William Stephens. All doing well.

Mr. and Mrs. Randall L. Jones' little son Carl is recovering nicely under the treatment of Dr. M. J. Macfarlane from his second attack of pneumonia the present season.

SUMMIT.

Summit, Utah, Mar, 18, 1914.

The weather is ideal for farming and the farmers are planting a larger acreage than for a number of years.

* * *

Pres. L. N. Marsden and Wilford Day, Walter and Morgan Richards, of Parowan, were present at the funeral services of Sister Mary Allen, and each had the privilege of speaking. Bro. Sylvester Jones of Enoch was also one of the speakers.

Nelson B. Dalley and family are home from Cedar City, where the boys have been attending school at the B. A. C. They are now busy on the farm.

* * *

Bro. John Beecroft will leave today for Holden and other cities in the northern part of the state.

* * *

Mr. and Mrs. Frank Jones have moved to Enoch where Mr. Jones will work for some time.

ANOTHER PIONEER ANSWERS SUMMONS.

Henry Elliker, a well known resident of Cedar City for a good many years, departed this life last Thursday morning at 1 o'clock. Pneumonia with which he was stricken last Monday, was the immediate cause of his death, though he has been practically bedfast for the last three years. Six months ago he was removed to the residence of his daughter Mrs. William Houchen, in order to receive the care that his infirm condition demanded. This is the last time that he was out of the house before his death.

Brother Elliker was born in Switzerland 85 years and six months ago and came to Cedar City in 1856 where he has resided the most of the time since. He was possessed of a wonderful physique during his prime, an illustration of which is shown by one incident of this part of his life. The deceased who was working at Beaver at the time, learned that his family then located at Toquerville were out of flour. He made the trip from Beaver to Toquerville on foot, and immediately started back to Cedar City carrying a bushel of wheat on his back. This he brought to the grist mill at this place, without any other means of locomotion that those supplied by nature, and returned to Toquerville with the flour in the same way.

The deceased, who had reached a ripe old age, leaves a wife and seven children as follows: William and John Elliker, Mary L. Houchen, Sarah T. Dover, Barbara Sherratt, Margaret Dover, and Minnie Baxter.

Funeral services will be held in the tabernacle, Sunday at 3 p. m.

Iron County Record
April 3, 1914

Cassie, the 10-year-old daughter of Mr. and Mrs. William Webster, Jr., fell off a plank while playing teeter last Tuesday and broke both bones of her fore arm. The injured member was given attention by Dr. Green, and the unfortunate chid is getting along nicely at this writing.

Little Onita Thorley, the six-year-old daughter of Mr. and Mrs. Robert A. Thorley, has lobar pneumonia, and while doing as well at this stage of the disease as could be reasonably expected, is at the same time a very sick child. Dr. Leonard is attending her.

Chauncy, the son of Caleb and Nellie Haight, was the victim of an accident which fractured his left leg, this week. His injury was caused by the fall of a horse upon which he was riding at the time. Dr. Macfarlane reports him progressing as well as can be expected at this time.

Iron County Record
April 10, 1914

Born: To Dr. and Mrs. R. Leigh, April 8, at the Southern Utah Hospital, a fine baby girl. Mother and child are doing well.

Onita, the little daughter of Dr. Robert Thorley, who has been suffering from an attack of Lobar pneumonia, is making a splendid recovery and Dr. Leonard reports that she will be around again within a few days.

Iron County Record
April 17, 1914

Dr. Leonard reports the birth of a boy to Mrs. Frank Kelsey of New Harmony, last Monday. All going well.

Dr. Macfarlane reports the arrival of a fine baby boy at the residence of Arthur Fife on Wednesday night. All concerned doing nicely.

Iron County Record
April 24, 1914

Mr. and Mrs. Dolph Andrus are receiving congratulations on the arrival of a fine eight-pound baby girl, born Tusday morning. Everything going smoothly, under the direction of Dr. Macfarlane.

Dr. Leonard was called to Hamilton's Fort last Monday to attend Mrs. James Clark, whom he delivered of a still-born babe. The mother though extremely ill, is progressing as well as can be expected.

Lamont Higbee the son of Mr. and Mrs. S. A. Higbee, underwent an operation for the removal of enlarged tonsils and adenoids, the operation was done at the Southern Utah Hospital by Dr. Leonard on April 17.

Iron County Record
May 1, 1914

Mr. and Mrs. Frank McConnell went to Parowan to attend the funeral of the infant child of John Evans. Mr. Evans is a brother of Mrs. McConnell.

Mr. and Mrs. George Nelson are receiving congratulations on the birth of a fine baby boy last Sunday. Dr. Leonard reports the interested parties all doing well.

The infant child of Mr. and Mrs. John Evans died with convulsions last Sunday, at Mr. Evan's ranch on the Cedar meadows. The little one was removed to Parowan for burial, where funeral services were held on Tuesday.

Mr. and Mrs. E. A. Cox are rejoicing over the arrival of a fine baby boy, born last Sunday at the residence of Mrs. Cox's mother, Mrs. Ann Thorley of this place. Dr. Macfarlane is in attendance and all going smoothly.

Iron County Record
May 8, 1914

B. F. Fnell, the popular proprietor of the Cedar City and Lund automobile line, has recently purchased a seven-passenger Caddelac car, and has traded his Stoddard Dayton machine for a new Overland, which will be a lighter car than any he is now using, and will be especially useful for side trips and service on the regular route when travel is light. The new Caddelac is now en route here from Salt Lake City.

SUMMIT.

Summit, Utah, May 6, 1914.

Mrs. Mary Green of Idaho is here for an extended visit with her parents, Mr. and Mrs. N. B. Dalley.

* * *

Our district school closed last Friday, after a most successful year, nearly all the children completed their grades.

* * *

Mrs. Etta Dalley is now hme again from Cedar City, where she has been for the past month.

* * *

Next Friday night the Summit appropriate to Mother's Day.

* * *

The last Sunday services were in charge of the bishopric and an excellent program was given. Next Sunday evening will be in charge of the Relief Society.

* * *

Nextt Friday night the Summit dramatic company will present the play entitled, "Comrades" in the amusement hall. It will be given for the benefit of the ward choir.

* * *

An athletic contest will be held here in the near future, between the married and the single men. A lively time is expected.

* * *

Pierce Cheney and family have moved to Will Lyman's farm, where they will be engaged this summer.

* * *

John H. Dalley will leave in a few days for a visit to Panguitch. Mr. Dalley goes as a missionary to France in June.

Iron County Record
May 15, 1914

Miss Annie McQuarrie from St. George is the guest of Mr. and Mrs. Randall L. Jones while visiting friends in Cedar City.

Use the classified advertising columns of The Record to effect the sale or exchange of your commodities. Our classified ads. bring results.

Dr. A. N. Leonard was called to Harmony Wednesday to officiate at the birth of a son that came to the home of Mr. and Mrs. William Chinn. Mother and babe are reported to be doing well.

An incipcient fire in the home of Miss Manie E. Perry was discovered just in time to save the house. Three or four coats hanging behind the front door in some way took fire and burned up.

Mr. James H. Clark was in from the sheep herd, having completed the shearing of his sheep and sale of his wool, a few days since. Mrs. Clark and children are also back from Panguitch, where they have been visiting for some time.

Mrs. Francis Middleton of Hamilton's Fort had the misfortune to dislocate one of her elbows last Friday. While stretching a clothes line, the rope broke causing her to fall with the above results. Dr. Macfarlane was summoned and placed the limb in a plaster of paris cast and it is apparently doing as well as could be hoped for at this time.

Iron County Record
May 22, 1914

Born to Mr. and Mrs. Lundell last evening a baby girl, reports Dr. Leonard. All is happiness and serenity.

Any persons desiring concessions from the city, such as licence for pool hall, city work, etc., would do well to apply to the Mayor at once. He is in the best of humor at present, due to the fact that a new "son" has risen at his domicile, which was ushered in last evening by Dr. A. N. Leonard. All doing nicely, and the Mayor has our congratulations.

Iron County Record
December 25, 1914

Last week we were so deeply engrossed with the work on our Christmas edition a number of local items escaped us, just as we were sure they would. One of these was the birth of a son and heir to Mr. and Mrs. Percy N. Wilkinson, born on the 18th inst., the child is thriving nicely under the professional care of Miss Belle Williams, a sister to Mrs. Wilkinson. Also a nice girl to the wife of Mr. Clifton McConnell. The young people have our hearty congratulations.

Mrs. Rowley, one of the Mexican refugees from Mexico, arrived in Cedar Wednesday to spend some time with her daughter and family, Mrs. Oscar Lunt.

JOSEPH S. SMITH ANSWERS CALL

Funeral Services Held Yesterday Afternoon in Tabernacle—Was a Familiar Figure Here.

Yesterday afternoon at 2 p. m. the funeral services over the remains of Joseph S. Smith, one of Cedar City's solid, stable citizens, were held in the local tabernacle.

Deceased departed this life on the 22nd inst. of diabetes. While his condition had not been robust no one had suspected that the end was so near. He was in attendance at the old folks' party on Thanksgiving day and was at that time apparently in his normal state of health.

For a number of years Mr. Smith has lived a widower, his worthy wife meeting death in a deplorable accident on the mountain road, when a defective brake caused the team Mr. Smith was driving to run away and capsize the wagon. There were three ladies on the load of lumber coming from their mountain dairies, all of whom were quite seriously injured, and Mrs. Smith killed.

A number of sons and daughters, all of whom are now practically mature, survive them.

A biographical sketch of the deceased's life will be published next issue.

Mrs. Emma Daugherty Smith of Milford is in town, having come to attend the funeral of her uncle, Jos. S. Smith, which was held yesterday afternoon,

Iron County Record
January 1, 1915

David Bulloch, one of the largest local growers of hogs, who has been in the habit of shipping the live animals to the Eastern or the Western markets, is this year having the animals that he has to sell slaughtered and cured at home by Messers. Reisig & Heine, who have opened a small packing house establishment at the I. C. Macfarlane farm in the North field. It is evident that Mr. Bulloch, after a careful investigation, has decided that there is more money in curing and marketing the hogs at home.

A wedding reception was held at the home of Mr. and Mrs. John M. Bladen last Tuesday evening in honor of Mr. Israel T. Neilson and Miss Margaret E. Cannon, who were united in the holy bonds of matrimony last week at Parowan. A large number of invited guests were present, and a most enjoyable evening is reported.

Mr. and Mrs. R. J. Williams of Kanarraville spent Christmas in Cedar with their daughter and family, Mrs. P. N. Wilkinson. Mr. Williams returned home Monday, his son Reese James coming up for him.

NADA.

Nada, Dec. 30, 1914.

How many New Year's resolutions have you made?

* * *

Best wishes for a happy New Year to the friends of "The Record" and all Iron county.

* * *

Three gentlemen from Deseret drove to Nada in quest of homesteads. They returned North Saturday.

* * *

The second invoice in history of Nada shows an encouraging increase of business. The stock is also somewhat larger.

* * *

Mr. Goddard and a friend from Los Angeles are spending the week looking over the country, but as yet have not made a selection.

* * *

Mr. I. L. Wade has returned to Kansas, after an extended visit with his children. John Wade was home from Enoch to spend the holidays.

Iron County Record
January 6, 1915

HAMILTON'S FORT.

New Year's Party.

Hamilton's Fort, Utah, Jan. 6, 1915.

A very pleasant surprise party was tendered Uncle John Urie, of Hamilton's Fort, last Sunday evening by the members of his family. A goodly number of his friends and neighbors, including a number of people from Cedar City, were invited and it was not until the guests began to arrive that the honored head of the family had any suspicions regarding the affair.

Mr. and Mrs. S. F. Leigh spent New Year's with the latter's parents at Hamilton's Fort.

* * *

Miss Lizzie Bulloch is spending a week or two in Hamilton's Fort the guest of Mrs. John Urie.

* * *

Mr. and Mrs. E. C. Cox spent New Year's Day and the week end with relatives and friends in Hamilton's Fort, returning last Monday.

* * *

Mr. and Mrs. J. H. Christensen returned Sunday from Circleville where they spent the holidays with relatives and friends.

Mrs. Thomas Wade, the unfortunate widow of the young man who was called hence last Tuesday, gave birth to a son Wednesday morning. The circumstance adds to the pitiable condition of the family, under the severe strain of circumstances in which they are placed, and moved Marshall Froyd to take up a collection for their assistance, by which means something over one hundred dollars was raised to assist them. The woman's parents, brothers and sisters are all very much moved by her afflictions and are doing everything in their power to assist in this hour of deepest gloom.

Yesterday afternoon at 2 p. m. the funeral services of Thomas Wade, a respected citizen of Cedar City, who passed away at 4 a. m. last Tuesday, the 5th, were held in the Cedar City tabernacle. Besides a large gathering of local friends and relatives of the deceased, two of his brothers and a sister were in attendance from Fillmore, Millard county, where deceased was born and reared.

According to the testimony of the attending physician, Dr. E. F. Green, deceased has been a sufferer for the past eight months from inflammatory rheumatism, and on December 15th was stricken with pneumonia, involving both lungs. Apparently he had passed the crisis of the disease, when other complications developed that resulted in his death.

Thomas Wade, who was the son of George and Margaret Wade, was born in Fillmore December 10, 1880, making him 34 years old at the time of his demise. His father is still living in Salt Lake City, his mother passed away two years ago. Three brothers and two sisters survive him.

Ten years ago last July he was married to Mary J. Leigh of this city, and five years ago they moved to Cedar City, where they have since resided. A number of small children, resulting from the union, are left without a bread-winner, as well as the dependent mother.

The speakers at the funeral were Bishop A. G. Matheson, Henry Leigh and William R. Palmer.

The grave was dedicated by Elder Jos. S. Fife.

During his sojourn among us the deceased was known for his industry, honesty and integrity, and had the respect of all who knew him.

A nice baby girl was added to the family group of Mr. and Mrs. William Grimshaw last Monday night. Everything going "nicely."

A girl was born to Mr. and Mrs. Whitney McDonald Wednesday night. The mother, who is staying temporarily with her parents in this place, is doing nicely.

The little baby of Mr. and Mrs. E. P. Jensen sustained quite a severe burn last week from setting down in a basin of hot water. It is getting along nicely at this time.

Dr. Leonard and Mrs. Pryor made a flying trip to Hamilton's Fort Wednesday night. As a result Alex and Ruth are the happy recipients of a dandy baby girl.

Wednesday of this week Jas. H. Clark was operated on by Dr. Leonard at the Southern Utah hospital. Henry is doing nicely and will be removed to his home soon.

Last Monday, while driving cattle, R. L. Fife met with a painful accident. His horse slipped on the frozen ground and fell, catching the rider's ankle beneath it. Dr. Leonard was summoned and reports a badly lascerated joint, but no bones broken. It will be some time before Lou can leave the house.

Tuuesday, January 26, Mr. and Mrs. Leonard Green were the happy recipients of a fine, big baby boy. Dr. Leonard reports mother and child as getting along fine.

KANARRAVILLE.

Kanarraville, Utah, Feb. 3, 1915. Wallace Williams has leased the Co-op. Store, not R. G. Williams, as was reported a few weeks ago.

* * *

Raymond Wiliams has been laid up with rheumatism for the past week or two, but is improving the last few days.

* * *

All the auxiliary organizations of this ward are in good working order, with an average increase of attendance of about 25 per cent.

* * *

John Adams of Cedar City camped here last night with a bunch of about 400 head of cattle. Albert Davis and D. Parker are in his employ.

* * *

Joseph Williams is suffering with rheumatism. It seems to be confined to his muscles and tendons, and does not affect his bones and joints.

* * *

Mayhew H. Dalley was called to Parowan the fore part of this week to perform some work upon the tax records of the county, prior to the compilation of the assessment rolls for the present season.

It is reported that there are a number of new cases of measles in town. Parents cannot be too careful about reporting any suspicious cases of sickness to the quarantine physician.

The people of Cedar City were greatly shocked and grieved Wednesday evening to learn of the sudden and unexpected demise of Miss Norine Bulloch, daughter of David and Sarah A. Higbee Bulloch of this city. Many were not even aware that the young lady was ill until the news of her death was circulated. She was one of the helpers in the nursery at the opening of the Round-up, and was taken ill immediately after, on February 4th, complaining of pains in her limbs, and a little later developing a fever that proved to be measles. Dr. Macfarlane was called and did all that he could for the patient, but she seemed imbued with the knowledge from the first that her call had come, and sank steadily day by day. For some months past at intervals she has been a sufferer from rheumatism, which had affected her heart, and it was thought to be due to the impaired condition of this organ that she was unable to rally from her bed of illness.

The young lady turned eighteen years on the 15th of last January. She was a prepossessing young person, pleasant, lady-like and refined. She was the idol of her parents, and had a wide circle of friends. A student of the Branch Agricultural College, pursuing the third year course, she is mourned by all the members of her class, as well as by the student body generally. Her death occurred Wednesday at 5 p. m.

The funeral services will be held in the Tabernacle next Sunday at 2:30, p. m.

The parents of the deceased are heart-broken over their sad bereavement. The mother is almost prostrated, and the father is all broken up and crushed. The Record joins with an entire community in offering condolence.

Iron County Record
February 26, 1915

ANOTHER OLD SETTLER CALLED TO OTHER SIDE

Mrs. Mary Sando Elliker Answers the Final Summons Today a Little Before 12.

- At 11:50 o'clock this morning, Mary Sando Elliker, wife of the late Henry Elliker, and one of the old settlers of Cedar City, passed away of old age and general debility. Sister Elliker's health had been steadily declining for a year or more, and particularly during the past eleven months since the death of her husband, but she has only been confined to her couch for two or three weeks.

The deceased was born in Paris, France, 74 years, 7 months and 1 day since, and came to Cedar City something more than fifty years ago. It is nearly fifty years since her marriage to Henry Elliker in this city, where they continued to reside until the time of their death.

A number of sons and daughters blessed their union, five daughters and two sons surviving them.

They went though all the hardships and privations incident to the settlement of a new country, being industrious, frugal and God-fearing people.

$1,000,000 California Money for Cedar Coal

That the California capitalists who are financing the development of the Dr C F. Green coal properties southeast of Cedar City, mean business is shown by the fact that articles of incorporation of a million dollar company, to be known as the Coal Creek Coal and Coke Company, will be filed with the county clerk of this county, at Parowan tomorrow, and immediately forwarded with the filing fees to the secretary of state at Salt Lake City. The capital stock of the corporation will be $1,000,000, which will be divided into 10,000 shares of the par value of $100 each. The company is being incorporated under the laws of the State of Utah, and the provisional board of directors will include the following: Jacob and Heber Weaver, of Los Angeles, Russell Berry of Portland, Oregon, James Toy and Heber Fife of Los Angeles, and Dr. C. F. Green of Cedar City, Utah, and the chief engineer is Charles C. Jones of Los Angeles

Heber Weaver and Herbert Fife of the provisional board are here assisting in the launching of the new company. The officers have not yet been named from the board of directors

Dr Green, who just returned from California yesterday, is authority for the statement that negotiations are pending with the American Steel and Wire company for the aerial tram with which the property will be equipped, and that active work on its construction will commence as early in the spring as practicable

A considerable portion of the stock is already subscribed and paid in, and the company will have a desirable harber frontage at San Pedro an extensive business site near the center of Los Angeles.

It is proposed at an early stage of the proceeding to erect extensive coke ovens near Cedar City and commence the manufacture of the bi-products of coal tar, including die stuffs, perfumes, extracts and the coal tar medicinal substances, such as acetanilid, antipyrine and others

Negotiations have already been entered into with the San Pedro Route for a branch line to the bins of the company to give an outlet to the coast for their product, and they have been assured of such a branch as soon as the company has the necessary tonnage ready for shipment They are guaranteed a daily market of 500 tons in Los Angeles as soon as they are ready to furnish it

This is an important announcement for Cedar City, and if the program is carried out as now planned it will mean the employment of an army of men and the distribution of a large monthly payroll that will have a most beneficial effect upon local financial conditions.

Dr Green states that it is the intention of the new company, as set forth in their articles of incorporation, to enter other fields of mining and manufacturing, and he predicts a great future for it He is also very hopeful for trade conditions in this country during the next five years, which he believes will be the most prosperous period this country has ever known

The writer was shown the certified checks from a California bank which will accompany the incorporation papers as filing fees, to cover the internal revenue expenses of the incorporation, etc. And the doctor stated that approximately $200,000 in cash and collaterals had already been advanced on the project —Iron County Record.

Iron County Record
March 5, 1915

Word comes from St. George by telephone of the birth there last Monday to Mr. and Mrs. W. W. McAllister of a fine girl. Mrs. McAllister was formerly Miss Katie Dalley of this place.

Iron County Record
March 9, 1915

NADA.

Nada, Utah, Mar. 9, 1915.
Miss Viola Matheson, whose brother and sister have recently become settlers here, arrived last Saturday evening and Monday went to Milford to file on land north of Lindeman's.

* * *

Mr. McQuire and son, an uncle and cousin of A. P. Murphy, spent a few days here, which ended in Mr. McQuire, Jr., going to Milford Monday evening and filing on section No. 17.

O. W. Holmes and Mr. Haus from San Joaquin valley spent Tuesday in looking for locations. They both said that after a week's stop the land here suited them better than any they had seen.

* * *

Dr. Hobbs of Los Angeles has filed on the south half of section 27. He has made several trips here and is very well pleased. A dentist from the same place is inquiring about land here. Prospects are that this section will continue to be settled by an intelligent class of people.

Iron County Record
April 2, 1915

Ashdown & Goddard intend leaving for the Eddards ranch above Quitchapa, the last of this week with their wood sawing plant, where they will make a stand and saw up a large quantity of wood, that is to be supplied by David Eddards and his sons. From there the wood will be hauled to town on the orders of their numerous customers. Persons wishing sawed wood should leave their orders.

NADA.

Nada, Utah, April 7, 1915.

Miss Viola Matteson now has a good well on her homestead. Water was struck at a depth of 21 feet. The house is nearly completed and she will move in this week.

Rev. Claton S. Rice of Cedar City conducted services here Tuesday evening. His sermon on "The Resurrection" was very helpful, indeed, and especially appreciated, being the first ever preached in Nada.

Sunday night a delightful shower was given in honor of Irwin Riddle and Miss Abbie Smith, who went to Parowan Saturday. The affair was in the nature of a surprise, and was managed by Clarence Riddle, a brother of the groom (?). The young people have the congratulations of The Record.

Uncle John Urie was up from Hamilton's Fort last Tuesday, and took occasion to renew his subscription to Southern Utah's biggest and best newspaper. Uncle John is carrying his age well, and little change has been noticable in him for the past eight or ten years. He is always jovial and entertaining.

Milo Corry, son of Sheriff and Mrs. John H. Corry, fell from a shed Sunday and fractured his arm just above the wrist. The limb as set by Dr. A. N. Leonard and the little patient is doing nicely.

Presbyterian Mission Services.

Next Sunday's services will be held as follows:

Preaching service at Cedar City at 8 p. m. The subject of the sermon will be, "Why I Believe in the Existence of God."

Sunday School and preaching service at Parowan beginning at 10:30 a. m. The subject of the sermon will be "Christian Liberty."

We invite you to attend.

CLATON S. RICE, Minister.

SUMMIT.

Summit, Utah, April 21, 1915.

Mr. Gregory of Las Vegas is here again at work on his farm.

* * *

Mr. Ed. Dalley is improving nicely under the care of Dr. E. Green.

* * *

Mr. and Mrs. John H. Dalley have gone to Panguitch for a few days' visit.

* * *

Angus Riggs is home again. He has been working for some time at Panguitch.

* * *

* * *

A very successful school year closed here last Friday.

* * *

Miss Bigley, the teacher of our Primary school, has returned to her home in Nephi.

* * *

Mrs. William Corry of Cedar City was the guest of Mrs. Fannie Farrow for a few days last week.

* * *

Mrs. John Farrow is running a boarding house at Rush Lake for the men who are shearing sheep there.

Iron County Record
April 30, 1915

KANARRAVILLE.

Kanarraville, Utah, April 28, 1915.

Last Monday evening a girl was born to Mr. and Mrs. Charles Parker, Jr. Mother and child doing fine.

* * *

The following is a list of the eighth grade graduates for the year 1915:

CEDAR CITY.

Alice Leigh, Richard Williams, Robert Simkins, Preston Wood, George Kleinman, Tena Sherratt, Carlos Fife, Idona Stewart, Van Dyke Jones, Ralph Perry, Karl Wood, Eula Lunt, Rilla Dalley, Roundtree Hunter, Lamont Higbee, Naomi Perry, Mary Hunter, Emeron Jones, Kumen Gardner, Loreen Haight, Ralph Adams, John Middleton, Vera Pratt, Verna Pratt, Rhoda Palmer, Ila Clark, Ellen Lunt, Gwen Walker.

The following seventh grade student passed the examination:

Mona Urie, Martha Urie, Avey Ryan.

PAROWAN.

Camilla Lowder, Elwood Jenson, Belle Skougard, Lannie Mitchell, Alfred Morris, Lucius Benson, Alice Taylor, Della Orton, Lucile Evans, Clifton Taylor, Arnold Orton, Thelma Rowley, La Verd Adams, Verna Orton, Marie McGregor, Caddie Orton, Orien Lyman, Frank Matheson, Mariam Burton, Bess Matheson, Ona Decker, John Wood, Walter Stevens, Natina Ward, Violet Rasmussen, Frank Matheson.

SUMMIT.

Jesse Dalley, Leo Farnsworth, Ermine Dalley, Virgie White, Letha Dalley, Florence Farrow.

KANARRA.

Fern Williams, Edith Pollock, Rulon Platt.

PARAGONAH.

Orson Talbot, Lowe Barton, Thelma McBride, Nolen Openshaw, Zola Robb, Ariana Barton, Elva Barton, Alva Barton.

HAMILTON'S FORT.

Katie Brown, Alfred Hamilton.

ENOCH.

Thornton Jones, Elroy S. Jones and Grace Jones.

Iron County Record
May 7, 1915

AUNT CHARLOTTE WALKER CALLED.

Answers Final Summons of the Grim
Reaper at 11 P. M. Last Monday—Funeral Yesterday.

At 11 o'clock last Monday night, Mrs. Charlotte Walker, or "Aunt Charlotte," as she was commonly called, answered the summons of the grim reaper and passed to a well-earned reward. She had been bed-fast for several weeks with a complication of diseases, including general debility, and while suffering severely, was seldom if ever heard to complain. Her sick-bed was attended by a brother and a sister, several of her children, besides other relatives and dear friends.

The funeral services were held in the tabernacle yesterday afternoon, and interment was made in the local cemetery. The speakers were Elders Jos. H. Armstrong, John Parry, William C. Mitchell, and William H. Corry. All bore testimony to the good character and amability of the deceased, and paid glowing tributes to her administrations among the sick and distressed.

Biographical Sketch.

Charlotte Chatterley was born on the 23rd of June, 1842, in Manchester, England, and when eight years old left her native land in company with her parents in the good ship North Atlantic for the United States. They landed in New Orleans October 31, and at St. Louis, Mo., November 8th following. Here the family remained until April, 1851, when they started for the valleys of the mountains, going by steamboat up the Churchill, and thence by ox team to Cedar City, where the subject of our sketch has since resided. They arrived here November 11th, 1851.

Ten years later Miss Charlotte was married to Thomas Walker, January 23rd, 1861, eleven children coming to bless their union, nine of whom are still living. Two sons preceded her to the other shore. The living children are: Thomas C., John H., Joseph, Morton C., Archibald, Carl C., Mrs. Edith Gregory, Mrs. Josephine Isbell and Miss Charlotte.

Iron County Record
May 14, 1915

Dr. Leonard reports the arrival of a fine girl at the home of Mr. and Mrs. Edwin R. Cox of Hamilton's Fort Monday night.

Iron County Record
May 21, 1915

Born.—Monday, May 17, to Mr. and Mrs. Arthur Bryant, a fine boy; and on the same day, to Mr. and Mrs. Samuel Fife, also a son. All parties concerned doing nicely.

Iron County Record
May 28, 1915

Mrs. Maggie Averatt of Washington came up for the funeral of her grandchild, the baby recently lost by Mr. and Mrs. Ray Cosslett, and remained a few days with relatives and friends.

Iron County Record
June 4, 1915

Dr. A. N. Leonard reports the birth of a girl baby to Mr. and Mrs. Will Wood Tuesday evening. This is their first born, and The Record extends congratulations.

KANARRAVILLE.

Kanarraville, Utah, June 2, 1915.

Tuesday, June 1, was a red letter day for Kanarraville, this being the date upon which the new through mail service went into effect. Quite a crowd of people collected at the post office to welcome the arrival of the first auto-truck. The band was out and furnished inspiring music. R. J. Williams, Jr., delivered a speech, expressing the appreciation of the people of the improved service, and welcoming the new contractors. Speeches were also made by two of the contractors, who thanked all present for the honor shown them by those present. The band was taken on the truck for a spin a mile north of town, where they were met by the south-bound car and returned home. The ride was a pleasing feature of the celebration.

Last Monday Dan Parker and Miss Effie Mulliner left for St. George to be married in the Temple. The groom is the second son of Charles Parker, Sr., while the bride is a daughter of Robert and Maggie Davis Mulliner, but who has been raised by Mr. and Mrs. Reese J. Williams from early childhood. They are both well respected young people of this place. A reception will be given in their honor at the home of Charles Parker Friday at 1 o'clock, and a dance in the evening. Mr. and Mrs. R. J. Williams accompanied the young couple to St. George, to be present at the marriage ceremony.

SUMMIT.

Summit, Utah, June 9, 1915.
Some of the farmers are commencing to cut their alfalfa, as it is getting quite rusty, as an effect of the excessive storms and cool weather.

* * *

Mr. P. D. Cheney has been very poorly, and found it necessary to go to Cedar City for medical treatment. He is a patient of Dr. Leonard.

* * *

Mrs. George Smith of Delta spent a few days here last week with her parents, Mr. and Mrs. Moroni Dalley.

* * *

Ed. Dalley is able to return to Pioche and resume his employment at that place in the mines.

* * *

Mr. and Mrs. William Hales of Junction, and Mrs. Fred Jones of Enterprise, are here for a short visit with relatives and friends

Mr. LeRoy Heap came down from Spry, Utah, bringing his wife, who will visit her mother, Mrs. Lottie Perkins, for a while.

W. W. Hall and family of Enterprise passed through Cedar City last Monday en route to Escalante, on a visit to relatives and friends.

Several of the citizens of Summit were here on Wednesday attending the celebration given in honor of the old folks. Aunt Lettie Dalley was one of the number, and she was admired by all present as she waltzed so gracefully around with the dancers.

Joseph R. Bentley is suffering from blood poisoning in his hand, caused from cutting the back of his hand on the rusty guard of a mowing machine knife. While trying to remove a burr the wrench slipped and the guard was driven into the back of his right hand.

Mrs. Stowalter of Panguitch is in Parowan spending a few weeks, visiting with her sisters, Mrs. Smith and Mrs. Evans.

* * *

M. H. Dalley and John Fife of Cedar City were in town Wednesday, meeting with the Board of Equalization.

Births for the month of June: A girl at the home of F. C. VanBuren, Philip Benson and John A. Evans; boys at the homes of Clark Orton and J. B. Dalton.

NADA.

Nada, Utah, June 16, 1915.
Howard Dinwiddie is making an extended visit with his ather and sisters.

Mrs. Stimson arrived here Wednesday to join her husband, who has the home in readiness.

Iron County Record
June 25, 1915

Miss Fern Williams and Thomas W. Adams of Kanarraville obtained a license from the county clerk on Friday, June 18th, and were married in the clerk's office. Pres. L. N. Marsden officiated. (Note.—The groom is a son of John H. Adams, who moved from Cedar City to Canada several years ago.—Ed. Record.)

Iron County Record
July 9, 1915

A baby girl at the home of Albert Mickleson July 4th was reported by Dr. Burton.

* * *

A nice boy was born to Mr. and Mrs. Grant Lowe last Saturday, reports Dr. James Green.

* * *

Births for the week: Mr. and Mrs. Frank Rutledge, boy; Mr. and Mrs. James S. Green, girl; Jennie Williamson, boy; Dr. Green in attendance.

Iron County Record
July 16, 1915

Dr. Green reports the arrival of a boy baby at the home of Robert Halterman.

George Durham had a relapse or recurrence of his attack of erysipelas the fore part of this week, and is still far from well.

Iron County Record
July 23, 1915

Dr. Burton reports the arrival of a girl at the home of Mr. and Mrs. George Harwood. All concerned doing nicely.

Iron County Record
July 30, 1915

Dr. Burton reports a visit of the stork to the homes of Mrs. Vinnie Redd and Vivian Decker. A girl at the home of the former, born July 23, a boy at Mr. Decker's, July 27th.

* * *

The little child of Tom Edwards of Paragonah was brought to Dr. Burton for medical attention a few days ago, having sustained a severe injury to one of its arms.

REAPER CALLS VALVABLE CITIZEN

Joseph M. Perry Passes Away Very Suddenly at the Age of 68, After Active Life.

JOSEPH M. PERRY.

At about 9 a. m. last Tuesday, Jos. M. Perry, on old and highly respected citizen of this place passed away very suddenly at the age of 68 years. He had been ailing for a few weeks but was not considered seriously ill by his family. He went about his work as usual, and no one suspected that he was in a serious condition. At the time of his death he was seated in a chair on the lawn and had just been talking and joking in his usual jolly manner, when he rose from the chair and fell forward upon his face in an unconscious condition, from which he never recovered, and was dead a few minutes later before a doctor could be summoned.

The funeral services were held in the tabernacle Wednesday afternoon, and were largely attended by relatives, friends and acquaintances. The tabernacle was nicely decorated for the occasion, and there were many floral offerings on the coffin. The speakers paid high tributes to the good character and worth of the deceased, and a long line of vehicles followed the remains to their last resting place.

BIOGRAPHICAL.

Joseph Moroni Perry, son of George and Susannah Ward Perry, was born in Wigan, Lancashire, England, on the 26th day of May, 1848. He emigrated with his parents and arrived in Salt Lake City in 1851, and in Cedar City in November, 1853.

As he grew in years he proved a great help to his parents, both in the field and home. He was a lover of children, nursing them with love and kindness, and taking much labor off his mother's hands. Grown to manhood, his childhood experience, hard work and poor living enabled him to accomplish the more ardous toil confronting him. His father was an industrious worker and kept Joseph busy, giving him a lasting experience which proved of much worth in his subseqent years of toil.

Joseph was a self-made man and proved an expert in many undertakings that fell to his lot. He took up the carpentry trade; a fair designer, fast worker, and his charges low. An honest, upright man of strong will power, original in his ideas and staid in his conclusions. He has done the carpenter work for many of the early homes built in Cedar City.

He was a prosperous farmer; vice-president of the Cedar Sheep Association; affable in counsel; a good citizen, a kind father and always surrounded by his children, who have grown to be industrious sons and daughters.

He was sealed to Elizabeth Jones, daughter of John Pidding Jones and Margaret Lee Jones, on the 2nd day of December, 1872, in the Endowment house at Salt Lake City, who preceded him to the grave, she having died 18 years ago. By this marriage six sons and four daughters were born; one son died in childhood. Five sons, four daughters survive him, who with a number of grandchildren, four brothers and four sisters, all living at Cedar City, deeply mourn his loss.

SUMMIT.

Mrs. Sargent of Panguitch is here with her daughter, Mrs. John H. Dalley.

* * *

The second crop of alfalfa is now ready to cut and grain is getting ripe very fast, so the farmers will be busy for a while again.

* * *

Bishop Charles Dalley, his brother Philip and Herbert White, with their families spent a few days on the mountain recently.

* * *

Mrs. Browning leaves tomorrow for Las Vegas, where she will spend the coming winter, returning in the spring to locate on their farm.

* * *

The Misses Cora and Theressa Hulet, Imogene Dalley and Luella Smith spent the 24th at Joseph Perry's ranch on the mountain, and were there when the news of his death at Cedar City reached them.

Iron County Record
August 13, 1915

Robert Mason was presented last Saturday with a bouncing boy by his wife.

Mr. and Mrs. Parley Dalley and Mr. and Mrs. R. L. Wrigley spent Sunday in the canyon. They report having had a splendid time and thoroughly enjoyed the beautiful scenery that abounds in Coal Creek canyon.

Iron County Record
August 18, 1915

NADA.

Nada, Utah, Aug. 18, 1915. John Wade went to Parowan last Thursday.

* * *

Mrs. L. H. Carpenter drove over from Parowan Tuesday.

A. B. Dinwiddie visited Beaver and Milford a few days last week.

* * *

W. A. Kirkman struck water at a depth of 24½ feet, and the water is fine.

Piano Tuning.

Mr. L. K. Stewart, a professional piano tuner who has been visiting Cedar City annually for the past few years, is again with us. Mr. Stewart guarantees strictly first class work and entire satisfaction. He has the highest possible recommendations from our greatest musicians and music houses. Leave orders for tuning at the Cedars Hotel.   Adv-1w.

Summit, Utah, Aug. 24, 1915.

The grain is nearly all in the stack and threshing will begin next Monday morning.

*   *   *

Next Friday Aunt Letty Dalley leaves for Twin Falls, Idaho, where she will spend the winter with her daughter, Mrs. E. Pratt.

*   *   *

Sam Fife has moved his family down to his farm about three miles north of town. He has a neat little bungalow and barn erected, and with his good well he has things very comfortable and convenient there.

*   *   *

Last Sunday we had a treat at the Sunday School and Sacrament services. Elders Mortensen and Bentley of Parowan and Brothers Jones and Matheson of Enoch were present and occupied the time and gave excellent instructions.

KANARRAVILLE.

Kanarra, Utah, Aug. 25, 1915.

George Davis moved his family down from the mountain ranch today.

*   *   *

Mrs. Dan Webster gave birth to a still-born baby girl today. Dr. Leonard was in attendance. Mrs. Webster is getting along fairly well.

*   *   *

Our silver band went to Hurricane today to be there for Peach Day. Quite a number of other people also went down.

*   *   *

George Berry and family are here again. Mr. Berry is looking after the interests that he still has in this county. Incidentally they are visiting with relatives and friends.

M. H. Dalley of Cedar City is surveying on the mountain for James Berry and Arnold Graf, who are trying to find a forty acres that does not belong to the coal company, which owns pretty much all the coal land on the Kanarra mountain.

Will Reeves and Ren Williams have been successful in opening up a new coal mine, which is close to the old one. Although only in 20 feet, the tunnel has revealed some very good hard coal. There will be a little improvement over the old mine: the coal will be dumped onto a screen and into the wagons, the water taking care of the screened coal.

Cedar City

Pete Bulloch is around on crutches as a result of an acicdent that befel him last week, while working in the hay. Something went wrong with the derrick fork with which he was unloading, and in attempting to go up on the fork to right the difficulty, he was in some way turned loose and fell with the fork, a tine of which was driven through his leg.

Iron County Record
September 3, 1915

Miss Nettie Mackelprang of Cedar City is here receiving treatment from Dr. Green for some constitutional ailment, and will shortly obtain her release.

* * *

Mrs. Lola Ollerton Turley, who has been visiting in Parowan for about three weeks, has returned to her home in the Salt River Valley, Arizona. She left Parowan last Monday.

The following list of births for the week are reported by Dr. Jas. Green: To Mrs. Cora Mickelson, a boy on the 22nd. To Mrs. Joseph Stevens, a girl on the 28th. To Mrs. Clara Robb, a boy on the 23rd. To Mrs. Albert Mortensen, a boy, which, however, lived only two hours.

Cedar City is to have another meat market again. This time it will be located in the old Houchen office, and will be conducted by Dan Perkins and Claud Urie.

PETIT JURORS FOR SEPTEMBER TERM

Names of Persons Drawn to Decide Cases at Approaching Term of District Court.

Parowan, Utah, Sept. 1, 1915.
Pursuant to an order by the Hon. Joshua Greenwood, Judge of the District court of the Fifth Judicial District, for twenty-five petit jurors for the September term of the said district court, and in accordance with the law in such cases, the County Clerk, County Treasurer and County Attorney met on August 31, 1915, and the names of persons to serve as such jurors were drawn as follows:

Henry Taylor, Parowan, Utah.
N. E. Jensen, Parowan, Utah.
Peter H. Gurr, Parowan, Utah.
Joseph Bentley, Parowan, Utah.
M. M. Decker, Parowan, Utah.
John Platt, Kanarraville, Utah.
Richard A. Thorley, Cedar City.
Chas. N. Corry, Cedar City.
Benjamin R. Lawrence, Summit.
Randall Lunt, Cedar City.
Caleb Haight, Cedar City.
Roy Urie, Cedar City.
John J. Hyatt, Parowan.
Daniel T. Leigh, Cedar City.
Wm. H. Orton, Parowan.
John H. Walker, Cedar City.
Alfred W. Lund, Paragonah.
William Tucker, Cedar City.
John R. Robinson, Jr., Paragonah.
R. G. Page, Parowan, Utah.
Lewis J. Balser, Kanarraville.
Robert Munford, Cedar City.
Ezra G. Thornton, Parowan.
George Esplin, Cedar City.
Samuel Ford, Kanarraville.
Duly certified to by the county officials named above.

Iron County Record
September 10, 1915

Miss Janie Wilkinson will leave today for Nephi, where she has been employed as a teacher in the public schools of that place.

The little child that was scalded to death at Summit yesterday was a niece of Parley Dalley of this place. He will go to Summit for the funeral.

Iron County Record
September 17, 1915

Mr. and Mrs. Will Murie have opened their bakery and restaurant for the winter season again, and are prepared to supply everything in the bakery and short order lunch line. Their advertisement will be found in another part of this issue of The Record.

NADA.

Nada, Utah, Sept. 21, 1915.—Mrs. Cliff McGinty and two children arrived from San Bernardino Monday evening, to join the lady's husband who shipped a car here a few weeks ago.

* * *

Mrs. B. Clein went to Cedar City on business Tuesday.

REAPER CALLS I. C. MACFARLANE

Death Comes as Happy Release from Long and Painful Siege of Severe Suffering.

At 7:30 o'clock last Sunday morning death released Isaac Chauncey Macfarlane from a long siege of suffering covering several years. He was a victim of some form of a malignant growth on his jaw, which was something of a puzzle to the doctors and surgeons who treated his case. Three different operations were performed for the removal of the growth, but it each time returned shortly after the wound of the operation had healed. He suffered intensely at times but was patient and for a long while remained cheerful.

The funeral was held in the tabernacle last Tuesday afternoon, and was attended by a large audience of the friends and acquaintances of the deceased. The speakers were Bishops Matheson and Foster, Wm. H. Corry and H. W. Lunt. The remarks were encouraging and sympathetic, and an excellent spirit prevailed. Special musical numbers were contributed by some of the best local talent. There were many floral offerings, and everything went to show the respect in which the community held the departed brother and friend.

"Chauncey"—this is the name by which he was familiarly known, was born in this city on the 29th day of March, 1856, making him 49 years of

age last March. He grew up in this place, and Cedar City has always been his home. His parents were Daniel and Keturah Macfarlane. The father preceded him to the other side a year or more ago, but the mother is still living. He is also survived by a wife, five children, and several brothers and sisters.

The deceased was a useful person in the community. Always possessed of a good voice, his sweet music has entertained local people upon many hundreds of occasions, and many a soul has taken its flight to the other shore on the sweet notes that he has furnished. He was possessed of exceptional dramatic ability, and was always a star in the local troupes when he took part, as he frequently did.

He was always generous, big hearted and kind. Was idolized by his family through all his suffering, and goes to a well merited rest.

The Record sympathizes deeply with his little family, left unprotected by his untimely death.

Mr. and Mrs. Roy Urie are receiving the congratulations of their many friends over the arrival of a fine girl, born September 20th.

Aunt Margaret Pryor is one of the contestants for the prize automobile. Sister Pryor is smart enough to see that an automobile would be mighty handy in her business.

Mrs. F. T. Craig, who has been residing with her parents, Mr. and Mrs. James Sherratt for a number of weeks past, gave birth to a fine daughter on the 18th inst. Mother and babe are doing nicely. The family has the congratulations of The Record. The father is at his work in Los Angeles.

James Bulloch has been ill the past three weeks with a severe attack of inflammation of the bladder. He is reported some better at this writing.

Mrs. John D. Williams presented her husband with a girl baby yesterday morning. Dr. Leonard was in attendance, and reports all concerned doing well.

Celebrates 81st Birthday.

Last Tuesday, Sept. 28th, was the eighty-first birthday of Brother Bengt Nelson, Sr., and in honor of the occasion a pleasant social gathering was held at his home in which the members of his family and the Swedish Colony of Cedar City participated. The evening was very pleasantly spent and delicious refreshments were conspicuous on the program.

Brother Nelson is an extremely well preserved old gentleman. He has been a hard worker all his life and is still capable of doing a fair share of labor when he cares to, which is, however, not at all necessary from a financial standpoint.

The Record wishes him many happy returns of the day.

DR. MACFARLANE TO LEAVE CEDAR CITY

Dr. M. J. Macfarlane, who has been practicing medicine and surgery in Cedar City for the past two years and upwards, will leave within the next two or three days for American Fork, where he has bought the home of Dr. Robison of that place, and where in connection with two other physicians he will launch a large hospital enterprise. Dr. Macfarlane states that his practice here has been very satisfactory, but he has a preference for surgery and the opening in Utah county offers much greater possibilities along this line.

Dr. Macfarlane has many warm friends in this vicinity who, while regretting his departure, will wish him all kinds of success in his new field.

The surprise of the week in social circles was the announcement that J. M. B. Higbee had been quietly married at Salt Lake City during conference week to a lady from Independence, Mo., with whom Mr. Higbee became acquainted while residing there. Particulars are lacking, but it is expected that Mr. Higbee will shortly return here, when we will make him "fess up."

James Bulloch is back from the L. D. S. Hospital, where he went with the expectation of undergoing a surgical operation. On careful examination his trouble was diagnosed to be some kind of a growth on the bladder, and the outlook for an operation was not deemed promising, so was not performed. Jim is up and around, and states that he is feeling very much better than he did a few weeks since. He says without any equivocation that he is going to get well, which is a strong point in his favor.

Uncle John Urie was up from Hamilton's Fort yesterday, shaking hands with friends and incidentally attending the old folk's party.

Dr. Leonard reports the birth of a son Sunday night to Mrs. Minnie Stevens Lang of Buckhorn, who is staying with her parents at Enoch. The lady and baby are progressing favorably.

MAGNIFICIENT PAIR OF DEER ANTLERS.

George Nelson was exhibiting the biggest and oldest pair of deer's antlers that we have seen brought into Cedar City for many a year last Tuesday. The horns represented the season's catch for George. The animal was killed over in the Miner's Peak country, or near Crystal, in the Gulch. Its age was estimated at 10 or 12 years, and it was certainly a fine head. George shot the animal in the hind quarters, only crippling it, and when he attempted to get up to the deer to cut its throat it showed a strong disposition to fight, and it was found necessary to shoot it again, this time through the neck.

Mr. Nelson was in company with Sam Bell and Ed. Houchen, and each brought in their deer the first of the week. The head and hind feet of Nelson's deer each touched the ground when laid across a fair sized saddle

MUNICIPAL PARTIES NAME CANDIDATES

The three local political parties—Republicans, Democrats and Socialists—held their precinct primaries last Saturday evening and each nominated a city ticket to be voted for at the coming election, November 2nd.

Republican Party Ticket.

The Republicans held their primary in the Library auditorium, and nominated the following ticket:

For Mayor—Richard A. Thorley.

For Councilman, 4-yr. term—Dr. A. N. Leonard.

For Councilmen, 2-yr. term—M. D. Higbee, Dr. Robert A. Thorley and H. H. Lunt.

Recorder—J. H. Arthur.

Treasurer—S. J. Foster.

Socialist Party Ticket.

The local Socialist party nominated the following ticket:

For. Mayor—George Urie.

For long term Councilman—Daniel T. Leigh.

Democratic Party Ticket.

The Democratic party placed the following ticket before the voters of Cedar City for their consideration at the polls Nov. 2:

For Mayor—J. M. B. Higbee.

For long term Councilman—Parley Dalley.

For short term Councilmen—Robert S. Gardner, William H. Corry, H. L. Jones.

Recorder—Maeser Dalley.

Treasurer—E. M. Corry.

Short term Councilman—O. P. Fretwell, Thomas S. Bladen, Albert F. Gower.

Recorder—Joseph G. Stevenson.

Treasurer—Gomer Cosslett.

PETER FROYD IS CALLED BY DEATH

Old and Respected Citizen of Cedar City Finds Relief from Long Illness in Last Sleep.

Yesterday morning at 7:30 o'clock the grim reaper called and gathered in to the ranks of the "great majority" Peter Froyd, an aged and respected citizen of Cedar City, who has been a patient sufferer for nearly two years from old age and general debility.

The funeral is being held this afternoon at 2 o'clock as we are preparing to go to press.

Peter Johnson Froyd was born Mar. 3rd, 1838, in Skabersjo, Sweden. He joined the Latter-day Saints church in his native land about 1868, and emigrated to America in 1880, coming direct to Cedar City, where he arrived in August of that year. He has been a devoted Church member ever since, and has always enjoyed the confidence and esteem of the community.

His family consists of two sons, Alfred and Henry, both of whom reside here. He also had two stepdaughters, one of whom died a couple of years ago in Rockford, Ill. The other is Mrs. Bengta Adams of Cedar City. These, with two sisters who are still in Sweden, are all the relatives he has, so far as known.

His last illness was a tedious and protracted one, but he was patient and uncomplaining through it all, and seemed anxious to give as little trouble and inconvenience as possible. For more than a year he has been with his son Alfred and family.

Iron County Record
October 29, 1915

WM. DOW VICTIM OF FATAL ACCIDENT

Father of the Dow Children Living in Cedar City, Meets Tragic Death at Pioche.

Three fatalities, within as many weeks, is the toll due to accidents recorded among the mines of this and adjacent districts. The first was Tom Grover, who met death by being crushed in a cave-in at Bristol, the next was Charley Gillen, the victim of a premature explosion in the Amalgamated Pioche mine; the last was Wm. E. Dow, who died early Tuesday morning as a result of an accident at the hoisting plant of the Yuba Leasing & Development Co., Sunday morning.

Dow was in the night shift, as engineer. It was about quitting time and just before hoisting the last man out of the mine, he put on his coat preparatory to walking down to his cabin. When the last skip was up,

Dow turned off the gasoline with his right hand and at the same time reached to turn off the oil cup suspended above the main shaft. Meanwhile, the ragged ends dangling from his coat sleeve became caught in the master gear and in almost a twinkling the engineer was drawn into the very jaws of death. Although the gas feed had been shut off, enough momentum was left in the wheels to do their fearful work, and Dow's arm was ground to a pulp in the immense cogs. He called for help, and the men whom he had just hoisted from the mine ran to his assistance. It took all the strength of four men to move the machinery backward, and even then it was necessary to use a pocket knife to cut mangled particles of clothing and flesh before the unfortunate man could be extricated from his precarious position. With his mangled arm dangling at his side; his collar and shoulder bones broken; his lungs pierced by broken ribs; besides other serious injuries and against the protestations of his associates. Dow in-

sisted on walking down to the hospital, where medical attention was soon available.

An examination of his injuries indicated that there was little chance for the patient to survive. However, Dow being a man of wonderfully strong physique, his friends hoped for the best; and they were quite encouraged Monday. But that night complications set in and at 4 a. m. Tuesday, the summons came.

The deceased had been a resident of Pioche for a number of years and during all that time followed mining as a vocation. He is survived by two small children, who are with their grandparents—Mr. and Mrs. W. D. Watts, at Cedar City, Utah.

Funeral services were held Wednesday afternoon under the auspices of Pioche Lodge No. 23, I. O. O. F. and interment took place in the Odd Fellows' cemetery. It was Dow's request to be buried here.

W. D. Watts, father-in-law of the deceased, was the only relative present at the obsequies.—Pioche Record.

Iron County Record
October 29, 1915

Mr. Don Coppin, one of our local business and mechanical citizens, is receiving the congratulations this week of his many friends and acquaintances on his marriage last Monday at Salt Lake City to Miss Edith Arbuckle, daughter of Bishop George Arbuckle of Emerson ward, Salt Lake City. Mrs. Coppin accompanied her husband back to this city, and they are now domiciled at the Wm. H. Corry Hotel, pending the undertaking of housekeeping on their own account.

The Salt Lake Telegram has this to say concerning the marriage that took place in Salt Lake:

"Miss Edith Arbuckle, daughter of Bishop and Mrs. George Arbuckle, 747 East Eleventh street, and Don W. Coppin of Cedar City, were married at noon today at the home of the bride's parents, her father performing the ceremony.

"Mr. and Mrs. Coppin will go on a short wedding trip, after which they will be at home in Cedar City, where Mr. Coppin is in business. Only the members of the family and a few intimate friends were present when the ceremony was performed."

A girl was born to Mr. and Mrs. George Corry last Tuesday morning.

This weather is delightful, but can we expect it to remain this way much longer?

Automobiles are getting so thick in Cedar City that it keeps one guessing to dodge them, and we sometimes stop to wonder whether this is good old Cedar City, or if we have been dropped off in Los Angeles or Pasadena.

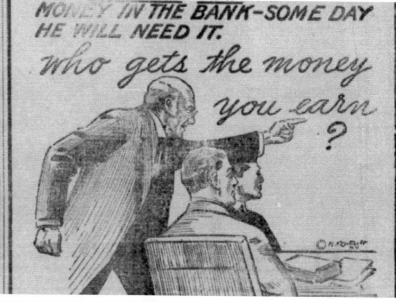

Iron County Record
November 5, 1915

Kanarra, Utah, Nov. 2, 1915.

John H. Williams' new bungalow is now ready for the plasterer. John H. Perry of Cedar City has the contract for this part of the work.

* * *

Dan Webster has bought the home of Parley Stapley. Parley is dissatisfied here and is going to Hinckley for the winter at least.

* * *

James Stapley lost a valuable work horse last night.

* * *

Mayhew H. Dalley of Cedar City has been spending considerable time here lately surveying a number of new lots which are being added to the town plats.

* * *

Sam Ford is remodelling his house and having cement walks and porches added, which will make it more attractive as well as convenient.

* * *

Joseph Williams has recently displayed a new sign, which reads as follows: "Joseph Williams, Groceries and Notions."

* * *

W. R. Davis, who has been a sufferer from rheumatism for a number of years, is now confined to the house

* * *

Mrs. Rebecca Sinfield of White River, Nevada, is here visiting with her brother, Mr. John Platt.

* * *

Alma Roundy, Sam Ford and Otto Reeves were the only lucky nimrods in Kanarra this year, each bringing home their deer during the open season.

The stork visited the home of Albert Kesler Monday night, leaving a baby girl. Dr. Green in attendance.

Iron County Record
November 19, 1915

Heber Holyoak is over from Milford for a short visit with his wife and little daughter.

* * *

Dr. Burton reports the arrival of a baby boy at the home of J. C. Robinson, Jr., Nov. 13th. All concerned doing nicely.

Washington County News
November 25, 1915

Marriages

Rex Mociac and Ivy George, Shivwits Indians, obtained a marriage licence from the county clerk Nov. 19 They were going to be married on the reservation, at Shem

Mr. Arthur D. Cox of Orderville and Miss Cora Haight af Cedar City obtained a licence on the 22nd inst. and were married in the temple here.

Iron County Record
December 3, 1915

Dr. J. F. Burton reports the arrival of a wee baby girl, weighing only 2½ pounds, at the home of Frank Norris, November 24th. All getting along nicely.

Harrison Goudge and Ivy Macfarlane of Cedar City were married at the home of Dr. James Green Tuesday evening. Mayor H. D. Bayles performed the ceremony.

Iron County Record
December 10, 1915

Born—To Mr. and Mrs. Jess Walker, a boy.

Bishop and Mrs. S. J. Foster have an increase in their family circle for this Christmas season, in the form of a nice baby girl, which Santa left the fore part of this week. While the old gentleman was a little early with his distribution of "dolls" this one is none the less welcome.

Iron County Record
December 17, 1915

The first case of chicken pox for Cedar City this winter, made its appearance at the home of Sam B. Jones this week, and yesterday Health Officer Leonard, after an investigation displayed a quarantine flag.

Miss Annette Webster left this afternoon with Leland Betttenson to spend the holidays in Circleville. Our reporter failed to learn whether it is the young lady's intention to return as Miss Webster or Mrs. Bettenson. But we suspect the worst.

Iron County Record
December 24, 1915

Mrs. Laura Bennett is here visiting her mother, Mrs. Emma Webb.

Born, to Mr. and Mrs. Frank Walker, a daughter, on Sunday, Dec. 19.

Mrs. Mary Hunter has been very ill with an attack of lagrippe for several days. Reports from her bedside this morning indicate that she is no better.

Miss Janie Wilkinson, who is teaching at Nephi, is home for a visit with friends.

Mr. Hillman Dalley and wife are here spending the holidays with M. H. Dalley and family.

Miss Sarah Gower, of this place, and Mr. Louis Burton, of Nephi, were married at Parowan, on Dec. 15. Both parties are well known here and have the good wishes of all.

Mr. and Mrs. George Bertoch, of Hunter, Salt Lake County, are visiting relatives and friends here, during the holiday season. Mrs. Bertoch is the daughter of Mrs. Sarah Leigh.

Born, to Mr. and Mrs. Lorenzo J. Williams of Kanarra, a boy, Thursday Dec. 23. All concerned doing nicely. Dr. Leonard in attendance.

Ray, the six-year old boy of Bishop A. G. Matheson, is rapidly recovering from an attack of pneumonia, and is now able to be around the house.

Miss Althea Dover and Mr. Kirby Estes surprised their friends last week by being quietly married at St. George. The happy couple have the good wishes of their many friends in the valley. Next March they will make their home in Oklahoma, where the groom has business interests.

Iron County Record
December 31, 1915

Born to Mr. and Mrs. Ernest Martineau Dec. 27, a boy. All doing nicely, and Dr. Leonard in attendance.

Iron County Record
January 7, 1916

Born, at Southern Utah Hospital, January 1, to Mr. and Mrs. Lehi A. Thorley, a girl. All doing nicely. Lehi says, "A fine New Year's gift."

Iron County Record
February 25, 1916

Born, to Mr. and Mrs. Ellis Christensen of Kanarra, a boy. Dr. Leonard in attendance.

Dr. Leonard reports the arrival of a fine baby at the home of Mrs. Ruth Gale. All concerned doing nicely.

Mr. Edward Cox, who has been suffering from a severe attack of sciatic rheumatism, is up from Hamilton's Fort taking the violet ray treatment, from Dr. Leonard.

Echoes From Cedar City Round-up

Practically every town in southern Utah has been represented at the Cedar City Round up which has held its sessions in the excellent rooms and well equipped laboratories of the Branch Agricultural College. The first weeks enrollment was 456 and Wednesday night of the second week it totaled 560

Hon Nathoniah Thomas in a lecture on water emphasized the importance of an organization in the operation of irrigation water. All the interests on every stream should organize and be directed from one representative board. Keep your water troubles out of the courts. Employ every other means of settlement before resorting to them. Appoint committees from each interest. Let them get together and thresh the differences out on a friendly basis. It saves a vast amount of money time and trouble

Mrs Nellie K Jones in her talk to the women on children advised that the delicate child be given plenty of fresh air fresh milk sensible clothing and individual care. No general rule can be applied to all children. Each child represents a problem which should be intelligently studied and its specific needs determined and provided for. This is a specialized study of the mother and should receive her best and most conscientious thought and effort

State Horticulturist J Edward Taylor lectured on the necessity of the home garden. In planting it a systematic arrangement should be followed. Determine the best thing to plant then set out to get a maximum yield from a limited area. It is usually best to plant rhubarb asparagus gooseberries or some other small fruit in the outside rows and arrange your other garden crops systematically on the rest of your small garden spot

The women of Cedar City have formulated a set of resolutions which will be presented to the city council promoting the movement for pure milk. They ask that an inspector of barns and corrals be appointed who shall see that they be kept clean and sanitary. They recommend the use of the regulation milk pail that the cow be curried and her udder and flanks, as well as the hands of the milker, be thoroughly washed before milking that all vessels used for milk be carefully sterilized that the house and milk cellars be well screened and that fly traps and other methods of fly extermination be extensively used

Miss Gertude McCheyne of the Utah Extension Division urged the women to get busy and make use of the opportunities offered for home demonstrations under the provisions of the Smith Lever law. These demonstrations will not be provided unless the women want them. Their especial work is to visit the women in their homes, help them to make lighter their work and help in every way possible in solving womans problems. These home demonstrators are women who are especially fitted to aid other women in their home life

ANOTHER NEW BUSINESS VENTURE IS LAUNCHED.

The quarters formerly occupied by the Cedar City post-office in The Record building, have been leased by Hayden Long and Royal Reid, and will be neatly fitted up as an electrical and plumbing store. Electrical conveniences for lighting, heating cooking and supplying motive power will be carried in stock, and there will be a modern display of plumbing materials as well.

March the fifteenth is the date mentioned for the opening up of the business.

Mr. Long is the gentleman who installed the heating, plumbing and ventilating system in the new district school building, and who now has the contract for the swimming pool and heating plant that is being installed in the Ward Hall. He is a conaractor and business man well known in the northern part of the state.

Royal Reid is by no means a stranger to Iron county. He has operated here and at Parowan, off and on, for a number of years, and is an electrician as well as a business man of reputation.

These gentlemen have shown good judgment in their choice of a town in which to engage in this business, and will nodoubt do well here.

NEW X-RAY MACHINE PROVES ITS VALUE.

William P. Barton, mail contractor between this place and Paragonah, residing at the latter place, is about the best pleased man we have seen in a long time. A few days ago his little son Kenneth had the misfortune to swallow a nickle, and since that time has been unable to swallow anything but liquid foods, and has suffered a great deal of pain and misery. He has been under the care of a physician in the northern end of the county, who was unable to locate the seat of the trouble.

As he did not seem to be making satisfactory progress, however, he was brought to Cedar City yesterday and Dr. Leonard took an X-ray picture of his throat and chest, showing very clearly the nickle well down in the esophagus. The child was then put on the operating table and after a general anaesthetic the coin was successfully dislodged and pushed on into the stomach. The child can now eat well, and there is little doubt of its speedy recovery. Mr. Barton is very thankful, indeed, that there is such an apparatus as the X-ray machine now in the county, as it clearly saved him hundreds of dollars and no end of inconvenience in this instance.

KANARRAVILLE.

Kanarra, Utah, March 22, 1916.

Last Friday night the drama, "Valley Farm," was presented to a well packed house under the auspices of the Relief Society. The characters were all well represented and the performance did those interested in its production great credit.

* * *

J. L. Davis is taking an X-ray treatment from Dr. Leonard for a cancerous growth on his nose.

* * *

Reese J. Williams, Sr., and L. J. Balser were home missionaries to Enoch last Sunday.

* * *

Elder Wilford Lawrence of Summit was here as a home missionary last Sunday, and addressed the people at the afternoon services on the subject of "Prayer." Elder John Platt occupied the remainder of the time in reporting the recent quarterly conference.

* * *

Last Monday we had a nice rain, lasting for about ten hours, falling in a gentle manner, with no wind accompanying to speak of.

* * *

Tuesday Dr. Leonard came down from Cedar City and delivered a lecture on "The Fly," using a chart to illustrate his subject, which was well received by an extra good turn-out, 170 people by actual count being present, not counting babies. It is hoped that the talk will result in good. Mrs. Leonard accompanied the Doctor and played two selections on the piano. Unfortunately the piano was out of tune, which embarrassed the performer, but of course we knew no difference, thinking that it was all in the music.

* * *

Sheriff Corry was in town today on official business.

* * *

Born—this morning at about four o'clock, twin girls to Mr. and Mrs. Wallace Pollock. Mrs. Hannah Williams officiated at the birth.

Mrs. Winnie Roche has been quite seriously ill for some time with La-Grippe and complications, but is reported some better at this time.

Dr. Macfarlane made a professional trip to Lund last Thursday and reports a baby boy at the residence of Mrs. Sam Barton of that place.

Mr. and Mrs. Gordon Matheson are receiving many congratulations on the birth of their first child, a girl, on the 20th inst. All concerned doing well. The young people are residing, it will be remembered, at Hurricane, Utah.

Dr. Leonard returned last night at a late hour from Kanarra and reports the birth of a son to Mr. and Mrs. Sam L. Pollock.

A baby girl came to the home of Mr. and Mrs. Clavenger Saturday night. All is reported favorable at the home.

With the approach of spring the "feathered tribe" begins to make its appearance. Among the rest the stork is very much in evidence, leaving a boy at the home of Mr. and Mrs. Wm. Webster March 27; a little girl with Mr. and Mrs. Naze Harris April 1; and a girl at the home of Mr. and Mrs. Mart Walker April 5. Dr. Leonard reports all of the above as doing nicely.

SWIMMING POOL TO BE READY IN TWO WEEKS.

The latest report on the new swimming pool is to the effect that it will be ready for use in two weeks. Mr. Hayden Long, the contractor, has kept things rolling from the start, and will apparently complete the job in record time. It is only a matter of two or three weeks at most until Cedar people will be enjoying this luxury. We use the word luxury advisably, for we are reliably informed that few towns of like population have swimming pools. Among the few Utah cities having public pools are Provo and Richfield. Both these places, and particularly Provo, are considerably larger than Cedar City, yet the Richfield pool is very much smaller than our pool and the Provo pool, which is just about the same size, is unprotected and available for use only in the warm weather.

It is equipped with a modern plant for warming the water, and can be used with comfort at all seasons of the year. It reflects credit upon the enterprise of the local community.

"For G—— sake, come quick!" was the startling message received by Dr. Macfarlane over the phone last Wednesday morning. The occasion for the excitement turned out to be the arrival of twin boys at he home of F. W. Middleton. All doing well.

Parley Dalley has spent several days recently in the Summit mountains locating potash deposits for himself and co-workers at the school. Mr. Dalley, from his knowledge of chemistry, is convinced that the strike is an important one and will mean a great deal for this section of the country.

The announcement has just been made by Messrs. G. R. Parry and A. T. Jones of the erection the present season of another large garage in Cedar City, which is to cost approximately $8,000, and will be an ornament to Main street. The new establishment is to be erected for Messrs. Parry & Jones by David Bulloch, on his ground just across the alley from the old Palmer residence on the west side of Main street, and will front on both thorofares. It is to have a plate glass front, heating plant, and all modern conveniences, providing garage for about 20 cars, besides the display and work rooms, which will accommodate a number more cars.

Architect Jones has the contract for the plans and specifications, and is already at work upon them. It is the purpose to push the construction right along as rapidly as possible.

The promoters and lessees of the garage announce their intention of carrying a full line of tires, accessories, gasoline, oils and grease, and to conduct a strictly up-to-date garage, where car owners can obtain the very most efficient service. They also state that as soon as the garage is ready they will handle all their cars for which they have the agency in co-partnership.

Mr. Bulloch, who is furnishing the investment for the undertaking, is one of the first pioneers of Cedar City. He was the first white boy, he states, upon the present site of the town, and is anxious to do his part towards the building up of the place. He has the ground and the money, and is willing to combine them in a state of productivity for a very reasonable return upon his investment.

With two garages already operating here, and with the announcement that Agent Fife, backed by the Ford company, will put up a $5,000 garage and service station, it looks as if car owners in this part of the country would be well cared for.

A party of four miners and prospectors, including Ed. H. Parry, Ern Walker, Rob. Arthur and Bert Nelson, started today to the sheelite deposits in Nevada, expecting to be away for some considerable time.

M. H. Dalley and son Hillman are in Parowan this week attending to some land business.

FOR SALE.—At reasonable prices, Idaho oats and Gem flour.—Alfred Froyd.

Mrs. Hattie Root, proprietor of the Lund hotel, was in town attending to business yesterday.

T. A. Thorley, accompanied by one of his little sons, is in Salt Lake City attending to some business matters.

Mrs. Annette Webster has resigned her position in the Cedar Sheep Association as clerk, and the vacancy has been filled by Miss Lulu Smith.

Mr. and Mrs. James Bulloch left the first of the week for their ranch near Newhouse, Beaver county, where it is their intention to conduct a dairy this summer.

SAHARA.

Sahara-Ford, Utah, June 7, 1916.
At the social gathering held at the home of Mr. and Mrs. Frank Hedrick, Sahara, Utah, May 12th, the welfare of the Sahara and Ford communities was discussed, the outgrowth of which was the organization of the "Get Together Club." The first regular meeting was held May 31, 1916, at the home of Mr. and Mrs. T. R. Prey, Sahara, with thirty-seven persons in attendance. The following officers were elected for the ensuing term: Mr. W. G. Burgess, president; Mrs. Gilbert Corn, vice-president; Mrs. T. R. Prey, secretary and treasurer; Mrs. James Baker, chairman, Mrs. Frank Hedrick, Mrs. Wallace G. Bumpus and Mr. Harry O. Willhide, members of the standing committee.

Following the musical and literary program, refreshments were served.

The next regular meeting will be on June 15th, at the home of Mr. and Mrs. A. H. Kendall, Ford, Utah. All

Keith Smith, the son of Mr. and Mrs. James Smith, was operated on Tuesday for hernia by Dr. Leonard. At this time the lad is reported to be getting along nicely.

We are informed that Mrs. Clifton of the California ranch, betwen this place and Lund, has purchased a new Dort car from J. David Leigh, who has the agency for Iron county.

There are persistent rumors afloat to the effect that Miss Della Smith of Cedar City and Mr. Topham of Paragonah are to be married on the 15th of this month. Wonder who can confirm the report.

Mrs. Murie and Mrs. Cunningham, of Salt Lake City, who have been visiting for a few days with their sister, Mrs. Richard A. Thorley and other relatives, will depart for their home today.

Cards are out announcing the marriage of Miss Florence Smith of this place and Mr. J. Johnson of Oasis, who were united in the holy bonds of matrimony in the Salt Lake temple June 2nd. They will be at home in Cedar City after June 9th. The Record congratulates.

The following account of the death of Sextus C. Johnson, who died recently at his home near Benson, Arizona, was handed to The Record by J. M. B. Higbee, of this place, who was well acquainted with deceased, and explains that he was the founder of Johnson's Fort, now known as Enoch, and that the settlement was named for him. Mr. Higbee further explains that Mr. Johnson is Mrs. George Lunt's father, who is a resident of Cedar City at the present time.

His death occurred on June 4th:

(From the Benson (Ariz.) Press.)

Sextus C. Johnson died Sunday morning last at his home about a mile north of Pemerene (Robinson) school house aged 86 years. The funeral took place Monday afternoon conducted by Elder M. P. Cosby, of the Church of Latter Day Saints, followed by other members of the church who spoke in eulogy of the deceased. Mr. Johnson came of Revolutionary stock, in which he took great pride. His grandfather was killed at the battle of Bunker Hill three days before his father's birth.

The deceased, who was born in Illinois in 1829, became the father of a large family, leaving a wife, five sons and seven daughters, besides a good many grand-children and a few great grand-children.

Mr. Johnson was leader of a large company of emigrants that crossed the plains from Missouri to Salt Lake City, Utah, in early days. He was captain of a company of minute men in the early Indian wars, but boasted of the fact that he never shed blood but that a way was always found to avoid it. His just way of dealing with the Indians made him many friends among them. Later he spent a good many years laboring among them and helped greatly to civilize some of the most vicious tribes of Southern Utah and Northern Arizona. Mr. Johnson was a pioneer and frontiers-man in the truest sense. He helped establish something like twenty-five settlements in Utah, Arizona and Old Mexico. Wherever Mr. Johnson went he was noted for planting fruit trees and beautifying the earth, and though seeming often to realize that he might not live to enjoy the fruit of his own planting, he nevertheless kept at his

good work. He was among the first settlers to go into the Mormon colonies of northern Mexico. He saw village after village spring up in the state of Chihuahua, but true to his calling of pioneer he pushed on out to the frontier again. At the time the Americans were called out of Mexico three years ago, Mr. Johnson was at Morelos, Sonora, where he had built himself a nice little home, seemingly content there to spend the last days of his life in ease. Coming out with the settlers, many of whom thought they were only

leaving for a month or two, but he had a clearer perception of what was in store for the colonists, for on leaving his little home with its cultivated tracts and orchard of ripening fruit, he seemed conscious of the fact that he was looking upon it for the last time. As he drove away he stopped and turning in the seat of his buggy took a last long look of regret at having to leave his home. Taking off his hat he said impressively and sadly, "Adios!" turned and came away.

Henry Nelson and Miss Irene Harris were quietly married in this city last Wednesday, only members of the immediate families being present.

The little daughter of Mr. and Mrs. Eugene Cripps of this place has pneumonia. Dr. Macfarlane is attending her.

On Tuesday, June 20th, Mrs. David Sharp presented her husband with a lovely girl. Dr. Leonard reports everything nicely.

Mr. and Mrs. Joseph Haslam have a son six years old ill with typhoid fever, but it is now in the third week and is doing nicely.

A new girl baby arrived at the domicile of Mr. and Mrs. Joshua Crosby last Friday. Dr. Macfarlane reports that mother and babe are doing well.

The Record acknowledges receipt of a card from Mr. and Mrs. J. O. Berry of Provo, Utah, announcing the birth of their first baby, an eight-pound boy, on June 14th. If we are correctly advised, this entitles our friend, Jos. S Berry, to the designation of grandfather. We congratulate all the way 'round.

Randall L. Jones, architect, has just placed his order for a new No. 10 Royal typewriter. This makes about eight or nine of these machines in use in Cedar City now, and all owners seem especially well pleased with them.

Last Monday while John Tait was doing work about his barn he had the misfortune to fall and do himself considerable bodily injury. At first he thought there was nothing very seriously the matter with him, and it was two days later that a physician was called in to find that he had two of his ribs broken, his spine injured and other bad bruises. He has been in bed all week practically, and it was found necessary to send for one of his married sisters to come and take care of him.

Mr Carl Heyburn and Miss Fliza Myrtle Bauer, both of Cedar City were married in the St George temple

Mr Orson J Bryan and Miss Elora Main Urie both of Cedar City obtained a marriage license here June 27th and were married in the St. George temple,

John Smith Walker was born on the 10th day of April, 1834, in the Iron district of Low Moor, near Bradford, Yorkshire, England. The oldest son of Joseph Walker and Betty Smith Walker. And after 82 years of mortal experience John departed to the vast unknown on the 16th day of June, 1916.

He was baptized in his native town, and when 15 years of age, emigrated with his parents and two brothers—William and Thomas—to Utah, under the presidency of Elder Orson Spencer, arriving in Salt Lake City in the early fall of 1849.

Father Walker bought a farm on Mill Creek, Salt Lake county, adjoining Jos. Wright's farm, who emigrated from Low Moor and was an old friend and fellow workman in the iron works of that place.

In the fall of 1850 Father Walker, subject to counsel of the Church authorities, left his wife and children on the farm and made a home in Parowan, Iron county. The following spring he sold his farm and moved his family to Parowan. Again directed by counsel of President George A. Smith, he pioneered with a small company and located a fort northwest of Cedar City cemetery, Matthew Carruthers presiding. President Geo. A. Smith, visiting the fort, counselled and advised a move to the south of the fort and surveyed a site for a city; this occurred in the spring of 1852. That fall a call was made by the presidency at the October conference for 100 families to strengthen Cedar City and labor at the iron works, located one-half mile above the walled city. In 1854, the month of May, President Young and company visited Cedar City, organized a stake, with Isaac C. Haight as president and Phillip K. Smith as bishop. He told the people they were in danger from the flood waters of Coal Creek, called a few brethren to follow him, directed his teamster and stopped on the present site of Cedar City. Placing the point of his staff on the northwest corner of the old I. C. Haight lot, he said, "Build west and south, but go no farther north."

Up to this time our friend John S. did a boy's part in the building up of the colony. He was then in his twenties, strong, hale and hearty. John was not an idler and his father and mother being industrious people found him something to do, which he did cheerfully. About this time he was ordained an elder and took an active part in the meetings of the quorum. The building up of a new town and surrounding the half mile square of the second town with a ten foot wall took every hand to the pick, shovel and ax.

The Legislature of 1853-54 granted Cedar City's charter, with Isaac C. Haight the first mayor.

To build homes lumber, shingles and lath were necessary. Father Walker and his son John were to the job and continued in the lumber business for many years. Father Walker, who had been a furnaceman in Low Moor, took hold and worked faithfully at the same kind of work for the Deseret Iron Company. The furnace costing three thousand dollars was located a few rods east of the present north bridge. The works shut down in the fall of 1857. The Walkers then turned to logging, lumbering and hauling to town.

On the 9th of August, 1864, our John took a wife, the lady we now call Aunt Maggie—her proper name, Margaret Augusta Pucell—and they were the parents of eleven children, six sons and five daughters. Sister Maggie, four sons, four daughters, 47 grandchildren and six great-grandchildren survive the deceased.

While logging one morning John was caught by a falling timber and received a dislocated hip and broken leg, and during the past eight years he has suffered more or less from that accident; he has also had two paralytic strokes, all of which tended to weaken his once strong body.

For 52 years Sister Maggie was a true, devoted helpmeet, and during his sickness was a comfort and consoler.

With all his strength he did not accumulate wealth, always satisfied with fair compensation for his work. He was a factor in pioneering Iron county, especially Cedar City. At the services held in the tabernacle his friends of long ago spoke in kind remarks of the departed.

BIOGRAPHICAL.

Edwin Charles Cox, son of Abraham and Frances Beard Cox, was born May 21, 1838, at Sommersetshire, England. At the early age of seven years he went out as page boy to Sir Edward Strode, one of the barrons of England. From the environment of this place he acquired most of his early education, and being among the titled and what is known as the gentry, he learned much of the grace and refinement of the higher circles of English society. When he became of an age to learn a trade he went as an apprentice to a landscape gardner at the same place. After completing his apprenticeship he accepted a position as landscape gardner at the Watley Rectory, where he remained for some years as gardner. From there he went to work in the coal and iron district of Wales, where he heard the gospel and was baptized into the Church of Jesus Christ of Latter-day Saints. He remained seven years in Wales, learned to read, write and speak the Welch language and for several years was secretary of the mission there. While in this work he became acquainted with Richard Palmer, who was there as a missionary. From the first he was an earnest worker in the cause he had embraced. Having acquired a good insight into music from Miss Strode, the old Barron's sister, he accompanied the missionaries to assist them with the singing and lated did missionary work himself, suffering persecution and mob violence for the gospel's sake.

After leaving Wales he again took a position as gardner at one of the large estates in London. There he met Mary E. Reid, who was cook at the same place and who afterwards became his wife. At the time of their marriage (June 8, 1865) Mary did not belong to the Latter-day Saint church, but through his earnestness and zeal she was soon converted and baptized. In the spring of '69 they set sail for

America, landing at Long Island in June. He secured a position as gardener and remained in the vicinity of New York for five years, then continued on to Utah, the home of his religion.

Arriving at Cedar City in the fall of '74 they went to live with his old friend, Richard Palmer. The market for garden produce in Cedar City was at that time very limited, so he took up carpentry with his brother Sam who had immigrated with him. He early organized a gardners' club, but owing to lack of market it met with but little success. He was battered from pillar to post, working at all sorts of things, as most people of the West did. In January, 1896, his wife died, leaving him with 8 of the nine children that had come to them. The following year his oldest child, Mrs. Joseph S. Smith, was killed in an accident on the mountain road.

In 1898 he went east to visit relatives and hunt up genealogy and in October of the same year was married to Julia A. Seaman of Sabula, Iowa. Together they made several visits to his family in Cedar City, and in 1908 he again made his home here. At the age of 70 years he began the erection of their home, which he himself has built and finished since, having also made several pieces of furniture.

All through his life he has taken pleasure in writing poems, a great many of which have been published.

January 24 of the present year, while sitting at his table after dinner, he was smitten with paralysis, completely disabling his left side. From then until the time of his death on June 24th, he endured great pain and suffering. However, at the last he passed away very quietly, with his

wife and five of his children at his bedside. He leaves, besides his faithful and devoted wife, the following named children: Mrs. Nelly Smith, Everard A. Cox, Mrs. Orson F. Tyler of Thatcher, Arizona, Mrs. Robert Mumford, Edwin R. Cox, Dr. W. C Cox of St. George and Mrs. Tinton Ahlstrom, 34 grandchildren and 9 great-grandchildren.

Iron County Record
July 13, 1916

Kanarraville, Utah, July 13, 1916.
Dr. Leonard was called last night to attend the baby of Mr. and Mrs. Raymond Williams, which is very ill with broncho pneumonia, having been sick for the past month.

* * *

Mr. and Mrs. Lois J. Balser went to Cedar City Wednesday with their daughter, Mrs. Adelia Wood, who has gone for treatment by the doctor.

* * *

Haying time is at hand. Those who did not cut their frosted alfalfa are now cutting a pretty fair crop; but those who did cut will be cutting again in about a week; in fact, some few are cutting again now.

* * *

The foundation is now completed for George Berry's new house, which is being erected on North Main street and is now ready for the carpenters

* * *

Thanks (?) to the rabbits, some of the farmers will not be at much expense in harvesting their grain crops this year.

* * *

Judging from the amount of goods being hauled in from the railroad, it appears that the home merchants are doing a good business.

Operations at Local Hospital.

Since our last issue Dr. Leonard reports the following operations at the Southern Utah Hospital:

George Adair from Orderville. Removal of bullet from his thigh. Mr. Adair was accidentally shot four years ago and has had a discharging sinus ever since that time. The doctor found the bullet with the aid of the X-ray, lodged against the bone. Mr. Adair is making a good recovery and will depart for home in a few days.

Elmer Taylor of Harmony was operated on July 8th for appendicitis. He will return home in good condition tomorrow.

June Williams was brought to Cedar during the night of July 8, by his brother-in-law, P. N. Wilkinson. Dr. operated before daylight. The appendix was in such a condition that it was found necessary to leave in a drain for a few days. June is reported to be doing fine at this time.

Mrs. Samuel Topham of St. George was operated July 11 for appendicitis and ovarian cist.

Marva Dunton, age 14, daughter of Mr. and Mrs. M. A. Dunton of Paragonah, was brought to the hospital. Drs. Leonard and Green performed the operation for appendicitis, and the little girl is getting along as well as can be expected.

Mrs. Rettie Wood, daughter of Mr. and Mrs. Balser of Kanarraville was brought to Cedar City last Wednesday. The doctor found her to be suffering from an acute attack of rheumatic fever.

A ten pound boy, which arrived last Friday, is reported at the home of Mr. and Mrs. Lawrence Clark. The folks couldn't do better, said Mr. Clark, in answer to our reporter's enquiry.

Mrs. Kate Adams Thomas from Nevada, is here visiting her father and other relatives, and was present at the funeral of her sister, Mrs. Chas. Stapley.

State Treasurer Jesse D. Jewkes, who was in the south on state road business, being a member of the State Road Commission, took occasion to pay a visit to Iron county, and spent Wednesday afternoon in Cedar City, going from there to Parowan. Mr. Jewkes informs us that his father was one of the first pioneers to the Cedar Valley. Incidentally Mr. Jewkes is feeling of the public pulse in a political sense and trying to get a line up on public sentiment on various questions in this part of the state. He may return with State Engineer Beers in a few days to look over various road changes and improvements under consideration in this locality.

SAHARA-FORD.

Sahara, Utah, July 19, 1916.

Mr. and Mrs. A. H. Kendall and family, accompanied by Mrs. Wallsmith of Ford, departed for California on the 13th via auto route.

* * *

Mr. Walter Jobart is spending a week with his parents, Mr. and Mrs. Charles Jobart of Ford, who are giving a dance in his honor this evening.

* * *

Mrs. Julia Smith, formerly of Ohio, is visiting her brother, W. H. Smith of Sahara.

* * *

Upon his return from haying at Newcastle, Mr. Howland, accompanied by Mr. and Mrs. D. A. Pearce of Sahara, departed for Antelope to visit Mrs. Pearce's sister, Mrs. Doone.

Mr. Clayton Phillips of Sahara is in California visiting his parents.

* * *

The next regular meeting of the Get-Together Club will be held at the home of Mr. and Mrs. Charls Jobart of Ford, Saturday evening, July 22. All invited.

* * *

Parry Mackelprang, en route from Nevada to Cedar City, spent the night at Sahara. We are always glad to see the boys.

* * *

Messrs. Ern and Doss Walker of Cedar City spent Tuesday at Sahara with A. E. Markwith.

* * *

Union Sunday School at Sahara 10:30 a. m. Mr. H. E. Rimmel, superintendent. All welcome.

A small son of Henry Eddards was brought off the mountain yesterday with a broken arm, received when he was dragged from the back of his cow pony by the limb of a tree. Dr. Leonard made an X-ray photograph of the limb and then reduced the fracture. Both bones of the fore arm were found to be broken.

Last Wednesday morning at 2 o'-clock Drs. Macfarlane and Leonard operated on little Hilma Lundgren, the three year old daughter of Mr. and Mrs. Charles Lundgren, for general peritonitis, due to appendicitis, the appendix having ruptured some days previous. The disease had progressed so far that little or no hope is entertained for the little one's recovery.

This is the banner year for broken limbs. The lates case reported is that of James Haslam, son of John Haslam, who was brought off the mountain last night with both the bones in his forearm broken. The limb was set by Dr. Macfarlane. The boy was injured by a horse he was riding falling with him.

SEE PARLEY DALLEY FOR LIVING ACCOMMODATIONS.

Students and other persons desiring accommodations for the winter should see or address Mr. Parley Dalley, Cedar City, Utah; and persons having rooms to rent, desiring boarders or having other accommodations to offer should report same to Mr. Dalley, who will be intrusted with the work of handling this matter.

Mr. Dalley states that while it is imperative that all the people who can furnish accommodations for students and others who desire to come here for the winter, still he does not anticipate any serious famine for accommodations, and he feels certain that he will be able to supply the demands.

Owing to the addition of one year of college work, it is expected that there will be a record attendance at the school this year, and everything looks propitious for an exceptionally interesting and successful school year.

Students coming here from the surrounding districts will receive a hearty welcome from the townspeople, as well as the faculty and resident students.

Iron County Record
August 11, 1916

Lafe McConnell is slowly recovering from his recent severe attack of illness and is now able to sit up and move about a little.

Little Keith Lambeth, whose life was almost despaired of last week, following an operation for ruptured appendix and peritonitis, is slowly improving. Dr. Macfarlane reports that unless unforseen complications arise, he will in all probability recover.

Born, to Mr. and Mrs. Ray Thomas, a fine baby boy, last Sunday. Mr. Thomas assures us that he is the finest ever.

Mrs. Harrison Green presented her husband with a baby girl Wednesday. This is their first, and The Record congratulates.

Dr. Macfarlane was called to Summit Monday to attend the infant of Mr. and Mrs. Wilford Lawrence, which had an abcess in its throat.

Dr. Macfarlane was called to Enterprise last week Friday to see Frank Terry's child, which has been sick for a number of weeks with some form of bladder trouble.

Mr. and Mrs. Dave C. Bulloch are the proud possessors of a fine baby girl, born last Wednesday morning. This is the first time for Mrs. Bulloch, so they may be excused for being a little egotistical over it. Dr. Macfarlane reports mother and babe doing well.

Mr. James Berry has joined the ranks of the motor car owners, having purchased one of the new model, 50-hp. Studebaker Sixes. Both Mr. and Mrs. Berry are learning rapidly to drive and handle the machine.

SAHARA.

We were indeed shocked at the unfortunate accident happening to Mrs. G. Corn Sunday evening at about 8 p. m., the accidental discharge of a gun injuring both her arm and leg. Mr. and Mrs. Frank Hedrick and Mr. H. Dougherty took her to Dr. Leonard's hospital at Cedar City, in the Hedrick's car, arriving about 12 p. m. the same evening. We are all anxiously awaiting her recovery, and hoping there will be no serious complications.

The Democrats of Iron County met in convention at the Library auditorium, in Cedar City, last Saturday and nominated a full county ticket and five delegates to the judicial district convention.

Ex-Prin. Geo. W. Decker heads the county ticket for the legislature, and the entire ticket is regarded as an uncommonly strong one.

The nominees for county offices are as follows:

For representative—Geo. W. Decker.

Long term commissioner—William Lund, of Modena.

Short term commissioner—Wm. P. Barton, Paragoonah.

County clerk—W. Warner Mitchell, of Parowan.

Treasurer—Lawrence J. Adams, of Parowan.

Recorder—Kate Taylor of Parowan.

Assessor—Maeser Dalley, of Cedar City.

Attorney—E. J. Palmer, of Cedar City.

Sheriff—Jos. S. Fife, of Cedar City.

Surveyor—Maeser Dalley, of Cedar City.

Delegates to Judicial Convention.

The following were chosen as delegates and alternates to the Judicial convention:

Delegates—Charles Adams, Parowan; Jos. S. Fife, Cedar City; J. W. Clark, Beryl; William Lund, Modena; Wm. P. Barton, Paragoonah.

Alternates—W. Warner Mitchell, Parowan; W. K. Granger, Cedar City; F. W. Middleton, Cedar City.

Last Sunday afternoon in the Cedar City tabernacle, commencing at 3 p. m., funeral services were held over the remains of Richard Palmer, one of the early settlers and a respected citizen of this place, who departed this life Saturday morning, Sept. 16th, at 7 o'clock, at the ripe old age of 88 years.

The casket was heavily laden with beautiful flowers, and the services partook more of the nature of a farewell love feast than of a funeral.

All members of the Stake Presidency were present upon the stand.

The speakers recited many of the incidents of the life of the departed, and all bore sincere testimony to the worthy and examplary life which he led. Those heard from on the occasion were, Elders David Bulloch, John V. Adams, Morgan Richards of Parowan, Dr. G. W. Middleton of Salt Lake City, Henry Leigh and Bishop A. G. Matheson.

By special request the song, "This World is Full of Beauty," was rendered by Gomer Cosslett.

The choir was present and rendered appropriate hymns.

A long line of automobiles and other vehicles followed the hearse to the cemetery, where interment was made. The grave was dedicated by President Wm. H. Lyman of Parowan.

BIOGRAPHICAL.

Richard Palmer was born in Aberdare, Wales, March 20, 1828. At the age of ten he began working in a machine shop, and from then until his young manhood was engaged in blacksmithing, engineering and working among metals.

He first heard of Mormonism at the age of fifteen, and five years later embraced the faith, becoming an active officer and member in the Welsh mission. In 1851 he came to America, and after working in St. Louis and vicinity for about a year, joined the A. O. Smoot company of Latter-day Saint emigrants and started across the plains in May, 1852. The trip proved to be a very hard one, as Salt Lake Valley was not reached until September and the subject of our sketch, though ill with chills and fever, had to walk nearly all the way.

After arriving at Salt Lake, he took up his trade of blacksmithing and worked at it until the "grasshopper year" of 1855, when the promise of a more plentiful supply of food stuff lured him to journey southward to the new settlement of Cedar City, or what is now known as the Old Fort. Here he again took up his trade among the early, struggling pioneers, and endured all the hardships of the arduous pioneering days of the section in which he has since lived.

In 1860 he went on a mission to Great Britain, where he held the position of president of the Monmouthshire conference, and where he met his wife, Johanna Rees Palmer.

Survived by six children, four sons and two daughters, and by his wife, whose untiring devotion and tender care of her aged husband was instrumental in prolonging his life to the ripe age he attained.

Richard was the only member of the Palmer family to join the Mormon Church and migrate to America. He was the eldest of a family of six, all of whom he survived by many years.

He died of old age and general debility. His last sickness was marked by the exceptional patience and cheerfulness that characterized his whole life, and particularly his recent years, during which time he was deprived of his eyesight.

He was possessed of a most remarkable memory, and up to the last hours of his illness, his intellect was as clear and active as that of a young man in health. Confronted by the last great change, ready for the final step from this stage of action, and fully cognizant of the fact that he had only a few days more to live, he was just as keen for the important news of the world and the local happenings as at any period of his life. Nor was he oblivious or unmindful of his most trivial obligations, and insisted upon his affairs being kept right up to the minute.

Like a leaf which had grown, not sear and yellow, on the stem, but as white as the driven snow, he finally let go his earthly support and dropped into the waiting lap of Mother earth, surrounded by relatives and friends who had gone before, and whom he felt the positive assurance of meeting and greeting once more.

Brother Palmer was a familiar figure in Cedar City. He was one of the landmarks, and he will be greatly missed and often thought of by those who are left behind.

A 10 pound baby boy was born to Mr. and Mrs. Arthur Bryant yesterday. Dr. Leonard reports that all concerned are doing nicely.

Born, to Mrs. Leland Bettenson, last Saturday, a boy. To Mrs. Henry Ashton, Tuesday, a boy. To Mrs. Wm. Sherratt, last Tuesday, twins, a boy and a girl. They lived only a few minutes.

Iron County Record
September 29, 1916

SAHARA.

Sahara, Utah, Sept. 29, 1916.

The regular meeting of the Sahara Center Civic club met with Mr. and Mrs. A. E. Markwith September 27th, in connection with the celebration of their eighth wedding anniversary, with the usual good attendance of club members. The following visitors from Newcastle were present: Mr. James Knell and daughters, Misses Mary and Iva, Miss Vera Pace, Mr. Claud Knell, Mr. Virgil Decker, Mr. A. T Jones and Mr. Robinson of Beryl.

One of the pleasant affairs of the past week was held at the home of Mrs. Arlie Fourman, on her wedding anniversary, September 20, 1916, from 10 a. m. to 4 p. m., which in reality was a stork shower in honor of Mrs. E. M. Magmussen. Following the dinner Mrs. Magmussen was the recipient of many useful and beautiful presents. Time passed quickly over the needle work and social chat. Those who participated were: Mrs. Frank Hedrick, Mrs. D. M. Pearce, Mrs. A. F. Markwith, Mrs. James Baker, Mrs. J. E. Fairley, Mrs. H. J. Patton, Mrs. G. Johnstone, Mrs. S. A. Davis, Mrs. T. K. Prey, Mrs. W. G. Bumpus, and Mrs. Chas. Jobert of Ford. Mrs. Fourman, who was assisted in serving by Mrs. Johnstone, proved a charming hostess. We all regretted Mrs. Corn's inability to be present.

SOCIALIST PARTY TICKET.

Following is a list of the nominees of the Socialist Party for county offices, as selected at a county convention held in Parowan on Saturday, the 23rd day of September:

For Representative, Robert G. Page, of Parowan.

Long term commissioner, Clark W. Lyman of Parowan.

Short term commissioner, Wm. H. Barton, of Paragonah.

County clerk, Jos. G. Stevenson, of Cedar City.

Treasurer, Isaac Bozarth, of Paragonah.

Recorder, Mrs. M. A. Gunn, of Parowan.

Sheriff, C. C. Bladen, of Cedar City.

Assessor, G. A. Gower, of Cedar City.

Attorney, A. F. Gower, of Cedar City.

MRS. W. W. DALLEY SUCCUMBS TO OPERATION.

Word has just been received here of the death at Salt Lake City of Mrs. W. W. Dalley of Summit, who was operated on for cancer, and died yesterday. The remains are being sent home for burial, and the funeral services will be held in Summit tomorrow afternoon.

Mrs. Dalley and her husband are among the old settlers of that place and are highly respected. Her many friends will be grieved to learn of her demise, and no doubt a number of people from Cedar City will be in attendance at the funeral.

One of the most harrowing and regrettable accidents that have happened in this locality occurred last Wednesday morning at an early hour to Will Urie of Hamilton's Fort, and which resulted in his death a little less than thirty hours after. The young man was unloading hay with a Jackson derrick fork, having risen early for the purpose, and in pulling the fork back out of the barn, it got to whirling as it descended and he was unable to avoid it. One tine struck him in the breast and penetrated his right lung to a distance of six or eight inches. Dr. Leonard was at once called and covered the distance of six miles to Hamilton's as quickly as possible, but found the unfortunate young man in a very precarious condition. He had bled profusely internally and his lung was filled with blood. He was weak and almost pulseless. He was rushed to the Southern Utah Hospital and everything possible done for him, but his wound proved fatal and he passed away at 10:30 Thursday.

The funeral services will be held in the Cedar City tabernacle tomorrow afternoon at 2 oclock, and interment will be made in the Cedar City cemetery.

William Urie was the son of John and Priscilla Urie of Hamilton's Fort, the aged father being in his 82nd year. That at this advanced age he should be required to witness the burial of one of his strong, robust sons seems to be an example of the irony of fate.

Deceased was 28 years of age, being born in Cedar City Sept. 10, 1888. It is rumored that he was to have been married in a month or so to one of Cedar City's attractive young women.

Will returned only about two years ago from a mision in Kentucky, being obliged to return a couple of months before the usual time on account of ill health. He was a sincere and upright young man of industrious habits and good character.

The Record sympathizes with the bereaved family in their affliction.

Iron County Record
November 17, 1916

Cannon-Corry Nuptials.

Next week Miss Lulu Corry will leave for the northern part of the state, where she will meet her fiancee in the person of Mr. Clyde Cannon of Logan, an electrician and the son of Architect Cannon of Salt Lake City.

The young people will proceed to Logan, where they will be married in the Logan Temple, after which they will return to Cedar City. As Mr. Cannon's employment requires much of his time in Milford and Frisco, it is probable that Mrs. Cannon will spend the winter or the greater part of it in Cedar City with her people.

Miss Corry is a highly respected young lady of this place, being the daughter of ex-Bishop and Mrs. W. H. Corry, and the groom is well spoken of by those having his acquaintanceship.

The Record extends congratulations and best wishes to the young people in advance of the auspicious event.

Washington County News
December 21, 1916

Mr Edgar C Jones of Cedar City and Miss Arletta Brinkerhoff of Glendale obtained a marriage license here on the 20th inst and intend being married at the St George temple

SAHARA.

Sahara, Utah, Jan. 3, 1917.

A New Year's dance was given at the Sahara school house Monday night with a large attendance. A number from Ford, Lund and Cedar City were present. Refreshments, consisting of sandwiches and coffee were served.

All departed in the wee sma' hours reporting a very enjoyable time.

A small party left Saturday morn-

...ltz and Butts, who are spending ... winter trapping there. The visit... found great sport in making the ...ounds of the traps, climbing peaks and taking pictures throughout the days. On Sunday evening a New Year watch party was held by the camp fireside. At the midnight hour the hosts served their guests with Dutch oven bread, cookies, pie and

Stage Passengers Have Nasty Experience

What came very nearly being a serious if indeed not a fatal accident, occured on the Cedar Lund road near Iron Springs last Sunday night One of David Leigh's autos left Lund with seven passengers about seven o clock in the evening but on account of trouble with the car were stranded some place on the desert for three or four hours in the blizzard which raged all through that memorable night The party was rescued from this predicament by one of the Knell Auto Line cars returning to Lund after leaving passengers at Cedar City This car was driven by Jimmie Worthington of Lund who found it impossible to hold the grade in the face of the driving blizzard and when in the vicinity of Iron Springs ran off the embankment into a reservoir

The party had to wade through the water to get out of the car and found considerable difficulty in making their way to the cabin at Iron Springs which they reached in a well nigh exhausted condition and where they had to spend the night being brought to Cedar early the next morning

Mr Knell learned by telephone of the disappearance of his car and wild with apprehension for the fate of the passengers spent the night in trying to get tidings of their whereabouts in order to render what assistance might be possible under the circumstances When sympathized with over the damage to his touring car Uncle Ben was so glad that no lives were lost that he could not talk about the car The party consisted of Mr and Mrs Sandberg and baby of Washington Miss Gubler Santa Clara James Cooper and Marcus Tegan Washington and Delos Hyatt of Parowan —Iron County Record

KANARRAVILLE.

Kanarra, Utah, Feb. 6, 1917.

A little 10 year old girl of Henry Pollock was stricken with appendicitis yesterday afternoon. Everything possible was done for her relief here, but without avail. On the advice of Dr. Macfarlane she was placed in an auto and hurried to Cedar City, where she was operated on about 8:30 this evening.

The twins of Mr. and Mrs. John W. Platt, which were born January 26, and for a time were very delicate, are thriving nicely now.

Some few days ago a coyote came to the home of Mr. W. W. Fee and engaged in a fight with his dog, which was bitten by the stranger, believed to be affected with rabies. Mr. Fee took no chances and shortly after killed the dog. We think the proposed dog tax will be a great benefit to the country, as it will do away with many of the worthless dogs, which aid the spread of rabies.

SAHARA.

Mr. Doc. Hoxie of Mountain Springs entertained a number of his friends at dinner Sunday, January 26, 1917. On the arrival of the guests one of the most delicious dinners was served. The afternoon was spent in taking kodak pictures and climbing Sugar Loaf mountain. Those who did not participate in the hike were amused by jokes and stories told by Mr. Hoxie. All agree that the host is a most excellent chef. and entertainer.

Those present were Mr. and Mrs. J. A. Baker, Mr. and Mrs. J. E. Fairley, Mr. and Mrs. Earl Freeman, Misses ___ and Carrie Hedrick, Taco-__ ___ ___ ___ Baker, Grace Magnussen and Mess. Wm. Shultz, Elvin Butts, G. C. Hutchison, A. F. Nelson, Frank Wright, F. Taylor, J. Franklin, nd E. Wunderlich.

Word was received in Cedar Wednesday of the death of Mr. Hyrum Perkins of Bluff. Mr. Perkins is a brother to the Perkins family of this place, and once resided here. His death is attributed to a bad fall which he had some time since, and which caused injuries from which he has been suffering all winter.

Born.—To Mr. and Mrs. J. U. Webster, March 15, an eight-pound boy. This is their firstborn, and they have our congratulations.

Cedar City Soon to Have Telegraph School.

On account of the recent eight hour law, there will be a great demand for Telegraph Operators. Young men and young ladies who are interested in this line of work and who wish to take a course in Telegraphy, can obtain full particulars by addressing Mrs. A. W. Johnson, Roy Croft Mail Box, Lund, Utah.—Adv.-1w.

The people of Cedar City were very much shocked and surprised to learn of the death of Mrs. Wiliam S. Smith, which occurred at her home in this city last Wednesday evening at 10:30 o'clock. Brights disease of several years standing, aggrivated by a severe case of measles, is stated as the cause of the lady's demise.

Mrs. Smith with her husband and family of seven living children came to Cedar City four years ago last July, and while they are in a sense new comers among us, Mrs. Smith made many friends and was well beloved and respe...l in the community. She was 41 years old on her last birthday.

With the exception of one daughter, Mrs. Dee Cox of Enterprise, her family is unmarried and reside at home.

The funeral services will be held tomorrow afternoon at 3 o'clock, it is thought, though all the arrangements have not yet been worked out.

The Record joins the community in extending condolence and sympathy to the stricken family.

KANARRA DISTRICT
SCHOOL NEWS PAPER

Mr. Henry Pollock and family returned home from Cedar City, where they have been for a month or so with their daughter "Lula" who has been undergoing an oppration for appendicitus.

Miss Mellonee Williams was taken to Cedar City, Sunday to have her toncils taken out. They have been troubling her for a long time.

Albert Davis'es second son "Dellle" got his arm dislocated he was taken to Cedar City and the Dr. set the displacement and put it in a plaster paris mold.

In Iron County on the first of may the County will give five cents bounty on rabbits and three cents on prairie dog's.

A flock of Seagulls were seen flying over town they were nearly white and made a very pretty sight.

WINNIE WILLIAMS, Editor.
CLAIR PLATT, Associate Ed.

Married

At the St George temple, Tuesday, March 27, Mr Samuel Stucki and Miss Ann Stewart Thorley The bride is a daughter of Mr. Richard A Thorley and the late Mrs Thorley of Cedar City, a very highly esteemed young lady The groom is a son of Mr. and Mrs John S Stucki of Santa Clara, a young man of sterling good qualities and exemplary character. They have the best wishes of a host of friends.

KANARRAVILLE.

Kanarra District School Paper.

Kanarra, Utah, April 4, 1917.

Mrs. Julia Wilkinson came from Cedar City yesterday to visit her father and mother, Mr. and Mrs. Reese Williams.

* * *

The mail truck was stranded down on the black ridge. The mail driver stopped the engine of his car while he put some water in the radiator When he looked for the crank he found he had lost it. Joel J. Roundy came along just then with a load of flour from Hurricane. He hitched on to the truck and pulled it a little way till the engine started; then the mail went on to St. George.

* * *

Arlan Davis, a student of the seventh grade of the Kanarra school, has quit school to drive the mail from Harmony to Kanarra, but found that he was too young, and now he is going to Harmony to work for Brother Prince.

The road men have hired some hands to haul gravel on the state road north of Kanarra. They will cap it so when it storms it won't be so hard to travel over.

* * *

Mrs. Emma Roundy, an old friend of the Kanarra people, was here visiting her friends and relatives recently.

* * *

Attorney E. H. Ryan was to have been down to explain incorporation to the people of Kanarra Sunday, but disappointed them by not coming.

* * *

Rebecca Platt, daughter of Mr. and Mrs. John W. Platt, has been ill for a week or so with erysipelas.

* * *

The Kanarra pupils had their quarterly examination, which the Superintendent sends out every two weeks.

CLAIR PLATT, Editor,
FAYETT PARKER, associate.

Pasture Treatment for Rabies Now Given in Cedar City.

Dr. A. N. Leonard, who went to Salt Lake City last week with a number of patients, including the S. R. Jones child to be treated for a bite from a rabid dog, returned the fore part of this week, bringing the child back with him. The Doctor states that he has been instructed in the administration of the pasteur treatment for rabies, and that he has been appointed Dr. Beatty's assistant to administer the treatment locally.

This will be good news to the people of this section of the country who may have occasion to obtain the treatment, since it will save them the expense of a trip to and prolonged stay in Salt Lake. The medicine, or virus, used is supplied by the government.

Miss Nellie Lunt entertained at luncheon Wednesday, in compliment to Mrs. Robertson, who is visiting here with her brother, Mr. George Hughes. Other guests were, Mrs. John Urie and Miss Ramona Clark.

Mr. and Mrs. Henry Ashton left last Sunday for Salt Lake City, where they will remain for a short time, when Mrs. Ashton will go on to Bluff and spend the summer with her mother.

Miss Lena Myers of Minersville is the guest of her sister, Mrs. Ray Thomas, of this city, for several weeks.

Miss Genevieve Ford is one of the latest victims of the measles, having come down with it Wednesday. However, she is not suffering a great deal from it.

Mr. and Mrs. S. J. Foster have a very sick child, their son Morris, as a result of complications developing from an attack of measles. For two or three days the little fellow's life has hung in the balance, but we are pleased to learn that he is a little better today.

The little three-year-old son of Thomas Stapley fell from a fence last Tuesday and broke his arm in the elbow joint. Dr. Macfarlane has the case in hand and states that it is a very serious break.

Bishop and Mrs. H. H. Lunt have the congratulations of The Record on the arrival of another son at their home April 23. Mother and babe are reported in prime condition.

Lunt-Dalton Nuptials.

Thursday of last week a very quiet wedding took place in Beaver court house, the contracting parties being Miss Aleen Dalton of Minersville and Mr. Walter Lunt of this place.

The bride is a daughter of Mr. and Mrs. T. W. Dalton, and is well respected and a popular young lady of high standing.

The groom is an industrous and well-respected member of one of the oldest and best known Cedar families, and will doubtless make a model husband.

After spending a few days in Minersville the young people will come on to Cedar City and will make their home here in the future.

SAHARA.

Mrs. C. H. Hunt and children from near Lund, are visiting Mr. and Mrs. Baker.

* * *

Mrs. Phillips, Mr. and Mrs. Baker, Mrs. Hunt and families were guests at "Doc" Hoxie Sunday. We will wager that they had an excellent dinner, as we can vouch for "Doc" being an A 1 cook.

Mrs. James Fairley is suffering from a badly swollen throat and glands under her tongue. She has tried various remedies without relief. The whole thing started apparently from a severe toothache.

Iron County Record
May 5, 1917

Born—To Mr. and Mrs. Joshua Walker, May 2nd, a girl.

A report has been received from the state bacteriologist confirming the suspicion of rabies in the coyote which visited one of the Sheep Association's flocks last week, killing 17 sheep and biting a number of others. All the sheep known to have been bitten by the animal and not already dead will be killed. The bitten sheep were separated from the remainder of the flock and were held pending the report on the coyote's head sent in.

Dr. Leonard reports that Morris Foster, the little son of Mr. and Mrs. S. J. Foster, who was so dangerously ill last week, is now recovering very nicely.

Mr. R. D. Adams has a child suffering from a severe case of St. Vitas Dance.

Thomas C. King, father of Mrs. R. B. Sherratt, with his family is moving from Coyote, Garfield county, to this place and wil in future make his home here.

Iron County Record
May 11, 1917

Tuesday night Dr. Macfarlane was summoned to Harmony to care for Mr. Sid Goddard, who was found to be suffering from an acute and serious attack of appendicitis. He was brought to this city and operated on at the Macfarlane hospital. It was found that the appendix had ruptured and formed a large abcess, and while the patient is doing as well as could be expected under the circumstances, his condition is exceedingly grave.

SAHARA

The emigrant car of Messrs. Burnes and Phillips arrived this week.

٭ ٭

Mrs. Pearce and mother, Mrs. McElroy, entertained Miss Hedrick, Mrs. Anderson and mother, Mrs. Nelson, and Mr. Shultz Sunday at dinner.

Guy Johnson reports Howland as better but far from cured. Howland is expecting to leave the springs for Los Angeles soon.

Iron County Record
May 18, 1917

Saturday an eight pound boy was born to Mr. and Mrs. J. N. Smith.

———×———

Fresh vegetables—asparagus, radishes, lettuce and onions at Leigh & Biederman's market.

Mrs. Wilford Fife has gone to Kanab to attend the funeral of her brother, who was accidentally shot while in Nevada.

———×———

Mr. and Mrs. George Ashdown are rejoicing over the arrival of a baby boy which came to their home a few days ago.

Mr. John Hamilton of Hamilton's Fort and Miss Genevieve Ford of this place, were married in the St. George Temple last Friday. The bride is a daughter of Mrs. William Ford of this place and is a well respected and talented young lady. The groom is the son of Mr. and Mrs. John Hamilton, and is a young man of high standing and of sterling qualities. The young people will make their home in Hamilton's Fort in the future.

Dr. Leonard Reports.

Mrs. Berry Williams of Kanarraville, who was operated upon last week for appendicitis, will be ready to leave the hospital the fore part of next week.

Miss Jean Urie, who was operated upon for appendicitis last Thursday, is improving very nicely.

Levona Parry, the little daughter of Mr. and Mrs. Isaac Parry, was operated on for appendicitis last Saturday, and is now ready to leave the hospital. This is the fifth operation that Miss Parry has undergone in the last six years, and it is certainly to be hoped that her health will be better from now on.

Dr. Leonard had a midnight call to

Harmony last Wednesday night to attend Mrs. Lawrence Prince, and the result was a fine baby boy at the Prince home Thursday morning.

Last week a fine baby girl was born to Mr. and Mrs. Will Wood of this city.

Iron County Record
Iron County Record
May 25, 1917

———×———

Born—To Mr. and Mrs. Thomas Bulloch Wednesday morning, a baby girl. All concerned getting along tip top.

———×———

Miss Rose Lunt, the fifteen year old daughter of Mr. and Mrs. Oscar Lunt, was operated on at the Macfarlane Hospital last night for acute appendicitis. The patient is progressing nicely from last reports.

Last Wednesday Milo Heyborne was thrown from a horse, breaking his collar bone. Dr. Macfarlane was called and reduced the fracture and made the patient as comfortable as possible.

———×———

Born to Mr. and Mrs. Thomas Mumford, a girl, last week.

———×———

KANARRA

Kanarra, Utah, May 30, 1917.

Mr. and Mrs. W. W. Roundy were up from their ranch last Saturday doing some shopping.

❀ ❀

John Stapley, Wallie Pollock and Ren Williams, with their families, have moved on to their farms south of town to be nearer their work.

❀ ❀

Ren Davis and family have also moved to their farm at Dry Creek to remain for a few days.

❀ ❀

Mr. and Mrs. John G. Smith returned home a few days ago from Salt Lake City, where they have spent the winter with their children. The girls live there and the boys found employment there all winter.

❀ ❀

Raymond Williams left Monday for his sheep herd northeast of Paragonah. David Davis went to the Stapley farm about four or five miles south of town to plant beans with his corn planter for Myron S. Roundy, Jr., last Monday. He expects to put in 25 acres, double-planting the rows.

❀ ❀

Mrs. Hannah Williams is having her house remodelled, the old porches torn away and new ones erected in their stead.

❀ ❀

George Roundy and his sister Lizzie were in town on a visit to their grandmother and other relatives, and also purchasing supplies for the sheep herd that George is working with.

❀ ❀

J. Wallace Williams went to Cedar last Monday with his wife, who was operated on at the Southern Utah Hospital. At last reports she was getting along fine.

❀ ❀

Last Monday evening Berry Williams brought his wife home from the Southern Utah Hospital, where she was operated on two weeks ago. She is rejoicing that she robbed the grave and is feelong as well as could be expected.

SAHARA.

Charles J. Hellings went to Enterprise for hay one day this week.

Mr. Earl Markwith has received his patent for his claim. We are glad of this, and we wish him the best of success in the years to come.

Messrs. Baker, Pearce, and Miss Laura Hedrick took dinner with Mrs. S. A. Davis Thursday.

❀ ❀

Mr. Reynolds is visiting his family this week.

W. J. Williams has been around town a few days, after having been out with the sheep all winter, for the Cedar Mercantile & Livestock Co.

❅ ❅

Arnold Graff is having his house finished up now, after a delay of several months. Thomas Perry of Cedar City is doing the carpentry work, and a Mr. Cottam of St. George has the contract for the plastering.

❅ ❅

Messrs. Cox and Merryweather, the plumbers, were here Monday and Tuesday plumbing George Berry's home on North Main street.

❅ ❅

Othello Roundy and family have moved here from Upper Kanab, and will make their home with us.

❅ ❅

Another rain today continuing nearly all afternoon. We will surely have some bumper crops if the spring weather continues much longer. The hay and grain crops look fine now, and the soil is in splendid shape for corn, beans, potatoes and garden truck.

❅ ❅

Registration Day June 5th seems to worry some of the young men, also some of the women don't feel any too well about it. They feel that if the men could do their scrapping on our own land it wouldn't be so bad.

❅ ❅

Yesterday the last child of Mr. and Mrs. Ren. Williams broke out with measles, after they had moved to the farm.

❅ ❅

Another rain today continuing nearly all afternoon. We will surely have some bumper crops if the spring weather continues much longer. The hay and grain crops look fine now, and the soil is in splendid shape for corn, beans, potatoes and garden truck.

❅ ❅

Registration Day June 5th seems to worry some of the young men, also some of the women don't feel any too well about it. They feel that if the men could do their scrapping on our own land it wouldn't be so bad.

❅ ❅

Yesterday the last child of Mr. and Mrs. Ren. Williams broke out with measles, after they had moved to the farm.

The above is a picture taken just before their departure of the three first young men to go from Cedar City for the purpose of investigating conditions and offering their services in the defense of their country. Reading from right to left they are Corlett Simkins, Gordon Hunter, Austin Merryweather.

WALTER HANSON.

MARRIES WIFE BEFORE ENLISTING IN THE NAVY

Last Monday evening at the home of Mr. and Mrs. Evan Wiliams a very quiet wedidng took place, when Miss Ruth Williams and Mr. Walter Hanson were united in marriage. Only the immediate members of the families of the bride and goom were present. Bishop H. H. Lunt performed the cermony. Later in the evening a reception was given in honor of the young people, which was attended by a large number of their friends and relatives.

The young couple left Wednesday for Salt Lake City, where it is the intention of Mr. Hanson to enlist in the U. S. Navy. Mrs. Hanson will remain with him until he leaves for San Francisco to join his company, after which she will return here to await his coming back from the war.

Both the bride and goom are popular and progressive young people in the community, and we regret the necessity that calls Walter away at this time. We wish to congratulate him on the step taken and also to commend him for being one of the first recruits from Cedar City. We join with his many friends in wishing him good luck while he is away.

War Spirit Reaches Cedar City.

Although Cedar City was rather backward in the furnishing of recruits for the army and navy, she is now rapidly making up for lost time. Within the last week there have been seven boys leave for Salt Lake City to proffer their services to the government. The first ones left here last Saturday afternoon. They were Mr. Austin Merryweather, Gordon Hunter and Corlett Simkins; early Sunday morning Eugene Woodbury and Pratt Tollestrup left in Gene's Saxon roadster to drive through to Salt Lake.

Catching the fever from the other boys who had gone, Lawrence Haslem hurriedly packed his grip and caught the train Sunday, and was the first to be honored with a uniform from Uncle Sam, from Cedar City. The other volunteer to complete the seven is Walter Hanson, who left yesterday to join the navy.

Iron County Record
June 8, 1917

Monday evening at the home of Bishop H. H. Lunt Miss Josephine Harris and Lionel Dover were united in marriage. Miss Alcione Dover and Moroni Smith acted as witnesses at the ceremony.

Dr. Leonard reports a baby boy at the home of Mr. and Mrs. S. R. Jones. All doing well.

Mr. and Mrs. Mosell of Latimer, this county, brought their little four-year-old daughter to the Southern Utah Hospital, in practically a dying condition with intestinal hemorrhage, last Monday afternoon. The little one was beyond relief and succumbed three hours after arrival. She was interred in the local cemetery, last Tuesday.

Tuesday, June 5th, Miss Naomi Perkins and Mr. Edwin Webb were married at the home of Mrs. Emma Webb, the goom's mother, Bishop H. H. Lunt officiating at the ceremony. Only the immediate members of the family were present. The bride is a daughter of Mrs. Lottie Perkins of this place, and is a well respected young lady in the comumnity. The groom is a son of Mr. and Mrs. Abe Webb and is also well respected, being an ambitious and progressive youth. The Record joins with their many friends in wishing them a long and happy life together.

Hunter Schoppmann Nuptials.

Mr. Washington Hunter and Miss Rebecca Schoppmann slipped quietly away to Parowan last Monday, where after a visit to the County Clerk's office they were united in marriage by Bishop Mortenson of Parowan. The party was accompanied by Mrs. Marcia Pexton, a sister of the groom, and were driven up by H. C. Bement.

The bride is one of Cedar City's estimable daughters, and well known in church circles.

The groom is the son of Mr. and Mrs. George R. Hunter and worthy of all the good luck there is coming to him.

The Record wishes the young people health, happiness and prosperity.

KANARRA

Kanarra, Utah, June 6, 1917.
Registration Day, June 5, was a day long to be remembered in Kanarra. A rousing meeting was held in the forenoon and some sports in the afternoon. It reminded people of Independence Day. All work was suspended and everybody was out and had a good time. 32 names were registered.

S. T. Ford has been to Cedar City the past few days learning to run his new Ford car, which he has just purchased from the local agent.

A few of the sheep shearers commenced shearing for James Berry today.

W. J. Williams went to Cedar today to consult Dr. Leonard about a bad sore that has been on his neck for the past three months. He phoned home to his wife that it would be necessary for him to undergo an operation which would be performed at 10 o'clock tomorrow. As a result his wife and father go to Cedar tonight to be at the operation.

The Misses Luella and Hattie Williams, also Miss Clara Mortensen left today on the mail car to take in the M. I. A. conference and enjoy an out. Miss Mortensen, who has been residing with Mr. and Mrs. Reese J. Williams, will remain in Salt Lake City for a while, at least, and the Williams girls will return in a few days.

After a long and distressing illness with goiter and complications involving the heart, Mrs. Hattie Gower, wife of Mr. A. F. Gower, was released from her bed of suffering last Tuesday. For the last several weeks her condition has been such that the hand of a merciful providence is acknowledged in her final release.

Harriet Jane Corry Gower was born in Cedar City, Dec. 25, 1860. She was the youngest child in a family of 12, five of whom survive her—three boys and two girls. She was married to John T. Gower in the St. George temple, October 8, 1879, and with her husband answered a call to help settle Bluff City, Utah. After a three years residence there, the failing health of her husband compelled their return to Cedar City, where Mr. Gower died in November of 1885. She was married to Albert F. Gower, a brother of her deceased husband, in September, 1904. Four children are living, the issue of her first marriage and six gandchildren.

Sister Gower was a faithful church worker as long as her health would permit, being a Relief Society teacher in the West ward for a number of years. She was a devoted mother, always considering her chldren before herself, and was always on hand to help any one in sickness and trouble.

The Record extends sympathy and condolence to all members of the bereaved family.

Funeral services were held in the tabernacle yesterday afternoon at 3 o'clock.

Opening prayer was offered by Joseph Armstrong and the closing prayer by Samuel T. Leigh. The scakers were Elders John Parry, Lehi W. Jones, Joseph T. Wilkinson and U. T. Jones. They spoke generally of the home-making qualities of the deceased, always found at her post and with only good to say about everybody.

Mrs. Elora Bryant, supported by the choir, rendered the vocal selection, "I Need Thee Every Hour."

Mr. Cassidy Root is employed at the Cedar Mercantile & Live Stock Company's store, while he is awaiting orders to report for duty at the training camps.

The litle son of Dr. Petty, who was injured in the automobile accident last week, is improving nicely, the critical period having been passed, though he will carry the scars to his grave.

Mr. and Mrs. John Dalley and family motored down from Summit yesterday, interviewing the business people of Cedar City.

The 16 year old son of Emanuel Jacobson entered the Macfarlane Hospital last Wednesday and had a 38 calibre bullet removed from his shoulder, which he received accidentally a number of years ago. The bullet had begun to trouble him of late, interfering with the motion of the muscles.

Mr. and Mrs. W. J. McConnell are spending a few days in town, resting after the severe ordeal they have been through in the death of their brother. They will return to LaVerkin next Sunday.

Miss Ina Leigh now occupies the position of head nurse at the Macfarlane Hospital.

Mr. and Mrs. Arthur Fife are receiving congratulations on the arrival of a fine boy on the 10th inst. Dr. Leonard should arrange his work so that he will be better able to observe the Sababth.

Roy McConnell, the fifteen-year-old son of Mr. and Mrs. George B. McConnell, was taken suddenly sick last Tuesday night while attending the picture show and had to be taken home for assistance. His symptoms gave strong indications of ptomaine poisoning. As he was at the camp with his father at the time his poisoning took place it is believed Roy's sickness was traceable to the same origin.

SHOCKING DEATH OF G. B. McCONNELL

Former Resident of this Place Falls Dead on Range at Night While Rounding Up Sheep.

In the demise of George B. McConnell, who was buried here last Monday, Cedar City is again called to mourn the passing of one of her native born sons, and under unusually distressing conditions. For the past two years George has resided in Hurricane, and was engaged in caring for a flock of sheep out in the vicinity of Antelope. Last Sunday evening Bert Anderson of Echo Farm came in as a special messenger conveying the information that Mr. McConnell had been missing from the sheep camp since Friday night, under peculiar circumstances. It seems that he had arisen in the night to round up the sheep which had left their bedding ground, telling his son and brother-in-law, who were with him at the camp, that he could get the sheep back alone, and for them to remain in bed. When they awoke in the morning, he had not returned and they started out to look for him, but the search proved unavailing. After searching for him all that day and the following night without results, Roy, the 15 year old son of the unfortunate man, was dispatched to Hurricane to obtain help. Sheriff Al. Hartley, Wilson Imlay, Dr. Wilkinson, W. J. McConnell, brother of the mising man, and a number of other citizens responded as soon as possible, but it was not until 6 o'clock on Sunday evening that Sheriff Hartley, accompanied by Roy, the boy, came upon the lifeless body, lying only about a mile and a half from the camp. The body was in such a state of decomposition through lying two days in Dixie's burning sun, that anything like a post-mortem was impossible, but the doctor pronounced ptomaine poisoning as the probable cause of death, through eating canned corn and jam for supper, and then as his tracks indicated, running after the sheep and becoming over heated, thus setting up a fermentation which hastened the work of the disease germs.

As soon as word was received here that the man was missing, LaFayette McConnell and Robert W. Bulloch, brother and brother-in-law, respectively, of the deceased, set out to assist in the search, but passed on an adjacant road the corpse already on its way to Cedar City, being conveyed by his brother Wiliam J. and Mr. Stout. They went only as far as Hurricane and returned, reaching here about five o'clock Monday morning.

Due to the condition of the body, funeral services were held Monday at 11 o'clock, at the residence of LaFayette McConnell. In the absence of Bishop Lunt, the services were conducted by Counsellor Calvin Pendleton. Opening Prayer was offered by Elder H. W. Lunt, and the benediction was pronounced by Elder Samuel T. Leigh. Vocal solos were beautifully rendered by Miss Helen Nelson and Mrs. Annette Bettenson. "Nearer My God to Thee" was given by the choir, led by Mr. Salt. The speakers were Bishop Matheson of the West Ward, Elder Jos. T. Wilkinson and Superintendent Nutall. Interment in the city cemetery was witnessed by a large circle of relatives and friends.

BIOGRAPHICAL.

George Barrett McConnell was born in Cedar City on March 4, 1875. He was the son of Henry H. and Eliza McConnell, the latter of whom survives her son, though in rather feeble health, and to whom the tragic death of her youngest living son, comes as a severe and almost unbearable trial.

He was married in 1901 to Miss Rebecca Pollock. Besides the widow, four minor children are left to mourn his loss, the eldest 15 and the youngest 8 years of age. He was devoted to his family, who feel his loss an almost unendurable affliction.

SOLDIER BOYS GIVEN OVATION

Big Automobile Parade and Patriotic Speeches Mark the Departure of Soldiers.

LADS SEE IMPORTANCE OF "GETTING IN RIGHT"

Last Monday, to Strains of Inspiring Music and With Old Glory Flowing on Every Side, Volunteers Take Leave of Families and Friends.

Last Monday, June 11th, was a day long to be remembered in the history of Cedar City, particularly by the volunteers leaving for the training camps, and by their many relatives and friends, and will not soon be forgotten by the people generally. It was an inspiring sight—the long line of automobiles which formed the procession that escorted the boys around town and beyond the outskirts of the city, to the inspiring music discoursed by the brass band, and amid the numerous flags and decorations with national colors.

After parading the principal streets the crowd drew up in front of the Co-op. Store, where a circle was left clear for the volunteers in front of the portico, from which the names of the patriots, not only from Cedar City, but two from Parowan and those from Washington county, were read, each being greeted with a round of applause.

Ex-Senator H. W. Lunt addressed those assembled.

At the close of the services, which were necessarily brief, in order to connect with the train at Lund, the procession accompanied the recruits beyond the city limits, after which the greater number of the automobiles returned home, a few, however, continuing on to Lund.

Following are the names of the volunteers sharing in the farewell proceedings:

From Cedar City.—Grant Walker, Erwin Walker, Brayner Wood, Arthur Haight, Ray Renshaw, Charles Pratt, George Corry.

From Parowan.—Orlando Adams, Wilford Bentley.

From St. George.—Brigham Randall, Clifford Hunt, Grant Grace, M. McMurtie.

From Toquerville.—Donald Forsyth and Kenneth Forsyth.

From Harrisburg.—Mr. ——Forsyth.

With the exception of two—Erwin Walker of this place and Mr. Forsyth of Harrisburg, the boys passed their final physical examinations, and are said to be the finest specimens of young manhood that have thus far mustered into service in this state.

A slight defect in one of his ears is said to be responsible for Erwin Walker being rejected, but we are of the opinion that the fact of his having a widowed mother and dependent minor sisters had much more to do with his being returned home.

The boys who have voluntarily enlisted have seen the advantage of "getting in right," for there is no question but that the man who volunteers his services to the government will receive the preference over the man who has to be drafted or forced into the service.

Corporal Ashby of the Salt Lake Recruiting Station, has been promoted to the office of sergeant, and is now in Cedar City again, accompanied by Corporal Leadbetter, also a Utah boy. These gentlemen can be found at the Cedars Hotel and will be pleased to explain all the conditions of the service and the advantage of enlistment over conscription to any young men interested.

Iron County Record
June 22, 1917

Miss Vera Rose was operated on at the Macfarlane Hospital for the removal of tonsils.

Mr. John H. Williams of Kanarra was in town yesterday and deposited a V with the Red Cross committee.

The friends of Miss Martha Langford and Mr. Erastus Jones will be pleased to learn of their marriage the first part of the week in the Salt Lake Temple. Both of the young people are well known in this community and are well respected. The bride is the daughter of Mrs. Lorena Langford of Summit, and is a graduate of the Branch Agricultural College. She is a talented musician. Mr. Jones is the son of Mr. and Mrs. Lehi W. Jones of this place, and is an ambitious and progressive young man. The young people were accompanied to Salt Lake by Mrs. Jones. They will return to make their home here.

SAHARA

Mr. J. A. Baker has accepted a position with Mr. Bawhes on the latter's ranch north of Sahara.

Guy Johnson went to Cedar City this week to have some teeth operated upon. He has our unbounded sympathy.

Mr. Peter B. Fife, accompanied by his daughter Emma and niece Miss Adrean Simkins left for Salt Lake City last Tuesday on a short visit.

Mrs. Parley Dalley and Mrs. Ed. Nisson, who were operated on at the Macfarlane Hospital last week, have sufficiently recovered to be moved to private homes.

Haight-Trimmer Union.

Miss Kathleen Haight, one of Cedar City's popular society girls, was married last Monday to Mr. Michael Trimmer. The bride is the daughter of Mr. and Mrs. Caleb Haight of this city. We are unable to get any definite information regarding the groom, but have sufficient confidence in the judgment of the young lady to predict a successful and happy voyage on the barque of matrimony, for the happy couple.

KANARRA

Kanarra, Utah, July 5, 1917.

Leland Stapley and Kumen and Wells Williams came in from the sheep camps to spend the Fourth.

Haying is on in earnest now, with the crop in general much better than for a number of years past. The water supply is keeping up fine, and all the crops look prosperous.

The Fourth passed very quietly here. The parade in the morning that was planned for failed to materialize. There should have been floats by the various organizations, but the only float seen was Old Glory.

Mr. and Mrs. George Wood and sister Jennie of Hurricane, Miss Mary Openshaw of Paragonah, Mr. and Mrs. Percy Wilkinson of Cedar City, besides a number of people from the outlying ranches were here to spend the Fourth.

The booze catchers could have made a good haul here on the 4th, but the local authorities were powerless to curtail the evil, because the only laws we have are the 1907 statute, and that does not apply to the present conditions.

THREE HURT IN AUTO ACCIDENT

Two Powerful Cedar City Cars Collide Head on Near Town July Fourth.

MRS. BULLOCH AND MRS SMITH ARE HURT

A very horrifying automobile accident, which although attended with quite serious results could, nevertheless have been much more terrible in its consequences, occurred on the afternoon of July 4th two or three miles west of this city.

As a result of the collision between two large machines loaded with passengers, Mrs. David C. Bulloch is in quite a serious condition with her cheek bone broken and caved in, Mrs. J. N. Smith has a smashed nose, and her little boy has a hole punched into his cheek just below his eye. None of the injuries are likely to prove fatal, but they are extremely painful and may result in serious disfigurement.

The two cars are quite badly demolished, but can be repaired.

It was after the games were over at the Fair ground that Delbert Smith was driving his mother, aunt and some children in their large gray National car west on the state highway in the direction of Lund, and was met by David C. Bulloch and family in their big seven-passenger Buick car. Mr. Bulloch had just passed up a Ford car and was on the left-hand side of the road when he met the Smith car. He was afraid of being "pinched" between the Ford car that was going in the same direction as himself and the National if he attempted to cross to the right-hand side of the road, and losing his head for a moment bore to the left. Mr. Smith in pursuance of the rules of traffic turned to the same side of the road and in a second, before anyone had time to think, the two big machines came together with a terrible impact, which was slightly reduced, however, by both drivers applying the brakes and meeting in a diagonal direction.

Other cars were soon upon the scene and assisted the unfortunate people to town, where at the local hospitals they received the best possible care.

The National car was able to make it into town on its own power, though very difficult to steer. The Buick was towed in by one of the garage men the following day.

Fortunately nobody was killed, and we trust that this accident, serious though it be, may prove as a warning to all drivers to use more care and perhaps prevent yet more serious accidents in the future.

Mrs. Joseph Williams of Kanarra was operated on at the Southern Utah Hospital last Monday for goiter.

———×———

Mrs. Annabella Schmutz Rencher of Pine Valley was operated on last Monday at the Macfarlane Hospital for female trouble.

———×———

Dr. Macfarlane reports that Robert Mumford, Jr., was the victim of an accident last week which resulted in the fracture of a thigh bone.

———×———

The little son of Mr. and Mrs. John H. Williams of Kanarra, was operated upon for Hernia last Monday by Drs. Middleton and Leonard at the Southern Utah Hospital.

———×———

Mr. Richard Bryant has been in a serious condition for the past few days, caused by a fall from the loft of his barn, breaking two ribs and causing other internal injuries. Dr. Macfarlane was called and now reports his condition as steadily improving.

———×———

Mrs. Ballard withstood the shock of the operation and rallied nicely from the anaesthetic, and appeared to be on the road to recovery until yesterday evening, when she seemed to be sinking. The most potent and powerful stimulants were employed, but appeared to have little or no effect, and she continued to sink, expiring shortly after six o'clock.

MAYBE MATHESON ACCIDENTALLY SHOT

Ball From 32 Cal. Pistol Passes Through Abdomen Piercing Intestine Five Times.

INJURIES REPAIRED AND BOY HAS CHANCE

Elder Brother Discharges Weapon While Trying to Remove Wet Cartridges from Magazine.

At the time of going to press word is received that Maybe Matheson has just died, dashing to the ground the hopes that had risen in the breasts of his parents and other relatives and friends for his ultimate recovery. No arrangements have been made yet for the funeral.

One of the most heroic fights for life that has been witnessed in Cedar City for a long time, is being put up over at the Southern Utah Hospital by Maybe Matheson, the 11 year old son of Mr. and Mrs. Dan. E. Matheson, who reside two or three miles from Enoch, in this valley.

Maybe and his brother Dwayne, who is a few years his senior, were watering in the field. The older boy had the pistol in his pocket and in turning the water it fell from his pocket into the stream. He picked it up and was in the act of removing the cartridges, his brother sitting on the opposite bank of the ditch, when the weapon was accidentally discharged, the ball entering the younger boy's abdomen in the vicinity of the naval and coming out through his hip bone.

The boy was rushed to the Southern Utah Hospital and was operated on by Drs. Leonard and Macfarlane, but not until between three and four hours had elapsed. It was found that the bullet had pierced the intestine in five places. The repairs were made as neatly as possible and every precaution known to modern surgery was taken, but at best it was conceded by such authority as Dr. Middleton, who was here the following day, that the boy had a very slim chance, indeed, for his life. However, five days have now passed and while the lad is in a desperate condition, with a general peritonitis, he appears to be holding his own, and every hour the chances are multiplying for his recovery. If he survives the next 24 hours Dr. Leonard states that he will feel very sanguine of saving him.

Miss Vera Bringhurst is spending a week or two in town visiting with Mrs. S. R. Wilkinson, her sister.

———————X———————

Painter and Paperhanger. T. F. Brady, Cedar City, Utah.

Mr. and Mrs. William Stewart of Alemo, Nevada, motored over to Cedar City the latter part of last week and picked up Mrs. J. P. Fuller, who is a sister of Mrs. Stewart, and continued on to Kanab for a week's visit. Mrs. Fuller is expected home shortly.

———————X———————

Mrs. R. W. Bulloch and children moved to their mountain ranch last Tuesday, to avoid the rest of the hot weather for this season.

Cedar City was in a state of excitement last Saturday over the absence from his parents and family of litle Kimball Haslam, son of Mr. and Mrs. Jos. E. Haslam, from the Haslam farm about 4 miles from town. The litle child was gone from 9 a. m. until 7:30 p. m., when he was found about a couple of miles from home by one of the Jenson boys.

There was quite a large searching party out looking for the lost child nearly all afternoon, and the search was in progress on a smaller scale much of the forenoon. The parents were well-nigh distracted.

The little chap was apparently none the worse for the experience when found.

———————X———————

Dr. Leonard reports a boy at the residence of Mr. and Mrs. Walter Harris born last Sunday and a boy to Mr. and Mrs. Lemuel Stevens last week.

Dr. Macfarlane was called to Harmony last Monday to attend the bedside of Mrs. Delbert Woolsey. After thoroughly diagnosing her case the Doctor pronounced it a 10-pound soldier for Uncle Sam.

———————X———————

Following is the order of drawing and the names corresponding to the first 202 numbers drawn at Washington, D. C., applicable to the Iron County Registration List. The numbers at the left of the columns show the order in which the serial numbers were drawn, the registration numbers not being given in this list. Iron County's quoto of the half million army to be raised, is 46 men, and twice this number is required to report for the first examination, which will be held next week by the local board. If these 92 names fail to yield 46 eligible soldiers, the board will go on down the list in the order here published until sufficient men are mustered to fill our quoto:

1—Thomas Lund, Modena.
2—Henry M. Jones, Enoch.
3—Archie Wilson, Heist.
4—Clarence Burger, Beryl.
5—George H. Lunt, Cedar City.
6—Geo. Albert Gower, Cedar City.
7—Edgar Mortensen, Parowan.
8—Horace Ray Skougard, Parowan.
9—Edgar A. Thornton, Paragonah.
10—Lawrence Clark, Cedar City.
11—Charles Mosdell, Hamilton's Fort.
12—Henry Webster Leigh, Cedar City.
13—Frank Parker, Kanarra.
14—William A. Olds, Kanarra.
15—Rowland Orton, Parowan.
16—Fred Wall (Indian) Cedar City.
17—Irvin R. Billingsley, Lund.
18—Edwin Webb, Cedar City.
19—Carlos Walker, Cedar City.
20—George C. Hamilton, Beryl.
21—Elias Leigh, Cedar City.
22—James A. Hyatt, Parowan.
23—Brayner Wood, Cedar City.
24—George Chidester, Pennsylvania.
25—Wilford Benson, Parowan.
26—Ellis Bentley, Parowan.
27—Joseph E. Topham, Paragonah.
28—Wilford E. Sylvester, Heist.
29—Silos Owen, Paragonah.
30—Ephraim Dailey, Paragonah.
31—Durham Morris, Parowan.
32—George Stanley Perry, Cedar City.
33—Gerald R. Eldridge, Beryl.
34—William Pucell, Cedar City.
35—William L. Evans, Parowan.
36—Pedro Ramier, Lund.
37—John Wade, Nada.
38—Claud L. Heist, Heist.
39—Corlett Simkins, Cedar City.
40—Lawrence J. Adams, Parowan.
41—Harvey Rosenberg, Cedar City.
42—Oliver Jenson, Cedar City.
43—William E. Thornton, Parowan.
44—Guy Caldwalder, Beryl.
45—J. Elmer Ray, Cedar City.
46—John S. Dalton, Parowan.
47—Stanley Benson, Parowan.
48—John Lewis Burton, Cedar City.
49—Kaleb A. Sparks, Cedar City.
50—Alvin Lloyd Couch, Lund.

51—George W. Koest, Parowan.
52—Arthur Thomas Marcell, Nada.
53—Norman Gouge, Cedar City.
54—Lewis A. Nelson, Cedar City.
55—Wilford Hunter, Cedar City.
56—William Archie Bond, Modena.
57—Peter Bulloch, Cedar City.
58—Reuben Jones, Enoch.
59—Tom W. Wright, Cedar City.
60—Miles Hunter, Cedar City.
61—Carter Ernest Lee, Beryl.
62—Herbert Fretwell, Cedar City.
63—Claud Harris, Parowan.
64—Bunichi Kumruira, Japan.
65—Charles Hendrickson, Lund.
66—William R. McGinty, Nada.
67—Joseph A. Ingram, Cedar City.
68—John L. Burton, Cedar City.
69—Sam. J. Whitney, Parowan.
70—Hart Hoxie, Lund.
71—Tom Fisher, Enoch.
72—Jesse C. Roundy, Kanarra.
73—Charles R. Graff, Nada.
74—Raymond Haight, Cedar City.
75—Edward Morgan Edwards, Paragonah.
76—Robert L. Halterman, Parowan.
77—Joseph H. Allen, Parowan.
78—Benjamin Harris Matheson, Nada.
79—Albert Spencer Benson, Parowan.
80—George O. Martineau, Cedar City.
81—John V. Schoppmann, Cedar City.
82—Marion Nephi Robb, Paragonah.
83—Erastus Heyborne Macfarlane, Cedar City.
84—David Otto Tullis, Newcastle.
85—Willard M. Perkins, Cedar City.
86—Oscar Julius Thompson, Lund.
87—William Hogan, Modena.
88—Joseph D. Foster, Cedar City.
89—Chester Harrison Hazelwood, Lund.

90—Parley Dalley, Cedar City.
91—James C. Pendleton, Cedar City.
92—Joseph Mitchell Dooley, Heist.
93—George tapley, Cedar City.
94—Fernleigh Gardner, Cedar City.
95—Frank Eugene Taylor, Parowan.
96—Charles F. Hulet, Newcastle.
97—Morris Burton Lyman, Parowan.
98—Mark C. McMullen, Cedar City.
99—Walter Hanson, Cedar City.
100—Frank L. Noyes, Parowan.
101—Ernest Calvin Robinson, Paragonah.
102—Hyrum T. Jones, Enoch.
103—Orson J. Bryant, Cedar City.
104—Ether Perry, Cedar City.
105—Rufus Bradshaw, Parowan.
106—John A. Booth, Cedar City.
107—James E. Worthington, Parowan.
108—Ed. G. Matheson, Parowan.
109—Thomas A. Robinson, Paragonah.
110—Leland C. Stapley, Kanarra.
111—Thomas A. Decker, Parowan.
112—Ervin Dustin, Cedar City.
113—Wilford Leigh, Cedar City.
114—George H. Corry, Cedar City.
115—John Ed. Houchen, Cedar City.
116—George Stanley Prothero, Paragonah.
117—Otto P. Dalley, Summit.
118—Treharne Leigh, Cedar City.
119—Kenneth Roylance, Cedar City.
120—Don Orton, Parowan.

121—Kumen Leigh, Cedar City.
122—Harold Mitchell, Parowan.
123—Oscar J. Thompson, Lund.
124—Conrad Hunter, Cedar City.
125—Willard Walker Jones, Enoch.
126—Glen Simkins, Cedar City.
127—George Tullis, Newcastle.
128—Ray S. Thomas, Cedar City.
129—John S. Mitchell, Parowan.
130—Delbert Farnsworth, Summit.
131—Wesley G. Bush, Prout.
132—Fred L. Biederman, Cedar City.
133—Cecil L. Pinder, Parowan.
134—David Sharp, Cedar City.
135—Elvid Williams, Cedar City.
136—C. B. Mannell, Lund.
137—William A. Haigh, Prout.
138—Frank C. Mitchell, Parowan.
139—Francis Dalton, Cedar City.
140—Wallace Davis, Kanarra.
141—Cal (Indian) Cedar City.
142—Joseph R. Webster, Cedar City.
143—Earl Urie, Cedar City.
144—Austin Barton, Paragonah.
145—Elmer Jasperson, Cedar City.
146—Clayton Perry, Cedar City.
147—Lionel Dover, Cedar City.
148—Gomer Cosslett, Cedar City.
149—Ivan Decker, Parowan.
150—Louis M. Davenport, Paragonah.
151—Robert L. Heyborne, Cedar City.
152—Erastus Jones, Cedar City.

153—Thomas Mosdell, Hamilton's Fort.
154—George M. Lewis, Lund.
155—Lehi M. Jones, Cedar City.
156—Wells A. Williams, Kanarra.
157—Wallace Hulet, Newcastle.
158—Henry Ashton, Cedar City.
159—Thomas O. Durham, Parowan.
160—J. S. Hyatt, Parowan.
161—Herbert Jackson, Parowan.
162—John R. Adams, Parowan.
163—George E. Roundy, Kanarra.
164—Maurice E. Wilson, Beryl.
165—Wilford Bergstrom, Cedar City.
166—Joseph Edwin Smith, Cedar City.
167—Robert Corry, Cedar City.
168—Roscoe M. Hailey, Sahara.
169—M. E. Trimmer, Lund.

170—James E. Carrie, Modena.
171—Leon Davis, Kanarra.
172—Harry Michels, Cedar City.
173—Albert N. Hodgson, Beryl.
174—Frank W. Hogan, Modena.
175—Thomas A. Topham, Paragonah.
176—John U. Hunter, Cedar City.
177—Victor L. Sylvester, Kanarra.
178—G. R. Parry, Cedar City.
179—Laban Burt, Parowan.
180—Robert O'Neil, Cedar City.
181—Leon Leigh, Cedar City.
182—Loren Sam Orton, Parowan.
183—William L. Melling, Cedar City.
184—Merl H. Gibson, Enoch.
185—John Yoeman, Beryl.
186—Bernard Guerro, Lund.

187—Millard Halterman, Enoch.
188—John Thomas Gower, Cedar City.
189—Henry Knight, Modena.
190—Lawrence F. Marker, Cedar City.
191—Alonzo Christensen, Newcastle.
192—Warren Mackelprang, Cedar City.
193—Edward A. Davis, Kanarra.
194—Orson W. Orton, Parowan.
195—Joseph Leroy Bauer, Cedar City.
196—Vernon Charles Bryant, Prout.
197—Ernest Isaac Lowe, Parowan.
198—Alma Esplin, Cedar City.
199—Oscar Edw. Frashke, Lund.
200—Jno. Wm. Murie, Cedar City.
201—James E. Dolan, Heist.
202—James Evan Eddards, Cedar City.

Iron County Record
August 3, 1917

CEDAR CITY SOLDIER EARNS RECOGNITION

Word is received here by the family of Lawrence Haslam, a Cedar City volunteer, of the distinction he has won in the marksmanship tests held, with light field artillery. Lawrence proved the best marksman of his regiment, and was awarded a silver medal for his good work. In writing home he enclosed a card bearing the following poem. Mr. Haslam is stationed down in Texas at one of the training camps

———×———

Dr. Leonard was called to Kanarra yesterday to wait upon Mrs. John Henry Williams. He reports the arrival of a son and heir. Mrs Wiliams is doing nicely and John H. is wearing a broad smile.

———×———

The arrival of a baby girl at the home of Mr. and Mrs. Jake Bergstroms on August 1st is reported by Dr. Macfarlane. All concerned doing nicely, and The Record congratulates.

———×———

A few days ago the 8-year-old son of John Dover was kicked in the jaw by a horse. The bone of the jaw was cracked and for a while it was feared that the ends of the jaw had been driven into the base of the brain. This probably was not the case, however, for Dr. Macfarlane reports that he is now convalescing nicely.

SAHARA

Mr. and Mrs. James Fairley, Mrs. Sam Davis and Master Bert were guests at dinner at the home of Mrs. Dave Pearce Sunday.

Iron County Record
August 10, 1917

Last Monday, Miss Winnifred Roche was thrown from a horse and painfully, but not seriously, injured.

Dr. Rufus Leigh of Provo has been in Cedar a portion of this week, at the bedside of his father, William D. Leigh, who is failing very rapidly of late.

Iron County Record
August 17, 1917

SAHARA

Mr. James Fairley made a business trip to Enterprise Friday.

Mr. Albert Nelson left Thursday to visit his parents in Washington.

Miss Florance Holmes left for Los Angeles, California, Saturday.

Mr. James A. Baker was home over Sunday to visit his family and mother.

Mesdames McElroy, Pearce and Davis took dinner with Mrs. Fairley Sunday.

George Koest of Parowan is visiting at the parental Koest home south of Sahara.

Messrs. Carlson, Wright and Casard were present at the club meeting Saturday night.

The citizens of this vicinity are now making a railroad crossing on the section line at Sahara.

Kanara, Utah, Aug. 16, 1917.

Mr. and Mrs. John Henry Williams have a fine son at their home.

✿ ✿

The farmers are busy harvesting their second cutting of hay, it being a good crop.

✿ ✿

David Davis erected a new hay shed last week, Noal Williams having charge of the carpenter work.

✿ ✿

George Berry is having a barn put up on his lot on North Main street. Ellis Christensen is overseeing the work.

✿ ✿

Mr. and Mrs. James Stapely have gone north to visit at Mona and Delta, where they have a son and daughter.

✿ ✿

Jew. Wood and Melba Reeves went to Cedar City to be operated on for appendicitis at the Southern Utah Hospital the first of this week.

✿ ✿

Noal Williams has moved into his new house, which he has erected entirely himself, with the exception of the plastering.

✿ ✿

A few of the young folks are going on the mountain for an outing today. They expect to be gone for two or thre days.

✿ ✿

Mrs. Hannah Williams, her sons Ray and Laliff Williams, took advantage of the visit of Dr. Stucki to the Southern Utah Hospital recently to have minor operations.

✿ ✿

Arthur Willis is another of our townsmen who has had a new hay shed erected on his premises. It has a lean-to on one side and is quite modern in construction. It will save its price for Mr. Williams in a few years.

———✕———

The following residents of Kanarra were noticed in town today: John Stapley, Sam. L. Pollock, Jesse F. Williams, John H. Williams, Joel J. Roundy, William R. Davis, George A. Berry, Berry Williams, Geo. A. Davis.

THE ANDERSONS HAVE SERIOUS AUTO ACCIDENT

Uncle Peter Anderson of Echo Farm, with his wife and daughter, Miss Laura, met with a distressing accident last week while on route to Cedar City. They were near the Berry farm between Kanarra and Hamilton's Fort, when the car which was being driven by Miss Laura, skidded off the grade and through some accident to the steering apparatus, became unmanageable. The car turned completely over, bruising the elderly couple considerably, and spraining both of Sister Anderson's wrists. Miss Laura received a broken shoulder bone on the left side, but very pluckily drove the rescue car into Cedar City with her one uninjured hand. Luckily Berry Williams of Kanarra, with two gentlemen passengers, was just behind the Anderson car when the accident occurred, so that the party was speedily rescued from their perilous predicament. Berry Williams drove the Anderson car into town, the top being badly smashed but not so badly damaged as to put it out of commission entirely.

Iron County Record
August 24, 1917

Another Cedar Girl Goes From Us.

In the marriage of Miss Nan Nelson, daughter of Mr. and Mrs. Bengt Nelson, Jr., to Mr. Claud Haws of Garfield county, Cedar City loses another bright and winsome young lady and one who will be geatly missed from her circle of friends and acquaintances.

The Panguitch Progress of the 17th has the following to say of this and two other weddings which had just occurred there:

"Mr. Claud Haws returned home from Cedar City with a bride. Quite a surprise to his friends. A very nice shower was held at the Haws residence Saturday evening. We think the bride was formerly Miss Nan Nelson of Cedar City. She is very beautiful and we welcome her to our town. We trust she will like it here. We wish the couple much happiness.

"Another shower was also given to Mr. Earsel Shirts and wife who was Miss Gotfredson of Circleville. We also wish them much happiness.

"Mr. Dwain Heaps and Miss Alvey were married Thursday. We wish them much joy.

"Three weddings this week good nothing like war to bring hearts together."

LIST OF OPERATIONS AT SOUTHERN UTAH HOSPITAL

Dr. W. M. Stookey, the eye, ear, nose and throat specialist, in connection with Dr. A. N. Leonard, performed operations at the Southern Utah Hospital for the following persons, the past week:

Mrs. James Smith, Cedar City.
S. A. Cram, Kanab, Utah.
Lilliff Williams, Kanarra, Utah.
Orson Haight, Cedar City.
Ray Williams, Kanarra.
Ellis Corry, Cedar City.
Ellen Smith, Cedar City.
Samuel Stucki, Santa Clara.
Hannah Williams, Kanarra.
Mrs. B. F. Knell, Cedar City.
Mrs. S. B. Jones, Cedar City.
Mr. and Mrs. J. G. Pace, Cedar City.
Miss Hattie Haight, Cedar City.
Mrs. Cora Cox, Short Creek, Ariz.
Mrs. Lettie B. Dalley, Summit.
Clifford Haight, Cedar City.

MEN WHO WILL FIGHT OUR BATTLES

Present Official List of Persons who Will Fill Iron County's Quota in Draft.

30 PER CENT TO REPORT EACH FIFTEEN DAYS

All Fathers Married Before Conscription Law was Passed Excused by Exemption Board.

Pres. L. N. Marsden of Parowan, who is a member of the county exemption board, was in Cedar City again yesterday on business connected with the filling of Iron county's quoto of the draft. The board takes the stand, in the light of recent rulings, that all fathers, married before the passage of the law calling the draft, should be exempted. This, with the failure of a great many to come up to the physical requirements, has necessitated the calling of a great many more men than had been anticipated, to fill the required quota.

Following is a copy of the latest list certified by the local board to the District Board for the State of Utah of persons who have been duly and legally called for the military service of the United States, and who have not been exempted or discharged.

Thomas Lund, Modena.
Henry Melling Jones, Enoch.
Archie Edward Wilson, Heist.
Edwin Webb, Cedar City.
Silas Sanford Owens, Paragonah.
Ephraim Dailey, Paragonah.
William Pucell, Cedar City.
John Wade, Nada.

Claude Leon Heist, Heist, Utah.
James Corlett Simkins, Cedar City.
Oliver Charles Jenson, Cedar City.
Guy Ruble Cadwallder, Beryl.
Stanley Forrester Benson, Parowan.
Alvin Lloyd Couch, Lund.
Herbert Dutton Fretwell, Cedar.
Charles Hendrickson, Sahara.
Jno. Ambrose Paramore, Parowan.
Hart Hoxie, Lund.
Jesse C. Roundy, Kanarra.
Benj. Harrison Matteson, Nada.
Albert Spencer Benson, Parowan.
Willard Mackelprang Perkins, Cedar
Wm. Basil Hogan, Modena.
George Stapley, Cenar City.
Fernleigh Gardner, Cedar City.
Frank Eugene Taylor, Parowan.
Ether Perry, Cedar City.
Leland C. Stapley, Kanarra.
Ervine Dustin, Cedar City.
Alma Wilford Richards, Parowan.
Oscar Julius Thompson, Lund.
John Sprouse Mitchell, Parowan.
Elved Williams, Cedar City.
Robert William Fowler, Parowan.

Earl Urie, Cedar City.
Lionel Charles Dover, Cedar City.
Louis M. Davenport, Paragonah.
Lehi Milton Jones, Cedar City.
Wells A. Wiliams, Kanarra.
Thomas Orton Durham, Parowan.
Geo. E. Roundy, Kanarra.
Wilford Bergstrom, Cedar City.
Roscoe Merrill Hailey, Sahara.
Michael Elsworth Trimmer, Lund.
Leon Davis, Kanarra.
Frank Walter Hogan, Modena.
Thos. Amenzo Topham, Paragonah.
Victor L. Sylvester, Kanarra.
Raymond Robert O'Neil, Cedar City.

The following named persons have not responded to the notiie from the Local Board to report for examination:

Carter Ernest Lee, Beryl.
Mercer Eugene Wilson, Beryl.
James Edwin Perry, Modena.
Wilford Carson Benson, Parowan.
John V. Schoppman, who has been married since May 18, was allowed exemption on account of a dependent widowed mother.

Iron County Record
August 31, 1917

BIOGRAPHY OF WILLIAM D. LEIGH

Short Synopsis of the Life of Old Settler Who Passed Beyond the Veil August 22nd.

William David Leigh, the son of Samuel and Ann David Leigh was born in the Parish of Llannelly, Carmarthanshire, South Wales, Great Britian, August 25, 1842. In 1849 he emigrated to America with his parents. They crossed the ocean in a sailing vessel, being eleven weeks on the sea. They landed at New Orleans and proceeded up the Mississippi and Missouri rivers. Near St. Joseph, Missouri the mother died. The family lived at Council Bluffs, Iowa for three years. In the summer of 1852 Samuel Leigh with his four motherless children crossed the plains to Salt Lake City by ox team, William walking most of the way. They remained in Salt Lake but three weeks then proceeded to Iron county remaining in Parowan the first winter. The following spring, 1853, the family moved to Cedar City where they established themselves permanently.

As a boy William Leigh experienced the hardships common to early life in the old Fort. He served as mail carrier in the early days to Santa Clara, experiencing many thrilling encounters with the Indians. He availed himself of all educational opportunities of the day and after maturity attended high school at St. George after which he taught in the public schools of Southern Utah.

July 9th, 1876, he joined in marriage, Elizabeth Wood of this city and from the union seven children were born, six sons and one daughter, two sons dying in early childhood. In 1912 his second son, Samuel G., died and the loss of this very dear and affectionate son was indeed a great trial. The children living are: W. H. Leigh, Ruby E. Leigh, Elias Leigh, of Cedar City and Dr. Rufus Leigh of Provo.

November 14, 1888 he left Salt Lake City to perform a mission for the church in Great Britian. His time, for the most part, was spent in and around Merthyr and also Llanelly, his birthplace, South Wales.

As Elder Joseph T. Wilkinson remarked at the funeral services, William D. Leigh was an all-around citizen. He was an Indian War Veteran, City Councilman for several terms, a faithful member and worker in the church continuing his activities as Ward Teacher until the time of his last illness. Farming and stock raising were his occupation and in this work he enjoyed good health until his final call. By nature he was kind and considerate of others always anxious to help anyone out of difficulty. As testiled by the speakers at his funeral, he was a man of great worth, his word always to be relied upon and his honesty above reproach.

Another young miller arrived at the home of Mr. and Mrs. William Matheson on the 28th inst. He came just in time to assist with the fall grind.

Otto, the young son of Sheriff Jos. S. Fife, was operated on at the Macfarlane Hospital today for the removal of his tonsils.

Mr. and Mrs. Henry Mathews of Price, Utah, were the guests of Dr. and Mrs. Macfarlane the fore part of the week. Mrs. Mathews is a sister to the Doctor.

"BISHOP" CORRY'S SUDDEN SUMMONS

Dropped Dead in His Home Last Tuesday Evening Without Warning; A Prominent Landmark.

Last Wednesday morning the people of Cedar City were shocked and surprised to learn of the sudden and unexpected death of "Bishop" William H. Corry, an early pioneer and for many years a prominent land mark in this city. The immediate cause of death was appoplexy. While his health has been failing somewhat for a year or more, and he has complained at times of feeling old and worn, he was in about his usual health on the day of his death, and had been to the

WILLIAM H. CORRY.

field for a jag of wood. In the evening at his home he was holding a business session with members of his family with whom he was con-

jointly interested in a large tract of land, and in attempting to walk from one room to another he was suddenly stricken and fell on his face to the floor. When his children attempted to raise him he said, "Don't touch me; I think my time has come." Before medical aid could reach him, his spirit had taken its flight.

Deceased was 67 years old, and has always lived a strenuous and active life.

Owing to the absence of some of his children who could not reach here earlier, the funeral is being held this afternoon, in the tabernacle, commencing at 2 o'clock.

BIOGRAPHICAL.

William Henry Corry was the son of George and Margaret Corry, and was born in Provo, Utah, July 30, 1850. With his parents he came to Cedar City in 1853, and has resided here ever since.

He passed through the trials and hardships of the early days, incident to the settlement of a new country.

He had little opportunity for acquiring an education, but when a young man he learned the trade of blacksmith which he followed for a number of years. He was of a strong robust type, of manhood, and capable of doing a prodigious amount of work. He had the reputation of shoeing more horses in a day than any other man in the country.

Vigorous and full of life, as a young man he was fond of outdoor sports and was noted as a "crack shot" with a rifle, rarely failing to bring down his deer or other game when he went for it.

On October 30th, 1871, he was married in the Salt Lake Temple to Elizabeth Parry, and 11 children came to bless and cement the union, of these four have died, leaving seven living. Those who preceded him to the other side of the veil are William Henry, George Edward, Arthur Edwin and Marion Parry. The living children are: Margaret Corry Roche, John P. Corry, of Ogden, Willard E., Elias M., Mary Jeanette Lunt, Lula Cannon, and Winnifred, the latter being the only one unmarried

In October, 1886, deceased left for a mission to the Southern States.

In December 1888, he was ordained bishop of the Cedar ward, and held the position until his resignation in October, 1901, at which time the city was divided in two wards. Afterwards he was made a member of the High Council of the Parowan stake.

In civil affairs he was also prominent, serving a number of terms as city councilman, member of the school board and filing other positions of trust. For about 12 years he was president of the Cedar Sheep Association.

He was always a liberal provider for his family, and a loving and indulgent father and husband. As bishop of Cedar ward he had the confidence and esteem of his constituency.

All the members of his family will be present at the funeral services, and the indications are that the attendance will be very large.

The portrait of deceased was taken something like 15 years ago while he was a member of the city council of Cedar City.

———×———

Rex Cheney, the little 8 year old son of Mr. and Mrs. D. P. Cheney, formerly of Summit but now residing in this city, fell from the fence onto the sidewalk causing a bad dislocation and fracture of the elbow joint. Dr. Macfarlane reduced the joint and the little boy is reported to be doing as well as can be expected.

———∧———

Mr. John P. Corry of Ogden and Mr. and Mrs. Cannon of Salt Lake City arrived on the auto from Lund yesterday to attend the funeral of their father, Wm. H. Corry, which is being held this afternoon, and W. E. Corry arrived from Idaho on to-day's passenger car. This completes the circle of the family of deceased, the others residing here.

Iron County Record
September 14, 1917

———×———

Francis, the youngest son of Mrs. May Condie has been bedfast the past week with rheumatism, but is on the improve at present.

———∨———

The following births are reported by Dr. M. J. Macfarlane: To Mrs. Key, of Twin Falls, Idaho, a boy yesterday; To Mr. and Mrs. David Eddards, last Monday, a boy; to Mr. and Mrs. Henry Nelson, last week, a girl, and to Mr. and Mrs. Lon Ahlstrom, also last week, a boy.

Last evening Dr. Leonard was called to Quitchapa to see Mrs. Hony, who was suffering from severe cramps at first indicating appendicitis, but the case responded to treatment and the lady was much better when the Doctor left her.

Iron County Record
September 21, 1917

Last Wednesday afternoon there was considerable life and animation on Main street on the occasion of the departure of the second contingent of 40 per cent of the conscripted men of Iron county. The street was lined with people anxious to shake the hands of the departing soldiers and to wish them God-speed and a safe return.

The boys were accompanied to the railroad by some of their parents and other relatives and friends.

Following is a list of those who made up the contingent:

Thomas Lund of Modena, who was in charge of the party.

Guy Ruple Cadwalder, Beryl.

Stanley Forreser Benson, Parowan.

Alvin Lloyd Couch, Lund.

Claude Emmet Harris, Parowan.

John Ambrose Paramore, Parowan.

George Stapley, Cedar City.

Frank Eugene Taylor, Parowan.

Leland C. Stapley, Kanarra.

Ervine Dustin, Cedar City.

Oscar Julius Thompson, Lund.

John Sprouse Mitchell, Parowan.

Elvid Williams, Cedar City.

Robert Fowler, Parowan.

Earl Urie, Cedar City.

Wells A. Williams, Kanarra.

Thomas Orton Durham, Parowan.

Geo. E. Roundy, Kanarra.

Jesse C. Roundy, Kanarra.

Lindsay Burton, Ely, Nevada.

(The latter was unable to reach home in time to accompany his contingent and under a ruling of the department was permitted to accompany the Iron county quota...

As the boys were lined up in the cars ready to start to the railroad at Lund, some of them began singing an old melody and all seemed to be cheerful and very willing to answer to the call of their country.

Iron County Record
September 28, 1917

KANARRAVILLE

Kanarra, Utah, Sept. 26, 1917.

The corn crop is now about harvested, but was not as good this year as last.

* *

The threshing is all done here except the lucerne seed which promises good returns this year.

* *

Reese J. Williams has in course of construction a three or four room addition to his house.

Dan. Webster has purchased the Jas. S. Berry home in Cedar City and has traded it to Mrs. Eva J. Reeves for her home in Kanarra. Mrs. Reeves expects to move to Cedar in the next few days.

* *

Four of our boys left for the U. S. training camps in Washington on the 19th. They were Jesse Roundy, Wells Williams, Leland Stapley and George Roundy.

* *

Mr. George Berry returned to his home in Salt Lake City last week in his private car, taking Mrs. Lydia Reeves and her two daughters as far as Venice. He was also accompanied through to Salt Lake by Mr. and Mrs. W. R. Davis, where Mr. Davis will receive treatment for rheumatism.

* *

Word has been received that Elder James L. Roundy of this place, now doing missionary work in Mississippi, has been sick for about a month with malaria fever. The latest report from him is to the effect that his fever has been broken and that he was gradually regaining his health again.

* *

A banquet was given the departing soldier boys the day before their entrainment at Lund. The old martial band was out in full force and a rousing meeting was held in the afternoon. Fruit and melons were served to all present, followed by a dance. The boys all expressed their appreciation of the honor shown them.

Iron County Record
October 5, 1917

Miss Sadie Dailey and Marion Dailey from Paragonah were in town last Wednesday, accompanying their brother Ephraim this far on his way to the training camp, where he will enter the service of Uncle Sam.

SALE OF CEDAR CITY DRUG STORE

And Merging With Palace Drug Store in One Corporation is Being Consummated This Week.

An important business deal, involving the consolidation of Cedar City's two drug stores under one management and ownership, is being worked out this week. The deal involves the purchase of the Cedar City Drug Store from Mrs. A. E. Pettigrew, its present owner, and the merging of this and the Palace Drug Store into one joint stock company. The deal is being put over by John Bladen, the proprietor of the Palace Drug Store, and Lafe McConnell, who has had experience in the drug business. But the ultimate intention is, we are informed, is to organize a joint stock company to operate and own the combined business, and that the stock of the company is to be quite widely distributed. The promoters have arranged for a first-class registered pharmacist, and for business connections with a northern wholesale drug house, and it is the intention to develop the business to the highest possible degree.

The inventory is being taken at this writing, and unless some unforseen hitch occurs the deal will be completed as above outlined within the next few days.

With the consolidation of the two stores Mr. Bladen will retire from the drug business, at least actively, and as soon as he can dispose of his other holdings here, will remove to Wyoming to take charge of a large cattle ranch which he purchased out there some little time ago.

THIRD CONTIGENT OF SOLDIERS GO

Iron County's 40 Per Cent of Quota, Consisting of 19 Men, Left Here Wednesday.

TEN OF THE NINETEEN ARE FROM CEDAR CITY

Many Touching Farewells, and Few Eyes are Dry as Boys Board Autos on Main Street Bound for Lund.

The Roll of Honor.

Following is the roll of honor that made up the party:

Lehi M. Jones, Cedar City, in charge
Henry Melling Jones, Enoch.
Edwin Webb, Cedar City.
Archie Edward Wilson, California.
Silas Sanford Owens, Paragonah.
Ephraim Daily, Paragonah.
William Pucell, Cedar City.
John Wade, Nada.
Herbert Dutton Fretwell, Cedar.
Benj. Harrison Mattson, Nada.
Fernleigh Gardner, Cedar City.
Hyrum Pidding Jones, Enoch.
Joseph Reese Webster, Cedar City.
Lionel Charles Dover, Cedar City.
Erastus Lunt Jones, Cedar City.
Wilford Bergstrom, Cedar City.
Oliver Chas. Jenson, Cedar City.
Adelbert Farnsworth, Summit.

Claud L. Heist of Heist, Utah, took the train at Modena in advance and will join the remainder of the recruits at Salt Lake City.

How Cedar City is Growing.

The following births are reported by Dr. M. J. Macfarlane for the past week: To Mr. and Mrs. Edwin Cox, a boy last week Thursday; to Mr. and Mrs. Sam Barton, a girl last Tuesday night; to Mr. and Mrs. James Parry, a girl Wednesday night; to Mr. and Mrs. Melborene Williams, a girl last Thursday ing; to Mr. and Mrs. Webster a boy today.

Summit, Utah, Oct. y1, 1917.

Hyrum Dalley of Cedar City was in Summit Saturday looking after his farm.

⁂ ⁂

Threshing here is over for this season, and the yield is the heaviest ever reported in the history of the place.

⁂ ⁂

Samuel L. Fife has sold his farm here to Thomas Davenport of Parowan and has acquired property there, where his future home will be.

⁂ ⁂

Summit's new school house is now completed and school is being held there. The quarters are much more pleasant and comfortable than the old building, a change that is greatly appreciated.

⁂ ⁂

Work is to be commenced at once on a splendid water system for Summit, by the aid of which this place will have one of the best culinary water supplies in the state. It will consist of a cement gravity line from the spring in the canyon to the supply tank, a distance of three-quarters of a mile. From this point pressure pipe will be used to town. It is expected that the system will be completed this year.

⁂ ⁂

From present indications and reports the population of our little town will be considerably decreased again this winter by the removal of families having children of high school age. Among these we learn of the following: Chas. R. Dalley and family are planning to spend the winter in Logan; Mrs. Lorena Langford and family intend moving to Cedar City, and Wm. W. Dalley and N. B. Dalley will likely move there also; Mrs. Letty B. Dalley will likely spend the winter in St. George.

KANARRAVILLE

Kanarra, Utah, Oct. 16, 1917.
Yesterday Roy Adams sheep camp burned completely up.

* *

Jesse Berry has gone to Loa, Wayne County with a load of grapes.

* *

Ether Wood of Hurricane was in town today and loaded a double outfit with coal.

* *

Arnold Graff now sports a new Ford and from all indications will enjoy his buy very much.

* *

Mrs. Sarah Reeves is on the sick list this week suffering with what the doctor terms Calls Bilious Boil.

Some where near 100 hogs have been taken to the lower basin to clean up the acorns. Some reports state that there are enough acorns to fatten 500 or 1000 head of hogs.

* *

The cattle men returned home last Sunday from the mountains reporting a fairly successful drive-out. Some of the cattle are still missing necessitating a repitition of the drive.

* *

The youngest son of Mr. and Mrs. Arnold Graff fell from a horse a few days ago fracturing his arm. The following day he was taken to Dr. Macfarlane at Cedar City where the unfortunate lad's arm was set and placed in a plaster of paris cast. The arm is progressing very nicely.

The eldest son of Berry Williams fell with a ladder which was dragging behind a load of corn and sustained a broken leg, the limb being fractured just above the ankle. Dr. Leonard was sent for and soon placed the limb in a cast. The boy does not seem to particularly care for his predicament.

* *

With the exception of a few white beans the threshing here is all completed, there having been three or four tons of alfalfa seed included in this year's seed crop. The Mexican Pinto was the first of the beans to ripen, ripening about September 15th while the white variety is scarcely ripe yet.

Sheriff Fife has gone to Lund today to investigate further the circumstances surrounding the death at 20 mile gap, of Harry J. Ashby, a homesteader whom a coroner's jury reported had come to his death last Sunday by his own hands. Circumstances have since come to light which tend to make residents of that section dissatisfied wih the verdict, and the widow of the deceased is anxious to have the stories of probable foul play investigated and set at rest.

The following births are reported by Dr. Macfarlane for the past week: To Mr. and Mrs. Bernard Leigh, last Monday morning, a boy; to Mrs. Oaroe Webb, Wednesday morning, a girl; to Mrs. Edgar Jones, Wednesday morning, a boy. The last named child is very delicate, being of premature birth, and will have a hard fight to pull through and retain its holt upon life.

Mrs. Frank Jones was brought in from Summit yesterday and last night underwent an operation at the Southern Utah Hospital. Her condition is now much improved.

Mrs. Silas Brinkerhoof underwent an operation yesterday at the Southern Utah Hospital for the removal of a large liporna tumor from her back; not of a malignant type. The patient is doing nicely.

Mrs. George Smith, who underwent a double operation at the Southern Utah Hospital a couple of weeks ago, is now convalescing rapidly and has been removed to the home of her father-in-law, Mr. James Smith. Her husband recently volunteered for service in the army.

CANFIELD AND WOODBURY MARRIED IN SALT LAKE CITY

The culmination of a courtship covering a number of years, and in which Miss Hortense Woodbury of this city and Willard Canfield of Enterprise, figure as the principals, was culminated this week in Salt Lake City, when the young couple were happily wedded in the Salt Lake Temple.

The groom has relatives in Cedar City, and is well known here, as he attended the local institution of learning for a number of years, and graduated from the high school department. He was prominent in school affairs here, being mayor of the school city and business manager of the school paper, "The Student." Mr. Canfield is a solid, substantial and progressive young man, and is fully dserving of the good fortune that has come to him in the winning of Miss Woodbury, who is one of Cedar City's sweetest and most accomplished young ladies.

Accompanied by her mother, Mrs. John S. Woodbury, and Mrs. Allie Knell, who is the groom's aunt, Miss Woodbury left Cedar last Monday af-ternoon and would be joined at Lund by her fiancee. Together they would go to the capital city and the wedding would probably take place Wednesday. After a short visit in the northern part of the state the happy couple will return to their friends in the south.

The Record has not been advised as to where the young people will make their home, but likely at Enterprise, that being the home of the groom.

We wish them health, wealth and happiness.

Iron County Record
December 14, 1917

FUNERAL SERVICES FOR MILTON SEVY

··· ⚜ ···

Speakers Pay Glowing Tributes to Integrity, Earnestness and Usefulness.

··· ⚜ ···

FLORAL OFFERINGS WERE MANY AND BEAUTIFUL

Milton H. Sevy was born Oct. 12, 1889, at Panguitch, Garfield county, Utah. He attended the district school at Panguitch and was a student one year at the Branch Normal school in Cedar City, Utah. In 1910 he was graduated from the Brigham Young high school at Provo. He entered the University of Utah in February, 1911, and was graduated with the degree of bachelor of arts in 1914. In 1913-14 he was president of the student body and in June, 1914, he was class valedictorian. He was a member of the Phi Delta Theta fraternity. Since leaving school he has been engaged with his father in the live stock business at Cedar City, near which he was fatally injured.

The surviving relatives include his father and mother, John L. and Mary H. Sevy; two sisters, Mrs. Warren Shepherd of Beaver, Utah, and Miss Merle Sevy, of Salt Lake; two brothers, Lyman E. Sevy, member of the national army and now on his way to France, and Heber M. Sevy, a student at the University of Utah.—Deseret Evening News.

The County Clerk issued a marriage license to Mr. Thurlow Gardner of Cedar City and Miss La Verda Chadburn of Central, on Dec 17.

Mr. and Mrs. Clyde Cannon are rejoicing over the arrival of a baby boy, born Monday, December 10.

Bishop John Dalley and wife of Summit were Christmas shoppers in Cedar City last Tuesday.

Operations at Southern Utah Hospital

The following persons were operated on at the Southern Utah Hospital last Monday:

Mrs. Joseph Williams of Kanarra, for appendicitis.

Miss Lola Williams, Kanarra, for removal of tonsils and adenoids.

Zelpha Wood, Cedar City, for removal of tonsils and adenoids.

WILSON LUNT WEDS
PAROWAN BELLE

Today in the Salt Lake Temple Wilson N. Lunt of Cedar City and Miss Agatha Day of this city, will be united in the hold bonds of wedlock.

The bride is a daughter of Mr. and Mrs. Wilford Day and a young lady of pleasing personality, and a lover of the home. She is known by hundreds of people of this section of the country and held in very high esteem by all who bear her acquaintance. She is sincere in all that she does, modest and unassuming and will make an ideal help-meet to her husband.

The groom is a son of Mr. and Mrs. Wm. Lunt of Cedar City, a young man who is well liked by his many friends, earnest and honest, and a young man who will make his way in the world and prove a loyal protector to the young lady who has given him her heart and hand.—Parowan Times.

Iron County Record
January 11, 1918

BANK REPORT

Made to the Bank Commissioner of the State of Utah of the Condition of "The Iron Commercial and Savings Bank," Located at Cedar City, in the County of Iron, State of Utah, at the Close of Business on the 28th day of December, 1917.

RESOURCES

Loans and discounts	$143,947.12
Overdrafts secured	7,192.28
Overdrafts, unsecured	1,159.72
Bonds, Liberty	1,100.00
Furniture and Fixtures	3,865.16
Checks and Cash items	1,740.62
Gold coin	740.00
Silver coin	1,117.76
Currency	1,239.00
Expense account	4,854.13
Interest and taxes paid	447.10
Capital stock subscriptions	1,260.00
TOTAL	$168,662.89

LIABILITIES

Capital stock subscribed	$ 50,000.00
Undivided profits, int. etc	4,253.61
Due State banks & bankers	307.26
Individual deposits	72,270.10
Certified checks	30.86
Cashier's checks	680.71
Savings deposits	12,904.50

IRON COUNTY'S SHERIFF PRAISED

Good Work in Apprehending of Power Line Thieves Told by the Owner.

VALUABLE SHIPMENT OF COPPER WIRE RECOVERED

Offenders are Now in Custody and One Has Serious Charge of Resisting an Officer With Deadly Weapon.

H. T. Johnson, general manager and one of the heavy owners in the Gold Springs Mining properties and the power line between that place and Modena was in Cedar City last Wednesday in company with Sheriff Froyd. Mr. Johnson, whose home is in Minneapolis, and who doubtless was regarded by the people in the western part of this county as a "tender foot" recently had a rather exciting experience with two tough characters—Clark and Alexander—who removed and tried to market some four or five thousand pounds of the heavy copper wire from the power line. The copper was taken down, cut into sections, taken to Milford and consigned through I. Cline, the Jew merchant of that place, to an eastern junk house.

Mr. Johnson gives a very interesting account of the discovery and tracing of the shipment, ending with the arrest of the two men, the last one, Alexander, being secured in Salt Lake City, in connection with which he gives our local sheriff credit for the principal role.

Mr. Johnson states that he was at old Springs at the time of the theft, and that they were using the power line to give telephone communication with Modena. Something went wrong with the line, and after trying for two or three days to get communica-

tion through, he started to investigate and found that a large section of the line had been removed. He at once sent messages to the principal offices along the Salt Lake Route to look out for the wire, and at the same time communicated with the Iron county sheriff at this place by telephone. Mr. Froyd explained that he had a meeting of the exemption board that afternoon, but that he would be out during the night or the following morning. "I did not believe him, said Mr. Johnson, "because some little time ago an automobile was stolen out there and it was three days before we could get the sheriff to come; I did not know that there had been a change in officers. Well, I went back up to camp, and the next day the sheriff obtained an automobile and came up to camp. But in the mean time he had communicated with his deputy at Milford, Mr. Baxter, and had located the shipment, and had instructed the Milford officer to arrest Clark, who was at that place.

"The sheriff wanted to get to Milford as soon as possible, and I obtained an automobile and we drove over. The Beaver county sheriff and Mr. Baxter had Clark under arrest, though he had made an attempt to get away from Marshal Baxter by covering him with a gun, but the sheriff returned just in time to prevent his escape. He was taken over to Beaver, where in connection with other prisoners he very narrowly missed making his escape by digging through the wall of the jail, where a stove had been built in.

"Without waiting for any rest the two sheriffs and myself boarded the train for Salt Lake, where we arrived just in time to prevent a shipment of 3,000 pounds of the copper from leaving for the east. One shipment had already gone. Then we hunted for four days for Alexander, Clark's partner in the affair. I finally discovered him in the act of getting some wood in a back yard to which clews had led us. By his connections in Salt Lake your sheriff was able to get valuable assistance from the police department and the Salt Lake county sheriff's office. He is a good officer and knows just how to proceed in cases of this kind."

Mr. Johnson was a grateful and highly pleased man. He stated that the value of the copper would be recovered from the merchant who handled the shipment. Clark is being held in Beaver county on a charge of resisting an officer and an assault with a deadly weapon, Alexander is in the charge of Sheriff Froyd at this place.

STALWART CITIZEN GETS FINAL CALL

Wm. P. Hunter Snatched from Family and Labors in Heighth of Mental and Physical Vigor.

The worst fears of his physicians, family and friends were realized in relation to Wiliam P. Hunter, who was in such a serious condition when we closed our forms on our last issue of The Record. The end came at 1:15 p. m. last Monday, and the funeral was held in the tabernacle yesterday afternoon at 2:00 p. m. The building was draped and decorated for the occasion, and there was a large attendance.

As mentioned in our last issue the cause of Mr. Hunter's illness and subsequent demise, was internal hernia, causing strangulation of the intestine. An operation was performed, but was delayed too long to save the patient's life. During his brief illness the patient suffered intensely, but retained his courage and fortitude to the last.

The speakers at the funeral were Elders R. A. Thorley, Henry W. Lunt, Andrew Corry, David Bulloch, Dr. M. J. Macfarlane, Principal Roy F. Homer, Bishop H. H. Lunt. A feeling

WILLIAM P. HUNTER

resolution of condolence from the Iron County Farm Bureau was read by Mr. Alma Esplin.

The opening prayer was offered by Bengt Nelson, Sr., and the benediction was pronounled by John V. Adams.

Two beautiful vocal solos were rendered by Bro. F. L. Hickman.

The speakers all referred to the life and character of the deceased with the highest degree of confidence and esteem.

BIOGRAPHY

The following brief sketch of the life of deceased is taken from the official Church biography:

Wiliam Pinnoch Hunter, a president of the 63rd quorum of Seventies, son of Joseph S. and Eliza C. Pinnoch, was born at Cedar City, Iron county, Utah, March 14, 1869. Was baptized Aug. 26, 1877, by Robert W. Heyborne, and confirmed by C. J. Arthur. Ordained a Deacon in 1881, a Priest in 1883, and a Seventy by Brigham H. Roberts, Sept. 21, 1890. He was set apart for a mission to Samoa by Apostle Abraham H. Cannon, Nov. 7, 1891, and left Salt Lake City a few days later. While on this mission he labored successfully in Toga, principally on the island of Tongatabu, and in the Haapai groups.

He returned home October 5, 1894.

June 24, 1896, he was set apart as a president of the 63rd quorum of Seventy by Johonathan Golden Kimball.

Married Charlotte Rountree of Nephi, April 23, 1897, in the Lalt Lake City Temple."

Four children, three sons and a daughter, were the issue of this marriage, all of whom survive their father, and none of whom are married. They are: Rowntree, Grant, William and Meriam.

Deceased was of a quiet, peaceful, retiring disposition. He never sought nor permitted his name to be used in connection with any public office, pre-ferring to be at home with his family. He followed farming and livestock as an occupation, and was fairly prosperous.

He was regarded as one of the solid and substantial citizens of the community and had a wide circle of acquaintances and friends, who mourn his untimely end.

Iron County Record
January 23-25, 1918

KANARRAVILLE

Kanarra, Utah, Jan 23, 1918

Ed. Young went to Washington this week with a grist for R. G. Williams.

* * *

The Groves Brothers lost one of their valuable team horses last Monday night.

* * *

Bert Davis has gone to Nevada with John A. Adams of Cedar City with a bunch of cattle.

* * *

George Berry of Salt Lake City is here again to look after his cattle and sheep interests.

* * *

Sam Pollock, Jr., of Tooele, was here about a week visiting relatives and friends.

* * *

Andy Berry went to St. George recently with coal and provisions for his mother, who now lives there.

* * *

Horace Roundy and Gustave Pingle are having about 40 tons of hay baled this week; principally grass hay.

* * *

Frank Anderson is a visitor here about every Sunday. The attraction seems to be about the R. G. Williams residence.

* * *

Hyrum Ford has sold or bargained his holdings here to a Mr. Sorenson of Idaho, and Victor Ford has sold his farm at this place to a Mr. Gardner of Idaho. Both gentlemen are brothers-in-law to Mr. Jesse B. Ford.

* * *

Myron Davis has been home from the sheep camp the past two or three days to be present at the marriage of his daughter Lorine to Joseph Hyatt of Parowan. The young people were married in Parowan last Monday.

* * *

It is reported that there is railing being placed on the Spring Creek and Camp Creek bridges, and a large culvert one-half mile south of Camp Creek bridges. These are road improvements which were very much needed.

Born, to Mr. and Mrs. Isaac Parry, Sunday, January 20th, at the Southern Utah Hospital, a girl. All concerned doing nicely.

NADA.

Nada, Iron Co., Utah, Jan. 30, 1918. Carlton Culmsee, son of Postmaster Culmsee of Nada, was astonished on Tuesday afternoon to see a coyote in front of his store and post-office. He immediately snatched his rifle and hurried after the animal until met by Robert Bonner, who fortunately was on his way to Nada, on horse-back. Soon they were joined by Herbert Stones, with a team and six-shooter. After a pursuit of several miles Mr. Coyote was pretty well exhausted and Mr. Bonner fiinally succeeded in getting near enough to shoot him. The head was sent to State Health Officer and all are anxiously awaiting re-sults as two valuable dogs were exposed to the coyote, which in the mean time are being kept carefully muzzled.

* * *

Michael P. McGuire, whose name is on the Iron county delinquent list of registrants, is our first volunteer. He joined the marines last August, went direct to Mare Island and has since written cheerful letters in praise of Uncle Sam as "boss." The last we heard of him was from the Philippine Islands. He wrote he was "still traveling"—somewhere in the Pacific.

Calvin R. Morrow, who is placed in class 1, took advantage of the call for volunteers in December and enlisted in the navy. While he was found to be color blind and not eligible for the signal corps, we understand he was retained in another branch of service for the government.

KANARRAVILLE

Kanarra, Utah, Feb. 5, 1918 Ed Young and John Stapley's families have German measles. They are of a light form quarantine being maintained only five or six days.

* * *

James S. Berry and family entertained the soldier boys at dinner this afternoon. Tomorrow the boys will be at Mr. and Mrs. George Davis home for dinner.

* * *

Monday morning Miss Christine Williams and Frank Anderson of Echo Farm left for Salt Lake where they will be married Wednesday, February 6th. They expect to be gone about ten days.

* * *

The soldiers bantered the rest of the town for a game of base ball which was to be played last Saturday. When the count was made the score was 19 to 26 in favor of the town. Again Tuesday a game was played which resulted in a victory for the town. The soldier boys took their defeat good naturedly.

SAHARA.

Miss Carrie Hedrick left February 2nd for Los Angeles to attend school. We certainly miss her and wish her the best of good fortune and a safe return.

Mr. Guy Johnson has resigned his position as postmaster and expects soon to turn over the office to his successor, Mrs. A. E. Phillips

Mr. Charles Magnussen and family have returned to Sahara. Mr. Magnussen is section foreman at this place. We certainly are glad to welcome these friends again.

Iron County Record
February 15, 1918

MORE SOLDIERS LEAVE
FOR TRAINING CAMPS

Many friends and relatives were on Main street surrounding the automobiles bound for Lund which were to carry away another small detachment of Iron county soldiers, Wednesday afternoon.

The automobiles were draped with flags, and there were tears in plenty when the boys took their departure.

Those going from Cedar City were:

Leon Leigh,
Logan Bryant,
William Mulliner,
Milo Heyborne,
Frank Jones,
Warren Mackelprang.

They entrained at Lund for Van Couver, British Columbia.

They were accompanied from this place by the following recruits from Parowan:

Lorin Orton.
Oscar Orton.
Lee Rowley.
Earl Skougard.

While the boys had been drafted, they were not required to leave at the present time, but volunteered to go into the service now.

Iron County Record
February 22, 1918

Dr. Leonard reports the arrival of a girl baby at the home of Mr. and Mrs. Kumen Leigh, born Feb. 20th. All doing nicely.

SAHARA.

Sahara, Utah, Feb 27, 1918.

Mr. W. A. Griffin went to Newcastle for hay this week.

* * *

Miss Grace Magnusen was visiting with Miss Bumpus at Ford this week and reports an excellent time.

* * *

Mr. H. Larsen, a new settler, has arrived and is establishing residence on his 160 acres southeast of Sahara.

* * *

Mrs. J. B. Reynolds has returned to work for the Salt Lake Route leaving for the north last Thursday evening.

* * *

Mr. Hal Griffin returned from Los Angeles Monday evening after several months absence in that city. Glad to have you with us again Hal.

* * *

Mrs. J. A. Baker has returned to her employment with the Salt Lake Route. We hope to record her return to Sahara for a permanant stay soon.

* * *

Chas. J. Hellings made the trip to Newcastle this week for hay. He reports the road to be in a very bad condition. His wagon sinking nearly to the axles in mud.

* * *

Mr. Geo. Griffin has just completed a well for Albert Nelson, getting good drinking water at about eighty feet. This makes a well on practically every homestead in the immediate vicinity of Sahara.

KANARRAVILLE

(Crowded out last issue.)

Kanarra, Utah, Feb. 21, 1918.

James S. Berry has been on the sick list for a number of days with quinsey.

Mr. Louis A. Rowe of Spanish Fork is here calling on his best girl, Miss Mae Williams. He has volunteered in the medical corps of the U. S. army and expects to leave in the near future.

Williams-King Nuptuals.

Miss Hazel Williams and a Mr. King of Escalante, Garfield county and a student of the B. A. C. of Cedar City, will be married today at about 3 o'clock. The bride-to-be is a daughter of Mr. and Mrs. J. H. Williams, and is a well-respected young lady, who will be greatly missed in the community when the young people leave for Escalante, their future home.

If there is any family in town that has not had or now has the German measles among them they are certainly few in number. The epidemic is supposed to have come from Millard county.

SIXTEEN MORE BOYS GO TO THE COLORS

Registrants Thwart Draft Call by Enlisting and Go to the Training Camps.

451—Albert Virgil Tollestrup, of Cedar City.

20—Jess Guyman, Parowan.

14—Ambrose Guyman, Parowan.

21—John Miller Gurr, Parowan.

570—David Clark Eddards, Cedar City.

316—Joseph LeRoy Bauer, Cedar City.

41b—George Murie Hunter, Cedar City.

491—Raymond Bengt Nelson Perry, Cedar City.

348—George Arthur Perry, Cedar City.

Sixteen more young men from Iron county responded to the call to the colors yesterday and bidding good-bye to their relatives and friends, took their departure for their various cantonments. The men included in the contingent and their serial numbers follow:

296—Thomas Mosdell, Hamilton's Fort.

472—Oley Adams Stapley, Cedar City.

566—Louis Franklin Farnsworth, Summit.

109—William C. Adams, Parowan.

146—William Austin Barton, Paragonah.

553—Jesse Osroe Webb, Cedar City.

397—Marion Wells Wilkinson, Cedar City.

The two last named go to the Engineer corps, Camp Fremont, Calif.

Iron County Record
March 8, 1918

Young Man on Horseback Collides With Light Pole in the Dark.

IMPACT BREAKS NECK AND FRACTURES SKULL

Lived Only About Fifteen Minutes—Funeral Held in Tabernacle Tuesday—Interment in Cedar Cemetery.

A most distressing accident occurred in Cedar City last Saturday night, which cost Alfred Hamilton, a young man from the village of the same name, his life. With another young man from the "Fort," Jack Middleton, he came up for the picture show. The electric plant was temporarily out of commission, so that there was no show, and the streets were in darkness. The boys had been to the residence of the unfortunate boy's brother, John C. Hamilton, Jr., and at about 8 o'clock were riding horseback from there to the home of Francis Middleton in the eastern part of town. In rounding a wagon that was on the street the horse Alfred was riding ran very near to a pole in the center of the street, and apparently did not see it until almost upon it. The supposition is that the horse shied, and threw the young man a little off his balance His head struck the pole and he was knocked to the ground and dragged a few yards before his companion could catch the horse and bring it to a stop.

The accident occurred on Center street, near the Dover residence, and the victim was picked up and carried into the rooms occupied by Mr. and Mrs. David Crosley, where first aid attention was given him and Dr. Macfarlane sent for. It was found that the young man's skull was fractured and his neck broken. He lived only about 15 minutes after the accident.

The funeral services were held in the tabernacle Tuesday at 10 a. m. The speakers were Elders Samuel F. Leigh, U. T. Jones, Charles Adams of Parowan, David Bulloch and Everard A. Cox. E. M. Corry sang the solo part in the choral anthem, "I Know that My Redeemer Lives." Interment was made in the Cedar City cemetery.

The young man is survived by his parents, John C. and Betsy A. Hamilton, and by a brother and five sisters, all of whom were present at the obseques. One sister, Mrs. Betsy Porter, came from Shelly, Idaho, for the services.

The young man bore a good character and was full of life and vim like most young men of his age, never stopping to consider danger in his exuberence of feeling.

The Record deeply sympathizes with the bereaved family on the sudden and shocking end of a promising career.

Iron County Record
March 15, 1918

Cupid's darts found vulnerable spots in the hearts of Mr. Joseph Mackelprang and Miss Eva Haslam, and as a sequence the young couple were married Wednesday, Mar. 13, the ceremony being performed by the County Clerk. The young people, who are receiving the congratulations of their many friends, will make their home in Cedar City, at least for the present.

Iron County Record
March 22, 1918

The little girls of Henry Mackelprang and Alma Esplin are improving nicely after their severe attacks of empyema.

Mr. John Dalley returned to Summit last Saturday, much improved in health, after his operation at the Macfarlane Hospital for empyema.

Born—to Mr. and Mrs. Ray Thomas Sunday, a boy; and to Mrs. Wallace Bracken a son the same day. Dr. Macfarlane reports all well. No wonder Mr. Thomas sang well in the opera this week.

Dr. Macfarlane was called to Kanarra last Saturday on the case of Mrs. Laron Williams, who gave birth to a boy, and to Mr. Joseph Ingram's on Monday, whose wife also presented him with a son.

Born, Mar. 19, to Mr. and Mrs. David Crosley, a 9 pound boy. Dr. Leonard reports the lady and baby to be doing well. Dave has not showed up at this office yet, however, and we fear the infant's hair wil not grow very well.

Iron County Record
March 29, 1918

Mrs. John Batts presented her husband with a son last Saturday night, Dr. Macfarlane reports that mother and infant are getting along nicely.

Mr. and Mrs. William B. Adams are receiving the congratulations of their many friends upon the arrival of a boy at their domicile last Wednesday.

SAHARA

Mrs. Hal Griffin has returned to Lund for an indefinite stay.

* * *

Mr. Jenkins of Beryl was a visitor at the ranch of C. J. Hellings one day this week.

* * *

Messers Guy Johnson, Athel Griffin and Hal Griffin went to Cedar City Friday on a short trip.

* * *

Miss Grace Magnussen made a flying trip to her home Sunday, returning to Lund on No. 2.

* * *

Mrs. Johnson has returned to her claim near Sahara and is preparing to do a bit of improving this coming season.

* * *

Mr. Jack Holland left Friday evening for Lyndyle, Utah, to enter the employ of the Salt Lake Route. Mr. Holland has filed on a claim south of Sahara.

* * *

"Doc" Hoxie, Charles Hellings and Guy Johnson drove to Lund Sunday to see Mr. Brooks in regard to the well. We expect to get Mr. Brooks and party to do our drilling.

* * *

We had a very fine rain ending in a two or three inch snow fall this week for which we are very thankful. There is lots of moisture in the ground now and this season's crops should be assured.

Concrete Highway

President E H. Snow of St George passed through Cedar City Wednesday on his way home from the general conference of the L D S at Salt Lake City. Seen by a representative of this paper, President Snow talked interestingly on the subject of good roads for this part of the state. "I am waiting for a report from the people of Cedar City on the analysis of the materials in your canyon for the making of Portland cement," said Mr Snow 'I believe that if the materials are all right, that there will be no trouble about financing a company to put in a 100 ton cement plant at Cedar City to supply cheaper cement to the southern counties of the state I believe that if Iron and Washington counties will subscribe one half the stock of the company, Charles Nibley and associates will do the rest and operate the plant The cost ought not to exceed $100 000.

"Then if the southern counties on the through state highway will bond for about $100,000 each, and the state will duplicate the appropriations of the counties, a good cement highway say nine feet wide, with turning places at needed intervals, could be constructed without imposing a serious burden upon anyone "

President Snow stated that he had talked this matter over a number of times with Charles Nibley, who is an important stockholder in the Red Devil cement plant, and that he was greatly interested in the matter.

President Snow fully appreciates the importance of cement in the development, on a substantial basis, of any country, and feels that there is nothing that local people can put money into that will mean more to the ultimate prosperity of the southern part of the state —Iron County Record.

ENOCH

Enoch, Utah, April 11, 1918.

Wm. J. Matheson of Midvalley who has been running the Cedar City Co-op Roller Mill for the past year has now accepted the same position under the Cedar City Milling Co.

* * *

Choir conductor Myron Jones is holding choir practice every Wednesday and Sunday nights in preparation for the dedication of the ward meeting house during conference.

* * *

Mr. Albert Biederman of Philadelphia, and brother of Fred Biederman, was here Sunday. This is his first trip west and we hope his opinion of the country will be favorable.

Dr. Leonard was called to Kanarra Wednesday. He reports the arrival of a son at the home of Mr. and Mrs. Andrew Berry.

A baby girl was born to Mr. and Mrs. Edwin Webb last Sunday evening. Mr. Webb is with the U. S. training camps or on his way to the front.

LETTER FROM OUR CEDAR CITY SAMMIES

Well, dear friends and folks, this will probably give you an idea of our daily life, but there is just one thing that we will add, and that is that our food does not contain much sugar and it is a well known fact that the system demands a certain amount of sugar. So we are in a position to handle as much candy or sweets as our friends wish to send us.

Your sons and Soldier Friends,

Company E: Marion W. Wilkinson, Jesse O. Webb, Orley A. Stapley, Geo. A. Perry, Raymond Perry, Thos. Mosdell, Parry Mackelprang.

Company D: Jack Gurr, Roy Bauer, Lew Farnsworth.

Address: 319th Engineers Co., Camp Fremont, California.

Headquarters Company: Clark Eddards.

Born, to Mr. and Mrs. John A. Loveless Sunday a boy; and to Mr. and Mrs. Samuel Bauer Wednesday, a boy. All concerned doing well.

Iron County Record
May 3, 1918

GRADUATION AT THE JUNIOR HIGH

Following is the list of graduates: Clara Bulloch, Selena Nelson, Jennie Middleton, Leo Palmer, Wallace Houchen, Leland Perry, Jane Lewis, Naomi Nelson, Fern Froyd, Rulon Wood, Karl Gardner, Ruth Cox, Thelma Brown and Ada Melling.

Born—To Mr. and Mrs. Leland Bettenson Tuesday, a girl. All concerned getting along nicely.

SAHARA.

Sahara, Utah, May 1, 1918.

Mr. and Mrs. Jeremiah Leavitt of Gunlock, Utah, were in Sahara one day this week. Mr. Leavitt brought over a lot of good things to eat to sell to our people.

* * *

Mr. H. C. Davis came home Sunday evening. All of Sahara were at the post office to extend a welcome to Bert. We are glad to have him with us again. He is a hustler and a regular fellow.

* * *

Mrs. Guy Johnson and Mrs. Earl Markwith returned home Monday night. We are glad to extend a welcome to these ladies. This about completes the list of absent ones, though we hear that S. A. Davis is contemplating returning to Sahara in about a week. Also Mr. J. E. Fairley is yet to come.

We are in receipt of a postal card from Mr. W. C. Jenkins of Beryl stating he has a Liberty Loan candidate corralled at Beryl, and will "we" come and sign him up. We will. We will lay down our shovel and our hoe and hike for Beryl tomorrow with pleasure. If we connect you will see his name in the honor roll from Beryl.

* * *

Saturday evening we had the misfortune not to attend the dance and missed meeting quite a party from Lund. Mr. and Mrs. J. D. Leigh, Mr. and Mrs. Green, Misses Haight, Gale, Ahlstrom, Grace Magnusen, Mrs. Hal Griffin, Mr. Ben Knell, Misses Gibson, Spillburg, Spendlove and others making up the party. We are glad to extend a welcome to our Lund friends and hope to see them again.

Iron County Record
May 10, 1918

OPERATIONS AT SOUTHERN UTAH HOSPITAL PAST WEEK

The following operations have been performed at the Southern Utah Hospital since our last report:

John Lundell, son of Mr. and Mrs. Albert Lundell, removal of tonsils.

Mrs. Orson Bryant underwent a critical instrumental delivery, the result being an 8 lb. boy. Mrs. Bryant and baby are doing nicely.

Mrs. Ernest Martineau was operated for appendicitis and the correction of female troubles.

Gordon Smith, son of Mr. William Smith, operated for appendicitis this morning.

Minor operations were performed for Mrs. Dan Webster of Kanarra and baby Gardner of Cedar City.

Iron County Record
May 24, 1918

Births Reported by Dr. Macfarlane.

The following births are reported by Dr. Macfarlane during the past week:

To Mr. and Mrs. J. M. Chatterly, Sunday, a girl.

To Mr. and Mrs. Wm. Stevens, Sunday, a boy.

To Mr. and Mrs. R. B. Sherratt, Monday, a boy.

To Mr. and Mrs. Hyrum Ford, Tuesday, a girl.

In Death of Mrs. Sarah Reese Walker Four Little Children are Bereft of Mother's Care.

Last Monday afternoon in the Cedar City tabernacle the funeral services were held over the remains of Mrs. Sarah Reese Walker, wife of Mr. . W. Walker, of this place, who succumbed to heart trouble, superinduced by goitre and other complaints. Mrs. Walker leaves four small sons, the oldest of whom is ten years and the youngest of which is not yet three.

Mrs. Walker was severely ill for about a month and in spite of all that her physician could do for her, grew steadily worse until death released her. Deceased was forty years old, and was the daughter of Hyrum and Elizabeth Reese, who resided in Cedar City until a few years ago when they moved to Mt. Carmel, and where, less than a year ago, Mrs. Reese died.

The tabernacle was appropriately draped and decorated with flowers for the occasion. Bishop H. H. Lunt presided, and the speakers were Jos. H. Armstrong, Andrew Corry, Fank Wood and Bishop H. H. Lunt. Professor Roylance directed the singing.

At the close of the very beautiful services, a number of relatives and friends followed the remains to their last resting place in the Cedar cemetery. The grave was dedicated by Bishop Thomas Jones of Paragonah, a relative of the family.

The sympathy of the community goes out to Brother Walker and the little children in their sad affliction, as well as to the father, brothers and sisters of the deceased, not all of whom were able to attend the services on account of the distances separating and the difficulty of travel.

The father and one sister, Rachel, of Mt. Carmel were here, returning home Wednesday.

Iron County Record
May 31, 1918

Dr. Leonard was called to Quitchapa on the 28th to attend Mrs. Hahne, who presented her husband with an infant.

Dr. Leonard reports a visit of the stork to the home of Mr. and Mrs. David Sharp on May 27, where a nice girl baby was left. Mrs. Sharp and the little Miss are doing nicely.

The little infant daughter of Mr and Mrs. George Foster died at noon today of pneumonia. The baby was just two weeks old and therefore not strong enough to withstand the ravages of the dread disease.

Mr. and Mrs. Joshua Walker claim the prize for the finest new-born baby in Cedar City this year. It is a boy and arrived on May 29th, tipping the scale at 15 pounds! Can anyone beat that. Dr. Leonard was in attendance.

Mrs. Kenneth Roylance received a visit while at the Southern Utah Hospital on the 28th. The new addition to the Roylance family is a boy. He already gives evidence of being a musician from the noise he makes, it is said. However, Mrs. Roylance and the boy are doing "just lovely."

SAHARA.

Sahara, Utah, May 27, 1918.

Mr. W. A. Griffin is up and around again after a three days illness.

* * *

James E. Fairly arrived home this week from his five months leave. We are glad to welcome him back to the colony.

Miss Agnes Bumpus was a visitor at Mr. and Mrs. Frank Hedrick's one day this week.

* * *

Messrs. Charles Hellings and Sam Davis contemplate going to Pocatello, Idaho, soon to engage in electrical work.

* * *

Mr. and Mrs. Guy Johnson entertained a party at their home Sunday. Guy left for Lyndyll Monday. Mrs. Johnson accompanied him as far as Lund.

ENOCH

Enoch, Utah, June 13, 1918.

Mrs. D. Grimshaw, who has been here visiting with her daughter, Mrs. M. S. Rogerson, returned home to Beaver last week, her son Randolph accompanying her.

Mr. and Mrs. Millard Halterman have rented Robert Mumford's home and are moving there this week. They have been living with Mrs. Halterman's parents, Mr. and Mrs. S. F. Jones the past winter.

REUNION OF LUNT= JONES FAMILIES

One Hundred Twenty-five Descendants of Thomas Jones and Henry Lunt Observe Birthday.

Some 125 people were in attendance at the reunion of the Lunt and Jones families held in this city Sunday evening, July 21, at the home of L. W. Jones. This included children, grandchildren and great-grandchildren of Thomas Jones and Henry Lunt, old pioneers of this end of the state, and widely known among the early settlers. A number of the families of posterity were not represented at the reunion, and in addition there are a number of others in the service of their Government.

It was a last request of Mary Ann Lunt that the two families which are very closely connected, meet once a year and the 20th of July was chosen as the most convenient time, being the birthday of both Thomas Jones and Henry Lunt. It was pos'p red one day this year, however, on account of the excitement attending the visit of the 145th regimental band. Appropriate speeches were given by Lehi W. Jones, who acted as chairman, Henry W. Lunt, W. W. Lunt, T. J. Jones; and Aunt Ann Macfarlane, who has been an intimate friend of both families forty years, gave some amusing incidents of pioneer days in her pleasing way. The speakers all related incidents attending the building up of Cedar City, the hardships and trials experienced by the pioneers and what they did for their children in coming to this country. An impromptu musical program was given by a number of the talented members of the families, and genealogical societies were organized; for the Thos. Jones Society, L. W. Jones was chosen president, Kumen Jones of Bluff City, vice president and T. Willard Jones, of Newcastle, secretary-treasurer. For the Henry Lunt Society, Henrietta L. Jones was chosen as president, Sarah Lunt, only surviving wife of Henry Lunt and who now lives in El Paso, Texas, as vice-president, and H. H. Lunt as secretary-treasurer. Light refreshments were served and the reunion adjourned until the 20th of July, 1919.

SAHARA

Sahara, Utah, July 21, 1918.

Mr. Harry Patten was home over Sunday.

* * *

Mrs. Reynolds has been on the sick list the past week, but is improving.

* * *

Mr. Joe Yeoman lost a valuable horse this week.

* * *

Mr. Hart Hoxie arrived from Los Angeles Tuesday evening.

* * *

Mrs. A. E. Phillips, post mistress of Sahara, drove to Lund on business the other day.

* * *

Mr. Ford Freeman is here from Kansas to stay with his mother, Mrs. C. E. Freeman.

Mr. Ray Ramsburg arrived from Los Angeles today. He reports that things are moving along nicely there.

* * *

Have you purchased your Thrift stamps at the post office? You had better do your bit.

* * *

Messrs. Bryant and Frank Hedrick were in Cedar City and surrounding country the past week selling horses.

* * *

Miss Grace Magnussen left for Wisconsin a few days since. She arrived safely and found the East changed considerably in six years.

* * *

Mr. and Mrs. Charles Jobert left for Salt Lake Friday. The community will miss them as they have been active members in our club and vicinity.

Cedar Boy Heroically Rescues Comrade

An act of heroism that won recognition from his colonel and regiment was performed recently by a Cedar City boy, particulars of which are contained in the following press dispatch

Camp Fremont, Palo Alto, Cal, June 15 — Two thousand men composing the 319th Engineers, presented arms this morning in the regimental parade grounds as a token of honor for the heroism of one of their number. Private Marion W. Wilkinson, who at the risk of losing his life yesterday evening dashed down a thirty-foot decline of "a dugout" and carried out private Maxwell N. Short, while dynamite blasts were going off around them. Colonel C. W Otwell, commander of the regiment, spoke warmly of the heroism displayed by Wilkinson.

The men were working on what is known as Company E's dugout, in the division system of trenches. Four holes had been drilled and these were loaded, Private Short remaining in the pit to fire the fuses One of the shots went off, and Short being missed, Wilkinson caught up a lantern and hurried down the incline after his comrade Half way down another blast extinguished the lantern. Wilkinson clambered to the surface, got another light and started down.

He found Short with both feet shot off, put him on his shoulder and carried him out as the other two shots went off. Wilkinson escaped with a few minor cuts There is a chance that Short will recover.

Vast Treasure Vault

Relative to the matter of proposed extensive development work on the large iron and coal deposits in the vicinity of Cedar City and the establishment of a big iron manufacturing plant on the shores of Utah lake, one of the engineers making an invistigation of the country, said to represent a large banking firm which may bid on the bonds for the building of a railroad, is quoted as follows: "I have covered the United States from coast to coast investigating proposed industries I have seen some pretty rich country, and I will frankly state that Utah has everything beat in the way of resources

"The territory which is covered by this proposed railroad is one vast treasure vault. Some of the greatest coal deposits known to the world are located there Mountains and mountains of iron ore of the highest grade, and it is all lying idle simply for the want of transportation to move it to the markets where it can be turned into steel and other commodities ' —Deseret News

Dr. Macfarlane reports the birth of a boy at the home of Mr. and Mrs. Treharne Jones Thursday, and to Mr. and Mrs. R. W. Bulloch the same day, also a son. All concerned doing nicely.

Miss Vera Pratt was operated on at the Macfarlane hospital Thursday for a badly ruptured appendix, resulting from appendicitis. Her condition is rather serious at present.

ENOCH

Miss Lila Gibson and Mr. John Gurr of Parowan were married August 6 at the home of the groom's parents. Mr. Gurr was here only 24 hours, being compelled to return to Camp Fremont where he was stationed, word being received that he was to be moved soon. We extend our congratulations to the couple and wish them success in this venture.

Iron County Record
August 16, 1918

Dr. Macfarlane reports a baby boy at the home of Mr. and Mrs. Bowler, new comers to this place.

Miss Nettie Urie of Hamilton's Fort has just returned from a three-months vacation spent in Salt Lake, Delta and Victor, Utah, most of the time in the two latter places with her sisters.

Iron County Record
August 23, 1918

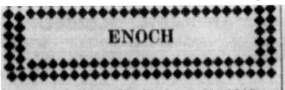

ENOCH

Enoch, Utah, Aug. 23, 1918.

Sunday the 18th, a girl was born to Mr. and Mrs. David Murie, and on Tuesday a girl to Mr. and Mrs. Robert Mumford.

Miss Ella Clark, daughter of Wm. Clark, was brought to the Macfarlane Hospital at midnight Saturday night suffering with acute appendicitis. The child was operated on but the appendix was found to have ruptured. After a stormy time for a few days the little girl is slowly recovering.

Mrs. Lottie Rosenberg received word last Tuesday that her son Harvey, who is in the fighting ranks in France, had been wounded. He received a flesh wound in his left hand and had the bones of his right ankle shattered by a piece of shrapnel. He is getting the best of care in a hospital and expects to be out very soon.

ELDERLY LADY CALLED HOME

Sister Mary Clark Higbee, at Ripe Age, is Summoned by the Angel of Death.

Sister Mary Clark Higbee, an old resident of this place, died Monday night, August 26th, after a rather protracted illness. She was the widow of the late John M. Higbee, and mother to a number of our prominent citizens, including S. A., M. D., Isaac C. and Edward Higbee, and Mrs. U. T. Jones, and Mrs. J. S. Woodbury.

Deceased was born in Ohio November 22, 1833, and came to Utah with the early pioneers, going through all the hardships and trials of that period. In crossing the plains, as a result of two of her brothers being called into the Mormon Battalion, she was left to drive an ox team with the company.

Was married to John M. Higbee in the fall of 1853 at Provo and arrived in Cedar City on her twentieth birthday.

Sister Higbee was the mother of 11 children, six of whom survive her, as do also 30 grandchildren and 22 great-grandchildren.

She has always been a devoted member of the Church of Latter-day Saints and was prominent in church work. For a number of years she was connected with the presidency of the Relief Society and did much good in that organization.

CEDAR CITY BOY CAPTURES 20 HUNS

Private Charles M Pratt of Cedar City, Sixth regiment of U S Marines, is in a French hospital with a machine gun bullet wound in his hip from which he will recover. The first time he "went over the top," he was unhurt, but was wounded the second trip Pratt captured 20 Huns in two days, the largest batch being found in a dugout.

Utah is gaining in coal production at the rate of 3564 tons a day according to figures compiled by the district representatives of the United States fuel administration During the first six months of 1918 the record was 2,334,580 tons

Cedar Soldier Takes Bride.

Mr. Earl Urie of this place, one of our Cedar City soldier boys who is working in a sawmill in Portland, Oregon, and Miss Pearl Whitney of Parowan, were married in Portland on August 24th. This marriage is the culmination of a courtship of several months, and it is believed that the young people had the wedding arranged before the departure of Miss Whitney and her mother for the Oregon lumber camps. Mr. Urie had applied for a furlough to come home, but his application was denied for the reason that he has been especially trained as a log scaler and there was no one to take his place.

Both Mr. Urie and Miss Whitney are well known here and their many friends will join us in wishing them joy and success in their new venture.

MORE IRON COUNTY BOYS GO TO COLORS

Hundreds Relatives and Friends Throng Main Street to See the Boys Off.

The Roll of Honor.

Following is a list of the men who entrain today for Camp Kearny from this county:

Jno. Franklin Wood, Paragonah.
Gerald Wilkinson, Cedar City.
Alfred S. Wilcock, Parowan.
Wallace Smith, Cedar City.
Frank S. Goddard, Cedar City.
Rulon Earl Barton, Paragonah.
Glenn Tullis, Newcastle.
Thos. E. Williams, Cedar City.
Thos. Gower Rosenberg, Cedar City.
Osmond Clair Lowder, Parowan
Jos. Ed. Schuman, Chicago.

Chas. Loyal Corry, Cedar City.
Arthur Frank Stapley, Cedar City.
Ebby Eddards, Cedar City.
Jno. Freeman Clark, Parowan.
Wm. Claud Edwards, Paragonah.
Rulon S. Dalley, Cedar City.
Orion Jones, Cedar City.
Harold McConnell, Cedar City.
Charles Leland Dalley, Summit.
Raymond Green, Cedar City.
Junior McConnell, Cedar City. (Included with the Washington county registrants.)

It is learned that Lynn Hunter of this place and Miss Gwen Burton of Parowan were married at the county seat last Wednesday, Sept 18. Apparently the wedding came as a surprise, even to their intimate friends. The Record wishes them joy and prosperity.

Mr. Ray Grimshaw and Marie Farrow of Summit were married at St. George last week and are receiving the congratulations of their many friends.

* * *

Robert Mumford and family have moved to their home in town after spending the summer on their farm. Mrs. Nellie Smith is staying with them on acocunt of the serious illness of Mrs. Mumford, who is her sister.

* * *

Miss Drucilla Grimshaw was taken to the Macfarlane Hospital at Cedar City Monday and had her right elbow straightened, which has been almost useless for a number of years.

❖❖❖ ENOCH ❖❖❖

Enoch, Utah, Sept. 19, 1918.

Mr. and Mrs. Millard Halterman have moved to their home at Midvalley, formerly belonging to J. W. Mendenhall.

* * *

We extend congratulations to Mr. and Mrs. Reuben W. Jones on the arrival of a fine baby boy at their home Sept. 12. This is their first boy, so is rather a pleasing event.

New Iron Co. Registrants

List of Names of Persons Between the Ages of 18 and 45 Years Who Registered for Military Service in Iron County September 12, and Whose Cards are in the Possession of Local Board

Reg. No.	NAME	Address.
1	Amos Fredrick Root,	Cedar City.
2	Daniel Brown Clark,	Cedar City.
3	Ralph Comer Adams,	Cedar City.
4	Arthur Francis Louis,	Cedar City.
5	William Heyborne,	Cedar City.
6	Angus Rosenberg,	Cedar City.
7	Bernard Moroni Hunter,	Cedar City.
8	John Harvey Ballard,	Cedar City.
9	Joseph Benjamin Bess,	Cedar City.
10	Grant Parry,	Cedar City.
11	Rex Perry,	Cedar City.
12	William Arthur Condie,	Cedar City.
13	DeLon Walker,	Cedar City.
14	Roe Middleton, Palmer,	Cedar City.
15	Grant Rountree Hunter,	Cedar City.
16	John Bryant,	Cedar City.
17	Lamont Higbee,	Cedar City.
18	Leland Leigh,	Cedar City.
19	George Vernon Lunt,	Cedar City.
20	Wallace Alma Flanigan,	Cedar City.
21	Thomas Chatterley Thorley,	Cedar.
22	Clarence Webster Heyborne,	Cedar.
23	Robert Bauer,	Cedar City.
24	Henry Herbert McConnell,	Cedar.

25—Wm. Edward Stevenson, Cedar City.
26—Herbert Riggs, Cedar City.
27—Mayhew Hillman Dalley, Cedar City.
28—Warrington W. McAllister, Cedar.
29—Francis Alonzo Brown, Cedar City.
30—James Ronald Urie, Cedar City.
31—Morton Chatterley Walker, Summit.
32—Thomas Roy Urie, Cedar City.
33—Horatio Owen Rice, Cedar City.
34—Clarence Isaac Haight, Cedar City.
35—David Wilson Woodard, Jr., Cedar.
36—Alonzo Pitt Ahlstrom, Cedar City.
37—Thomas Jones Higbee, Cedar City.
38—David Claud Urie, Cedar City.
39—Ozias Hanie, St. George, Utah .
40—William Howell Warrington, Cedar.
41—Eugene Angus Cripps, Cedar City.
42—Thomas Oscar Stokes, Preston, Ida.
43—George Henry Gower, Cedar City.
44—Elias Moroni Corry, Cedar City.
45—David Dunn Sherratt, Cedar City.
46—Oscar Mayo Willis, Lund, Utah.
47—Ora Alexander Martin, Cedar City.
48—John Albert Loveless, Cedar City.
49—Louis Snyder Alexander, S. L. City.
50—John Aaron Batt, Cedar City.
51—Henry Lunt Jones, Cedar City.
52—Conroy Bryner Wood, Cedar City.
53—Edward Hahne, Cedar City.
54—Alonzo Jones Higbee, Cedar City.
55—Mitchell Monroe Smith, Cedar City.
56—James Lawrence Bess, Cedar City.
57—George Kenneth Urie, Cedar City.
58—Menzies John Macfarlane, Cedar.
59—Walter Smith Harris, Cedar City.
60—Roy Fisher Homer, Cedar City.
61—John Henry Fife, Cedar City.
62—James McDonald Hamilton, Cedar.
63—Francis Webster Leigh, Cedar City.
64—Frank Richard Lambeth, Cedar City.
65—George William Perry, Cedar City.
66—Tipton Pitt Ahlstrom, Cedar City.
67—Robert Aldridge Thorley, Cedar City.
68—Samuel Webster Leigh, Cedar City.
69—David Robert Condie, Cedar City.

70—Kumen Lunt Jones, Cedar City.
71—Wm. Franklin Jordan, Cedar City.
72—John Edward Westerhold, Cedar City
73—Ontonio Luca—Cedar City.
(Care of James Smith.)
74—Ambrose Lorenzo Watson, Cedar.
75—William Sherratt, Cedar City.
76—Joseph Smith Thompson, Cedar City.
77—Israel Taylor Neilson, Cedar City.
78—John Alexander Condie, Cedar City.
79—Wm. John Matheson, Cedar City.
80—Edwin Reid Cox, Hamilton's Fort.
81—Samuel Leigh Fife, Parowan, Utah.
82—Henry Aldridge Thorley, Cedar City.
83—Henry Jenson, Cedar City.
84—Charles Edwin Adams, Cedar City.
85—Samuel Fife Leigh, Cedar City.
86—Howard Chamberlain, Cedar City.
87—John Sixtus Haslam, Cedar City.
88—Thos. William Mumford, Cedar City.
89—Frank Aldridge Thorley, Cedar City.
90—Archibald Swapp, Cedar City.
91—Ellis Melbourne Colvin, Lund.
92—Wm. Chatterley Macfarlane, Cedar.
93—John Abner Adams, Cedar City.
94—Wm. Wallace Flanigan, Cedar City.
95—Charles Hallman, Cedar City.
96—Wm. Rees Palmer, Cedar City.
97—Donald Clyde Urie, Cedar City.
98—Joseph Adam Kopp, Cedar City.
99—James Mashburn, Cedar City.
(Care of James Smith.)
100—John Perry Fuller, Cedar City.
101—Adelbert Bywater, Cedar City.
102—Carl Otto Lundgren, Cedar City.
103—George Wood Urie, Cedar City.
104—Corydon Walker, Cedar City.
105—Preston Wood, Cedar City.
106—Charles Stevens, Enoch.
107—Guss Chatterley Pendleton, Cedar.
108—Donald Parry Mackelprang, Cedar.
109—Erwin David Rhead, S. L. City.
1384 S. 14th East St.
110—Morgan Rollo, Cedar City.
111—Vernon Gronway Parry, Cedar City.

112—Alfred Christian Stucki, Cedar City.
113—Herbert Price Haight, Cedar City.
114—Lloyd Martinose McArthur, Cedar.
115—Archie James Gale, Cedar City.
116—Jas. Whittaker Thornton, Cedar City
117—Jas. Alexander Tweedie, Cedar City.
118—Robert Snow Gardner, Cedar City.
119—Chas. Franklin Ross, Cedar City.
120—John Stephen Christenson, Cedar.
121—Frank Henry Petty, Cedar City.
122—Millard Don Watson, Cedar City.
123—Joe William Walker, Cedar City.
124—Joseph E. Haslam, Cedar City.
125—Randall Lunt Jones, Cedar City.
126—James Corlett Parry, Cedar City.
127—Thomas Willard Jones, Newcastle.
128—Wm. Cameron Murie, Cedar City.
129—Charles William Bechtol, Cedar City.
130—John Cuttler Carpenter, Cedar City.
131—Wm. Edward Elliker, Cedar City.
132—John Taylor Bulloch, Cedar City.
133—William Henry Leigh, Cedar City.
134—James Bulloch, Cedar City.
135—Thomas Dix, Cedar City.

136—Hyrum Chandler Ford, Cedar City.
137—Chas. Pitman Clifton, Lund, Utah.
138—Wm. Benjamin Haslam, Cedar City.
139—Jas. Whittaker Chatterley, Cedar.
140—Geo. Webster Esplin, Enoch.
141—Horton David Haight, Cedar City.
142—Wm. Bailey, Adams, Cedar City.
143—Geo. Clarence Goddard, Cedar City.
144—Daniel Enoch Matheson, Enoch.
145—Andrew Nevan M. Rollo, Cedar City
146—Karl Wood, Cedar City.
147—Golden Haight, Cedar City.
148—Carlos Lee Jones, Cedar City.
149—Thomas Gordon Smith, Cedar City.
150—Paul Carroll Seegmiller, Cedar City.
151—James Darwin Nelson, Cedar City.
152—Francis Rollo, Cedar City.
153—Samuel Charles Bell, Cedar City.
154—Solon Junius Foster, Cedar City.
155—Wm. Henry Clark, Cedar City.
156—Jacob Nephi Smith, Cedar City.
157—Daniel Fife Leigh, Cedar City.
158—Fred Garfield Burkholder, Lund.
159—William Stephens, Cedar City.
160—Edward Horton Parry, Cedar City.
161—Robert Durias Adams, Cedar City.
162—Wm. Ernest Corry, Cedar City.
163—William McDonald, Lund.

164—John Corry Gower, Cedar City.
165—Jeddiah Francis Woodard, Cedar.
166—Samuel Arthur Davis, Sahara, Utah.
167—Albert Urie Nelson, Cedar City.
168—Chas. Rountree Hunter, Cedar City.
169—Arnold Lamar Graff, Kanarra.
170—Kimball Jenson, Cedar City.
171—John Karl Carpenter, Cedar City.
172—William L. Jones, Cedar City.
173—Joseph Carlos Fife, Cedar City.
174—Fred Bywater, Cedar City.
175—Charles Cram Bulloch, Cedar City.
176—Martin Frank Jacobson, Cedar City.
177—Charles Rupert Dalley, Summit.
178—Benj. Raymor Lawrence, Summit.
179—John Farrow, Summit, Utah
179—John Farrow, Summit.
180—Benjamin H. Smith, Jr., Sussex, N.J.
181—Graham Brown McAllister, Summit.

182—Christain Peterson, Summit.
183—Sumner Clarence O'Donnal, Summit.
184—Niels Christian Madsen, Summit.
185—John Ronald Lowe, Summit.
186—Alexander Dalley, Summit.
187—Charles Clarence Smith, Summit.
188—Isaac Chamberlain, Summit.
189—John Henry Dalley, Summit.
190—Oscar Jones Hulet, Summit.
191—Jesse Ernest Dalley, Summit.
192—Lloyd Dalley White, Summit.
193—Virgil Streator Owen, Summit.
194—Thomas Henry Rowley, Parowan.
195—Clayton Ellsworth Trimner, Parowan
196—Earl Munford Decker, Parowan.
197—Eloyd Battenson Burton, Parowan.
198—George Alma Lowe, Jr., Parowan.
199—Wm. Thomas Morris, Jr., Parowan.
200—Wm. Francis Whitney, Parowan.

201—John Herbert Corry, Cedar City.
202—Joshua Walker, Cedar City.
203—Evelyn Connay Parry, Cedar City.
204—Lehi Aldridge Thorley, Cedar City.
205—Edward James Higbee, Cedar City.
206—George Albert Lunt, Cedar City.
207—George Henry Macfarland, Cedar.
208—Howard Claud Lewis, Cedar City.
209—Ernest A. Walker, Mesquite, Nev.
210—Francis W. Middleton, Cedar City.
211—Peter Taylor Neilson, Cedar City.
212—Joseph Edgar Perry, Cedar City.
213—Thomas Horace Glaze, Summit.
214—John Peter Bayles, Parowan.
215—Martin Lazelle Skougard, Parowan.
216—Orian Burton Lyman, Parowan.
217—John William Taylor, Parowan.
218—James Leech Adams, Parowan.
219—Chas. Allen Hollinghead, Parowan.
220—Edward Mitchell Dalton, Parowan.
221—Nathan Benson, Parowan.
222—Archibald Benson, Parowan.
223—Frank King Gurr, Parowan.
224—Frank Anderson Matheson, Parowan
225—Hyrum Lester Fix, Parowan.
226—Thomas Owen Taylor, Parowan.
227—James Alma Benson, Parowan.
228—George Henry Durham, Parowan.
229—Wm. Anthony Hawkins, Parowan.
230—Andrew F. Neilson, Henrieville, Utah
231—John Horace Miller, Parowan.
232—Wm. Sylvester Monson, Parowan.
233—Jasper George Stubbs, Parowan.
234—Robert Davenport, Parowan.
235—Mark Carlyle Roberts, Parowan.
236—Bart Ward Mortensen, Parowan.
237—Calvin Crane Connell, Parowan.
238—Alphonso Lowe, Parowan.
239—William Glenn Clark, Parowan.
240—Joseph Ervin Stevens, Parowan.
241—David Phillip Barton, Parowan.
242—Enoch Orton Rasmussen, Parowan.
243—Garfield Merritt Clark, Parowan.
244—Hugh Leech Adams, Parowan.
245—George Harwood, Parowan.

246—George Bettridge, Parowan.
247—Joseph Rasmussen, Parowan.
248—Geo. Tompkins Cason, Parowan.
249—John Geary Page, Little Pinto, Utah.
250—Ephraim Williams Perkins, Cedar.
251—Jesse Turner Forsyth, Newcastle.
252—Frank Knell, Newcastle
253—Edmund Leroy Grant, New Harmony
254—John Hardman Tullis, Newcastle.
255—James Claudius Knell, Newcastle.
256—Parley Maybe, Enterprise.
257—Chas. Woodruff Tullis, Newcastle.
258—Neil Donald Forsyth, Newcastle.
259—John McMurtrie Tullis, Newcastle.
260—Joseph Ernest Eldridge, Pinto, Utah.
261—Thos. Whittaker Forsyth, Newcastle.
262—Joseph Leon Eldridge, Pinto, Utah.
263—Robert Platt, Newcastle.
264—Vodo Del Vecchio, Newcastle.
265—Richard Edward Tullis, Newcastle.
266—Roy Pack, Enterprise.
267—Heber Eldridge Harrison, Newcastle.
268—John Henry Perry, Cedar City.
269—Daniel Geary Page, Pinto, Utah.
270—James Newberry Connell, Parowan.
271—Jess Franklin Lowder, Parowan.
272—Henry Alfred Mitchell, Parowan.
273—John Arthur Evans, Parowan.
274—James Green, Parowan.
275—Jorgen Andrew Jensen, Parowan.
276—Edward Ambrose Burton, Parowan.
277—Edward Reeves Liston, Parowan.
278—Albert Moroni Ogden, Parowan.
279—John Raymond Lee, Parowan.
280—George Ence, Parowan.
281—Eugene Meeks Dalton, Parowan.
282—Willard Andrew Wood, Parowan.
283—John Melvin Ward, Parowan.
284—Chas. Augustas Orton, Parowan.
285—Samuel Amasa Halterman, Parowan.
286—William John Gurr, Parowan.
287—Thomas Bennett, Parowan.
288—William Leech Adams, Parowan.
289—William Joseph Lowder, Parowan.
290—Clarence Edgar Dalton, Parowan.

291—Amil William Witte, Parowan.
292—Alvin Richard Benson, Parowan.
293—William Delbert Smith, Parowan.
294—Charles Henry Heap, Parowan.
295—Marion Andrew Simkins, Parowan.
296—Jos. Marion Halterman, Parowan.
297—John William Bentley, Parowan.
298—John William Benson, Parowan.

299—Lawrence L. Davis, Kanarra.
300—Le Roy Myers, Parowan.
301—Clark Wilford Ograin, Stateline.
302—Ether Leroy Carter, Lund.
303—Leslie Archie Hiestand, Lund.
304—Wallace Taylor Couch, Lund.
305—Julius Theodore Hunt, Lund.
306—Leo Arthur Slayman, Lund.
307—John David Leigh, Lund.
308—John Ray Brown, Lund, Utah.
309—Andrew J. Lewis, Nada.
310—Henry Vandervord, Lund.
311—Domingo Lopez, Nada.
312—Frank Joseph Sanfellco, Lund.
313—William Adam, Lund.
314—Peter Thompson Keillor, Nada.
315—Oliver Ira Burkholder, Lund.
316—Robert Minnis Stafford, Lund.
317—Job Franklin Hall, Lund.
318—Russell Edwin Anderson, Lund.
319—Thomas Raymond Canova, Lund.
320—Carl Putman Casad, Sahara.
321—Hugo Hunt, Lund.
322—Joseph Elvert Pierce, Lund.
323—Fred C. Waldschmidt, Lund.
324—Ralph W. Sanders, Nada.
325—Charles Warren Booth, Lund.
326—Ernest Le Roy Carter, Lund.
327—John H. Johnston, Lund.
328—Henry Edward Smith, Nada.
329—Asa Grant Brooks, Lund.
330—John Willard Green, Salt Lake City.
1830 Lake Street.

331—John Frith, Parowan.
332—George Frith, Jr., Parowan.
333—James Samuel Green, Parowan.
334—Albert Matheson Marsden, Parowan.
335—Geo. Rasmus Mickelson, Parowan.
336—George Homer Thornton, Parowan.
337—John Henderson Pendleton, Parowan.
338—Thomas Wendell Bayles, Parowan.
339—Hans Jorgon Mortensen, Parowan.
340—John William Mortensen, Parowan.
341—George Stevens, Parowan.
342—George Bernard Fowler, Parowan.
343—Claud Charles Hollberg, Parowan.
344—Geo. Walter Rasmussen, Parowan.
345—Thomas Edward Fowler, Parowan.
346—William Richards Adams, Parowan.
347—Arnold Orton, Parowan.
348—William Jewell Wilcock, Parowan.
349—Clark Ward Lyman, Parowan.
350—George Chester Gunn, Parowan.
351—Wm. Clarence Pendleton, Parowan.
352—Joseph Richard Lister, Parowan.
353—Alvin Alexander Benson, Parowan.
354—William Martell Eyre, Minersville.
355—James Le Roy Hyatt, Parowan.
356—Joseph Rasmus Bentley, Parowan.
357—Frank M. Rasmussen, Parowan.
358—Paul Mensoe Adams, Parowan.
359—Edgar Merion Stubbs, Parowan.
360—Silas Taylor Orton, Parowan.
361—Stanley Walter Roberts, Parowan.
362—Leonidas Bertram Johnson, Parowan.
363—Clarence Richards, Parowan.
364—Walter William Stubbs, Parowan.

365—Thomas Knott Holyoak, Parowan.
366—Sidney Pynor Pritchard, Parowan.
367—Jullon Evans Rolling, Parowan.
368—Alma Earl Hyatt, Parowan.
369—George Smith Wimmer, Parowan.
370—Delbert Ward Mortensen, Parowan.
371—Alfred Serenus Morris, Parowan.
372—Thomas Davenport, Parowan.
373—Jas. Corey Robinson, Jr., Parowan.
374—Wm. Henry Orton, Parowan.
375—Clifton Taylor, Parowan.
376—Jos. Ferguson Holyoak, Parowan.
377—Joseph Stevens, Parowan.
378—Joseph Rueben Mortensen, Parowan.
379—John Burrough Davenport, Parowan.
380—Joseph Bartlette Dalton, Parowan.
381—Vernon William Heap, Parowan.
382—Blanchard Eli Whitney, Parowan.
383—Joseph Moroni Jensen, Parowan.
384—Marcus L. Guymon, Jr., Parowan.
385—John Logan Lowder, Parowan.
386—Ellis Threlkeld Orton, Parowan.
387—Joseph Clayton Mitchell, Parowan.
388—Lucius Marsden Benson, Parowan.
389—Herbert Harold Trimmer, Parowan.
390—Clifford Holmes Benson, Parowan.
391—George Leo Enee, Parowan.
392—Ray Bentley, Parowan.
393—Wayne Monroe Guymon, Parowan.
394—Frank Elwood Jensen, Parowan.
395—Thomas Ward Bettridge, Parowan.
396—Junius Dewey Bentley, Parowan.
397—Jesse Rowley, Parowan.
398—Reuben Wesley Gould, Parowan.
399—Bruhn Dwain Decker, Parowan.
400—Melburn Benson, Parowan.
401—Charles Herbert Knell, Newcastle.
402—Thomas James Holyoak, Parowan.

403—Peter Hanson Gurr, Parowan.
404—Marion Edgar Lowder, Parowan.
405—David Albert Matheson, Parowan.
406—John Henry Jensen, Parowan.
407—Jesse Edward Clark, Parowan.
408—George Ellis Bentley, Parowan.
409—George Louis Burton, Parowan.
410—Ernest Johnson Orton, Parowan.
411—Lawrence Johnson, Parowan.
412—ElRoy Smith Jones, Enoch.
413—Thornton Armstrong Jones, Enoch.
414—Wm. Franklin Armstrong, Enoch.
415—Myron Simkins Jones, Enoch.
416—Nephi Stevens, Enoch.
417—Owen Matheson, Enoch.
418—Robert Mumford, Enoch.
419—Ray Grimshaw, Enoch.
420—Lorenzo Matheson, Enoch.
421—John Alvin Davenport, Enoch.
422—William Henry Grimshaw, Enoch.
423—Oliver Carlos Stevens, Enoch.
424—Charles Franklin Stevens, Enoch.
425—Kenneth Haight Macfarlane, Cedar.
426—Francis B. Webster, Cedar City.
427—John Calloway Isbell, Cedar City.
428—William Leroy Jesperson, Cedar.
429—Wilford Dover, Cedar City.
430—John Herbert Melling, Cedar City.
431—Berry Mulliner, Cedar City.
432—John Edward Dover, Cedar City.
433—Myles Adams, Cedar City.
434—Thomas Adams Bladen, Cedar City.
435—Lorenzo Lunt Hunter, Cedar City.
436—Robert Abel Arthur, Cedar City.
437—William George Wooley, Cedar City.
438—Frank Leslie Gower, Cedar City.
439—Richard Williams, Jr., Cedar City.
440—Roger Harris, Cedar City.

441—Robert William Bulloch, Cedar City.
442—Heleman Parson Webster, Cedar.
443—David Murie, Cedar City.
444—Ralph James Wilcock, Spry, Utah.
445—Isaiah Bozarth, Paragonah.
446—Esperidion Flores, Modena.
447—Pedro Martimer, Modena.
448—Sabastian Enriques, Modena.
449—Patricio Gutierres, Modena.
450—Carlos A. Castillo, Modena.
451—Anastrio Terijo, Modena.
452—Celestian Cruz, Modena.
453—George Kiyomon Takai, Modena.
454—Joseph James Wilson, Modena.
455—Sextus Johnson, Modena.
456—Carl Ludwig Kittleson, Prout.
457—William Lund, Modena.
458—Melvin Dewitt Heist, Heist.
459—Carl Robins, Prout.
460—David Waugh Bloater, Modena.
461—Frank Conner Peckles, Modena.
462—Coleman T. Ayers, Lampoc, Calif.
463—Charles John Eridson, Modena.
464—Harmel Jacob Bauer, Cedar City.
465—Frank Gilbert Webster, Trout.
466—William Daniel Dooley, Heist.
467—Thomas John Dooley, Heist.
468—Edward James McGrath, Modena.
469—Lonie Elsworth Paddock, Modena.
470—Merlin June Topham, Parowan.
471—David Merrill Edwards, Paragonah.
472—Newton Floyd McBride, Paragonah.
473—Stephen Burrows Barton, Paragonah
474—Jesse Lowe Barton, Paragonah.
475—John Nolon Openshaw, Paragonah.
476—Claudius L. Robinson, Paragonah.
477—William Milton Robb, Paragonah.
478—Jesse William Topham, Paragonah.
479—Morgan Bell Edwards, Paragonah.
480—Milton Luther Dailey, Paragonah.
481—Archie M. Lamoreaux, Paragonah.
482—Franklin K. Williamson, Paragonah.
483—Rudolph Salazer Garcia, Paragonah.
484—Wm. Thomas Davenport, Paragonah.
485—Benj. Wm. Openshaw, Paragonah.

486—Hyrum Banks Robinson, Paragonah.
487—Stephen Smith Topham, Paragonah.
488—Thomas Alex. Edwards, Paragonah.
489—Edwin W. Williamson, Paragonah.
490—John B. Topham, Jr., Paragonah.
491—Thomas Wm. Robb, Paragonah.
492—John Calvin Barton, Paragonah.
493—John Seeman Haight, Cedar City.
494—Gnacia Birton, Cedar City.
495—John Edward Edwards, Paragonah.
496—David A. Lamoreaux Jr., Paragonah.
497—Marius Alfred Dunton, Paragonah.
498—Albert Daily Robb, Paragonah.
499—Marion Dailey, Paragonah.
500—David James Edwards, Paragonah.
501—Archie Price Spilsbury, Cedar City.
502—John Edward Davis, Cedar City.
503—Thomas D. Pryor, Cedar City.
504—John Henry Williams, Kanarra.
505—Jesse Payson Gee, Parowan.
506—Von Willard Watts, Cedar City.
507—Leada Glenn Williams, Kanarra.
508—Joseph S. Williams, Kanarra.
509—John William Berry, Kanarra.
510—Lewis Merill Groves, Kanarra.
511—William Andrew Berry, Kanarra.
512—Reese James Williams, Kanarra.
513—Charles Parker, Jr., Kanarra.
514—Herbert Henry Wood, Kanarra.
515—Golden Parrish Roundy, Kanarra.
516—Lester Williams Ford, Kanarra.
517—Wm. Wallace Pollock, Kanarra.
518—Alonzo Lazeli Stapley, Kanarra.
519—William Jones Williams, Kanarra.
520—James Sylvester Berry, Kanarra.
521—Ceylon Davis, Kanarra.
522—Jesse Arthur Berry, Kanarra.
523—Jos. Henry Pollock, Jr., Kanarra.
524—Earl Fisher Smith, Kanarra.
525—Jesse Berry Ford, Kanarra.
526—Samuel Lorenzo Pollock, Kanarra.
527—Albert Davis, Kanarra.
528—Byron Napoleon Pollock, Kanarra.
529—Jesse Franklin Williams, Kanarra.
530—Samuel Thomas Ford, Kanarra.

531—Jones Preston Wiliams, Kanarra.
532—Harry Jay Patten, Sahara.
533—James Acia Baker, Sahara.
534—Henry Terrel Griffin, Sahara.
535—Herbert Clarkson Davis, Sahara.
536—Charles Mart'n Magnussen, Sahara.
537—Charley Rufus Couch, Sahara.
538—Michael Rilley, Sahara.
539—George Elmer Griffin, Sahara.
540—Ross Adrian Brown, Sahara.
541—Norman Scott Beeler, Beryl.
542—Lucio Axgona Duxascano, Beryl.
543—Nicholas Megia Chocon, Colton, Cal.
544—Bert Rinson Frasure, Prout.
545—Samuel Miner Alison, Prout.
546—Numzio Fucarino, Enterprise.
547—Jasper McPherson Sweeney, Beryl.
548—William Evans Pryor, Cedar City.
549—Isaac W. Parry, Cedar City.
550—Thomas Gilbert Barton, Toquerville.

551—Thomas Bulloch, Cedar City.
552—Royal S. Gardner, Cedar City.
553—Arthur James Bryant, Cedar City.
554—Ralph Crane Watson, Cedar City.
555—Samuel Vincent Mulliner, Cedar City.
556—Lemuel William Willis, Cedar City.
557—Alfred Dover Klingonsmith, Cedar.
558—William A. Tucker, Cedar City.
559—Joseph Forest Haws, Cedar City.
560—David William Webster, Cedar City.
561—Horace Alvin Dover, Cedar City.
562—Reuben Herbert Walker, Cedar City.
563—Chas. Christian Bowler, Cedar City.
564—De Quincey Wix, Cedar City.
565—Moroni Corry, Cedar City.
566—John Middleton, Cedar City.
567—William Henry Bess, Cedar City.
568—Ernest Webster, Cedar City.

569—Charles S. Wilkinson, Cedar City.
570—Franklin Bryner Wood, Cedar City.
571—John Moody Foster, Cedar City.
572—Alfred John Elliker, Cedar City.
573—Henry Tibs Ashdown, Cedar City.
574—Thomas Lawrence, Cedar City.
575—Daniel Urie Webster, Cedar City.
576—Robert Bulloch Simkins, Cedar City.
577—Archibald Walker, Summit.
578—John Urie Webster, Cedar City.
579—Robert Burns Sherratt, Cedar City.
580—Frank Jackson Ashdown, Cedar City
581—Henry Hunter Lunt, Cedar City.
582—Joseph Mackelprang, Cedar City.
583—Willam Thomas Hunter, Cedar City.
584—David Dix, Cedar City.
585—Ralph F. Perry, Cedar City.
586—Francis H. Middleton, Cedar City.
587—John Goodfellow Holland, Cedar.
588—Chris Ashdown, Cedar City.
589—Cornelius Wanner, Cedar City.
590—Wm. Henry Fretwell, Cedar City.
591—Fred Barnson, Cedar City.
592—James Wm. Middleton, Cedar City.
593—Walter Murie, Cedar City.
594—Calvin C. Pendleton, Cedar City.
595—George Albert Wood, Cedar City.
596—John Middleton, Cedar City.
597—Erastus Bertleson Dalley, Cedar.
598—Joseph Perkins, Jr. Cedar City
599—Carl Augustus Burkholder, Cedar.
600—J. William Walker, Cedar City.
601—Alfred Terry Lund, Paragonah.
602—Geo. Alvin Williamson, Paragonah.
603—Jonathan David Prothero, Paragonah.
604—Geo. Albert Robinson, Paragonah.
605—James William Barton, Paragonah.

606—John Lewis Dalton, Paragonah.
607—Joseph Hansen Lund, Paragonah.
608—George Nelson Holyoak, Paragonah.
609—William H. Boardman, Paragonah.
610—Richard Neilson Lund, Paragonah.
611—John Henry Prothero, Paragonah.
612—Clarence G. Paramore, Parowan.
613—John H. Williamson, Paragonah.
614—David Evans Pryor, Cedar City.
615—Wm. Henry Sawyer, Cedar City.
616—Peter Fife Leigh, Cedar City.
617—Daniel Stephens, Cedar City.
618—John Campbell Macfarlane, Cedar.
619—George Hyrum Corry, Cedar City.
620—Roston Hilton Bryant, Cedar City.
621—Henry Mackelprang, Cedar City.
622—Roy Edwin Kelsey, Cedar City.
623—Lot Marion Pexton, Nephi, Utah.
624—Caleb William Macfarlane, Cedar.
625—John R. Robinson, Jr., Cedar City.
626—Preston Swapp, Cedar City.
627—Paul Sanford Pierson, Lund.
628—Jose Villa, Cedar City.
629—Clarence Lynd, Beryl, Utah.
630—Don Carlos Thornton, Parowan.
631—Arthur Merrill Willis, Kanarra.
632—Jonathan Davis Morrill, Modena.
633—Louis C. Stilwell, Modena.
634—Freeman W. Pendleton, Jr., Parow'n
635—George Oliver Taylor, Parowan.
636—Joe Ayerdi, Cedar City.
637—James Richard McGinty, Parowan.
638—Dave Cannon, Moccasin, Arizona.
639—Marion W. Brown, Parowan.
640—Peter Frederick Bruhn, Parowan.

Iron County Record
September 27, 1918

FUNERAL RITES FOR ELIZA McCONNELL

BIOGRAPHICAL.

Eliza Williams McConnell was the daughter of Thomas Williams and Ann Jones Williams. She was born at Smansee, Wales, April 28, 1838, and came to this country when she was only eight years old. She endured the hardships of pioneer life in Utah. Deceased was born of an influential and well-to-do family, but was left an orphan at a tender age and was obliged to make her own way in the world. She was brought to America by her stepmother. They made their way to Utah after a long and tedious journey and settled in Lehi. It was there that she later met her husband, Henry McConnell, to whom she was married in the year 1856. After five years of married life the family moved to Cedar City, where they helped to build up the new community.

Sister McConnell was always very industrious and for many years kept a dairy in the Cedar mountains. She was the first white woman who ever went into these mountains. When her husband was called on a mision to the Eastern States she took up the burden of supporting her family, when her dairy still stood her in good stead.

She was skillful in the use of herbs and medicines and spent a good deal of her time in her younger days assistitng her sick neighbors.

As old age and infirmities crept upon her she worried because she was not able to do as she had done in her younger days. She was generous to a fault, giving away things she needed herself, to help others.

Deceased was the mother of eight children, three of whom preceded her to the other world, as also did her husband, five years ago. The living sons and daughters are: Mrs. Eliza Ann Sawyer, Wiliam J., LaFayette and Thomas F. McConnell, and Mrs. Minta M. Bulloch.

Iron County Record
September 30, 1918

SAHARA

Sahara Utah, Sept. 30, 1918. Mr. Harry Patten was home over Sunday.

* * *

Mrs. Hobbs and Arvilla Root went to Lund Friday night, returning Sunday night.

* * *

Mrs. Hall Griffin is home for a few days and tells us that her husband got his foot mashed in Lynndyl.

* * *

Messrs Bert Davis and Bert Reynolds came home Saturday from the Bishop Bridge Gang and returned Sunday.

Mike Riley came in Sunday night on No.4, returning on No.3. He certainly made a flying trip and states that he enjoys his work at Coma.

* * *

Our farmers are taking advantage of the nice rains we have had the past week by getting some of their fall plowing done.

* * *

Mr. J. A. Baker received a car load of fence posts from the R. R. to build the fence on the railroad right of way running through his land.

* * *

The school children are doing their bit picking up peach pits and other shells to make masks from.

Iron County Record
October 18, 1918

Born—To Mr. and Mrs. Kenneth Macfarlane Tuesday, a girl. All doing nicely.

Mrs. Bert Gower was operated on last Monday at the Macfarlane Hospital for appendicitis.

Mr. and Mrs. Charles Mosdell, Jr., of Hamilton's Fort are happy over the arrival of a baby girl at their home the first of the week.

———— ✦ ————

Miss Estelle Parry who volunteered her services as a nurse to Uncle Sam has received her call and will leave soon for Camp Kearney, California

FUNERAL RITES FOR CHASE WILLIAMS

Impressive Services Held at Kanarra for Remains of Boy Who Met Death in Auto Accident.

Kanarra, Oct. 21, 1918.

The funeral services of Chase Williams who died last Wednesday at Cedar City from injuries received in an auto accident, was held here last Friday at 3 o'clock. The ward choir furnished the music. Prayer was offered by Elder John Sorenson and John W. Platt pronounced the benediction. Miss Bateman sang the solo,

"Face to Face." The speakers were Elders Riley G. Williams, Joel J. Roundy and Bishop Berry. There were many beautiful floral offerings, which covered the casket. The class mates of deceased from the B. A. C. sent to Salt Lake City for a nice bouquet of flowers, which, however was delayed in transit and did not arrive until the next day; but the parents appreciated the gift of the students and their token of love for their son. The pall bearers were Earl Smith, Glen Williams, Elden Reeves, Ray Williams, Cecil Parker and Ceylon Davis. The grave was dedicated by J. W. Williams.

Glen King, a son-in-law of Mr. and Mrs. John H. Williams, came from Logan, where he was in training at the school, to attend the funeral of his brother-in-law, Chase Williams.

* * *

Mrs. Fern Adams of Canada, daughter of Mr. and Mrs. John H. Williams, arrived in town today. She came expecting to be present at the funeral of her brother, but was too late. She will visit here for some time.

Iron County Record
November 15, 1918

ENOCH

Enoch, Utah, Nov. 14, 1918.

Three members of David Gibson's family are down with the flu.

* * *

Mr. Owen Matheson of Midvalley has purchased a car which will aid him greatly in his well drilling work.

* * *

Mr. Bert Mason and family of near Lund are living on Wm. J. Matheson's farm at Midvalley, which Mr. Mason has rented.

* * *

The post office is now in first-class running order under the management of Mrs. M. S. Rogerson, the new official.

Mrs. Flora Mumford who has been very critically ill for the past month, passed away Wednesday morning at 9 o'clock. This is a particularly sad affair, due to the fact that she leaves a husband and three small children, besides a three-months old baby. Mrs. Mumford was the daughter of the late E. C. Cox of Cedar City and has a host of relatives and friends to mourn her loss. Mr. and Mrs. Mumford have been residents of this place for a number of years and Mr. Mumford and his family have the sincere sympathy of the entire ward. Funeral services were held on the meeting house grounds at 11 o'clock Thursday

A baby girl was born to Mr. and Mrs. Leonard Haight of Midvalley the fore part of this month. This is the first offspring of this union and the happy parents are receiving the congratulations of their many friends.

WORLD PEACE HAS COME AT LAST

Armistice Terms Signed Last Monday Morning, Hostilities Ceased at 11 A. M.

ISRAEL ABBOTT
Reported ' missing in action, Oct 4 "

Mrs Abbott, who is staying with her father in this city, received a phone message Tuesday morning from Enterprise, where she had been teaching school, that a letter had arrived there for her from her husband bearing the "censor's" mark and date ' Oct 24," 20 days later than the date he was reported missing Mrs Abbott phoned back, "open the letter and see date when written," only to receive the discouraging reply ' Letter remailed to you via Cedar City " So it will be Thursday night before Mrs Abbott can have her mind set at rest It looks reasonable to suppose that the letter was written after the date when Abbott was reported "missing," and Mrs Abbott has great hopes that all is well with her husband

————W.S S————

Iron County Record
November 29, 1918

BREAD WINNER TAKEN FROM WIFE AND TOTS

William Elliker is Another Victim of Influenza Epidemic, Leaving Wife and 3 Children

It is always sad to see a wife and family of helpless children deprived of the assistance of the bread-winner and made to face the cold world with but little protection from want. Such a bereavement results from the death of William Elliker of this city, who went down a victim of influenza on November 20th, having contracted the disease at the new Lunt Coal mine, in connection with some four or five other workmen. The disease ran its usual fatal course of about a week, pneumonia developing as a complication, and nothing that could be done appeared to stay the advance of the disease.

Deceased was a man over forty years of age, had been twice married, but only his last wife bore him children, of which three survive him. His present wife was formerly Miss Ethel Vanarsdel.

The mother was herself seriously sick with influenza at the same time as her husband and was unable to take care of him or to accompany the remains to the cemetery.

Deceased was a native of this place, being born and raised in Cedar City, although a part of his life was spent in mining at various places.

Mrs. James Stapley is a recent victim of influenza.

————W.S.S.————

Isaac Nelson and family have fallen victims to influenza.

————W.S.S.————

Carl Burkholder and family have just been released from quarantine, after a "family" helping of the "flu." Carl thinks it is no joke.

————W.S.S.————

Miss Mildred Adams, the seventeen-year-old daughter of Mr. and Mrs. Lorenzo Adams, is reported by Dr. Macfarlane to be the only patient in Cedar City at present who is giving him serious concern. The doctor is very much worried about Mildred's case, which fails to respond to treatment. Her temperature remains very high in spite of all that can be done for her.

Miss Mildred Adams, Daughter of Mr. and Mrs. Lorenzo Adams, is Last Victim in Cedar City.

We have another sad death to record this week as a result of the dreaded influenza, complicated with pneumonia. We refer to the demise of Miss Mildred Adams, daughter of Mr. and Mrs. Lorenzo Adams, who answered the final summons on Tuesday, Dec. 3rd. Mildred was taken ill with influenza Nov. 28 and was very bad from the start.

Mildred Adams was born Sept. 16, 1901, making her 17 years of age at the time of her death. She was an exceptionally bright and lovable girl, and was liked by every one who knew her. She was an excellent student in school, graduating from the district shool in 1915, and was a third year high school student at the time of her death.

The funeral services were held at the cemetery Tuesday at 4 o'clock. The speakers were Bp. H. H. Lunt, Bp. Wm. R. Palmer, and J. H. Pendleton. Mr. and Mrs. Adams wish to sincerely thank all who were so kind as to give assistance or proffer assistance in their sad trial.

The family of Isaac Chamberlain at Summit has influenza. Dr. Macfarlane is giving them medical care

Born—To Mr. and Mrs. Frank Anderon last Friday, a boy. Dr. Macfarlane reports all doing nicely.

Miss Mary Urie, after having practically recovered from the "flu" suffered an attack of appendicitis, but is on the road to recovery at present.

Miss Lula Heyborne, eldest daughter of Mr. and Mrs. Chas. H. Heyborne, has pneumonia. At this writing she is doing as well as could be expected.

On recent visits the stork has left babies at the following homes: Mr. and Mrs. James Bulloch, Mr. and Mrs. Joseph Perkins, Mr. and Mrs. Lem. Stephens and M. and Mrs. William Pryor.

Born Tuesday morning to Mrs. Frank Jackson a boy. Mrs. Jackson was formerly Miss Marcella Matheson and her husband is now in Camp Meade, Maryland.

Monday morning a baby boy was born to Mr. and Mrs. Angus Bulloch.

Park Westover and family, who reside in a portion of the Ray Cosslett residence, all have the influenza. At this writing Mrs. Westover, who was the first to take down, is recovering rapidly and the other members of the family are apparently gaining. Mrs. Ray Cosslett also has a mild attack of the disease.

Mrs. Kunz, instructor in English at the B. A. C., is a recent victim of influenza. She also has a son and daughter down with the disease. This is the last of the families residing at the Ray Cosslett home to contract the disease, the other two families occupying the building already having come down with it.

William Smith, Prominent Live Stock Grower, Succumbs to Fatal Disease After Short Illness.

It is the unpleasant duty of The Record this issue to chronicle the death of William S. Smith, one of the solid, enterprising citizens of this place, who has fallen another victim to influenza-pneumonia. Mr. Smith was afflicted with influenza about two weeks ago, and after the influenza had subsided, pneumonia set in and he has been desperately sick ever since. He made a hard fight, and apparently was passing the crisis of the disease some days ago, but took a relapse and gradually sank to his final rest, the end coming at 5:40 Thursday morning.

The funeral service is being held at the residence this afternoon, begining at 2 o'clock.

William S. Smith was born June 24, 1870, and resided the greater part of his life in Kane county, where he engaged in the livestock business. He was married to Catherine Carpenter, and seven children survive him, as the issue of the marriage. Mrs. Smith preceded her husband to the other side of the vail in March of 1917. The family moved to Cedar City about six years ago, and Mr. Smith has been in the sheep business during his residence here. He was a builder and a substantial citizen, whose word was as good as his bond.

About ten years ago he returned from a mission to Great Britain, in which capacity he served for two years.

The orphan children of Mr. Smith are Lulu Smith Cox, wife of Mr. Dee Cox; Wallace, now in training at Camp Kearney; Gordon, Lamar, Wilford, Elda and Dee, all of whom reside at home with the exception of those noted above, and were at the death-bed of their father.

Deceased was 48 years of age at the time of his demise.

An affectionate and indulgent father always, he will be greatly missed by the children, who, however, are left well provided for and with the aid of their uncles and other relatives will not suffer for material things, but will greatly miss the companionship and watchful care of their only remaining parent, snatched from them by the relentless and unmerciful pest that is ravishing the country.

The Record extends sincere sympathy and condolence to the bereaved family and other relatives.

SAHARA

Sahara, Utah, Dec. 9, 1918.

Mrs. Davis and Little son Bert left for Los Angeles Tuesday.

* * *

Some snow storm we have been having.

* * *

It sure seemed like living on a farm to see four nice hogs hung up Saturday. Mr. Couch, Mr. Baker and Mr. Magnussen did the work.

Iron County Record
December 20, 1918

Young Married Man of Cedar City Dies After Week's Illness—3 Children Left Fatherless.

Influenza claimed its eighth victim in Cedar City last Sunday, Dec. 15, in the death of Conrad Hunter, a young man 27 years of age with a family consisting of a wife and three children.

Conrad was one of the men who contracted influenza while working at the Iron County Coal Company's mine, and was brought home Sunday, December 8th, and developing pneumonia, died just one week later.

He seemed very sick from the start and his case was regarded as serious.

He leaves, besides his wife and three small children, a father and mother, a brother and two sisters to mourn his departure.

The funeral services were held at the home of his mother, Mrs. Beatrice Hunter, who has not fully recovered from a severe attack of influenza-pneumonia that she passed through herself a few weeks ago. The speakers were Elders Samuel F. Leigh and Henry W. Lunt.

The sympathy of the community goes out to the bereaved family and especially to the little fatherless children in their loss of a father's care and support.

Born—Wednesday morning to Mr. and Mrs. Gordon Matheson, a girl. All is reported well with them.

Born—To Mr. and Mrs. Dan Seegmiller this morning, a girl. Mrs. S. has been ill with influenza, but at present is recovering from the effects of the disease.

Wallace Smith, who was here for the funeral of his father, William Smith, returned to Camp Kearney Thursday where he will secure his release and then return home permanently.

Willard Canfield, Dave Tweedie, Loyal Corry and Herman Bement are the latest arrivals from the various training camps. We are glad to welcome the boys back again.

BORN.—To Mr. and Mrs. Walter Hanson, last Saturday, twins, one of the babies dying at birth. To Mr. and Mrs. J. A. Adams Sunday, a girl.

Miss Anile Stewart Thursday, for acute appendicitis.

Miss Geneva Anderson, Saturday, for removal of tonsils.

The small daughter of Mr. and Mrs. Francis W. Leigh Wednesday, for removal of tonsils.

Dr. Macfarlane now estimates that he will be leaving Cedar City for study in the East about the 15th of this month.

SAHARA

Sahara, Utah, Feb. 9, 1919.

Mr. and Mrs. J. E. Fairley and Mr. and Mrs. C. R. Couch are spending over Sunday with Mr. and Mrs. Fourman at Modena.

* * *

Mrs. George Griffin went to Eccles to be with her husband as he has a foreman's job on the station.

* * *

We had a wood-cutting bee at the school house Saturday. After the work was finished, a tasty lunch was served.

Mrs. Violet Hobbs returned to Lund after a few weeks visit with her mother, Mrs. N. B. Hobbs.

* * *

Mrs. Baker returned to Nada Monday to join her husband.

* * *

Mr. and Mrs. Hall Griffin have accepted positions with Mr. Webb on the rail road.

* * *

Mr. Reynolds was home over Sunday.

KANARRA

Kanarra, Utah, Feb. 12, 1919.

Another soldier boy has returned home. He is Elmer Davis and arrived last Friday. He looks and feels fine and is proud of his experiences while in Camp Lewis. Also, another of our misionaries is back—Elder Lorenzo Roundy. He came in on the passenger car last Thursday. He has only the highest of praise for the missionary labors, but of course is glad to be home again after 27 months in the mission field.

The following births were attended this week by Dr. Bergstrom: To. Mr. and Mrs. John Davis Saturday, a boy; to Mr. and Mrs. George Hunter Wednesday, a boy.

Dr. Bergstrom attended births this week as follows: Mrs. Glen King, a boy, Mrs. Lehi Thorley a boy, Mrs. Rone Gilles of Newcastle, a boy.

John Parry and William Walker Answer Reaper's Summons—Were Both Old Residents.

JOHN PARRY

Hon. John Parry, whose obsequies were held at the family residence last Wednesday afternoon, was born in New Market, Flenstshire, North Wales, November 13, 1841, making him 77 years old on his last birthday. When about seven years of age he was miraculously healed by prayer. This was a factor in his parents investigating and joining the Church of Jesus Christ of Latter-day Saints.

Fifteen years later the family came to Utah, crossing the plains with handcarts, and locating in Cedar City in 1856.

In 1863 he recrossed the plains, going to Missouri by ox team for immigrants and in 1866 he responded to a call to go to Long Valley with other young men to guard the settlements from the attacks of Indians. In 1869 he married Mary Ann Haight, and they are the parents of ten children, nine of whom are living. In 1875 he was called on a mission, being sent first to Pennsylvania and later to England.

Through his pioneering experience he developed a capacity and willingness for discharging a large amount of service in the interest of the public. He was three times elected mayor of Cedar City and three times a member of the state legislature.

Among his tastes and ambitions was a profound interest in education. He truly appreciated the value and joy of learning, and was for a long time a member of the Board of Education of the Parowan Stake Academy. Later he was instrumental in securing the location of the Branch Normal School at this place, and in his capacity of county representative in the legislature, aided that institution in various ways.

Deceased was a most public spirited citizen, often neglecting his own affairs to render various services to the community at large.

He died quite suddenly March 17th, from the results of a stroke, being ill only a few days and suffering practically no pain.

The speakers at the funeral were: Supt. L. John Nuttall, Elders David Bulloch and Alex G. Matheson. All bore testimony to the good character and useful life work of the deceased.

The singing was by the choir, under the direction of Mr. Frisby.

A public funeral was prevented by reason of the order of the Board of health, but there was a large number of relatives and immediate friends in attendance and a profusion of pretty flowers, the long procession that followed the remains to their last resting place in the local cemetery bearing witness to the respect in which the community held the deceased.

One by one the older settlers are leaving us, and of assurity we must look on the other side of the vale now for the big majority.

WILLIAM WALKER

Yesterday afternoon at 4 p. m. at his home in this city, death relieved William Walker, a pioneer and respected citizen of this place from a long and trying bed of suffering from cancer, which attacked him some three years ago.

William Walker was a conspicuous figure in this locality for many years during the early settlement and development of this part of Utah.

Born in Sheffield, England, on Feb. 22, 1836, he emigrated to America in his early teens, crossing the ocean in the ship Setland, and landing in St. Louis. With his parents he made his way to the Salt Lake Valley, and was a member of the first pioneer company to this county, settling first at Parowan and then accompanying the first company of pioneers to this valley, where he has since resided.

As a young man he was noted for his athletic attainments, being a foot racer, jumper and broncho rider.

He made a number of trips into Southern California over the old Mormon Trail to San Diego, while Los Angeles was still little more than a village, for supplies, and was one of the first residents of this place to own and drive horse teams. He was also the first man in Cedar City to own and operate a mowing machine here.

He was married to Janet Corry on Christmas Day, 1862, and nine children were the issue of the union, seven sons and two daughters. Mrs. Walker died on the fiftieth anniversary of their wedding, or their golden wedding anniversary. The children are: Wm. V. Walker, George H. Walker, and Joshua Walker of this place, James and Ernest Walker of Nevada, Mrs. Will Macfarlane of this place, and Edwin Walker and Mrs. Peter B. Fife who have preceded their father to the other world.

William Walker was one of the sturdy old veterans who took a live part in the subduing of this once forbidding spot, and helped to make it a desirable place to live. He was a home man, and never took much stock in politics or religios activities, though he was a sincere and consistent member of the Latter-day Saint church.

During his last illness, by reason of the nature of his disease, he has been a great sufferer, but has been wonderfully patient and resigned through it all.

Acocrding to present plans the funeral will be held Saturday afternoon at 2 o'clock. His two sons are expected from Nevada and his grandson, Ernest Fife, from Garfield county.

Interment will be made in the local cemetery.

DIXIE POWER CO. ACQUIRES CEDAR CITY ELECTRIC PLANT

A L Woodhouse, president of the Dixie Power Co , and Miss Ada Gardner the stenographer for the company returned Wednesday from Cedar City, where they had been fixing up contracts, etc , required in the transfer of the Cedar City electric plant to the Dixie Power Co.

The purchase price and terms are not known to us

The Dixie Power Co, will extend it's service from Glen Cove and take care of Cedar City and other towns in Iron County.

JOHN PARRY

Old resident and prominent citizen of Cedar City, and conspicuous public worker and educator, who died in this city March 17th from a paryletic stroke at the age of 77 years.

WILLIAM WALKER

Pioneer and builder of Cedar City, who died March 20th, at the ripe age of 82 years.

Four Deaths as Result of Recent Outbreak of "Flu" and its Deadly Aftermath, Pneumonia.

HAZEL FLANIGAN

Hazel Flanigan was the only daughter of Mr. and Mrs. William Flanigan of this city. She was born June 2nd, 1903, at Springdale, Washington Co., and moved to Cedar City with her parents in September, 1910. She was seized by influenza on the night of March 15th, and developing pneumonia, when apparently over the "flu," died March 24th, and was buried Mar. 25th. The funeral was held at the residence the speakers being Elders E. J. Palmer, H. Claud Lewis, Sam. F. Leigh. The opening prayer was offered by Bro. John Chatterley, and the benediction was pronounced by Elder William Lunt. Miss Luke very beautifully rendered the solo "Sweet Rose," and the choir sang "Nearer My God to Thee" and "We Need Thee Every Hour."

Owing to the quarantine regulations, relatives at Hurricane, Springdale, Virgen City, Fillmore, Hinckley and Circleville, including grandparents, uncles, aunts and cousins, were unable to attend, though a number expressed their desire of doing so.

As above stated, the deceased was the only girl in the family. The boys are: Wallace, aged 19; Glen, aged 13; Elsworth, aged 11, and LaVar, aged 4.

Hazel was one of the type of girls seldom seen now-a-days. She was trustworthy, industrious and responsible, being more like a matured woman than a girl. Yet withal she was gentle, affable and pleasant, and had a wide circle of friends who will miss her greatly.

The parents are all broken up over their great loss.

VERA ADAMS

Miss Vera Adams, daughter of Mr. and Mrs. William B. Adams of this city, who was claimed last Tuesday by the influenza plague which broke out anew in this city a few weeks ago, was born in this city Christmas Day, 1898, making her 20 years of age last Christmas. She was an attractive and lady-like girl, and was beloved by all who knew her. A student of the B. A. C. the present winter, she was held in the highest regard by her classmates and the faculty of the school, as attested by the beautiful floral offerings which they carried to her funeral.

The Adams family took down with the "flu" March 8th, the entire family being affected. As is so often the case, the young lady apparently recovered from the attack of "flu" and then developed pneumonia, the deadly aftermath of this plague. Everything possible was done for her, but to no avail. She seemed to have been marked by the Grim Reaper for his own, and death came last Tuesday at about noon, as stated.

A quiet funeral was held at the family residence Wednesday afternoon at 4 p. m., the speakers being John V. Adams, grandfather of the young lady, Elders S. F. Leigh, Frank B. Wood and Jethro Palmer.

All the speakers gave words of comfort and consolation to the bereaved family.

A long line of automobiles followed the hearse and a company of boys and girls, the classmates of the deceased, to the cemetery, where interment was made.

MRS. CHRIS ASHDOWN.

There is nothing more harrowing and heart-rending that the separation by the angel of death of a mother from a husband and a flock of small children, and the sympathy of the community goes out this week to Mr. Chris Ashdown and his little group of six motherless children, as a result of a visitation upon them by the dread scourge of influenza.

Deceased was 42 years of age, and was the daughter of Mr. and Mrs. Daniel Pendleton of this place. Death came when the atack of influenza through which she was passing turned to pneumonia.

The funeral services were held at the residence yesterday afternoon, Bishop H. H. Lunt presiding.

Opened by singing "Sometime We'll Understand," and "I Know That My Redeemer Lives."

The speakers were H. W. Lunt, S. F. Leigh, who spoke of the excellent character and life of deceased, and gave comfort to the bereaved ones.

Choir sang in closin, "Deepening Trials."

Deceased was a devoted wife and mother and lived and moved very largely in the realm of her own home.

Besides her husband and children, deceased leaves a father and mother, several sisters and two brothers to mourn her untimely death.

MORANE ADAMS

The fourth death from influenza-pneumonia during the present epidemic, occurred Wednesday night, when Morane Adams, aged 11 years and the daughter of Mr. and Mrs. William B. Adams, who had already lost their eldest daughter, passed away, after a hard fight for her life.

Morane was a little unfortunate, being slightly abnormal in some respects, but these misfortunes appealed all the more to the sympathy and parental instinct of the father and mother, and being the second death in their family within two or three days made it all the more pathetic. Mrs. Adams was completely prostrated by the double bereavement, and the entire family having been afflicted with influenza made it a most harrowing experience for them.

Iron County Record
April 4, 1919

Sister Stapley of Kanarra, a lady 72 years old, is at the Macfarlane Hospital with a fractured hip and seems to be on the improve.

Samuel Stucki, while assisting with the branding of some colts at the Thorley ranch near Kelsey's, had his hip severely strained and at first it was feared that his thigh was broken. The young man was rushed to town in an automobile, but on examination his injury was not found to be as bad as was at first feared. He is recovering slowly, though his injury is quite painful.

The following births are reported by Dr. Bergstrom for the past week: To Mr. and Mrs. Thuro Gardner, last Tuesday night, a son; to Mr. and Mrs. Joseph Hyatt of Kanarra, Wednesday morning, a girl; to Mrs. Gray, at the local hospital Saturday, a boy, and to Mr. and Mrs. Ray Brown at Iron Springs Sunday, a son.

Iron County Record
April 11, 1919

Walter Hansen, Mrs. Jos. B. Dalley and Kathleen Jenson are Toll of Week in Cedar City.

WALTER HANSEN

It is always distressing to see a young man or woman in the full vigor of life and apparently with everything before them, snatched away by the messenger of death. This is the condition which surrounds the demise of Walter Hansen, a young married man of this place, who died at 1:20 Monday afternoon, April 7th.

Walter was a physical giant and scarcely knew what it was to be sick a day in his life, until while in Salt Lake a couple of weeks ago he was attacked by influenza. He returned home and developed as a complication gastroid intestinal trouble, resulting in a ruptured bowel. Dr. McGregor of St. George was called into consultation with the local practitioner on his case, but the deadly peritonitis continued to progress, until the entire abdomen became lifeless and the death of the patient followed.

Deceased was the son of Andrew Hansen and Eliza A. Houchen Hansen, and was born in this city Mar. 15, 1896. He was a graduate of the high school department of the B. A. C., and took a lively interest in athletics and basket ball while in school, being a member of the basket ball team in 1916 when they won the state championship.

On May 28, 1917, he was married to Miss Ruth Williams, daughter of Mr. and Mrs. Evan E. Williams, of this place, and one child, a daughter of two months, survives him, as well as his wife, one brother and several sisters.

The funeral services were held at the residence Wednesday afternoon, Bp. H. H. Lunt presiding. The choir was present and furnished the singing, which included the following anthems: "Abide With Me," and "I Need Thee Every Hour."

Principal Roy F. Homer was the first speaker. He recalled the excellent record of deceased while in school and of his various school activities. Spoke words of comfort to the bereaved wife and family.

Elder H. W. Lunt spoke of the hope of a future meeting, and of what a comfort it is to Latter-day Saints.

Elder Samuel F. Leigh also gave comfort and assurance to the bereaved ones and urged them to study the Scriptures, and be in a position to mingle with loved ones in a future existence.

Mr. Christensen, coach at the B. A. C., spoke of the regard in which he held the deceased, who was always eager to help his friends and do his share in school activities.

The benediction was pronounced by Hunter Lunt, and in closing the choir sang "Some Time We'll Understand."

The floral decorations were very beautiful, many of which were contributed by loving friends. There was a large attendance and the services were very beautiful throughout.

The remains found a last resting place in the local cemetery.

MRS. JOS. B. DALLEY

Friends and acquaintances of Mr. and Mrs. Joseph B. Dalley of Summit were greatly shocked and surprised Tuesday morning to learn of the sudden death of Mrs. Dalley, who was formerly Miss Sarah Ann Heyborne of this city, and for some time a teacher in the public schools of this county. Mrs. Dalley has not appeared strong for some years, but few people knew that she was in a dangerous condition until about the time of her death. Her trouble was endocorditis, though this may have been aggrivated to some extent by an acute atack of appendicitis, which she suffered about a month ago, but from which she had fully recovered. At that time she was brought to Cedar City and placed in the care of Dr. Bergstrom, and was intending to return home the present week, but was taken suddenly last Sunday with a heart spell from which she did not revive, but slowly sank until the end came at 6:40 Tuesday morning.

Sarah Heyborne Dalley was born February 16, 1878, in Cedar City.

She was educated in the public schools of this place and was one of the first students to enter the Branch Normal School when it was established here. She was closely connected with the work of the Y. L. M. I. A. and the Primary organization in Cedar City.

She was married to Bishop Joseph B. Dalley of Summit June 26, 1913, and was again closely associated with the Y. L. M. I. A. and Primary organization at Summit.

She has suffered greatly of late years from a complication of heart and kidney complaints.

KATHLEEN JENSON

A very sad death occured at 2:15 a. m. April 4th when Kathleen, the beatiful young daughter of Mr. and Mrs. Heber C. Jenson passed away. Some weeks previous to her last illness she suffered an attack of influenza, but recovered sufficiently to resume her school work. Being of a very persistent nature she continued her activities contracting one cold after another, until she was finally sent home from school with a distinct fever. A six weeks seige of pneumonia followed during which time she showed exceptional patience and faith in her recovery. Kathleen was in her eighteenth year, being born on the 18th of August 1900. She was a beautiful girl, her outward charm being a reflection of a very fine and sympathetic nature. She showed exceptional talent in many lines being of a very artictic temperament. She was unusually generous and affectionate and was the inspiration of the entire family. Besides her grief stricken parents she leaves three brothers and one sister to mourn her untimely loss.

Impressive funeral services were held Sat. afternoon at 2.00 o'clock at the home of Mr. and Mrs. Thos. J. Webster, uncle and aunt of the deceased with whom she had been very intimate. Dr. Bergstrom spoke of her character and the patience and kind consideration she had for others which characterized her long illness. Bishop Palmer told of his acquaintance with her as a little child and Bp. Lunt spoke words of consolation to the family and behalf of the family thanked all those who had in any way assisted in the sickness of Kathleen.

Exceptionally fine music was furnished by Mr. Johnson, violinist, Mr. Frisby, vocalist and the choir. Her high school class and a large gathering of friends and relatives followed her remains to the cemetery.

Iron County Record
April 25, 1919

Mr. and Mrs. D. Wilson Woodard are rejoicing over the arrival of a fine baby boy Apr. 15, Mrs. Woodard is at the Esther Apartments, Salt Lake city under the care of her sister, Miss Roundy who is a trained nurse.

BENGT. NELSON AND JOHN VORLEY ADAMS

Brother Adams Speaks at Funeral of His Friend and in Less than Two Hours is Himself a Corpse—Short Biography of Brother Nelson.

BENGT. NELSON.

Cedar City hadn't a more genuinely good, sincere, kind-hearted and loveable old man that Bengt. Nelson. If he had an enemy, we have failed to learn of it. Honest as the day is long, upright and charitable, he was beloved by all who knew him. His demise came suddenly last Tuesday, and was the result of an accident which befel him two or three days earlier. He was engaged in making some improvements about his home, and was struck by a plank in the abdomen. A hernia of years standing was caused to strangulate, and death ensued. It is a coincidence that Mrs. Nelson's death, which occurred a few years since, was also due to an accident, and this notwithstanding the fact that they were quiet, careful, home-folks.

Had Bengt Nelson lived until the 28th day of next September he would have been 85 years old, yet he was comparatively spry and active and enjoyed working in proportion to his physical strength. He was a mason by trade and he leaves a number of monuments in the form of homes and public buildings in Cedar City of his thrift and industry.

He was tender hearted as a woman, and at funerals, where he was a frequent speaker, he almost invariably broke down and shed tears. He leaves a family of four sons and one daughter, and one son and two daughters have preceded him to the beyond. The names of the children, and the order of birth, follow:

Caroline Nelson, born in Cedar City Dec. 22, 1857, married Sam'l T. Leigh Dec. 19, 1878, died May 3, 1885.

Bengt Nelson, Jr., Born March 11, 1860, married Sarah C. Hunter, resides in Cedar City.

Ellen D. Nelson, born Mar. 21, 1862, married Thos. W. Perry; resides in Cedar City.

Henry A. Nelson, born Feb. 3, 1864, died July 8, 1864.

John P. Nelson, born Jan. 19, 1893, married Hannah N. Orton of Paro-wan; resides in Cedar City.

Anna M. Nelson, born Nov. 9, 1868, died June 25, 1883.

Isaac A. Nelson, born May 8, 1871, married Sarah H. Arthur; resides in Cedar City.

Charles A. Nelson, born Nov. 6, 1873, Married Clara Taylor; resides at Salt Lake City.

Bengt Nelson was born in Lomma, Sweden, about three miles west of Lund, Sept. 28, 1834. His grandfather, Andres Anderson, was a dragoon in the Swedish army and was in the war with Napoleon in 1807. Bengt was educated in the common schools of Sweden, the family being in moderate circumstances. He would help his father on the farm in summer and go to school in the winter.

As he was approaching his 'teens the boy worked for a short time as apprentice to his cousin, who was a good blacksmith. Later he worked with another relative for three years, learning the trade of bricklayer. At the end of three years he went to work with a master mechanic at Lund, where he perfected himself in his chosen trade.

Was baptized into the Church of Jesus Christ of Latter-day Saints on April 15, 1854. On the 19th of November, 1854, with his brother-in-law and two sisters, who had also joined the Latter-day Saints, he boarded a small steamer bound for Copenhagen, and on the 24th of November, with about 300 others set sail for Liverpool, England. After much delay from storm and winds, they arrived in Liverpool Dec. 24. Rested in Liverpool for several days and on Jan. 11, 1855, boarded a sailing vessel for New Orleans, where they landed on the 23rd of February. Next morning boarded a river steamer for St. Louis, arriving on the 7th of March.

He crossed the plains with ox teams in Capt. A. O. Smoot's company, arriving at Salt Lake City Nov. 9, 1856.

He was married Nov. 16, 1856, to Ellen Johnson, a Swedish girl and a friend of his sister's who crossed the plains with them.

"The council at that time was for those who had no employment to move into the setlements, so I decided to take the first chance I could get to leave the city. Bishop Woolley thought it best to go south. The first man I found was Bishop Klingon Smith from Iron county, who was up to get people to go to Cedar City to help build up the iron works, which had already been started. So in company with the Bishop and others we left for the south.

On our way we suffered a good deal with the cold. In Round Valley, now Scipio, we were lost in a fearful snow storm and could not find the road leading to the canyon. Reaching a clump of cedars on the west side of the valley we camped for the night, and next morning it had cleared up, but we had about two and a half feet of snow. During the whole of that day we had to walk ahead and break the road in front of the teams as they could not go through it. These were the two worst days we had on the journey; we had some snow and cold weather after that but it was not so bad. We finally reached Cedar City November 29, 1856.

"Winter was approaching and the weather was cold. I was very anxious to find something to do to provide ourselves with the necessities of life; we were strangers, without friends and feeling very lonely. Of course, it was not long before we found friends, and good ones, too."

BROTHER JOHN V. ADAMS DROPS DEAD IN YARD

"There is no occasion to mourn over the death of such a man as Brother Nelson; he has lived to a ripe age and has earned his reward. And there will be no occasion to mourn when I leave this existence, which will not be long now." These in substance were the words of Brother John V. Adams, as he addressed the friends who had assembled to do last honors to that worthy person. In less than two hours his lifeless body was being prepared to receive his shroud. After the funeral he had a little coughing spell, and was given a cough lozenger and went into the open air. He was seen to stagger and fall in the yard at the rear of the house, and those near hurried to his assistance. He was dead in a few seconds, apparently having ruptured a large artery in the region of his heart. It all happened so quickly that the family could not realize that the end had come, and when the truth had dawned the good wife was completely unnerved and shocked most cruelly.

While John V. Adams was nearing 90 years of age and perhaps the oldest person in Cedar City, he was a remarkably spry and well preserved. He took his daily walk and kept his lot and garden a model of beauty and neatness. He was gentle, kind and considerate of the feelings of others, an excellent neighbor and a true and loyal citizen. His death was totally unexpected and the entire comumnity was shocked with the news.

The majority of his children reside here and soon they had gathered at the residence, but too late to see their father in life. He was spared all the pain of a separation as well as all sufferings of a physical nature.

The funeral will be held at the tabernacle tomorrow (Saturday) afternoon, at 2 p. m.

John Varley Adams was born in Raunds, Newhampshire, England, on August 17, 1832, so that had he lived until the 17th of next August he would have been 87 years old. He was the oldest resident of Cedar City, and possibly of Iron county.

SAHARA

Sahara, Utah, Apr. 14, 1919.

Harry J. Patten of Cedar City was a visitor in Sahara Sunday.

Mr. and Mrs. J. A. Baker of Nada were visitors in Sahara over Sunday.

Dr. Hobbs of Latimer spent Sunday with his wife, Mrs. Hobbs who is the school teacher here.

Mr. Olaf Lee of Beloit, Wis., is a guest at the home of his cousin, Mrs. C. M. Magnussen.

Mrs. Chas. Anderson arrived home last week, having spent the winter in Los Angeles.

Mr. Guy Johnstone was home over Sunday. He is working in Milford at present.

Mr. N. L. Meades came home for a weeks visit from Ogden where he is employed.

Word has been received from H. O. Daughtery stating that he would be home soon.

Washington County News
May 1, 1919

DIXIE POWER COMPANY
BUILDS GOOD LINE

The new line being constructed west from Cedar City by the Dixie Power company over which to transmit the high tension current from their Santa Clara plant for supplying this valley, is a most substantial affair and should stand for half a century practically without attention The poles are all of imported cedars, of generous size and about 30 feet in length above the ground They have charred butts, and bear two cross arms, for taking care of the heavy duty copper lines and a telephone system

It is quite evident that the Dixie Power Company is here to stay and is not doing things on a temporary, make-shift basis The wire and insulators are arriving, and the management announces the expectation of having the line completed and connected up with the main plant by the 15th of June

In the mean time the company is giving Cedar City a very much more efficient and dependable service with the old plant than we enjoyed before their coming here. It is a matter of "every fellow to his trade"

Making and supplying electricity is the business of the attaches of the Dixie Power company, who are specialists in that line —Iron County Record

Iron County Record
May 2, 1919

Mr. Hugh Matheson of Parowan is spending a few days in Cedar City, assisting to care for his fater, Alex Matheson, who is at the local hospital.

Iron County Record
May 9, 1919

LIFE SKETCH OF JOHN V. ADAMS

J. V. Adams was born Aug. 17, 1832 at Raunds, Northampshire, England. Became a member of the L. D. S. Church June 25, 1850. Feb. 9, 1853 he bid adieu to kith and kin, leaving England to gather with the people of his religious convictions, as with the other converts of that period. His travels were full of experiences and incidents that were alike trying and joyous. The natural wonders of America's topography, filled his being with admiration as the writings of his travels evidence. With his company he reached Salt Lake City Oct. 10, 1853. Mary Anne Bailey became Brother Adams' wife Apr. 9, 1857, and was the mother of his eleven children, five of whom with their mother preceded him to the home eternal.

April 1863, Bro. Adams again crossed the plains with ox teams to assist other converts to the promised land. Hardships and suffering visited the company but his keenest sorrow was the death of his brother Thomas whom he was bringing to his southern home, but his body was buried at Round Valley.

Sept. 1899, Bro. Adams married Bengta F. Nelson whose untiring and wifely devotion has no doubt preserved her husband's life as since his sight failed him her every effort was to see that his joys in living should not grow less. His mind remained active, he was always interested in civic and religious affairs, had maintained positions of trust, such as member of City Council, mayor; taught in the public and sabbath schools, had belonged to the Soldiers Rifle Co. in early days, and was a lieutenant at the time of the Indian disturbances. He had been a citizen of Cedar City for over 60 years.

The funeral services bespoke the deceased's pure guileless greatness. The attendance, music, flowers, sentiments all were significant of the love and regard entertained by neighbors and friends of John Vorley Adams.

Herbert Fretwell is another Cedar City Sammie who returned home this week, after having seen active service at the front in France.

Margaret, the baby daughter of Mr. and Mrs. Ray Cosslett was taken severely ill Wednesday with what Dr. Bergstrom pronounces to be pneumonia, and Mr. Cosslett was sent for from the sheep herd near Iron Springs early yesterday morning. The little one appears to be better at this writing.

Engineer J. E. Eddards, who has been negotiating the sale of a large group of iron claims to a California investor, expects a representative here the last of this month to close up the deal. The almost certainty of the railroad building from Lund in the immediate future is stimulating interest in the mineral deposits of this locality, and some important developments are expected in the very near future.

A little son of Grant Lowe underwent an opearation at the local hospital Friday of last week for the removal of tonsils and adenoids.

Yesterday, May 22, Miss Blanche Lunt of this city and Mr. Henry P. Dotson of Minersville were married in the St. George Temple. Miss Lunt is the youngest daughter of R. W. Lunt and is well liked and respected by her many friends and acquaintances in this city. She is winsome and loveable and will make an ideal helpmeet. The groom is well known in Beaver county, is of a good family and has the respect of a host of friends in his home town, and also of this place. He was with the 145th infantry in France and will make a devoted husband, we have no doubt. The young people have the best wishes of The Rcord in their new and important venture.

Our soldier boys are gradually returning home, Wm. L. Melling being the latest arrival from overseas service.

Mrs. Martha Alexander of Washington is in Cedar City visiting her daughter, Mrs. C. S. Wilkinson, and other relatives during the hottest part of the summer.

The following births are reported in Cedar City since our last account: To Mr. and Mrs. Webster Leigh, a girl; to Mr. and Mrs. John M. Foster, a boy; to Mr. and Mrs. Wallace Lunt, a girl; to Mr. and Mrs. Jos. Thompson, a boy; to Mr. and Mrs. Thomas Mumford, a girl. 12 hours after the confinement of Mrs. Mumford it was found necessary to perform an operation to relieve an obstruction of the bowel. The operation was successful, and Mrs. Mumford is doing nicely at this writing. Dr. Macfarlane officiated at the births and was assisted in the operation by Dr. Bergstrom.

Iron County Record
June 13, 1919

A Live Wire Turn Loose.

The prospective construction of the road has attracted considerable attention to the district, while the presence of a real live wire in the community has done much to stir up interest in the situation. This is E. J. Eddards, whose intersting history already has been told in the Telegram, but the following from the original story can appropriately be reproduced:

"After an absence of twenty-five years almost to a day, E. J. Eddards, known to old time mining men of Utah and Nevada as 'Death Valley Joe,' has returned to his original stamping ground in Iron County.

"Not only has Mr. Eddards 'come back' in the physical sense, but in a financial way, and with the prospect in the latter construction of becoming one of the captains of the mining industry.

"When 'Death Valley Joe,' which appellation Eddards does not resent because of his present and prospective success, discovered the Barefoot mine in the Death valley on Nevada-California line, he was barefoot and wore gunnysacks in lieu of leather footwear to protect his pedal extremities from the hot desert sand, and because of this fact the mine took the name by which it has been favorably known for a number of years. Today he left in his own touring car on a business trip to Salt Lake.

"When, also, he left Cedar City a quarter of a century ago, he was not a miner in the true sense of the word and he was not aware of the existence in Iron county of any minerals except iron, some copper, which he came across in working on the iron deposits, and of coal.

"His return with a practical knowledge of mining and of geology as it pertains especially to cinerology, having during the period comprising a third of man's allotted span of three score years and ten, since leaving Utah visited or operated in practically all of the celebrated mining districts of the world.

Outside Capital Interested.

Eddards has accomplished much since his return. He has created syndicates of holders of various kinds of mineral lands and is interesting outside interests in the properties. Thus far he has made several deals, one of them involving iron lands, which were acquired by big San Francisco interests for $250,000. Development work on this property already is in progress under the supervision of Mr. Eddards, who also has employed a force to begin the development of the coal land holdings of the Old Capitol Fuel & Iron Company. Both of these projects have been started as the result of positive assurance of the construction of the railroad.

Eddards also has interested mining men in the district, with the result that a company known as the Ora Del Rey has been formed and acquired extensive holdings at the mouth of what is known as Bullion Canyon, and soon will start development operations in a big way.

Iron County Record
June 20, 1919

Following is a list of the names selected to serve as jurors for Iron Co., to serve at the term of court setting in Parowan June 26th, by the County attorney and treasurer, who form the jury commission:

Hugh Matheson, Parowan.
Monroe Benson, Parowan.
Oscar M. Lyman, Parowan.
Arthur Jones, Cedar City.
Webster Leigh, Cedar City.
E. A. Cox, Cedar City.
Charles Bryant, Cedar City.
John Tullis, Newcastle, Utah.
Daniel Seegmiller, Cedar City.
Charles Adams, Parowan.

Isaac Haight, Cedar City.
William Edwards, Paragonah.
O. P. Fretwell, Cedar City.
James C. Robinson, Parowan.
Joseph Mortensen, Parowan.
John Bauer, Cedar City.
John Macfarlane, Cedar City.
William B. Adams, Cedar City.
Henry W. Taylor, Parowan.
Carlos Stevens, Enoch.
Gates Burt, Parowan.
Thomas S. Bladen, Cedar City.
C. E. Peak, Stateline.
Isaac Nelson, Cedar City.
Hans J. Mortensen, Parowan.

Mr. and Mrs. R. R. Reid are here on a short visit to Mr. and Mrs. J. A. Kopp. Mr. Reid has a lot in Cedar City and intends building a home here next spring.

Rulon Dalley returned last evening from Camp Kearney, California, where he has been serving Uncle Samuel as a secretary in the office of the Judge Advocate General. He looks well and states that he enjoyed the work and and we have a vision of a busy man in an office across the way who has been looking wistfully forward to the return of his favorite stenographer and typewriter, whose congestion of work will now be relieved. One by one they are getting back to us.

Iron County Record
June 27, 1919

Born.—To Mr. and Mrs. William Webster last Friday night, a boy. All concerned doing nicely.

John H. Williams of Kanarra, was a Cedar visitor Wednesday.

The latest arrivals from overseas service are Glen Macfarlane, Virgil Tollestrup, William C. Adams, Edwin Webb. Mr. Webb was accompanied home by his wife and mother-in-law, who met him in Salt Lake.

GOLDEN WEDDING CELEBRATION

Relatives and friends of Mr. and Mrs George Mace gathered at their home at Kanab on June 21st to celebrate the fiftieth anniversary of their marriage. They were married in the Salt Lake Temple June 21, 1869, after journeying from Washington in this county by mule team. A month was required to make the round trip.

Shortly after their marriage they moved from Washington to Kanab and were among the earliest settlers at that place They have spent about 45 years in the old home where their wedding was observed Their family numbers seven children and twenty-three grandchildren The children are Wandle H, George G, Mrs. R J. Watson of Glendale, Chas A, Wm M. of Cedar City, Mrs. Joel H Johnson, Jr, and Mrs. Nephi M. Johnson.

Dinner was served at noon to members of the family and at 4 o'clock p. m many of the lifelong friends and neighbors of the couple gathered on the lawn to do them honor. A specially prepared musical program was rendered after which the time was spent in recounting stories of the "early days" in southern Utah while refreshments were being served.

With departure of the guests at dusk all expressed themselves as having spent an unusually pleasant day and one to be long remembered Friends and relatives join in wishing the honored couple many more happy years together.

Brother and Sister Mace were residents of Dixie for a number of years previous to their removal to Kanab Just previous to his marriage Bro. Mace was called to assist in bringing emigrants to Utah who were too poor to provide outfits for themselves and for this purpose he drove an ox team from St. George to a point on the Missouri river and back During this trip he and Chas. F. Foster of this city were messmates.

Wife of Prominent Citizen Succumbs to Operation for Removal of Goiter from Neck.

This (Friday) afternoon the funeral services are being held over the remains of Mrs. M. D. Higbee, who died at the local hospital following an operation for the removal of a goitre. The operation was performed by Dr. Middleton, who has specialized in this class of cases and is acknowledged to be one of the best in the state, but on account of the frail condition of the patient she could not recover from the shock and died the next day after the operation.

The sympathy of the people of the community goes out to Mr. Higbee and family in their hour of gloom and sorrow, over the loss of a faithful wife and a devoted mother.

BIOGRAPHICAL

Julia A. Higbee, daughter of Isaac C. Higbee and Elizabeth Summers, was born in Cedar City July 2nd, 1862, and was married to M. D. Higbee March 22, 1882. They had a family of seven children, two boys and five girls, three of whom have preceded their mother to the great beyond. Her living children are Mary E. Thorley, wife of Dr. R. A. Thorley, Zina Bryant, wife of Charles Bryant, Myron F. Higbee and Ruth Seegmiller, wife of A. C. Seegmiller. She has six grandchildren.

Deceased was a faithful Latter-day Saint, and served as counsellor in the Relief Society for nearly six and a half years, which position she held up to two weeks ago, when she resigned on account of ill health. She was full of faith, devoted to her religion and family, and fond of administering to the needs of others who were in trouble or want. In this work she frequently did more than her strength warranted.

SUMMIT

Summit, Utah, July 23, 1919.

Miss Eleanor Hulet, daughter of S. C. Hulet of Cache county, is here visiting with relatives.

* * *

Hyrum Dalley has gone to the mountains to spend the 24th with his family, who are at the Herbert White ranch on the Mammoth.

* * *

Charles Dalley is recovering from a severe attack of sickness. It was feared he was coming down with typhoid fever.

* * *

Mr. and Mrs. John H. Dalley and family, also Wm. W. Dalley, have gone to Panguitch to spend the 24th with relatives and friends.

* * *

The rains we have had recently have done a great deal of good to the growing crops and in keeping the irrigation water up to normal.

* * *

Sumner O'Donnell, who has been employed by the Commission Lumber Company at their saw mill in Cedar Canyon, is home for a short visit.

* * *

George H. Durham, Parowan's efficient music teacher, has taken a class of pupils in vocal and instrumental training and comes here twice each week to give lessons

* * *

Wilford H. Lawrence, who is employed by the Southern Utah Bee & Honey company, has gone to Cedar City to assist in the extraction of honey again.

* * *

Mr. and Mrs. Roy Grimshaw from "See More" ranch, near Enoch, have been visiting with Mrs. Grimshaw's parents, Mr. and Mrs. Farrow of this place.

* * *

Isaac Chamberlain and family have gone to the mountains for a fishing trip. The mountains seem to have an especial charm this summer, as there are very few people in town who have not taken a trip.

SAHARA

Sahara, Utah, July 22, 1919.

Mr. J. B. Reynolds and V. M. Carlson came home for over Sunday.

* * *

Mrs. V. M. Carlson spent a few days with Mr. and Mrs. G. Corn in Lund.

* * *

Mr. and Mrs. C. R. Couch made a trip to Enoch Saturday to visit Mr. and Mrs. J. E. Fairley.

* * *

Mrs. J. E. Fairley returned home with Mr. Couch Monday. She expects to visit for a few days in Sahara, then go to Enterprise for the 24th.

Word has been received from Mr. H. O. Dougherty to the effect that he is about ready to start to Sahara with a well outfit. We hope he will soon have a good pumping plant in operation.

* * *

Mr. Michael Rilley died Thursday, July 17, at the home of Mr. and Mrs. V. C. Carlson. Deceased was a native of New York, 46 years of age. Death was due to cancer of the stomach. Mr. Rilley had made his home in Sahara for nearly four years and his death was quite a shock to the community, as he had only taken to his bed three days before his death. He left no known relatives.

Death Calls Joseph T. Wilkinson at Early Hour This Morning—His Active, Unique Life.

By William R. Palmer.

Joseph T. Wilkinson, one of Cedar's aged and most respected citizens, passed peacefully away at an early hour this morning. In his demise the community and the church of his adoption lose a unique and useful character.

Joseph Thomas Wilkinson was born in Manchester, England, March 26, 1847. He, in connection with his parents and other members of the family, became members of the Church of Jesus Christ of Latter-day Saints and emigrated to Utah when Joseph was nine years of age. From this early period he has been associated with the Mormon people in all their struggles and hardships in establishing themselves in this country.

December 31, 1868, he was married to Elizabeth Emily Wells in St. George, Utah. To this union five children were born, four of whom still survive. These are Mrs. Emily Mc Connell, Mrs. Sadie Buckwalter, and Editor Charles S. Wilkinson, all of Cedar City, and Joseph T. Wilkinson, Jr., of Cane Beds, Arizona.

In July, 1880, his wife died and was buried in Leeds, Utah, which was then the family home.

Later Bro. Wilkinson married Jane S. Wells, a half sister of the first wife, and with her he has been blessed to live out the remainder of his days. Nine children have been the result of this union, eight of whom still live. They are Dr. H. H. Wilkinson, Percy N. Wilkinson, Gerald Wilkinson and Elizabeth Wilkinson of Cedar City, Raymond A. Wilkinson of St. Joseph, Arizona, Stephen R. Wilkinson of Milford, Utah, Jane W. Wilkinson of Salt Lake City, and Marion Wilkinson of Hurricane, Utah.

From the two unions he leaves behind him a large and respected posterity to perpetuate his name on the earth.

Bro. Wilkinson has lived an active and useful life. Civilly and ecclesiastically he has filled many important and responsible positions and his duties have always been discharged with fidelity and ability. He possessed a legal mind and was admitted to the Bar of Utah. Before coming to Cedar City he served as justice of the peace for years in Leeds, through the turbulent days of Silver Reef. In his court many a lawless character was given his lesson in respect for the magesty of the law. He permitted nothing but the orderly processes of law and when the bully attempted to override the proper regulations of his court he departed from it a sadder but a wiser man.

Since his residence in Cedar he has held the positions of mayor of Cedar City, justice of the peace, prosecuting attorney for Iron county, city recorder, and others.

Ecclesiasticallf he was first counsellor to Bishop Crosby in Hebron and afterward held the same position to the same Bishop in Leeds, Utah. He was for a long time Sunday School superintendent in Leeds and held the same position in Cedar after his removal here.

It can truly be said of Bro. Wilkinson that he was "a self-made man;" and I might go a step further and say that he was a self-educated man. The only scholastic training he received was in the schools of England prior to the time he was eight years of age ,and six weeks spent when a young man in a private night school. Yet when eight years of age he had read the Bible from cover to cover to his mother who unfortunately lacked this acomplishment, and before his death had accumulated a library second to none in the county and was perhaps the most copious reader in Cedar City, possessing a world of information on nearly every subject. Books were his hobby, and he would deny himself anything else to obtain the works he coveted. Notwithstanding the fact that he had so little schooling he was himself a very successful school teacher for a number of years in Leeds, and it is related of him that his pupils never failed to make rapid progress in their studies. A sequel to this progress may have been found in the ample hickory stick which was never lacking his desk, and was marked "exhibit one." Yet while he was exacting in the discipline within his school, on the playground he never failed to lead the boys in their athletic sports, such as ball, steal-sticks, "old sow" guinnea peg.

Failing health has ripened him for the separation which death must inevitably bring, but has not effaced the recollections of happy days spent with a fond and indulgent parent, who could play as well as work, from the minds of his family.

The funeral services over the remains of Bro. Wilkinson will be held in the Cedar City tabernacle next Sunday afternoon at 2 o'clock.

NADA

Mrs. Della J. Hedges has issued most unique and tasteful cards announcing the marriage of her daughter, Ruth, to Mr. Silas J. Owens at Salt Lake City, July 3, 1919.

Mrs. Owens has resided here for a number of years and is one of our most popular young ladies, and by her lovable disposition and pleasant manners has made a host of friends who wish her many years of happiness..

A large number of friends of the young couple from Lund and Nada serenaded them at the home of Mrs. Hedges. A mose delightful evening was spent with music, games and conversation. Mrs. Owens delighted her guests with several songs, playing her own accompaniment on the piano.

Mr. and Mrs. St. George Wells, with their seven sons and daughters, Mrs. Thomas Andrus and Mrs. Effie Judd all relatives of the deceased, came up from St. George to attend the funeral of Joseph T. Wilkinson last Sunday.

Mrs. George Angell of Leeds, was in Cedar City last Saturday and Sunday to be present at the obsequies of her brother, Joseph T. Wilkinson.

DR. LEONARD HAS BUSY STAY IN CEDAR CITY

Dr. A. N. Leonard spent a few days in Cedar City the first of this week, performing a number of operations for the correction of nasal and throat troubles, as follows. On—

Ada Watson of Glendale, tonsils and adenoids.

Ervine Watson, Glendale, ditto.

Small son of Mr. and Mrs. Bert Anderson of Echo Farm, tonsils and adenoids.

William Gower, City, nasal pollyps.

Max Pace, Helen Pace, Mrs. Lulu Cannon, Claude Smith, Phoebe McConnell, City, for tonsils and adenoids.

Glen W. Williams, Kanarra, tonsils and adenoids.

Hannah Williams of Kanarra, tonsils and adenoids.

Dr. Leonard went from here to Arizona, where he has enough nose and throat operations to keep him busy practically all the month of September, after which he will go to New York and take post graduate work for several months.

MARRIAGES

Mr Benjamin Cameron, Jr, and Miss Effie Cannon were married in the St George temple on October 1 The bride is a daughter of David H Cannon, Jr, of this City, a highly respected young lady who has been employed in the office of the Dixie Power Co since its formation The groom is the bishop of Panguitch

Henry Marvin Jones of Cedar City and Miss Lucy Esplin of Orderville obtained a marriage license here yesterday and intend being married in the St George temple today.

Marriage licenses were issued on the 30th ult to Mr. Desmond Hall and Miss Gladys Sarah Drake, both of Enterprise, and to Mr Raymond Albert Stahell and Miss Thelma Truman, both of Enterprise

CUPID GETS BUSY OUT OF SEASON

Sly Scamp Catches the People Napping and Works Overtime With the Following Results:

Lunt-Ashton Nuptials.

Yesterday morning Mr. and Mrs. H. W. Lunt and daughter Corris left for Salt Lake City with Mr. A. T. Jones, who was driving through in his private car. Miss Lunt will meet Mr. Elmer Ashton of that place, who returned last spring from a mission to the Southern States, and they will be married October 8th. They will make their home in Highland Park in the beautiful residential district of Salt Lake City. Miss Lunt is a native born daughter of Cedar City and has a very wide circle of friends and admirers. She has been a prominent figure in the younger social set. Mr. Ashton, while not so well known to us, comes of a good family and has made many friendes while here on brief visits, who will extend congratulations to the young people and best wishes for a happy married life.

Jones-Esplin Now Benedicts

The following paragraph from the Washington County News received here today arrested our attention, and the statement is confirmed by parents of the young men here: "Henry Marvin Jones of Cedar City and Miss Lucy Esplin of Orderville obtained a marriage license here yesterday (Oct. first) and intend being married in the St. George Temple tomorrow." The young people are both well known to Cedar people, having been students of the B. A. C. and active in school and social affairs. The groom is the son of Mr. and Mrs. T. J. Jones of this city and has a large number of relatives and friends here. Miss Esplin is almost as well known here through her attendance at school and they will be extended the heartiest congratulations and well wishes for their future welfare.

Ann Smith Gets Wright.

A romance which began when the 145th Artillery Band was here a year ago last June culminated Sept. 24 in the marriage of Mr. Jack Wright of Bingham and Miss Ann Smith of this city. The bride is the daughter of Mr. and Mrs. James Smith, one of our best-off families and is well known and highly respected iin the community. Mr. Wright is not so well known to local people, but has been here a number of times since his return from France early this spring. They are making their home in Bingham.

The Record joins with the many friends of Miss Smith in wishing her a joyous voyage on the matrimonial sea.

Harris-Hanson Union.

Miss Irene Harris and Ralph Hanson of Salt Lake City were married in Parowan last Wednesday. Miss Harris is well known here having worked in public places for a number of years, and was employed at Blakely's Drug Store at the time of her marriage. Mr. Hanson, who has resided here the past summer, is an employee of the Jordan & Brown Transportation line, is liked by all his acquaintances, and they both have a large circle of friends who will wish them success and God speed.

Perkins-Harris Also Take Leap.

Miss Anna Harris and Willard Perkins, both of this city, were married in Parowan last Friday. They are well known here and their friends will wish them success and happiness. Mr. Perkins received his discharge from military service early this summer.

Iron County Record
October 10, 1919

Lawrence Haslam of this city, one of the first volunteers from the state and the first from this county, arrived home from France October 4th. Lawrence saw a lot of action on the battle front in the artillery division and received a service star for bravery in risking his life to save a wounded comrade. He left for France in May, 1917, and returned on the 4th of September, arriving in Cedar City on the 10th as above stated.

Sergeant Haslam received his training at Ft. Bliss, Texas, and was with the 5th Field Artillery of the First Division. It was the intention of Mr. Haslam's relatives to give a party in honor of their son the day following his arrival, but owing to him suffering a sudden attack of tonsilitis the affair was delayed until last Monday. About 100 guests were there to do him honor and the home was tastefully decorated in the national colors. A most enjoyable evening was spent and a delicious buffet luncheon was served at midnight.

Iron County Record
October 17, 1919

Gower Resenburg and Itha Harris, both young people of this city were married last Wednesday and their friends here will wish them all the joys of married life. Miss Harris was well known here although she has not lived here but a short time. Mr. Rosenburg is a native son of this place and served in the army at Camp Lewis receiving his discharge early in the spring.

Ray Perry of this city and Mildred Thayne of Washington were married last Monday. The bride has spent the greater part of the summer here and has made many friends who will wish her success. The groom is the son of Tos. Perry of this city and has been honorably discharged from service in the U. S. Army. Their friends here are extending congratulatons to the happy pair.

The Jesperson family who have lived here since they were forced to leave Mexico are leaving for Arizona in the near future where they will stay until it is safe for them to return to their old home in Mexico. They still have hopes of returning to Mexico but the prospects at present look pretty slim.

Alger L. Renshaw and Miss Tena Sserratt both of this city were married Wednesday, the 15. The groom is the son of W. R. Renshaw of this place and has some very interesting experiences in France where he served with the A. E. F. He returned some few weeks ago. The bride is the daughter of D. D. Sherratt of this city and is well respected here and will make an excellent helpmeet for her husband. A reception was tendered the young couple Wednesday evening and a most enjoyable time is reported. The Record joins with their friends in extending congratulations.

Iron County Record
November 7, 1919

Mr. Clarence Cripps and Miss Mable Dover, both of this city, were married Wednesday in Parowan. Mr. Paul C. Blakely took the young people to the county seat for the purpose of obtaining the license and having the knot tied. The bride is the eldest daughter of Mr. and Mrs. Horace Dover and is a bright and attractive young person. The groom is one of the Cripps brothers who came to Cedar City some two or three years ago. He is an industrious, mind-your-own-business type of young man and should make a devotel husband. The Record extends best wishes.

A force of men has been working for some time past opening a new coal mine in the Canyon under the direction of J. E. Eddards. It is reported that the mine is looking well, and that it will soon be producing a fair grade of merchantable coal, at close proximity to town.

Make Clean Sweep and Elect Entire Ticket—Some Big Majorities of More Than Two to One.

The battle of the ballots is over for another year, and as the smoke lifts from the scene of carnage, it is discovered that in Cedar City it is the Democrats who have been vanquished. There is not a single survivor on the ticket. Like the Alimo of old, there was not a survivor left to tell the tale; and strange to say, the Republicans lost not a single man (or woman either, for that matter.)

The election was lively, but peaceful. The streets were alive all afternoon with people, and the vote was much heavier than is usual at a city election. It was predicted during the day that there would be an unprecedented number of scratched ballots, but the count revealed that more than usual ballots had been voted straight.

The result of the election was a surprise to everyone. Democrats expected at least half of the places on the ticket, and few Republicans expected to elect all their candidates. No one, Republican or Democrat, expected such heavy majorities as were given, particularly shown in the vote for mayor.

The ticket as elected, follows:

For Mayor—Arch Swapp.

For Recorder—J. H. Arthur.

For Treasurer—Sadie Buckwalter.

For Councilman, 4-year term—S. J. Foster.

For Councilmen—2-year term, J. G. Pace, John P. Fuller and T. J. Jones.

The vote on the nominees was as follows:

For Mayor			
Name	Dis. 1	Dis. 2	Total
Swapp (R)	187	196	383
Jones (D)	46	98	144

For Recorder.			
Arthur (R)	175	189	361
Dalley (D)	57	100	157

For Treasurer.			
Buckwalter (R)	146	132	278
Houchen (D)	84	157	241

For Commissioner, 4 Yr. Term.			
Foster (R)	148	140	288
Dalley (D)	82	144	226

For Councilmen, 2 Yr. Term.			
Jones (R)	159	179	338
Pace (R)	163	171	334
Fuller (R)	152	182	334
Williams (D)	75	112	187
Bulloch (D)	64	115	179
Corry (D)	73	101	174

MRS. RICKARDS GETS RELEASE

Years of Suffering Terminate in Death Last Monday, Nov. 24, In This City.

The sympathy of the community goes out to Mr. J. R. Rickards in the sad bereavement which has come to him in the loss of his life partner. For while the deceased has been an invalid for a good many years and more or less of a burden on the family, she leaves the world empty and lonely for the husband who is forced to tread the remainder of life's shady decline alone.

Death released Mrs. Rickards from her afflictions last Monday, November 24th, her age being 77 years. Her health has been poor for the past 12 years, and for ten years she has been practically an invalid and bed-fast, her trouble being rheumatism.

The funeral was held in the Cedar City tabernacle last Wednesday, and was largely attended.

Julia A. Hales Rickards was born in Navoo, Ill., July 17, 1842, and coming with the L. D. S. immigrants to Utah, was married in December, 1893, to J. R. Rickards. No children have resulted from this union, but they have raised Julia Rickards and Sarah H. Davis to womanhood. Deceased was always a kind, industrious and patient woman, enduring her long and trying ordeal with much fortitude, and almost without complaining. The husband did everything possible to restore his wife to health, and last winter the greater part of their time was spent in southern California.

The remains were interred in the Cedar City cemetery.

Following is a list of the jurors selected by the jury commission to serve during 1920:

Adams, William, Parowan.
Adams, Charles D., Parowan.
Adams, James L., Parowan.
Eyre, Herbert, Parowan.
Abbott, Samuel, Paragonah.
Ashdown, Chris, Cedar City.
Adams, Frank B., Cedar City.
Anderson, James E., Cedar City.
Adams, Lorenzo, Cedar City.
Arthur, Robert A., Cedar City.
Allen, William, Summit.
Armstrong, John M., Enoch.
Adams, Ancel, Parowan.
Bayles, Herman D., Parowan.
Burton, Sydney R., Parowan.
Bentley, Joseph R., Parowan.
Bentley, William, Parowan.
Bentley, George, Parowan.
Bennett, Thomas, Parowan.
Benson, Richard H., Parowan.
Barton, David P., Parowan.
Benson, James A., Parowan.
Benson, Edgar, Parowan.
Bentley, Charles, Parowan.
Barton, William P., Paragonah.

Barton, John S., Paragonah.
Barton, John S. P., Paragonah.
Bleak, Leonard, Paragonah.
Bulloch, Warren, Cedar City.
Bettenson, Leland, Cedar City.
Bergstrom, O. P. W., Cedar City.
Bulloch, John T., Cedar City.
Berry, James S., Kanarra.
Bauer, Samuel, Cedar City.
Biederman, Fred L., Cedar City.
Balser, Louis J., Kanarra.
Hansen, Andrew, Cedar City.
Urie, John Jr., Cedar City.
Perry, George E., Cedar City.
Higbee, S. A., Cedar City.
Leigh, Francis W., Cedar City.
Corry, Moroni, Cedar City.
Haight, Herbert P., Cedar City.
Wood, George H., Cedar City.
Lunt, Raymond H., Cedar City.
Jones, Ashton, Cedar City.
Williams, William, Cedar City.
Watson, Ralph, Cedar City.
McMullen, Mark, Cedar City.
Corry, E. M., Cedar City.
Parry, John G., Cedar City.
Webster, Herbert W., Cedar City.
Thorley, Thomas A., Cedar City.

Palmer, Jethro, Cedar City.
Nelson, John P., Cedar City.
Nelson, Bengt, Jr., Cedar City.
Simkins, William, Cedar City.
Gardner, Royal S., Cedar City.
Lunt, William W., Cedar City.
Pace, John G., Cedar City.
Pendleton, Calvin C., Cedar City.
Wilkinson, Chas. S., Cedar City.
Kopp, Joseph A., Cedar City.
Matheson, Gordon, Cedar City.
Parry, Evelyn C., Cedar City.
Gardner, Robert S., Cedar City.
Dalton, Robert E., Parowan.
Durham, Thomas T., Parowan.
Davis, Edward A., Parowan.
Dalton, Jos. B., Parowan.
Evans, John A., Parowan.
Gurr, William H., Parowan.
Gurr, John H., Parowan.
Gunn, George R., Parowan.
Harwood, George, Parowan.
Hoyle, Benjamin, Parowan.
Arthur, Joseph, Parowan.
Berry, Andrew, Kanarra.
Williams, James W., Kanarra.
Parker, Charles, Jr., Kanarra.
Williams, John L., Kanarra.

Pollock, Joseph H., Kanarra.
Stones, Daniel, Paragonah.
Topham, Thomas, Paragonah.
Robb, Samuel, Paragonah.
Dalley, Nelson B., Summit.
Dalley, Charles R., Summit.
Lawrence, B. R., Summit.

Jones, Myron S., Enoch.
Jones, Sylvester F., Enoch.
Tullis, John H., Newcastle.
Knell, Claude, Newcastle.
Robinson, James C. Jr., Paragonah.
Decker, Joseph O., Parowan.
Ward, Silas J., Parowan.

NADA

Nada, Utah, Jan. 5, 1920.

Lee, the six year old son of Mr. and Mrs. H. Linderman, passed away at their home here at 10:30 a. m. Sunday after an illness of a week with bronchial pneumonia. hTe death of little Lee is a sad blow to the parents sisters and aunt, Mrs. A. J. Lewis, who spared nothing in the care and nursing of their dear one. A doctor was called from Parowan, but in spite of all that medical aid and nursing could do, the young life passed on to the great beyond. The sympathy of the community is extended to the bereaved family. Interment will take place in Parowan.

* * *

Mrs. Chas. Galpin and two children left Sunday for Castle Gate, Utah, to join Mr. Galpin who is working there. The oldest son will remain here with his aunt, Mrs. H. E. Smith and attend the Nada school.

GORDON HUNTER AND MISS NETTIE WEBB, WED

Last Sunday, Jan. 4, Mr. Gordon Hunter of this place and Miss Nettie Webb of Murray, Utah, but who has spent the last six months in Cedar City and who has been attending the B. A. C. this winter, sprung a surprise on their many friends and relatives, outside of the groom's immediate family, by hieing themselves to Parowan, procuring a marriage license, and having Bishop H. J. Mortensen of that place tie the knot which made them man and wife.

The groom is the son of Mr. and Mrs. J. H. Hunter and was a volunteer in the recent war. He has been employed for some months in the Leigh Furniture & Carpet Company, where it has been a part of his duty occassionally to outfit young couples who entered housekeeping on their own account, and it may be that this has furnished a part of the inspiration which developed and ripened so happily.

Miss Webb has made many friends here since coming to Cedar City, and enjoys the confidence and esteem of all who know her.

The young people are very conservative and have decided to postpone their honeymoon until a future date, and are going right on with their daily routine of work as though nothing unusual had happened. The Record joins with their friends in wishing them joy and happiness.

Born—to Mr. and Mrs. Albert Kays December 31, a girl. All doing well.

Sister Mary Anne Parry, Pioneer, Dies of Pneumonia After Successful Operation

Last Wednesday afternoon 3 p. m. Mrs. Mary Ann Parry passed away at the local hospital as a result of pneumonia cotnracted after undergoing an operation for the removal of gall stones. The operation was performed by Dr. Middleton with the assistance of Drs. Macfarlane and Bergstrom. The operation was apparently entirely successful and the patient's condition was hopeful until Tuesday afternoon, when pneumonia developed and thre patient succumed in twenty-four hours.

Sister Parry follows closely her life partner, John Parry, who departed this life on the 17th of last March, as a result of a paralytic stroke.

Mary Ann Haight Parry was born in Salt Lake City, May 5, 1850, her parents, Isaac Chauncy and Eliza Ann Haight, with two sisters, Caroline Arthur and Keturah Macfarlane Parry, were pioneers, entering Salt Lake Valley in September, 1847.

In 1853 her father was called to Cedar City to take charge to the iron works. At the age of three years she came here with her parents, and has resided here ever since.

Sister Parry knew all the joys and sorrows of poineering a new country. The fortunate thing of her life was that she remembered the joys and saw the good in every incident, person and thing she met. As a girl she took part in the social life and was a member of the choir and other organizations.

On January 11, 1869, she was married to John Parry. They were the parents of ten children, five sons and five daughters, nine of whom survive them.

At the time of her husband's death, March 17, 1919, she was suffering from a severe attack caused from gall stones. The grief caused by the parting with a noble companion and the constant trouble with her ailment prevented her from getting strong. Early in December she suffered the second severe attack. When she recovered sufficiently she wanted to have an operation to remove the cause of her trouble, but after a successful operation pneumonia set in as above stated and her death followed quickly.

Sister Parry was one of the best respected ladies in the comumnity and for a long while when in her prime was a prominent figure in social and ecclesiastical circles. She is survived by a large progeny of highly respected children and the sympathy of the entire community goes out to them in the loss of their mother.

Mr. and Mrs. Herbert Haight are receiving the congratulations of their many friends on the arrival of a son and heir at their domicile Tuesday, January 13th. Mrs. Haight and the baby are doing nicely, and it is believed that with careful nursing Herbert may pull through.

L. E. Whitmore, cashier of the First National Bank of Price, Utah, was in town a few hours yesterday on his way to St. George to visit with relatives for a day or two, before continuing his journey on to California. It will be of interest to old timers in Southern Utah to know that the cashier of the Price bank is a grandson of "Doc." Whitmore, who was killed by the Indians out near Kanab in the early settlement of the country. He is a nephew of Mrs. Nixon, who resides ot St. George, and he is a cousin of the Whitmore Brothers of Nephi, prominent in banking and commercial circles there.

✦ ✦ NADA ✦ ✦

Nada, Utah, Jan. 19, 1920.

C. D. Kieth has purchased H. M. Couche's Ford.

* * *

Vernon Johnson's colts are missing since the big storm.

* * *

A. J. Lewis, H. Linderman and Joe Warren motored to Parowan this week.

* * *

Mr. Karl Mertin of the Nada Milk Goat Farm, has had exceptionally good luck trapping lately.

* * *

One of our section men were reported "down to bed rock" last Saturday night. Rumors are conflicting— better ask Leo McGuire if there were rocks in his bed, that is perhaps nearer the truth.

Gerland Lash is relieved and happy once more. He has received a letter from his mother, stating that she is recovering from her recent illness and able to bid goodbye to the nurse who has cared for her several weeks.

* * *

Mr. and Mrs. Adolph Sahm who moved to Santa Barbara, Calif, last year have returned to Utah to live. Mr. Sahm says that he prefers life on his homestead, as work in Santa Barbara was not to be had. He is a painter by trade.

* * *

Mike Schoof of Escondido, Calif. and Mr. Wright from Kansas were here last week. They are both in the market to buy some Nada land. Their brothers own land in this vicinity and they feel that it is a good time and place to invest.

Farmers Round-up at Cedar City, Feb. 9-14

Principal Homer announces Sessions twelfth annual farmers' round-up and housekeepers' conference for Southern Utah, at Cedar City, Feb 9 to 14 inclusive

What gives promise of a rare treat for the progressive farmers and housewives of the South is heading this way It is none other than the Twelfth Annual Farmers' Round-up and Housekeepers' Conference at the Branch Agricultural College of Utah. If the statement be true that the past determines the future, the success of the approaching Round up is assured For the attendance of the good people of Southern Utah at the Round ups has been of most gratifying order. President John A Widtsoe, President E G Peterson, and Professor John T Caine III have all made the statement more than once that for attendance and interest in proportion to population, the Round-ups of Southern Utah have established world records.

That farmers should make some stir when their important gatherings come along is not to be wondered at, for they are accustomed to making "dirt fly" It is a common thing for them to ' move the earth," to turn at least some of it "upside down," and also to ' bust up' and "knock to pieces' until the object of their wrath is thoroughly ground down and pulverized.

When such men get together and in addition bring with them their wives who have ' trained them to it" for years, something indeed worth while is about to happen When to this is added the prospect of addresses by some of the leading authorities in America and several experts from the Utah Agricultural College and the Branch Agricultural College on the identical subjects in which the farmer is interested—his farm problems—it may safely be assumed that the farmer will be here with both eyes open, with ears alert, and with an active tongue

Professor John T. Caine, 111, Director of the Extension Division of the Utah Agricultural College, says,

"The annual Farmers' Round-up and Housekeepers' Conference of the Utah Agricultural College is coming to be an institution, and every year the interest and attendance increase. We are preparing a better program for 1920 than we ever have had in the past, and from reports which we have received from field agents throughout the State we have reason to look for a record-breaking attendance

"The Round-up and Conference really comprise a college for grown-ups who, because of their other duties, are unable to attend the regular college courses and who are desirous of learning the latest and best methods in their respecive lines of work The meetings are held at a time of year when it is convenient for the farmer to go to the college, when his mind is sufficiently free from other cares to enable him to devote his thoughts to this concentrated form of education which we prepare for him, By close application to the lectures, demonstrations and practical training afforded by the college staff at the Round-up, he can go home with a thorough knowledge of the latest agricultural, stock raising, horticultural or dairying methods that have been developed within the preceding twelve months "

Work will be given in Hygiene for the School Child, Hygiene for the Pre-school Child, Management of Farm Equipment Irrigation Equipment, Farm Buildings and Equipment, Poultry Equipment and Management, Heat, Light, Water, Plumbing and Sewage, Home Dairying, Household Repairs, Home Furnishing and Decoration, Short cuts in Sewing, and Short cuts in cooking, Automobiles and Tractors, etc.

These classes will be conducted by members of the Branch Agricultural College, members of the Utah Agricultural College faculty, and national experts from various parts of the country.

DIXIE POWER CO. ISSUES STATEMENT

Operating Income and Expenditures Covering 11 Months of 1919.

INCOME

Sale of current	$25,293.14
Sale of Mdse. and Labo	6,195.59
Total	$31,488.73

EXPENDITURES

Operation of plants	$ 5,909.53
Operation transmission, etc.	460.15
Operation distribut'n system	8,141.06
Consumption expenses	299.36
Commercial expenses	693.09
Promotion of business	250.93
General expense (including interest and taxes)	12,549.27
Net Income	3,285.34
Total	$31,488.73

It is interesting to note that the net income for January, 1919, was $284.53, while the net income for November reached $1,207.02.

Until the plant at Cedar City was dismantled, we operated for several months under conditions productive of but little profit.

With the removal of the pipe from Cedar City plant to our No. 1 plant and re-installed there, that plant will be in condition for very economical operation. This work should be finished by February 1st, 1920.

CUSTOMERS

The output of our plant is distributed to customers located as follows:

St. George	342
Washington	48
Santa Clara	32
Hurricane	151
Toquerville	51
Enterprise	83
Gunlock	17
Cedar City	362
	1096

There are balances due from customers of $10,482.94, distributed as follows:

St. George Division	$ 3,581.90
Hurricane	2,916.28
Enterprise	817.76
Cedar City	3,176.00
	$10,482.94

Respectfully submitted,

A. L. WOODHOUSE,
President and Manager.

A statement of assets and liabilities follows as of November 30, 1919:

A statement of assets and liabilities follows as of November 30, 1919:

ASSETS

Property and Plant to January, 1919,	$212,959.31
Additions this year to date	156,325.63
Cash	1,330.27
Customers' acc'ts receivable	10,482.94
Miscellaneous acct's rec'ble	300.00
Material and supplies	15,274.87
Investments	250.00
	$396,923.02

LIABILITIES

Funded dept	$142,000.00
Notes payable	18,743.60
Accounts payable	44,590.42
Capital stock outstanding	183,407.54
Accrued interest	2,999.75
Extensions account	151.34
Surplus	4,048.37
Depreciation	982.00
	$396,923.02

Born.—To Mr. and Mrs. James Parry a girl, and to Mr. and Mrs. Roice Nelson, a boy, last Wednesday. All concerned doing nicely.

ENOCH

Enoch, Utah, Jan. 22, 1920.

The school at Midvalley is making excellent progress under the efficient tutorship of Miss Estelle Jones who accepted the position after the holidays, the Midvalley pupils having attended school here up to that time.

* * *

Strict quarantine has prevailed here since the outbreak of the flu and it is hoped that the dread disease may escape us. The only cases so far reported are the three oldest children of Wm. Grimshaw who have been attending school at Cedar City, but they are getting along nicely without any serious complications.

We are very pleased to report that Aunt Susannah Jones who has been very ill for the past two months is slowly but surely improving. On her return from St. George the latter part of November she was stricken with paralysis and with other complications has had a very hard time of it but with careful and patient nursing she is able now to sit up and it is sincerely hoped by the whole community that she may very soon regain the use of her limbs.

Iron County Record
February 6, 1920

Josiah Eddards returned from the Goldstrike district of Washington Co. the first of this week, after a very strenuous trip in the mud. He reports, however, that the country down there looks better to him than ever, and brought back some very rich samples of gold-bearing ore, in which it is no trouble to see the free gold without the aid of a glass.

LUND-CEDAR ROAD IS THE WORST IN ITS HISTORY

Mr William Perry, the mail contractor between Lund and St George, via Cedar City, is playing in hard luck these days The road between this place and Lund is the worst in its history It takes a big strong team all day to make it from Lund to the Sarver ranch, a distance of barely 12 miles with a ton of mail or express Motor vehicles of all kinds are practically useless on the other end of the road near Lund Mr Perry has had to resort to teams and wagons to move the rapidly accumulating parcel post mail He has one load on the way which should arrive some time Saturday and has started two more teams to Lund for mail matter The first, second and third class mail is being hauled to Sarver with horses and there loaded on trucks and transported the remainder of the distance

Passenger autos are experiencing all sorts of difficulties in getting through, having to be pulled through in many places by horses Some get stuck in the mud and passengers have in some cases had to walk several miles

For the past two years there has been talk of concrete, hard surfaced and combination roads between this place and Lund and enough money has been spent between the State and Federal government road departments in engineering and in see saw-ing to have surfaced the worst of this road and made it passable the year round, but still we are right where we were when they started The ever present talk of a railroad, too, has had its effect in holding back improvement of the wagon and auto road, but it is about time we got down to 'brass tacks' and did something besides talk It should be remembered that 10,000 people are dependent upon this thirty odd miles of road for their mail, express, freight and passenger service During the month of December last year the mail contractor handled 40 tons of mail over this route And to think that we must continue year after year to drag all this business in wet weather through a bog hole, and in dry weather through an ash-bed of silt, is a disgrace to the state, to the people of this district and to the federal government which professes to be doing something for the improvement of post roads throughout the country.

The condition must not be permitted to maintain another season —

W. G. Platt of Kanarra, who was up last Tuesday for medicines and supplies for the sick at Kanarra, reported that there were 300 cases of "flu" at Kanarra. Nearly everybody was sick, he said, and not enough well ones to look after them. Mr. Platt said he was the only well person in his father's family at home, and that he had had no sleep for four nights. He had influenza while in the mission field a year or more ago and apparently is immune.

Cedar City Couple Play Prank on Friends and Public—Secret Out at Last.

"Their little secret is out, Here's what it all is about:" We don't know which of the young people was so ashamed of the venture as to wish to keep it a secret all this while, but it now develops and is acknowledged to be a fact that Stanley Parry and Miss Vera Pace, both of this place, were quietly married last December. There was a report in circulation at the time that they were either married or about to be married, but when Miss Pace was asked in relation to the matter she treated it as a huge joke, neither affirming or denying the story but giving out the impression very strong that there was nothing to it.

The fact that she continued her position at the Iron Commercial and Savings Bank, while the groom(?) pursued his studies in the north, served to add evidence to the commonly accepted verdict that the marriage was only a myth.

But now the whim has lost its romance and the young lady has "fessed up." Under the circumstances we believe that a dose of good old-fashioned "shiveree" would about fit their case, but it ought not to be administered until the groom is here to bear his part of the humiliation.

Well, the young people are both respected members of this community, from good families, and at this late date The Record takes pleasure in whishing them much joy, though we are unable to explain how they are going to find it in the way they are starting out.

A party of mining men consisting of E. J. Eddards, Henry, Will and Willard Eddards and Allwin Bradley, left for Alamo, Nevada, this week to developing some mining property. It is the intention to leave two of the boys there for the summer, the remainder of the party returning soon to work in the Goldstrike country.

Elderly and Much Respected Lady of Cedar City Succumbs to Influenza-Pneumonia.

In the death of Marion Brown Arthur. which occurred February 17th, Cedar City loses another of its old and respected ladies, the cause of her death being pneumonia, superinduced by an attack of influenza.

Funeral services were held at the residence of her daughter, Mrs. Thomas King, in order that Mrs. King, who is just getting over a spell of illness, might attend. Beautiful and appropriate songs were rendered by the choir, and the speakers, Lehi W. Jones and Myron D. Higbee, paid due tribute to the deceased. Bishop H. H. Lunt conducted the services and made a few closing remarks. Floral offerings were quite profuse considering the season of year, and were very artistically arranged.

The members of the immediate family of the deceased who were in attendance, were her son David Dunsire, daughter Mrs. Elizabeth King, brother, Robert Brown, with his son and daughter of Greenville; also members of the family here. Two sisters of the deceased, Janet Adamson of Salt Lake City, and Christina Warner, of oyote, Utah, were not able to attend.

Interment was made in the city cemetery, Elder William V. Walker dedicating the grave.

Marion Brown Arthur was born at Halbarth, Fifeshire, Scotland, July 2, 1844; emigrated to this country, arriving at Salt Lake City July 4, of Coyote, Utah, were not able to at- 1872. With her two children and other members of her father's family, she moved to Greenville, Beaver county. She was married to Christopher J. Arthur in November, 1875, since which time she has made her home in Cedar City.

✛ SAHARA ✛

Sahara, Utah, Feb. 21, 1920

Messrs Pete Corn, J. B. Reynolds. and J. E. House were home to spend Sunday with their families last week.

* * *

Mrs. J. B. Reynolds has moved to her home on the ranch after spending a couple of weeks with her daughter, Mrs. G. E. Griffin.

* * *

Mr. Earnie House came home to spend a few days with his mother and sister who are living on their ranch here.

* * *

Mrs. J. A. Baker came down from Nada on Tuesday to attend the funeral of Mr. Benton, she returned to Nada Wednesday accompanied by Mrs. Gilbert Corn.

Mrs. V. M. Carlson and little daughter arrived home from Cedar City on Feb. 8, the little girl has not been feeling well until the last few days, but at this writing she seems to be on the improve.

* * *

Mr. Louis Benton a resident of Sahara for over three years. passed away on February 15 at his home here. The news of his death was a shock to all, though he has never been very strong, his affliction being a weak heart. Mr. Benton was a good kind hearted neighbor and friend, honest and upright in all his dealings. The community extends heartfelt sympathy to the bereaved wife and son who remain to mourn his loss. Theh remains were sent to Salt Lake City February 17 for burial.

MRS S. J. FOSTER PASSES

It is the sad duty of The Record this issue to chronicle the death of Mrs Jessie Foster, beloved wife of Cashier S J. Foster of the Bank of Southern Utah, which occurred yesterday evening, Thursday the 19th, at 6 o clock p m

Mrs Foster was taken ill of influenza nearly two weeks ago, and developed pneumonia, but while being in a most critical condition for two or three days, successfully passed the crisis of her attack a week ago and everybody had the impression that she was on the sure road to complete recovery

A valvulatory trouble of the heart greatly complicated her disease and made her case more serious than it would otherwise have been from the first, and this handicap finally decided the battle for life against her

Mrs Foster was a very intelligent, competent and examplary wife and mother She was prominent in social circles, and was respected by all who knew her Her husband is a prominent and progressive young man who, besides being cashier of the bank named is a member of the City Council, the president of the Commercial Club, and for several years was bishop of the Cedar East ward

Deceased leaves a family of five children who will be denied a mother's care and guidance The sympathy of the community goes out to them and to the suffering husband in their hour of gloom and sorrow

Funeral services will be held in the Tabernacle Sunday afternoon at two o clock —Iron County Record

Emma Jessie Morris was born in St George on Feb 2, 1879, a daughter of Mr and Mrs R A Morris She lived here until her marriage to S. J. Foster in this city May 29, 1905, after which they moved to Cedar City. She was the mother of six children, the eldest 14 years, the youngest 18 months, all of whom survive her The two youngest children were brought to this city by the mother of deceased, who went to Cedar City to look after her daughter on learning of her serious illness The other children will remain with their father.

Funeral services were held in the Cedar City tabernacle at 2 p m last Sunday, conducted by Bishop William Palmer. The choir furnished the singing. Consoling remarks were made by Elders Uriah T. Jones, Myon Higbee and Joseph Armstrong Bishop Henry Lunt read the sentiments of Herbert Webster (the nearest neighbor for years) who could not attend owing to being quarantined with "flu." Elder Lyle Coray rendered a solo, and Elder Erastus Anderson pronounced the benediction.

Interment was made in the Cedar City cemetery. The grave was covered with beautiful flowers, many of which had been sent from Salt Lake

R. A. Morris and daughters, Miss Orpha and Mrs Agnes Atkin, went to Cedar City last Friday to attend the funeral. They returned Monday evening accompanied by the two youngest children of S F. Foster who will for the present make their home with their grandparents S J. Foster brought them home and will spend a day or two here.

Mrs Maggie Paxman, mother of S J Foster, came to Cedar City from Salt Lake to attend the funeral She is a sister of J. M. Moody of this city,

KANARRA

Kanarra, Utah, Feb. 25, 1920.

On the 9th inst. Aunt Orilla Williams passed away as a result of paralysis. It is thought that she also had a touch of the "flu."

Whooping cough has developed at the home of J. S. Stapley, Mr. Stapley's son Parley and family came from Helper about the middle of January, but they have no idea as to where the child contracted the disease.

By actual count we have had 196 cases of influenza here. Four cases of pneumonia developed, but no deaths. If the cases here were deemed to be of a light form, however, we certainly do not want to have a severe epidemic of the disease.

Manager Woodbury of the Telephone Company has been more than usually cordial and obliging to the patrons and employees of the company recently. When it is known that on last Wednesday evening he became a grandfather, the explanation is quite clear. Mrs. Hortense Canfield is the mother of a fine eight-pound son, and the father, Willard Canfield, is as happy as a king. Mother and child are doing nicely, and the family has the congratulations of The Record.

SUMMIT

Summit, March 4, 1920.

Alex Dalley and family have moved to Delta where they expect to make their home.

* * *

Miss Leone Dalley went to Beaver this week to visit with her sister, Mrs. Imogene Cowdell.

* * *

Harold Smith who has been at the sheep herd for some time is home again visiting among friends.

* * *

Clarence Smith and family have recovered from their seige of the flu sufficiently to return to Parowan.

We are glad to report that Summit is now entirely free from flu. There was a total of 14 cases here, 12 of those being at the Winn Farm.

Mrs. Mary C. Dalley who has just recovered from the flu expects to return to Cedar City soon to take care of her sons Jessie and Orien who are attending the B. A. C.

All public gatherings as well as school have reopened this week with a good attendance at school. Mrs. John H. Dalley is teaching the grammar grades in place of her husband who is ill.

Iron County Record
March 9, 1920

NADA

Nada, March 9, 1920.

Miss June Lindeman is staying with Mrs. H. E. Smith for a short time.

* * *

David McKnight, Honorable Mayor of Minersville was a Nada caller last Thursday.

* * *

Oscar Reiner was over from Cedar City last Sunday talking pumps and engines to Nada citizens.

* * *

Anthony Stephenson came down from Milford last week and is now at work on the section as are also Ray and Dewey McGinty.

The Thermo section crew has been working with the Nada crew again, as part of the Nada section was under "slow-down-to-five-miles-an-hour" orders.

* * *

E. R. White has quit work in Milford and has now commenced his deep well. His tractor plow has arrived and when the roads permit, he will bring in his new International tractor.

* * *

The better service predicted with the return of the railroads to their owners is already evidenced by prompt freight shipments. Efficiency will be restored with a wholesome competition.

Iron County Record
March 18, 1920

SUMMIT

Summit, March, 18, 1920.

The stork visited the home of Mr. and Mrs. John Farrow March 8, leaving them a fine baby boy.

Jos. B. Dalley and Herbert White have exchanged homes, and the two families have been busy moving this week. Mr. Dalley's mother and sister, Mrs. Pratt are with him now.

SUMMIT

Mr. and Mrs. Vernon Dalley who have been living in LeGrande, Oregon are here visiting with Joseph B. Dalley. It is reported that they expect to make Summit their home.

Tuesday afternoon the Relief Society members took lunch and spent a social hour with Aunt Lettie Dalley. She has been confined to her room for several months but is feeling quite well considering her condition and she enjoyed the visit very much.

The six-year-old child of Mr. and Mrs. James Clark died Thursday at about noon following a severe attack of wooping cough. The little one contracted the disease about a week ago. Milton, a brother, is expcted home today from Nevada, where he has been working.

JOHN DUTTON

LAST RITES SAID FOR JOHN DUTTON

Aged and Useful Citizen of Cedar City Passes On At Ripe Old Age of Eighty-Six.

Funeral services for Mr. John Dutton, who died in this city at an early hour April 2nd, were held in the tabernacle last Sunday at 3 p. m. There was a large attendance of the friends and acquaintances of the deceased, who was in his 86th year when the grim reaper claimed him. The speakers at the funeral were E. J. Palmer, Henry Leigh, and Jos. H. Armstrong. Bro. John Chatterley also contributed some sentiments in the form of a paper which was read, the author's voice being too poor for personal expression. The choir was present and furnished the music.

The deceased lived to a ripe old age and has been gradually failing for a year or more past. He lived an active, industrious and useful life and was one of the old land marks in the history of the municipality. Until his health became too feeble to permit, he was one of the most efficient coal mine operators locally. Of late years he has devoted him self more to clerical work and has served a number of years as precinct justice of the peace and as registrar of vital statistics.

He is survived by four sons and daughters. His wife and other children have preceeded him to the other side of the veil. The survivors are: Thomas Dutton, Mrs. O. P. Fretwell and Mrs. F. B. Adams of this place, and Hyrum Dutton of Idaho.

BIOGRAPHICAL.

John Coben Dutton was born Oct. 12, 1834, in England. He received a common school education and also learned the trade of coal miner.

He was married to Margery Cooper at Stoke Upon Trent Protestant Church Aug. 5, 1854, by the Rev. Wm. Duck. They emigrated to America in 1865, leaving Liverpool May 18 and arriving in New York June 14, but on account of the presence of smallpox on shipboard were not permited to land until the 17th. They stayed in Williamsburg until the following December, when they moved to St. Nicholas, Skuykill county, Penn., where he worked in the anthracite coal mines until December, 1875. Then they left for Salt Lake City on the 21st of December. From Salt Lake they moved to Mt. Pleasant, San Pete county and remained there until in March, 1876, when they started for Cedar City, arriving here March 19, of that year, and resided here until their demise, doing their share of the pioneer work in a new country.

All the sons and daughters of the deceased were present for the funeral.

Born—to Mr. and Mrs. Gower Rosenburg a fine baby boy, Monday, April 5th.

Mr. and Mrs. Stratton of San Francisco arrived here last Saturday to visit for a few weeks with their daughter, Mrs. Clark Eddards.

The Biederman Market has received part of the material for their new ice and cold storage plant.

Mr. Caldwell, the father of Mrs. E. J. Eddards left Cedar Monday for home. He has been visiting in Texas and visited here a few days on his way home.

Thorley-Harris Nuptials

Martin Thorley and Miss Rachel Harris went to Salt Lake last week accompanied by Mrs. David Thorley. The young people were married while there. Miss Harris worked in the Blakely Drug Store the past year and is well liked and respected by all who know her. The groom is the eldest son of Mr. and Mrs. David Thorley, prominent citizens of Cedar City, and the young man is a conscientious, industrious young man. The young people will receive the congratulations of a large circle of friends here on their return.

Iron County Record
April 30, 1920

Born.—To Mr. and Mrs. Ray Cosslett, a fine baby girl Saturday, April 17th. All concerned doing nicely.

Born—To Mr. and Mrs. Grant Lowe last Wednesday, a fine girl.

Iron County Record
May 14, 1920

BORN.—To Mr. and Mrs. Andrew Tidwell last week a fine boy. Mr. Tidwell was formerly Miss Myrtle Walker of this place. This confers the title of grandfather of Mr. Frank Walker, and he is right proud of the cognomen.

◆ N A D A ◆
◆◆◆◆◆◆◆◆◆◆◆◆

Nada, May 11, 1920.

There are contests and rumors of contests in this vicinity of late.

* * *

Robert Bonner went to Milford Monday to attend to shipping his wool.

* * *

Nada school closes May 14, after a successful year's work with an enrollment of eight at present.

* * *

Heavy showers fell Monday and Tuesday. Needless to say they were welcome as the top of the ground was beginning to dry out.

Word has been received here of the marriage of our former neighbor, Clinton Myers to Miss Mable Western, both of Milford. Congratulations and best wishes extended.

* * *

Mr. and Mrs. O. H. Moore, Mr. and Mrs. D. L. Barnes and Elizabeth Barnes motored to Minersville Sunday. They brought with them a quantity of wild trees and bushes to plant on their homesteads.

* * *

H. M. Couch and sons, A. L. and Wallace took advantage of the rain today when the ground was too wet to work, and motored from Latimer, via Nada to J. F. Dinwiddie's to have some blacksmith work done.

MARRIAGES

Mr Benjamin Bringhurst of Garfield and Miss Bernice Gates of this city were married May 25 in the St. George temple he bride is a daughter of Mr. and Mrs Jed Gates, a young lady held in very high esteem by a large circle of friends, who has been teaching school here They intend leaving today for Garfield to make their home there

Mr. Verdon James Coleman of Delta and Miss Vilate Stahell of Enterprise were married in the St. George temple, Friday, May 21.

Mr. Moroni Perry and Miss Flora Seegmiller, both of Cedar City, were married, Friday, May 21, in the St. George temple.

A baby boy arrived at the home of Mr. and Mrs. Adam Seegmiller last Friday.

Born this week to Mr. and Mrs. Reese J. Williams of Kanarra, a boy.

Born—To Mr. and Mrs. Jonathan Hunt, a fine girl Tuesday. All concerned doing nicely.

SUMMIT

Mrs. Rose Simpkins and children of Circleville are here visiting with her parents, Mr. and Mrs. Moroni Dalley.

It is reported that Joseph Dalley's property in town is for sale. Whether he intends to remain in town or move elsewhere is not known at present.

We are pleased to report that Mr. John H. Dalley is improving since his recent operation and is now able to be out attending to some of his duties again.

KANARRA

Last week two interesting weddings occurred which included three young people from this place, Mr. Wm. B. Stapley and Miss Sophia Parker were married in the St. George temple Wednesday and Mr. Wm. Isom of Hurricane and Miss Vaughn Pollock of this place were married at the same place Thursday. Their many friends here will wish them success in their new undertaking.

Iron County Record
June 24-25, 1920

SUMMIT

Otto and Jesse Dalley were Salt Lake visitors this week.

Miss Margaretta Dalley is home again after spending the winter in Panguitch with her sisters, Mrs. Mildred Riggs and Mrs. Rula Housten.

Mrs. Wm. H. Dalley, who has been here the past month making final preparations to move left for Delta yesterday where the family has purchased a home.

Cedar City

Last Tuesday a girl was born to Mr. and Mrs. George Crofts.

Iron County Record
July 2-7, 1920

CEDAR CITY BOYS FIND LIFE MATES

—o—

Mr. Grant Walker and Miss Delchia Mathie were married in Salt Lake City Tuesday, June 17th. Miss Mathie is the daughter of Mr. and Mrs. William Mathie of Huntington, and is a very popular young lady in the section where she is known. Mr. Walker, the son of Mr. and Mrs. William V. Walker of this place, served two years during the late war as a marine, most of the time among the South Sea Islands and along the Asiatic coast. Thursday evening a wedding party was given them at the home of Mr. and Mrs. Thomas Bulloch, which was attended by more than eighty of their friends.

SUMMIT

Summit, Utah, July 7, 1920.
Mrs Lettie B. Dalley and daughter,
Mrs. Ann Pratt, will leave tomorrow
for an extended trip to Idaho, visiting
relatives in several towns and cities.

Iron County Record
July 16, 1920

SUMMIT

Mrs. George Smith and children are
here to spend the summer with her
parents, Mr. and Mrs. Moroni Dalley.
They have been residents of Delta for
some time, but have sold out their
possessions there.

Miss Lucile Huntington of Beaver
was a visitor here last week. Her
cousin, Leone Dalley, returned with
her for a short stay in Beaver.

Washington County News
July 29, 1920

DALLEY·PACE

Mr Rulon S. Dalley and Miss
Martha Pace were married at the
home of the bride's parents July 23,
Elder John E Pace officiating

The bride is a daughter of Mr. and
Mrs John E Pace of this city, and is
a highly respected young lady who
has a large circle of friends

The groom is said to be a young
man of exemplary character, a resident of Cedar City

The many friends of the young
couple join in wishing them happiness

Iron County Record
July 30, 1920

FIRST SETTLERS OF CEDAR CITY

Intrepid Band Faces Winter Hardships in Answer to Call of President Young.

SENTIMENT BEGUN SEVENTY YEARS AGO

Pioneer Day Audience Listens to Interesting Tale of Cedar City's Birth and Childhood — Story Reads Like Fiction Now.

(Given by Miss Agnes Brown at the Pioneer Day Celebration.)

We are all familiar with the story of how our people were driven from their homes in the east, and were led westward by President Brigham Young, arriving in Salt Lake valley in 1847, just seventy-three years ago today, but few of us are familiar with the story of the coming of our own pioneers to Cedar Valley. The story of our own pioneers should be more interesting to us even than that of the first pioneers because we are acquainted with so many of the characters.

To Sister Alice and Brother David Bulloch, two of our remaining pioneers, I am indebted for the information I have, but since I have attempted to condense seventy years of history into a ten minute talk I have had to omit many of the interesting incidents they told me.

President Brigham Young must have been a very wonderful leader indeed for he seemed to know just exactly what wealth was in each part of Utah and what people were best suited to develop it. He had early discovered the vast mineral deposits in our county and especially was he interested in the iron. So in the winter of 1850, just three years after the arrival of the pioneers in Utah, he called a company of twelve families to come down and build a town in this valley. These families were all Scotch people who had traveled all the way from their native country together. They had been in Utah only a week or two when they received the call to come down here. President Young knew that they had all worked in the iron and coal foundaries of their own country so he sent them here to develop Iron County.

This body of people had been known as the "Scotch Independent

Company" and their high ideals and sincerity in their religious beliefs is evidenced by their posterity of splendid citizens and by the kind of town they built.

We think nothing of running into Salt Lake in less then a day now, but just imagine the strength of character it took for that little group of people to start out on a three hundred mile trip in the middle of winter, with ox teams that travelled at most not more than twelve miles a day, travelling into a country where there were no roads other than trails, and where the Indians were anything but friendly.

Under all of these difficulties it seems that the peoples' spirits would have been at a very now ebb and yet this was not the case for they came along happily knowing that they were performing a duty. Even though they often only travelled a distance of six miles in a day they were not discouraged, but sang and occasionally danced by the light of campfires in the enclosures made by their wagons.

After many long, weary days the pioneers finally arrived in the valley and found Henry Lunt, George Woods and Joseph Walker here before them. These men had reached the valley a month or two before and had commenced work on a town located on the north side of Coal Creek below what is now our cemetery. Here the pioneers built homes, although they only consisted of dugouts or the wagon boxes supplemented with a lean-to made from willows, and they cleared land and made farms.

This thrifty, industrious little body of people lived here about two years then as more people began to move into the town they decided to move across the creek away from the hills and built a fort to protect themselves from the Indians. The houses in the new town was built of cottonwood logs which were brought from the bottoms and the entire town was surrounded by an adobe wall about eight feet high and 1½ feet thick. In each side of this wall a guard house was built in order that the Indians might not attack them unawares. When the houses were ready the entire town moved from the first site, a distance of one and a quarter miles in one day.

During the next five or six years the pioneers cleared new land and cultivated it; they mined iron ore at Iron Springs and coal in the canyon and brought it to the smelter at the Fort where they made pig iron and Iron castings. The iron industry was finally abandoned because they found it was not profitable, so the pioneers turned their entire attention to farming and stock raising.

More people moved into town each year and finally it was necessary to move again so this time they moved up nearer the hills and built where our town now stands. Here the pioneers again had to clear new land for their farms and go through all the hardships of building a new town.

The first site was called "Coal Creek."; the second was called the "Fort," but the third town was given the name of Cedar, selected because of the many cedar trees which then grew in the valley.

In 1853 when the California gold fever was at its height a great many people decided to leave Cedar and follow the lure of gold. President Young advised them against such a move and begged them to stay on their farms. He said "If you go down to California you will forget your religion and apostatize from the church, and you will not prosper." And his prophesy was fulfilled for most of the people who did leave, drifted away from the church, and many of them not only were financial failures but were broken down in spirit and health.

However, quite a number who left in 1853 moved back again in 1857 when the call for volunteers came to meet the advance of Johnson's army.

During the early years it must have required a vast amount of courage and energy for the pioneers to meet and conquer the wilderness to which they had migrated. They were hundreds of miles from the nearest store and had to rely upon nature to furnish them the necessities of life. All of their clothing was made from wool grown by their flocks and woven by the women, or from cotton which was raised in Dixie. A tannery was one of the first attempts at manufacturing, and all of the shoes the people wore if they were fortunate enough to have any were made there.

They soon learned that an excellent substitute for sugar was the honey dew that fell each evening, and that oose root could be used to wash with. Nor was all their time devoted to hard work. They had a band which they all claim was a very fine one, too, and they had a choir that would rival our own choir today.

About the first thing the pioneers did was to establish a school, which, although the text book was often only the Bible, and the school lasted only three months during the year, yet it gave them a desire for education, and there was surprisingly little illiteracy among the pioneers.

But the great fundamental thing that held the pioneers together was their religion. They had sacrificed much for it and it entered into their every day life.

Doctor Winship, the prominent Boston educator, said in Salt Lake last winter, 'The strength of the nation lies in the strength of the community, and science is just coming to realize that the nucleus of a successful community MUST be religion. Your Mormon leaders seem to have known this instinctively.

And so we love and respect "Our Pioneers" who have made it possible for Utah to be recognized as a leader in education and moral uplift.

Iron County Record
August 6, 1920

Mr. and Mrs. Jack Worthen are the parents of a brand new baby girl.

Mr. and Mrs. E. J. Eddards, who have been at Goldstrike during the past season, are visiting in Cedar

SAHARA

Sahara, Utah, Aug. 3, 1920.

Mrs. V. M. Carlson and little daughter, Mrs. A. T. Griffin and Mrs. N. L. Meads and children were callers at Magnussen's on Tuesday.

* * *

The rain and bad roads prevented several persons from going to Nada last Saturday evening. Those who went up on the train were: Misses Tacoma Baker, Luella Magnussen and Bessie House; from Beryl were Mrs. Valburg Magnussen and Harlin Magnussen. All report a dandy good time, and lots of cake, ice cream, punch and fruit. They all say they are going again.

Mr. and Mrs. J .E. House and daughter Bessie, and Mrs. A. E. Phillips and Miss Tacoma Baker, spent Tuesday night with Mrs. Forncrook at the Lund Hotel.

* * *

Mr. and Mrs. Jas. A. Baker and daughter Blendine Sundayed with Grandma Phillips.

* * *

Mrs. A. T. Griffin called at Magnussen's on Tuesday.

* * *

Mr. V. M. Carlson is on the sick list at present.

Iron County Record
August 17, 1920

NADA

Nada, Aug. 17, 1920.

J. C. Harter is over from Wah Wah valley doing assessment work on his claim.

* * *

The Misses Bertha and Irene Kesler went to Milford last Sunday to visit for the opening of schohol. They will be greatly missed, especially among the young people.

* * *

Mrs. H. Lindemann and daughters autoed to Minersville yesterday. They report a great scarcity of fruit there.

* * *

Collie Huntington of Beaver has filed on a homestead near J. H. Harter's We are glad to welcome new settlers. Always room for one more.

* * *

Mr. and Mrs. George Bentley were over from Parowan last Thursday to visit at the Kesler home.

Ray McGinty came up from Caliente for an over Sunday visit with home folks.

* * *

S. S. Owens of Cedar has rented the Lewis ranches for range for his sheep.

Iron County Record
August 27, 1920

Mr. and Mrs. Ernest Cripps lost their newly born child last Saturday. Mrs. Cripps, who was in a very serious condition Sunday, is now recovering.

Mr. M. H. Dalley and daughter Ora are back from Salt Lake. Mr. Dalley was called to his daughter, who has been ill and when he returned he brought her with him.

It was a great surprise to the people of Cedar City to learn of the death of Thomas Walker of this place, which occurred last Monday morning at 8 o'clock, as a result of uremic poisoning. Deceased was sick only from Wednesday until the following Monday. He was a man 57 years of age, having been born in Cedar City November 20, 1863. He never married, but leaves a number of brothers and sisters to mourn his departure.

The funeral services were held in the Tabernacle Wednesday, the speakers being Pres. H. W. Lunt, Andrew Corry and Herbert W. Webster. The choir was present and rendered appropriate music.

Floral tributes were profuse, and interment was made in the Cedar City cemetery.

Thursday, Sept. 30th, at the home of Mrs. Houghton, aunt of the bride, at Salt Lake City, the ceremony was performed that united Dr. J. W. Bergstrom of this place and Miss Clara Pond of Salt Lake City in the holy bonds of wedlock.

Dr. Bergstrom is too well known in Cedar City to require any introduction from us. He is a successful and climbing doctor, with splendid prospects.

Miss Pond is a graduate of the L. D. S. Nurse School and has been well acquainted with Dr. Bergstrom for some time. She is a very capable and talented young person.

The young people arrived here last Monday, after a short honeymoon trip in the northern part of the state, and for the present are domiciled at the home of Mr. and Mrs. Thomas Webster. Their future home will of course be in Cedar City.

The Record joins their many friends in best wishes for a long and happy married life.

Matrimony has been epidemic and apparently contagious to some extent in Cedar City the past few days, and October has not been one whit behind June, so far as the activities of Friend Cupid are concerned.

Among other notable weddings this week is that of Cashier S. J. Foster of the Bank of Southern Utah and Miss Helen Nelson, for some years an employee of that same institution.

whose marriage took place in the Salt Lake Temple Thursday. The happy couple is now in Salt Lake attending the state fair and enjoying a honeymoon trip. They will be at home to their friends here within a few days.

Both are highly respected in the community, and the Record extends congratulations and best wishes.

That well known ally of Old H. C. of L., the stork, brought Mr. and Mrs. Will Dobson a new girl Monday morning. Both mother and child doing well.

A wedding party is being given today at the home of Will Adams in honor of Mr. and Mrs. Oscar Orton. Mrs. Orton, formerly Miss Mamie Stapley, is Mr. Adams' niece.

SAHARA

Sahara, Oct. 6, 1920.

We enjoyed a large attendance at the dance the club held Saturday eve. We expect to have some more good times in the future and hope to see our friends and neighbors with us.

* * *

Mr. Russel Conner took a trip to Hamblin Valley recently to look after his homestead.

* * *

Mr. C. M. Magnussen and Messrs H. O. Dougherty and H. C. Davis took a business trip to Parowan Monday.

* * *

Mr. V. M. Carlson is shipping Mrs. J. B. Reynold's household goods to her as they have decided to spend a year where they now are in Michigan.

Lawrence Meades enjoyed a very pleasant surprise on his birthday given by a number of his friends here.

* * *

Mrs. A. T. Griffin has been appointed librarian of the Sahara library.

* * *

The Messrs. Markwith, Boghosian and Yoeman were Parowan visitors Tuesday.

* * *

Mr. N. L. Meades has accepted a position with the B. & B. Dept. on the S. L. R. R.

* * *

Mr. Adams of Sevier is in the neighborhood, staying with Mr. E. Markwith.

* * *

Mr. J. B. Morris returned to Sahara the other day after a long absence.

NADA

Nada, Utah, October, 5, 1920

J. C. Houghton and son Dudley of California Ranch came in on No. 4 Tuesday evening to look over their place here and visit with their friends.

* * *

Charley Workwell, of Salt Lake City is now employe of the Nada section. As all the men Workwell, he will be no exception.

Miss Elizabeth Barnes, who has spent the summer in Denver, has returned and is attending school in Milford.

* * *

C. D. Keith came in from Milford Saturday afternoon and his son Cecil returned with him. They expected to make a trip to the county clerk's office before returning, so the wedding bells will soon be ringing.

Last Sunday evening, November 14, the golden wedding anniversary of Mr. and Mrs. Hyrum L. Perry was celebrated by a family gathering and banquet prepared by Mrs. Don Urie and the Misses Bertha, Louie and Minnie Perry, all nieces of the honored guests. The wedding ceremony which was commemorated on Sunday in Mr. and Mrs. Perry's home on second west, was performed in the Endowment House in Salt Lake City by Pres. Joseph F. Smith. The journey from Cedar City to Salt Lake was made by the bride and groom by team, there not being any railroad line at all south of Salt Lake City. It took nine days to go and as the happy couple stayed a few weeks in Salt Lake City visiting relatives of the bride, more than a month was consumed in the wedding trip.

There are only two persons in Cedar City today who have been here longer than Mr. Perry. He was born in England and came directly from there to Cedar, stopping in Salt Lake City only a short time on the way.

His present home, when he built it, was in his field and there were no houses near it and very few west of what is now Main street at that time. The two tall pines in front of the Perry home are all of forty years old and have themselves seen many surprising changes in their surroundings. Before her marriage Mrs. Perry was Naomi Perkins, daughter of William and Jane Perkins of Wales, Great Britian, where Mrs. Perkins was born. The couple have lived in Cedar the whole fifty years, and most of the time in the same home. Being of a retiring nature, both of them objected very strenuously to the ward celebration planned by some of their friends in honor of their wedding anniversary and were so insistent that the plan was finally given up. Both insist that the fifty years of married life have passed very happily and seemingly cannot be made to realize that it is a notable achievement to have reached the fiftieth milepost together. Many friends and relatives attended the banquet in their honor, and felicitations have been coming to them from many others who could not attend.

◆ **NADA** ◆

◆ ◆ ◆ ◆ ◆ ◆ ◆ ◆ ◆ ◆ ◆ ◆ ◆ ◆

Nada, Utah, Nov. 23, 1920.

While the Nadaites are not too busy to remember to be thankful, they are too busy this year to plan anything in the social line, so Thanksgiving Day will be observed in a very quiet manner.

* * *

J. W. Dinwiddie, who has been employed with the B. & B. Gang is at home for a while.

Mr. Cartwright of Beaver was a Nada caller last Thursday.

* * *

Mrs. R. R. McGinty is slowly convalescing from her recent siege of pneumonia. Her daughter, Mrs. C. R. Keith has returned to her home.

* * *

A large number of Indians from Indian Peak, Pine Valley, camped here last Saturday, en-route to Minersville and Beaver.

One of Cedar's pioneers, Henry Leigh, passed away at an early hour Thursday morning. Of the deceased's seventy-seven years of usefulness on earth, sixty-nine were spent in Cedar, and the name of Henry Leigh is so closely interwoven with the life of the community that a history of the city of Cedar would be incomplete without it. In the business of the community he was connected with the Co-op store, the oldest surviving business house here, for twenty-one years, a good share of the time as manager. At the time of his death he was president of the Cedar Sheep Association, one of the strongest institutions of the town.

But his most useful contribution to the public welfare was in his record as public official. He has at various times been mayor, treasurer and councilman of the city corporation, was county superintendent of schools for two years, and was counselor to Stake President Uriah T. Jones during the entire period of President Jones' service in that capacity.

Henry Leigh was the son of Samuel Leigh and Ann Davis Leigh, and was born in South Wales, December 30th, 1843. At the age of eight years he was brought to Utah by his father, his mother dying on the way, a victim of the plague of cholera which used to rage in the "states" in those unscientific and unsanitary days.

In May of 1879, he married Amy Webster of Cedar City, and is the father of seven children as follows: Mrs. Kumen Jones, Samuel W. Leigh, Francis W. Leigh, Miss Jennie Leigh, Webster Leigh, Mrs. Wallace Lunt, and Wilford Leigh. All except Miss Jennie Leigh are residents of Cedar. Miss Leigh is Assistant State Home Demonstration Leader, with headquarters at Logan, Utah.

Mrs. Leigh, wife of the deceased, is still alive and an active member of various community organizations.

BRYANTS OBSERVE GOLDEN WEDDING

Saturday, December 18th, the sons and daughters of Mr. and Mrs. R. J. Bryant, with their families, celebrated the golden wedding anniversary of their father and mother at their home in Cedar City. The celebration took the form of a banquet with music, singing and a general good time following. Br. Richard Bryant and wife from Bingham, Mr. Ras Bryant and wife of Park City, Mrs. William Taylor of Salt Lake City, all made special trip to Cedar to attend the family celebration. The sons and daughters and families of Cedar who attended are: Mr. and Mrs. Frank W. Leigh, Mr. and MrMs Horace Dover, Mr. and Mrs. Charles Bryant, and Mr. and Mrs. Abner Perry,

At least forty years of the married life of the honored couple has been spent in Cedar City, the earlier years having been spent in Saint Louis.

Iron County Record
December 31, 1920

1921 JURY LIST FOR IRON COUNTY

Also List of Jurors to Serve in District Court at January Term

Adams, Thomas D. Parowan.
Adams, Orlando W. Parowan.
Allen, Hyrum B. Parowan.
Adams, William B. Cedar City.
Ashdown, Frederick. Cedar City.
Brickert, Edwin. Parowan.
Bayles, John P. Parowan.
Benson, Phillip. Parowan.
Barton, James W. Paragoonah.
Barton, John C. Paragoonah.
Boardman, William H. Paragoonah.
Bullock, Robert W. Cedar City.
Bryant, Charles J. Cedar City.
Berry, John W. Kanarra.
Bauer, John. Cedar City.
Biederman, Albert. Cedar City.
Bond, William A. Modena.

Carpenter, John C. Cedar City.
Corry, John H. Cedar City.
Cox, Everard A. Hamiltons.
Dalton, John S. Parowan.
Dalton, Harley. Parowan.
Daily, Wilson. Paragoonah.
Davenport, James B. Paragoonah.
Dalley, Joseph B. Summit.
Davis, Albert. Kanarra.
Evans, Veltis, Parowan.
Edwards, Morgan B. Parowan.
Esplin, George W. Cedar City.
Ence, Lewis W. Cedar City.
Eldridge, Clarence G. New Castle.
Fowler, Thomas E. Parowan.
Flannigan, Wm. W. Cedar City.
Fuller, John P. Cedar City.
Forsyth Richard H. New Castle.
Fife, Samuel L. Cedar City.
Farnsworth, Adelbert. Summit.
Ford, Hyrum C. Cedar City.
Fisher, James. Enoch.
Gurr, Peter H. Parowan.
Gardner Robert B. Cedar.
Gower, John C. Cedar.
Gibson, David W. Enoch.
Goulding, Arthur J. Beryl.
Gleason, John. Heist.
Hyatt, Herbert S. Parowan.
Holyoak, Joseph F. Parowan.

Halterman, Samuel. Porowan.
Haight, Isaac C. Cedar City.
Higbee, Edward J. Cedar City.
Hunter, Wm. T. Cedar City.
Houchen, Pratt. Cedar City.
Hulett, Charles F. Summit.
Hulett, C. F. Jr. Newcastle.
Isbell, John C. Cedar.
Jones, Thomas W. Paragoonah.
Jones, Alma T. Cedar City.
Jones, Charles E. Enoch.
Jones, Reuben W. Summit.
Jones, Orion. Cedar.
Jenson, Heber C. Cedar City.
Jenkins, Wm. C. Beryl.
King, Thomas C. Cedar City.

Knell, Frank. New Castle.
Jenson, John E. Parowan.
Taylor, Thomas. Parowan.
Lyman, Oscar M. Ptrowan.
Pollock, Samuel L. Kanarra.
Lowe, George A. Parowan.
Lowder, Louis M. Parowan.
Lund, Richard N. Paragoonah.
Leigh H. Webster. Cedar City.
Lunt, Wallace H. Cedar City.
Leigh, J. David. Lund.
Lundell, Albert. Cedar City.
Lang, Parley. Buckhorn.
Lawrence, Wilford. Summit.
Mickelson, Joseph. Parowan.

Keith, Wm. J. Buckhorn.
Limb, Urban V. Buckhorn.
Mitchell, J. Harold. Parowan.
Mitchell, Walter C. Parowan.
Matheson, David A. Parowan.
Mortenson, Samuel C. Parowan.
Marsden, Nelson. Parowan.
Mumford, Thomas W. Cedar City.
Macfarlane, Erastus H. Cedar City.
Middleton Francis W. Cedar City.
Mosdell Charles M. Hamiltons.
Murie, David. Cedar City.
Orton, Orson. Parowan.
Orton, John P. Parowan.
Prothero, John H. Paragoonah.
Pendleton, James C. Parogan.
Palmer, Edward J. Cedar City.
Perry, George W. Cedar City.
Prince, William E. Cedar City.
Platt, W. Kanarra.
Fowles. Parowan.
Rasmussen, George W. Parowan.
Cobb, Albert. Paragoonah.
Robinson, Hyrum B. Paragoonah.

Roosevelt, Lewis. Cedar City.
Stubbs, William. Parowan.
Stevens, Joseph. Parowan.
Smith, Jacob N. Cedar City.
Stucki, Alfred C. Cedar City.
Stevens, Carlos. Enoch.
Taylor, George F. Parowan.
Topham, Simon T. Paragoonah.
Thorley, Frank A. Cedar City.
Tollestrup, A. Virgil. Cedar City.
Thornton, Edmund T. New Castle.
Tullis, Edward R. New Castle.
Ward, William G. Parowan.
Whitney, Samuel J. Parowan.
Williams, John H. Kanarra.
Williamson, Franklin K. Paragoonah.
Wood, Conroy. Cedar City.
Walker, William V. Cedar City.
Williams, Richard. Cedar City.
White, Herbert. Summit.
Wilcock, William S. Parowan.
Ward, David W. Parowan.

Jurors for January term of District Court:

1.—John Bauer, Cedar City, Utah.
2.—Samuel L. Fife, Cedar City.
3.—Everard Cox, Hamilton's Fort.
4.—Parley Lang, Buckhorn, Utah.
5.—John H. Prothero, Paragonah.
6.—Thomas C. King, Cedar City.
7.—Lewis W. Ence, Cedar City.
8.—Hyrum C. Ford, Cedar City.
9.—William W. Flannigan, Cedar.
10.—Herbert S. Hyatt, Parowan, Ut.
11.—Harley Dalton, Parowan.
12.—Edward T. Thornton, New Castle.
13.—Albert Davis, Kanarra, Utah.
14.—John E. Jensen, Parowan, Utah.
15.—Simon T. Topham, Paragonah.
16.—Richard H. Forsyth, New Castle.
17.—Frank A. Thorley, Cedar City.
18.—J. David Leigh, Lund, Utah.
19.—George Rasmussen, Parowan.
20.—William E. Pryor, Cedar City.

Mr. and Mrs. George M. Hunter, Jr. who were married last week in the Saint George Temple, are at home this week at the residence of the groom's parents, Mr. and Mrs. George M. Hunter. Mrs. Hunter, the bride, is the daughter of Mr. and Mrs. George

Aged Pioneer and Mother of Large and Highly Respected Family Passes

Mrs. Mary Hunter one of Southern Utah's pioneers, passed away in Cedar City, Saturday, January 8th at 11:30 p. m. Sister Hunter, who was 90 years old, had been confined to her bed for the past five years. Her descendants form a considerable and highly useful and respected group in the community, the surviving children being as follows: Walter Murie and David Murie of Cedar City, Elizabeth Hunter of Saint George, Mrs. Ellen Chaffin of Idaho Falls, Idaho, children of her first marriage, and Mrs Mary Ann Leigh, George M. Hunter, Joseph A. Hnter Mrs. Rose H. Lunt and James Hunter, all of Cedar City, Utah, the children of her second marriage.

Funeral services were held Tuesday afternoon, January 11th, at the Tabernacle, Bishop William R. Palmer presiding. Bro. John Chatterly offered the invocation, and Andrew N. Corry, Alex G. Matheson, John Chatterly and Pres. H. W. Lunt were the speakers. The many hardships she endured in early day pioneering and proofs of her great faith in her religion and devotion to her children and neighbors were related. H. H. Lunt gave the benediction and Samuel T. Leigh dedicated the grave.

LOYAL CORRY WEDS MISS GWEN. WALKER

Last Wednesday, Loyal Corry and Miss Gwen Walker were married at Cedar City. Mr. Corry is the son of Mr. and Mrs. Charles N. Corry and the bride is the daughter of Mr. and Mrs. Jorn H. Walker, and has been employed for some time in the Golden Rule store. Bride and groom are both prominent and popular among their circle of friends in Cedar City.

"Uncle" Peter Anderson of Echo farm was painfully injured and narrowly escaped death last Thursday, the 13th inst. Although he is nearly 81 years of age, his 81st birthday being Feb 18 next, he had been plowing that morning and was returning home when the straw upon which he was riding slipped forward, throwing "Uncle Pete" on his head between the team he was driving. He talked to the animals, one or both of which are mules, to keep them quiet while he endeavored to place himself so that the wagon would pass over without injuring him, but was not quite successful, one of the broad-tire wheels passing over his right ankle and that portion of the leg just above it, cutting through the flesh to the bone and severing the tendons. Medical aid was summoned and he was brought to this city.

He is comfortably located at the home of his daughter here, Mrs John Pulsipher, and his eldest son, J E Anderson of Cedar City, is here looking after him. He is in good health and cheerful, standing the pain well for a man of his great age.

He is one of the oldest living, if not the very oldest Dixie pioneer, having settled at Bellevue in 1868. his early years were spent as a fisherman in his native country, Denmark, and he has all the characteristics of that sturdy race. He homesteaded an apparantly worthless piece of land, literally covered with rocks and by diligent and unremitting labor transformed it into the best fruit farm in the Dixie country. The old home is known as Anderson's ranch or Echo farm.

The many friends of the sturdy and industrious veteran join with The News in wishing his complete recovery.

PIONEER OF IRON COUNTY ....
PASSES AT HAMILTON'S

Word is received of the death of John Urie Sen. of Hamilton's Fort, this afternoon. Funeral services will be held in the Cedar City tabernacle Sunday afternoon at 2:00 p. m. An account of Brother Urie's life will be published in the Record next week.

Mrs. Mary C. Dalley of Summit was in Cedar City yesterday on business, part of which was the securing of supplies for work in the Summit Primary of which Mrs. Dalley is president.

John Urie was born in Airdrie, Lanark County, Scotland, April 28th, 1835. At about the age of eighteen he came to America. The trip and later events are recorded in the letter already mentioned, of which the following are extracts:

"My voyage from Glasgow to New Orleans was a protracted one. Being eleven weeks, it gave me time for reflection. The result was a shaving of some considerable extent of my zeal and enthusiasm on religious matters and a settling down to subjects of a more material nature. I stayed in New Orleans three days and came to the conclusion that I had seen better places. Proceeded up the great Missouri river to Keokuk, occupying some ten or eleven days. Stopped there three days and proceeded thru the state of Iowa a distance of 350 miles with ox-train to Kanesville, occupying some four weeks, an experience that shall never be forgotten. Some of the most pious saints got through with the religious business of their lives and dropped off on the road, not seeing the necessity of traveling such a hard road to heaven. They were generally disagreeable, dishonest men whose firmness and grit had no foundation. Some were English and some Welsh, but, honor to my country, no Scotch. They were bent to see the end if there was any end.

Encamped with about thirty-six wagons and about 150 head of oxen and cows on the banks of the Missouri opposite Omaha. Twenty years ago was quite different to what it was today. We were three weeks crossing the river on a flat-boat of our own construction, landing where Omaha now stands. It was a labor of great magnitude, and your oldest son played a prominent part, being young, strong and healthy and a good swimmer. My part of the labor was in much demand and no doubt I was imposed upon. This three weeks will be demanded on my old age to the extent of three years. The subsequent trip to Salt Lake City, over rivers and mountains during eleven weeks was one to me of hard service, and will also be required of me in my last days. Indeed, now at the age of thirty-eight I begin to feel the effects of my intemperance in youth caused by hard fare, hard labor and exposure.

Arriving at my destination on the 23rd of Sept., 1853, without friends or acquaintances, no money in pocket, an extreme youth, and disdaining to beg, I began to feel the dependence of my situation. But nothing daunted my courage. I had come here for a purpose. To pursue that was my firm determination.

I had come to a desert country, whose few inhabitants were wrestling and battling under all the circumstances attending the settlement of a new country 1,000 miles from the confines of civilization, and such a country. There was poor and in no condition to help the stranger who came into their midst. Under these circumstances I entered Salt Lake City, but I found friends who were strangers to me, who fed me and gave me shelter, who had commisseration for their coreligionists. In this I could see and feel the practical form of a religion that fed the hungry and clothed the naked. I began to understand that Mormonism was practical and material and that long and exhaustive sermons on the Godhead and on our future existence, although first in our hopes and future prospects, were secondary to the object of building up a society here on earth wherein men could enjoy a little of that heaven that was always taught us to be beyond time and beyond space, ever ahead of us and never arriving there. I believe that if I ever enter heaven it will be one of my own make.

Went to California, arriving in Sacramento July 7th, 1854 with $40 in my pocket, the result of my labors on my trip as blacksmith for the company. That journey was a hard one, and indeed all such journeys at that time bore this character.

Staying but a few days in Sacramento, then a small place, I made my way into the mines, worked three or four months, made about $350, and came to San Francisco on my way back to Salt Lake City, although having serious thoughts of returning to Scotland. But the idea of being baffled in my pet idea of religious principles, and of you my parents and also my acquaintances having the laugh on me, turned my course toward Salt Lake City. I took shipping to San Pedro, 450 miles down the coast, and from thence to San Bernardino, a distance of 90 miles on foot with my budget on my back. Stayed three weeks and worked for my board. Bought three horses, two to ride and one to pack, and for the first time in my life bestrode a horse. And by-the-bye, it was only half tamed, on a journey of 800 miles to Salt Lake City. You may guess my feelings, but my hopes and firm resolve bore me up under all circumstances.

For 500 miles a more wretched country is not under the sun. Arriving in Cedar City the 13th day, the first settlement on the route. I met an acquaintance and resolved to push my fortune in this place. I was hardly twenty years of age when I arrived here.

My experience in this place for the following eight years was extraordinarily hard, often without food for three or four days at a time. At one time four months without bread of any kind, living on roots and weeds of different kinds. This was in consequence of the grasshopers, bad harvests, etc.

I married when twenty-one and lost my wife in childbed one year after; and in 1857, Jan. 16th, I was married to my present wife, a day that shall ever be remembered by me, as one that began my days of prosperity.

Here I am with eight boys and girls with their mother to look after them.

Space will not allow the printing of much as we would like of John Urie's history. He raised a large and respected family in Cedar City and was ever a useful and faithful citizen and church member.

SUMMIT

Mrs. Laurena Langford and son Bertrand of Cedar City were the guests of Mr. and Mrs. Moroni Dalley a few days last week.

Last Friday evening a social was given at the home of Jos. B. Dalley in honor of Mrs. N. C. Madsen's birthday. A jolly crowd of married people were present and enjoyed the evening very much.

Iron County Record
February 25, 1921

Dixie Pioneer Turned Desert Waste Into One of the Biggest and Most Productive Orchard Farms In Southern Utah

On Friday, February 18, funeral services were held at St. George, Utah, over the remains of Peter Anderson, widely known in all the settlements of southern Utah as one of Dixie's pioneers. On the 20th, memorial services were also held at Toquerville.

Peter Anderson has the distinction of having owned and operrated the first telephone line in Utah's Dixie. He was one of the first to install a complete water system for culinary water. The well-known Anderson orchard at his home, called Echo Farm, is the largest privately owned orchard in Dixie.

The deceased was born in Falster, Denmark, Feb. 18, 1840. Due to the death of his parents, he was compelled to leave home while only a boy. He followed the sea for many years, seeing most of the world. He came to Utah in 1863, locating in Manti, where he married Anna Iorgenson. He moved to Salina later and was in the Blackhawk war in 1866. He lived at Gunnison, Nephi and Payson successively before moving to Dixie in 1868. He located at first at Belleview, but in 1884 established the present Echo Farm, perhaps better known as Anderson's Ranch, where he resided until an accident led to his death. Jan. 6th, he slipped from a load of straw and the wagon wheel ran over his ankle dislocating it. The shock was too much for his vitality, and he died at St. George, Feb. 15th. The surviving children are:

Jas. E. Anderson of Cedar City, Mrs. H. L. Naegle of Toquerville, B. F. Anderson of Echo Farm, Mrs. Laura Pulsipher of St. George, Albert Anderson of Echo Farm, Mrs. J. A. Hougaard of Manti, and Miss Anna Anderson, who is teaching in Utah county.

Last Saturday Morris Hopkins, the 12-year-old son of Mr. and Mrs. John D. Hopkins of this place died of heart trouble aggravated by a recent attack of pneumonia. Funeral services were held last Tuesday at 2:00 p. m. Mr. and Mrs. Hopkins moved to Cedar City last fall to enjoy the superior school facilities, and recently purchased the former home of S. J. Foster on second east street.

W. W. LUNT GOES TO TAKE NEW POSITION

William W. Lunt of Cedar City, who has recently been appointed superintendent of the State Prison Farm, is now in Salt Lake City to take up the duties of his new job. His family will probably remain in Cedar until the schools close for the year in order to give the children opportunity to get their promotion certificates, then they will move to Salt Lake City.

Mr. Lunt is a practical farmer, better known nowadays as a "dirt farmer", and has always been a useful and highly rspected member of the community. He is by disposition and training well fitted for the work he is undertaking, and those who know him best look for a most successful administration of the farm.

MRS. E. B. HARRIS IS LAID TO REST

Was Earnest and Capable Public Servant and Devoted Wife and Mother

LEFT HUSBAND AND CHILDREN

Funeral Services Held Tuesday For Victim of Dread Pneumonia

Last Tuesday afternoon at two o'clock the funeral services were held for Mrs. Ebenezer Harris, of Cedar, who died of pneumonia last Sunday. Mrs. Harris was Anna Hallman, sister of Charles Hallman of this city, and was born in Sweden on the fourth day of July, 1875.

When she was only twelve years old, she left Sweden for America, with her little brother who was only ten. The two of them came across the ocean and over the plains to Utah by themselves. They came to Cedar and Mrs. Harris has resided in this place ever since. At the age of twenty she married Ebenezer Harris, better known as "Naze" Harris, and has been a competent and devoted mother and loving wife. She was highly respected in the community as a faithful, efficient public worker, good neighbor and useful citizen.

The husband and ten children are left to mourn the loss of the mother. Five of the eight girls in the family are married. They are: Mrs. Irene Hansen of Salt Lake, who came to attend the funeral and is still in Cedar, Mrs. Vera Nelson, Mrs. Ann Perkins, Mrs. Rachel Thorley and Mrs. Inez Dover, all of Cedar City.

Of the five children still at home, Miss Oral is oldest. Naze, the next oldest, is 14, then there are Rex, Norma and Erma. Miss Oral was in Salt Lake to attend school when her mother was stricken, and came home with her sister, Mrs. Hansen.

Bishop Palmer of the West Ward presided at the funeral services. The choir sang, "Though Deepening Shodows Throng Thy Way". After which the opening prayer was offered by Pres. Henry Lunt. Mrs. Annette Bettenson was assisted by the choir in singing, "Long I Have Dreamed of a Beautiful City." Senator U. T. Jones spoke. The choir sang, "Beyond the Hills." Talks were given by Calvin Pendleton, Samuel F. Leigh and Bishop Palmer. The closing song by the choir was, "Shall we Meet Beyond the River?" Prayer by T. J. Jones. The grave was dedicated by W. H. Leigh.

Iron County Record
April 22, 1921

KANARRA

Kanarra, Utah, Apr. 19.

A couple of weeks ago Lazell Stapley had a narrow escape for his life. While turning loose some horses he had taken from the R. A. Thorley corral on the Roundy farm on Ash creek, his foot caught in some way in the coil of a long rope which was on an unbroken horse. The animal started to run, dragging the boy through rocks and brush and over ditches. He was badly bruised and scratched, and was unconscious for some time, but finally found his way to the house. Mr. Thorley, who was just leaving for Cedar, put the boy in his car and brought him home, where his head was washed clean of blood and dirt. He is getting along well now.

Miss Viola Davis has gone to Price, Utah, to work for her aunt who lives there. She expects to be gone for the summer.

Owing to various kinds of sickness in Laverkin and Toquerville, Mrs. Hattie Stapley did not stay there as long as she expected.

Word was received at Cedar City last week announcing June 17 as the date upon which the Brooklyn Eagle excursion to Zion National park will arrive in Cedar City, and setting the number in the party at 125.

Iron County Record
May 6, 1921

MRS LETITIA CORRY ENDS USEFUL LIFE

Beautiful and Impressive Funeral Services for One of Iron County's Pioneers

EIGHT CHILDREN ARE LIVING

Left Her Girlhood Home In England to Settle With Saints

Funeral services over the remains of Mrs. Letitia Corry, wife of Andrew Corry, were held last Sunday at three o'clock p. m. in the tabernacle, Bishop Parson Webster officiating.

Mrs. Corry was the daughter of Charles and Mary A. Newcombe and was born at Fillongley, Warwickshire, England, January 26, 1843. She left her home for the sake of her faith in the gospel when only a girl. In 1868 she came to America. She became acquainted with Andrew Corry on her way across the plains, and was married to him in the Salt Lake Endowment house, on the 22nd day of April, 1870, settling in Cedar with him the same year. She is the mother of ten children, two of whom are deceased. The living children are: Charles N., William N., George H., Moroni, Mrs. Margaret C. Webster, Mrs. Emily C. Haight, and Mrs. Ida C. Macfarlane. Two surviving sisters live in Cedar: Mrs. Jane Lambeth and Mrs. William Tucker. Another sister, Mrs. Mary A. Dover, died in Cedar City, on Christmas day last. There are 36 grandchildren and 5 great-grandchildren in the family. Mr. Corry, her husband, is still hale and hearty, though getting well along in years.

Iron County Record
May 13, 1921

Three Cedar City girls will graduate this year from the nurses' course at the Latter-day Saints Hospital in Salt Lake City. Miss Nell Lunt, one of the graduates, is the daughter of President H. W. Lunt, another Miss Mary Hunter, is the daughter of George M. Hunter, and the third, Miss Ina Leigh, is the daughter of Samuel T. Leigh.

Arizona Supreme Court Denies the Right To Assess Stock Of Other States

The case of the State of Arizona against James Smith of Cedar City, in which Mr. Smith resisted the attempt to collect 25 cents a head for the privilege of grazing his sheep in Arizona has been decided by the Supreme court of Arizona in favor of Mr. Smith. This decision, declaring the law which attempted to levy such tax unconstitutional, is a gratifying victory for Mr. Smith and for every sheepman and cattleman of Southern Utah who uses Arizona range.

It is also a victory for Attorney E. H. Ryan, who has represented Mr. Smith through the whole fight for his rights, up to the time attorney Ryan was laid up from pneumonia. Mr. Ryan's brief before the Supreme Court of Arizona was printed in the Record office last summer, and made a fair-sized pamphlet. That it was an able effort is proved by the decision of the court, which follows Mr. Ryan's argument closely. Associated with Mr. Ryan in the case was Judge D. N. Straup of Salt Lake City, one of the ablest lawyers in the West today."

Mr. Smith took his sheep on their accustomed range in Arizona, refused to pay the tax of twenty-five cents a head, was arrested and applied for writ of habeas corpus. This was denied by the lower court, and appeal was made to the Supreme court attacking the constitutionality of the law under which he had been arrested. The appeal has been under consideration for a long while, and it is a relief and satisfaction to the stockmen to get a decision. Besides the ten thousand head of sheep Mr. Smith took on the Arizona strip, from which the Arizona officials tried to collect a revenue of $2,500, other herds to the amount of about 200,000 head have been taken into the same territory, and under the law would have had to pay $50,000 to the state. Cattle were assessed 50 cents a head, and though not so many cattle as sheep were involved, the tax would have amounted to a good many thousand dollars, and would have amounted to a prohibitory tariff on stock, a form of taxitation that is prohibited not only by the

constitution of the United States but by that of the state of Arizona as well.

Many other stockmen besides Mr. Smith were under arrest for violation of this law, and are now freed by this decision. Mr. Smith had run sheep in Arizona during the winter months for over thirty years, and others have done the same, and all have paid general taxes on their

herds in both Utah and Arizona. In some cases stockmen have paid the excessive tax under protest, and it is likely that their money will now be refunded.

The law as it stood, had it been declared constitutional by the Arizona court and the Supreme court of the United States, would have been a death-blow to stockraising along the Utah-Arizona line.

BOULDER DAM PROJECT IS CAUSE OF OPTIMISM

Mr. Don Coppin is home from a trip to Las Vegas and St. Thomas, Nevada, where he has been to close a deal to furnish a carload of Cletracs to be used to haul borax from the newly developed deposits 28 miles from St. Thomas and 49 miles from Las Vegas. The opening of these deposits is causing considerable activity in that section, but perhaps the greatest source of cheer to the people of Las Vegas is the promise of development to come from the building of the great Boulder Dam on the Colorado river, which will water an immense area in Arizona, Nevada, and California, and will be one of the greatest reclamation and power projects in the West. Las Vegas will profit most from this project, which is now being surveyed by engineers. but Cedar City and St. George will feel the direct stimulus of the new influx of population to the territory to be irrigated. Los Angeles to the south and Cedar City to the north are the only outlets to that section. Mr. Coppin says the people of the towns just visited are much enthused over the prospects for the great irrigation system.

R. S. GARDNER GOES SUDDENLY

Robert Snow Gardner was born January 25, 1884 at Pinevalley, Washington County, the son of R. B. and Bernella Gardner, who survive their son and are living at present in Cedar City. At the age of 14 years he came to Cedar City and attended the then B. N. S., going to the University of Utah after completing the work here, and taking out a bachelor's degree in electrical and hydraulic engineering.

From 1906 to 1909 he filled a mission in Germany, where he was very successful in his work.

On his return from his mission he taught one year at the B. N. S., then spent another year at school at the University of Utah.

He next went into Provo Canyon and superintended the construction of a power plant for Uncle Jesse Knight. He was married December 21, 1910, to Ann Jones, daughter of Mr. and Mrs. Lehi W. Jones, and moved to Cedar City and took a position as teacher in the B. A. C. his subjects being higher mathematics and mechanical arts. He taught in the school until the spring of 1919, but all the time was devoting part of his time to engineering projects outside of school, one of these being the surveying and mapping of the Coal Creek Irrigation system, which he did for the State engineer. There are many reservoirs and water projects throughout the county which were surveyed and figured by Mr. Gardner during this period. One in the Parowan mountains, another at Paragonah, a big one at Enterprise, and others might be mentioned. The engineering work for the new water system in Cedar City was done by Mr. Gardner.

November 15, 1918, while wiring a transformer here in Cedar City, Mr. Gardner received the charge from a high tension line, which burned his hands severely and only by a miracle left him still alive. For five months his hands had to be bound up so he could not use them, and the shock of the current left him in a bad condition. But he went right on teaching school, while having to be dressed and fed and otherwise waited on by his wife and relatives. And because he made no complaint, and kept at his work determinedly, few people realize the seriousness of the accident he had met.

The press of engineering work forced him to give up his teaching and open up an office in the Sheep Store building, which he has occupied to the present time.

May 14th, Mr. Gardner, who had been working too hard, was taken with what appeared to be a nervous collapse. He was taken to the best obtainable aid in the state, but on the 15th became seriously ill and died on the 16th at Salt Lake City.

He leaves his wife and three small sons, J. Scott, aged 9, Sage aged 7 and Lehi Robert aged 3. A sister, Mrs. Jessie Whitehead, is living in Saint George. Four other sisters, unmarried are Bernida, Mamie, Thelma and Luree, and two brothers, Arthur and Fernleigh all live in Cedar City. His grandmother, Mrs. Ann Snow of Pine, alkv survives him, and just left Cedar City a few weeks ago after a visit here.

Iron County Record
May 27, 1921

HULET-WALKER WEDDING

Mr. Oscar Hulet of Summit and Miss Violet Walker of Cedar City, daughter of William V. Walker, were married Thursday, May 19th, in the St. George temple. A wedding reception was given at the home of the bride's parents Friday evening, May 20th. The bride and groom are both popular and useful members of well-known families, and have the good wishs of a host of friends for the safe and happy voyage on the choppy sea of matrimony.

KANARRA

Kanarra, May 25, 1921.

Carl Smith returned from Salt Lake a few days ago bringing with him a new Ford touring car, also his sister Sophia, and two of his sister Mae's children.

* * *

William B. Williams and Jones Williams came home yesterday on the passenger auto from the South.

* * *

Miss Lenna Stapley, Plom and Cleo Williams, and Clement Pollock, who have been attending school at Cedar City, have come home for the summer.

Bishop R. J. Willams has bought the L. J. Bolser home and is having it repaired and remodelled. The house needs plumbing and wiring in addition to other repairs.

* * *

Cecil and Fay Parker are the owners of a Ford car.

* * *

Joseph S. Williams and wife,, Mrs. Hulda Webster and Miss Velma Williams left yesterday for Monroe, where the Wiliams' family will buy a new home if conditions suit.

* * *

Joseph H. Pollock, who has been making Monroe his home since last October , came here about two weeks ago on a visit. He looks and feels lne for a man of his age He is making his home with his daughter. Mrs. Rosella Christensen.

Mrs. R. G. Williams returned home last Sunday from Salt Lake with her daughter, Melonee, who has been attending school there this winter.

* * *

Mrs. Susie Wiliams is in Logan visiting two of her daughters living there.

* * *

D. Claude Urie, County Road Supervisor, returned to Cedar yesterday after repairing the road between Cedar and the county also grading the lane through the field toward New Harmony.

TWENTY-NINE GET B. A. C. DIPLOMAS

President Widtsoe Delivers Address to Graduating Class Tuesday

PAYS TRIBUTE TO PRIN. HOMER

Baccalaureate Seimon is Delivered By Senator Joseph Quinney in Tabernacle.

There were twenty-nine graduates from the Branch Agricultural College this week, as follows:

Home Economics Dept.

Irene Chamberlain, Cedar City, Alberta Day, Parowan, Jane Lewis, Cedar, Vera Macfarlane, Cedar City, McNone Nelson, Cedar City, Elizabeth Smith, Glendale, Annie Chamberlain Esplin, Orderville, Alice Palmer, Cedar City.

Agriculture.

Irvin Eyre, Minersville, Grant R. Hunter, Cedar City, ElRoy Jones, Enoch, Golden Roundy, Kanarra, Henry Webster, Cedar City, Rulon Wood, Cedar City.

Mechanic Arts.

Karl Gardner, Cedar City, Waldo Higbee, Cedar City, Leo Palmer, Cedar City, Grant Parry, Cedar City, Leland Perry, Cedar City.

PARRY-WOOLLEY UNION.

Vernon Parry, son of John H. Parry of Cedar City, was married last week to Miss Velma Woolley, daughter of Mrs. Vangie Woolley of Parowan. The young couple will make their home in Cedar City. Their many friends wish them much happiness.

Washington County News
June 2, 1921

OBITUARY, I. C. MACFARLANE

Isaac Chauncey Macfarlane died at his home in this city on May 23, 1921. He was born at Cedar City, Utah, on November 3, 1855, a son of John Menzies and Ann C. Macfarlane His father was called to the Dixie mission in 1968 and his family accompanied him to Dixie in that year. At an early age I. C. Macfarlane learned the gospel of work and he practiced it throughout his life till failing health limited his physical activities When 13 years old he carried mail between St George and Pinto on horseback, on one occasion being so badly frostbitten near Pinto that when he arrived there he had to be lifted off his horse and rubbed with snow to get the frost out of him He knew what hardship and hard living meant His father was an engineer and music instructor but devoted so much of his time to public service that he did not possess much of this world's wealth, consequently his family knew what hard living meant and they all had to work hard.

I C Macfarlane was married in the St George temple to Hephzibeth Smith, January 5, 1877; after bearing him five children, four of whom are living, his wife died, March 6, 1891. On March 16, 1892, he married Christina Forsyth in the St George temple, and by this wife had three children, two of whom are living Besides his wife he is survived by his mother, who was 84 years old on the 3rd of March last, and the following children; Mrs. Nellie Frost, Coalville; Mrs Maud Judd, LaVerkin; I C. Macfarlane, St. George; Mrs. Heppy Milne, St. George; Mrs. Samuel Bleak, St. George, and Donald C. Macfarlane of St. George; also surviving are 17 grandchildren and the following brothers and sisters: John M Macfarlane of Salt Lake City, Mrs David H Morris, S. A Macfarlane, Mrs. Andrew N. Winsor, Mrs David R Forsha and R Urie Macfarlane, St. George, Miss Ann Macfarlane, W. C. Macfarlane,

Dr. M. J. Macfarlane and Erastus Macfarlane, Cedar City; Mrs. Clarence Clark, Fillmore, Mrs. J. C. Benson, Enterprise; Miss Jennetta Macfarlane, Salt Lake City, and Hubert Macfarlane of Ogden

I. C. Macfarlane was called for a mission to Europe in 1888, but Apostle Erastus Snow raised objections as his services were required so much here that he could not be spared and he was released.

He served the public in many capacities, his first big work being as engineer and supervisor of the Washington dam and canal. He was afterwards engineer for the La Verkin tunnel and canal, the Hurricane dam and canal, and the Enterprise reservoir and canal. He was also county engineer for many years, and city engineer, holding this office at the time of his death. As an engineer he proved his good judgment, questioned sometimes but always vindicated; he gave cool and careful deliberation to his work and when decided went ahead. He served as mayor of St. George, city councilman, county commissioner, member of the first state land commission, under Governor Wells, school trustee, and on nearly all committees to locate roads, etc.

Ecclesiastically he was a member of the stake high council, was superintendent of Sunday schools, under Bishop James Andrus when St. George was all one ward, was a M. I. A. officer many years and was identified with all church organizations He was bishop of the St George East Ward for 18 years, being released a short time before his death on account of failing health

He took stock in every home enterprise started here and never refused or shirked in any move made for the development of the Dixie land he loved so much.

Bishop Macfarlane was a splendid type of man. He was very blunt and straightforward, and this bluntness repelled many at first who afterwards became his warmest friends when they discovered the goodness within him of which speech was no indicator. When he could not agree with anyone on any matter after consideration, he disagreed and there was no hope of changing his opinion. He was one of Nature's rough diamonds, gentle and kind, honest and true, of unswerving loyalty to God, his country, his friends and all just principles. His memory is revered and blessed by many who remember his kindness to them, and by many others who loved him for his manly qualities

Just recently he built a beautiful home, hoping to spend a few years with his devoted wife and children whom he loved so much, but it was not to be and he answered the call to a better and more beautiful home than any on earth where he will later have the great joy of meeting those he loved on earth never to be again parted from them.

He was a true son of "Dixie," dependable at all times, and has left behind him work that stands as a monument to his memory. His work was well done, even to the end.

The Mesdames Wallace Lunt and Ray Lunt entertained at a card party at the home of Mrs. Wallace Lunt Thursday afternoon in honor of Mrs. Stanley Parry. Those present included Mrs. Parry, Mrs. Florence Higbee, Mrs. Lafayette Canfield, Mrs. Gwen Matheson, Mrs. Annette Bettenson, Mrs. Blanch Jones, Mrs. Lula Cannon, Mrs. Jennie Lunt, Mrs. Abbie Corry, Mrs. Lola Watson, Mrs. Ellen Bulloch, Mrs. John U. Webster, Mrs. Helen Foster, Mrs. Jack Christensen, Mrs. Claude Lewis, Mrs. Mary Williams Thorley, Mrs. Frank Leigh.

SUMMIT

Mrs. Rula Houston and her sister, Miss Margaretta Dalley of Panguitch, are here for a visit with relatives and friends.

Mrs. Imogene Cowdell with her two children are here from Beaver, the guests of her parents, Mr. and Mrs. J. Philip Dalley.

NADA

Mr. and Mrs. J. W. Brown are rejoicing over the arrival of a lovely daughter born Saturday, May 28th. Dr. H. C. Hunter of Milford was in attendance.

* * *

Mrs. E. M. Colvin and Jack Goff visited at the Smith home today.

* * *

Miss Lola Eyre of Minersville is spending a few days with her sister, Mrs. Robert Bonner.

Mr. Craven, representing the Bundy project at Thermo, transacted business in Nada last Saturday. While they are not doing much at present, Mr. Craven expects to make final proof on his desert claim some time in the future.

* * *

We learn that Glenn Barnes and Florence Kemp were married in Milford last week. Accept our congratulations.

SUMMIT

Reuben Jones has gone to Idaho to shear sheep.

Oscar W. Hulet, in company with Mr. Beiderman of Cedar City, has gone to the mountains for a fishing trip.

Messrs. Jones and Price, who have been testing cattle for tuberculosis found two milk cows here affected with the disease. The animals were killed and their bodies destroyed by fire.

William Smith received word last week that his little grand daughter, child of Mr. and Mrs. Fred Jones of Enterprise, had died of the whooping cough.

Otto P. Dalley, who has a homestead right in Summit mountains, has moved to his claim to make proof on his land.

Last Thursday the Sunday school enjoyed an outing in the canyon.

Mr. and Mrs. Ross Simpkins with their family motored from Circleville last week to spend a few days with Mrs. Simpkin's parents, Mr. and Mrs. Moran Dalley.

Iron County Record
June 24, 1921

MARRIED.

Miss Fern Ashworth of Beaver, and Edward Houchen of Cedar, were married at the home of the bride's parents, Mr. and Mrs. O. E. Ashworth, Thursday evening of last week at 7 o'clock. They were attended by Mr. and Mrs. John Ashworth, a brother and wife.

Bishop Paice of the West ward, performed the ceremony.

A reception was given at 8 o'clock, when thirty guests were present. The home was beautifully decorated, the color scheme of pink and white being carried out thru all the rooms. The tea table had as a centerpiece a large white wedding cake, trimmed in pink. At the top was a beautiful basket filled with bleeding hearts and white daisies. Pink and white ice cream with dainty cookies was served.

The young couple will make their home in Cedar City.—Beaver Press.

Iron County Record
July 1, 1921

Kanarra Correspondence.

Sheriff Leigh and Geo. Hunter came down last Monday in response to a letter received from here, evidently from a mother, but with no name signed to the letter, saying that a fifteen gallon keg of home brew was cached in Camp Creek canyon. The letter gave so clear a description of the spot where the keg was concealed that the sheriff had no trouble in locating it. He took the hooch back to Cedar with him.

Mr. and Mrs. George Wood of Hurricane are here visiting Mrs. Wood's mother, Mrs. Hannah Williams.

Mr. and Mrs. King of Escalante, Garfield county, were visitors here the first of the week. They returned Tuesday, taking Mr. King's daughter-in-law, who was formerly Miss Hazel Williams, back with them.

John Wallace Williams is with us again after having been gone for eleven or twelve years. He says that he is glad to be back again with relatives and friends.

Iron County Record
July 22, 1921

Wells Williams of Kanarra spent Wednesday in Cedar visiting with his sister, Mrs. P. N. Wilkinson.

Mrs. M. Dalley of Summit spent the latter part of last week in Cedar, visiting at the home of her daughter, Mrs. L. Langford.

Mr. and Mrs. Evelyn Parry's oldest daughter was taken to the hospital Tuesday and operated on for appendicitis. The girl is rapidly recovering and within a few days will be able to be removed to her home.

Sahara Correspondence.

Mr. and Mrs. V. M. Carlson announce the birth of a nine pound baby boy.

Mr. C. M. Magnussen purchased a fine cow of W. R. Palmer at Cedar City.

Mrs. J. A. Baker is a visitor at the A. E. Phillips home for a few days

Mr. and Mrs. L. Burascano together with Mrs. Wm. R. Palmer and son of Cedar City, called at the Magnussen home on Wednesday.

The section gang has been moved to Ford. The crew now consists of thirty men.

Mrs. A. E. Phillips has resigned as postmistress in favor of Mrs. F. F. Howland.

Little Pearl Carlson and Miss Dorothy Meads are staying with Mr. and Mrs. H. F. Griffin.

Rus Connor is in the dairy business. He was around with a good supply of fine butter on Sunday.

Mrs. A. F. Griffin is busy taking a course in dress making.

Master Kenneth Davis is up from Hermosa Beach, visiting his father, H. C. Davis and family. He will return home on July 31.

John Lunt Loses His Life by Being Thrown From Wagon Near Three Creeks.

Saturday afternoon the people of this city were shocked to receive news of an accident which happened that morning at 9 o'clock on the Cedar mountains at the head of Three Creeks, about thirty miles from Cedar City, when John Lunt was so severely injured that he succumbed Sunday morning.

John and his wife were out on a fishing and business trip in the mountains and were driving to Three Creeks, where they intended to make camp, when the accident occurred. Mr. Lunt was driving a four-horse team, when suddenly they ran into a deep washout which threw the horses off their balance and pitched John and his wife from the seat to the ground. Mr. Lunt held to the lines and was drawn under the rear wheel, which was locked, and was dragged a short distance and badly crushed. He was hurt internally and lost considerable blood, which welled from his mouth at every breath.

The injured man's wife took one of the horses and altho badly bruised and with a broken rib, rode for a considerable distance for water, meeting a sheep herder who assisted her. How the lady managed the ride in her injured condition is a mystery.

Mr. Roy, a close friend of Mr. Lunt's, who was driving some horses a little ways behind the wagon was on the scene a few seconds after the accident and assisted the injured man to a shady spot and administered first aid, until the arrival of Dr. Bergstrom, who had been sent for in the meantime. The doctor arrived as quickly as automobiles and horses could bring him and did what he could. removing Mr. Lunt from the scene of the accident to the local hospital in Cedar.

At the hospital everything was done that was possible to relieve the suffering man, but his condition was such that he could not repond to treatment and succumbed Sunday morning about noon.

Funeral services were held Tuesday afternoon in the Tabernacle and a large concourse of friends and relatives was present to pay their last tribute of respect.

The speakers were Alex G. Matheson, Lehi W. Jones, Samuel F. Leigh and U. T. Jones. H. L. Frisby rendered in a touching manner the beautiful solo, "Since He Went Away." Prayer was offered by John Chatterley and benediction pronounced by T. J. Jones.

Mr. and Mrs. Wm. Adams announce the birth of a baby boy.

Dr. Bergstrom reports the birth of a lovely girl to Mr. and Mrs. Claud Eddards, Tuesday.

Mrs. Malinda P. Roundy is here from Salt Lake City, visiting for a few weeks with her daughter and family, Mrs. D. Wilson Woodard. Mrs. Roundy is well acquainted with the older people of Cedar City.

Mr. and Mrs. Wm. Lunt were called from Salt Lake City, Sunday, because of the death of their son, John, due to an accident he sustained at Three Creeks the day before. Mr. and Mrs. Lunt will leave for the metropolis tomorrow.

Iron County Record
August 19, 1921

Nada Correspondence.

V. C. Johnson and J. E. Moore were Milford visitors last week.

Mrs. Maude Parrent and two children arrived Tuesday evening from Puenta, Calif., to make an extended visit with relatives and friends.

Mrs. Mary B. Lewis went to San Francisco via Salt Lake Sunday morning. She will visit her daughter and many friends in northern California for a few months.

B. Henschke and two children, who have spent the summer here, will return to their home in Salt Lake this week.

J. W. Dinwiddie spent Sunday at his home here. He returned to Islen, Nev., Monday morning.

De Wix has purchased a windmill of H. E. Smith, who expects to move to California this fall.

Iron County Record
August 26, 1921

A baby was born Sunday to Mr. and Mrs. Henry Jones.

Mrs. W. J. Coppin and daughter Lenore, of Salt Lake City, are spending a week with Mrs. Coppin's son, Don.

TERRIFIC FLOOD IN CEDAR SATURDAY.

Inundates.. Northern .. Part of City--Sweeps Through Fields.. —Much Damage Done.

Last Saturday afternoon at about 6 o'clock one of the heaviest local storms ever known visited Cedar City and adjoining mountains, reaching as far east as Maple canyon in the main canyon.

The rain fell in torrents for an hour and a half until every wash, guly and small canyon carried large volumes of water which centered in the main creek causing it to overflow its banks from the mouth of Coal Creek on north and west to the fields where the water spread thru the fields sweeping away grain and alfalfa in large quantities.

From Maple down damage was done at every turn, four county bridges being destroyed and swept away.

In the northern part of the city for three blocks in width the water flooded gardens and inundated cellars, doing great damage.

On the north side of the creek the most damage was done. The W. Webster and Caleb Haight residences were flooded to a depth of three feet, which destroyed much of the househoih effects contained in both places. One wall of the kitchen of the Caleb Haight residence was washed away which allowed the water to carry away all the contents of the room

After passing these places the flood spread through the North field dividing, part going directly west and the other part, the greater of the two, going through what is known as the "Bull Dog" field, flooding practicallf every alfalfa field and depositing mud and debris to a considerable depth.

Just below the mouth of the main canyon at the Mrs. J. G. Webster residence the water cut into the corral and stack yards at the rear and carried away the corral, 300 cedar posts and several pigs and chickens. Will Walker, a neighbor on the north of the Webster place, suffered a similar loss, losing his entire stack of hay in addition to his corral.

In addition to the flood down the main canyon there was a heavy one from the "Squaw Cave" country which divided just south of town, half going through the South field and the other half down main street. The damage done in the South field can't be estimated, but will run into the thousands of dollars, as will the damage to crops in the North field and "Bull Dog" field.

So far as we are able to learn the greatest single loss will be to the county and state in the destroying of the four bridges, and it is estimated that to replace them will necessitate the expenditure of six or eight thousand dollars.

A. G. Anderson, manager of the So. Utah Bee and Honey Co., states that the flood reached his bee colony on the Wm. Hunter farm north of town and practically destroyed 30 stands of bees besides killing all the brood and destroying the honey contained in the combs. Mr. Anderson estimates the loss to the company at about $2,500.

The flood was the heaviest and most dangerous that has visited this section in the history of the oldest citizens, doing more damage than any half dozen floods that Iron County has had in 60 years' time.

Iron County Record
September 9, 1921

Mr. and Mrs. Williard Canfield entertained Mr. and Mrs. Joe Whitmer at 500 Tuesday evening.

The Misses Clara Bullock, Jennie Middleton, Thelma and Nellie Brown left today for different points in Wayne county, where they have been engaged to teach school this winter.

Miss Vera Macfarlane is back at her position with the Cedar City Drug company, after an absence of two weeks recovering from an operation for appendicitis.

ENOCH.

James Fisher and family have moved here from Rush Lake and will make this place their permanant home. Mr. Fisher recently purchased the Rogerson residence.

Raymond Jones, who met with an accident while working on the thresher, is now able to walk on crutches.

The funeral services over the remains of the baby of Mr. and Mrs. Nephi Stevens was held Friday afternoon.

Mr. and Mrs. John Lee Jones are doing work in the St George temple

Stanley Smith and family have moved from Summit to Enoch. They have been taking care of the Herbert White Farm during the summer

We are pleased to announce that George W. Jones has decided it would be lonesome to live the balance of his life alone. He was married to Henrietta Cox Wednesday in the St. George temple. They will make their home in Cedar City for the present.

Wm. Reeves of Kanarra was in Cedar on business Wednesday.

Arnold Graff of Kanarra was a business visitor in Cedar Wednesday.

Mr. and Mrs. Rulon Dalley are the proud parents of a baby boy, born Saturday morning, September 17th.

Commissioner Berry Williams of Kanarra was here Wednesday to meet Governor Mabey and party.

Mrs. John H. Smith, formerly Miss Agnes Brown of this city, has returned from northern Utah and is now visiting her mother, Mrs. Amy Brown of Hamilton's Fort. Mrs. Smith will return to Salt Lake soon, where she will join her husband, who is at present in Idaho.

Mr. and Mrs. H. Peyton Johnson of Sandy are annoucing the birth of an 8½ pound baby girl, born to them September 13th. Mr. Johnson will be remembered as having taught in the music department of the B. A. C last year, and Mrs. Johnson, before her marriage, was Miss Floss Gardner of Cedar.

SAHARA.

Mr. and Mrs. Sanflecie of Nada ralled at Magnussen's on Sunday.

Mr. H. O. Dougherty has been digging his potatoes. He reports a good crop.

Mrs. H. C. Davis and little daughter Romaine is spending a week with her parents.

Mr. and Mrs. F. F. Howland took a trip to Enterprise on Sunday.

Mr. Mathews, the well driller from Barclay. Nev., has been in this neighborhood for a few days this week.

Mr. and Mrs. L. A. Burascaus returned from Cedar City on Sunday after spending a few days visiting at that place.

STEEL CORP. CLOSES DEAL FOR IRON CO. ORE

The Utah Steel Corporation of this city and Midvale has completed a deal with the Milner corporation, owner of 3,000 acres of valuable iron ore deposits in Iron county, and a big tract in Washington county, whereby the former becomes assured of an unlimited supply of ore as soon as the Steel people are ready to handle it.

A. C Milner, president of the Milner corporation, sizing up the immense prospect ahead for the proposed branching out of the Utah Steel corporation and the advantage promised for the state, as a future great steel and iron manufacturing center, made it easy for the steel company to handle the ore by putting the purchase on a royalty, instead of a commercial purchasing basis The ore is soft, and so easily mined that it can be operated by steam shovel like the Utah copper and cost not over 50 cents a ton to load it on the cars,

The Iron county deposit, is a little north of a direct line between Lund and Cedar City, about 28 miles from Lund, and the steel company has assurances from the Union Pacific, through Vice-President H. M Adams, that the railroad will co-operat> to the fullest requirements, noticeably in the way of building a spur road from Lund to the iron deposits Mr. Milner says analyses of the ore show it of a quality superior to that of the Great Lakes region, and contains a minimum of sulphur which will be readily absorbed by the limerock used in fluxing.

Sales Manager H. G Parcell said the purposes of the company include installation of a blast furnace at the Midvale plant to cost $1,500.000, which, with the addition of four more open hearth furnaces to the two already in use, will increase the capacity of the enlarged plant to 25,000 tons of manufactured steel products a month The present capacity is 6,000 tons per month It is also proposed to install mills turning out galvanized and plain steel sheets for manufacturing into a wide variety of steel products by other manufacturing concerns which will establish themselves in this vicinity so as to be able to secure their raw material immediately at hand without paying freight on this material from distant points, For instance, the freight on such commodities between Pittsburg, Pa, and this city is $33 30 per ton.

Contracts for Supply

The steel corporation has contracted with the Utah Fuel company for its supply of coke as will be seen from the following communication just received by the steel people from the coal company!

' Morris Rosenblatt, general manager Utah Steel Corporation· This confirms our heretofore positive assurance that we will indefinitely protect your coal and coke requirements at prices based upon actual cost plus a reasonable profit, and in every other way continue to co-operate with your interests to the fullest extent "
(Signed)   "A. D. PIERSON,
"General Sales Agent
"A. H. COWIE,
"Vice President "

Mr. Parcell said it is the intention to begin construction of the enlargement at the earliest possible moment. He emphasized again a statement made this morning, by General Freight Agent J. A. Reeves of the Oregon Short Line, that by the looks of things he should say there is a strong likelihood of Salt Lake county being made the location of a second Colorado Fuel & Iron company, though Mr. Parcell contends that the Utah proposition will far exceed the Colorado corporation because of the immense advantage enjoyed here in having the raw material right at the doors, while the Colorado company is obliged to ship in from a long distance.

Iron County Record
October 14, 1921

KANARRA.

Last Thursday a farewell party was given in honor of Golden Roundy who left last Sunday for a mission to Oklahoma.

Quite a few Kanarra men and teams are at work on the Cedar-Lund post road.

September 30 Earl Smith made a hurried trip to Monroe, returning October 2 with a bride in the person of Miss Verda Williams, daughter of Mr. and Mrs. Joseph S. Williams. Their friends wish them happiness and success.

SUMMIT.

Mr. and Mrs. George Dodge of Toquerville have moved to Summit and are now living at the home of Wm. W. Dalley.

Marion Alldredge and N. C. Madsen have gone to Delta to work in the sugar factory.

O. W. Hulet, Otto P. Dalley, Sumner O'Donnel, Wilford H. Lawrence, Wm. W. Dalley and Virgil Owen expect to leave today or tomorrow for various points in the mountains to spend a few days deer hunting.

Mrs. B. R. Lawrence returned yesterday from Salt Lake where she has spent the last week.

Harold Smith and B. R. Lawrence are leaving today for Delta. Several others expect to go there soon to seek employment.

Iron County Record
November 25, 1921

Samuel Ford of Kanarra was in Cedar Thursday.

Mrs. Eldridge of New Castle was a Cedar visitor Wednesday.

Assessor Hillman Dalley spent Monday in Parowan attending the commissioners' meeting and going over some matters pertaining to his office.

Mr. Earls, representing the railroad, spent Friday in Nada.

Mr. and Mrs. Frank Sanfelice left Monday for northern Utah, where he will take charge of a section gang. Mr. Sanfelice has been in charge of the Nada section for several months.

Mr. and Mrs. D. L. Barnes will entertain their children, Mr. and Mrs. H. G. Barnes and Miss Elizabeth Barnes of Milford on Thanksgiving day.

Mr. and Mrs. H. R. Moore will give a family dinner on Thanksgiving day, the guests to be Mr. and Mrs. Max Moore, Miss Helen Moore, Master Kenneth and J. E. Moore.

Iron County Record
December 2, 1921

SAHARRA.

In spite of the bad weather sixty people gathered at the school house to enjoy the Thanksyiving supper given by the Sahara Civic Center club. After supper the evening was spent in dancing and a very good time was reported by all.

Maxwell Magnussen has been on the sick list for about a week, but is improving at this writing.

Mr. and Mrs. McHenry and daughter, Miss Ruby, arrived lately from Pasadena, Calif. They expect to be permanently located in our neighborhood.

Mr. and Mrs. H. C. Davis who left for Colorado Springs, not long ago to visit Mr. Davis' mother and sister, were heard from, writing that their little daughter was taken sick with scarlet fever. They will not be able to return when they expected on account of the quarantine.

LIST OF JURORS FOR 1922.

The following are the citizens who have been drawn for grand and petit jurors for the year 1922:

John A. Adams, Cedar City.
George A. Ashdown, Cedar City.
Herbert C. Adams, Cedar City.
Dolph Andrus, Cedar City.
Charles Adams, Parowan.
David C. Bullock, Cedar.
James L. Bess, Cedar.
Orson Bryant, Cedar.
Samuel Bauer, Cedar.
Joseph Benson, Parowan.
Gates Burt, Parowan.
David P. Barton, Parowan.
Wm. A. Berry, Kanarra.
Howard Chamberlain, Cedar.
Elias M. Corry, Cedar.
Charles L. Corry, Cedar.
Joseph D. Cox, Cedar.
Calvin C. Connell, Parowan.
David P. Chenney, Summit.
Victor M. Carlson, Lund.
David Dix, Cedar City.
John E. Dover, Cedar.
Rulon S. Dalley, Cedar.
Jos. O. Decker, Parowan.
Alvin Decker, Parowan.
Robt. Davenport, Parowan.
Hyrum Dalley, Summit.
Wm. W. Dalley, Summit.
David L. Davis, Kanarra.
Henry O. Dougherty, Lund.
Samuel A. Davis, Lund.
H. J. Doolittle, Lund.
Alma Esplin, Cedar.
Leonard Evans, Cedar.
Thos. Edwards, Paragoonah.
Jos. S. Fife, Cedar City.
Arthur R. Fife, Cedar.
Alfred Froyd, Cedar.

George W. Foster, Cedar.
John H. Fife, Cedar.
Samuel T. Ford, Kanarra.
Nathanal Gardner, Cedar.
Wm. J. Gurr, Parowan.
Jas. S. Green, Parowan.
Wm. Grimshaw, Enoch.
Arnold Graff. Kanarra.
Myron F. Higbee, Cedar.
Samuel L. Heybourne, Cedar.
John G. Holland, Cedar.
John Hamilton, Cedar.
Henry Houchen, Jr., Cedar.
Joseph E. Haslam, Cedar.
John J. Hyatt, Parowan.
Thos. J. Haycock, Parowan.
O. G. Hutchings, Buckhorn.
Erastus L. Jones, Cedar.
Samuel B. Jones, Cedar.
Thos. J. Jones, Cedar.
Jos. M. Jensen, Parowan.
Mark Jackson, Parowan.
Jos. R. Lister, Parowan.
Wm. H. Lyman, Parowan.
J. J. Jones, Paragoonah.
Thos. C. King, Cedar.
Raymond H. Lunt, Cedar.
Francis W. Leigh, Cedar.
Joseph E. Lister, Paragoonah.
Alfred W. Lund, Paragoonah.
D. A. Lamoreaux, Paragoonah.

Thomas Lund, Modena.
Joseph Melling, Cedar.
August Mackelprang, Cedar.
E. H. Macfarlane, Cedar.
Wm. C. Murrie, Cedar.
Geo. R. Mickelson, Parowan.
Wm. C. Mitchell, Parowan.
L. N. Marsden, Parowan.
S. A. Matheson, Parowan.
Robt. T. Miller, Parowan.
Robt. Mumford, Enoch.
J. C. Muldoon, Modena.
Thos. F. McConnell, Cedar.
E. M. Owens, Cedar.
Ellis Orton. Parowan.
Isaac Parry, Cedar.
John H. Perry, Cedar.
Frank H. Petty, Cedar.
F. W. Pendleton. Parowan.
Abner Perry, Cedar.
Alex H. Rollo, Cedar.
James C. Robinson Jr., Parowan.
Thos. H. Rowley. Parowan.
George W. Rasmussen, Parowan.
John R. Robinson Sr, Paragoonah.
Alexander Robb, Paragoonah.
Kenyon D. Robinson, Paragoonah.
Wm. C. Reeves, Kanarra.
Wm. W. Roundy, Kanarra.
Arch Swapp, Cedar.
James Smith, Cedar.

Archie P. Spillsbury, Cedar.
George Stevens, Parowan.
Walter W. Stubbs, Parowan.
Peter Skougard, Parowan.
Ray Stones, Paragoonah.
Nephi Stevens, Enoch.
David A. Thorley, Cedar.
Wm. E. Thornton, Parowan.
John B. Topham, Paragoonah.
J. Turner Forsyth, New Castle.
John H. Tullis, New Castle.

James A. Thornton, New Castle.
Thomas Urie, Cedar.
George K. Urie, Cedar.
J. M. Ward, Parowan.
Granville H. Warren, Parowan.
Lucia A. Burascano, Modena.

John Hamilton of Hamilton's Fort, spent Thursday in Cedar on business.

Mr. and Mrs. Orson Haight are rejoicing over the arrival of a paby girl at their home Monday, November 28.

MARRIED.

The marriage of Miss Mary P. Knell, daughter of Mr. and Mrs. R. C. Knell of Cedar City, and Heber Sevy of this city, took place Wednesday in the Salt Lake temple. The ceremony was performed by Apostle Stephen L. Richards. A wedding dinner was served at the home of the bridegroom's parents, Mr. and Mrs. John L. Sevy, on Douglas avenue. Mr and Mrs. Sevy will make their home in Cedar City. —Salt Lake Tribune.

Enoch.

"Baby Scott" was presented by the Enoch Dramatic company last evening. Much credit is due those who took part. It was well attended and a short dance was given after the play which was enjoyed by all.

Mrs. Emma Wood is a visitor at the home of Mr. and Mrs. Hyrum Jones.

Chester Jones from St. George and Vertis Wood from Cedar City, are spending the holidays with Mr. and Mrs. M. S. Jones.

Nelson Dalley of Summit was a Cedar visitor Thursday.

Reuben Jones of Winns was a business visitor in Cedar Thursday.

SUMMIT.

Delbert Smith and family of Parowan were visiting yesterday with his parents, Mr. and Mrs. Wm. Smith.

Charles Dalley has sold his flock of range sheep and expects to replace them with full blood Rambouletts.

Stanley Dalley, who has been teaching school at Wallsburg, Wasatch county is home for the holidays.

Quite a number of our citizens have just received from the business houses of Cedar City, a beautiful calendar illustrating the Cedar Breaks. It is a work of art and is appreciated by those fortunate enough to receive one.

Last Friday evening the Primary association gave an interesting program. The proceeds were given for the Primary hospital fund.

The Paragonah basket ball team played the Summit team last night resulting in a score of 28 to 31 in favor of Summit. The two teams will play again next Friday evening in Paragonah.

Special Christmas services were held here Sunday afternoon, the music being furnished by a quartet, consisting of Mr. and Mrs. Otto P. Dalley, Letha Dalley and Reuben Jones. The speakers were Otto P. Dalley and Harold Smith, who spoke on "The Divine Mission of the Savior," and Joseph Smith, respectively.

A. T. Lawrence spent Christmas in Cedar with his brother Thos. Lawrence.

Mrs. Elzina Hulet entertained her daughters and their families at Christmas dinner Sunday afternoon.

Oscar J. Ireta and Orvilla Hulet Letha, Marcella and Helen Dalley, Afton Madsen, Alice Allen, Lucy Farrow, Weston Cheney, Jessie Orion and Marie Dalley and Herbert White are home from the B. A. C. to spend the holidays.

Iron County Record
January 13, 1922

Arnold Graff of Kanara was a business visitor in Cedar Wednesday.

A girl was born to Mrs. Mary (Knell) Spencer Tuesday night.

A girl was born Thursday, to Mrs. George Croft.

The Stork left a lovely baby girl at the home of Mr. and Mrs. Earl Merryweather Wednesday.

Ben Davis of Beaver was in Cedar a few days last week attending to business.

Mr. and Mrs. Croft are happy over the arrival of a lovely baby at their home this week.

Mr. and Mrs. Walter Spencer are giving loving attention to a new baby that was born to them this week.

Iron County Record
January 20, 1922

In the death of Mrs. Sadie Buckwalter which occured last Saturday morning, Cedar losses one of its useful citizens, a woman of many and varied talents. She had a wide circle of friends, because she always found something to like in everyone she met.

She was an enthusiastic worker, doing her full share at all times and doing it promptly. Although a sufferer from a very severe heart trouble for the past year, she kept on with her work to within a week of her death.

Sadie Wilkinson Buckwalter was born in Hebron, Utah, April 10, 1872, the daughter of Joseph T. and Elizabeth E. Wilkison, both deceased. She came with the family to Cedar City in her early youth, where she secured all the education available, and entered the teaching profession. She followed this for several years when she went to Salt Lake City and became a bookkeeper and accountant, in which she attained a high degree of efficiency and skill. In 1907 she was was married to R. E. Buckwalter of Salt Lake City, after which they moved to Rexburg, Idaho. While in Rexburg Mrs. Buckwalter held important positions in the church, particularly the Mutual Improvement Association. In 1914 she returned to Cedar City where she taught again, later accepting a postioin in the Iron Commercial Bank. She was elected City treasurer in 1919, being re-elected last City election, which position she held at the time of her death. She served as president of the Young Ladies' East Ward Mutual for three years, but was oblidged to resign in 1921 because of ill health. She leaves a son, eight brothers and three sisters to mourn her departure.

Funeral services were held in the tabernacle January 16, at 2 p. m. with Bishop Bengt Nelson conducting.

The services were opened by the Choir singing an appropriate hymn, after which prayer was offered by Elder Wm. R. Palmer. Mrs. Webster Miss Gardner and Mr. West rendered a beautiful trio, and were followed by the following speakers, all of whom spoke of the excellent worth of the deceased: Elder S. J. Foster, Elder A. G. Matheson and Pres. Henery W. Lunt. Benediction was pronouced by Elder David Bulloch.

The floral offerings were many and beautiful and completely covered the casket in which the mortal remains of Mrs. Buckwalter were enclosed.

Iron County Record
February 10, 1922

Bentley-Tucker.

The many friends of Mr. Ray Bentley will be glad to learn of his marriage on Friday night of last week to Miss Mabel Tucker of Cedar City. Ray is a son of Mr. Edward Bentley, and is an industrious well thought of man, and should make a good life partner for the lady of his choice Miss Tucker is a daughter of Mr. and Mrs. Wm Tucker and is highly respected by those who know her We join with their many friends in wishing them a long and happy life.

Parowan Times.

Sumner O'Donnel expects to leave with his family the first of next month to make his home in Mexico.

SAHARA.

F. T. Howland is again employed by the Salt Lake Route at Beryl.

The whole Magnussen family are on the sick list, having a hard seige of the grippe.

Little Romaine Davis came up from Beryl with her auntie, Miss Valberg Magmussen, on Thursday and stayed until Sunday.

A good time was spent at the club meeting and dance last Saturday eve. A crowd from Lund came to help us be merry.

A new baby boy was born to Mr. and Mrs. George Nelson recently.

Mr. and Mrs. Milbourne Williams are happy over the arrival of a baby boy at their home.

Mrs. Oscar Hulet, Jr., was operated on at the local hospital Monday for appendicitis. She is recovering rapidly.

Mr. and Mrs. J. V. Adams are rejoicing over the arrival of a new baby at their home, which was born yesterday.

SUMMIT

Mr. and Mrs. Levi Alldredge expect to move to the Winn farm soon, where Mr. Alldredge has employment from Reuben Jones for the summer.

Mr. and Mrs. Herbert White, Mrs. Mary C. Dalley and Wm. W. Dalley returned Saturday evening from St. George where they have been doing temple work.

Mrs. Chas R. Dalley, Mrs. O. W. Hulet, Mrs. N. C. Madsen and Mrs. John Farrow who have been in Cedar taking care of their children who contracted the "Flu" while attending the B. A. C. have all had a siege of the same, but are on the improve.

The "Flu" has found its way into quite a number of homes here, and though no quarantine law has been enforced the malady seems to be pretty well confined to its present limits, as no new cases have developed the past day or two, and we are pleased to report no serious cases so far.

SAHARA

Mrs. H. C. Davis of Beryl called on Mrs. A. T. Griffin Wednesday afternoon.

Mrs. Arlie Fourman and Alice spent the week end with Mr. Fourman, down on the ranch.

Mrs. H. C. Davis, Romaine and Mrs. Magmussen were callers at Mrs. Reynolds' on Tuesday afternoon.

Mr. Lee F. Doyle arrived over-land from his home in Cavina, California. We are glad to have Mr. Doyle with us again.

The Messers Doyle, Magmussen and Reynolds spent Wednesday afternoon with Russel Courer, they report a pleasant visit.

Word has been received that we can look for Mr. Clayton Philips at any time. He has a standing welcome with his old friends and neighbors.

Branch Agricultural College Basket Ball Team.

THE PLAYERS.—Reading from left to right—Luke, D. Webster, West, H. Webster, Hunter, Haight and Wood.

KANARRA NOTES.

A girl was born to Mrs. Henry Polloch, March 1.

Dr. E. Green of Cedar City was in town yesterday on buisness of his profession.

Word was received here Monday that Mr. and Mrs. Lewis E. Rowe, now of Overton Nev. are the proud parents of a fine girl, thus making Mr. and Mrs. R. G. Williams grand parents for the first time. Mr. and Mrs. Rowe went to Overton last fall to teach school, as Mr. Rowe was accepted as Supt of the Muddy Valley schools.

NADA

Our section crews have been working with the Lund section men the last few days.

Ray Stancliffe who has been building a house on his place south of Nada, went to Milford Monday.

Mr. and Mrs. A. D. McGinty accompanied by Mrs. H. Linderman and Miss June motored to Milford last Friday. They went by the way of Minersville.

Sunday morning the spirit of Mrs. Margaret J. M. Hamilton took it's flight to realms above after a lingering illness, and funeral services were held in the tabernacle Tuesday afternoon.

The deceased was born in Indiana May 8th, 1838, and while just a child went with her parents to Nauvoo, Illinois, leaving the latter place for Salt Lake City in 1843. While living in Nauvoo, she knew the prophet Joseph Smith and was there at the time of his martyrdom.

After coming to Salt Lake City she with the family came to Parowan, arriving in 1853. It was at Parowan she became the wife of Samuel Hamilton, in 1857, who preceeded her to tre spirit world several years ago.

From Parowan a few years later she and her husband moved to Cedar, living here for a short time, then going to Hamilton's Fort. In 1863 the deceased went to live in Dixie, where she resided until six years ago when she again came to Cedar where she resided the balance of her life.

Mrs. Hamilton from the time of her youth has always been an ardent Latter-day Saint, living the principles as closely as was humanly possible. She was devout, earnest and was held in esteem by a large circle of friends and acquaintances.

The deceased leaves four children to mourn her departure, one son and three daughters.

At the funeral services over the remains of the deceased, prayer was offered by Bp. E. M. Corry, the speakers being, Elder A. G. Matheson, Elder Chas. Adams of Parowan, and Councellor M. D. Higbee. Benediction was pronounced by Elder E. J. Palmer.

Appropriate singing was rendered by the choir under the leadership of Director Jas. West. Solos were sung by E. M. Corry and Gordon Matheson.

The following babies are reported to have arrived this week: a boy to Mr. and Mrs. Gordon Hunter; a girl to Mr. and Mrs. Moroni Perry; a girl to Mr. and Mrs. Heleman Webster; a boy to Mr. and Mrs. Jas. Parry.

ENOCH

Mr. and Mrs. Wm. Grimshaw went to Delta Wednesday on business.

A baby boy was born March 17th to Mr. and Mrs. Dolph Grimshaw.

Mr. Joseph Smith of St. George is visiting with his daughter Mrs. C. E. Jones.

Mrs. M. S. Jones in company with the Bee Hive girls took a horse back trip last Saturday to Mrs. Esplin's. A pleasant afternoon was spent and a dainty lunch was served by the hostess.

The family of Alonzo Ahlstrom is particularly unfortunate. The third child having developed pneumonia as a result of the epidemic of influenza.

The case of Diptheria reported in Mayor Dalley's family is now recovered and the family released from quarantine.

SIMKINS--ASHDOWN.

Thursday a cermony was performed uniting in wedlock Robert Simkins and Miss Ellen Ashdown of this city.

The bride is a daughter of Fred Ashdown, and is known favorably. being a charming young lady of winning personality.

The groom is a son of Mr. and Mrs. Wm. Simkins, highly respected by a large number of people in this end of the state. He is an earnest and sincere young man. and his many friends will be pleased to learn of his venture into the holy bonds of wedlock.

The Record tenders sincere congratulations to the bride and groom.

We are called upon again to record the passing of a Cedar citizen from that dread disease pneumonia.

Thos. Williams, after suffering from influenza for two weeks, was stricken with pneumonia, from which he was unable to rally and succumbed Tuesday afternoon.

The deceased was 68 years of age, well known and respected. He originally came from Wales to this city, arriving here in his early manhood and made his home here from that time until his death.

Mr. Williams was a hard working man, inoffensive, minding strictly his own affairs, honest and upright. Although not a man who professed religion or took part in civic affairs, he was held in esteem by a large number of people of this city, and many in adjoining towns.

The deceased leaves his wife, three daughters and two sons, besides several brothers and sisters to mourn his departure.

Funeral services were held yesterday in the tabernacle.

Washington County News
March 30, 1922

Funeral services were held in the Santa Clara Ward meeting house Thursday March 23 at 2 p m The speakers were Elders Samuel Wittwer Arthur K Hafen Prof Reid Theo Graff John Hafen and Bishop E R Frei

The first speaker talked of the wonderful companion that she was to her husband throughout her entire life He said he had become well acquainted with her in the early pioneer times and that she was ever willing to sacrifice that her own might be comfortable and happy

Bro Arthur K Hafen spoke of her good example to us all and said that though she lives no more in the flesh yet long does she live in our memories

Sisters Erma Reber and Cecila Tobler sang Whispering Hope

Prof Reid then spoke saying that although he did not know the departed one personally that she must have been a devoted and influential mother because of the honorable family she had reared

Bro Theodore Graff then spoke of the honorable family that Brother and Sister Stucki reared stating that her family was among the most honorable in the Church

The deceased is survived by her husband one brother John Pauman twelve children thirty-one grandchildren and three great grandchildren The surviving children are Barbara Tobler Zahner of Washington Utah John M Stucki Bertha Graff Hulda Wittwer Ernest Stucki Joseph Stucki all of Santa Clara Utah Ferdinand K Stucki who is filling a mission in the Northern States, Herman W Stucki instructor in the high school at Delta Utah William T Stucki who is attending the University of Utah Samuel B Stucki of Cedar City Utah and Mrs Leona Ray of St George Utah

Her loss as a kind and affectionate mother guide and counselor will be keenly felt by all her children who have been so well directed by her untiring hand her love patience perseverance and peaceful disposition

ENOCH

Born April 2, a boy to Mr. and Mrs. Stanley Smith.

George and Thornton Jones have gone to Arizona to shear sheep.

Mrs. Selma Jones is spending a few days visiting with relatives in Cedar.

Millard Halterman has been sick for a few days but is able to be around again now.

Mrs. Viola Taylor from New Harmony is visiting with her parents Mr. and Mrs. John Armstrong.

John A. Davenport went to Lund Monday to haul cement for the Cedar Lumber and Commmission Co.

A number of the people went to Cedar Tuesday to attend the funeral of Mrs. C. G. Bell.

Mr. H. C. Lewis and Mr. Parker, one of the members of the Clinic delivered an interesting and profitable lecture and also showed ilustrated pictures of tubeculosis which was appreciated by all present.

HENRY EDDARDS DIES SUDDENLY

The people of Cedar were astounded Saturday evening to learn that Henry Eddards, who had gone to Nevada a few days before, was brought home dead.

So far as we are able to learn the particulars are about as follows:

The deceased with his brother, Joe, went to Nevada Wednesday previous to look over some mining prospects, and upon returning Saturday about seven miles west of Antelope Spring was stricken with a severe pain in his left arm while driving the car in which they were riding. The pain became so intense that Henry was compelled to let his brother take the wheel. Soon after he complained of severe pains in the region of his heart, and upon arriving at Antlope Spring was in a serious condition.

Neither man had anything that could give relief to the suffering man, consequently Joe drove hurriedly toward Cedar, but had not gone far when Henry suddenly straightened out, gasped a few times and succumbed.

The brother of the deceased came on to Cedar with the body and called a physician to see if he could determine the cause of death, which was pronounced as being a contraction or cramp of the heart.

Funeral services were held Tuesday afternoon in the tabernacle at which a large number of the people of Cedar were in attendance. The services were impressive; the choir rendering appropriate music; the speakers delivering excellent addresses, and speaking of the estimable character of the deceased. Floral offerings were many and beautiful.

The deceased was well known here, having made Cedar his home for many years. He was considered to be upright, honest and sincere, and was held in respect by a large circle of friends. He leaves a wife and six children tl mourn his untimely departure.

Wm. Eddards of Delta arrived in Cedar Sunday night, having been called here on account of the sudden death of his father, Henry Eddards. The gentlemen left for Delta Wednesday, accompanied by his father-in-law, Mr. Lee, who came with him to attend the funeral services which were held Monday afternoon.

KANARRA

Funeral services over the remains of the little two year old child of Mr. and Mrs. Pollock who died in Cedar City April 3 were held in the Ward Chapel Wednesday of this week, Bp. R. J. Williams presiding.

The invocation was offered by Norman Barrick of the ward bishopric, the music was furnished by the ward choir, a selection by Mrs. Ruth Williams and Mrs. Sadie Williams. The speakers were: Jas. S. Stapley, John W. Platt, John W. Berry and Bp. Williams. A large congregation was in attendance although the heavy snow which had been falling all day prevented but few to go with the remains to the cemetery where Bp. Williams dedicated the grave.

Mary M. Stones.

N. H. Barton has commenced work on his new cement house.

* * *

Mrs. D. B. Edwards went to Cedar Thursday to see Dr. Macfarlane.

* * *

Mrs. Lizzie Lamoreaux who has been sick for two weeks is better again.

Mrs. Lucy J. Williamson who has been visiting her daughter Mrs. Jay Jeffers in Milford is home againe.

* * *

Last Monday morning Mrs. S. E. Savage's store was burned to the ground. It is not known how the fire started.

John Benson of Enterprise spent Wednesday in Cedar tending to business and visiting with friends.

* * *

Born to Mr. and Mrs. John Condie Wednesday, a girl. Dr. Macfarlane in attendance.

Joshua Walker is sufficiently recovered from his operation that he can now be removed from the hospital.

* * *

Born—A daughter to Mrs. Velma Studhone, and a daughter to Mr. and Mrs. Jas. Bess.

Mr. and Mrs. Don Coppin are rejoicing over the arrival of a bouncing baby boy that came to their home Wednesday morning. Don says that the lad is "hitting on all cylinders" and boosting to beat the band for the "light six" Studebaker.

JOHN CHATTERLEY DIES AT AGE OF 87 YEARS. WAS ACTIVE MAN IN PUBLIC AFFAIRS BEFORE AGE CREPT ON HIM.

We regret the announcing of the passing away of one of our old residents and pioneers Tuesday night, after having been ill since January.

He was stricken with Flu in December, recovering from that, seemingly, but being so weakened that he was unable to withstand the after effects because of his advance age, which was 87 years.

The deceased has lived here since the early days of the settling of Cedar City, has been in his younger days a public spirited man, and associated in public affairs much of his time. He was also very devout in religious matters and until he became handicapped by infirmities of age he was a constant attendant at church.

We are unable this week to give a biography of his life, but will endeavor to do so next week.

Funeral services will be held in the Tabernacle next Sunday, and David H. Morris of St. George, E. J. Palmer of this city and others will be the speakers. Special musical umbers appropriate to the occassion are being prepared.

John Chatterley was born in Manchester, England, July 4th. 1836. The oldest of a family of four, viz: John, Ann, Charlotte and Morton. Was educated in the Manchester schools, having a finished education at the age of 14. Was very thorough in all the common branches.

At the age of fifteen, he with the balance of the family left their comfortable home, sacrificed much of their property in order to join the latter-day Saints, who were begining to feel a desire to gather to Zion. On the third of September, 1850, they boarded the "North Atlantic," which landed them in New Orleans late in October. During the voyage a very severe storm came up and the captain lost his bearings and was very much worried when there suddenly appeared a very bright light in the sky, enabling him to see that the ship was drifting close to the corral reefs near the West Indias. He quickly changed his course, and said that henceforth he would try to always have a company of Latter-day Saints on board. During the first day out, there were only five out of 356 passengers who were able to be on deck, John Chatterley being one of the five.

From New Orleans they took the river steamer Sultana, arriving in St. Louis, Nov. 8th.

The family stayed in St. Louis about five months, building wagons to carry them across the plains to Utah. His father, Joseph Chatterley being an expert wheel-wright and mechanic. Fourteen wagons were made, eleven of them being used by the family and six other families that Bro. Chatterley was bringing with him.

Leaving St. Louis in April, 1851, they made their way as best they could with their ox teams to Utah, arriving in Salt Lake City in the fall of the same year. They had been in Salt Lake only a short time when they with a number of other families were called to settle Southern Utah and help start the iron works. They willingly took up the march again, traveled as far as Parowan which was then a small place settled only a few months previous. Bro. Henry Lunt was the leader of the small company that came on to Cedar City, arriving on the 11th. of Nov. 1851. They endured with fortitude the hardships incident to pioneering a new country, and subduing the Indians who were then rather hostile toward the whites. Bro. Chatterley stood his own, and often times his father's share of guarding against the Indian depredations, although only sixteen years of age. He finally became quite a friend to the redmen. On one occasion he with others were sent over the mountains on an important errand and they encountered many dangers and privations, being without of food for some time except rabbit meat as they were able to procure it. He was always willing to do whatever he was called upon to do by those placed in authority, and he went to meet and assist a company of emmigrants who were coming across the plains, while suffering quite severely from rheumatism. But he felt that the Lord would help him in his endeavor, and came back very much improved in health. John Chatterley was always a public spirited man, and was very active in both civic and social affairs in the early days of Cedar. He held at various times almost every office pertaining to city government. And was for some time leader of the Choir and Brass Band; Also manager of the home dramatic, giving his time willingly and without recompense.

Bro. Chatterley was very fond of good reading, and possessed a splendid library, which he was always willing to share with his friends. He taught school in Cedar City for quite a number of years, while still quite a young man. He was married to Sarah Whittaker on the 12th day of March, 1862. Nine children being born to them, four having preceded him to the great beyond.

The five remaining are as follows: Sarah E. Haight of Los Angeles, Cal., Lottie C. Perkins, Nancy C. Walker, John M. and James W. Chatterley, all of Cedar City. There are also eighteen grand children and fourteen great-grand children.

WATSON-SWAPP

April 22, 1922, a ceremony was performed in Cedar, Bp. E. M. Corry officiating, that united in wedlock H. C. Watson and Miss Delna Swapp.

Few of the friends of the young couple were aware that they had contemplated being joined in marriage that day, and were agreeably surprised to learn of the event.

Miss Swapp is the eldest daughter of Mr. and Mrs. Archie Swapp, and is well known and much thought of by a great many people of this city and of Kanab, the latter place being her home before coming to Cedar with her parents a few years ago. She is a winsome young lady, intellectual and highly cultured, a lover of home and surroundings.

The groom is a young man of estimable qualities, having while residing in Cedar the past two years, gained many friends by his manly and upright way of living.

The woung couple have the best of wishes for their success in matrimony from their many friends.

A daughter was born to Mr. and Mrs. Peter Leigh yesterday. Mother and babe doing nicely.

* * *

Clay Watson is at present in Ogden on business, but is expected back within a few days.

Mrs. Nellie Haight, daughter of John Chatterley, came up from her home in Los Angeles this week, because of the death of her father. Mrs. Haight will remain a week or two after the funeral before returning to California.

Mr. and Mrs. Fred Biederman are happy over the birth to them of a bouncing baby boy, the first in the family. The little chap is being waited on as though he were a king, and the parents are happy to have the privilege of doing homage to him.

Iron County Record
May 2, 1922

A boy was born to Mr. and Mrs. J. T. Bullloch Sunday night. Mother and babe doing nicely

Mr. and Mrs. Earl Skougard are happy over the arrival of a baby boy at their home last Tuesday.

* * *

Tuesday morning a baby boy was born to Mr. and Mrs. Sterling Seegmiller.

Mrs. Cathy Johnson, daughter of Mr. and Mrs. Wm. Webster, gave birth to a baby boy Wednesday. Mother and babe doing nicely.

Tuesday morning a baby boy was born to Mr. and Mrs. Sterling Seegmiller.

* * *

Miss Annie Corry left for Salt Lake City yesterday where she will spend a week visiting with friends.

Miss Gladys Arbuckle of Salt Lake City is here visiting with her sister, Mrs. Don Coppin.

* * *

Mrs. Cathy Johnson, daughter of Mr. and Mrs. Wm. Webster, gave birth to a baby boy Wednesday. Mother and babe doing nicely.

—oo—

Saturday a bouncing boy was born to Mr. and Mrs. Moroni Smith. Mother and babe doing nicely.

View of Canal on Thorley Project Below Kanarra.

The above is a view of the canal leading from Ash creek to the Thorley project lying just north of the Black Ridge, and a few miles south of Kanarra, being located in Washington County. The canal is six feet wide at the bottom and about ten feet at the top, with an average depth of two feet, capable of carrying 12 cubic feet of water. It is four and a half miles long, and conveys water to every part of the 2500 acres of fertile land owned by Richard A. Thorley of his city. At present the canal is supplying more than enough water for all irrigation purposes and on land that is producing excellent wheat, corn, beans, alfalfa, fruit and vegetables. Persons doubtful of the immense proposition that Mr. Thorley is putting over should take the time to make a trip there, because an actual sight gives a better idea than words or pictures can possibly do. People who know, have stated that this project is the best, if not the largest, of its kind in the state of Utah.

Iron County Record
July 7, 1922

Try Our Home-Made

SANDWITCH BUNS

Just an instant to halve them through and spread in the filling of butter, jelly, cheese or meat.

Every family that goes on picinics will want to be introduced to our Sandwich Buns—the making of any picnic luncheon.

Count the number going and then multiply by three or four—it's a mighty poor picnicker who won't enjoy that many.

G. & H. BAKERY

Baked Goods Fresh and Delicious

No 27

"No wonder the American Eagle is always pictured as screaming"

And the American dollar goes a lot farther if you spend it at the

CEDAR MERCANTILE CO.

Iron County Record
July 14-21, 1922

Riley and Wallace Williams of Kanarra were business visitors in Cedar Wednesday.

Last week Elias Leigh and Miss Alene Walker were united in wedlock, the affair being very quiet and unostantatious.

Mr. Leigh is a son of Mrs. Elizabeth Leigh, and the bride a daughter of Mrs. Nancy Walker, both of this city.

The couple have the well wishes of their friends for success and happiness in their union.

SUMMIT

Miss Afton Madsen is visiting in Salt Lake City.

Miss Thelma Huntington of Beaver is visiting with relatives here.

Mrs. Reuben Jones spent last week in Parowan with her mother, Mrs. Connell.

Mr. Charles Radford of Iowa is here to spend the summer with his brother Merle.

Mrs. Ordena Dalley is home again after an absence of nearly two months in Provo.

Last Sunday Mrs. Lucy Farrow entertained about thirty relatives in honor of her birthday.

Mr. and Mrs. Dan Cameron have returned to Panguitch after a three weeks stay in Summit.

Miss Leone Dalley and sister, Mrs. Imogene Cowdell and children are here from Beaver visiting with their parents, Mr. and Mrs. Philip Dalley.

Wm. W. Dalley and son, Bp. John H. Dalley and children have gone to Panguitch to spend two or three weeks with relatives.

Elder Leland Dalley who recently returned from a mission was the principal speaker in sacramental services Sunday. His remarks were very instructive and interesting.

Mr. and Mrs. Dee Cox are happy over the arrival of a lovely baby girl at their home this week.

Iron County Record
July 28, 1922

A baby boy was born to Mrs. Rilla Jesstison last week. All concerned doing nicely.

Mr. and Mrs. Myron M. Higbee are rejoicing over the arrival of a lovely baby girl at their home this week.

Mr. and Mrs. Angus Rosenberg are devoting their undivided attention to a beautiful baby girl that arrived at their home recently.

Mr. and Mrs. Mark McMullin are joyfully spending their time waiting on a bouncing baby boy that came to bless them.

Iron County Record
August 18, 1922

Mr. and Mrs. Dean Cuttler are the proud parents of a baby boy, born to them Sunday.

Mr. and Mrs. Karl Wood are rejoicing over the arrival of a lovely baby girl, which came to bless them nearly two weeks ago.

Born a son to Mr and Mrs John M Lang July 29 The baby is doing nicely but the mother died the same day leaving a husband and family to mourn The remains were taken to Cedar City Sunday for burial The family formerly lived at Buckhorn in Iron county Much sympathy is felt here for the bereaved husband and family

LIGHTNING STRIKES KANARRA FAMILY

——oo——

MRS. REN WILLIAMS AND TWO CHILDREN RENDERED UN- CONCIOUS. CHILDREN BAD- LY BURNED.

——oo——

Last Saturday the people of Cedar were startled to learn that at about 5 o'clock that morning, Mrs. Ren Williams of Kanarra, and two of her children were struck with lightning

It appears upon inquiry that the lady with her three children were in bed, one boy, the eldest, sleeping with her, and the other two, a boy and a girl, were together in another bed, both beds being in the same room.

At the time a terriffic thunder storm was on with much lightning, and a ball of fire was noticed coming under the screen door of the room, jumped to the corner, ran along the wall and flashed to the bedstead near the childrens' heads. The storm had awakened the children and the mother, and they were keenly alive to the peril of ligtning striking, and were positive of seeing the ball of fire, about 6 inches in diameter, coming into the room until it reached the bed when it struck the children rendering them unconscious, and the jar reaching the bed of the mother, rendering her unconscious. The bolt seemed to strike the electric light globe, knocking out the fusing. In a short time the mother regained her senses sufficiently to grope to the bed where the children were, being able to see only as flashes of lightning came. She found the children dead as she supposed, neither show- ing any signs of life. She, frantic from fright, sent the eldest boy for

from fright, sent the eldest boy for help, and the little chap went two blocks and a half to his grandparents and got them to come to the home, where they found Mrs. Williams moaning over her children, thinking them dead.

A messenger was immediately sent to Cedar for a physician and when he arrived on the scene the children were resusitated, and at present they are doing nicely, as is also the mother.

The boy was burned from his left elbow up the arm to the shoulder then around to the back of his head, where the bolt burned the hair en- tirely off. The little girl, three years of age, was struck on the right side of the abdomen, ranging up the side to the shoulder, around the throat and up to the forehead and around to back of head, with the hair being badly burned. The width of the burn on each child is about 1¼ inches. The little girl received bad burns on the left leg and left heel.

At the present writing the victims of the lightning's vindictiveness are feeling all right, other than slight pains from the burned parts on their bodies.

Jake Smith now sports a sport model of the Buick, recently purchased from the local agent, J. A. Kopp.

—oo—

Dr. and Mrs. J. W. Bergstrom have gone to Bringham City to attend the Peach Day celebration being held at that city.

Golden Haight now sports a new Chevrolet car, recently purchased from Leonard Green, local agent.

—oo—

Miss Lucile Kunz left for Salt Lake Wednesday where she will attend the U. of U. this winter.

—oo—

Assessor Hillman Dalley spent Wednesday in the northern end of the county on business connected with his office.

PERRY-NELSON

—oo—

Two weeks ago in the Salt Lake Temple Leland Perry and Miss McNone Nelson, both of this city, were united in the holy bonds of wedlock.

The couple arrived home Tuesday afternoon, and were given a reception at the home of the bride by her parents, at which several members of both families were present.

The bride is a lovable young woman, the daughter of Mr. and Mrs. Bengt Nelson, courteous and ladylike at all times, a lover of the home.

Mr. Perry is the son of Mr. and and Mrs. John Perry, and is held in high esteem by a large number of people in this city and adjoining towns. He is a bright, engergetic and progressive young fellow.

—oo—

SUMMIT

—oo—

Oscar J. Hulet has gone to Hamlin Valley where he will teach school this winter.

—oo—

Mr. Ralph Adams and his young wife, (formerly Miss Ireta Hulet), left Sunday for Lund where Mr. Adams will teach school.

—oo—

Isaac Chamberlain and family, former residents of Summit who have been living in Kane County several years returned last week to make their home here.

—oo—

The Misses Leone, Letha, Marcella, and Helen Dalley, Afton Madsen, Ellen Allen, Lucy Farrow, Arvilla and Marie Dalley have begun at the B. A. C. Several others expect to register within the next week or two.

William Otto Reeve of Kanarra and Miss Wealth Millett of Cedar City Sept 18 married in the St George temple

Clarence Goddard and family, after a couple of years in northern Utah, have returned to Cedar, and are convinced that this city is as good, if not better, than any other place they have seen while away.

Berry Williams of Kanarra, was a business visitor in Cedar Monday. Mr. Williams is county commissioner, and upon being asked by a Record scribe as to whether or not he was a candidate for re-election he stated that if the party desired his services further he had no objection to making the race.

SAHARA

—oo—

Dr. Boghosian and wife were Sahara visitors.

—oo—

Mr. and Mrs. Dans of Modena visited at the Baker home Sunday.

—oo—

Mrs. Burton Reynolds went to Modena to visit her daughter Mrs. Geo. Guffrie.

—oo—

Mrs. J. A. Baker and Mrs. H. T. Griffrie went to Parowan Saturday.

Mrs. Foreman and daughter Alice moved to Lund to have Alice attend school.

—oo—

Mr. Burton Reynolds came to Sahara Saturday night and returned Sunday.

—oo—

Mr. H. C. Davis was taken to Salt Lake City Friday for an operation of appendicitis, he is 'diing nicely.

—oo—

Mr. Lewis passed through Sahara on his way to see about some of the schools.

Iron County Record
October 20, 1922

Program For

IRON COUNTY HOSPITAL DEDICATION

3:30, P. M. Sunday, October, 22, 1922.

1—Music by the Cedar City Band.
2—Selection .... Quartet.
3—Dedication Prayer .... President M. D. Higbee.
4—Selection .... Quartet.
5—Talks .... Pres. Henry W. Lunt,
.... Dr. J. Macfarlane
.... Mr. L. A. Marsden,
.... Mr. Lehi W. Jones,
6—Selection .... Cedar City Band.

With completion and dedication of the Iron Couny Hospital, the people of Southern Utah have at their command one of the best equiped and convenient hospitals in the state. Every citizen is envited to be present at the dedication and to visit the hospital at any time within the prescribed hours. IT IS YOUR HOSPITAL. Make it so by giving it your support.

The following babies are reported the last week: To Mr. and Mrs. John M. Chatterley, a boy; to Mr. and Mrs. Mont Hunter, a girl at the County hospital; Mr. and Mrs. Joshua Walker, a boy; Mr. and Mrs. Urie Williams, a girl.

The little daughter of Archie Lamoreaux of Paragonah, was brought to the hospital Monday night with acute appendicitis. She was operated on during the night and is recovering rapidly.

NADA

Sim Resler who has spent the last few years near here, has moved to Milford with his cattle.

—oo—

Mr. D. L. Barnes went to Milford and brought back his wife and baby who have spent a few months under the care of Dr. Hunter.

—oo—

Alvin Couch, Oscar Stephenson and Carlton Culmsee spent Sunday at home and returned to their various occupations.

R. McGinty and C. R. Keith who are working in Minersville spent Sunday at home.. Mr. Keith reports a lucky catch in one of his traps—a huge gray wolf.

—oo—

Mr. and Mrs. DeWix left Friday for Placentia, California where Mr. Wix has a position in the oil fields for the winter. They made the trip in their Ford and have made plans to return in April.

Iron County Record
November 3, 1922

LIST OF NOMINATIONS, GENERAL ELECTION, NOVEMBER 7, 1922.

Constitutional Amendment NO. 3 — A joint resolution proposing to amend Section 9, of Article VI, of the Constitution of Utah, relating to Compensation of the Members of the Legislature.	For the Amendment to Section 9, of Article VI, of the Constitution of the State of Utah.
	YES	NO

Constitutional Amendment NO. 1 A concurrent resolution proposing to amend Section 1, Article XIV, of the Constitution of Utah, relating to State Indebtedness.	For the Amendment to Section 1, Article XIV, of the Constitution of the State of Utah.	Constitutional Amendment NO. 2 — A resolution proposing to amend Sections 2 and 3, of Article 13, of the Constitution of Utah, relating to Property Subject to Taxation and Rates of Tax.	For the Amendment to Sections 2 and 3, of Article XIII, of the Constitution of the State of Utah.
	YES	NO		YES	NO

REPUBLICAN TICKET

For United States Senator ERNEST BAMBERGER	
For Cong. Representative 1st Dist. DON B. COLTON	
For Justice of the Supreme Court JAMES W. CHERRY	
For Supt. of Public Instruction DR. C. N. JENSEN	
For State Senator DAVID HIRSCHI	
For State Representative RANDALL L. JONES	
For Co. Commissioner, 4-yr. Term HUGH L. ADAMS	
For Co. Commissioner, 2-yr. Term GEORGE B. WILLIAMS	
For County Clerk JOHN W. BENTLEY	
For County Treasurer W. CLAIR ROWLEY	
For County Sheriff J. TREHARNE LEIGH	

For County Recorder KATE TAYLOR	
For County Attorney GEORGE HUNTER LUNT	
For County Surveyor HILLMAN DALLEY	
For County Assessor HILLMAN DALLEY	
For Precinct Justice SAMUEL T. LEIGH	
For Precinct Constable ANDREW HANSEN	

DEMOCRATIC TICKET

For United States Senator WILLIAM H. KING	
For Cong. Representative, 1st Dist. MILTON H. WELLING	
For Justice of the Supreme Court E. E. CORFMAN	
For Supt. of Public Instruction D. C. JENSEN	
For State Senator CHARLES B. PETTY	
For State Representative U. T. JONES	
For Co. Commissioner, 4-yr. Term. H. D. BAYLES	
For Co. Commissioner, 2-yr. Term. HEBER E. HARRISON	
For County Clerk W. L. ADAMS	
For County Treasurer JAS. C. PENDLETON	
For County Sheriff MORONI CORRY	

For County Recorder KATE TAYLOR	
For County Attorney JOHN M. FOSTER	
For County Surveyor M. H. DALLEY	
For County Assessor E. H. MACFARLANE	
For Precinct Justice MORONI URIE	
For Precinct Constable ANDREW HANSEN	

SOCIALIST TICKET

For United States Senator C. T. STONEY	
For Cong. Representative, 1st Dist. JOHN Q. WATERS	
For Justice of the Supreme Court	
For Supt. of Public Instruction RUBY LINDSAY WEBBER	
For State Senator	
For State Representative	
For Co. Commissioner, 4-yr. Term.	
For Co. Commissioner 2-yr. Term.	
For County Clerk	
For County Treasurer	
For County Sheriff	

For County Recorder	
For County Attorney	
For County Surveyor	
For County Assessor	
For Precinct Justice	
For Precinct Constable	

Iron County Record
November 10, 1922

ELECTION RETURNS OF IRON COUNTY FROM EACH VOTING DISTRICT

	Enoch	Summit	Kanarra	—and No. 1	Cedar No. 1	Cedar No. 2	Stockborn	—and No. 2	Paragonah	Modena No. 1	Modena No. 2	—rowan	Newcastle	Stateline	TOTAL	MAJORITY
United States Senator																
Ernest Bamberger, R	34	26	84	7	215	272	2	23	70	11	15	271	17	15	1052	480
Wm. H. King, D	11	15	22	7	101	136	4	22	30	15	6	175	21	7	572	
Cong. Representative																
Don B. Colton, R	27	25	85	8	214	284	3	22	72	10	17	276	20	15	1076	535
Milton H. Welling, D	8	16	18	6	100	125	3	21	30	15	5	168	19	7	541	
Justice of Supreme Court																
James W. Cherry, R	26	26	88	8	221	288	2	22	78	10	15	282	18	15	1099	559
E. E. Corfman, D	9	17	18	7	95	124	4	21	30	15	6	160	21	7	540	
Supt. Public Instruction																
Dr. C. N. Jensen, R	25	25	90	7	221	283	3	22	76	11	15	297	18	15	1109	591
D. C. Jenson, D	10	16	17	7	95	123	5	21	30	15	6	146	21	7	517	
State Senator																
David Hirschi, R	26	26	85	7	196	250	2	20	71	11	16		17	15	1027	398
Chas. Petty, D	9	17	16	9	124	170	4	25	47	14	1		25	7	629	
State Representative																
Randall L. Jones, R	32	25	75	9	210	245	2	17	81	11	16	272	18	15	1026	405
U. T. Jones, D	3	18	35	7	108	167	4	28	24	15	5	171	21	7	621	
4 Year Commissioner																
H. L. Adams, R	22	31	89	5	224	311	5	28	90	10	16	376	22	15	1224	740
H. D. Bayles, D	13	12	36	10	94	111	1	17	27	13	5	131	17	7	484	
2 Year Commissioner																
George B. Williams, R	28	28	71	00	214	289	3	11	80	9	15	259	6	15	1031	401
Heber Harrison, D	6	15	36	15	104	133	3	35	36	20	4	183	33	7	630	
County Clerk																
John W. Bentley, R	31	36	76	10	227	310	6	3	93	12	17	267	27	15	1120	593
Will L. Adams, D	4	7	29	5	92	111	0	23	30	14	3	190	12	7	527	
County Treasurer																
Clair Rowley, R	28	32	75	9	223	295	6	26	85	12	17	322	22	15	1167	673
James Pendleton, D	7	11	31	6	96	125	0	20	10	3	5	119	17	7	494	
County Sheriff																
J. T. Leigh, R	30	29	80	10	210	327	5	30	72	15	14	300	18	15	1155	648
Moroni Corry, D	5	14	26	6	109	97	1	16	46	9	8	142	21	7	507	
County Recorder																
Kate Taylor, R & D	35	43	106	14	317	425	6	46	119	25	22	436	38	22	1654	1654
County Attorney																
G. H. Lunt, R	26	27	74	10	200	279	2	23	83	8	16	294	17	15	1074	484
J. M. Foster, D	9	16	31	6	118	147	4	23	35	18	5	149	22	7	590	
County Surveyor																
Hillman Dalley, R	30	28	92	10	235	321	4	27	88	12	16	297	25	15	1290	734
M. H. Dalley, D	5	15	13	6	84	104	2	19	30	14	6	149	12	7	466	
County Assessor																
Hillman Dalley, R	30	31	99	10	227	315	4	28	92	13	18	302	24	15	1298	750
E. H. Macfarlane, D	5	12	6	6	93	107	2	18	28	15	4	141	13	7	458	

Iron County Record
November 24, 1922

NEWS FROM KANARRA

—oo—

Jerry Williams has been making some improvement on his premises.

—oo—

Lester Ford left yesterday for Delta to work in the sugar factory.

—oo—

Bp. Williams went to Parowan last week on business.

—oo—

Otto Reeves and wife moved to Cedar last week to make their home there.

—oo—

The greater number of the swine that were on the mountain this fall were snowed in and had to be trailed out.

—oo—

Joe Ingram and family passed through town last week, calling on Mrs. Ingram's mother, Mrs. Eliza Wood, then continued their journey to Castle Gate.

—oo—

SUMMIT NOTES

Charley Miles is home again after an absence of several months in Yellowstone Park and northern Utah.

Mr. and Mrs. Delbert Smith and family of Parowan spent Sunday with relatives here.

Mr. and Mrs. Obadiah Farrow, and Mrs. Ray Grimshaw are doing temple work in St. George.

Heber Dalley of Cedar is spending a few days at the home of his brother Hyrum Dalley.

Joseph Dalley returned this week from Logan and other points in the northern part of the state.

Arvilla Hulet, Afton Madsen and Marie Dalley were home from the B. A. C. to spend the week-end.

SAHARA NEWS

Mr. Geo. Griffin and family was a caller at Hall Griffin's over Sunday.

Mr. A. T. Hobbs of Lund was in Sahara Sunday.

Mrs. Dr. Boghossian has been nursing Mrs. Howland for a week.

Jim Baker is busy building a barn for his stock this winter.

Hall Griffin has been working on Dr. Boghossian's well.

The McHenrys of Ford were callers at the Howland home Monday.

Mrs. Foster Howland is on the sick list at this writing she is some better.

Mr. Tullis who is building the bunk house at Beryl attended the dance at the schoolhouse Saturday night.

Mr. and Mrs. Burns moved back to Sahara from Mr. Burascano's place.

We had a club meeting Saturday night to arrange for Thanksgiving. Everybody invited to join us.

Iron County Record
December 8, 1922

As we announced last week we were obliged to hold over until this week the biographical sketch of the life of Thos. Perry, deceased, and who was laid to rest in the Cedar Cemetary last week. We publish it this week as follows:

Thomas Ward Perry was born at Cedar City, Utah, March 30, 1858, the sixth child of George and Susannah Ward Perry, well known pioneers of Cedar City, now deceased, and has made his home here all his life. He was married March 20, 1884, to Ellen Dortea Nelson. In his early manhood he freighted from Silver Reef to York in Juab County, Utah, then a railroal junction.

Due to poor health of his wife he turned to carpentry as an occupation that he might be at home. He worked as an apprentice to George Ashdown and later as a partner of his brother Joseph M. Perry.

He was also a member for many years in the Old Brass Band.

Being of a retiring disposition, seeking no worldly honors, his life was not of a public nature although he was repeatedly nominated as a delegate to conventions, aking a deep interest in the civil life of the community, refusing to accept nominations for office to which his party wished him to run.

His religious life was better known to his family than any one else. No church works or church history that he could obtain that he hadn't read and he knew exactly where to lay his hand on any passage of scripture he desired. He had a firm faith in the gospel which his parents embraced in their native land, England.

He leaves a wife and seven children all grown to maturity, he being the first to break the family circle. The children are Susannah Ellen, wife of Andrew F. Olsen of Ephriam, Abner Ward Perry, Raymond Bengt Nelson Perry, George Arthur Perry, of Cedar City; Dora, wife of Daniel K. Olsen, of Ephriam, Ralph Fiske Perry, and Marcella, wife of Fred A. Slack, and six grand children.

WORTHY KANARRA COUPLE CELEBRATES GOLDEN WEDDING IN ROYAL STYLE—TOWN PARTICIPATES.

—oo—

On November 24th, at Kanarra, Utah, Mr. and Mrs. R. J. Williams, Sr., celebrated in royal style their Golden Wedding Day, at which there were present besides the honorable couple, 5 great grand children, 44 grand children and 79 friends, in fact practically the whole population of the town of Kanarra.

A splendid time is reported and the affair consisted of a sumptuous dinner, with appropriate program which was rendered while refreshments were being served. After the guests had been abundantly satisfied with good things to eat, they were invited to the amusement hall of the town where a delightful dance was indulged in. Old and young "tripped the light fantastic" until the early morning hours.

Mr. Williams is a man known by hundreds of people of this section of the state and was one of the early pioneers here, and has been held in high esteem ever since his arrival by all who has become acquainted with him. He was born at Council Bluff, Iowa, July 17, 1851. He was married to his wife, Martha Maria Davis, November 24, 1872. To this union were born ten children, 6 boys and 4 girls all of whim are living and married, except the youngest. Mr. Williams was the son of Rees James Williams and Elizabeth Davis Williams who embraced the gospel of the Latter-day Saints in South Wales and came to America with other saints. living at Council Bluff a year during which time his father made wagons for the pioneers to cross the plains to Salt Lake City. The family crossed the plains in 1852 arriving in Salt Lake City in October of the same year. The father of the subject of our sketch was accidently killed in working at a saw mill in Little Cottonwood canyon May 27, 1860. After the death of his father Mr. Williams, then only a boy of nine years, moved to Iron County with his mother and the balance of the family. They lived at Fort Harmony a while, finally moving to Kanarra where the family have made their residence ever since. During the early life of Mr. Williams he with other pioneers suffered all the trials and hardships incident to early settlement of the country, and he, even when a boy, took his turn with the men in guarding the town and cattle from the depredations of the Navajo and Pied Indians.

The honored and loved wife of Mr. Williams, Martha Maria Davis, was the daughter of John J. Davis and Maria Davis, who also embraced the gospel in South Wales and emigrated to America. Mrs. Williams after liv-ing in several places in Northern Utah, until the Black Hawk war broke out, when she and her parents were forced to move, going to Kanarra, where they assisted materially in the settlement of that place, Mrs. Williams standing her part faithfully in the hardships of pioneer life. Here she met her husband who loved and wedded her, and has lived a happy and contented life for fifty years.

The names of the ten children of the esteemed couple are as follows:

Mrs. Wallace Williams, R. J. Williams, Jr., Mrs. S. T. Ford, W. J. Williams, John Henry Williams, Mrs. J. W. Prince, James Williams, Mrs. P. N. Wilkinson, Kumen Williams, Wells Williams, besides an orphan reared by the honored couple, Mrs. Dee Parker.

Iron County Record
December 15, 1922

KANARRA NOTES

Wm. J. Williams has gone to Parowan on business.

—oo—

A moving picture show will be installed in the school this week.

—oo—

Leland Sullivan was seen in town this week on his way to Cedar.

—oo—

Adlia Wood was in town one day last week from Castle Gate to see relatives and friends.

—oo—

Our School Principal with the janitor and 9th grade students are making benches for the school auditorium.

—oo—

James S. Stapley is erecting a hay shed on his farm 4 miles South of town.

—oo—

Mr. Rossell Christensen, formerly Miss Pollock, is here visiting with her brothers and sisters.

—oo—

Reli: Society gave a social to members of the Bishopric this evening which was a success in every respect.

—oo—

Basket Ball playing will be the main sport at school this winter. We will expect to challenge or be challanged before the school term is out.

—oo—

Wallie Pollock and son Clemet came home from Castle Gate last week, and moved the family up there for an indefinite stay.

—oo—

John Meredith of Salt Lake is visiting with A. Stephenson.

—oo—

C. Roper is at home after working for some time on the B. & B. gang.

—oo—

H. C. Eyre of Minersville was in Nada Monday and reported the roads in bad condition.

—oo—

Mr. Stubbs and son C. J. of Paro-
wan brought a bunch of sheep over last week.

—oo—

Ray Stancliffe who has been herding for Bob Bonner has returned to his work in Milford shops.

—oo—

Mrs. Max Moore is making an extended visit at the home of her son Bob, in Milford.

—oo—

Mrs. R. R. McGinty returned last Sunday night from a short visit in San Bernardino.

Cedar City Utah Dec 7
Editor Washington County News

About the middle of March 1863 Apostle Erastus Snow of St George received a call from President Brigham Young to send a train of 40 ox wagons back to Florence Nebraska to bring a number of emigrants to Utah

Apostle Snow received the letter late at night Early next morning he called on me to go as a teamster, which I cheerfully did and so was the first man called on Pres Young nominated Daniel D McArthur as captain of the company James Andrus as assistant captain or wagonmaster

There were two younger men in the train than myself Geo H Crosby and Albert Stratton and I confess to being the least experienced ox driver

We were divided into messes from six to ten in a mess The calf messmen were Alex Meade captain of the mess David Hirschi Charles Wilson Anthony Paxton Alex Matheson Frederick Bleak Richard Hawkins and Joseph Harmon

There were four mounted men who guarded the cattle at night Erastus McIntire Solomon Wardell, 'Bill' Lytle and Wm Alexander There were four yoke of oxen to each wagon.

We left St George on April 1, 1863 arrived in due course at the Missouri and had to wait there some six weeks for the emigrants to come up the river The nearest railroad was at St Joe down the river 200 miles We started on the return trip about July 24th and out travelled every other ox train on the plains that year so that we were called hell-saving Dixie As an instance of our energy, every man would have his eight head of oxen picked out of over 300 head and ready to start in 20 minutes from the time they were driven into the corral, this of itself was no small matter Everything was well ordered and good counsel was always given and generally accepted Prayers were never neglected no matter how busy we were

There were enough discomforts in crossing the plains in those days that very few people wanted to go back Obituary articles often say, 'She walked all the way across the plains " Quite so, as there were 12 persons to each wagon to haul their bedding and baggage the chances to ride were ngligable

Well I am an old man now, and there are very few of those old Wagas left I would like to know how many and preadventure to eat an old fashioned slapjack with good Dixie molasses with them on April 1st 1923 (Deo Nolante)

With kindly salutations for my old comrades of sixty years ago

Alexander Matheson.

Santa Claus' Workshop

ENOCH NEWS.

Merl Gibson is seriously ill in a Salt Lake Hospital.

A splendid cottage meeting was held at Arthur Bryants. Elder Grant Walker was the speaker.

Mr. Owen is building a barn down in his farm. A Mr. Haycock of Panguitch is living there.

Over twenty young people of the Enoch precinct are in Cedar City schools this winter leaving so few at home that no Mutuals are held.

Mrs. Anna Adams is very energetic in caring for the new school house and grounds, cleaning up, mending fences, and planting bulbs and trees.

Elder Golden Haight departed for a mission in the Central States, December 4. The support given him by his friends before leaving was much appreciated.

The street running east and west through Midvalley has been greatly improved in the last year by grading, culverts bridges while on man toward Iron Springs is using it for a reservoir.

Iron County Record
December 23, 1922

H. W. Leigh, our enterprising furniture dealer, is exceptionally happy this holiday season, because of the fact that his wife presented him with a lovely baby girl last Friday. Mother and babe doing nicely.

Mr. an Mrs. Roy Bauer are rejoicing over the arrival of a bouncing boy at their home on 3rd. East. It's the first to come to bless them, and of course they are very happy over the event.

Mrs. Amy Brown of Hamilton's Fort spent Thursday in Cedar on a Christmas shopping expedition.

Iron County Record
December 29, 1922

Tuesday noon the people of Cedar were again startled and shocked at the report of a life coming suddenly to an end without warning.

George Perry, a man well known and respected in this city, was going about his daily duties when he was suddenly stricken with contraction of the heart muscles and ceased to live within a moment or two. The attack came without warning, although the deceased had been slightly ill with an attack of indigestion.

He had just attended to some chores outside the home and entered when he was stricken, falling upon a sofa, and expired before a daughter who was in the house could render any assistance or call for help.

It will be remembered that a brother of the deceased, Thos. Perry, passed away in a similar manner while plowing in the field, appoplexy being credited as being the direct cause of death.

The deceased was a man whom honest and upright man, in whom his friends placed trust. ....

He will be sadly missed by the children who are left to mourn his sudden and unexpected departure.

Funeral services were held in the Ward Hall yesterday and the building was taxed to capacity to seat the relatives and friends who had gathered to pay their last tribute of respect to the departed.

The services were conducted by Counsellor Samuel F. Leigh of the West Ward, prayer being offered by Elder A. G. Matheson. The speakers were Elders Parley Dalley and H. Claude Lewis, each of whom told of the excellent character of the deceased and spoke many words of condolence to the mourners. Benediction was pronounced by Counsellor Myron D. Higbee.

Iron County Record
January 5, 1923

We have been informed that Miss Ella Matheson, daughter of Mr. and Mrs. A. G. Matheson, was married ried last week to George Foster in the St. George temple.

The young couple have the well wishes of a host of friends for their happiness and success as man and wife.

The bride is a young lady who has won the respect of many people by her high ideals of life, honor to her parents and devotedness to duty, both in the home and the church to which he belongs.

The groom is a well known and highly respected citizen of Cedar who came from St. George several years ago to make his home in Iron County. In both places he is well liked and respected, is a capable, honest and courteous young man.

. The Record tenders sincere congratulations to Mr. and Mrs. Foster.

Iron County Record
January 12, 1923

KANARRA
——oo——

Hartley Woodbury has gone to California in search of work.

——oo——

Charles Parker, Jr. returned from California for the Holidays. He and his family moved to California last July .

——oo——

Mrs. Erland Flowers gave birth to a fine girl Jan. 4th. From reports they are getting along fine.

——oo——

Bp. Williams and wife went to Provo for the holidays. While there the Bp. bought a new piano for our church.

——oo——

Rulon Platt left last Saturday for a mission to the Southern States. A farewell party was given in his honor by the town. A purse of $58.00 was given him by the committee who had the affair in charge.

——oo——

A petition was circulated Saturday and Sunday asking the County Commissioners to put electric lights on poles long main street. Only two persons refused to sign. We are earnestly awaiting their action.

SAHARA

Joe Yoeman was up from Beryl Sunday.

Mr. Ence came back from Cedar Thursday.

Theo and Leonard Griffin have been very sick with bad colds.

H. I. Dougherty is drilling a well on the north side of his homestead.

Mr. Donald Burns spent New Years with Mr. and Mrs. R. Burns.

Mr. Arthur Crawford of Enterprise has been delivering hay and grain to Sahara.

Mr. and Mrs. Athol Griffin returned from Mammoth, Utah, where they had been called on account of the Death of Mrs. Griffin's brother.

Iron County Record
January 19, 1923

SUMMIT

Peter Gurr and Marlow Topham of Parowan are here laboring as missionaries.

Leland Dailey and Wilford Lawrence will leave tomorrow for a two weeks mission in Cedar City.

Bros. John P. Orton, and George Rowley of Parowan were speakers at Sacramental meeting Sunday.

A cottage meeting was held Thursday evening at the home of Obadiah Farrow. The house was filled to overflowing and a splendid time enjoyed by all present.

Mrs. Radford of Iowa, mother of Merl Radford of this place is expected to arrive here tomorrow to make her home. Another son, Charles, is also on his way, coming in his own car.

Hyrumn Dalley of Summit spent Tuesday in Cedar attending to some matters of a private nature. Mr. Dalley says that everybody in Summit is well, and that the people generally have passed the winter so far without serious sickness.

SERVICES FOR JOHN DAVIS HELD

—oo—

Services were held Monday for John Davis of this city, who passed from this life Saturday last after a lingering illness. The deceased passed away at the home of his mother, Mrs. Nancy Davis.

We are informed that Mrs. J. C. Hamilton of Hamilton's Fort is very ill at present. The lady has been a sufferer for a considerable time, and does not seem to improve under careful nursing and medical treatment.

NADA

Mike Schaaf went to Minersville to buy a bunch of hogs last week.

Mr. and Mrs. M. Minagi and children were in Salt Lake last week.

Mrs. N. Barnes has recovered from her recent illness.

Beaver county assessor, James Rollins is in Nada and vicinity on official business.

Carlton Culmsee returned to Reed, Sunday after spending the week end at home.

.... SUMMIT.

—oo—

George Smith left Tuesday with about 50 head of steers which he has been fattening for the California market.

—oo—

Chas. Radford. arrived here last week from Alboka, Iowa. Mr. Radford has leased the Reuben Jones farm at Windom for four years.

—oo—

Mr. and Mrs, Ralph Adams are happy over the arrival of a baby girl Monday Mrs. Adams is at present at the home of her parents, Mr. and Mrs. O. W. Hulet.

Next Friday evening a basketball game will be played between the married and single men under the auspicies of the Civic Improvement Club.

—oo—

Farmers are jubilant over the prostpects of an abundant water suply for next sumer as the recent storms have piled up a great deal of snow in the mountains.

—oo—

Last Friday evening the daughters of Elzina Hulet entertained at a social in honor of their mother's 62nd birthday. About 30 of the older married people were present and enjoyed themselves with games, music, etc. Refreshments were served.

Last Monday the spirit of Denton Jones, 15 year old son of Mr. and Mrs. T. W, Jones, passed on to other realms after suffering for a considerable time from strangulated hernia followed by peritonitis. During his entire illness he was patient and willingly submitted to the treatment for his illness that the skilled physicians and nurses at the county hospital could give.

For a time after peritonitis developed he seemed to rally, but another complication set in which was too much for his weakened system and the lad succumed peacefully to the Grim Reaper.

Charles Franklin Stevens, of whose life the following brief account is but a synopsis, was born in Little Cottonwood, south of Salt Lake City, on Dec. 27th, 1853, and died at his home north of Cedar City, Utah, Feb. 24th. 1923.

Almost his whole life has been devoted to pioneering work of the southern part of Utah. He spent the greater part of his youth at a place called Shonesburg in the extreme Eastern part of Washington County, where he met and married Olive DeMills by whom he had at this place the following children. Franklin, Carlos, Minnie, Nephi, Olive, Ida, and Myrtle. After this the family moved to Orderville, where the following children were

Franklin, Carlos, Minnie, Nephi, Oliva, Ida, and Myrtle. After this the family moved to Orderville, where the following children were born; Oscar, Majorie, Benjamin, Rosswell and Isabelle. The two last died in infancy as also had one in their former home making three whom he had lost during their earliest infancy.

In 1909, the two sons Carlos and Nephi camee over from Orderville and began the preparations for a home in this valley previous to the moving of the family which they did in te summer of 1911

Bro. Stevens went through many trials after he came here in the loss of so many of his family. His good wife was an invalid from the time of the birth of the son Carlos, and suffered bodily pain and misery through the many years of raising her family, but through it all and the fact of that indomitable blood of the true hardy pioneer and the further fact that he had the unshakable conviction of right, it was always his first

duty to is wife and family to see that all he could was done and done willingly for their welfare. Towards the latter part of her life the good wife suffered many bodily ills and finally succumbed on March 10, 1913. The daughter Marjorie volunteered to take a mission some time latter and while in the work of the Lord gave up her life to the grim reaper while in the field with headquarters at Denver, Colorado, Nov., 5th., 1918. On April 21st, 1919, the eldst son came into the yard after doing some work out in the field and dropped dead without any struggle and before he could be carried into the house. On July 29th, 1922, while at St. George where her husband and she were at work in the Temple at that place and had been living for several years, the oldest daughter Minnie Stevens Lang gave up her life leaving a husband and four children.

Bro. Stevens during all this and many other troubles of minor nature has never been heard to utter ont word of cofplaint and his testimonies, of which he had a great

many, were always of the strongest in regard to the Gospel and in which he was always an earnest worker and he has never in all his life shirked any duty that he was called to perform by those in authority. Frank, as he was always familiarly called by all his ssociates was a pioneer in the truest sense of the word and was always a producer and not a social parasite. He earned every dollar he ever had and if that saying is true that "An honest man is the noblest work of God," then this earth is the better by far from his having lived in it, for it can be truly said of him that he never wilfully injured any living man. He was at the St. George Temple when he took his last sickness which turned to

pneumonia of the most verulent type which terminated in his death as stated above. He leaves behind him seven children and over forty grand children and two great-grand children.

Many men have testified that in more than forty years of their acquaintance with Frank Stevens they have never heard him speak ill of his fellow man.

Funeral services were held at the Enoch Tabernacle February 26th, 1923. The speakers were Elders Lorenzo and Owen Matheson, Bp. C. E. Jones of the Enoch ward and L. W. Jones of Cedar. Interment was made in the Cedar cemetery.

WOMAN CIVIL WAR VET. ANSWERS LAST ROLL CALL

Emma Winans a Civil War veteran widow of A J Winans passed away after a long siege of illness at the home of William Brooks March 7 1923

Deceased was born at Richibucto New Brunswick Canada March 17 1832 Her maiden name was Emma Pine On Sept 30 1850 she was married to John J Gifford and of this marriage she became the mother of three children Mr Gifford lost his life in a shipwreck The Rock Roy going down with all of her crew of which he was one in January 1857

In the year 1863 Mrs Gifford enlisted at a recruiting station in Waterton N Y as a cook in the 11th Infantry and was sent to Fort Independence Boston Harbor There she met A J Winans who was principal musician in 11th U S Infantry, and married him in the fall of 1863 she continued as cook all during the war They were discharged in Richmond Va on expiration of term of service and they both reenlisted in the same regiment An order from Washington disbanded all bands in the army excepting the Marine band There was a consolidation of the 11th Infantry and others forming the 16th Infantry They were stationed and served in nearly all of the important camps in the Southern States

In all Mrs Winans and her husband were in the U S military service for nearly twenty years as cook and musician respectively, receiving their final discharge from the army at Fort McKavett, Texas March 23 1883 She had been in receipt of a pension for several years

They then moved to Idaho then to Ogden, Utah, then to Cedar City, Utah, then to St George Utah, at which place they remained until death called them, Mr Winans dying several years ago

Mrs Winans is survived by one son William B Gifford of Mainville, Ill, and one granddaughter Miss Samie Gifford of Berkely, California

Funeral services were held in the Stake Tabernacle at St George Utah under direction of Bishop F G Miles The building had been decorated for the occasion and there was a good attendance of friends to show their last respects to the veteran

The speakers were Elders John D Pace, David H Morris, and F G Miles Choir sang 'Rest For The Weary' and other hymns and there was a violin solo Interment was made in the city cemetery, deceased being laid alongside the remains of her husband

SUMMIT

———oo———

Leroy Smith of Minersville is here visiting with his brother George Smith.

Reuben Jones moved his family to Lund last week where he has employment.

George Smith who is representing a California packing plant bought a half carload of hogs in Summit last week.

Mr. and Mrs. Obadiah Farrow and daughter Mrs. Marie Grimshaw returned last week from St. George where they have been doing Temple work.

Mr. and Mrs. Wm. Smith entertained Friday in honor of Mr. Smith's 69th birthday. A large crowd of married people were present, and report having had a splendid time.

In the death of Eva Mae Pace, eight year old daughter of Mr. and Mrs. J. G. Pace of this city, the fond hearts of the parents are stricken with grief, as is also the hearts of their many friends in Cedar and nearly every town and hamlet of southern Utah.

Her demise occurred Saturday, March 24th. after the young girl had suffered since January 2nd from heart trouble. Everything that the family physician could do was done, as well as the most careful and conscientious nursing by loving hands, but the disease had gained such a hold upon the young girl that all was of no avail.

Funeral services were held Sunday afternoon at 3:30 and a large gathering of sympathizing relatives and friends were present. Bp. E. M. Corry officiated, the speakers being Elders S. F. Leigh and Wm. R. Palmer. A beautiful solo was given by Elder H. L. Frisby and the choir rendered appropriate music.

The floral offerings from friends were numerous and beautiful.

KANARRA

Mrs. Flower of Idaho is here visiting her daughter, Mrs. John Stapley.

Will Olds has rented Mrs. Mary J. Williams' farm for this season.

Mr. and Mrs. C. A. Thompson and family were down Sunday night to the drama.

R. G. Williams is having some new fence put up on his residence lot on main street.

Irvin Williams and Sam Ford have gone to work on the railroad near Lund.

Horace Roundy and Gus Pingle are putting up a house each. Roundy on west street and Pingle on his farm one mile north of town.

The piano committee put on another play Sunday night. "Peg O' My Heart", to a well filled house. The characters were well taken and well presented. The actors did credit to themselves and satisfied the patrons. The proceeds go to paying for the new piano which is installed in the meeting house.

SAHARA

Miss Tacoma Baker went to Modena Monday.

Earl Marwith and Bryant Hedrick spent Thursday in Sahara.

Mr. and Mrs. L. A. Burascano passed through Sahara enroute to Cedar City.

Mr. and Mrs. Dave Empy and daughter passed through Sahara enroute to their home. They spent the night at the home of Mr. and Mrs. J. A. Baker.

A crowd of 50 attended the dance at Sahara Saturday night. Those from out of the town were Mr. and Mrs. Bruce and children of Utana, Miss Morehouse of Utana. Mr. and Mrs. H. C. Davis and daughter; Miss Opal Gott and Leon Gott. Mr. Lohf, Kelley Brothers and Mr. and Mrs. Webster of Beryl. The pies brought a good price and everybody says Sahara for a good time. It also being the birthday of one of our Sahara Club membebra, Mr. Earl Markwith, the people gove him a surprise of a nice birthday cake.

Iron County Record
April 6, 1923

GARDNER-LEIGH

The friends of Arthur Gardner and Miss Ina Leigh will be pleased to learn of the marriage of the young couple in the St. George Temple, Tuesday of this week.

The groom is a highly respected young man of this city, and counts his friends by the score. Mr. Gardne is the cashier of the Iron Commercial Bank, and has the entire confidence of the officials of that institution. He is a learned, capable young man, and entitled to the well wishes of his friends.

The bride is the talented daughter of Mr. and Mrs. S. T. Leigh, a lady who has been identified in a public way in Cedar for several years, being a nurse in local hospitals, and for several months had charge of the county hospital nursing force. Through her activities as a professional nurse she has made many friends, each of whom will wish her success and happiness throughout her married life.

NADA NEWS

J. D. Leigh is moving the house from the old Wix homestead.

Max Moore visited with the home folks over Sunday.

Mrs. O. H. Moore has returned from Reed to her home here.

Alvin Couch returned Sunday night from Caliente for a three months stay at home.

A good rain fell here on Tuesday. It was more welcome than the dust storm last Friday, needless to say.

Mrs. Ollie M. Couch went to Modena last Saturday to make final proof on her homestead, before U. S. Commissioner Lund. Her father, J. F. Dinwiddie and Mrs. L. A. Culmsee accompanied her as witnesses.

The Service Star Legion ladies are very desirous of securing the names of all the soldiers from Cedar City who served during the late world war, and will appreciate it if any person that knows of any young man who was called or volunteered for service will hand in the name to the secretary of the organization. The list the Service Star has at present is incomplete, and is as follows:

Adams, William C.
Burns, Hubert, Gold Star
Bryant, Logan H., Gold Star
Bryant, Danial H.
Bauer, J. Leroy
Bauer, Samuel
Bauer, Ervin
Bergstrom, Wilford
Brown, John M.
Barton, Alma Ross
Bryant, Erastus J.
Corry, George Heyborne
Corry, Robert U.
Corry, C. Loyal
Carpenter, John Karl
Cox, Dee T.
Clark, John F., Gold Star
Clark, James Milton
Cosslett, Gomer D.
Dover, Charles Lionel, Gold Star
Dustin, Ervin
Dalley, Rulon

Dalton, Arthur
Davis, William
Davis, Thomas S.
Edwards, James Clark
Edwards, William D.
Eddards, Evan
Eddards, Ebenezer
Fretwell, Herbert D.
Fife, Louis R.
Grimshaw, George U.
Grimshaw, Randolph
Green, Raymond
Gardner, Thurlow
Gardner, Fernleigh
Granger Walter K.
Gardner J. X.
Gibson Merrill H.
Heyborne, Milo L.
Haight, Arthur C.
Hunter, George W.
Hunter, Lamont W.
Hunter, Gordon L.
Haslem, Arthur
Haslem, Lawrence
Jasperson, Elmer, Gold Star
Jones, Harry M., Gold Star
Jones, George W.
Jones, Orien Robert
Jones, Lehi M.
Jones, Erastus L.
Jones, William L.
Jones, Jared Franklin
Jones, U. Ashton

Jones, Emron H.
Jensen, Charles Oliver
Kaze, John
Lunt, John Henry
Leigh, Leon
Leigh, Elias W.
Leigh, Wilford
Leigh, Leland
McConnell, Harold, Gold Star
McConnell, L. Junior
Macfarlane, Glen
McDonough, George
Mackelprang, Warren P.
Mackelprang, Melvin Parry
Mulliner, William T.
Melling, William L.
Moore, Roy
Mosdell, Thomas W.
Middleton, Francis H.
Murio, Bernard
Merryweather, Austin
O'Neil, Raymond R.
Olsen, Pard
Olsen, Alfred
Perry, Arthur N.
Perry, Raymond
Perry, George Ether
Perry, Hyrum L.
Pucell, William Lloyd
Perkins, Willard M.
Parry, Stanley Haight
Pace, Legrand
Parry, Gronway G.

Parry, Chauncey
Pendleton, William Carlos
Palm, George Stapley
Palm, Merlin Larson
Pratt, Charles M.
Rosenburg, Harvey G.
Rosenburg, Thomas G.
Root, John Cassidy.
Roche, William
Reed, Ervin D.
Rollo, Ezra S.
Rollo, Morgan
Renshaw, A. Lee
Ray, J. Elmer
Sherratt, Merdell E.
Smith, Moroni Klingon
Smith, George Albert
Smith, James D.
Smith, Wallace
Smith, Heber Edwin
Simkins Vergene
Simkins, James Corlett
Stapley, Arlie Adams
Stapley, Arthur A.
Smith, Gordon
Sawyer, Fremont M.
Schmutz, Eldon
Thorley, Lester R.

Thorley, Alldredge R.
Thorley, Morton C.
Tollestrup, A. Virgil
Tollestrup, Pratt
Tweedie, David Hume
Urie, Arthur P.
Urie, Earl G.
Webster, Wilford
Webster, Joseph R.
Woodbury, Eugene
Williams, Thomas Evan
Williams, Elvid
Wilkinson, Marion W.
Wilkinson, Gerald
Wood, Ulrich Bryner
Walker, John Erwin
Walker, William Grant
Webb, Edwin
Webb, Jess O.
Worthen, Mark

SUMMIT NOTES

Mr. and Mrs. Oscar J. Hulet were in from Hamlin Valley to spend the week end with home folks.

Isaac Chamberlain is home again after working for several weeks with a force of men at Cedar Breaks.

Mrs. O. W. Hulet has gone to Lund for a few days visit with her daughter, Mrs. Ralph Adams.

Mr. and Mrs. Arthur Jones and family, Sylvester Jones, and Joseph E. Jones of Enterprise were visitors last week at the home of their sister Mrs. O. W. Hulet.

Two parties of prospectors have been at work in Summit mountains the past week.

WOOD-MERRYWEATHER

Tuesday Preston Wood and Miss Zylphia Merryweather of this city were married, the announcement of the marriage causing consideable surprise among the friends of the young people.

The bride is a daughter of Mr. and Mrs. F. H. Merryweather, and is thought a great deal of by a large number of friends and acquaintances, as well as numerous people in Provo, the home of the Merryweathers before coming to Cedar three or four yeas ago.

The groom is a son of Mr. and Mrs. Geo. H. Wood, and is well known and respected in Cedar.

We understand the young people will make their home in Cedar.

The Record extends sincere congratulations to Mr. and Mrs. Wood.

NADA NEWS

Mrs. Jane Keillor, aged 70 years passed away last Thursday, April 19 at the home of her son. The body was taken to Milford for burial, funeral services were held on Friday, April 20. The sympathy of the entire community goes out to the bereaved family.

Mrs. S. E. McGinty, Ray, Grace and Bennette left last week for San Bernardino when they will spend the summer.

C. L. Robinson and Mr. Topham left for Minersville Tuesday. When they remain until after the M. I. A. day Saturday and for shearing.

S. B. Robb brought in a bunch of young sheep for a month's stay on the range here.

BORN—to Mr. and Mrs. D. C. Bulloch a boy, Wednesday.

—oo—

Charles Esplin came in from his ranch yesterday suffering from an attack of appendicitis.

—oo—

Mrs. Maria Bulloch, who has been very ill for some time past of a complication of diseases, is reported today improved.

Edwin Higbee of Toquerville purchased this week a lot in the Dalley-Urie Subdivision west of town and contemplates erecting a neat bungalow thereon as soon as materials can be secured.

Mrs. Amy Brown of Hamilton's Fort spent Tuesday in Cedar on a shopping tour, and visiting with relatives.

—oo—

Mr. and Mrs. Hunter Lunt entertained a number of friends at a bridge party Saturday night, the guests enjoyed thoroughly the hospitality of the host and hostess.

The following have been operated at the county hospital the last week. Preston Swapp, Athens Thompson, Mrs. David Eddards, Miss Hendrickson of Parowan, Mrs. Edward Carroll of Orderville and Mrs. John A. Adams and Howard Kunz. All are reported doing nicely.

Tuesday afternoon hundreds of friends and acquaintances met at the tabernacle to pay their last tribute of respect to Mrs. Maria Bulloch who departed this life Saturday after suffering intensely from a complication of diseases.

Construction of the Lund Cedar Branch of the Salt Lake Route is going forward so rapidly that the road is built to Iron Springs already and at the rate they are working they will be in Cedar City with trains in fourteen more working days.—Paro

A prominent Cedar young couple are to be married in the Salt Lake Temple next Wednesday.

The happy contracting parties are Parson Webster and Miss Evelyn Palmer, both well known and held in very high esteem by scores of people of Cedar and Southern Utah.

Their host of friends will wish them a long, happy and prosperous life as man and wife.

Willard Canfield was in town a few days last week, on his way back to Salt Lake City, from Enterprise where he had been to attend the funeral services of his mother, who was buried last week. He returned to the University, where he has been attending school, to finish up his graduation work.

After spending three years on a successful mission in Australia Elder Gordon Smith has returned home.

The young man has enjoyed his labors in promulgating the gospel, and arrives home looking and feeling splendid.

The many friends of the young man are very pleased to again greet him.

Mr. and Mrs. Warren Bulloch are happy over the arrival of another child to bless them. It's a boy, healthy and well developed.

SUMMIT NOTES

—oo—

...Mr. and Mrs. Obadiah Farrow spent Sunday with friends in Cedar.

—oo—

Miss Virgie White, who has been teaching school at Elsinore, returned home last week.

—oo—

Mrs. Isaac Chamberlain is enjoying a visit from her mother, Mrs. Cram of Kanab.

—oo—

Otto Dalley has gone to his ranch on the mountains where he will keep his sheep for a short time.

—oo—

John Philips and Charles Dalley, who recently sold a bunch of sheep to Mr. Thorley of Cedar, have just returned from the Kanarra mountains where they went to deliver them.

—oo—

Mr. and Mrs. Wallace Jones of Overton, Nev. are here for a visit with Mrs. Overton's parents, Mr. and Mrs. Isaac C. Haight.

Stanley Dalley is home again after spending the winter teaching school at Wallsburg.

—oo—

Charles Radford has gone to Aboka, Iowa for a short visit with relatives.

—oo—

Bernell, Madsen, Charley Miles and Marion Alldredge have gone to work on the railroad grade near Lund.

—oo—

Mr. and Mrs. Oscar F. Hulet have returned from Hamlin Valley where Mr. Hulet has been employed as school teacher the past winter.

John L. Sevy spent the week in Cedar attending to business matters.

—oo—

Monday, last a baby boy was born to Mr. and Mrs. John Smith.

—oo—

Mr. and Mrs. Willard Canfield are the proud parents of a baby girl, born May 28th.

Albert Biederman, Evelyn Parry and Gon Parry, members of the local Rod and Gun Club have recently received appointments as game wardens under the State Fish and Game Commissioner.

...SAHARA NEWS NOTES.

—oo—

June 10, 1923.

—oo—

Mr. and Mrs. J. A. Baker went to Cedar Ctiy on Decoration Day.

—oo—

William Griffin spent the week's end at Minto with his son.

—oo—

Mrs. Guy Phelps of Modena spent Saturday and Sunday here.

—oo—

H. A. Dougherty and W. A. Brown are putting up a windmill for Dr. Boghossian.

—oo—

Mr. Sprague of Cedar City was a Sahara caller Friday on piano business.

—oo—

Mr. Irvine of Salt Lake City was in Sahara Saturday on private business.

Salt Lake Tribune
June 11, 1923

Cedar City June 11 —This has been a big day for Cedar City for it marks the beginning of railroad transportation N A Williams general superintendent of the Los Angeles & Salt Lake railroad brought the first train over the branch line from Lund on the main line to this town today It was an important event and seemed to meet with the approval of all living in this neighborhood

The mayor and a committee of the whole was on hand The entire country in this vicinity turned out and men women and children were on the receiving line In the special party with Mr Williams were Marius de Brabant assistant traffic manager of the Union Pacific system T C Peck general passenger agent at Los Angeles Randall L Jones assistant park engineer for the system and his son Carl and a large crowd of business men from Salt Lake and Los Angeles Duncan MacVichie consulting engineer for the Columbia Steel corporation and a few others came as far as Iron Springs and stopped there

There was a mass meeting at noon, immediately following luncheon at which short talks were made by some of the visitors the mayor and others Following this there was a trip to the canyon the party returning to Lund at 6 o clock this evening —Salt Lake Tribune

The friends of Reuben Walker and Kate Bloomgren were agreeably surprsied Saturday last to learn of their marriage in Parowan.

The couple are well and favorably known and are receiving the sincere congratulations of a large circle of frie..ls.

Nellie T. Pace, daughter of Amas and May W. Thornton, was born in Pinto, Washington County, Utah, Feb. 18, 1870, and there her childhood and young womanhood was lived. She was married to J. Granville Pace Sept. 18, 1895, She was the mother of nine children, four of whom preceded her to the other world.

She was a member of the Stake Relief Society and had also worked as an aide in the Stake M. I. A. and local organizations. Was corresponding secretary for the organization of the Daughters of the Pioneers; Twice President of the Economic Club; a worker in Service Star, and never a call was made of her in any capacity but she responded with pleasure. She was a devoted Latter-day Saint, a gifted speaker with charm of manner and language; her winning smile was a joy to all. She was of a highly spiritual and intelectual mind, taking advantage of every opportunity for learning. She was a student of the B. Y. University; taught school for a number of years in Washington and Kane counties, also during the time her husband was on a mission. She was a true and devoted wife, a tender mother, a loving daughter and sister. His family can take comfort in the thought that "not death is strong enough to part asunder, Whom life and love hath joined."

Her friends are legion, she was an inspiration in time of joy or sorrow. She loved humanity and lived it in her daily life. A few lines from a poem of Bro. Brimhall, expresses her heroic womanhood:
"A mind that soared above the dust,
A heart that throbbed for duty,
A hand that shared the frugl crust,
And touched the world with beauty."

Tuesday a ceremony was performed in Redmond, Utah, uniting in matrimony Mr. Vernon Nelson of that city and Miss Elizabeth Smith of Cedar.

The young bride is a daughter of J. C. Smith of this city and is well known and respected.

The many friends of the young lady will be pleased to learn of her venture and wish her every success in her journey through life with the man of her choice. *

MARRIED

We learn that Stanley Roberts and Miss Clara Bulloch were married Monday at Delta.

The young couple have many friends here who will be pleased to learn of their union and will wish them much joy and a long and successful life as man and wife.

Iron County Record
June 29, 1923

Wednesday the gentle spirit of Mrs. Eva Lunt Jones of this city took its flight to its Maker from when it came sixty-two years ago.

The departed was well known to all old residents of this city, and to hundreds of the younger people, and was held in very high esteem by them all. She was born in Cedar February 7, 1861, the daughter of Henry Lunt and Mary Ann Lunt, both of whom preceded their daughter to the spirit world several years ago.

Eva Lunt Jones was a devout Latter-day Saint and during her whole life took much joy from living up to the precepts of the church of which she was a member. Her life throughout was sincere, earnest and devoted to her parents, and her husband and children. She went through all the trials and hardships during the early pioneer settlement of Cedar.

Eighteen years ago her health became undermined, and she grew worse as time went on, until finally death came as a boon to relieve her of suffering.

She leaves a devoted husband and the following children to mourn her departure: Randall L. Jones. Mrs. Sadie Thorley, Mrs. Mame Ballentyne, Mrs. Cora Stucki. Jed Jones, Marvin Jones, Elton Jones and Preston Jones.

Samuel Kelsey, a man everybody that bore his acquaintance respected, succumbed Wednesday afternoon to the dread disease of cancer of the stomach.

He had suffered for a long time, and everything that medical science could suggest for his release from pain and suffering was done. but the disease prevailed and caused death at the time above stated.

The deceased was about 67 years of age, and leaves to mourn his departure several children.

Funeral services were held in the tabernacle today, and there was a large number of sympathizing friends and acquaintances of the bereaved family present.

MARRIED. ....

Last week Loyal U. Millett of this city, and a daughter of Mr. and Mrs. Thornton Hepworth of Springdale, were married in the St. George temple.

The young couple returned to Cedar Sunday and intend making their home here.

The groom is a son of Mr. and Mrs. Marion Millett, and is well and favorably known. He has many friends who will be pleased to learn of his matrimonial venture, and will wish he and his wife a pleasant voyage on the matrimonial sea of life.

Mr. and Mrs. Moroni Smith were made happy by the arrival of a lovely baby girl last Saturday. Mother and babe doing nicely.

Iron County Record
July 6, 1923

Sunday evening the people of Cedar were startled and surprised to learn that a well known and respected citizen has passed from life.

Christian E. Mackelprang, aged about 77 years, who has been in Somewhat feeble health the past winter and spring, was suddenly stricken with heart failure and collapsed just as he was retiring for the night,

The deceased had been able to be around the house and yard, although feeling feeble, and did not feel sickness or pain. Sunday evening he was seemingly feeling all right, and just before retiring at about 9:30 decided to place a lamp on the parlor table so that members of his family who were out would not have to enter the home in darkness.

His wife had already retired, and after Mr. Mackelprang had placed the lamp in position proceeded to join his wife, and upon reaching the bed side, he suddenly sank to the floor. His wife called to him, and arose and upon going to his side found that he had expired.

Funeral services were held Tuesday afternoon in the tabernacle, and a large number of relatives, friends and acquaintances were present to pay their last respects to a good man, and one that does not have an enemy among the hundreds of people with whom he was acquainted.

Christian E. Mackelprang, was the oldest child of Peter and Margaret Mackelprang, both having preceeded their son in death several years ago. The deceased was born at Rodby Malrbo, Denmark, February 16, 1846.

When he was ten years of age he with his parents emigrated to Utah. They traveled by ox team to this land and for years endured all the hardships incident to pioneering a new country. Ten years after the family arrived Christian went back east and brought out another party of emigrants, at which time he met Lenora Bailey, whom he married June 15, 1868. Eight children was born of the union.

The deceased took part in the Black Hawk war, serving one month at Little Creek in this county, where the most dangerous part of services were rendered. He was called to go with the first party to San Juan county, and assisted in planting the first fruit orchard at that place. He was also called later to go and explore the Dixie country for probable location for colonizing, the country explored by him being what is known as the "Muddy."

He served for three years as minute man before the telegraph system was installed, and gave excellent service, being always ready to carry messages to any part of the southern part of the territory.

He was a member of the Church of Jesus Christ of Latter-day Saints, and although not an office seeking man did whatever he was called upon to do in a church capacity. He was a devout husband and a kind and loving father who will be missed greatly.

Christian Mackelprang leaves a wife and several children to mourn his departure, yet they know full well that he is entitled to a glorious reward for honest and upright living, and this fact lightens the pain of the separation.

Iron County Record
July 13, 1923

SUMMIT NOTES

The first cutting of hay is almost harvested. While not so heavy as last year, the crop is almost normal.

Reuben Jones of Lund has been in town putting up hay this week.

Miss Jessie Jordon formerly of Summit but now of Delta, is visiting here with old time friends.

Mrs. S. L. Fife and family of Cedar City spent Sunday with friends in Summit.

Mr. and Mrs. N. C. Madsen went to Milford Monday evening, bringing home their son Bernell, who became ill while working on the railroad there.

Cedar City—Regular train service on the branch line of the Union Pacific system from Lund to Cedar City commenced July 1, with two trains each way daily.

—oo—

Work on the J. C. Penny store is being rushed, and the contractor, Mr. Ashton, expects to have it completed by August 1st.

—oo—

The new Cox and Merryweather building is nearing completion. The owners expect to open for business by the 24th.

Following is a list of the Pioneers now living in Cedar City:

Joseph H. Armstrong, 1847, A. O. Smoot Company; Andrew Corry, 1847, Edward Hunter Company; Keturah M. Parry, 1847, Horace Eldridge Company; David Bulloch, 1851, Scotch Independent Company; Ann Elizabeth Perry Arthur, 1852, James Jeppson's Company; Hyrum Perry, 1852, James Jeppson's Company; Margaret Bladen Heyborne, 1852; Alice Bladen Bulloch, 1852; Daniel T. Leigh, 1852, born on Plains, Welch Company; Daniel S. Pendleton, 1852; Timothy Adams, 1855; Mary A. Smith-Armstrong, 1855, Milo Andrus Company. Tillie Heyborne Macfarlane, 1856; Charles Heyborn, 1856, Augustus Farnham Company, from Australia via California; Edward Parry, 1856, Capt. Bunker Hand Cart Company; Christina C. Brown, 1856; August Mackelprang, 1856, Knud Peterson's Company; Amy Webster Leigh, 1856, born on Plains, Martin's Hand Cart Company; Jane Arthur Corry, 1860; Zepher Kelsey Nexon, 1861; Alexander Matheson, 1862, Homer Duncan Company; Margaret Pryor, 1862, Homer Duncan Company; Jane E. Pryor, 1862, Homer Duncan Company; Joseph Melling, 1863; Eliza E. Bladen, 1863; Johana Palmer, 1863, Capt. McArthur's Company; E. M. Owens, 1863, John R. Murdock Company; Catherine Judd Carpenter, 1864, Capt. Warren's Company; Hannah Ahlstrom, 1863, Capt. Thompson's Company; William Tucker, 1866, worked way from Kentucky; Nora B. Mackelprang, 1866, Capt. Thompson's Company Emily Crane Watson, 1868, John R. Murdock Company; Albertina Sandin, 1868; Melissa Rollins, Lee Heyborn, Joseph Perkins, Eliza Stephens.

KANARRA NOTES

July 25, 1923.

Pioneer Day passed off very satisfactory. Kanarra and New Harmony joined in the celebration with each furnishing parts of the program. R. G. Williams gave a very good Pioneer talk. Juanita Davis gave the oration which was well presented then there were songs, music and reciting. In the afternoon the sports consisted of racing by married and single men and boys; also by the maried women and girls. There were two saddle horse races, dismount saddle and and return to line for a purse. Take it all in all the day was a success due to live and energetic committees from both towns. Today there has been horse and foot racing all day, and quite a number from New Harmony came over to join in the sports.

R. J. and W. J. Williams have their homes repainted which is a credit to them as well as to the town.

J. W. Prince and family of St. George are here visiting Mrs. Prince's parents and friends.

The crops are looking fine, altho we have had no rain, but live hope of having some in the near future.

Mrs. Amy Brown of Hamilton Fort was a visitor in town Monday, having come to see her daughter, Mrs. Smith, off to Salt Lake City. While Mrs. Bdown was in town she took occasion to visit with her brother, F. W. Middleton.

Mrs. John Henry Smith and son left for Salt Lake City Monday. The lady has been in Cedar and Hamilton Fort for the past several months, greater part of the time being spent at the fort with her mother, Mrs. Amy Brown was in town she took occasion City to join her husband.

Iron County Record
August 3, 1923

Many people of Cedar were grieved to learn of the death of Mrs. Mary Ann Armstrong which occured last Saturday after two years of suffering.

She was a woman who had won the admiration, love and respect of a host of people in southern Utah, and was known far and wide as a lovable wife, mother and friend.

Her passing leaves a vacancy that can never be forgotten by those who knew her best and by those she leaves behind to mourn.

Mary Ann, was the daughter of Joseph H. Smith and Maries Stanford, and was born December 27, 1844, at Bromley, Stafforshire, Enland, ad crossed the ocean on the old ship "Curling" landing in New York May 22, 1855.

She came to the Salt Lake Valley with the Milo Andrus company, walking the entire distance across the plains, arriving in Salt Lake Oct. 26, 1855. She remained in Salt Lake one year, her parents coming to Cedar, raching here Dec. 5, 1855.

The deceased was married to Joseph H. Armstrong in the old Endowment House in Salt Lake City, Oct. 9, 1866, by Wilford Woodruff.

As a result of the union she became a mother of seven children, 4 boys and 3 girls, J. S. and L. S., of Rigby, Idaho, Mrs. Jane A. Jones, John M. and W. F. of Enoch, Utah, Mrs. Mabel Macfarlane of this city, one girl preceeding her to the other side.

She took Lucy Belle, (Daughter of John T. Joseph and Elizabeth Elliker, (at the death of her mother) when only 9 days old, to whom she gave a mother's full love.

She also took at the death of their mother, three of the brother's children, one of whom she kept until she married C. E. Jones, new bishop of the Enoch ward; also raised Mrs. Emma Wood of Montecello, Utah.

Mary Ann Armstrong was an active worker in the Relief Society all her married life, and was first counsellor to Sister Ann Thorley for 8 years.

The deceased leaves 47 grand children and 27 great-grand children.

Mrs. Chas. S. Noble, wife of the Fuller Brush Co. representative, and two children arrived in Cedar City Wednesday and they are now domiciled in the Alice Bulloch home on First West street.

SUMMIT NOTES

—oo—

August, 4th. 1923.

Bp. John H. Dalley and family returned last week from a visit to Panguitch, and a fishing trip to the lake.

—oo—

Miss Helen Dalley is home again after a visit in Salt Lake City with her sister Letha who was recently married to Bert Farnsworth.

—oo—

Mrs. Velma Anderson and her two young children are here from south Dakota for a visit with her parents, Mr. and Mrs. James Owens.

—oo—

Henry Dalley of Preston, Idaho, surprised his many relatives and friends last week by a friendly call. He has been away from Summit for 24 years.

—oo—

Mr. and Mrs. Oscar J. Hulet and sister Arvilla are home again after a week's trip to Cedar Breaks and vicinity.

SAHARA NEWS

—oo—

Mr. and Mrs. L. A. Burascano were in Sahara Monday.

—oo—

Marshal Glover is working at Sahara.

—oo—

Miss Opal Gott and brother were Sahara callers Sunday.

—oo—

The section gang has increased to 11 men.

—oo—

Mr. and Mrs. Jones of New Castle called on H. T. Griffin Sunday.

—oo—

Mr. and Mrs. Hal T. Griffin spent a few days in Cedar the guest of Mr. and Mrs. Craig.

—oo—

Mr. and Mrs. Romberger and son George and Kate Moore stopped at Sahara enroute to Cedar.

—oo—

Mr. Lambert and family went to Cedar City to take their daughter to the doctor.

—oo—

Every body will be at the Big Box social Saturday night, good music and a good time.

—oo—

Mr. Kirkham of the Gum Supply Co. of Salt Lake City was a caller at the section house Monday.

—oo—

Mr. and Mrs. Willard Canfield leaves tomorrow for Coalville, Utah, where Mr. Canfield will be employed as instructor in the High school.

Last Tuesday Timothy Adams, one of the old, sturdy pioneers of this city, passed on after having lived for nearly 89 years.

He has been one of the men who in early days helped to fight the Indians and to conquer the wilderness to make it blossom as the rose and to become a beauty spot of plenty for the posterity of those determined men and women who left Missouri with Brigham Young, the noted Mormon lead- who directed the colonization of Utah. ___ ___ ___ ___ ___ ___ _____

Timothy Adams was a man of jolly disposition, honest and upright, and though he was imbued with some of the failings of men he was considered, and proved himself to be a sturdy and self reliant man whom everybody liked.

Funeral services were held in the tabenacle Wednesday afternoon, the speakers being Andrew Corry, A. G. Matheson, S. F. Leigh, each of whom told of the many good qualities they had observed in the departed pioneer.

and friends to emigrate to Utah, Feb. 15, 1855. He crossed the ocean in the ship Sidons arriving in Philadelphia, April 10, 1855, after a voyage of nearly 8 weeks. From Philadelphia he went by railroad to Pittsburg. From Pittsburg he went by boat, Polar Star, to St. Louis, thence to Atichson. From there he crossed the plains by ox train to Salt Lake Valley. He arrived in the fall of 1855.

He was ordained an Elder by Bishop Henry Lunt. Became a member of the 73rd Quorum of Seventies. R. R. Birkbeck presiding. He was chos-

BIOGRAPHICAL

Timothy Adams was born in the village of Raunds, Northhamptonshire, England, Sept. 11, 1834. During hsi boyhood, was educated by attending Sunday School which was the only schooling he had. He joined the Mormon Church, was baptised, and confirmed as a member of the Raunds Branch of the Churrh of Jesus Christ of Laterday Saints, by Henry Bailey and Ekin Lovell, Elders in the Bedfordshire conference, Feb. 1853. He left all his relatives

en with others to go back to the missiouri river to help the Saints out to Utah. Here he met Louisa Houchen from Norfolk, England, who became his wife. They were married in Salt Lake City, Oct. 1866. From there he came to Cedar City, and has lived here since. His wife preceeded him to the great beyond, almost 20 years ago.

Nine children were born to them, five are dead and four are living in Cedar City.

He died Aug 21, almost 89 years old.

RETURNS TO CEDAR

Dr. C. B. Hobbs, well known to quite a number of Iron County residents, and who has a large tract of land near Nada, is back in Cedar again after a three years absence in Texas.

Monday morning the four year old child of Mr. and Mrs. Roy Mackelprang sucumbed to the dread disease membranous croup.

The child had been ill for a week and everything possible was done for the litle one, but of no avail and death came to relieve the child of its sufferings.

Funeral services were held at the family residence, with Bp. E. M. Corry officiating.

The many friends of the bereaved parents extend heartfelt sympathy to them in the loss of their loved one.

Miss Sophia and Josephine Roundy of Kanarra will be in attendance at the Golden Spike celebration and Rodeo with their mother. Mrs. Roundy will be remembered as an old resident of Cedar City and a patron of the Branch Normal.

GOLDEN SPIKE CELE-BRATION AT CEDAR

There was a very large number of people present at the Golden Spike celebration and Harding Memorial service at Cedar City Wednesday The editor was unable to attend and is indebted to Mr Henry T Atkin of this city for this account There was a large number of people present from Washington county Hurricane being very strongly represented Among those present from St George were Mr Atkin chairman of county commissioners Mayor A E Miller and Jos S Snow

The special train carrying the not ables from Salt Lake was delayed and did not arrive at Cedar until about two o clock

The ceremony of laying the golden rail was very impressive It was laid on the spot where President Harding s car stood The four spikes were driven by Governor Mabey representing the State of Utah Dan S Spencer representing the rail road company District Forestor R H Rutledge representing the forest service and David Bullock one of pioneers of Cedar City representing Iron county

Rain stopped the program after Senator Smoot and President Heber J Grant had finished their addresses the vice president of the Union Pa cific being in the midst of his address at the time

There was a very large delegation of California people present

The many friends of Mr. and Mrs. E. B. Dalley extend their sympathies and condolences to them in their loss of their loved daughter Vilate, aged 10 years, who died Sunday morning from peritonitis, superinduced by ruptured appendix.

During the early part of last week the young girl was taken seriously ill, but it was not thought that she was afflicted with ruptured appendix, and not until Friday of last week was her case pronounced such.

She was taken to the hospital where an operation was performed in the hopes that her life might be saved but all that was done was of no avail and she passed away as above stated.

She was a loveable young girl, her mother's standby in the home, and a little lady that everybody who knew her loved. She will be sadly missed, not only by her parents, brothers and sisters, but by a large number of girl and boy friends, as well as many grown friends.

Funeral services were held Monday afternoon in the tabernacle, Bp. Bengt Nelson officiating.

SAHARA NEWS

—oo—

Mr. and Mrs. Glover were Sunday callers at Sahara.

—oo—

Wallace Couch was a caller at Sahara Sunday.

—oo—

Sahara has a moving time, several more families have moved here for school.

—oo—

Leon Gott and Galen Kelley are patients at the Boghosslan Sanitarium, both getting along nicely.

—oo—

Tacoma Baker was kicked on the arm by a horse. It is very painful but no bones were broken.

—oo—

NADA

—oo—

Mrs. L. A. Culmsee and son Carlton visited Lund last Saturday.

—oo—

V. C. Johnson and D. L. Barnes motored to Milford Tuesday. Mr. Johnson will fill a position in the depot.

—oo—

Miss Helen Moore will teach the Nada school this year. The pupils are in readiness to begin as soon as the supplies arrive.

—oo—

Ray, Grace and Bennette McGinty returned from an extended stay in San Bernardino, California.

Our corps of teachers,, together with their assignments is as follows:

CEDAR CITY, JUNIOR HIGH SCHOOL AND ELEMENTARY GRADES:

Frances B. Fenton, Principal; Eula Fletcher, English; Ethel Perry, reading and literature; Elna Froyd, Home economics; E. B. Dalley, geography and mathematics; Warren Pendleton, manual training; Marvin Jenson, science and civics; S. Y. McAllister, mathematics and physical education; Miss Morimon, sixth grade; Ether J. Stuckl, sixth grade; Oscar Hulet, fifth grade; Effie Robinson, fifth grade; Vera Macfarlane, fourth grade; Rhoda Palmer, fourth grade; Lucile Thorley, third grade; Janet Sharp, third grade; Mildred Lewis, grade; Mary W. Chidester, first grade; Thelma Chidester, first grade; second grade; Alice Palmer, second LaVerne B. Dalley, first grade.

PAROWAN HIGH SCHOOL AND ELEMENTARY GRADES.

Robert L. Fenton, principal, Smith-Hughes Agriculture; V. B. Decker, mathematics, farm mechanics; Irene Thorley, Smith-Hughes Home economics;; Scott Matheson, history and social science; Adele A. Matheson, reading and English; J. D. Thomas, English; Clifford Empey, geography, English, Civics; Gracia Robinson, sixth grade; Bertha Reynolds, fifth grade; Virgie White, fourth grade; Mary Orton, fourth grade; Laurel Decker, third grade; ....second grade; Fae N. Benson, first grade.

PARAGONAH SCHOOL.,

Amasa Stones, principal, seventh and eighth grades; Merrill Lund, fifth and sixth grades; Glenna Marsden, third and fourth grades; Ila C. Barton, first and second grades.

KANARRA SCHOOL.

Kumen Williams, principal, seventh and eighth grades; Winnie Williams, fourth, fifth and sixth grades; Alenna Stapley, first, second, third grades.

SUMMIT SCHOOL.

D. L. Thomas, principal, grammar grades; Alice Allen, primary grades.

NEWCASTLE SCHOOL.

LaVar E. Green, grammar grades; Maude Austin Moyle, primary grades.

ONE TEACHER SCOHOLS.

Ethel Terry, Modena; Aida Tollestrup, Enoch; Ralph Adams, Midvalley; Elene Smith, Lund; Clyde Obray, Hamlin Valley; Ethel Hatch, Yale; Zoella Palmer, Hamiltons Fort; Sahara.

Mr. Orren Taylor of this place and Miss Alice Allen of Summit were married September 1st. Orren is the son of Mr. and Mrs. James C. Taylor and all are highly respected residents of New Harmony. The many friends of the young couple wish them a happy and prosperous life.

Iron County Record
September 28, 1923

Emron Jones and Jennie Cox are receiving the congratulations of scores of friends on their marriage which occured in the St. George temple Wednesday of last week. ___ ...

The groom is the son of Mr. and Mrs. U. T. Jones, a young man who is honorable and upright, being held in high esteem by a large number of people of this city and surrounding towns. _____ ___ ___ ___ ___ ___ ___

....The bride is a daughter of Mr. and Mrs. J. D. Cox, a lady who is widely known among old and young of this city, and is thought a great deal of. She is a loveable and pleasing young woman and will make a stauch and true life companion to the man of her choice. ___ .... ___ .... ___ ___ ......

....The Record extends sincere congratulations to the young couple, and wishes for them a long, happy and useful life as man and wife.___ ___ ...

Mrs. Thos Holyoak who was operated on last week for a gangreuous appendix is recovering rapidly.

Born to Mr. and Mrs. Orson Haight a girl, September 24, and to Mr. and Mrs. Vernon McBride a girl, September 25th.

Mr. and Mrs. Elmer Sprague both of whom were injured in the auto accident last Monday, the former suffering a back injury the latter a fracture of the skull and lacerations about the limbs are slowly recovering. Mrs. Sprague lay unconscious for 12 hours, her condition being considered very ccritical. We understand, however, that with complete quiet and rest for a few more daays she may be recovered sufficiently to be removed from the hospital.

Iron County Record
October 5, 1923

Again we are called upon to chronicle the death of a resident of Cedar City. This time that of Thomas Urie, who was sumoned to his home in the spirit world suddenly Friday, succumbing to the grim reaper within a few minutes after being stricken with contraction of the heart muscles.

The deceased was at work on a grain stack on his son's farm assisting in the threshing, and after working for about 20 minutes complained of feeling ill. He was taken to the house and after being placed in a bed was taken with a chill, and began to vomit. He also complained of pain in his chest. Restoratives were given him and in a few moments he said he felt better, and advised his son Roy to go ahead with the work saying he would be out in a short time.

Roy went out, but in a very few moments was called back as his father had taken worse. Upon enterng the house Roy saw that his father was desperately ill, and called the doctor by phone. But before anything could be done for the deceased, or a physician arrive, he had breathed his last. The physician upon arrival at the house gave the cause of death as being cramping of the muscles of the heart.

The body was brought to town from the farm and prepared for burial at the home of the deceased. Services were held Sunday afternoon in the tabernacle, which was filled to overflowing with relatives, friends and acquaintances. The speakers were Pres. Henry W. Lunt, Alex G. Matheson and U. T. Jones, each of whom told of the departed as they had known him, saying that he was a faithful worker and always did his duty as he saw it. He was a city marshall here for 12 years, and water master 7 years, and gave entire satisfaction to his constituents, and to the public generally. The speakers referred to his faith in the principles of the gospel of the L. D. S. church, and stated that he was an ardent believer and worker.

The singing by the choir was appropriate, the floral offerings beautiful.

In the passing of Thos. Urie Cedar has lost a man who always worked for the best interests of the city, who was loyal to his friends, and who believed in the educating of our young people along proper lines. He was industrious in the extreme, and took great pleasure in keeping himself busy. He was earnest in all he did, and nothing done by him was half hearted.

He was born in this city Jan. 19, 1863, his parents being John and Sarah Ann McMullin Urie, both of whom preceeded him to the great beyond a number of years ago. His mother was born in Waterford, Ireland, and his father in Glasgow, Scotland, both coming to this part of Utah during the pioneering days.

Thos. Urie was married to Catherine in April, 1884, eight children resulted from the union, six of whom are living, Mary, Roy, Earl, Milton, Moroni and Martha.

In addition to the children above mentioned he leaves a devoted wife to mourn his departure, and the sincere sympathy of scores of friends is extended to her in her hour of sorrow.

Sunday Mrs. Milton Urie presented her husband with a lovely girl baby.

—oo—

Mrs. J. J. Pace presented her husband with a bouncing baby boy Sunday. All concerned doing nicely.

Iron County Record
October 12, 1923

THORLEY-BULLOCH

—oo—

This week the many friends of R. A. Thorley and Miss Lizzie Bulloch were agreeably surprised to learn that the couple have joined the ranks of married people.

We are informed that they were married in the St. George Temple and after their marriage remained in that city to do some temple work before returning to Cedar.

The groom is a man well known to the people of southern Utah, especially to the people of this city. He is a man whom, everybody that meets him likes and respects, and they find him true to his friends, straight forward and sincere.

The bride is a lady of high ideals respected by scores of people of this section of the state, an earnest lady-like woman and her friends will wish for her a happy and contented life with the man of her choice.

The Record extends sincere congratulations to Mr. and Mrs. Thorley.

SHERRATT-LAMB

—oo—

Monday Wm. Sherratt of this city, and Mrs. Lamb of Toquerville were united in the bonds of wedlock, and they are now receiving the congratulations of friends of this city and those of the bride in Washington county.

The Record extends sincere congratulations to the couple and wish them success and happiness in their union.

Iron County Record
October 19, 1923

—oo—

Word has been received that Miss Rilla Dalley, daughter of Mr. and Mrs. Mayhew H. Dalley, was married to Mr. Bernell J. Hansen of Spanish Fork. The couple were married in the Salt Lake Temple Wednesday Oct. 10, and immediately after the ceremony the couple came to Cedar and spent a few days visiting with the parents and brothers of the bride.

The friends of Mrs. Hansen who live in this section of Utah will be pleased to learn of her venture and wish her a long, happy and successful life.

The groom is a young man respected by a large circle of friends in Spanish Fork, and is a prosperous farmer and livestock grower.

On Oct. 17, at Parowan, Utah, a ceremony was performed by Justice of the Peace, Geo. Morris of that city, by which Chas. W. Heyborne of Cedar, and Miss Grace Stubbs of Parowan were united as man and wife.

The groom is a son of Mr. and Mrs. Samuel Heyborne, and the bride is a daughter of Mr. and Mrs. Walter Stubbs of Parowan.

Thursday morning of last week the little five months old child of Mr. and Mrs. David C. Bulloch passed away, the direct cause of death being bowel trouble.

The sympathy of the many friends of the bereaved parents is extended to them in their sorrow.

A marriage ceremony was performed by Bishop H. L. Adams on Monday evening which united Mr. Earl B. Clark, former resident of this City and Miss Iva Knell of New Castle. Earl is the son of Mr. and Mrs. Collins W. Clark, both deceased, and was born and reared in this community. He attended school at the B. N. S. where he met Miss Knell ten or twelve years ago, and we suspected then that he thot she was about the only girl in the world. Since then he has seen army service during the war and after receiving his discharge he located in Kane County where his brother Kenneth was, and he has been there practically every since.

Miss Knell is the charming daughter of Mr. and Mrs. James Knell of New Castle, a very refined and accomplished young lady.

As we go to press we learn that Oliver Jenson of this city and Miss Ellen Smith of Glendale were married in the St. George Temple this week.

The groom is a son of Mr. and Mrs. Heber Jenson, and is very well known and highly respected by a large circle of people in this end of the state. He is a solid, earnest young man whom it is a pleasure to meet, and counts his friends by the score.

The bride is a young lady of winning personality, home loving disposition, and a lady who wins the respect of those who bear her acquaintance.

Last week a Mr. Chadburne of Washington County, and Miss Leah Bauer of this city were united in the bonds of wedlock.

The bride is a daughter of Mr. and Mrs. Jos. Bauer, and is well known in this city and has a large circle of friends who will wish her success and happiness during her married life.

The couple are at present in California where they will spend a few weeks visiting.

Word has been received here that Mrs. J. L. Heap of Spry recently gave birth to her fifth boy, and that mother and babe are doing famously. Mrs. Heap is a daughter of Mrs. Lottie Perkins, and her many friends in Cedar will be pleased to learn of the recent addition to the family circle.

Wednesday at the home of the bride a ceremony was performed by Bp. E. M. Corry, which united as man and wife Wallace Flannigan and Miss Nettle Walker.

The groom is a son of Mr. and Mrs. Wm. Flannigan, the bride being a daughter of Mrs. Nancy Walker, both young people being well known and respected.

As soon as the bishop pronounced the young couple man and wife the invited friends of the couple showered them with rice and expressed sincere congratulations.

Preston Wood acted as best man to the groom, while Mrs. Irissa Nelson acted as best lady to the bride.

The evening following the marriage was spent in a very pleasant manner by the young married couple and the relatives and close friends of the couple the time being spent in singing playing games, reading and chatting.

November 16th, Kimball Jenson and Elene Smith were married not knowing that their brother and sister (the Smith girls are twins) were to be married the same day.

Mr. Kimbal Jenson is a successful cattleman and farmer and a big hearted honest fellow, whose word is as good as his bond. Miss Smith is a graduate of the B. A. C. (as is also her sister) and was a prominent member of the debating team last year, having won the school medal for debating. Success and happiness to them.

Saturday Kimball Jenson and Miss Elene Smith were married and since have been receiving the congratulations of their friends.

The groom is the second son of Mr. and Mrs. Heber Jensen, well known and liked by all who know him.

The bride is a daughter of Mr. and Mrs. D. A. Smith of Glendale, favorable known and highly respected.

The young couple have the well wishes of everyone who know them for their success and happiness as man and wife.

The patients this week at the Iron County Hospital are: Mrs. E. G. Ellison of Caliente; Orna Burton, little daughter of Dr. Burton of Parowan; and Mrs. Alma Esplin and Mr. Elmo Corry of Cedar City. All have undergone operations and are improving rapidly.

Dr. M. J. Macfarlane was called to Orderville this week by William Brinkerhoff. Mr. Brinkerhoff's little son was seriously burned. Dr. Macfarlane accompanied by of the hospital nurses, Miss Pauline Walker, made the trip n record time and did their best to save the child but their efforts were of no avail. The little one died a few days later.

Iron County Record
November 30, 1923

Master Knell son of R. C. Knell of Newcastle was brought in the hospital with a serious fracture of the leg, sustained when the horse he was riding fell. As the bone protruded thru the skin the fracture is necessarily considered more serious.

Born to Mrr. and Mrs. Geo. Hunter a boy last Friday.

—oo—
Born to Mr. and Mrs. Lehi Jones
Thursday a baby girl.

—oo—
Born to Mr. and Mrs. Arthur Fife
a boy last Saturday.

Iron County Record
December 7, 1923

Last Tuesday Miles Adams and Miss Nola Hall were united in the bonds of wedlock.

The groom is a son of Mr. and Mrs. Frank Adams of this city, and the bride is a daughter of Mr. and Mrs. Wm. Hall, who are now domiciled on the Watson ranch just north of Kanarra.

The young couple have the best wishes of many friends for their success and happiness as man and wife.

SAHARA

—oo—
Ray Kelley went to Milford Thursday night to consult a doctor. He returned Friday feeling fine.

Miss Hatch and Marion Carter motored to Lund Tuesday where Miss Hatch caught No. 4. She will spend the Thanksgiving with her people at Woodcross. She returned Monday to resume her school work.

Mr. Bruce and family moved to

Modena. We are sorry to loose them because they were a credit to Sahara.

Mr. and Mrs. Robert Burns, Mr. Doughterty, and Elmer Phleps went to Modena Monday. Mr. Burns proves up on his homestead.

Mr. and Mrs. Kelley went to Modena Monday. Mr. Kelley relinquished his grazing claim and Mrs. Kelley filed in a desert claim.

Mr. Galen Kelley while going to Mr. Gott's place ran into a tractor and wagon that had stopped along the road and smashed his car up considerably.

Marshal Glover and Ray Kelley went to Cedar City Wednesday for some repairs.

Oscar Stephenson of Milford spent Thanksgiving day at Sahara.

Washington County News
December 13, 1923

WOMAN BOOTLEGGER
CONDEMNED AT CEDAR CITY

Excitement was so intense and feelings so roused at the liquor trial at Cedar City of Miss Zella Carter postmaster of Beryl and her brother Marion that it was necessary for Sheriff J T Leigh to arm his deputies according to information brought here today by Mark Ryan undercover man of the prohibition enforcement force

Both were convicted The woman was fined $299 Her brother was fined a like amount and sentenced to six months in jail

Mr Ryan said that sympathy seemed to be for the defendants Ryan was named assistant prosecutor He said crowds seeking entrance were so large that the trial was transferred to the city library auditorium Two hundred women attended

Four wittneses for the defense were arrested on charges of prejury

Miss Carter will go to trial in the federal court here Monday Dec 3 on a charge of violating the federal prohibition law She was tried once before on the same charge the jury disagreeing —Deseret News

The friends of Mr. Daniel Webster and Miss Rhoda Palmer will be pleased to learn of their marriage which took place in the St. George Temple Thursday.

The groom is a son of Mrs. Eliza Webster, and the bride a daughter of Mr. and Mrs. E. J. Palmer.

The yong couple are very well known to the majority of the people of this city, are highly respected and have the well wishes of everyone for a long, useful and happy life as man and wife.

N. B. Dalley of Summit was operated last week for hernia and is recovering rapidly.

Baby boys were born to Mr. and Mrs. H. E. Petersen nad Mr. and Mrs. Lester Ford at the County Hospital this week.

BORN—To Mr. and Mrs. D. L. Sargent, a girl.

Mrs. J. M. Armstrong of Enoch was operated Saturday night for an acute appendix.

On January 1st. Bp. E. M. Corry united in wedlock William Stevenson and Miss LaVern Evans, the event transpiring at the home of Mr. Charles Halfmen.

The young couple are well respected by a large number of people who are tendering them sincere congratulations and well wishes for their happiness and success in their union.

A large number of people in this section of the state, especially of this city, will be grieved to learn of the death of Grandma Jesperson, whose death occurred recently in Colonia Chuichupa, Mexico.

Mrs. Jesperson was a resident of this city during the war period, and was respected and admired by all who became acquainted with her.

Readers of the Record will remember that Mrrs. Jesperson lost her grandson, Elmer Jesperson, who was killed in action in the world war.

Word of the death of the lady was received in this city by Mrs. Peter B. Fife, who was a close friend of the deceased while she lived here.

We are called on to chronicle the passing of Indian Captain Pete, who passed from this life last Saturday and was buried Monday in the Cedar cemetery on the Indian Plot of ground.

Captain Pete was a gentleman in every sense of the word and held in very high esteem by not only the members of his colony of Indians, but nearly every man and woman in this part of Utah.

He was bright, broad-minded and congenial Indian, who ruled his followers with justice, and they were always willing to listen to his cousel and profited much thereby.

In the passing of Captain Pete we have lost a real man, one of "nature's noblemen," and one that was extremely friendly to the whites, of a devout religious turn of mind, believeing strongly in the "Great Spirit," and that the Indians were as much the children of the Great Father as are the white people.

May his spirit rest in peace, and his reward be glorious for the many good deeds he has done among his people.

—oo—

Mr. and Mrs. Ray Lunt are happy over the arrival of a bouncing baby boy, born at the County hospital New Years Day. Mother and babe are reported as doing nicely.

ASSESSOR INVADES NADA

—oo—

MAKES HIS REGULAR YEARLY ROUNDS—PAROWAN CITIZEN VISITS DESERT COMMUNITY.

Word was received here Tuesday that Mrs. Susannah Jones of Enoch had passed away Monday night at the home of her daughter, Mrs. O. W. Hulet of Summit. Funeral services and interment were held at Enoch Wednesday.

The deceased was the wife of Sylvester F. Jones, and was a woman very highly respected by scores of people of this county. She was a sincere woman, a devout Latter-day Saint, and was known as a big-hearted, sympathetic and generous friend to the sick and needy.

Sister Jones not only held the love and respect of the white people with whom she was acquainted, but by her kindness to the native Indians had won their love.

The deceased believed strongly in temple work for the dead and she year after year spent weeks doing vicarious work for the dead. She was also a devoted member of the Relief Society of Enoch, and besides attending to her duties in a church way, lived the principles of the gospel she espoused in a way that entitles her to a great reward in the Kingdom of God.

The deceased came to Utah with her parents in 1863, and moved to this county from Salt Lake City shortly after her arrival and has lived here ever since. She was married to Sylvester F. Jones about 50 years ago, 11 children resulting from the union, 8 of whom, besides her husband are living.

SAHARA.

January 19, 1924.

The number of children attending school is increasing every week.

Miss Mabel Harris is staying with Mrs. Fourman and attending school here.

Mr. and Mrs. J. A. Baker and other visited Mr. and Mrs. Gott on Sunday.

Elmer Phelps spent a few days with Mr. and Mrs. Burns the fore part of the week.

Horace Phelps of Modena was in Sahara a few days visiting his brother Elmer.

SUMMIT NOTES

Miss Belva Hulet of Morgan County, Utah, who is attending school at the B. A. C. spent the week end visiting relatives in Summit.

Wm. W. Dalley, Mr. and Mrs. Obadiah Farrow and Mrs. Marie Grimshaw returned last week from St. George, where they have been working in the temple the past two weeks.

Obadiah Farrow who has been quite ill since his return from St. George is reported some better.

Otto P. Dalley left Tuesday to fill a two week's mission in Parowan.

KANARRA NEWS
January 15, 1924.

Last Friday the married people of this ward were entertained by the old folks committee. At 2 o'clock they commenced to gather at the meeting house, and at 3 o'clock 75 per cent of the married people sat down to a sumptuous dinner, after which a good program was given. At night a dance was given, consisting of old time quadrills, reels, marches, etc. to old time music furnished by Sam Pollock, violin, Arnold Graff, guitar, Layron Williams, mandolin, and Junius Williams, piano. All in all it was a grand success.

John G. Smith is having his house repaired, by adding a porch and putting on a new roof.

NADA
January 15, 1924.

Mr. Lonergan, the new road master got in touch with the section foremen in an inspection trip last week. H. R. Moore, section foreman at Thermo, brought him to Nada in his car.

Thrusday and Friday is wood haulers day for the church houses. A big dinner will be served to all who get wood or deposit $2.00 for a ticket.

Our amusement hall is nearly completed, all that remains to be done s a little plastering.

Lawrence Prince is here visiting his mother for a few days.

Bp. Berry has purchased Jas. Berry's home and has recently moved into it.

Arnold Graff received word this week that his sister Mrs. Barbara Gray, of Santa Clara had died Sunday.

Mrs. Geo. B. Williams who is under Dr. Wilkinson's care at Hurricane is slowly improving.

Iron County Record
January 25, 1924

Last evening Miss Ruth Middleton, daughter of Mr. and Mrs. F. W. Middleton, was severely burned, caused by her dress catching fire from a heater by which she was standing.

The girl's dress was of silk and blazed rapidly, and although members of the family quickly tore the burning fabric from the young lady, the flames burned her limbs very severely.

She was taken to the county hospital where medical treatment was given, and though suffreing intensely from the burns she is doing very nicely.

Iron County Record
February 1, 1924

Monday evening at the home of Mr. and Mrs. Ray Wood, Bp. E. M. Corry united in matrimony Morgan Rollo and Miss Mary Jane Jones.

The groom is the second son of Mr. and Mrs. Alex H. Rollo, who has many friends that are very pleased to learn of his venture, and are tendering many sincere congratulations and wishing him a long and happy married life.

The bride is a daughter of Sam. B. Jones, a young lady of pleasing personality, well known and very highly respected by a large number of people who will be pleased to learn of her union to the young man of her choice. The best wishes of the young lady's friends are that she may enpoy years of happinesss and success in her union with the groom.

On the 16th of January a ceremony was performed in the St. George Temple that united in wedlock Francis Laney and Miss Ruth Cox.

The groom is a well known resident of Washington County and has many friends who will be pleased to learn of his marriage to Miss Cox, who is a daughter of Mr. and Mrs. Everard Cox of Hamilton's Fort, and a young lady of winsome personality and high ideals.

The couple will make their home in St. George.

The Record joins with their numerous friends in wishing them success, long life and happiness as man and wife.

NADA NEWS

—oo—

January 28, 1924.

T. J. Norris is at Lund, in charge of the garage while O. M. Norris is in Caliente selling automobiles.

—oo—

L. A. Culmsee finished putting up ice last week.

—oo—

A car load of ice for the Nada section was put off at the switch and the crew has been busy unloading. The quality is excellent this year.

—oo—

Mr. and Mrs. C. R. Keith announce the birth of a son, Harry Robert, January 25, at San Bernardino, California.

Iron County Record
February 22, 1924

Last Friday night the little daughtre of Mr. and Mrs. Monte Hunter passed away, the immediate cause of death being pneumonia.

Funeral services were held at the home of Mr. and Mrs. J. N. Smith grandparents of the child, last Sunday afternoon.

The services were impressive and attended by scores of friends and relatives, whose sympathies were with the bereaved parents because of their untimely and terrible loss.

We received word the fore part of hte week that a son of Mr. and Mrs. Nat. Gardner died in Salt Lake City Monday.

The lad had been taken to that city for treatment for diabetes. He received the best of medical attention but the disease had such a hold on him that medicines could not counteract the disease.

—oo—

The death on February 14 of Alton Claud Thompson took from our midst a bright young man and one whom everybody that knew him liked and respected.

The young man's death was caused by diphtheria as was announced last week. His body was interred in the Cedar cemetery, funeral services being held at the home of Mr. and Mrs. E. J. Palmer, where the young man succumbed to the dread disease.

No one was allowed to enter the house, and the body was not removed to the open until time for interment. The assembled sympathizing friends and neighbors held services outside the home.

The diseased was born in Green River, Utah, July 15, 1905, and was the son of Alton R. and Rhoda Gillis Thompson. He was a young man of high ideals and was an active worker in all activities of life, both temporally and spiritually. He was a clean young man in all walks of life.

—oo—

At the county hospital Tuesday, Mrs. Roy Mackelprang gave birth to a boy. The child is doing nicely, while the mother, who has been somewhat ill for several weeks past in reported as being rather weak, but seemingly on the improve.

Iron County Record
February 29, 1924

KANARRA NOTES.

—oo—

Farmers are busy plowing and putting in grain these days.

—oo—

Mrs. James S. Stapley has gone to Castlegate, Utah to visit with her two sons, William and Leland.

—oo—

Mrs William Hall who was burned very severely by her clothing catching fire is in a very bad condition.

—oo—

The Primary officers put on a play or entertainment last P. M. which was a perfect success in every way. Their sale of tickets amounted to $14.00.

—oo—

Elder L. Glenn Williams returned home February 20, from Californai Mission where he has been laboring for the last 27 months.

—oo—

Bishop Williams has been working in Cedar for the past ten days. On his return home he will commence on his service station he will put up on north main street.

Iron County Record
March 7, 1924

John T. and Angus Bulloch returned Tuesday from the Lower Herd country where they had been to take a bunch of cattle. The gentlemen report that feed in that section of our mountains is beginning to show, there being no snow to retard its growth. They report also a shortage of snow at the head of the Coal Creek Canyon and the summit.

SUMMIT

L. N. Marsden and Walter Mitchell were home missioners to our ward last Sunday.

The Summit Water System Company has had quite a force of men at work this week on the main.

Alex Dalley has gone to Springdale to bring his family who have been there for several weeks.

Wm. H. Dalley and son Alex, who have been living in Delta for several years have returned to Summit to make their homes.

County Agent, Alma Esplin called a meeting here Saturday evening for the purpose of promoting the Farm Bureau work.

Last Friday evening the four act drama "Mr. Easyman's Niece" was presented here by the B. A. C. Dramatic Club. All who saw it enjoyed it immensely.

Yesterday morning at the county hospital the five year old child of Mr. and Mrs. Edwin Hamblin died, the immediate cause being pneumonia.

The sympathy of the people is extended to the bereaved parents in the loss of their little one.

Funeral services will be held Saturday at 1 P. M.

KANARRA NEWS

March 10, 1924.

About four inches of snow fell here Monday night.

Aunt Eliza Wood was completely over come when she heard of the Castlegate explosion, knowing she had a son and son-in-law in the mine and has since been confined to her bed. The end is looked for at any moment. All her children are now here, this being the first time they have all been together for over twenty years.

Those who attended all or part of the Conference at Cedar from here were as follows: Bp. R. J. Williams, Mr. and Mrs. R. J. Williamson, Mrs. Louoie Stapley, Mr. and Mrs. L. J. Williams and son Max, Mr. and Mrs. W. C. Reeves, Mr. John W. Platt, and daughter Rebecca.

The funeral services over the remains of Mrs. Alice Jane Urie held in the Tabernacle last Sunday were impressive. The first speaker was Elder Sam F. Leigh, who touched on the life and charactcd of the diseased and told of the beautiful life lived by her; that she was a home maker in the fullest sense of the word and that her first and filial duty was to her family. She was ever to be found at home in the line of her duty, as she had never been one of the public seeking kind of women but many were the things of beauty in her life to make the heart of many glad by the things she did of an unostentatious nature, and which left in the hearts of the recipients a warm spot of love. She has spent all her life in this community and comes of that old sturdy stock of the early history of Cedar City. He spoke of the great sacrifice made by her and her parents in the old country when they affiliated themselves with the then unpopullar religious sect known as Mormons, and what they had to go through in their early battles of pioneering.

BIOGRAPHICAL

Alice Jane Parry Urie was born at Cedar City, May 14, 1856. She was the second daughter of George and Susannah Perry. In her girlhood days she figured prominently in the social activity of the day and her sweet voice singing in the ward choir will be remembered by her old friends.

She married George Urie Feb. 16, 1881 in the St. George temple. To them were born six children all of whom survive her.

She has been an active Relief Society worker and was head of the quilt committee for a number of years She and her husband acted for many years as members of the "Old Folks Committee". She was a devoted wife and mother and her loss will be keenly felt by her family.

On the morning of March 21st she arose as usual prepared the morning meal and went about her household duties until near eleven o'clock, when she complained of feeling a little sick, but not serious. At twelve-thirty o'clock she was changed in a twinkling of an eye from mortal to immortal not knowing the taste of death.

KANARRA NOTES.

The Raleigh construction company has commenced grading on the highway adjoining the town on the north.

After three feet of snow which has fallen here since March 13th, we are now able to do a little work.

W. J. Williams was home from his sheep herd the fore part of the week.

Last week boys were born to Mr. and Mrs. Dee Parker and Mr. and Mrs. Kumen Williams. All concerned doing fine.

Aunt Eliza Wood, who has been so seriously ill for the past three weeks. is reported to be somewhat improved, and is now able to take a little nourishment.

—OO—

We are glad to learn that Uncle Joel J. Roundy who was operated at the county hospital, was not afflicted with ulcers of the stomach as was feared. His trouble was caused by a diseased appendix, which was removed. He is reported as getting along nicely.

Iron County Record
April 11, 1924

—OO—

Sunday last the people of Cedar were grieved to learn of the death of Mrs. Elizabeth Ashdown, who quietly passed beyond after suffering from dropsy for a period of several months.

Elizabeth Jackson Ashdown was born April 29, 1846 in Pratts Bottom, Chelsflel, Kent, England. She with her husband emigrated to Utah in 1877, arriving at Nephi where they remained several weeks, and finally came to this city about December, 1977. They were converted to the L. D. S. faith in England but did not join this religious sect until June 29th, 1878.

SUMMIT NOTES

—OO—

Dr. Parker and others of the Utah Health Association gave a lecture with moving pictures to a very appreciative audience here last Thursday.

—OO—

Mr. Andrus and Mrs. M. J. Macfarlane of Cedar City occupied the time at the sacramental meeting Sunday. They were here in interest of M. I. A. day.

—OO—

Members of the Gun and Rod Club of Parowan met with the people here Sunday for the purpose of enlisting new members.

Mrs. Martha Allen Dalley, wife of Moroni Dalley died at her home here Tuesday, after a long illness. Mrs. Dalley was a faithful Latter-day Saint and for many years was president of the Relief Society of Summit Ward. She leaves a host of friends to mourn her loss, besides a husband and four daughters. Mrs. Larena Langford of Cedar City, Mrs. Nora Simpkins of Circleville, and Mrs. Mae Simpkins of Hinckley, and Mrs. Ann Smith of Summit. Also a number of grand children. Funeral services was held here Wednesday at 2 P. M.

—OO—

Miss Lillian Farrow, daughter of Mr. and Mrs. John Farrow was married last week to Bernette Fartheringham of Milford.

—OO—

Mrs. Larena Langford of Cedar has been here the past week assisting in the care of her mother Mrs. Martha Dalley.

SAHARA NEWS

—oo—

Mr. R. F. Brannon went to Cedar City to work for Jack Smith on the carpenter gang.

—oo—

Those who attended the oil meeting at Beryl Wednesday night were Mr. and Mrs. A. Fourman, Mr. and Mrs. A. J. Russel, Mr. and Mrs. J. A. Baker, Mr Boghossian, Mr. J. Del Vecchio.

The Pie supper given by the Sahara Civic Center was well attended Saturday night.

—oo—

Mrs. Del Vecchio and children spent the week end on the ranch with Mr. Del Vecchio.

—oo—

Mr. A. T. Hobbs of Cedar was a caller at Sahara Sunday.

—oo—

The section crew has increased their gang to eight.

Iron County Record
April 18, 1924

MARRIED

—oo—

We are informed that Sunday Leo Palmer and Miss Irene Chamberlain went to Salt Lake City where they were married in the Salt Lake Temple Wednesday.

The many friends of this popular young couple will be pleased to learn of their union and wish them a long happy and successful life as man and wife.

Both the contracting parties are well known and are held in rsepect by the people here. The groom is a son of Mr. and Mrs. E. J. Palmer, the bride being a daughter of Mr. and Mrs. Howard Chamberlain.

The Record tenders the young couple congratulations, and wishes that their journey through life on the barque of matrimony may be one prolonged trip of happiness.

Iron County Record
April 25, 1924

As proof that the fire truck recently purchased by the city from J. A. Kopp is an efficient fire fighting machine we need but call attention to its work at a fire that started in the rear of the John Elliker home.

When the fire was noticed there was no one at home and it had got a good start on the walls of the kitchen and the flames had crept half way up the roof.

Mr. Kopp, as chief fireman assembled his crew of workmen in record time, mounted the truck and arrived at the fire in one minute from the time the alarm was sounded.

The chemical apparatus was trained on the fire and in four minutes after the flames were out.

Had it been necessary to have waited until the old fire hose could have baeen secured and fastened to the fire hydrant the building would have been entirely consumed.

The fire fighting machine is exactly what we have needed, but a greater efficiency in fighting fire could be had did we have a crew of men trained in the handling of the machine, ready at any minute to respond to the alarm of fire.

SUMMIT NOTES

April 23, 1924.

The Stake Officers of the Relief Society were visitors at the regular meeting Tuesday.

Mrs. Harold Smith and baby are visiting for a few days with relatives in Minersville.

John Brown of Hamilton's Fort was a business visitor in Cedar Monday.

Arnold Graff of Kanarra was a business visitor in Cedar Monday.

Mr. and Mrs. F. L. Beiderman and family of Cedar City were visitors at the home of O. W. Hulet, Sunday.

Mrs. Leland Dalley who is just recovering from a recent operation is spending a few weeks with her mother, Mrs. Carter in Minersville.

The school grounds have been thoroughly cleaned by teachers and pupils, and trees will be planted this week around three sides of the lot.

Mrs. Lucy Stapley of Summit was in Cedar Tuesday on a shopping expidition.

Miss Lola Williams of Kanarra who has been desperately ill of pneumonia at the hospital is recovering.

Iron County Record
May 9, 1924

Dr. Macfarlane reports the following births at the County Hospital: Mrs. Robert Simkins a boy; Mrs. Bert Gower, a boy; Mrs. David Lister, a boy; Mrs. John V. Schopmann, a boy.

NADA

George Meyers went to Minersville Sunday on business. Misses Elizabeth and Louise White accompanied.

Linford and Showalter, J. R. and J. M. Robinson, Tebbs Bros. are leaving for Minersville where the three latter will shear, while the former go to Panguitch shearing corrals.

Zabrsky and Jameson of Minersville are shearing for Bonners and Culmsees this week.

Carlton Culmsee spent Friday and Saturday in Milford.

Following is the list of Junior College and Fourth Year graduates.

JUNIOR COLLEGE

Thelma Brown
LaVerne B. Dailey
Fern Froyd
Annie Gale

Mary Muir
McNone N. Perry
Agnes Wilson
Ruby Woodard

HIGH SCHOOL

Elizabeth Ashdown
Sidney Ashdown
Mary Ashton
Thora Bauer
Genevieve Chamberlain
Thelma Chidester
Gui Clark
Edrie Corry
Marva Corry
Iris Decker
Lucy Farrow
Roma Foster
Beryl Froyd
Maxine Froyd
Laura George
Charles Griffin
Arvilla Higbee
Loran D. Hirschi
Alexander Horsley

Carlos T. Jones
Vernon Jones
LaVera Leigh
Roma Middleton
Ellen Murie
Merle Pace
Pearl Pace
Alice Parry
Annie Porter
Carlyle Smith
Nola Smith
William R. Thorley
Ruth Tollestrup
Gertrude Walker
Clara Webster
Mary Williams
Mayne Williams
Plorn Williams

Iron County Record
May 16, 1924

—oo—

Work on the Cedar-Kanarra road project is going along in splendid shape. Those who should know claim that Mr. Raleigh and his crew fo workers are skilled and will make of this strip of highway one of the best in the southern end of the state.

NADA

Edgar Norris, the youngest son of Mr. and Mrs. T. J. Norris, passed away at the Milford hospital last Thursday night of typhoid fever after an illness of about three weeks.

Edgar was twenty years old last September. He leaves his father and mother, two sisters and two brothers, besides several neices and nephews to mourn his early death.

His death came as a shock to the entire community, as his health had been always exceptionally good. He was a young man of good habits, honest and upright in all his dealings and beloved by everyone..

The funera was held at Milford last Saturday.

The whole community attended the services at that place offering sympathy and consolation to the grief stricken relatives.

Junior High Graduatec, 1923-24

Afton Adair
Iva Adams
Grace Ahlstrom
Ella Armstrong
Waldo Adams
Cora Armstrong
Marvel Arthur
Marjorie Ashdown
Leonard Ashdown
LaPreal Barnson
Camilla Bauer
Wesley Bauer
Magness Bauer
Marie Billingsly
Clifford Bryant
Arthur Bulloch
Violet Chatterley
Millie Chidester
Ella Corry
Virginia Corry
Douglas Corry
Theo Corry
Ruth Cox
Otto Dover
Noah Edmundson
Shirley Gudmundsun
Helga Hanson
Rex Harris
Rex Holland

Mirla Houchin
Claude Houchin
Gwen Hunter
Edwin Jacobsen
Faun Jensen
Lynn Jones
Verda Jones
Ivor Jones
Edwin C. Jones
Lillis Jones
Marie Kopp
Howard Kunz
Vivian Leavett
Wilma Leigh
Roberta Leigh
Amy Leigh
Marjorie Lewis
Clella Luke
Virginia Macfarlane
Owen Matheson
William Matheson
Annis Munford
Kathryn Murie
Hunter Nelson
Helen Pace
Leslie Pace
Keturah Parry
Edward Parry
Christina Pendleton

Daniel Pryor
Mary Robinson
Dora Robinson
Sherman Russell
Margaret Sherratt
Bert Smith
Ima Smith
Vergene Stewart
Jessie Stewart
Athens Thomspon
Wesley Thorley
Esther Tollestrup
Ross Urie
Gerald Wade
Alice Walker
Elma Walker
Myles Walker
Theon Watson
Zella Webster
Lettie Webster
Elroy Webster
Echo Webster
Vernon Williams
Wanda Woodard
Lucile Wood
Lynn Wood
Virtis Wood
Willard Wood

Iron County Record
May 23, 1924

We failed to report last week the marriage of Von Watts and Miss Elizabeth Imlay. However, we are pleased to make the announcement at this late date and tender congratulations to the young couple.

The groom is a son of Mr. and Mrs. W. D. Watts of this city, the bride is a daughter of Mr. and Mrs. Imlay of Panguitch, Utah.

The young couple are well respected and have the well wishes of numerous friends for their success and happiness in married life:

The Sprague Music Company is moving their piano into the new Cedar Hardware Company's store. Mr. Sprague expects to be out of town most of the summer and during his absence Mr. A. T. Jones will look after his Cedar sales.

The people of this city were grieved deeply Tuesday to learn that LaDean Leigh, the nine years old daughter of Mr. and Mrs. Kuman Leigh had passed away, following an attack of appendicitis, which turned to peritonitis.

She was taken to the hospital Sunday and an incision made in the hopes that the poison could be drawn from her intestines and her life saved.

Everything possible was done by the surgeons and nurses to save the life of the child, but the disease had made such ravages on her system that nothing that was done was any avail.

—oo—

Last Friday a small son of Mr. and Mrs. Wallace Bracken had the misfortune to have his left arm broken. It appears he and a companion were swinging on the lower limbs of a tree when his companion let go the limb he was holding to which switched back striking the Bracken boy on the arm, with the result above stated.

Mrs. John Smith, of Salt Lake City, daughter of Mrs. Amy Brown of Hamilton's Fort, was a visitor in Cedar Monday. The lady has been with her mother for about a month, and decided to spend one day in Cedar visiting acquaintances and relatives. She will remain in Iron County for the summer, while her husband is working at Bingham, Utah.

SUMMIT

—oo—

z   May 28, 1924.

Miss Helen Chamberlain returned last week from Kanab High School the past winter.

—oo—

The farmers are jubilant over the prospects of good crops since the storm this week.

—oo—

Mr. and Mrs. Leland Dalley are visiting in Minersville for a few days.

—oo—

Some of the Primary Stake officers were in attendance at the Ward Primary Conference here last Sunday.

—oo—

Merl Radford and Miss Theresa Hulet were married last Friday. Mr. Radford is a native of Iowa, but has lived in our community for a number of years and has won many friends. The bride is the daughter of Mrs. Elzina Hulet. She is a true home maker, and is held in the highest respect by all who know her. The young couple have the best wishes of all, for their future happiness.

We are informed that Andrew Corri, Jr. of this city, and Miss DeWolf, were married Monday at Parowan.

The groom is a son of Mr. and Mrs. Wm. N. Corry, and has the well wishes of his friends for success and happiness with the lady of his choice.

We are not acquainted with the bride, but have been informed that she is a lady of excellent character and respected by a large circle of friends and acquaintances.

BORN—At the county hospital to Mr. and Mrs. Oscar Hulet of Summit, a boy on Wednesday, May 30.

—oo—

Mrs. Rass Macfarlane presented her husband with twin boys last Sunday, June 1st. They are "regular fellers."

—oo—

The Stork seems very busy. He left a boy with Mr. and Mrs. William Wood Saturday, May 31.

SUMMIT

Alex Dalley and family have returned from Delta where he was called on account of the serious illness of his father Wm. H. Dalley, whom, he reports is greatly improved.

Mr. and Mrs. Oscar Hulet are happy over the arrival of a new son at the Iron County Hospital last Saturday.

Ronald Dalley with his wife and family are here from Escalante, visiting for a few days with his parents, Mr. and Mrs. Nelson B. Dalley.

Mr. and Mrs. John Farrow have gone to Mammoth for a visit with their daughter Mrs. Jack Berry.

Mr. and Mrs. Oscar J. Hulet are home again after spending the winter in Cedar City where Mr. Hulet has been teaching school.

Iron County Record
June 13, 1924

URIE-HUNTER

In the St. George Temple Tuesday Moroni Urie and Miss Mary Hunter, both of this city, were united in the bonds of wedlock Tuesday.

The groom is well known to the greater number of people of this section of the state, and is held in very high esteem. He has been prominently identified in a public way for several years in eccleasitcal work, and has had the honor of successfully filling a mission- promulgating the truths of the L. D. S, Church. He has held several important church positions with credit to the community and himself. At present he is clerk of the Parowan Stake of Zion, which position brings him in contact with practically all the people of this section, and through his geniality, honesty and gentlemanly conduct has won a host of warm friends who will each and all wish for he and his bride the happiness as man and wife which is their just due.

The bride is a winsome daughter of Mr. and Mrs. G. M. Hunter, a young lady of home lovink tendencies, vivacious, courteous and lovable in every respect and will make an ideal helpmeet to her husband. Her scores of friends will be pleased to learn of her venture into the matrimonial world.

We have always thought that Hillman Dalley was one man in the county that would not boast, but we find we are wrong. He is now saying that his wife presented him last Friday with the very best and handsomest baby girl that every arrived in Cedar City. Mother and babe at county hospital and doing nicely.

Fred Smith is rejoicing over the arrival of a beautiful girl that arrived Wednesday. This is the first girl to be born to them, they having welcomed four boys. The little miss is receiving undivided attention from her parents. Mother and babe doing nicely.

URIE—MILES

Yesterday at St. George, Wood Urie was united in the bonds of wedlock to Miss Anna Miles of that city.

The many friends of Mr. Urie's residing in this section of Utah will be pleased to learn of his matrimonial venture and wish him a long and happy wedded life. The groom is a son of Mrs. Lillian Urie, well respected by scores of people throught southern Utah.

The bride is one of St. George's winsome young ladies, and has a host of friends and acquaintances that hold her in very high regard, each of whom will wish for her continued happiness throught her married life.

THURMAN HIGBEE MARRIED

Wednesday in the St. George Temple, Thurman Higbee of Cedar City was married to Miss Thelma Miller of Panguitch. After the ceremony the young couple left for Zion National Park to spend a week or ten days before returning to Cedar to make their home.

Thurman is a son of Mr. and Mrs. E. J. Higbee, and well known to nearly all Cedar people. The young lady has spent two winters here attending school at the Brnach Agricultural College and is known by a large number of Cedar people.

Their many friends will wish them much happiness as man and wife.

SUMMIT

June 25, 1924.

Mrs. Larena Langford of Cedar City was a visitor at the home of her father, Moroni Dalley this week.

Mr. and Mrs. Skye Cowdell and children and Mr. and Mrs. Lynn Cowdell of Los Angeles are having an extended visit with the ladies' parents, Mr. and Mrs. J. Philip Dalley.

Mrs. Harlod Smith and baby are visiting with relatives in Mineraville.

Funeral services were held here Monday morning for William H. Dalley, a former resident of Summit, who died at his home in Delta last Saturday night. He is survived by his wife, Mrs. Catherine Dalley, three sons, Edward, Alex and Leonidas Dalley of Delta and a daughter, Mrs. Sadie Hales of Ogden. A son-in-law, Jesse Gifford of Springdale, with his parents and sister; also Mayhew H. and Heber Dalley of Cedar City, brothers of the deceased, were in attendance at the funeral.

DALLEY-HIGBEE

Although rather late in reporting we are nevertheless pleased to announce the marriage of Ray Dalley to Miss Lila Higbee of Toquerville on June 23.

The groom is a well known young man of this city whose scores of friends will wish him happiness and success with the young lady of his choice, who is a well known and highly respected lady of Toquerville.

The Record joins in wishing the young couple a long and happy life as man and wife.

SAHARA

Marshal Glover transacted business in Cedar Monday.

Mr. and Mrs. Hall T. Girffin of Cedar were in Sahara Tuesday on business.

Mr. R. B. Bishop, supervisor of the B & B department called on Mr. Baker and family and he reports a fine baby girl arrived at his home.

The Enoch Troup of the Boy Scouts and the Bee-hive girls left Wednesday for a ten day trip to Cedar Breaks and vicinity where two camps will be operated, one for boys and one for girls under the supervision of the mothers and Scout Masters.

SUMMIT

Mr. and Mrs. Leland Dalley are visiting with relatives in Minersville.

Mr. and Mrs. Marion Alldredge and Mr. and Mrs. Levi Alldredge and children left for Las Vegas Tuesday after visiting several weeks at the home of the ladies' parents Mr. and Mrs. Hyrum Dalley.

Mrs. Susie J. Hulet was rushed to the hospital Monday morning after suffering all night with an accute attack of appendicitis. She was operated upon, and is reported to be getting along sa well as can be expected.

Mr. and Mrs. Hummell returned Monday from a trip to Bryce Canyon.

Mrs. J. Philip Dalley left last week for a visit with her daughters in Los Angeles.

SUMMIT.

Mrs. Sausie Y. Hulet returned yesterday from the Iron County hospital where she recently underwent an operation for appendicitis.

Miss Afton Madsen is spending a few days visiting in Salt Lake City.

Mr. and Mrs. Jessie Shurtz and children of Escalante are here for a few days visit with Mr. and Mrs. N. B. Dalley, parents of Mrs. Shurtz.

Mr. and Mrs. Wm. Allen and daughter Melba motored to Salt Lake City Tuesday, for a week's visit with their daughter, Mrs. Alice Taylor.

Among those who have gone to the mountains for an outing this week are Bp. John H. Dalley and family, Isaac Chamberlain and family, Mrs. Stapley and family, Miss Hazel Hammell, and Mr. U...el ...nell M-dson.

David Eddards and sons have been here putting up hay for W. J. Knell.

DAN AHLSTROM DIES AT BAKER, NEVADA

Daniel E. Ahlstrom, who was severely injured at a rodeo at Baker, Nevada, July 24, (as reported in this paper of the 31st ult.), succumbed to his injuries last Thursday, July 31, the remains being brought home to his sorrowing wife and family last Saturday forenoon.

Daniel E. Ahlstrom was born at Cedar City, Utah, December 16, 1877, a son of Mr. and Mrs. Charles M. Ahlstrom; he married Minnie Seegmiller at St. George, July 25, 1906, and of this union there are three children, all living, Miriam, age 17, Jack, age 15, and Howard, 3 years of age.

Dan came to St. George a few years before his marriage and worked for Charles F. Foster, attending to cattle, etc. He was a man of very cheerful temperament, fond of outdoor sports, always jolly; he was of a very kindly disposition, a good neighbor, willing at all times to give a helping hand in the public service; his heart was big, and his cheerful smile will be missed by everybody who knew him. He took much pride in his home and family, and expressed regret, to a friend, R. A. Morris, that he had to leave to earn money, remarking that when he had cleared off his obligations he would stay at home with his family. The esteem in which he was held was fully attested by the very large attendance at his funeral, and the profusion of beautiful flowers which adornd the casket and the stand and which were later laid on the grave.

Funeral Services

Funeral services were held in the Stake Tabernacle at 6 o'clock Monday evening, presided over by Elder John H. Cottam of the East Ward bishopric. Services commenced with singing "Some Sweet Day" by the choir under direction of Mrs. Emma Squire. Prayer was offered by Elder Jos. T. Atkin. A cornet duet, "Some Time, Some Where," was given by the Bleak Bros., Earl and Samuel.

Elder Richard A. Morris spoke of his early acquaintance with Bro. Dan and the love and affection between them. When Dan left for Baker (where he met his death) he had a premonition that something was going wrong. Dan's life in this community was an open one. He had a bigger heart for his friends than anyone I ever knew. He was a great hand to play pranks in camp and was always jovial. He loved his home and his family and told me he had obligations to meet which was his reason for leaving home. His life was full of noble actions. The speaker paid a high tribute to the 15-year old son of the deceased, Jack.

Elder Albert E. Miller said this large gathering was a manifestation of our love for Dan. I have worked for him, with him, and he had worked for me, and I knew him as a friend to everyone, and everyone was his friend. He was as true and as kind-hearted as it is possible for man to be.

John Sumner, the seven year old son of Ed. Sumner, owner of the Sumner Bottling Works, died Sunday noon at the Iron County Hospital. The child received a fracture at the base of his skull on being thrown from the side of a car on July 31, and tho he was fully conscious until just a short time before his death he had no chance for recovery.

Funeral services were held Tuesday at three o'clock in the tabernacle and were in charge of Bishop Corry. Reverend Davis, of the Presbyterian Church delivered the sermon and the music was provided by the choir. The dedicatory prayer at the cemetery was offered by Joseph H. Armstrong.

Mr. and Mrs. Sumner have not been in Cedar City very long but they have the sincere sympathy of the Cedar people in their sad bereavement.

KANARRAVILLE

—oo—

Sixteen children in Kanarra ra who were exposed to measles have been quarantined for the past two weeks, but as they have showed no signs of developing tho disease the quarantine is to be lifted.

Laron Williams is making an addition of two rooms to his house.

The second cutting of hay is now on and is fairly good considering the dry hot weather and the small amount of water available.

—oo—

Glen Macfarlane has been receiving treatment at the hospital for a severe case of erysipelas.

Mr. and Mrs. C. B. Maxwell have a daughter born Sunday, at the local hospital. Mother and child are doing well.

—oo—

Mr. and Mrs. Larsen, newcomers to Cedar City, are the parents of a boy born Monday at the Iron County Hospital. The baby and the mother are both geting along nicely.

SUMMIT

—oo—

Mr. and Mrs. Angus Riggs of Panguitch were visitors last week at the home of Mrs. Riggs' brother, Bishop John H. Dalley.

Miss Afton Madsen returned Monday from a three week's trip to Salt Lake City and Morgan County.

Miss Lucile Huntington of Beaver spent last week visiting with relatives in Summit.

Mrs. Albert C. Dalley and family enjoyed a ten days visit with relatives and friends here, on their return to Idaho. They have been in Southern California the past year where Mr. Dalley will remain until autumn.

Miss Claire Bennion, daughter of Dean Milton Bennion, of Salt Lake City was married in the Salt Lake Temple, Thursday, August 14th., to William Lunt Jones of Cedar. After their marriage in the Temple, Mr. and Mrs. Jones were given a reception at the Bennion home. They left soon afterward for a honeymoon tour of Southern Utah.

Mrs. Jones taught Domestic Science in the Branch Agricultural College last year and was quite well known in Cedar City. "Bill" Jones, as he is best known to Cedar people has always lived here. Both of the young people are well thot of by all who are acquainted with them, and sincere good wishes are extended by their many friends.

After the trip is finished the couple will make their home in Cedar City.

Summit.

—oo—

Miss Marie Dalley is going to Las Vegas this week for a visit with her sister, Mrs. Levi Alldredge.

—oo—

Mrs. J. Philip Dalley returned home Monday after an extended visit with her daughters, Mrs. Imogene and Mrs. Lena Cowdell.

—oo—

Mr. and Mrs. N. C. Madsen and son Elmer, and Miss Hazel Hammell motored to Salt Lake City this week.

—oo—

The second cutting of hay is almost harvested and the grain cut. The crops this year are considerably below the average.

KANARRA

—oo—

August 14, 1924.

Born Monday to Mr. and Mrs. Charles Parker, Jr., a boy and to Mr. and Mrs. Earl Smith, a girl. Drs. Macfarlane and Green were in attendance. Mother and babies doing fine.

—oo—

Mrs. Naomi Ingram who has been here with her children and staying with her mother, Mrs. Eliza Wood, left here yesterday for Salt Lake City where she has bought her a home.

—oo—

Mrs. Emma Roundy Christensen and daughter left here yesterday for Provo. She has been here for the past month or so visiting her son Horace Roundy and family.

—oo—

Gus Pingel has sold his farm and animals to Berry Williams. He is going north somewhere to hunt him a new home.

—oo—

The grain is all cut and will soon be ready for the thresher. Good crops are reported.

—oo—

Mr. and Mrs. Ren Williams and family and Jennie Reeves are on a fishing trip down at Pintura Creek.

SUMMIT NOTES.

——oo——

Mr. and Mrs. Bert Farnsworth of Salt Lake City are here for a visit with Mrs. Farnsworth's parents., Mr. and Mrs. Chas. Dalley.

Stake Pres. Henry W. Lunt and counselor M. D. Higbee were visitors at scaramental meeting Sunday and gave us some good instructions.

Millard Halterman of Midvalley is expected here next week with his threshing outfit.

Mrs. Isaac Chamberain and family returned from the mountains last week where they spent most of the summer with Mr. Chamberlain who has a position with the government forest reserve.

Mr. and Mrs. Oscar W. Hulet and Mr. and Mrs. Oscar J. Hulet returned a few days ago from a fishing trip to Fish Lake. They report having had an enjoyable time.

Mr. and Mrs. Leonidas Dalley of Delta were visiting here with relatives Tuesday, on their way to attend the rodeo at Cedar City.

Mr. and Mrs. George T. Cottam celebrated their golden wedding day Tuesday with a big dinner in the Tabernacle basement which was attended by a large number of relatives of this highly respected and estimable couple. They have nine children living, all of whom were at the dinner as well as 43 grandchildren. There was a big time at the Cottam residence at night which was enjoyed to the full by everybody present.

Mr. and Mrs. Cottam are counted among the foremost citizens of St. George. Brought up here among the pioneers of Dixie they have developed strength of character and worth that places them easily in the most-to-be depended upon citizens, industrious, capable, God-fearing and upright. May they be blessed with health and strength to the end of their days is the sincere desire of their many frieds.

Those who attended from a distance were Dr. and Mrs. Frank Petty and family of Cedar City, Mr. and Mrs. Charles B. Petty and family of Hurricane, Mr. and Mrs. Frank B. McIntire and family of Price, Mrs. Albert Pace and family of Price, Mr. and Mrs. Antone B. Prince and family of New Harmony, Mr. and Mrs. J. Milton Cottam of Los Angeles, Cal., and Bishop Frank Holt of Gunlock.

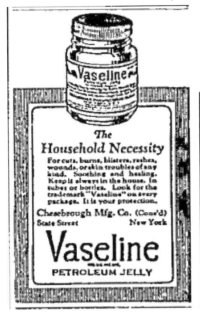
The announcements of the marriage October 8th, of Arthur Stapley of this city, and Miss Lulla Tullis of Newcastle, are out.

The marriage will take place in the St. George temple.

Mr. Stapley is a son of Mr. and Mrs. Thos. Stapley, a young man well known to the people of this city. The young lady is a daughter of Mr. and Mrs. John Tullis of Newcastle.

The friends of the couple will be pleased to learn of their contemplated union.

Chiropractic

Corrects the Cause

QUESTION—"One of your lady patients tells me you are able to handle Chronic Appendicitis without an operation. Is this true?"

ANSWER—If you suffer with so-called Chronic Appendicitis, you should submit to a Spinal Analysis to find the CAUSE. We do not advocate the use of drugs or surgery for this ailment. We believe no organ was placed in the body that should be removed by operation. If an organ becomes diseased, it is because Nature's means of repair, the nerves, are injured or pinched where they leave the spinal cord, and by adjusting these misplacements in the spine we are able to prove that Chiropractic gets you well—WITHOUT SURGERY. Remember, the appendix was placed in your intestinal tract for a purpose. Keep it; you will need it in the years to come. Have your spine adjusted and the appendix will continue to be useful to you. If you would avoid this operation, we urge you to—

HAVE YOUR SPINE EXAMINED

O. F. WALDRAM, D. C.

Office on 1st. East St. Across from Ward Hall.

Cedar City, Utah, Phone 18.

USED CARS

Buick 7 Passenger	$600.00
Buick Six Roadster	$900.00
Buick Six Touring	$300.00
Chevrolet Touring	$385.00
Maxwell Touring	$300.00
Dodge Truck	$450.00
Ford Touring	$125.00
Ford Touring	$100.00
Crevrolet Delivery	$250.00

Kopps Garage

"Guaranteed Workmanship"

Reliable Accessories

CEDAR CITY - UTAH

Phone 139F2

J. A. KOPP, Prop.

Last Wednesday at the county hospital Clarence Lamareaux was operated for appendicitis. He is doing very nicely.

This week Parry Mackleprang and Miss Noami Perry went to Salt Lake City to be united in marriage.

The young man is a son of Gus Mackelprang and is well known to the majority of the residents of this city.

Miss Perry is a sister of Miss Bertha Perry, and young lady who holds the esteme of scores of friends.

The Record joins their many friends in wishing them a long and happy life as man and wife.

ADAMS—HUNTER

Monday at the home of the bride Wallace Adams and Miss Nola Huntre were joined in the bonds of wedlock.

The groom is a son of Mr. and Mrs. Herbert Adams, and the bride the daughter of Mr. and Mrs. James Hunter.

The young couple have the best wishes of their many friends for a long and happy life as man and wife.

Wednesday Zeal Murrie, 10 year old son of Mrs. and Mrs. David Murie, died from the effects of blood poisoning.

A week ago the boy stepped on a rusty nail whch was embeded very deeply in his foot. Immediate attention was given to the wound by the boy's parents, but infection set in and blood poisoning resulted, which could not be abated, the result being the death of the lad as above stated.

Funeral serivces were held in the Enoch Ward chapel. Many of sympathizing friends of Cedar, as well as the entire Enoch ward were in attendance at the funeral services Thursday. Interment was made at the Enoch cemetery.

The friends of Orson Fretwell were surprised and pained to learn Tuesday that he had passed away, succumbing to four convulsions that attacked him early that morning.

Some time ago he suffered a partial paralysia, and apparently recovered from it, although the attack had somewhat weakened his mind. His physical condition seemed strong, and it was with considerable surprise to his wife and children that convulsions came and ended his life.

Orson Fretwell came to Cedar in the early settlement of the town, coming from England with his brother John, who died here several years ago. In England he joined the L. D. S. Church and has been a devout believer in its principles ever since. He has held important positions in the church quorums of whch he was a member, has acted as ward teacher, Sunday school class leader, quorum class leader, and was always willing to act in any capacity that the authorities desired him.

He has also acted in a civil capacity at different times during his life, and always filled the position assigned to him with promptness and dispatch. He was a conscientious, hard working, and honest man, and was respected by scores of people hereabouts who knew him ever since he came to this city.

Funeral services will be held this afternoon at the tabernacle and interment will be at the Cedar Cemetary.

The Record joins with the many friends of the wife and children in tendering sympathy in their loss of a devoted husband and father.

Cards are out announcing the marriage of Miss Maude Hunter of this city, and Mr. J. Erie Bennett of Parowan, to take place October 25.

Miss Hunter is a daughter of Mr. and Mrs. G. M. Hunter, a young lady well known here, and who holds the esteem of a large number of the people of Cedar, in fact of all who bear her acquaintance.

Mr. Bennet is a young man who is well liked by the people of Parowan, and is upright, honest and industrious.

The Record joins with their friends in wishing them happiness and prosperity will follow them through life.

—oo—

The following births are reported from the county hospital for the month of October up to the present date:

Oct 5, to Mr and Mrs. Chas. Hunter, a boy; Oct 4, to Mr. and Mrs. Thos. D. Little, a girl; Oct. 19, to Mr. and Mrs. Mart Worthen, a girl.

Wm. H. Lyman and family of Parowan have moved to Cedar and will make their home here for the winter at least..

—oo—

Everything has its good points. Taking a deep breath for a long kiss develops a girl's lungs.

Iron County Record
November 7, 1924

REPUBLICANS CAPTURE EVERY COUNTY OFFICE AND CAST HEAVY MAJORITY FOR STATE AND NATIONAL OFFICES.

—oo—

For President—
Calvin Coolidge, Rep. _____ 1202
John W. Davis, Dem. _____ 544
Robert M. Lafallotte, Ind. _____ 227
For Vice-President—
Charles G. Dawes, Rep. _____ 1202
Charles W. Bryan, Dem. _____ 544
Burton K. Wheeler, Ind. _____ 227
For Congress Representative—
Don B. Colton, Rep. _____ 1427
Frank Francis, Dem. _____ 555
For Governor—
Charles R. Maybye, Rep. _____ 1377
George H. Dern, Dem. _____ 630
For Secretary of State—
H. E. Crocket, Rep. _____ 1417
James W. Funk, Dem. _____ 575
For State Auditor—
John E. Holden, Rep. _____ 1421
Daniel O. Larsen, Dem. _____ 572
For State Treasurer—
John Walker, Rep. _____ 1416
Joseph Ririe, Dem. _____ 571
For Attorney General—
Harvey H. Cluff, Rep. _____ 1412
J. William Robinson, Dem. _____ 571

For Supt. Public Instruction—
Dr. C. N. Jensen, Rep. _____ 1421
Dr. Hugh H. Woodward, Dem. 572
For Justice Supreme Court—
Daniel N. Straup, Rep. _____
A. J. Weber, Dem _____
For State Representative—
Wm. H. Lyman, Rep. _____ 1068
Walter K. Granger, Dem. _____ 952
For District Judge—
Thos. H. Burton, Rep. _____ 1109
O. A. Murdock, Dem. _____ 837
Wm. B. Higgins, Ind. _____ 100
For District Attorney—
G. Hunter Lunt, Rep. _____ 1286
Grover A. Giles, Dem. _____ 711
For 4 Year Commissioner—
Evan E. Williams, Rep. _____ 1174
Edward J. Palmer, Dem. _____ 811
For 2 Year Commissioner—
Lyman E. Sevy, Rep. _____ 1166
Thos. W. Jones, Dem. _____ 841
For County Attorney—
Reuben J. Shay, Rep. _____ 1240
John M. Foster, Dem. _____ 750

KANARRA NOTES

The H. E. Club held a meeting Oct. 31 at the home of Mrs. Sade Williams.

The first book lesson was given by Mrs. Vilda Davis and the constitution for the club was read by the president Mrs. Ruth Williams. There was nine members and three new joiners present. Mrs. Williams and Mrs. J. T. Raliegh served a fine lunch at the close of the meeting.

The same evening the officers gave a Hallowe'en party at the home of Mrs. Mabel Williams. The room was nicely decorated, games arranged and a lunch of squash pie, sandwiches, cokies, olives and hot cocoa was served. Every one seemed to enjoy themselves and have a very good time.

Nine Commandments For Motorists

If all motorists would observe the following "nine commandments" there would be a great reduction in the number of accidents on the highways.

1. Drive on the right side of the road; it's just as good as the left.

2. Slow down when approaching a cross road; it is nearly as dangerous as a railroad crossing.

3. Look out for children. You can never tell what they will do, and you are always in the wrong when you hit one.

4. Be sure that your lights are not defective or glaring; it's no joke driving into a blinding glare, as you yourself know.

5. Read and obey the warning signs; they are not put up as ornaments.

6. If you've got to speed—do it where you don't kill anybody but yourself.

7. When making minor repairs get to the side of the road and stop where your car can be seen from both directions; otherwise you may stop longer than you anticipated.

8. Speeding around corners is a straight route to the hospital. Don't race past a stopped car. Some day the jury will call it manslaughter.

9. Use discretion. The fact that you had the right-of-way, won't bring anybody back to life, least of all yourself.

BIRTHS AT HOSPITAL

Births at the county hospital for the past two weeks are as follows: To Mr. and Mrs. Frank Jackson, a girl; Mr. and Mrs. H. Clay Watson, a girl; Mr. and Mrs. H. Tidwell, a girl; Mr. and Mrs. J. A. Young, a boy.

SAHARA

Bryant Hedrick had a valuable cow killed by the train Saturday.

Mr. and Mrs. J. A. Baker were in Parowan and Cedar day last week.

Mr. H. O. Dougherty was in Beryl Monday on business.

Mr. Arlie Fourman went to Cedar Sunday.

Mr. J. J. Lippincott went to Los Angels; he intends bringing his wife back when he comes.

Mr. Pollock of Kanarra was canvasing our town Soturday. He is agent for ready to wear clothes.

MARRIED

Saturday last Miss Fannie Walker and Mr. Butler of this city were joined in wedlock.

The bride is well known in this section of the state, particularly in Cedar, and is held in esteem by scores of people. The groom, who came to Cedar about a year ago, is a steady, conscientious gentleman, who is well liked by those who bear his acquantance.

The Record joins with the friends of the couple in wishing them long life and happiness as man and wife.

Dr. Bergstrom, Fred Biederman, Leonard Green and Wallace Smith returned Saturday from the Kaibab forest with twelve fine deer. Strung up, those big bucks were a sight to stir the heart of any hunter. The party agree it is the finest hunt they have ever enjoyed.

Iron County Record
December 5, 1924

RECENT BIRTHS

To Mr. and Mrs. Delbert Woolsey, a boy; to Mr. and Mrs. Frank Kelsey, a boy; to Mr. and Mrs. Thos. Myers, a girl; to Mr. and Mrs. Geo. Smith, a girl; to Mr. Mrs. Geo. Prothero, a boy.

Mrs. Arthur Lewis of Lynndyl, Utah, spent the last week in Cedar visiting with her mother, Mrs. Mary Jane Wade.

BORN—To Mr. and Mrs. Ezra Rollo, Saturday morning, a lovely girl. Mother and babe doing nicely.

New babies at the hospital this week are a son to Mrs. Stanley Prothero of Paragonah; a daughter to Mrs. Horace Roundy of Kanarra, and a girl to Mrs. Thornton Jones.

SUMMIT NOTES

Mr. ad Mrs. Charles Dalley and family returned Monday from Salt Lake City, after a few days visit with their daughter Mrs. Bert Farnsworth.

Mrs. Alice Taylor who has been employed as Primary Grade teacher here, resigned her position and returned last week to Salt Lake City, where her husband has employment.

Mr. and Mrs. Walter K. Granger of Cedar City spent Thanksgiving with Mrs. Ganger's parents, Mr. and Mrs. N. B. Dalley.

Mr. and Mrs. Ralph Adams came in from Newcastle to spend the Thanksgiving holidays with relatives here.

Mrs. Carter of Salt Lake City is teaching the Primary Grades here this week, until a permanent teacher can be secured.

Mrs. eorge Smith was operated on Tuesday at the County Hospital for the removal of goitre. She is reported as getting along nicely.

N. C. Madsen left unday for Los Angeles where he will take a course in automobile mechanics.

A real live base ball game was played Thanksgiving day between the married and single men, the score being in favor of the married men.

—oo—

Wm. W. Dalley left last week for St. George where he was married in the temple to Miss Hulda Wittwer of La Verkin.

Iron County Record
December 26, 1924

CAPTAIN PETE'S WIDOW DIES

—oo—

This morning "Lucy Pete" (Indian) widow of Capt. Pete, died from pneumonia. So far as we are able to learn the deceased was ill for two weeks, and that every attention was given her that could be, but the disease had gained such a hold on her system that medicines were of no avail.

Burial will be had tomorrow in the Indian plot of the Cedar Cemetery.

MRS. PERRY HAS LEG BROKEN

—oo—

Last Monday while Mrs. Ellen Perry was out at the rear of her home she accidently slipped and fell, suffering a compound fracture of the left leg below the knee.

Surgical attention was given the lady immediately and she is now resting easily.

RUNS KNIFE IN EYE

Monday night while playing with a knife a son of Wallace Bracken accidently ran the knife in his eye. Although serious, it is believed that the sight has not been inpaired.

SAHARA NEWS

—oo—

Effective January 1, 1925 the Sahara Post Office will be "Zane."

Mr. and Mrs. Arlie Forman returned from Cedar. They will spend the holidays in Los Angeles.

Mr. and Mrs. M. E. Glover went to Cedar City this week.

Ray Kelley has been on the sick list, he has a very sore knee caused by a sprain.

Mrs. Del Vecchio and children went to Salt Lake City to spend the holidays.

You people in Cedar may have stray cattle, but we certainly have our share of them. We think it would be a good plan to have a general round up and every one take care of the stock he owns and not impose upon some one else.

NADA

In January 1925 marks the 11th anniversary of the Nada Post office and inspires the question:—How many patrons has the office? 1925 finds the population of Nada not much greater than in 1914. There are 28 families, with a total of 66 persons, so we are holding our own while other offices established during that period of the developement of the Escalante desert have all been discontinued, we are informed.

The friends and acquaintances of Taylor Thornton, of Newcastle, and Hilda Hunter of this city, will be pleased to learn of their marriage, the ceremony being performed in this city last Wednesday.

The groom is well known and respected by a large number of people of this section of the state, while the bride is known and respected equally well.

The Record joins with the friends of the couple in wishing them happiness and success as man and wife.

Hirshel Urie, the five year old son of Mr. and Mrs. Milton Urie is in the hospital following a serious accident due to the explosion of a giant cap with which the unfortunate child was playing. The explosion tore off the thumb and three fingers from his left hand and another wound of the eye seriously endangered his sight. We are pleased to report that the vision will not be seriously impaired and that he is resting comfortably at present.

Mrs. Christina B. Chatterley and Mrs. David Thorley are visitors in Lehi, the guests of Mr. and Mrs. Ben Harris. Mrs. Harris is a daughter of Mrs. Chatterly, and a sister of Mrs. Thorley.

Saturday night Mr. and Mrs. David Thorley gave a reception in honor of the marriage of their son Thomas to Miss Beth Fox, the marriage taking place recently in Salt Lake City.

A large number of relatives and friends were in attendance and a very enjoyable evening passed. Music, games and partaking of delicious refreshments was the order of the evening.

The newly weds were tendered a generous supply of household necessities, and some of the luxuries, as presents by the guests.

Mr. and Mrs. Paul Arns are happy over the birth of a baby boy that arrived Monday. Mother and babe progressing nicely.

(Parowan Times)

A midnight wedding on Thursday of last week, at the home of Mr. Edward M. Dalton of this city, and Miss Lola Cox of Cedar as husband and wife; the ceremony was performed by Mayor J. Clayton Mitchell

The groom is the oldest son of Mr. and Mrs. Robert E. Dalton, a cheerful, industrious and likeable young man. The bride is a daughter of Mr. and Mrs. J. D. Cox of Cedar City, and is one of the prominent young ladies of that community. What their plans are for the future, we have been unable to learn.

With their numerous friends here and elsewhere, we join in wishing them joy and happiness on their journey through life.

James Bulloch of Delta spent the fore part of the week in Cedar visiting relatives. Mr. Bulloch was accompanied by his family and was on his way home from Kanab where they had been visiting.

Iron County Record
February, 1925

Today we received information that Mrs. Mary Alice Jones, wife of Sylvester F. Jones of Enoch, passed away yesterday at the home of her daughter in Summit.

Funeral services are to be held in Enoch tomorrow, a report of which, together with a biography of the life of the diseased will be furnished to the Record for publication next week.

Tuesday the little spirit of the 16 days old child of Mr. and Mrs. Marion Lauretzen passed away, succumbing to an attack of bronchial pneumonia. Funeral services were held at the family residence Wednesday afternoon.

The sympathy of many friends goes out to the parents in their hour of sorrow and bereavement.

The little son of Mr. and Mrs. Parley Dalley is nursing a broken arm, the result of a fall. Surgical attention was given shortly after the accidently, and reports at present are that the patient is doing ncely.

Saturday night last the people of this city, a great many of them at least, were startled by a slight earthquake at about nine o'clock; then again they were disturbed at about 12 o'clock, or shortly after. Sunday morning at 6 and 9 o'clock the earth again trembled, while at about 1:30 there was a severe jolting that frightened the people considerably.

From that time on until Tuesday morning there were other tremblors, until the number totaled 11.

The little daughter of Mr. and Mrs. Wallace Lunt had the misfortune to break her leg the other day. She was swnging in a hammock and somehow caught her foot on the frozen ground, snapping it just above the ankle and tearing the ligaments of the foot quit severely. Surgical attention was given immediately and the little one is now progressing nicely.

ZANE (SAHARA)

Mr. and Mrs. McHenry of Ford was in Zane looking after their cattle.
—|o|—
Mrs. Del Vecchio and children returned from Salt Lake where she has been visiting her relatives for six weeks.
—|o|—
They have increased the Laborers on the section which makes it good for people who are hunting work.

It is rather fortunate that Mr. Nortis has a tractor. It keeps him busy pulling automobiles out of the mud.
—|o|—
A shower, dance and oyster supper was given for Mr. nad Mrs. Harion Carter Saturday night. We had a very nice crowd considering the bad roads.
—|o|—
Mrs. T. R. Prey of Lund was in Sahara Saturday returning Sunday.

SUMMIT

Mr. and Mrs. Loland Dalley, Mrs. Harold Smith and Miss Helen Chamberlain returned Tuesday from Minersville where they have been visiting the past week.

—|o|—

Elder Scott Day of Parowan who has recently returned from a mission to Great Britian, was the speaker at Sacramental meeting here Sunday. His address was much appreciated and enjoyed.

—|o|—

The annual stockholders' meeting of the Summit Irrigation Company was held Monday for the purpose of electing two new board members. George I. Smith was elected president, and Charles R. Dalley, secretary of the company.

—|o|—

Quite a number of towns people attended the funeral services of Mrs. Mary Alice Jones at Enoch last Saturday.

—|o|—

Samuel L. Fife of Cedar City was in town Tuesday attending to business matters.

—|o|—

Mrs. George Smith and children are visiting with her sister Mrs. Laurena Langford at Cedar City.

KANARRA

—|o|—

There is quite a bit of sickness among the children and a few adults.

—|o|—

Elmer Davis, Earl Smith and Gus Pingel came home today. They have been working for Doughterty and Black on their road contract. The grading is now about completed from the county line to ash creek bridge.

—|o|—

Layron Williams was in from the sheepherd last week end.

—|o|—

Herald Stapley came home last week from Daugherty and Black road camp suffering with pneumonia.

—|o|—

Rass Anderson was in town last week buying cattle.

—|o|—

Mrs. D. T. Thomas left last week for Salt Lake City. She expects to be gone about a month.

—|o|—

G. Berry Williams and Albert Davis had their tonsils removed Tuesday by Drs. Macfarlane and Bergstrom.

—|o|—

Mr. and Mrs. R. J. Williams, Sr went to St. George last Sunday to attend a birthday dinner with their daughter Bell Prince. Ocassion being her 40th birthday.

NADA

Weather reprot for January 1925. Precipitation .23. Total snow fall 2.5 inches. On ground the 15th 5.5 inches.

Alvin Couch accompanied by a Mr. Anderson spent Sunday at the home of the former, returning to Delta where they are employed.

Another periodic revival of interest in the Dead Man's Secret Mine on Blue Knoll.

On February 5th, Frank Petty, father of Dr. Petty of this city, passed peacefully away after an extended illness. He was 68 years of age, and came to the Dixie country in his early boyhood. Te was one of the very earliest of thesettlers in the up-river country in Washington county, and was known as a man of high ideals, honest and upright in his dealings with his fellowmen.

The deceased was known as a man who believed in the educating of his children, and has the distinction of having had four children graduate from the D. N. S. and B. A. C., one of them being a surgeon, two dentists and the fourth a merchant, now a member of the Utah legislature.

He was a devout Latter-day Saint, and always received much joy and satisfaction by living the precepts of that faith.

His son, Dr. Petty, of this city, on being notified of the serious illness of his father, went immediately to Hurricane on the 5th and was at the bedside of his parent at time of death, remaining in Hurricane until after the funeral.

Mr. and Mrs. Chas. Bryant are happy over the arrival of a beautiful baby girl that came to bless them Sunday. Mother and babe reported as doing nicely.

Last Sunday the spirit of Mrs. Anna Anderson, mother of our fellow-towns man, J. E. Anderson, passed on to the spirit world from whence it came 77 years ago.

Sister Anderson was well known to a large circle of people of this city and county, and was known as a devout woman, who lived the life of a saint, winning the love of all with whom she came in contact by her graciousness, big heartedness and charitable disposition.

She was one of the early settlers of Utah, and she with her husband, now deceased, made their home, and raised a large family at what is now known as Echo farm in Washington county.

She passed away at the home of her son in Cedar , and the body was taken to Hurricane where funeral service were held, after which it was taken to St. George where interment took place.

Iron County Record
March, 1925

The infant born to Mr. and Mrs. Willard Perkins last week died last Monday.

Funeral services were held at the home Monday afternoon, quite a large number of sympathizing friends being present. The sympathy of the friends of the bereaved parents goes out to them in their hour of srorow.

s Williams of Kanarra was in Monday, having come up to is wife, who last week present- with a lovely daughter. Wells d and happy, and the mother be doing nicely. The Cedar s of Mr. Williams were very d to congratulate him on the of his daughter.

Sunday afternoon the funeral services over the remains of Mrs. Annie Christina Williams, who died from Bright's Disease last Friday, were held in the tabernacle with Bp. F. B. Wood officiating.

The choir was in attendance and rendered some appropriate singing for the occasion, under the direction of Mr. Manning, who also sang a beautiful solo, very gratifying and encouraging to the mourners.

The speakers were Elders A. G. Matheson and Samuel F. Leigh, each of whom spoke of the excellent character of the deceased, stating that although she was of a retiring nature she was generous and kindly, and was a firm believer in the gospel. The speakers gave much encouragement to the children who are left to mourn, and admonished them to follow in the paths of religion that their beloved mother had followed.

There were numerous floral offerings contributed by kind friends which tended to brighten the feelings of the mourners in the knowledge that friends sincerely extended sympathy to them in their loss.

The deceased was a daughter of Jence Anderson, who proceeded her to the Beyond some twenty years ago, and the wife of Thomas Williams, who departed this life three years ago. She was born in Cedar 59 years ago; and during all that time has been identified with the Church of Jesus Christ of Latter Day Saints and believed firmly in the principles thereof.

She was of a retiring disposition, warm hearted, honest and upright, a devoted mother to her children, and a woman who was liked by those who bore her acquaintance for her upright and honest character.

SUMMIT
—|o|—

On account of so many attendng the exercsies of the Relief Society Annual Day at Parowan on the 17th, the program here was postponed until the evening of March 21st.

A large crowd assembled at the home of Pres. Lillian R. White where an inpromptu program and social was held, and a splendid time enjoyed by all.

Mr. and Mrs. Otto P. Dalley are receiving congratulations upon the arrival of their first son last Sunday morning.

N. C. Madsen returned last week from Los Angeles where he has been taking several months training in automobile mechanics.

Saturday an interesting baseball game was played here between New Castle and Summit, the score being 30 to 21 in favor of New Castle. In the evening the same teams played a game of basket ball, Summit winning an easy victory.

Mr. and Mrsr. Ralph Adams spent the week end wth Mrs. Adams' parents, Mr. and Mrs. O. W. Hulet. Mr. Adams accompanying his students from Newcastle who played ball.

There seems to be an epidemic of colds and sore throats here. Little Shirl Chamberlain is quite seriously ill at present with throat trouble.

Mrs. Wm. Allen returned last week after a two weeks' visit at Salt Lake City with her daughter. Mrs. Alice Taylor and her first grandson who arrived recently.

MARRIED

——|o|——

Last Saturday night at Parowan Ross Benson of that city and Miss Mae Bauer of this city were united in the bonds of wedlock, Mayor J. Clayton Mitchell officiating.

The young couple are well known in Cedar and are respected by a large circle of friends, who will be pleased to learn of their union.

The Record joins with friends in wishing them happiness and success.

Sunday the little four year old boy of Mr. and Mrs. Calvin Pendleton fell from hte second story window of their home sustaining a fracture of the skull. The little fellow was taken to the hospital and surgical attention given him. The patient is reported as recovering nicely.

NADA

——|o|——

Weather report for February. Precipitation .44 inches. Greatest in 24 hours .28; date 21. Just a trace of snow.

——|o|——

W. L. Davis and son of Greenville are putting in 40 acres of rye for A. Stephenson.

——|o|——

Mrs. Oscar Stephenson and J. O. Stephenson are spending a few days in Milford this week.

L. N. Marsden of Parowan returned to his home, after a few weeks stay at his ranch near hear.

——|o|——

Mrs. Mike Schoaf who is visiting at her old home in Illinois will return this week.

——|o|——

M. B. Edwards of Paragonah and Silas Owens of Cedar City were here recently, attending to business matters and calling on friends.

Iron County Record
April, 1925

Granddaughter of Mrs. Haight Dies

——|o|——

Last week Mrs. David Haight, Golden Haight, and Mr. and Mrs. Geo. Esplin went to Richfield to attend the funeral of a 13 year old daughter of Mrs. Mary Poulson, grand daughter of Mrs. Haight.

The child died suddenly, giving no indication that there was anything seriously wrong with her. She had been suffering somewhat with a severe cold, and the evening of her death had been given some medicine to quiet her nerves, and put to bed Sometime after retiring she had awakened and called her mother, who went to the bed and asked what was wanted. The child seemed to have been only partly awake and went back to apparent sleep again. Still later her mother went to see if the girl was sleeping and found that death had come. No cause has been assigned for the sudden death.

Saturday afternoon about 3 o'clock the home of Myron Jones was completely destroyed by fire. It is thought that the fire started from a defective flue. The fire was not discovered until it had made good headway. The fire department at Cedar City was called, but due to the heavy wind that was blowing they were unable to do anything to stop the fire.

It was a frame house and burned so quickly that nothing was saved.

SUMMIT

Special to the Record.

Mrs. Lillian Fartheringham of Frisco is here visiting with her parents Mr and Mrs. John Farrow.

Last Saturday night the Boy Scouts entertained at a social and dance. Hot dogs were sold, the proceeds to apply on the purchase of uniforms for the boys.

Mr. and Mrs. Obadiah Farrow and daughter Mrs. Marie Grimshaw have gone to St. George to work in the Temple for about two weeks.

Mrs. Imogene Cowdell and little daughters of Los Angeles are here for an extended visit with her parents, Mr. and Mrs. J. Phillip Dalley.

George Smith who has been operating the engine for the road construction company in Washington county this winter has completed his job and returned Tuesday with the engine which belongs to the Summit threshing machine company.

Mrs. Harold Smith has returned from Minersville where she was called last week on account of the serious illness of her mother, whom she now reports as improving.

Mrs. Isaac Chamberlain returned Monday with her baby daughter from the county hospital feeling fine.

Joseph Fife, son of Samuel Fife was hurried to the hospital Wednesday and operated on for acute appendicitis.

45 Students to Graduate From B. A. C.

The graduating committee has voted (subject to the approval of the Faculty) t o graduate the following students next May, provided all work for which they have been registered this year and are now pursuing, is satisfactorily completed, a n d provided also that any "incomplete" or "conditioned" work, upon the satisfactory completion of which graduattion has been indicated as conditional, is so completed:

High School Division.

Meta Adams,
Willie Adams,
Durrel Corry,
Marie Dalley
Romola Dalley,
G. Wayne Esplin,
Morris Foster,
Melva Froyd,
Eula Gardner,
Thurman R. Gardner,
L. De Vere Hall,
Gwen Heaton,
Spencer Isom,
Idona Jackson,
Bernard Johnson,
Afton Madsen

Lydia Matheson,
Vervene Neagle,
William Palmer, Jr.,
B. Fayette Parker
Furl Porter,
Thurman Pryor,
Cora Riddle,
Freda Robinson,
Caddie Rollo,
Alice Rollo,
La Preal Thorley,
Grant V. Twitchell
Zilpha Urie,
Earl Whittaker,
Lu Zene Wilkinson,
Annie Wilkinson,
Alice Williams,
Cathie Williams
Wavie Williams,
Eva Dean Wood,
Sylvia Woodard,
Virginia Spencer,

College Division.

Mrs. M. Adams Burton,
Alice Higbee,
Merle Pace,
Alice Palmer,
Ruth Walker,
William H. Wood,
Claire V. Woodard.

MIDVALLEY

Raymond Jones, son of Bp. Chas. E. Jones, leaving for a mission to the Central States, and Golden Haight, just returned from the same mission, were the speakers at Enoch Sunday March 29.

Owen Matheson is drilling a well for Leonard Haight.

Mr. and Mrs. David Murie are improving nicely. Both having undergone operations at the Iron County Hospital recently.

Mrs. Fred Carrol of Orderville spent two weeks at the home of her brother Geo. W. Esplin.

BORN—To Mr. and Mrs. Jed Woodard, April 12, a girl. Mother and babe doing nicely.

Berry Williams of Kanarra was a business visitor in Cedar Wednesday.

Antone Pryor, the nine year old son of Mr. and Mrs. Wm. Pryor, died yesterday after a month's illness from plural pneumonia.

The boy six weeks ago contracted an attack of flu, that developed into plural pneumonia, which medical skill and careful and conscientious nursing failed to curb, death resulting as above stated.

Ernest Judd was operated at the hospital Wednesday night for acute appendicitis. He is reported recovering satisfactorily.

Iron County Record
May 1925

The people of this community were grieved to learn Wednesday evening that Mrs. Johanna Palmer passed from this life after suffering for some time from pneumonia.

The deceased was 82 years of age, and so weakened that she was unable to battle successfully against the insidious disease. She passed peacefully away and has gone to a well earned rest.

She was one of Cedars most highly respected pioneers, having passed through all the hardships incident to the early settlement of Cedar City.

She was a most devout Latter Day Saint and her heart was ever warm for those who suffered, and her hand was always liberal in bestowing assistance to the needy.

Funeral services will be held Sunday afternoon in the tabernacle, commencing at 3:30.

Next week we hope to be able to publish a biographical sketch of the life of this good woman who bears the love of every person that became acquainted with her during her sojourn upon this earth.

Following is a brief biographical sketch of the life of Sister Joanna Reese Palmer, who passed from this life last week, one of nature's most noble women, for whom score of people of Southern Utah held deep love:

Joanna Reese Palmer was born in Pontypool, South Wales, August 6, 1842. She, with her entire family, joined the Mormon Church while still in Wales, and in 1863, at the age of twenty-one she emigrated to America. The ocean trip on a slow sailing vessel consumed seven weeks, and on the trip across the American continent to Utah the young girl saw the land east of the Mississippi ravaged by the Civil War, and to the west she saw a thousand mile, bison dotted Indian infested wilderness, over which she tramped most of the way afoot.

On her arrival in Salt Lake City she was married to Richard Palmer whom she had met while he was on a mission to Wales, and they took their honeymoon trip to Cedar City in Southern Utah, where the rest of their life was spent. The deceased, though frail of body, was a person of great energy, and by tireless work and a natural aptitude for handicraft, she mastered the arts of pioneering and made a comfortable home for her family in the wilderness.

Last Saturday at Winns Hollow the 18 year old son of Mr. and Mrs. W. M. Grimshaw was accidently shot with a rifle.

The accident happened when a brother of the injured young man, got up from the meal table and sat down upon a cot on which the gun was lying, dislodging it. The gun in falling exploded and sent the charge of shot into the hip of Geo. Grimshaw who was seated at the table.

Fortunately the bullet had been withdrawn from the cartridge and small bird shot substituted just a little while before the accident.

The young man was brought to the county hospital where his wound was dressed and he is now getting along nicely, and unless infection sets in will soon be able to be around as was his wont before the accident.

Following an operation at the county hospital performed about two weeks ago, Joseph Walker passed away Wednesday night.

The deceased was 45 years old, and has been a sufferer for over a year, having undergone three operations for correction of the trouble but it seems that his vitality has been brought so low by the inroads of the disease that he was unable to withstand the shock of the last operation.

Funeral services will be held in the tabernacle this afternoon.

The deceased was unmarried. He leaves several brothers and sisters to mourn his departure.

The eldest son of Mr. and Mrs. Warren Bulloch was operated on for appendicitis at the county hospital Tuesday. Reports from the hospital are that the lad is rapidly recovering from the shock of the operation.

SUMMIT NOTES.

Most of the local sheep owners have finished shearing their flocks.

Mr. and Mrs. Nelson D. Dalley are enjoying a visit from their daughter, Mrs. Ada Schurtz and children, of Escalante, Utah.

Lawrence Grimshaw of Midvalley is spending a few days at the home of his brother Ray.

Mrs. Lillian White has received word of the death of her sister Mrs. Lena Jones of Big Horn Wyoming. Mrs. Jones was a former resident of Summit.

Mr. and Mrs. Herbert White went to Beaver Tuesday to attend the funeral of Mr. White's cousin William White of that city.

GENERAL LIVE STOCK DEALERS

JOHN A. ADAMS
Rancher and Shipper
Telephone 170W

J. E. ANDERSON
General Livestock Merchant
Telephone 75R

WARREN BULLOCH
General Livestock Merchant
Telephone 44W

WALTER K. GRANGER
General Livestock Merchant
Telephone 128W

J. E. HASLEM
Rancher and Shipper
Telephone 1128W

LEHI M. JONES
General Live Stock Merchant
Telephone 181W

F. W. MIDDLETON & SONS
Rancher and Shipper
Ranch 90J4   Res. 148R

LEIGH BROS.
Rancher and Shipper
Telephone 117

J. G. PACE
Rancher and Shipper
Telephone 63

JAMES SMITH & SONS
Rancher and Shipper
Ranch 91W3   Res. 59

J. N. SMITH
Rancher and Shipper
Telephone 36

JOHN S. WOODBURY
Rancher and Shipper
Telephone 4

JOHN C. WRIGHT
Rancher and Shipper
Telephone 216

J. D. HOPKINS
Rancher and Shipper
Telephone 151W

A. P. SPILSBURY
Ranchers and Shippers
Telephone 125

ARCH SWAPPP
Ranchers and Shippers
Telephone 183

T. A. THORLEY
Ranchers and Shippers
Telephone 166R

DAVE THORLEY
Rancher and Shipper
Telephone 109J

ALPHABETIC INDEX TO ADVERTISERS

Cedars Hotel and Restaurant — Office Stage Lines
Cedar Lumber Co. — All Builders Supplies
Cedar Milling Company — Flour and Cereals
Cedar Mercantile Company — General Merchandise
Cedar Mercantile Company — General Office
Cedar Mercantile Company — Farm Machinery
Cedar Mercantile Company — Blasting Powder
Cedar City City Garage — General Repairs
Ceadr City Laundry — General Work
Ceard City Plumbing Company — General Work
Christensen-Jones Company — General House Furnishings
Cooper Electric — All Appliances
Hunter Bros. — Gent's Furnishings
Craig, Mrs. S. D. — Cleaning and Pressing
Dalley and Judd — Driveit Yourself Co.
Dixie Power Co. — Power and Light
Don's Garage — General Service, Studebaker Specialities
Doolittle Co., H. J. — General Wholesale
Doolitte Company — PEP and VICO
Electric Cafe — Eletric Cooking
El Escalante Service Station — General Service
Ford Motor Company — J. H. Fife
Forbes & Dalley — Real Estate and Insurance
Foster, J. M. — Attorney
Foster and Corry —General Insurance
Fuller's Golden Rule Store — Dry Goods and Apparel
Freitag, Mac. — Lawyer
Gordon, W. H. — Jeweler and Watchmaker
Hancock and Barnes — Attorneys
Hardy, A. Y. — Abstractor
Holland, Louise, — Ladies' Fitter, Cedar Mercantile Co.
Hunter Barber Shop.— Service and Baths
Independent Harvester Co. — Cedar Mercantile Co.
Iron Commercial & Savings Bank — General Banking
Iron County Record — Job Printing
Iron County Record — Iron County Record
Irene Models — Mary Palmer
Johnson Mercantile Co. — Blasting Powders, Milford, Utah
Johnson, Dr. A. C. — Deputy State Veternary

Kopp's Garage — General Service Buick Specialties
Knell, B. F. — Stage Line
Leigh Furniture & Carpet Co. — Res. & Of. Furniture & Equip
Lowery Cash Store — General Groceries
Mammoth Plaster and Cement Co. —
Macfarlane John C. — Dairy
Macfarlane and Bergstrom — Physicians and Surgeons
Middleton and Sons, — Ranchers and Farmers
Navajo Indian Trading Post —Blankets, Baskets and Curios
Palmer, Jethro — Harness Shop
Palmer, Wm. R. — Nationail Secretary and Treasurer Canyon C
Penney Company — Department Store
Parry, Evelyn —Lime Manufacturer
Peterson Drug Co. — Curios, Sodas, Drugs
Petty, F. H. — Cedar Nash Motor Co.
Rhoden Booterie — Ladies' and Gentlemen's Shoes and Hosiery
Radiator Welding Company — Acetylene Welding
Sargent, Dr. A. E. — Chiropractor, Mercantile Bldg.
Shay and Lunt — Attorneys

Sprague Music Company — Musical Instruments
Standard Supply Company — General Merchandise
Star Service Station — General Service
Southern Utah Plumbing Company — General Plumbers and Sup
St. George Stage — Cedars Hotel
Southern Utah Cleaning and Pressing Company
Thorley Theatre — Movies
Tourist Cafe — Restaurant
Thorley and Byrnes — Fertilizers, Cedar Mercantile Company
U. S. Forest Service — In case of Forest Fire Call
Urie, G. K. — General Meat Market
Undertakers — Cedar Lumber Company
Varonos Jim — Candy Store and Sodas
Winterrose, R. E. — Embalmer
Wood, F. B. — Wood's Toggery
Zion Candy Kitchen — Candy Factory

———o———

Robert Adams, son of Mr. and Mrs. Adams, left Tuesday for a Mission to England. He will be set apart for the mission in Salt Lake City at the headquarters of the L. D. S. Church.

The friends of Elder Adams wish him success and pleasure while he is proselyting the gospel.

———o———

The 11 months old child of Mr. and Mrs. Pectral is at the county hospital where it was taken for correction of telescoping of the bowels. The patient is doing nicely.

Mr. and Mrs. Aldridge Thorley are rejoicing over the arrival of a beautiful baby girl, born at the county hospital.

———o———

Mr. and Mrs. Royce Nelson are happy over the arrival of a new baby at their home, born this week. Mother and babe doing nicely.

———o———

100,000 Trout For Duck Creek

———o———

Al Biederman, president of the Cedar City Gun and Rod Club announces that 100,000 trout have been shipped from the Glenwood fish hatchery, and taken to Duck Creek where they were planted this week.

The fish were taken in a regular tank truck built for the purpose, with a capacity of 100,000, and insures the delivery of the fish in good condition, much better than has been the case in the old time cans, holding from 500 to 1000 each.

Mr. Biederman states that it was first intended to plant the trout in Navajo Lake, but because of the low water in the lake this year it was deemed unsafe to plant them there, consequently Duck Creek was chosen, which has a never failing supply of water, and sufficient for several times 100,000.

Mr. Biederman also states that this is the first shipment of several that is to be made to this section of the state this year.

ONE KILLED, TWO IN-JURED IN ACCIDENT

The Misses Mary and Audrey Atkin and their brother; Don were seriously injured last Saturday night when a motorcycle with sidecar in which they were coming home ran into a wagon with hayrack on it near Hamiltons Fort, Miss Audrey dying from her injuries the next morning.

Miss Mary had been teaching school at Hinckley and last Thursday Don and Audrey went there to bring her home. They were on their way home when, about 8 p. m. Saturday, the motorcycle ran into the rear end of a hayrack on a wagon. So far as can be learned here, no one saw the accident. It was not quite dark at the time and the dust is said to have been very thick, which would account for the wagon not being seen until too late to avert the accident. Audrey is believed to have been riding on Mary's lap and therefore was the more seriously injured. All were taken to Cedar City to receive treatment, and efforts were made to communicate by telephone with the parents here, but the Bell telephone line was out of commission and no word was received here until about 12 hours after the accident, when Mayor Atkin took the mother to Cedar City while a messenger went out to notify the father who was at Short Creek, Arizona.

Audrey recovered consciousness about two o'clock Saturday morning, asked for a drink and inquired how badly she was injured but soon relapsed into unconsciousness and passed away about six o'clock Sunday morning, ten hours after the accident. Mary's most serious injury is a fractured leg, the right one, the knee being badly shattered, and she has numerous cuts and bruises on her head. Don's jaws are broken in four places, one hand broken, one knee badly cut and minor injuries. Their sister Lillian is with them at Cedar City.

Audrey Atkin was 19 years of age on the 22nd of December last, and was engaged to be married to Herbert Blake, a young man of Hinckley, on the first of September next. She was a sweet, lovable girl, and her untimely passing is not only a severe blow to her parents and relatives but is also a sad shock to the community.

The parents arrived home from Cedar City at 10 p. m. Sunday with the remains of their dear child.

Funeral Services

Funeral services were held in the Stake tabernacle at 3 o'clock Tuesday afternoon, conducted by Bishop James McArthur. There was a great abundance of beautiful roses and other flowers on the stand which were later used to cover the grave. There was a very large attendance.

The speakers were Pres. Thomas P. Cottam, Pres. Edw. H. Snow and Bishop McArthur. The musical numbers were "Lead Me Gently Home," by the choir; "He Shall Feed His Flock," trio; "Father in Heaven," vocal solo by Sister Hettie Bentley; a violin solo by Sister Vera Seegmiller, and "Tho' Deepening Trials" by the choir. Invocation was by Bishop F. G. Miles; benediction by Elder H. L. Reid.

Pres. Cottam said in part, this large gathering shows the deep sympathy felt by the entire community for Bro. and Sister Atkin. This terrible accident filled our hearts with sorrow. He desired that our Heavenly Father would comfort the hearts of Bro. and Sister Atkin. Our sister's sweet spirit has returned to God, who gave it. It is our duty to so live each day that when our summons comes we should be prepared to go. Felt to caution all against this awful speed mania; had often watched cars pass his home and felt the drivers did not realize their great danger. If we are faithful we shall come forth from the tomb and receive an inheritance that has been prepared for us. Prayed God to bless Bro. and Sister Atkin that they be faithful and keep His commandments. Life is uncertain; we know not when the Lord will require our life and we may be called home any time. Prayed God to pour the holy oil of consolation on the hearts of Bro. and Sister Atkin.

Pres. Snow: I feel to express the great love and sympathy felt by the community for Bro. and Sister Atkin; felt the desire to lighten their burdens

of grief and sorrow; if ever there is a time when we need our friends it is when sorrow overtakes us. Felt impressed by the wonderful love and great sacrifice of Jesus Christ; the liberality of the voluntary offer— "Father, here am I, send me;" other volunteers would have taken away mans free agency, but Christ gave man his free agency; God accepted His plan and He became for us a lamb slain before the foundation of his world. We are all free agents, as the poet has said:

"Know this that every soul is free,
    To choose his life and what he'll be;
For this eternal truth is given,
    God will force no man to heaven."

We may do as we please in this life but in the resurrection we will remember our actions and be our own accusers; there are no pangs like the pangs of conscience. We grow through adversity; sweet are the uses of adversity. If we do not live the laws of health we suffer; we know how gloomy everything looks if we

are sick and how much brighter if we are well; it is a law decreed of heaven that every blessing is predicted on obedience. We must obey the law laid down by our Father; we cannot blame the Lord for our own folly. Damnation is falling short of our glory; God is just, mercy may not rob justice nor justice mercy. We have been given a knowledge of right and wrong, let us try to work out our own salvation. We must remember the commandment chosen as the M. I. A. slogan, "Honor thy father and thy mother;" our boys and girls need that slogan; we live in an age of speed. Advised parents to avoid too many "dont's;" parents should not refuse innocent pleasure, but we should teach obedience. God is the Father

of us all and we must obey Him; this life is our opportunity to do His will. May the sweet life of our departed sister be an inspiration to those left behind.

Bishop McArthur spoke of his sympathy and his sorrow at Audrey's death. We must live so we may be worthy to meet her again. We do not understand the purposes of the Almighty, but we cannot get away from the fact that if it is His will it is best. Invoked His blessing on those called upon to mourn, and thanked all who had come to their assistance in their hour of need.

Interment was made in the city cemetery, the grave being dedicated by Elder Martin L. McAllister.

Following are recent births recorded by the register of vital statistic at Cedar City; To Mr. and Mrs. D. B. Hopkins, a girl; Mr. and Mrs. Burrus Barton, a boy; Mr. and Mrs. Alldridge Thorley, a girl; Mr. and Mrs. Martin Walker, a boy.

Records in the County Clerk's office at Parowan show the issuance of marriage licenses during the week to John M. Brown of Cedar City and Althea Lund of Paragonah, and to Grant Jones and Geneva Robb, both of Paragonah.

JURORS FOR JUNE TERM

Pursuant to an order from Judge Burton, dated May, 20, that thirty five jurors be drawn for the June term of the District Court which convenes here on Tuesday, June 23rd at 2 o'clock p. m., the following names were drawn on Monday of this week by the Clerk , Treasurer and Attorney, and the venire placed in the hands of the Sheriff, with instructions to withhold services until further orders from the Court.

Albert E. Adams, John P. Orton, Albert Mickelson, John T. Mitchell, George W. Rasmussen, Wm. Adams, Hartley W. Dalton, George W. Decker and Wilford Day of Parowan.

Rolce B. Nelson, Kumen L. Jones, Evelyn C. Parry, Richard Williams, Thos. J. Webster, John H. Perry, Donald C. Urie, Samual A. Higbee, August Mackelprang, David A. Thorley, David Murie, John G. Pace, Robert W. Bulloch, Warren Cox, H. J. Doolittle, Samuel Bauer, John C. Carpenter, John S. Woodbury and Calvin C. Pendelton of Cedar City.

James G. Knell, of Newcastle.

Wallace Williams, Leon Davis and Reese J. Williams of Kanarra.

James W. Barton and Wm. P. Barton of Paragonah.

Oscar J. Hulet, of Summit.

Mrs. Lannie Hoyt Here.

Mrs. Lannie Hoyt of Snowflake, Arizona is here visiting with relatves and friends. The lady had been to Salt Lake City attending the M. I. A. Jubilee, and decided to call at Cedar on her way home.

Mrs. Hoyt is a sister of John, Isaac and Edward Parry, and is known by scores of people in this locality. While a resident of Cedar before her mariage to Mr. Hoyt of Kanab, she was publically identified in several church capacities and was always an enthusastic and willing worker in any line of endeavor she undertook.

The friends of Mrs. Hoyt are very pleased to greet her again.

Takes His Plunge.

—|o|—

"Posey," whom all Cedarites know well, took a plunge in the pool at the Dave C. Bulloch ranch on the mountan last Sunday, and scared all the fish so badly that not one bite has been recorded by any fisherman since.

It appears that "Posey" was standing on a small log at the edge of the pool, holding his rod and line waiting patiently for a fish to "strike., None took the trouble; however, and "Posey" half turned to reach the bank, saying "I'm going."

And go he did, head first in the water, takng an involuntary plunge. He scrambled to shore and went gasping to camp a short distance away, stripped his wet garments, hung them to dry, and remained in bed during the process, having no dry clothing to change to.

According to the boys who were near, the plunge was one of the most artistic possible, being for more graceful than any ever. taken by the diving beauties of Coney Island.

Up From Kanarra.

—|o|—

Riley G. Williams of Kanarra was a business visitor in Cedar Wednesday.

Mr. Williams announces that crops are very good in and around Kanarra, but there will be a shortage of corn, because of the fact that the apparent drought that seemed to threaten the country prevented the farmers from seeding as much as usual.

Outside of a shortage of corn, the vicinity will raise an average of every other crop usually raised there.

—|o|—

Last Tuesday a son of Mr. and Mrs. Ras Macfarlane was operated on for appendicitis. The boy is reported as doing well.

—|o|—

J. V. Adams, son of Mr. and Mrs. Wm. Adams is at the County hospital suffering from an attack of pneumonia. The patient is reported as doing nicely.

—|o|—

It is reported that Mr. and Mrs. David C. Bulloch are rejoicing over the arrival o a bouncing baby, born to them this week.

Last Friday afternoon in Parowan Harmel Bauer and Miss Fern Ashdown were united in wedlock.

The groom is a son of Alowis Bauer, a young man of quiet and unassuming pretensions, of stirling character, whose many friends in Cedar are well pleased to leran of his advent into matrimony.

The bride is the eldest daughter of Chris Ashdown, a home loving girl, who holds the high esteem of scores of people of her acquaintance.

The young couple will make their home in Cedar, and have the well wishes of everybody for a long, happy and useful life as man and wife.

SUMMIT

—|o|—

The Sunday School Ward Conference was held here last Sunday with a good attendance. Several of the Stake Sunday School officers were present.

—|o|—

Mrs. Charles R. Dalley returned Saturday after a month's visit with her daughter, Mrs. Letha Farnsworth of Salt Lake City. Mrs. Farnsworth and baby daughter returned with her for a visit with relatives and friends in Summit.

—|o|—

Isaac Chamberlain went last week to Cedar mountains where he has a position as Government Forest Reserve Rider.

—|o|—

Quite a force of men were employed here last week by the road construction companies, locating gravel suitable for use in the building of the Parowan-Winn Hollow road which will begin in a few days.

First Grandson

—|o|—

Mr. and Mrs. Dan E. Matheson are proudly telling friends that they have one of the finest grandsons (the first for them) to be found in this fair state of Utah.

The boy was born to their daughter Mrs. Ervin Stevens last Friday evening. Mother and babe are reported as progressing nicely.

—|o|—

NADA

—|o|—

Mr. and Mrs. Alvin Couch of Milford visited friends in Nada last Sunday.

—|o|—

LaMar Pree, county agent, of Beaver County was here organizing an association of farmers with flocks of sheep.

—|o|—

Carlton Culmsee has hauled his wool to Milford and sold with the Beaver Co. pool.

—|o|—

Miss Mable Brumfield arrived from West Virginia to visit her cousins, Oscar and Anthony Stephenson.

—|o|—

Miss Nell Morris who spent a few weeks with Mrs. Oscar Stephenson, returned to Greenville.

—|o|—

Little Jane Moore fell from a rocking chair and broke her left arm last Wednesday. She was taken to Beaver for X-ray photographs and Dr. set the broken member.

Like our Facebook page NewsClippingsFromThePast for articles, pictures, contests and coupons.

A complete list of News Clippings Books can be found on our website www.newsclippings.net

All of our books are available on Amazon.com

Thank you for reading this News Clippings Book, if you enjoyed it please take the time to leave positive feedback on Amazon.com. Your feedback and word of mouth really does make a difference and are our main source of advertising.

Thank you,

David Andersen & Kaylene Canfield

44687959R00280

Made in the USA
Charleston, SC
07 August 2015